Ōoku

THE INNER CHAMBERS

by **Fumi Yoshinaga**

VOL. **14**

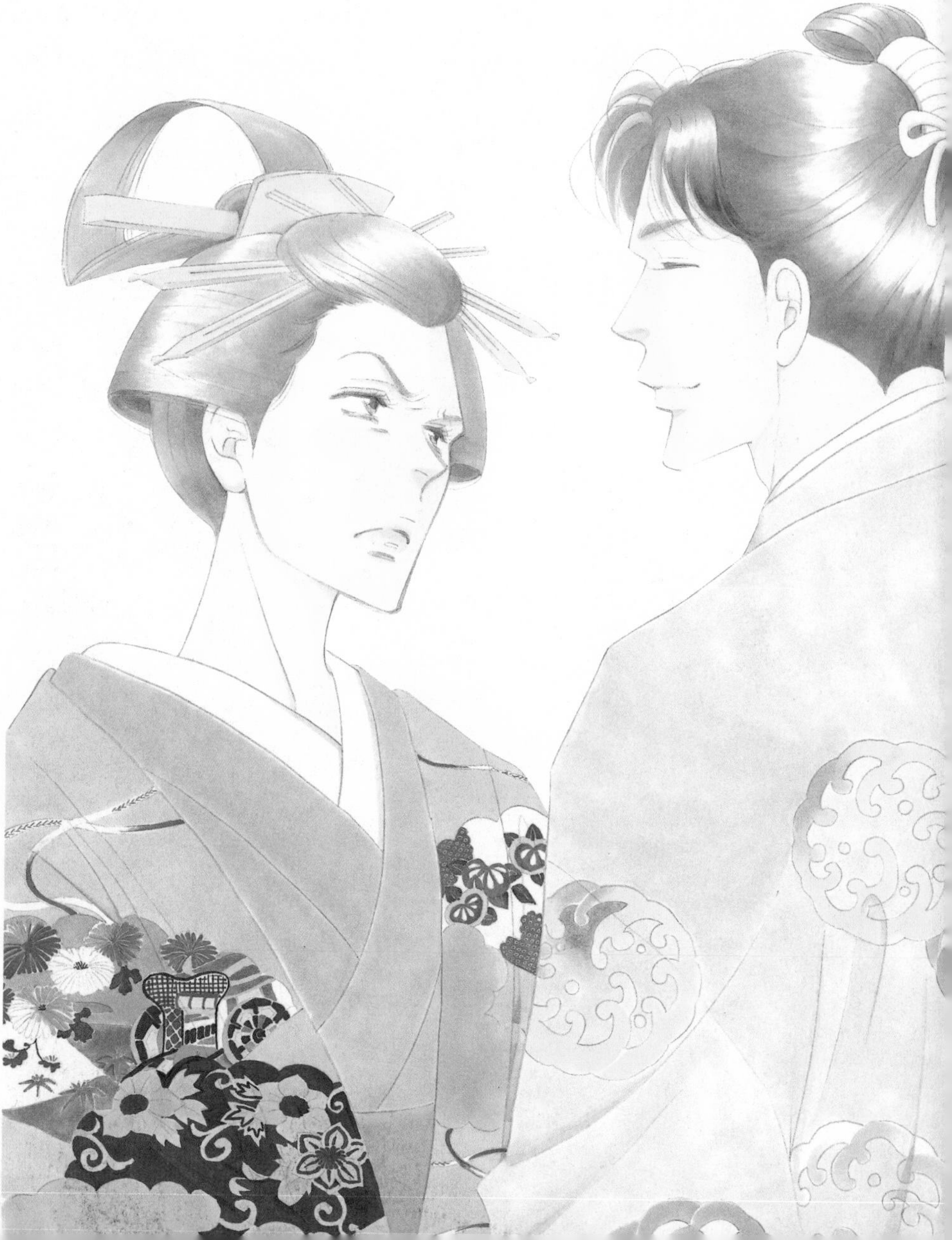

TABLE *of* CONTENTS

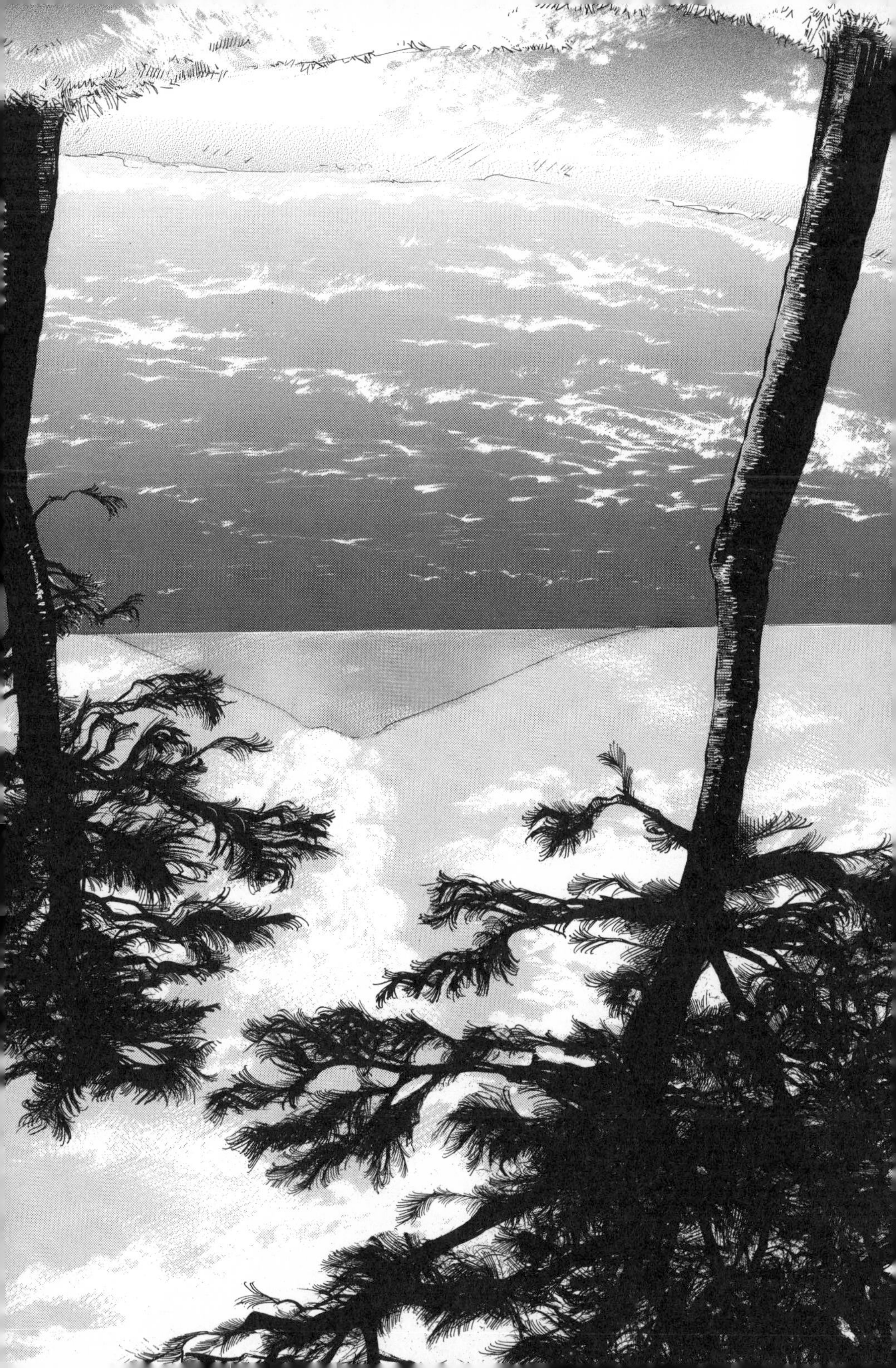

THE INNER CHAMBERS

CAST *of* CHARACTERS

From the birth of the "inverse Inner Chambers" to its zenith, to eradicating the Redface Pox, and now to the end of Tokugawa rule…?

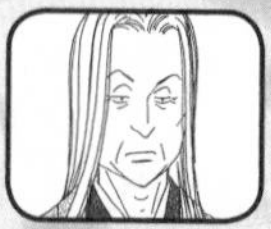

SENIOR CHAMBERLAIN

LADY KASUGA

↓

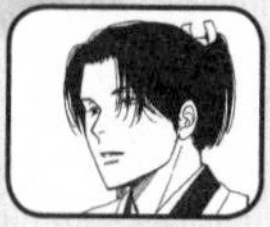

MADE-NOKOJI ARIKOTO

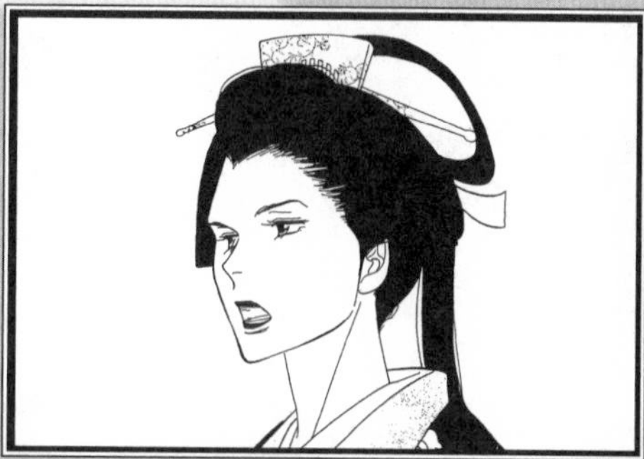

TOKUGAWA IEMITSU (III)

Impersonated her father, Iemitsu, at Lady Kasuga's urging after he died of the Redface Pox. Later became the first female shogun.

TOKUGAWA IETSUNA (IV)

Iemitsu's eldest daughter, known as "Lord Aye-do-so."

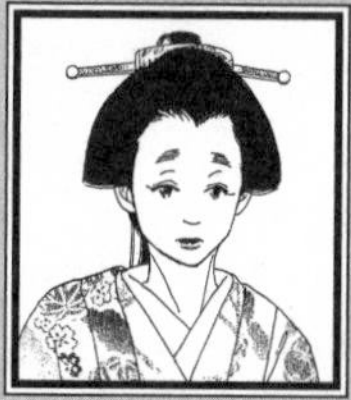

TOKUGAWA TSUNASHIGE

TOKUGAWA IENOBU (VI)

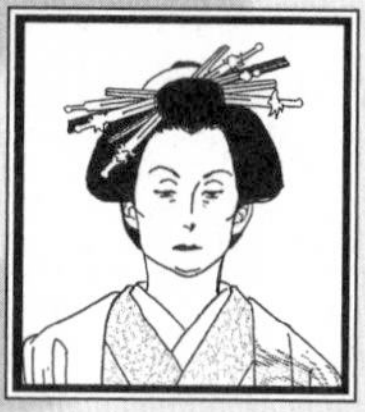

A ruler of sterling character but poor health, who died soon after assuming office.

TOKUGAWA IETSUGU (VII)

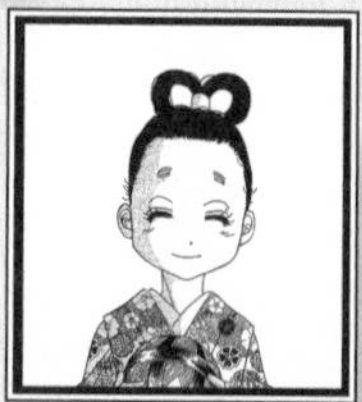

Died in childhood.

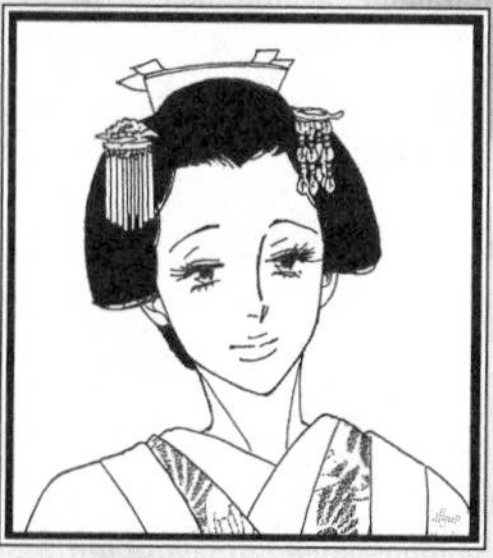

TOKUGAWA TSUNAYOSHI (V)

Endowed with both intellect and beauty, she did her best to rule wisely, but became known as "the Dog Shogun" due to unpopular policy mistakes later in her reign.

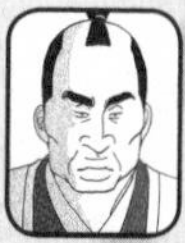

SENIOR CHAMBERLAIN

EJIMA

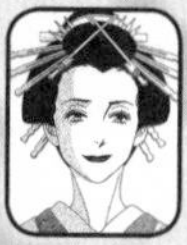

PRIVY COUNCILLOR

MANABE AKIFUSA

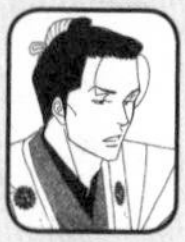

SENIOR CHAMBERLAIN

EMONNOSUKE

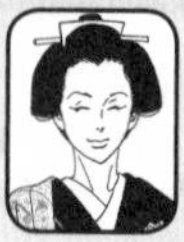

PRIVY COUNCILLOR

YANAGISAWA YOSHIYASU

RACED TO FIND A CURE FOR THE REDFACE POX UNDER TANUMA OKITSUGU

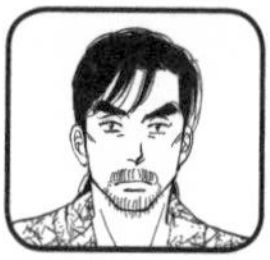

KUROKI RYOJUN

Continued working as a doctor following Aonuma's death.

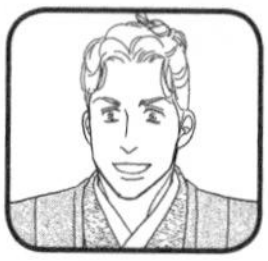

AONUMA

Mixed-race physician of Western medicine. Sentenced to death following the downfall of Lady Tanuma.

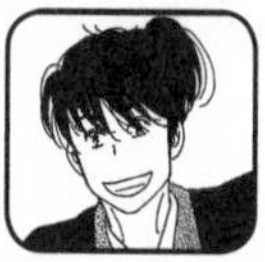

HIRAGA GENNAI

Multitalented genius.

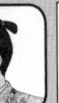

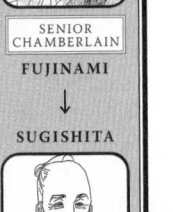

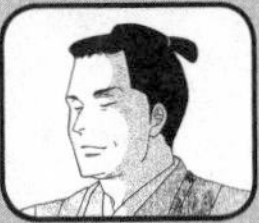

SENIOR CHAMBERLAIN

FUJINAMI

↓

SUGISHITA

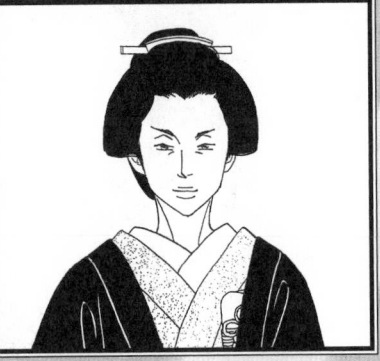

TOKUGAWA YOSHIMUNE (VIII)

Third daughter of Mitsusada, the second head of the Kii branch of the Tokugawa family. Acceded to domain lord and then, upon the death of Ietsugu, to shogun. Imposed and lived by a strict policy of austerity, dismissing large numbers of Inner Chamber courtiers and pursuing policies designed to increase income to the treasury.

PRIVY COUNCILLOR

KANO HISAMICHI

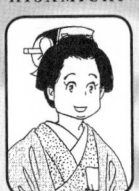

MUNETADA (HITOTSUBASHI BRANCH)

Yoshimune's third daughter

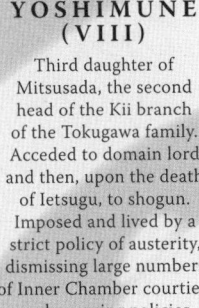

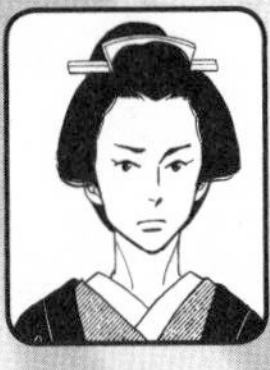

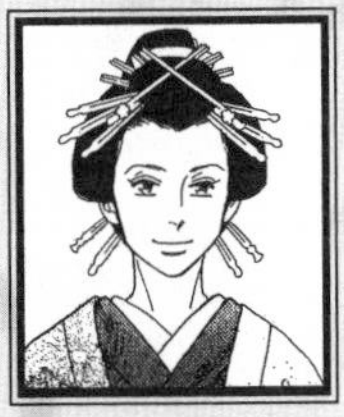

TOKUGAWA HARUSADA

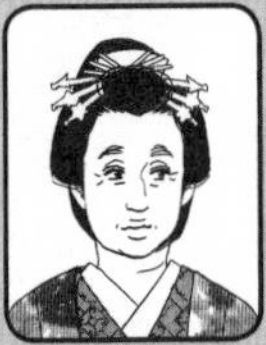

"Monster" who ruled Edo Castle through murder by poison.

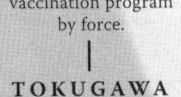

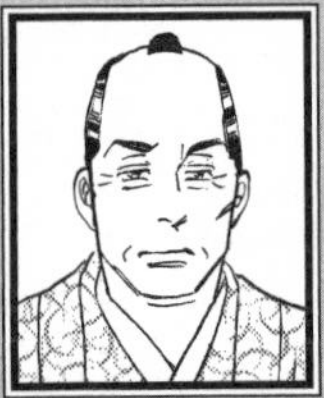

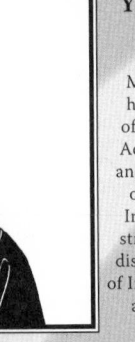

TOKUGAWA IENARI (XI)

Became shogun at mother's behest. Carried out nationwide vaccination program by force.

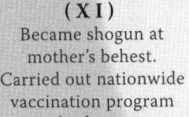

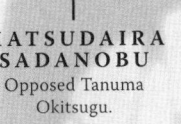

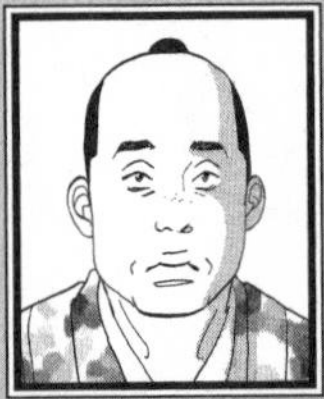

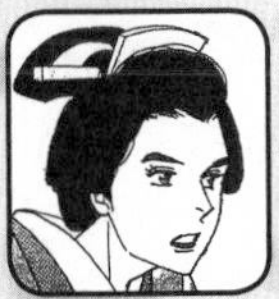

TOKUGAWA IEYOSHI (XII)

Became shogun at age 45. Perversely obsessed with his daughter, Iesada.

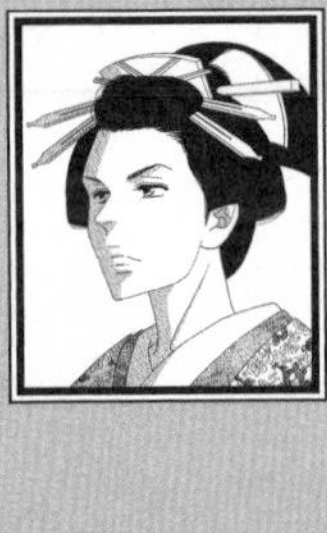

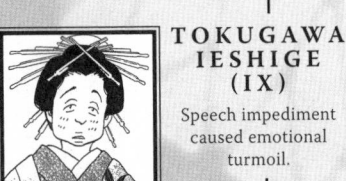

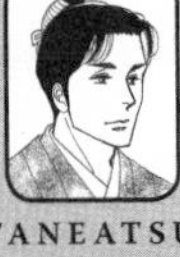

TOKUGAWA IESADA (XIII)

Sexually abused by her father for years. Her consorts were poisoned by him.

MUNETAKE (TAYASU BRANCH)

Yoshimune's second daughter

MATSUDAIRA SADANOBU

Opposed Tanuma Okitsugu.

TOKUGAWA IESHIGE (IX)

Speech impediment caused emotional turmoil.

TOKUGAWA IEHARU (X)

Intelligent but somewhat brittle.

CHAMBERLAIN ↓ SENIOR COUNCILLOR

TANUMA OKITSUGU

Active under Iesada and later Ieharu. Devoted efforts to eradicating the Redface Pox.

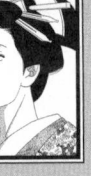

TANEATSU

Iesada's third consort.

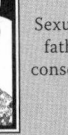

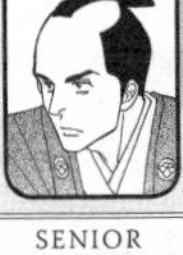

SENIOR CHAMBERLAIN

TAKIYAMA

Kagema courtesan of samurai stock, discovered by Masaharu and brought to the Inner Chambers.

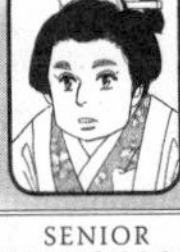

SENIOR COUNCILLOR

ABE MASAHIRO

Committed politician, deeply trusted by Iesada.

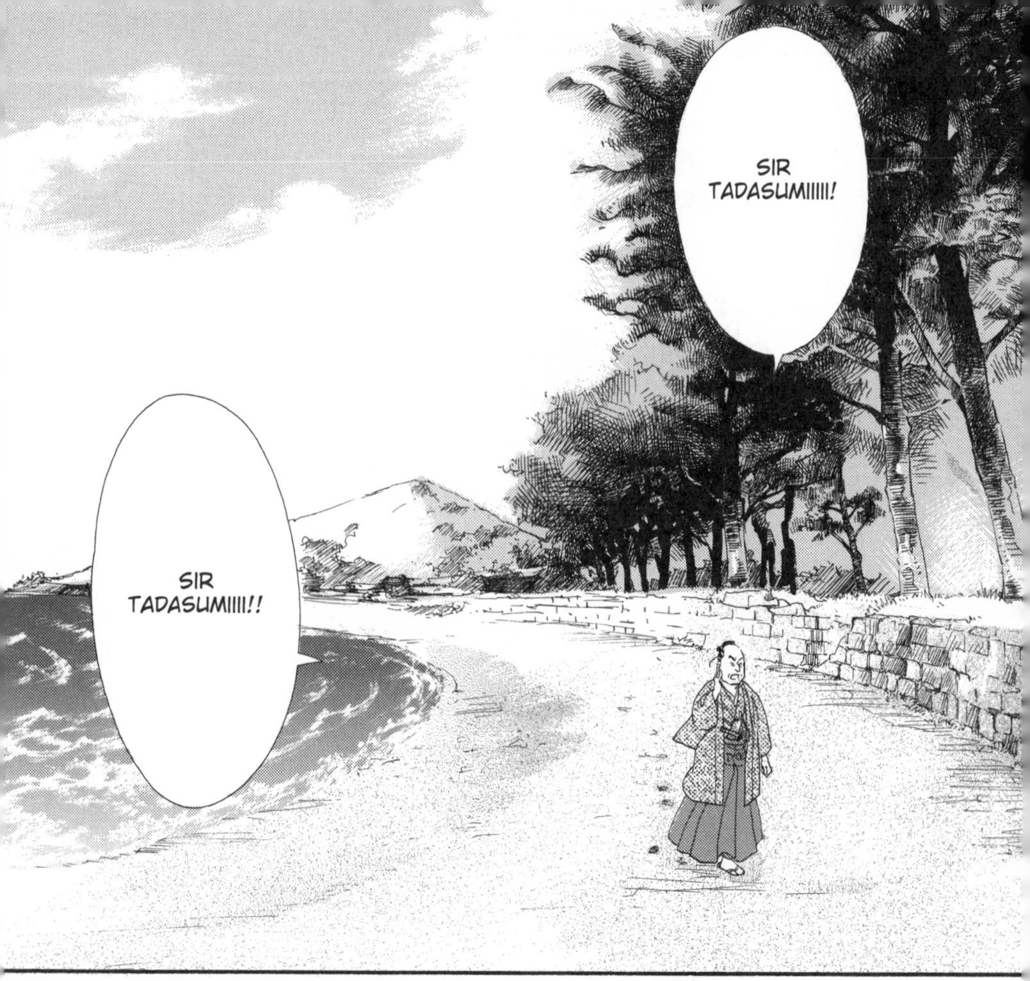
SIR TADASUMIIIII!
SIR TADASUMIIII!!
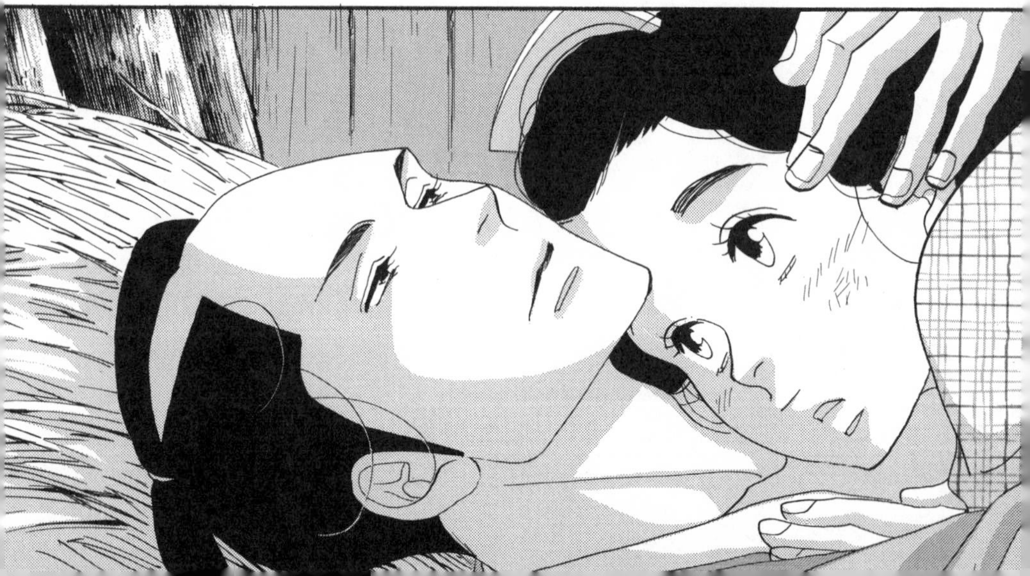

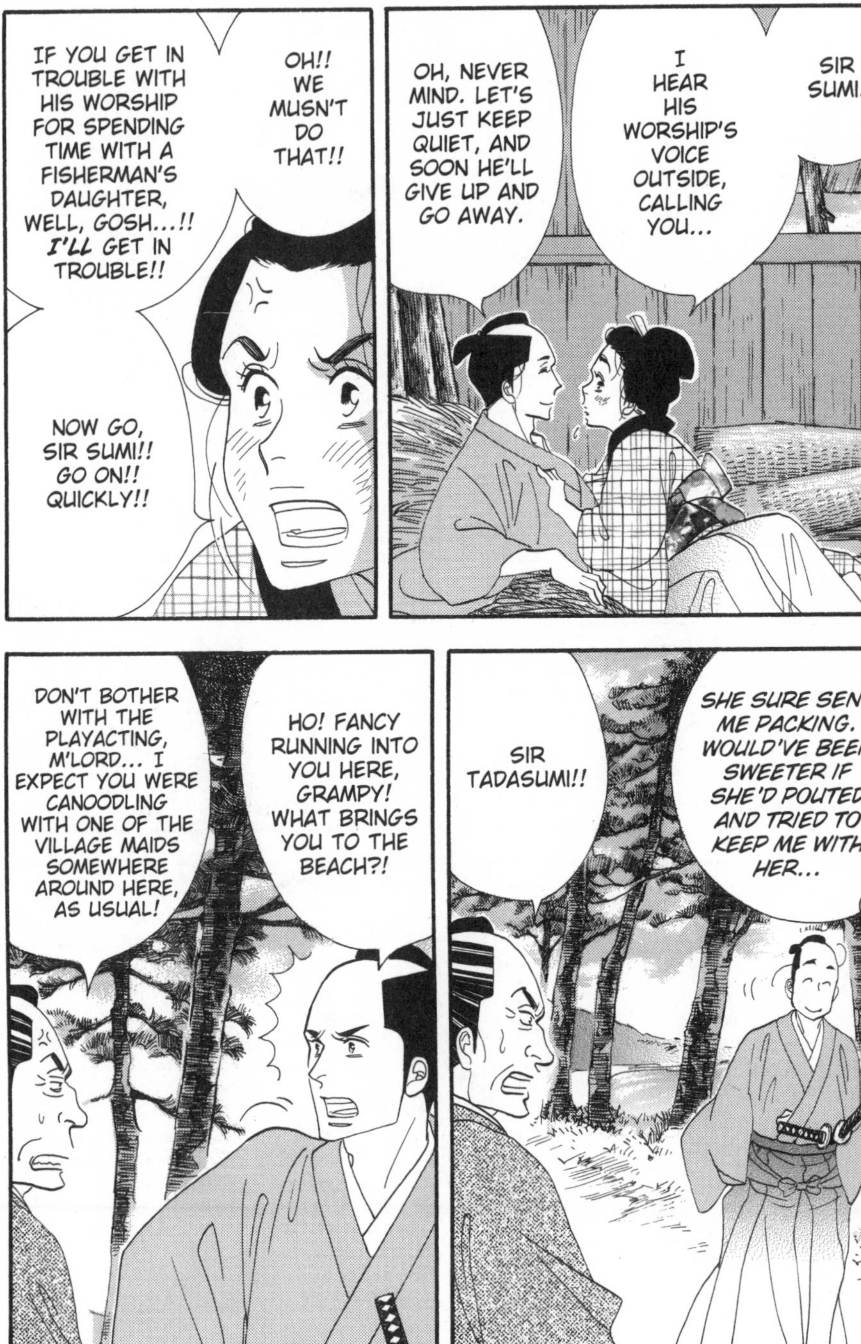
SIR SUMI.
I HEAR HIS WORSHIP'S VOICE OUTSIDE, CALLING YOU...
OH, NEVER MIND. LET'S JUST KEEP QUIET, AND SOON HE'LL GIVE UP AND GO AWAY.
OH!! WE MUSN'T DO THAT!!
IF YOU GET IN TROUBLE WITH HIS WORSHIP FOR SPENDING TIME WITH A FISHERMAN'S DAUGHTER, WELL, GOSH...!! I'LL GET IN TROUBLE!!
NOW GO, SIR SUMI!! GO ON!! QUICKLY!!
SHE SURE SENT ME PACKING. WOULD'VE BEEN SWEETER IF SHE'D POUTED AND TRIED TO KEEP ME WITH HER...
SIR TADASUMI!!
HO! FANCY RUNNING INTO YOU HERE, GRAMPY! WHAT BRINGS YOU TO THE BEACH?!
DON'T BOTHER WITH THE PLAYACTING, M'LORD... I EXPECT YOU WERE CANOODLING WITH ONE OF THE VILLAGE MAIDS SOMEWHERE AROUND HERE, AS USUAL!

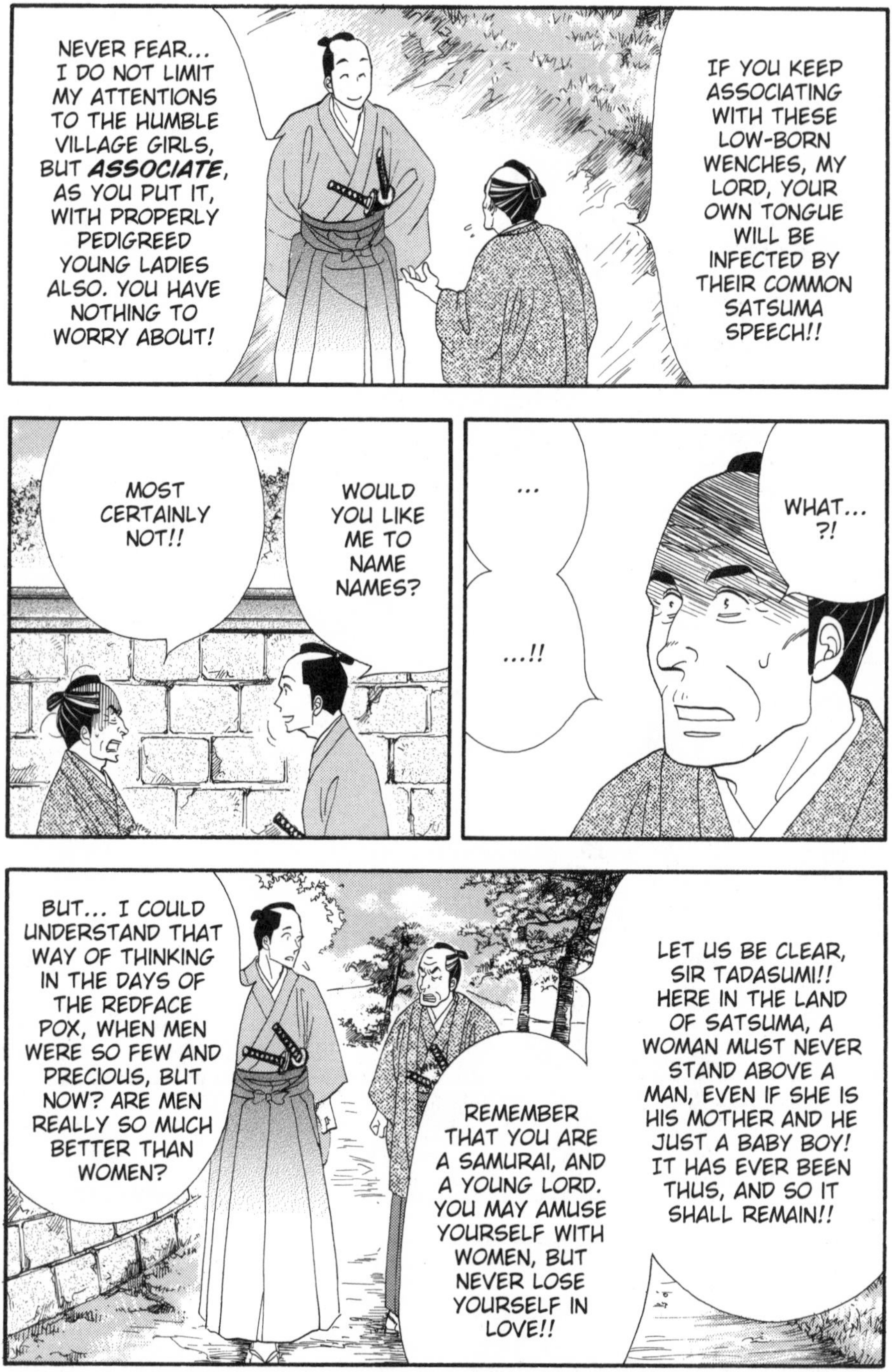
IF YOU KEEP ASSOCIATING WITH THESE LOW-BORN WENCHES, MY LORD, YOUR OWN TONGUE WILL BE INFECTED BY THEIR COMMON SATSUMA SPEECH!!
NEVER FEAR... I DO NOT LIMIT MY ATTENTIONS TO THE HUMBLE VILLAGE GIRLS, BUT ***ASSOCIATE***, AS YOU PUT IT, WITH PROPERLY PEDIGREED YOUNG LADIES ALSO. YOU HAVE NOTHING TO WORRY ABOUT!
WHAT... ?!
...
...!!
WOULD YOU LIKE ME TO NAME NAMES?
MOST CERTAINLY NOT!!
LET US BE CLEAR, SIR TADASUMI!! HERE IN THE LAND OF SATSUMA, A WOMAN MUST NEVER STAND ABOVE A MAN, EVEN IF SHE IS HIS MOTHER AND HE JUST A BABY BOY! IT HAS EVER BEEN THUS, AND SO IT SHALL REMAIN!!
REMEMBER THAT YOU ARE A SAMURAI, AND A YOUNG LORD. YOU MAY AMUSE YOURSELF WITH WOMEN, BUT NEVER LOSE YOURSELF IN LOVE!!
BUT... I COULD UNDERSTAND THAT WAY OF THINKING IN THE DAYS OF THE REDFACE POX, WHEN MEN WERE SO FEW AND PRECIOUS, BUT NOW? ARE MEN REALLY SO MUCH BETTER THAN WOMEN?

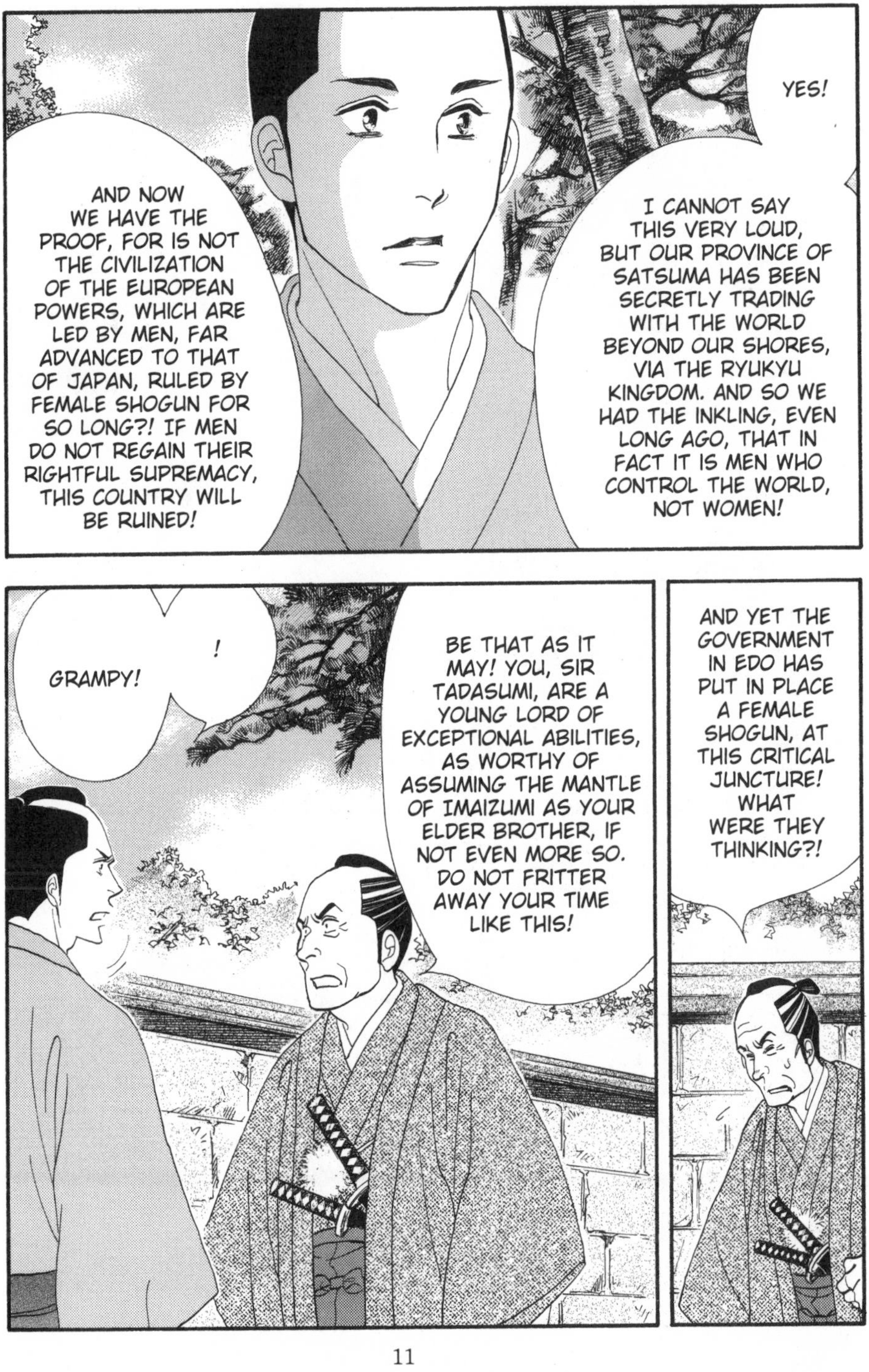
YES!
I CANNOT SAY THIS VERY LOUD, BUT OUR PROVINCE OF SATSUMA HAS BEEN SECRETLY TRADING WITH THE WORLD BEYOND OUR SHORES, VIA THE RYUKYU KINGDOM. AND SO WE HAD THE INKLING, EVEN LONG AGO, THAT IN FACT IT IS MEN WHO CONTROL THE WORLD, NOT WOMEN!
AND NOW WE HAVE THE PROOF, FOR IS NOT THE CIVILIZATION OF THE EUROPEAN POWERS, WHICH ARE LED BY MEN, FAR ADVANCED TO THAT OF JAPAN, RULED BY FEMALE SHOGUN FOR SO LONG?! IF MEN DO NOT REGAIN THEIR RIGHTFUL SUPREMACY, THIS COUNTRY WILL BE RUINED!
AND YET THE GOVERNMENT IN EDO HAS PUT IN PLACE A FEMALE SHOGUN, AT THIS CRITICAL JUNCTURE! WHAT WERE THEY THINKING?!
BE THAT AS IT MAY! YOU, SIR TADASUMI, ARE A YOUNG LORD OF EXCEPTIONAL ABILITIES, AS WORTHY OF ASSUMING THE MANTLE OF IMAIZUMI AS YOUR ELDER BROTHER, IF NOT EVEN MORE SO. DO NOT FRITTER AWAY YOUR TIME LIKE THIS!
!
GRAMPY!

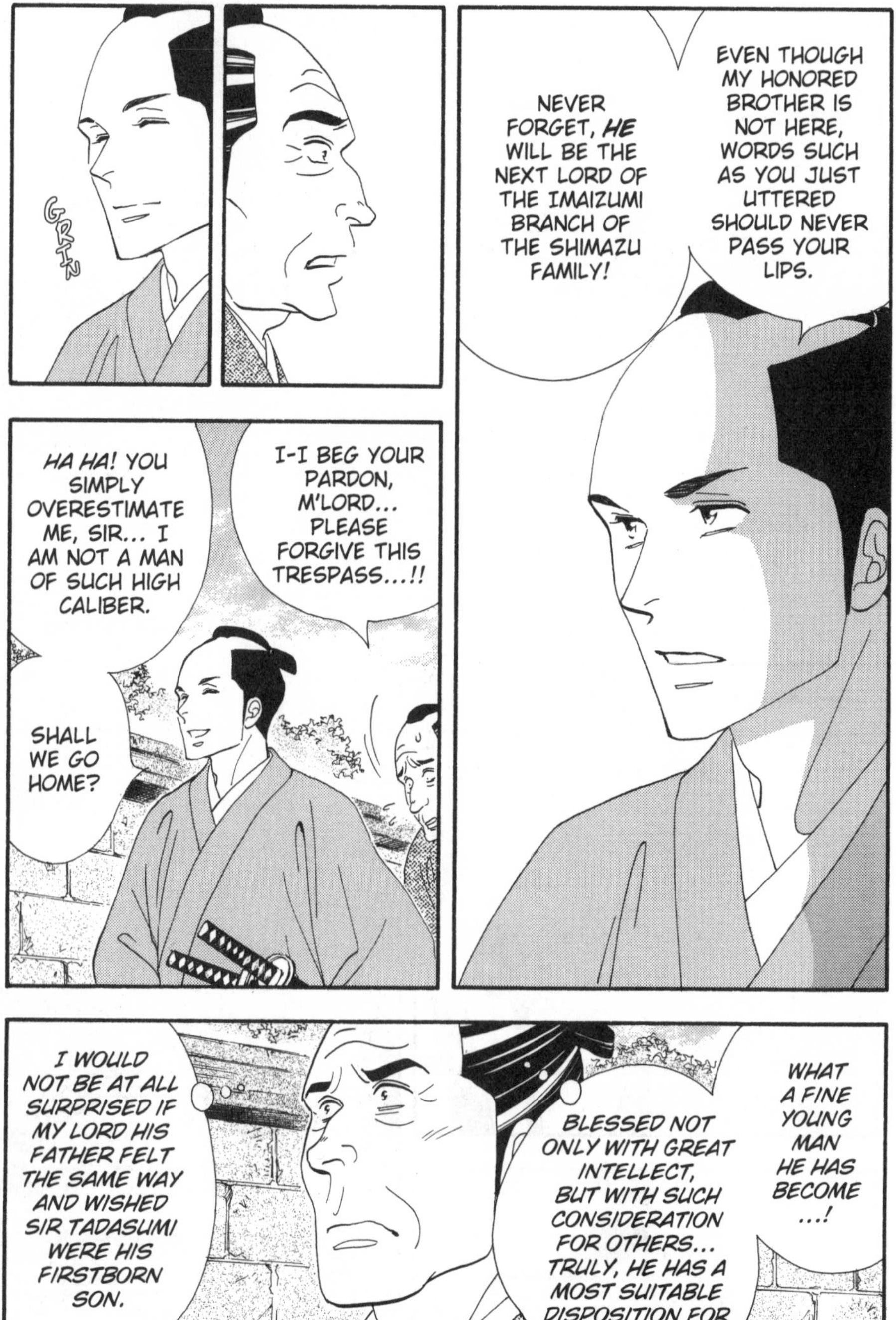
EVEN THOUGH MY HONORED BROTHER IS NOT HERE, WORDS SUCH AS YOU JUST UTTERED SHOULD NEVER PASS YOUR LIPS.
NEVER FORGET, *HE* WILL BE THE NEXT LORD OF THE IMAIZUMI BRANCH OF THE SHIMAZU FAMILY!
GRIN
I-I BEG YOUR PARDON, M'LORD... PLEASE FORGIVE THIS TRESPASS...!!
HA HA! YOU SIMPLY OVERESTIMATE ME, SIR... I AM NOT A MAN OF SUCH HIGH CALIBER.
SHALL WE GO HOME?
WHAT A FINE YOUNG MAN HE HAS BECOME ...!
BLESSED NOT ONLY WITH GREAT INTELLECT, BUT WITH SUCH CONSIDERATION FOR OTHERS... TRULY, HE HAS A MOST SUITABLE DISPOSITION FOR A LEADER.
I WOULD NOT BE AT ALL SURPRISED IF MY LORD HIS FATHER FELT THE SAME WAY AND WISHED SIR TADASUMI WERE HIS FIRSTBORN SON.

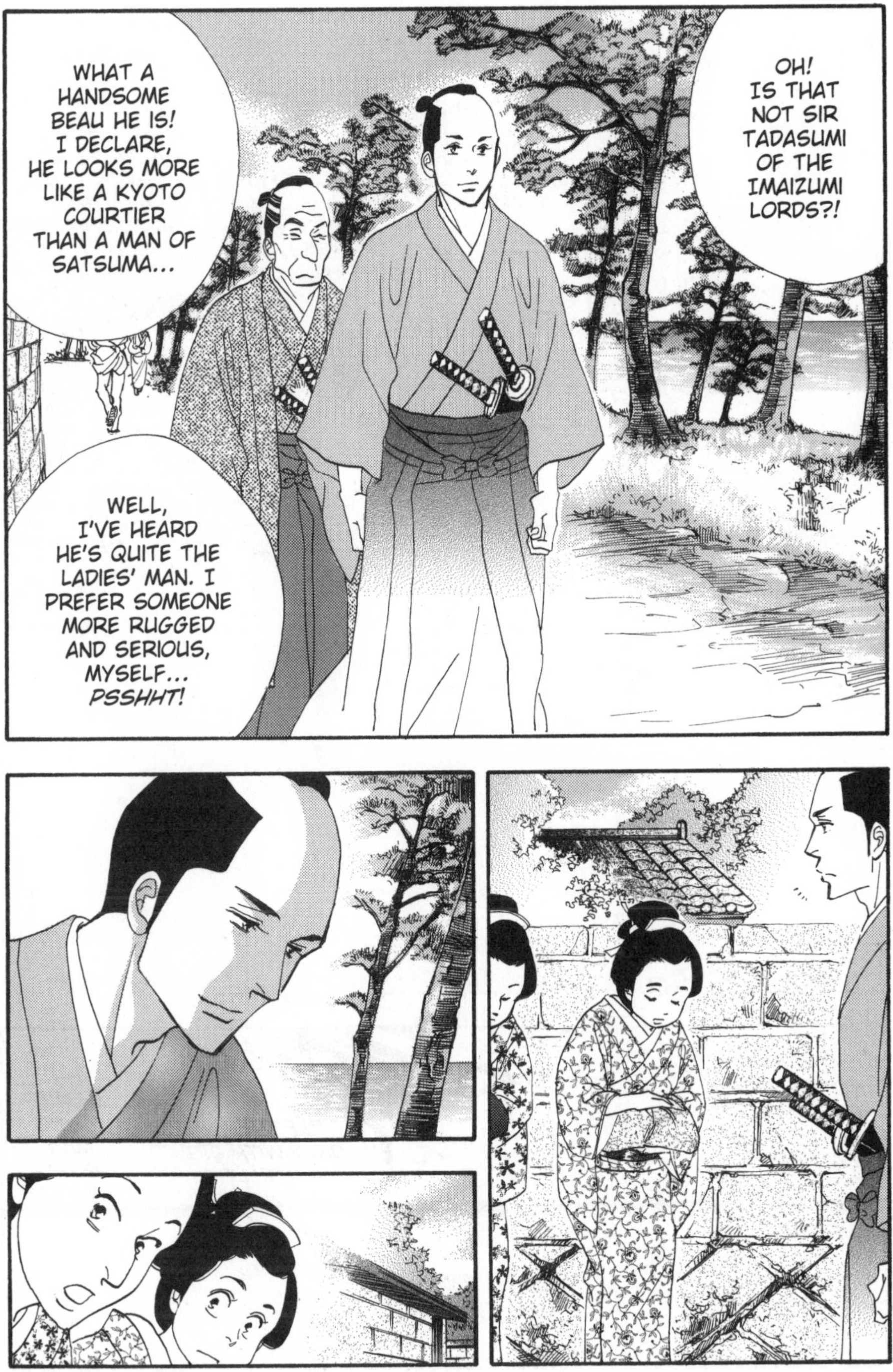
OH! IS THAT NOT SIR TADASUMI OF THE IMAIZUMI LORDS?!
WHAT A HANDSOME BEAU HE IS! I DECLARE, HE LOOKS MORE LIKE A KYOTO COURTIER THAN A MAN OF SATSUMA...
WELL, I'VE HEARD HE'S QUITE THE LADIES' MAN. I PREFER SOMEONE MORE RUGGED AND SERIOUS, MYSELF... PSSHHT!

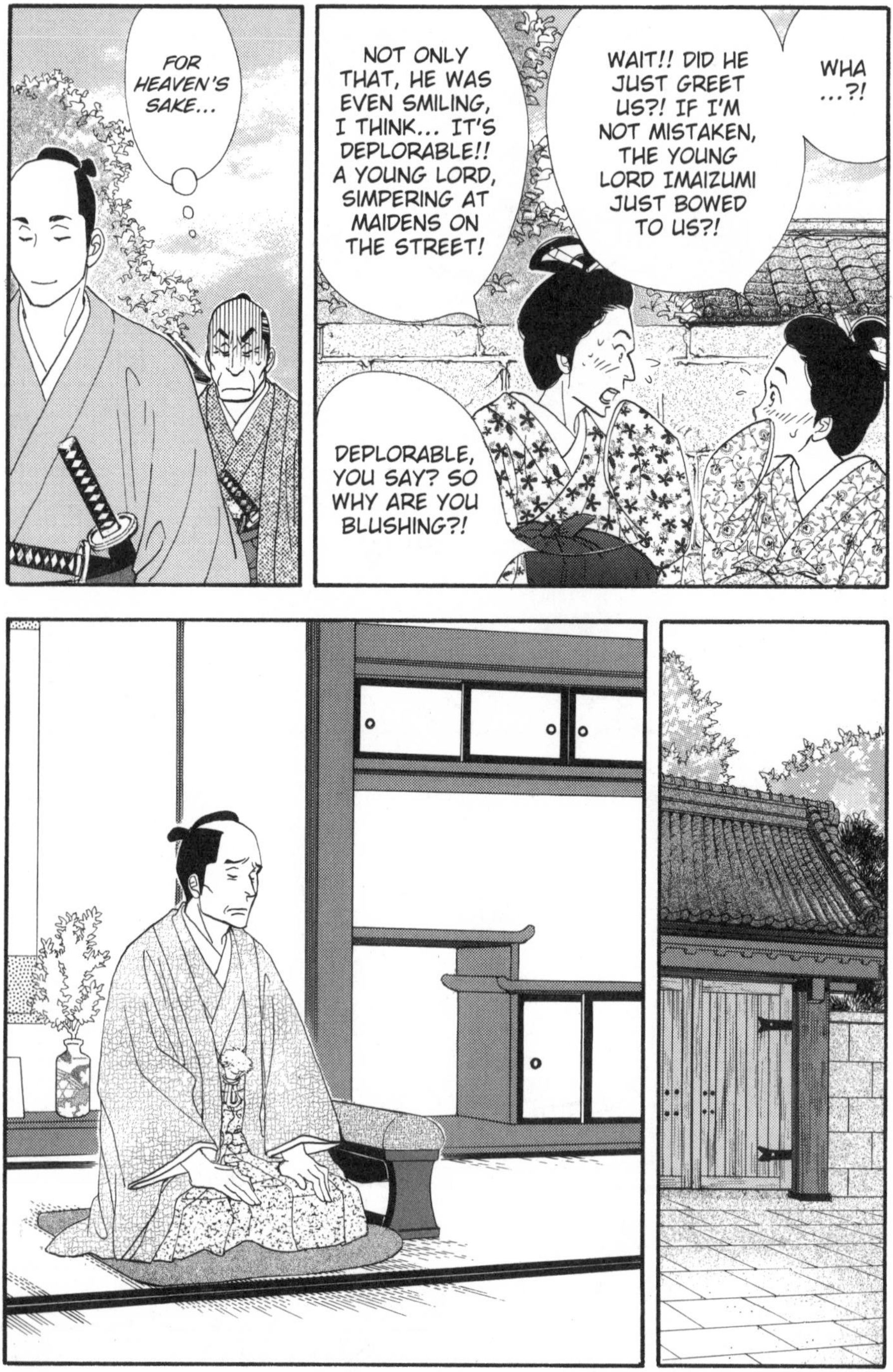
WHA ...?!
WAIT!! DID HE JUST GREET US?! IF I'M NOT MISTAKEN, THE YOUNG LORD IMAIZUMI JUST BOWED TO US?!
NOT ONLY THAT, HE WAS EVEN SMILING, I THINK... IT'S DEPLORABLE!! A YOUNG LORD, SIMPERING AT MAIDENS ON THE STREET!
DEPLORABLE, YOU SAY? SO WHY ARE YOU BLUSHING?!
FOR HEAVEN'S SAKE...

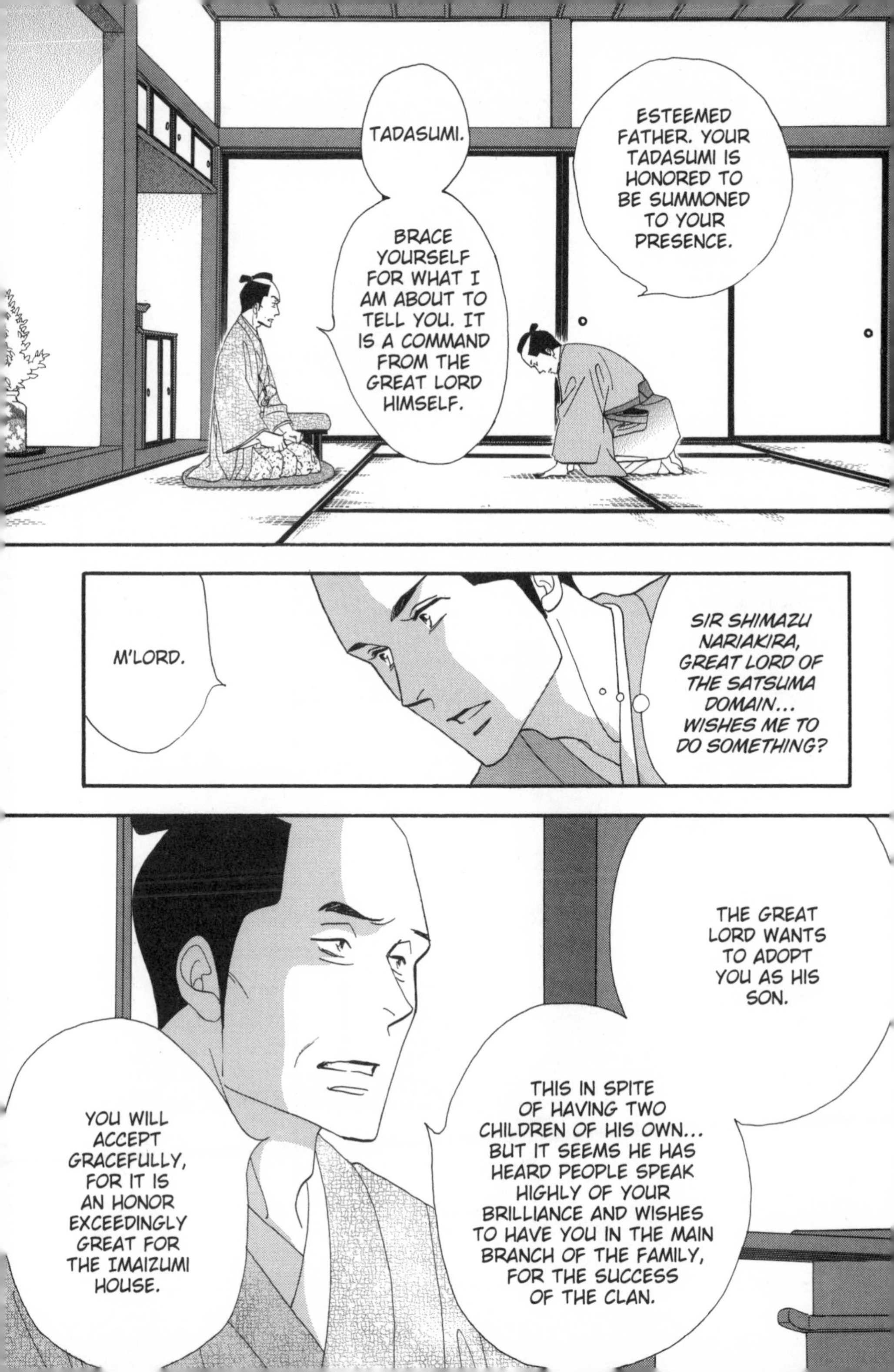
ESTEEMED FATHER. YOUR TADASUMI IS HONORED TO BE SUMMONED TO YOUR PRESENCE.
TADASUMI.
BRACE YOURSELF FOR WHAT I AM ABOUT TO TELL YOU. IT IS A COMMAND FROM THE GREAT LORD HIMSELF.
SIR SHIMAZU NARIAKIRA, GREAT LORD OF THE SATSUMA DOMAIN... WISHES ME TO DO SOMETHING?
M'LORD.
THE GREAT LORD WANTS TO ADOPT YOU AS HIS SON.
THIS IN SPITE OF HAVING TWO CHILDREN OF HIS OWN... BUT IT SEEMS HE HAS HEARD PEOPLE SPEAK HIGHLY OF YOUR BRILLIANCE AND WISHES TO HAVE YOU IN THE MAIN BRANCH OF THE FAMILY, FOR THE SUCCESS OF THE CLAN.
YOU WILL ACCEPT GRACEFULLY, FOR IT IS AN HONOR EXCEEDINGLY GREAT FOR THE IMAIZUMI HOUSE.

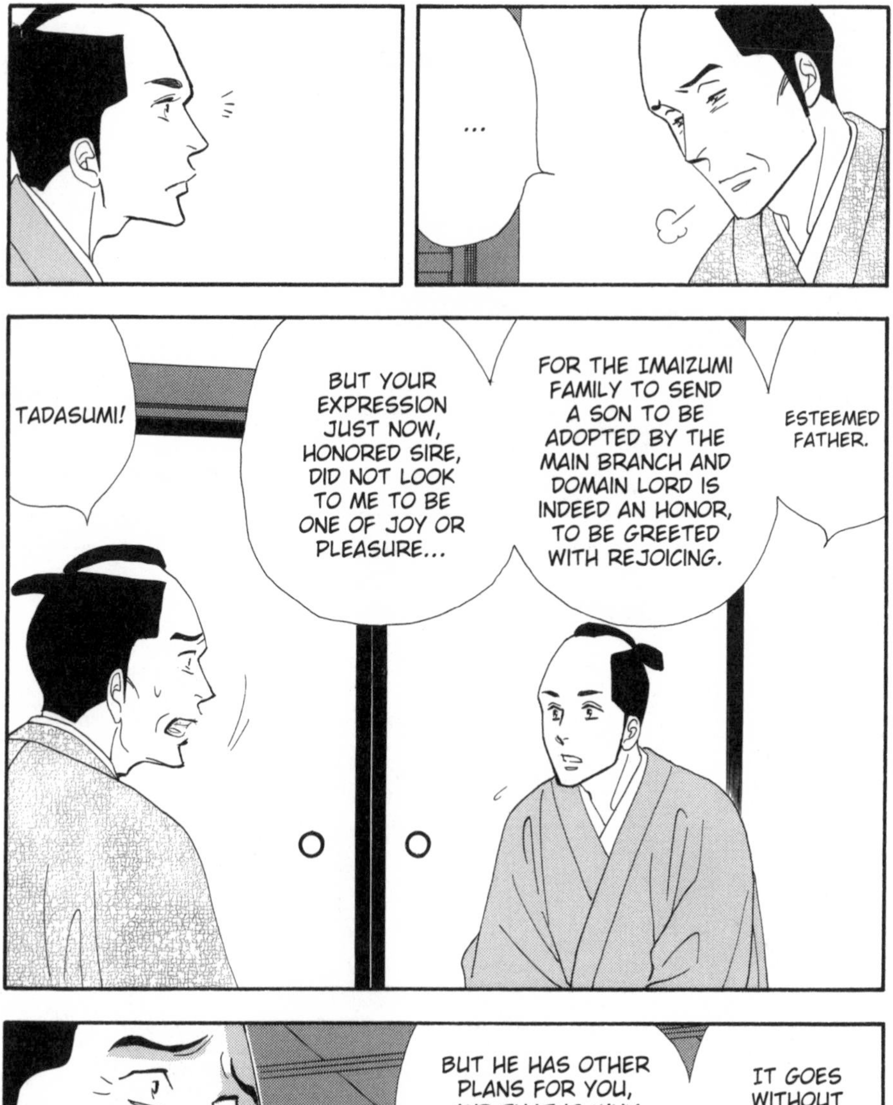
...
ESTEEMED FATHER.
FOR THE IMAIZUMI FAMILY TO SEND A SON TO BE ADOPTED BY THE MAIN BRANCH AND DOMAIN LORD IS INDEED AN HONOR, TO BE GREETED WITH REJOICING.
BUT YOUR EXPRESSION JUST NOW, HONORED SIRE, DID NOT LOOK TO ME TO BE ONE OF JOY OR PLEASURE...
TADASUMI!
IT GOES WITHOUT SAYING THAT IF YOU WERE SIMPLY TO BECOME THE GREAT LORD'S ADOPTED SON, I WOULD BE JUMPING FOR JOY!
BUT HE HAS OTHER PLANS FOR YOU, AND THAT IS WHY I CANNOT HIDE MY DISMAY. LORD NARIAKIRA IS SAYING THAT AFTER HE HAS ADOPTED YOU, HE WILL SEND YOU TO EDO TO BECOME THE CONSORT OF THE TOKUGAWA SHOGUN!!

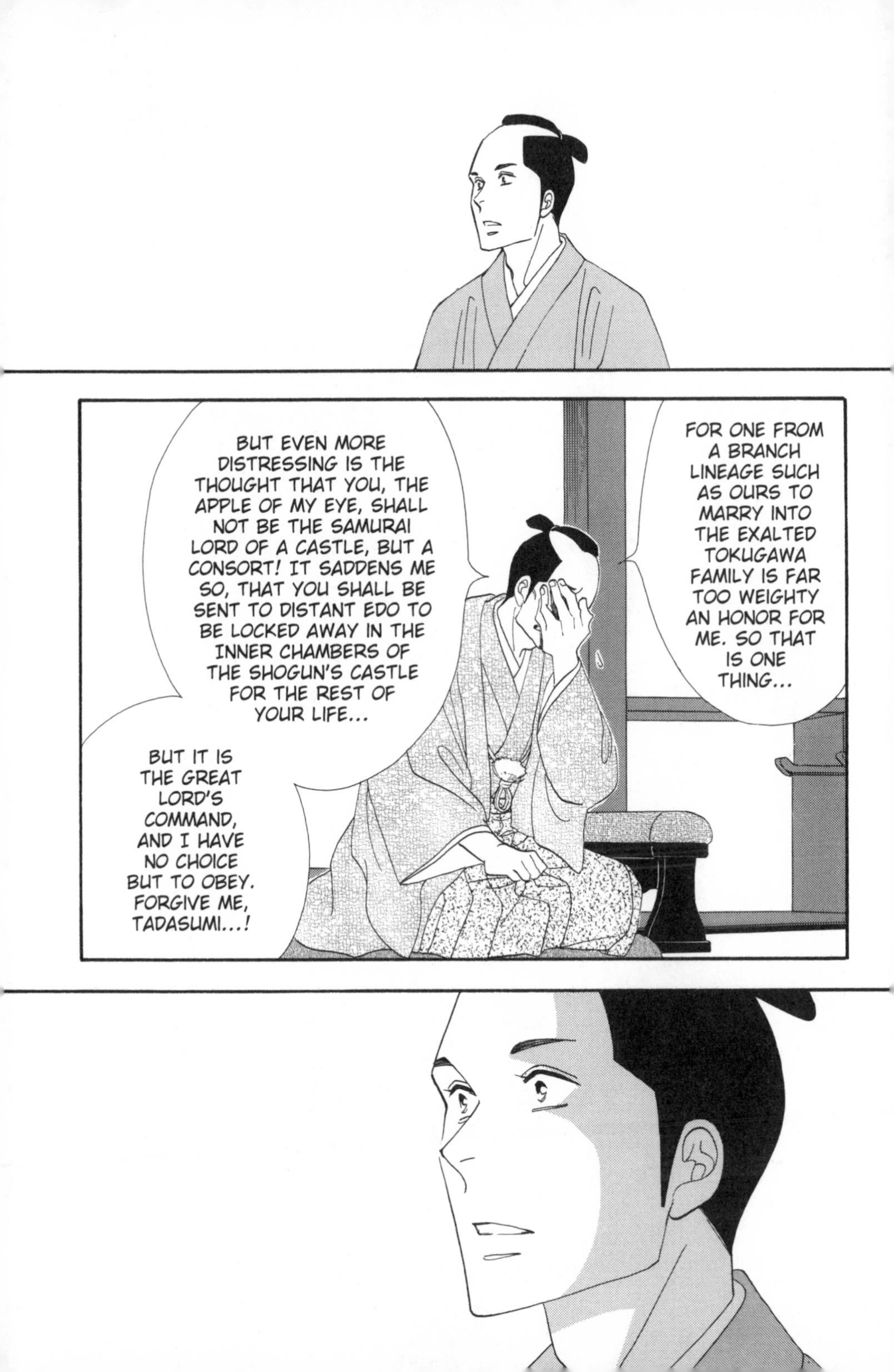
FOR ONE FROM A BRANCH LINEAGE SUCH AS OURS TO MARRY INTO THE EXALTED TOKUGAWA FAMILY IS FAR TOO WEIGHTY AN HONOR FOR ME. SO THAT IS ONE THING...
BUT EVEN MORE DISTRESSING IS THE THOUGHT THAT YOU, THE APPLE OF MY EYE, SHALL NOT BE THE SAMURAI LORD OF A CASTLE, BUT A CONSORT! IT SADDENS ME SO, THAT YOU SHALL BE SENT TO DISTANT EDO TO BE LOCKED AWAY IN THE INNER CHAMBERS OF THE SHOGUN'S CASTLE FOR THE REST OF YOUR LIFE...
BUT IT IS THE GREAT LORD'S COMMAND, AND I HAVE NO CHOICE BUT TO OBEY. FORGIVE ME, TADASUMI...!

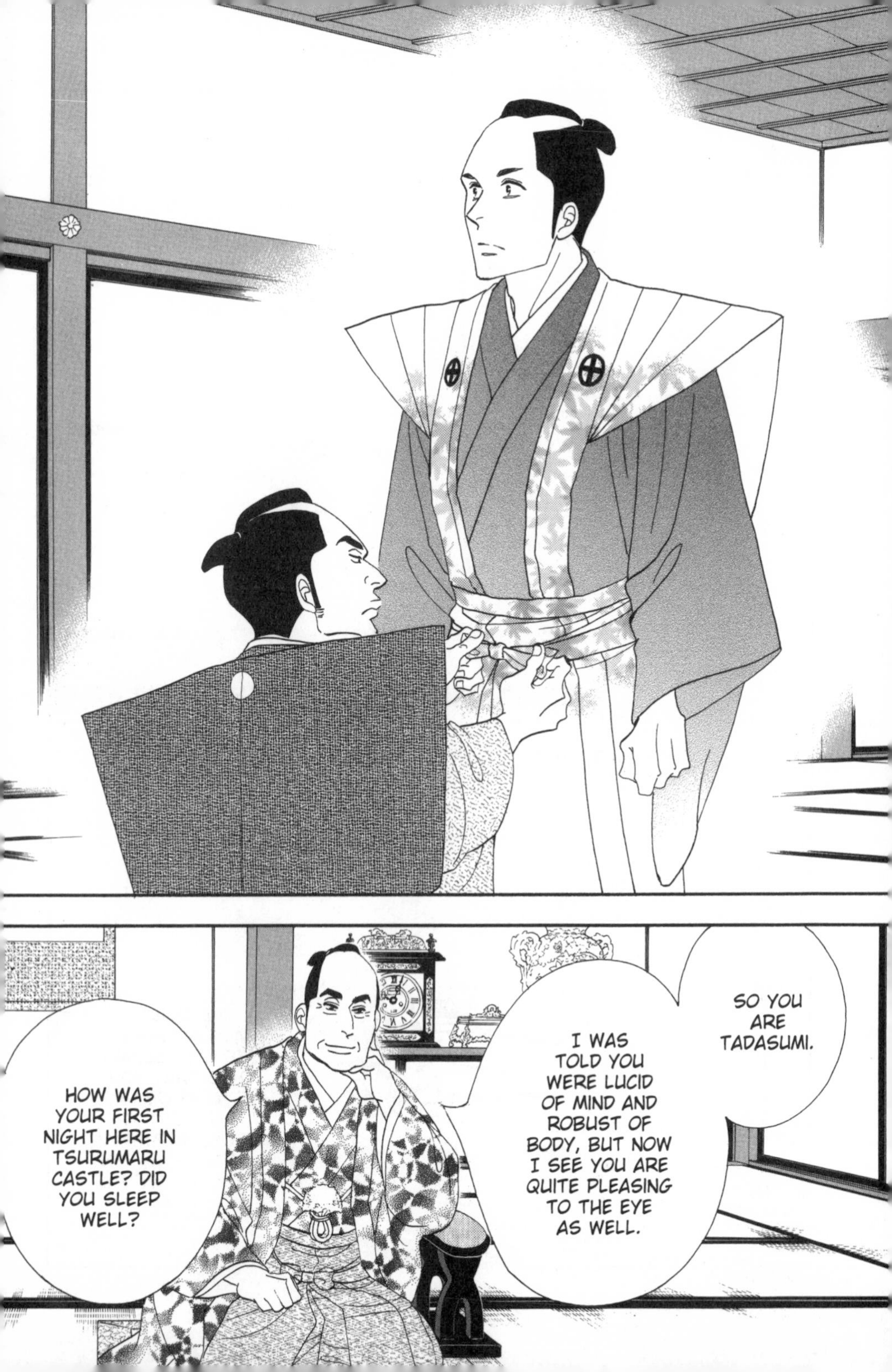
SO YOU ARE TADASUMI.
I WAS TOLD YOU WERE LUCID OF MIND AND ROBUST OF BODY, BUT NOW I SEE YOU ARE QUITE PLEASING TO THE EYE AS WELL.
HOW WAS YOUR FIRST NIGHT HERE IN TSURUMARU CASTLE? DID YOU SLEEP WELL?

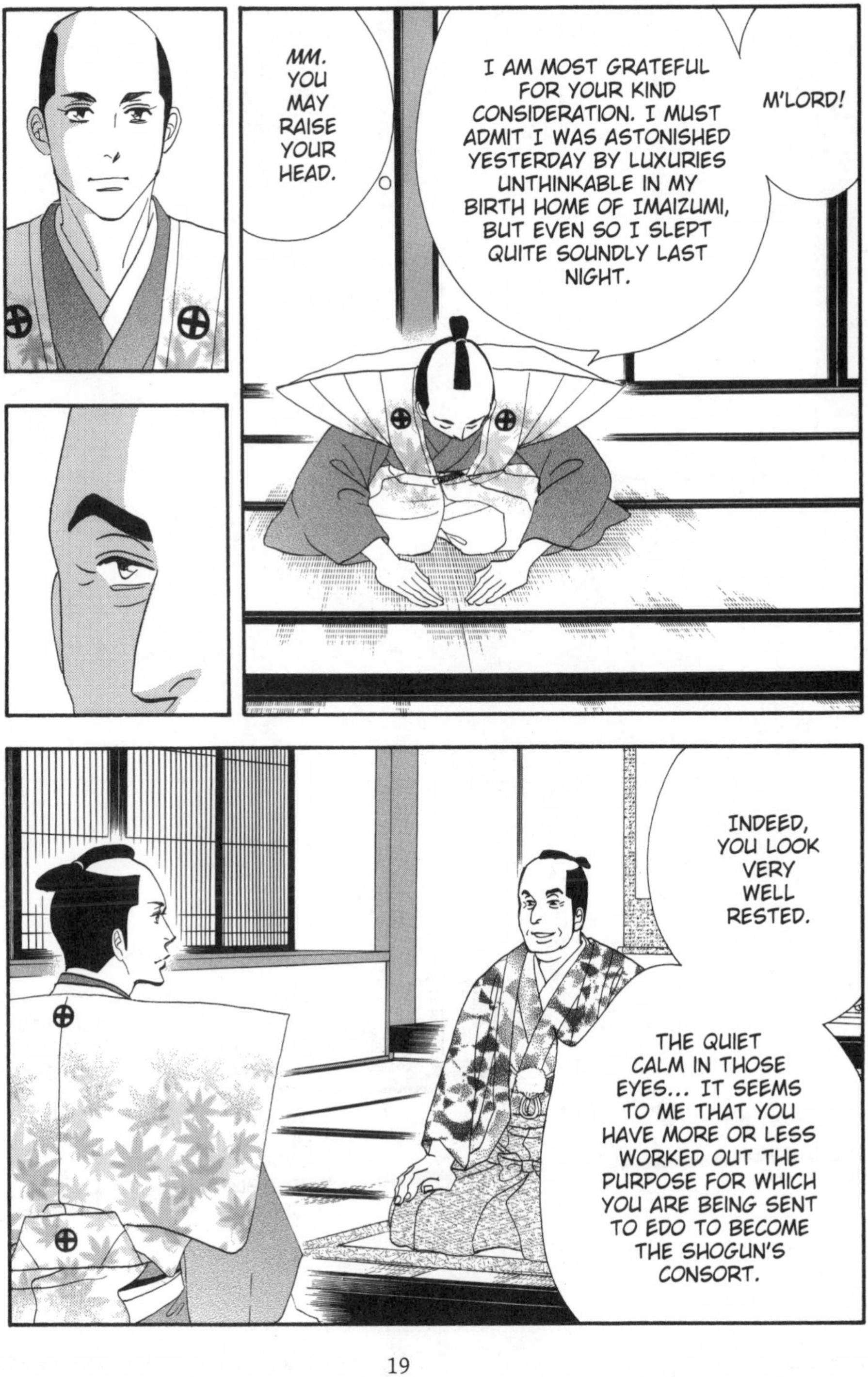
M'LORD!
I AM MOST GRATEFUL FOR YOUR KIND CONSIDERATION. I MUST ADMIT I WAS ASTONISHED YESTERDAY BY LUXURIES UNTHINKABLE IN MY BIRTH HOME OF IMAIZUMI, BUT EVEN SO I SLEPT QUITE SOUNDLY LAST NIGHT.
MM. YOU MAY RAISE YOUR HEAD.
INDEED, YOU LOOK VERY WELL RESTED.
THE QUIET CALM IN THOSE EYES... IT SEEMS TO ME THAT YOU HAVE MORE OR LESS WORKED OUT THE PURPOSE FOR WHICH YOU ARE BEING SENT TO EDO TO BECOME THE SHOGUN'S CONSORT.

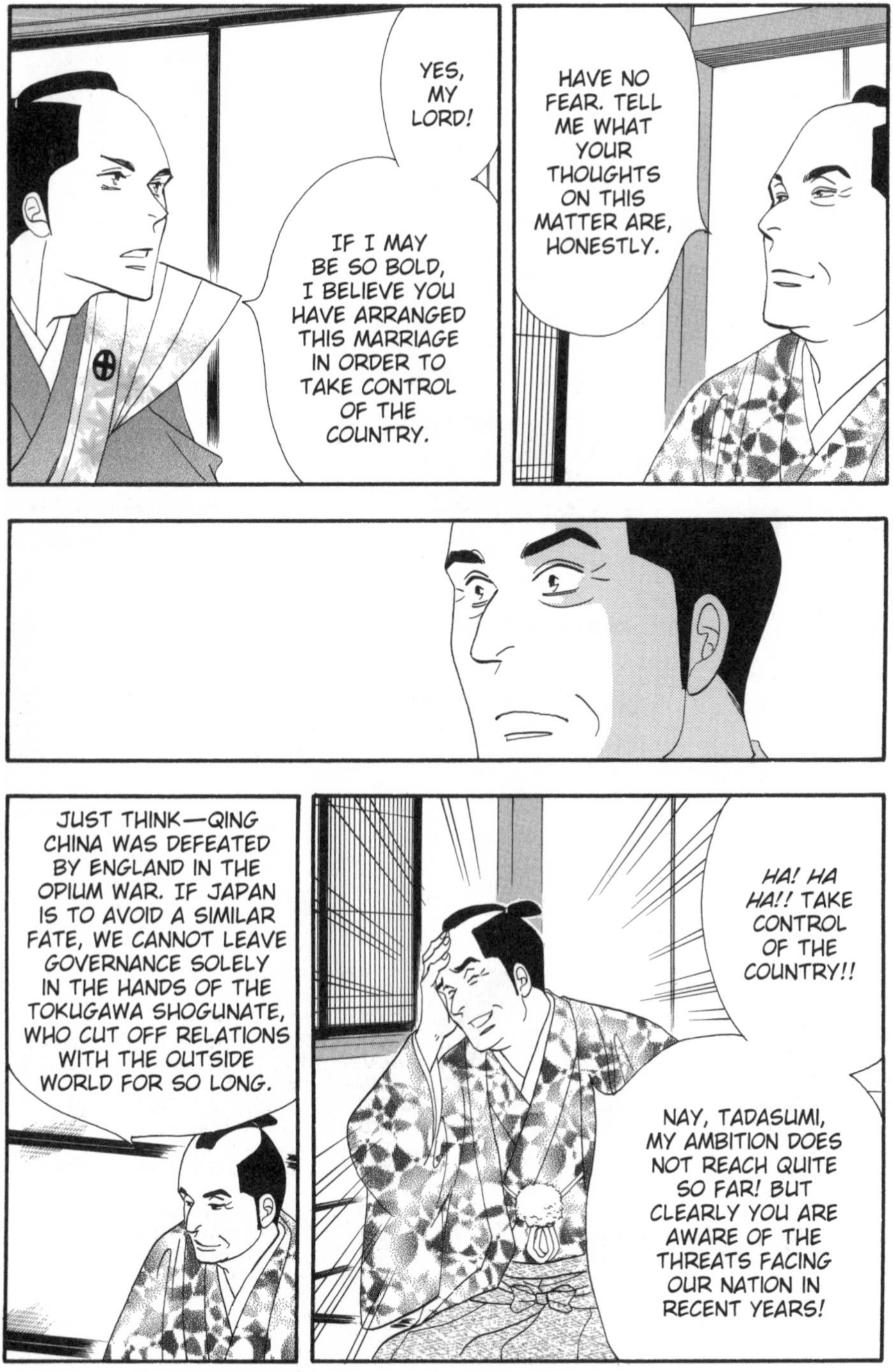
HAVE NO FEAR. TELL ME WHAT YOUR THOUGHTS ON THIS MATTER ARE, HONESTLY.
YES, MY LORD!
IF I MAY BE SO BOLD, I BELIEVE YOU HAVE ARRANGED THIS MARRIAGE IN ORDER TO TAKE CONTROL OF THE COUNTRY.
HA! HA HA!! TAKE CONTROL OF THE COUNTRY!!
NAY, TADASUMI, MY AMBITION DOES NOT REACH QUITE SO FAR! BUT CLEARLY YOU ARE AWARE OF THE THREATS FACING OUR NATION IN RECENT YEARS!
JUST THINK—QING CHINA WAS DEFEATED BY ENGLAND IN THE OPIUM WAR. IF JAPAN IS TO AVOID A SIMILAR FATE, WE CANNOT LEAVE GOVERNANCE SOLELY IN THE HANDS OF THE TOKUGAWA SHOGUNATE, WHO CUT OFF RELATIONS WITH THE OUTSIDE WORLD FOR SO LONG.

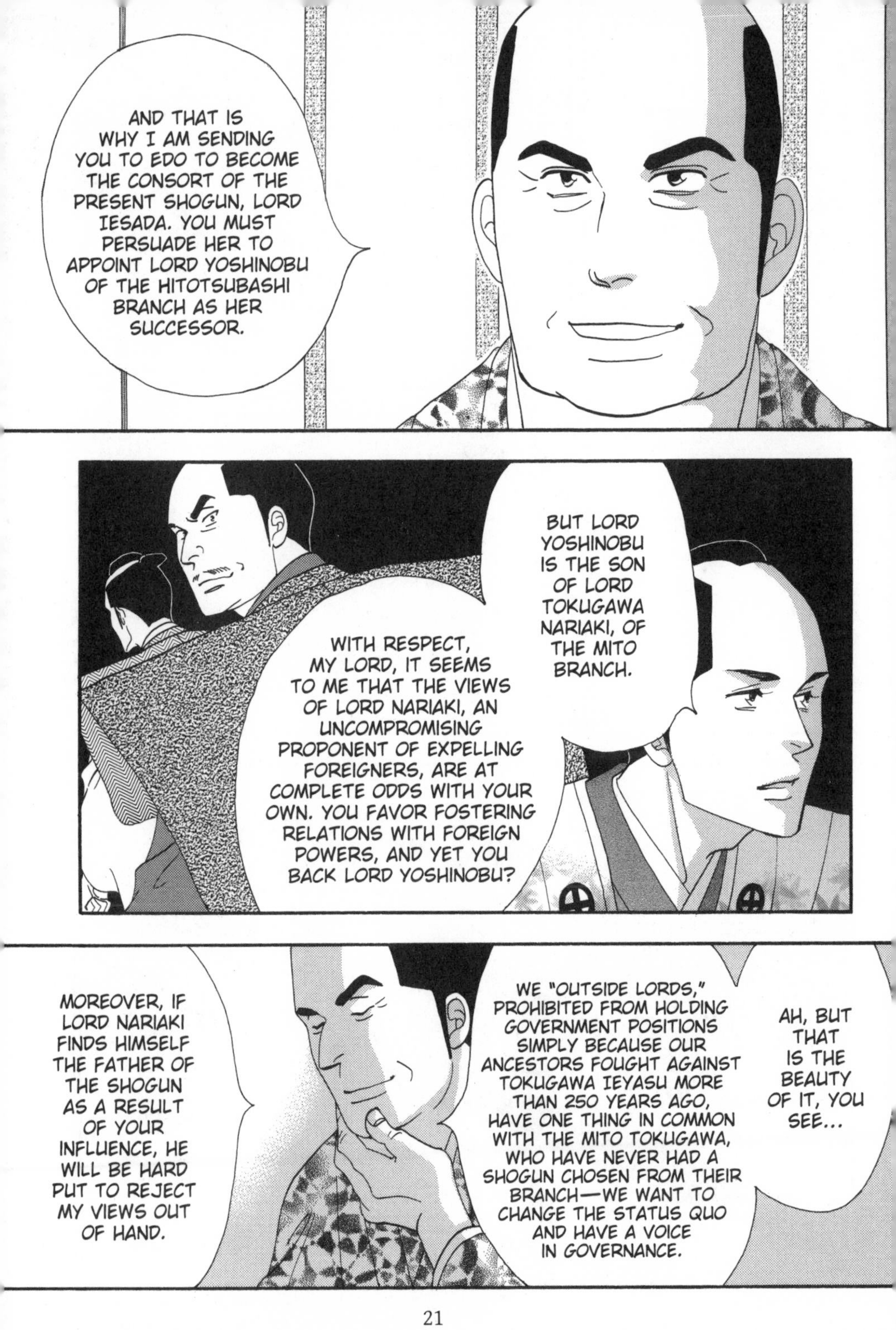
AND THAT IS WHY I AM SENDING YOU TO EDO TO BECOME THE CONSORT OF THE PRESENT SHOGUN, LORD IESADA. YOU MUST PERSUADE HER TO APPOINT LORD YOSHINOBU OF THE HITOTSUBASHI BRANCH AS HER SUCCESSOR.
BUT LORD YOSHINOBU IS THE SON OF LORD TOKUGAWA NARIAKI, OF THE MITO BRANCH.
WITH RESPECT, MY LORD, IT SEEMS TO ME THAT THE VIEWS OF LORD NARIAKI, AN UNCOMPROMISING PROPONENT OF EXPELLING FOREIGNERS, ARE AT COMPLETE ODDS WITH YOUR OWN. YOU FAVOR FOSTERING RELATIONS WITH FOREIGN POWERS, AND YET YOU BACK LORD YOSHINOBU?
AH, BUT THAT IS THE BEAUTY OF IT, YOU SEE...
WE "OUTSIDE LORDS," PROHIBITED FROM HOLDING GOVERNMENT POSITIONS SIMPLY BECAUSE OUR ANCESTORS FOUGHT AGAINST TOKUGAWA IEYASU MORE THAN 250 YEARS AGO, HAVE ONE THING IN COMMON WITH THE MITO TOKUGAWA, WHO HAVE NEVER HAD A SHOGUN CHOSEN FROM THEIR BRANCH—WE WANT TO CHANGE THE STATUS QUO AND HAVE A VOICE IN GOVERNANCE.
MOREOVER, IF LORD NARIAKI FINDS HIMSELF THE FATHER OF THE SHOGUN AS A RESULT OF YOUR INFLUENCE, HE WILL BE HARD PUT TO REJECT MY VIEWS OUT OF HAND.

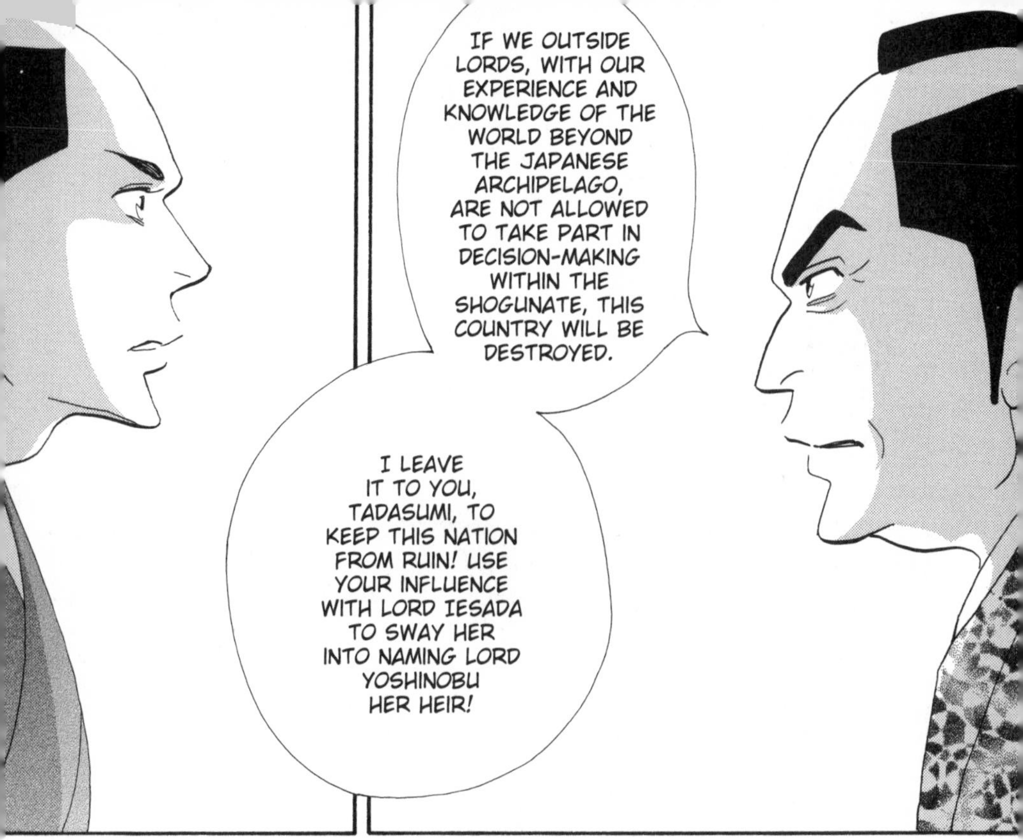
IF WE OUTSIDE LORDS, WITH OUR EXPERIENCE AND KNOWLEDGE OF THE WORLD BEYOND THE JAPANESE ARCHIPELAGO, ARE NOT ALLOWED TO TAKE PART IN DECISION-MAKING WITHIN THE SHOGUNATE, THIS COUNTRY WILL BE DESTROYED.
I LEAVE IT TO YOU, TADASUMI, TO KEEP THIS NATION FROM RUIN! USE YOUR INFLUENCE WITH LORD IESADA TO SWAY HER INTO NAMING LORD YOSHINOBU HER HEIR!
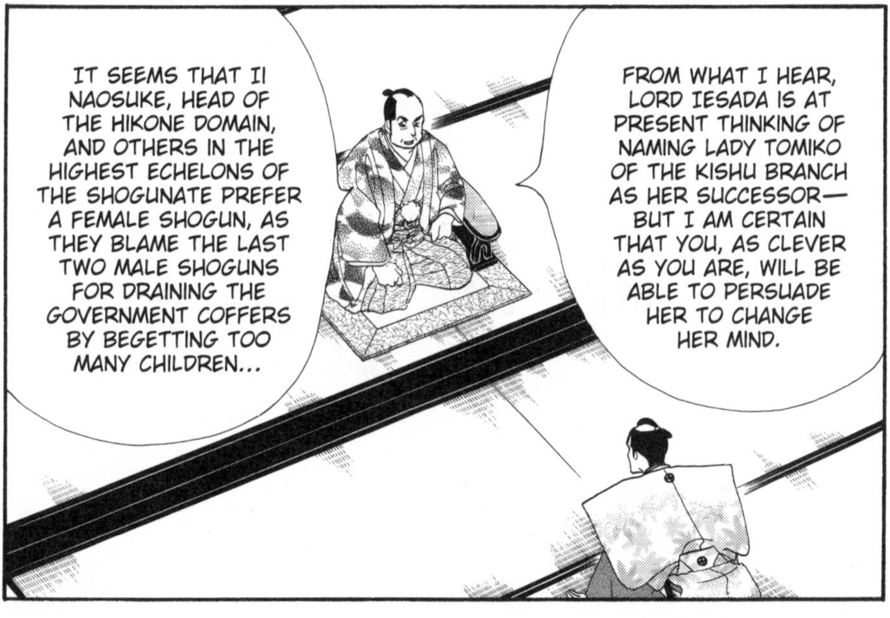
FROM WHAT I HEAR, LORD IESADA IS AT PRESENT THINKING OF NAMING LADY TOMIKO OF THE KISHU BRANCH AS HER SUCCESSOR—BUT I AM CERTAIN THAT YOU, AS CLEVER AS YOU ARE, WILL BE ABLE TO PERSUADE HER TO CHANGE HER MIND.
IT SEEMS THAT II NAOSUKE, HEAD OF THE HIKONE DOMAIN, AND OTHERS IN THE HIGHEST ECHELONS OF THE SHOGUNATE PREFER A FEMALE SHOGUN, AS THEY BLAME THE LAST TWO MALE SHOGUNS FOR DRAINING THE GOVERNMENT COFFERS BY BEGETTING TOO MANY CHILDREN...

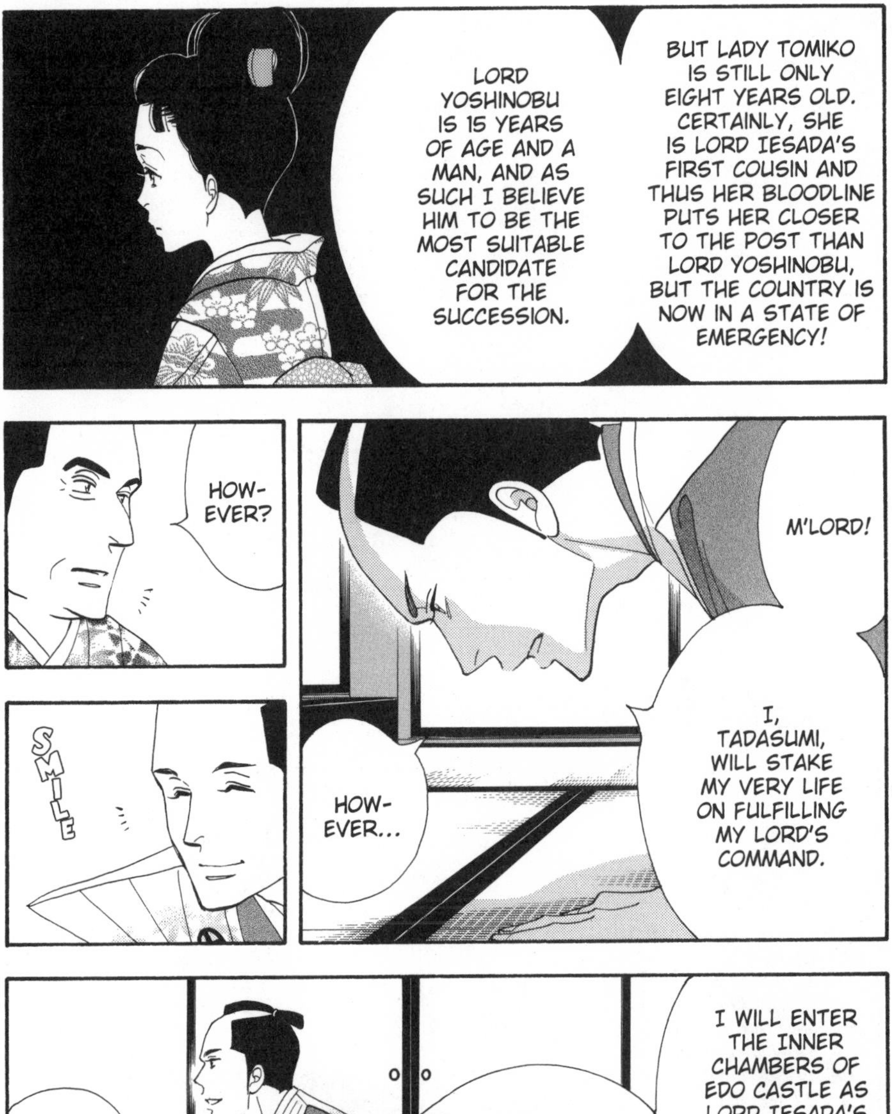
BUT LADY TOMIKO IS STILL ONLY EIGHT YEARS OLD. CERTAINLY, SHE IS LORD IESADA'S FIRST COUSIN AND THUS HER BLOODLINE PUTS HER CLOSER TO THE POST THAN LORD YOSHINOBU, BUT THE COUNTRY IS NOW IN A STATE OF EMERGENCY!
LORD YOSHINOBU IS 15 YEARS OF AGE AND A MAN, AND AS SUCH I BELIEVE HIM TO BE THE MOST SUITABLE CANDIDATE FOR THE SUCCESSION.
M'LORD!
I, TADASUMI, WILL STAKE MY VERY LIFE ON FULFILLING MY LORD'S COMMAND.
HOW-EVER...
HOW-EVER?
SMILE
I WILL ENTER THE INNER CHAMBERS OF EDO CASTLE AS LORD IESADA'S CONSORT...AND MY DUTIES WILL PRIMARILY BE IN THE MARITAL BEDCHAMBER.
MY LORD DOES ME GREAT HONOR TO BELIEVE THAT I AM SOUND OF MIND, BUT EVEN MORE THAN THAT, I AM QUITE HALE OF BODY. IT IS THEREFORE A DISTINCT POSSIBILITY THAT I SHALL GET LORD IESADA WITH CHILD.
WHAT SHALL I DO THEN?

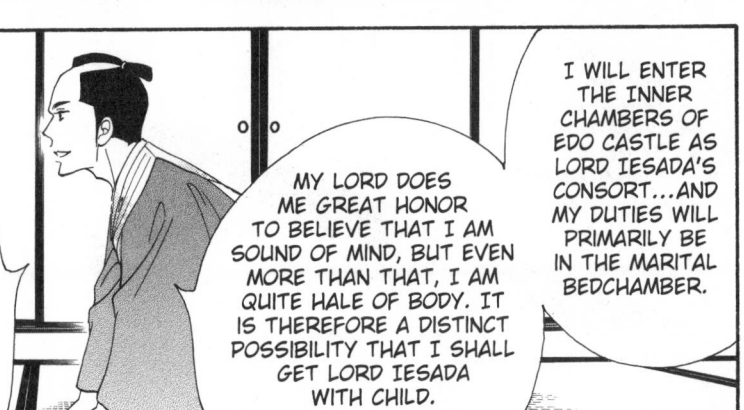

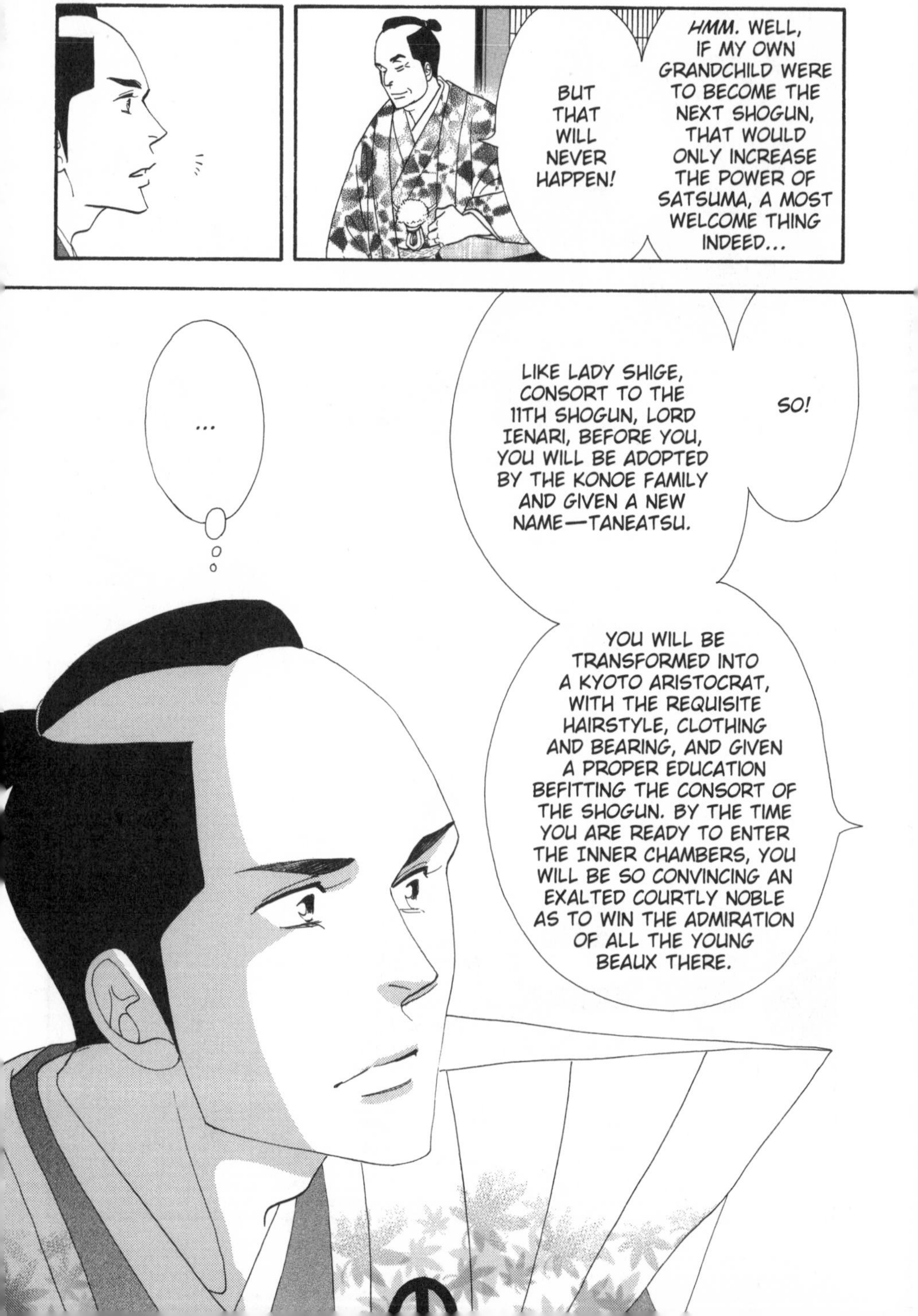
HMM. WELL, IF MY OWN GRANDCHILD WERE TO BECOME THE NEXT SHOGUN, THAT WOULD ONLY INCREASE THE POWER OF SATSUMA, A MOST WELCOME THING INDEED...
BUT THAT WILL NEVER HAPPEN!
SO!
LIKE LADY SHIGE, CONSORT TO THE 11TH SHOGUN, LORD IENARI, BEFORE YOU, YOU WILL BE ADOPTED BY THE KONOE FAMILY AND GIVEN A NEW NAME—TANEATSU.
YOU WILL BE TRANSFORMED INTO A KYOTO ARISTOCRAT, WITH THE REQUISITE HAIRSTYLE, CLOTHING AND BEARING, AND GIVEN A PROPER EDUCATION BEFITTING THE CONSORT OF THE SHOGUN. BY THE TIME YOU ARE READY TO ENTER THE INNER CHAMBERS, YOU WILL BE SO CONVINCING AN EXALTED COURTLY NOBLE AS TO WIN THE ADMIRATION OF ALL THE YOUNG BEAUX THERE.
...

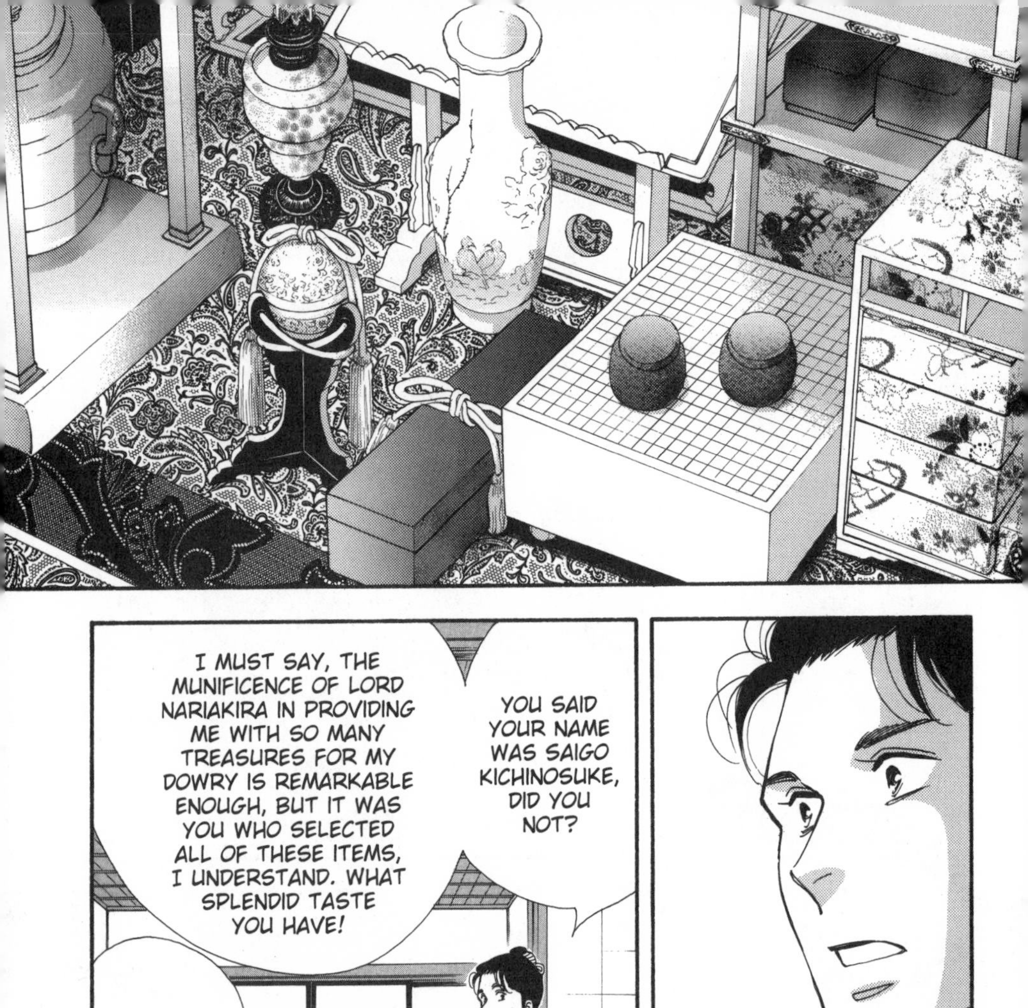
WHOA...!!
YOU SAID YOUR NAME WAS SAIGO KICHINOSUKE, DID YOU NOT?
I MUST SAY, THE MUNIFICENCE OF LORD NARIAKIRA IN PROVIDING ME WITH SO MANY TREASURES FOR MY DOWRY IS REMARKABLE ENOUGH, BUT IT WAS YOU WHO SELECTED ALL OF THESE ITEMS, I UNDERSTAND. WHAT SPLENDID TASTE YOU HAVE!
N-NOT AT ALL!!

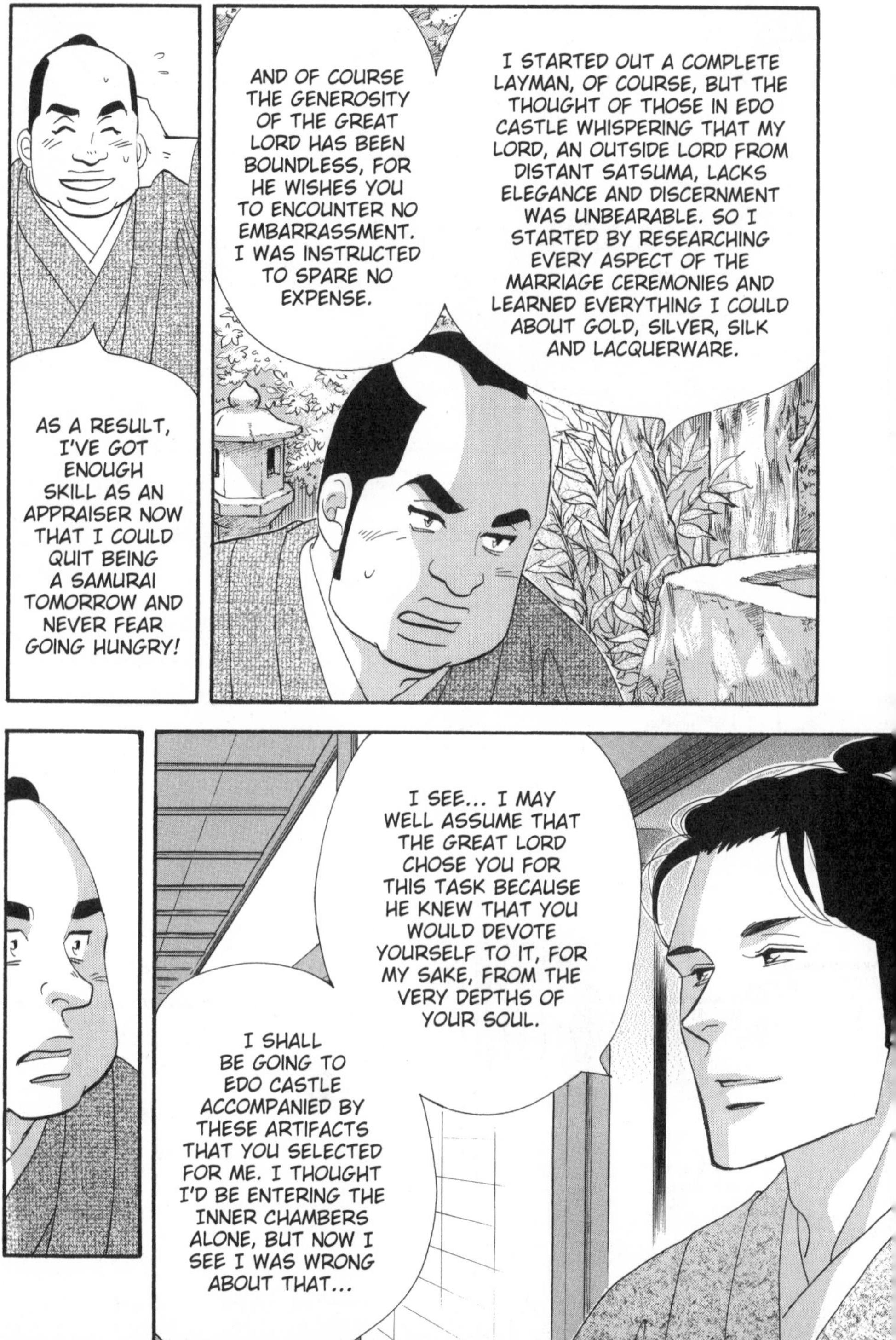
I STARTED OUT A COMPLETE LAYMAN, OF COURSE, BUT THE THOUGHT OF THOSE IN EDO CASTLE WHISPERING THAT MY LORD, AN OUTSIDE LORD FROM DISTANT SATSUMA, LACKS ELEGANCE AND DISCERNMENT WAS UNBEARABLE. SO I STARTED BY RESEARCHING EVERY ASPECT OF THE MARRIAGE CEREMONIES AND LEARNED EVERYTHING I COULD ABOUT GOLD, SILVER, SILK AND LACQUERWARE.
AND OF COURSE THE GENEROSITY OF THE GREAT LORD HAS BEEN BOUNDLESS, FOR HE WISHES YOU TO ENCOUNTER NO EMBARRASSMENT. I WAS INSTRUCTED TO SPARE NO EXPENSE.
AS A RESULT, I'VE GOT ENOUGH SKILL AS AN APPRAISER NOW THAT I COULD QUIT BEING A SAMURAI TOMORROW AND NEVER FEAR GOING HUNGRY!
I SEE... I MAY WELL ASSUME THAT THE GREAT LORD CHOSE YOU FOR THIS TASK BECAUSE HE KNEW THAT YOU WOULD DEVOTE YOURSELF TO IT, FOR MY SAKE, FROM THE VERY DEPTHS OF YOUR SOUL.
I SHALL BE GOING TO EDO CASTLE ACCOMPANIED BY THESE ARTIFACTS THAT YOU SELECTED FOR ME. I THOUGHT I'D BE ENTERING THE INNER CHAMBERS ALONE, BUT NOW I SEE I WAS WRONG ABOUT THAT...

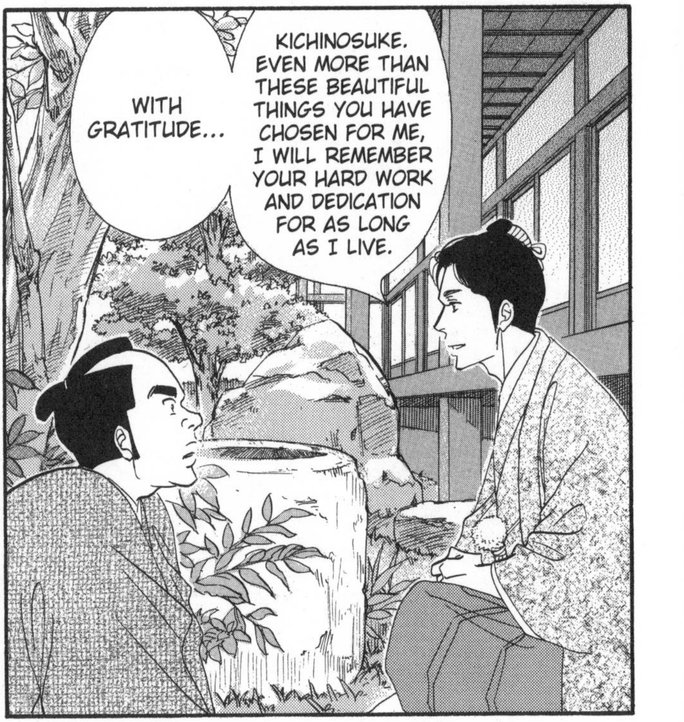
KICHINOSUKE. EVEN MORE THAN THESE BEAUTIFUL THINGS YOU HAVE CHOSEN FOR ME, I WILL REMEMBER YOUR HARD WORK AND DEDICATION FOR AS LONG AS I LIVE.
WITH GRATITUDE...
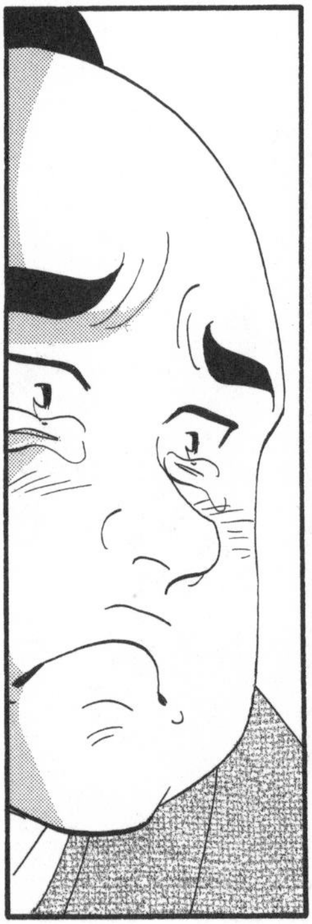
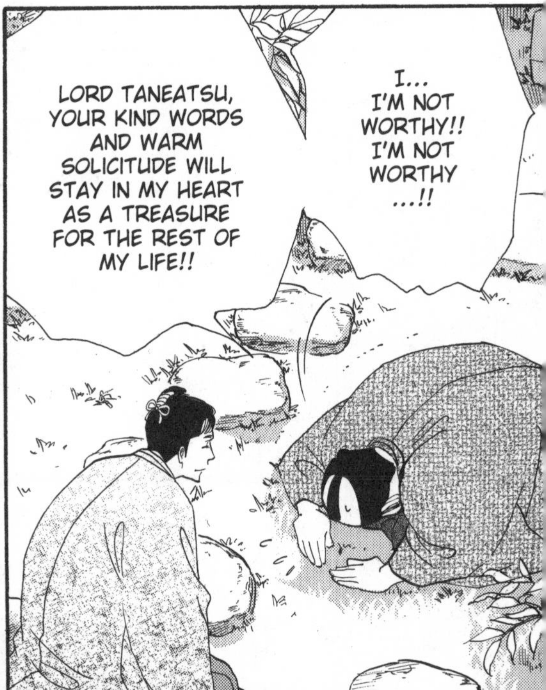
I... I'M NOT WORTHY!! I'M NOT WORTHY ...!!
LORD TANEATSU, YOUR KIND WORDS AND WARM SOLICITUDE WILL STAY IN MY HEART AS A TREASURE FOR THE REST OF MY LIFE!!
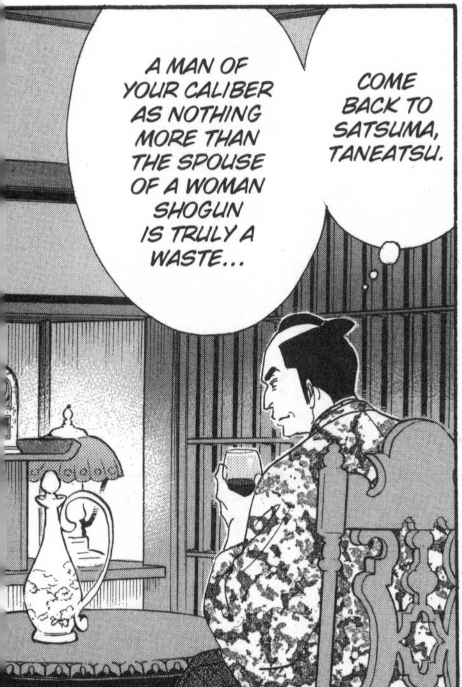
COME BACK TO SATSUMA, TANEATSU.
A MAN OF YOUR CALIBER AS NOTHING MORE THAN THE SPOUSE OF A WOMAN SHOGUN IS TRULY A WASTE...

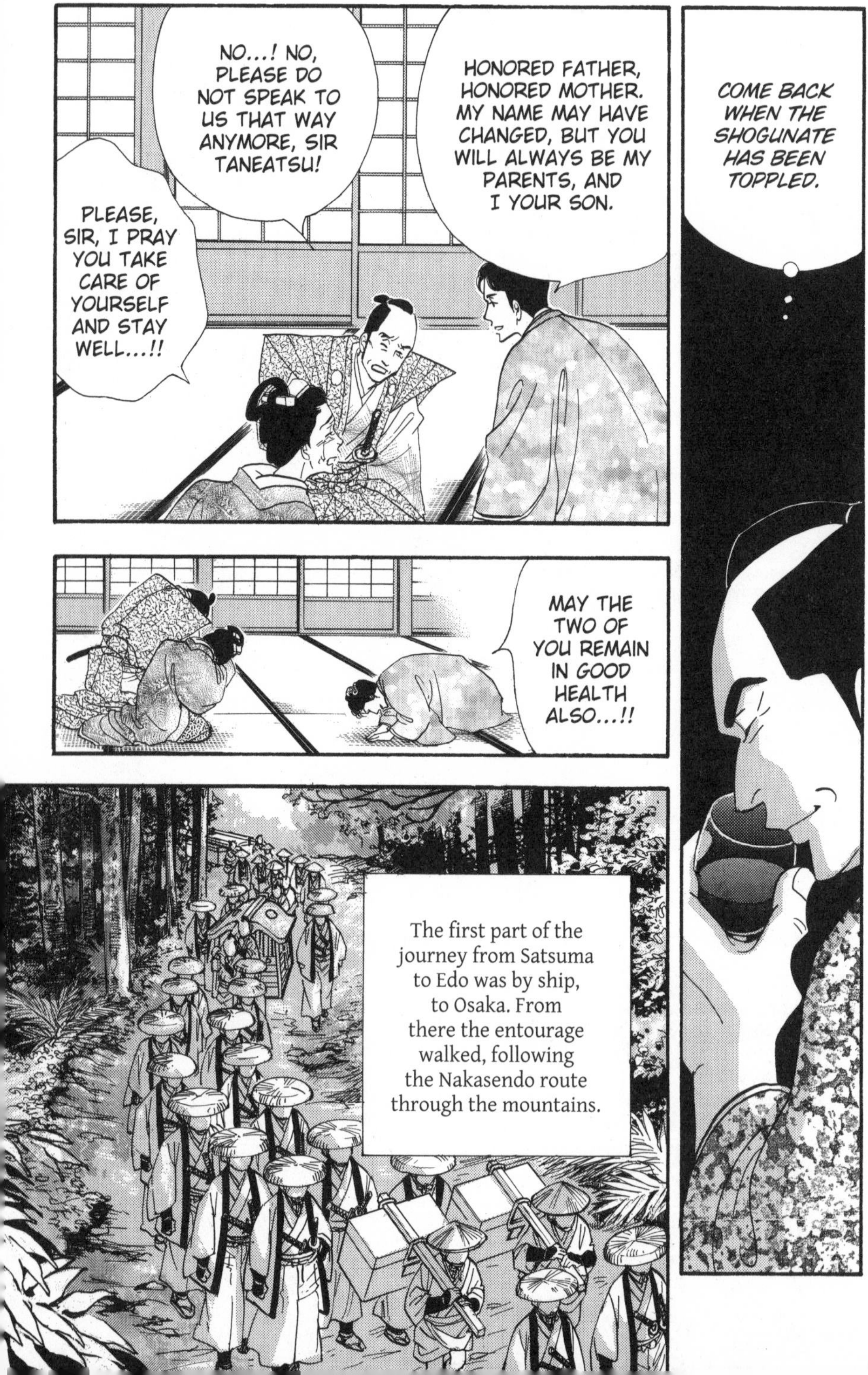
COME BACK WHEN THE SHOGUNATE HAS BEEN TOPPLED.
HONORED FATHER, HONORED MOTHER. MY NAME MAY HAVE CHANGED, BUT YOU WILL ALWAYS BE MY PARENTS, AND I YOUR SON.
NO...! NO, PLEASE DO NOT SPEAK TO US THAT WAY ANYMORE, SIR TANEATSU!
PLEASE, SIR, I PRAY YOU TAKE CARE OF YOURSELF AND STAY WELL...!!
MAY THE TWO OF YOU REMAIN IN GOOD HEALTH ALSO...!!
The first part of the journey from Satsuma to Edo was by ship, to Osaka. From there the entourage walked, following the Nakasendo route through the mountains.

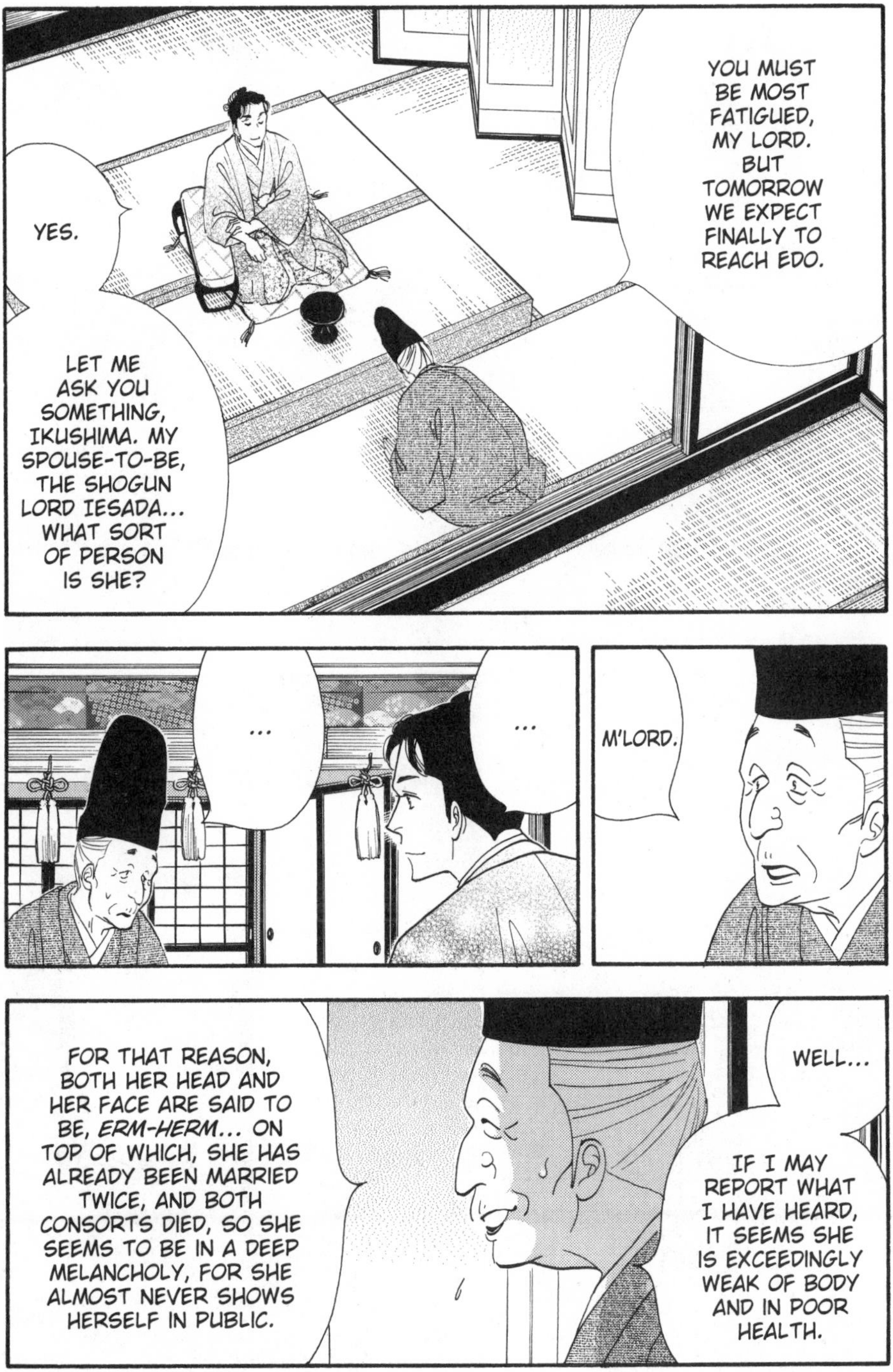
YOU MUST BE MOST FATIGUED, MY LORD. BUT TOMORROW WE EXPECT FINALLY TO REACH EDO.
YES.
LET ME ASK YOU SOMETHING, IKUSHIMA. MY SPOUSE-TO-BE, THE SHOGUN LORD IESADA... WHAT SORT OF PERSON IS SHE?
M'LORD.
...
...
WELL...
IF I MAY REPORT WHAT I HAVE HEARD, IT SEEMS SHE IS EXCEEDINGLY WEAK OF BODY AND IN POOR HEALTH.
FOR THAT REASON, BOTH HER HEAD AND HER FACE ARE SAID TO BE, *ERM-HERM*... ON TOP OF WHICH, SHE HAS ALREADY BEEN MARRIED TWICE, AND BOTH CONSORTS DIED, SO SHE SEEMS TO BE IN A DEEP MELANCHOLY, FOR SHE ALMOST NEVER SHOWS HERSELF IN PUBLIC.

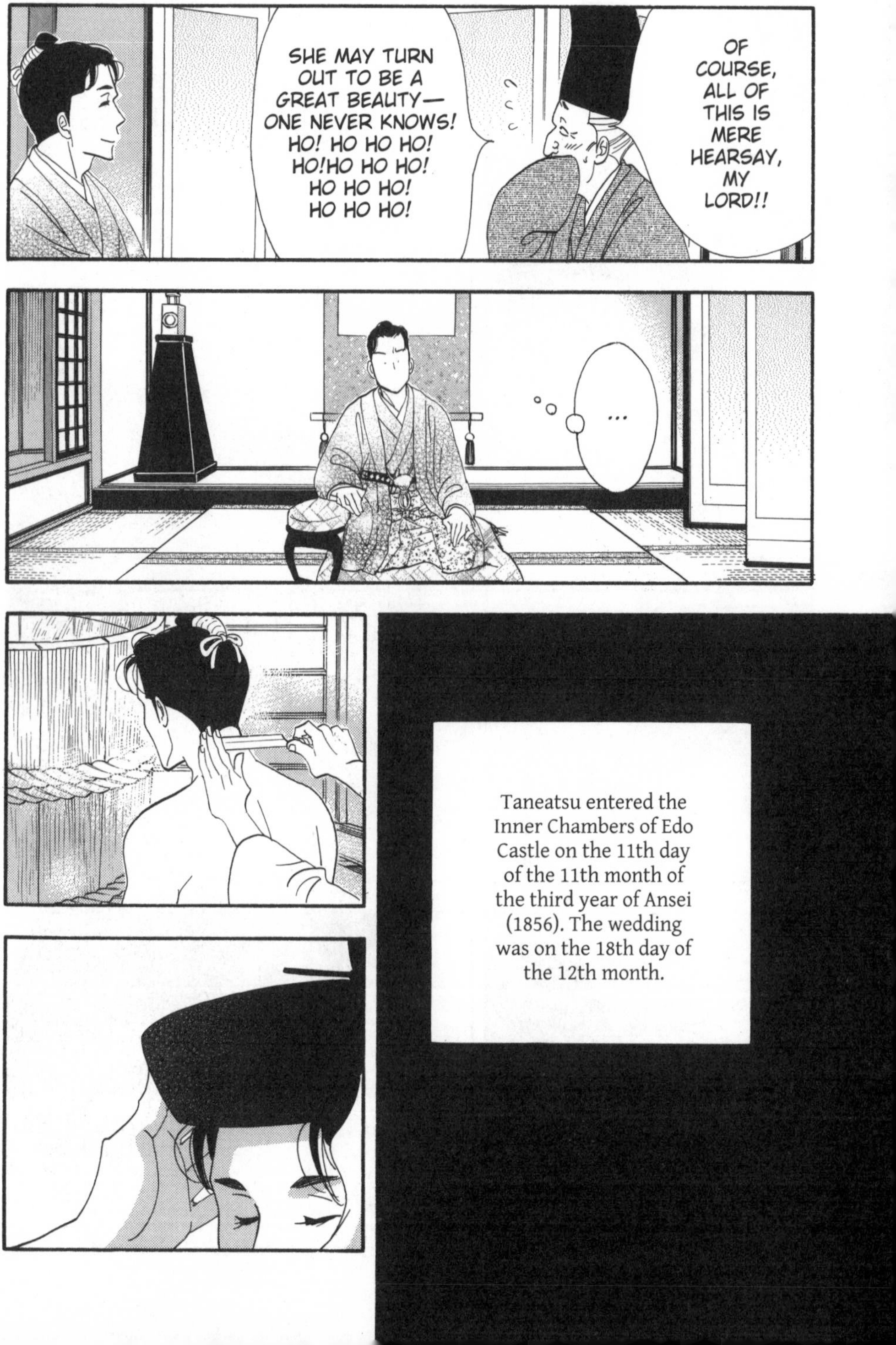
OF COURSE, ALL OF THIS IS MERE HEARSAY, MY LORD!!
SHE MAY TURN OUT TO BE A GREAT BEAUTY— ONE NEVER KNOWS! HO! HO HO HO! HO!HO HO HO! HO HO HO! HO HO HO!
...
Taneatsu entered the Inner Chambers of Edo Castle on the 11th day of the 11th month of the third year of Ansei (1856). The wedding was on the 18th day of the 12th month.

NOW...

I WILL FINALLY SEE WHAT SORT OF LADY THE VERY "ERM-HERM" SHOGUN IS.

JUST ON THE OTHER SIDE OF THIS DOOR...

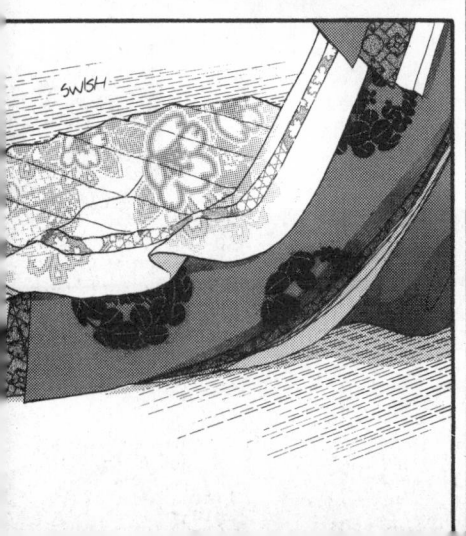

SWISH

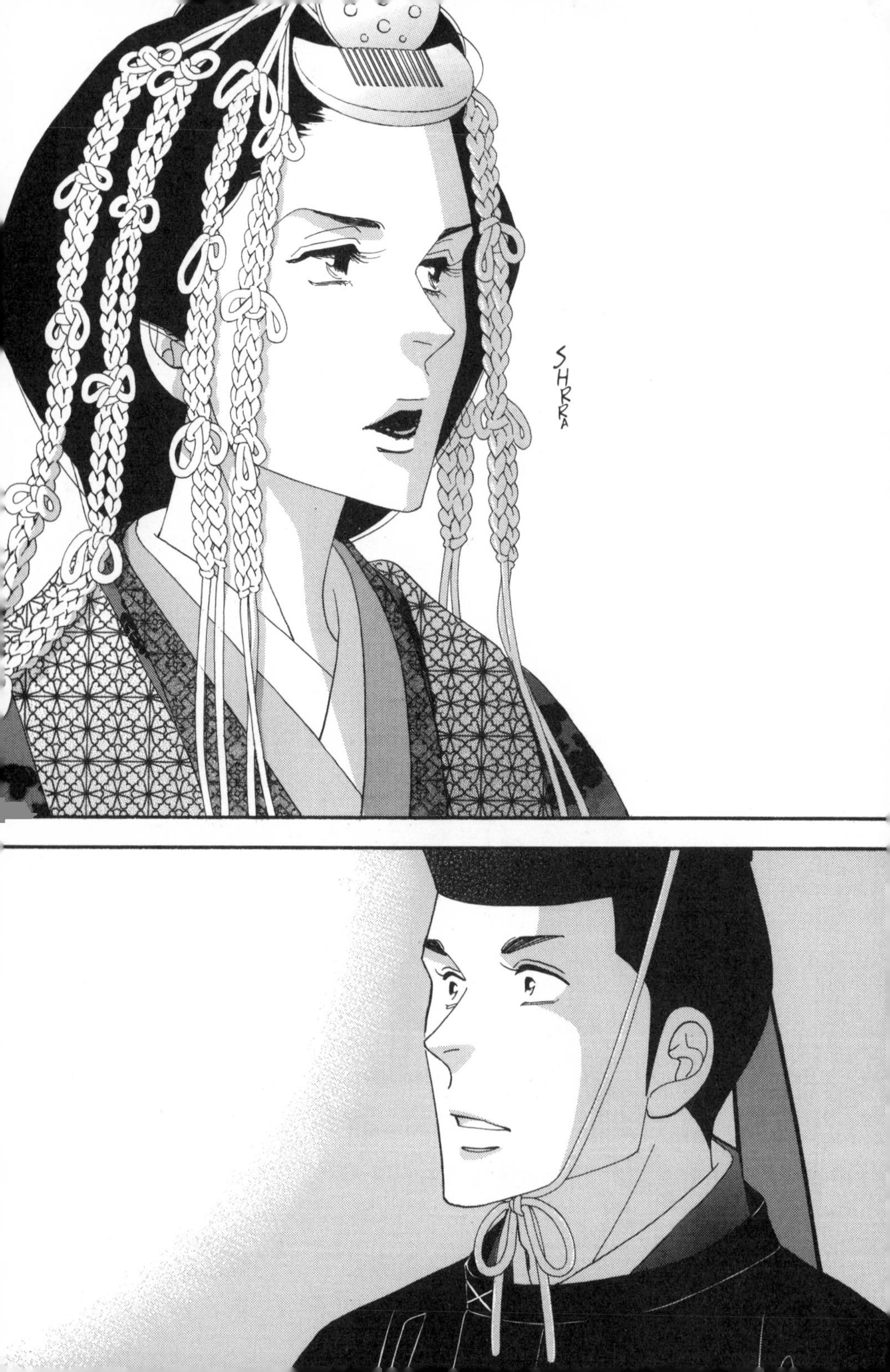
SHRRA

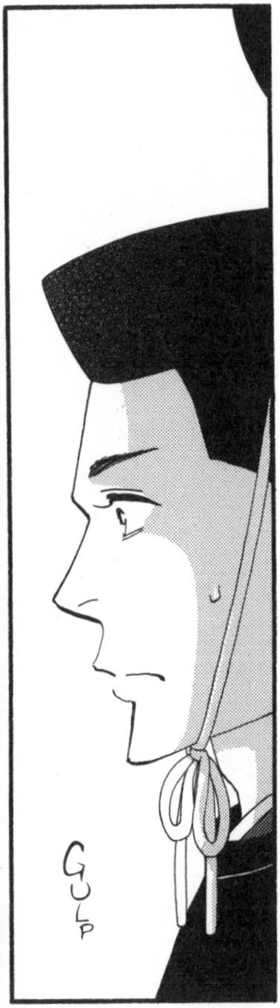
GULP

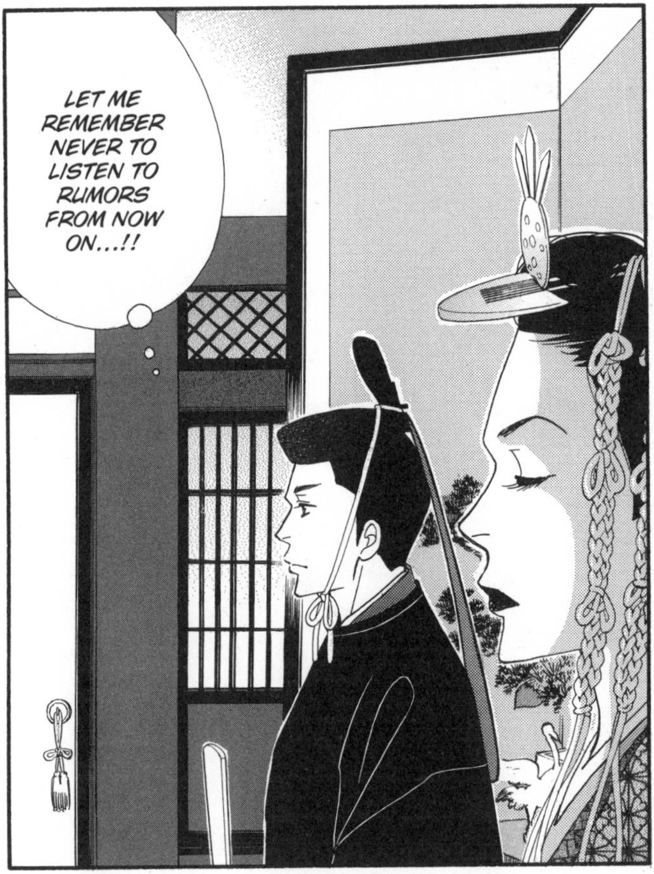
LET ME REMEMBER NEVER TO LISTEN TO RUMORS FROM NOW ON...!!

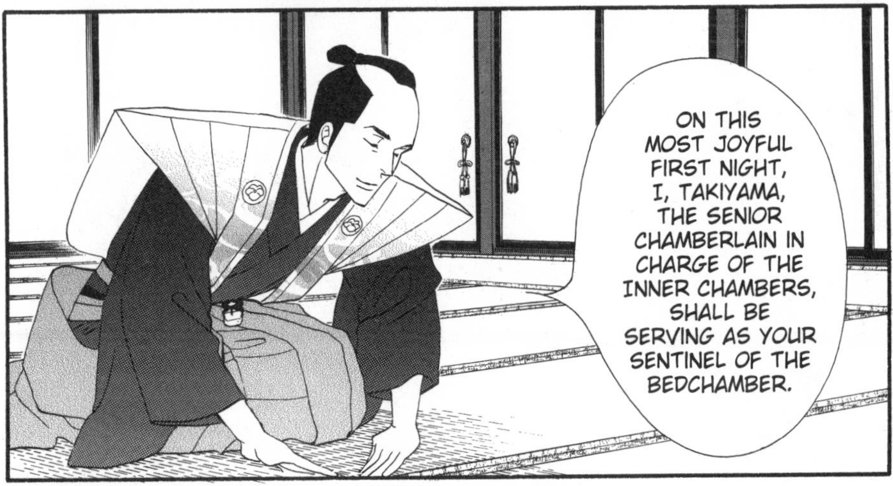
ON THIS MOST JOYFUL FIRST NIGHT, I, TAKIYAMA, THE SENIOR CHAMBERLAIN IN CHARGE OF THE INNER CHAMBERS, SHALL BE SERVING AS YOUR SENTINEL OF THE BEDCHAMBER.

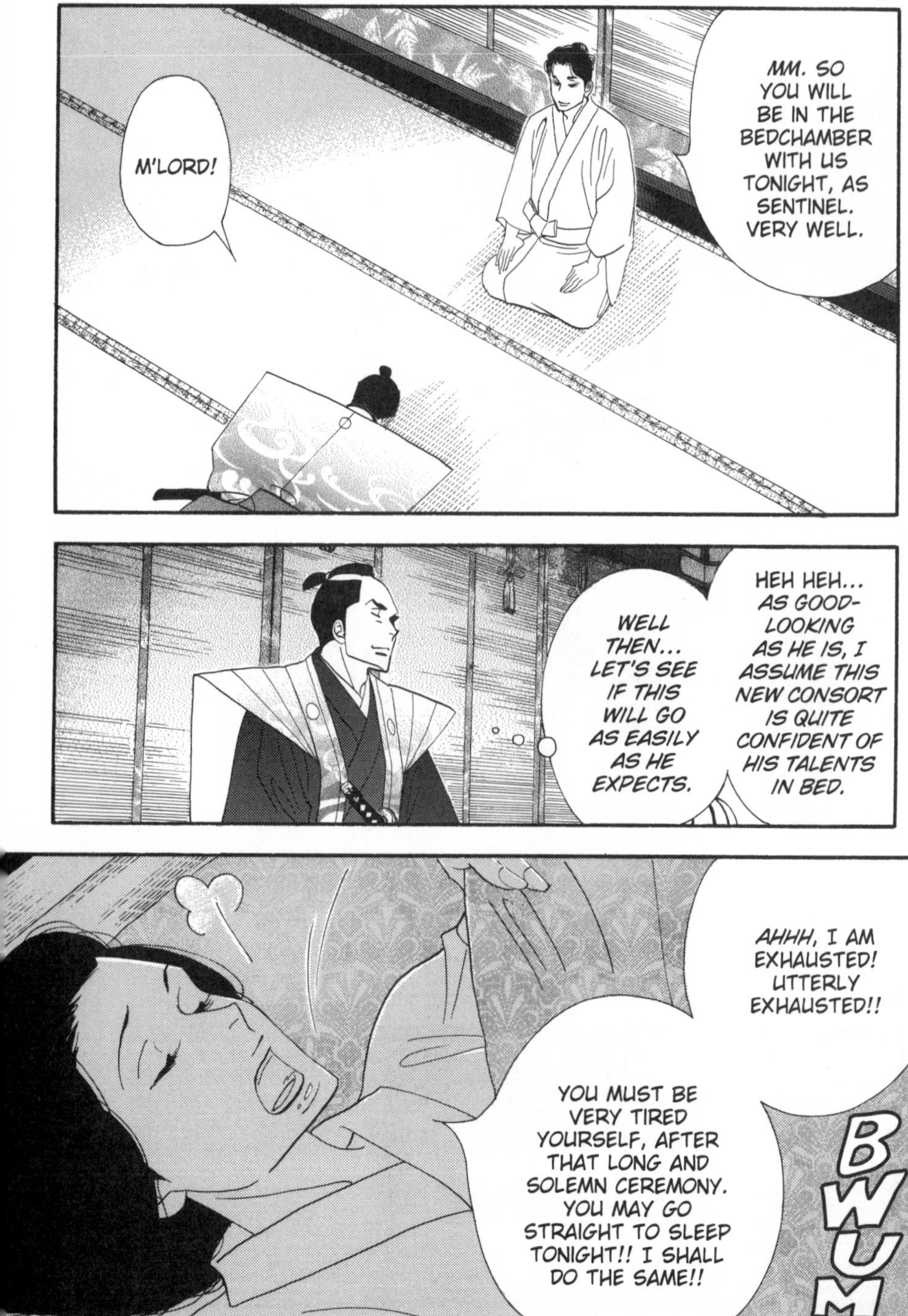
MM. SO YOU WILL BE IN THE BEDCHAMBER WITH US TONIGHT, AS SENTINEL. VERY WELL.
M'LORD!
HEH HEH... AS GOOD-LOOKING AS HE IS, I ASSUME THIS NEW CONSORT IS QUITE CONFIDENT OF HIS TALENTS IN BED.
WELL THEN... LET'S SEE IF THIS WILL GO AS EASILY AS HE EXPECTS.
AHHH, I AM EXHAUSTED! UTTERLY EXHAUSTED!!
BWUMPH
YOU MUST BE VERY TIRED YOURSELF, AFTER THAT LONG AND SOLEMN CEREMONY. YOU MAY GO STRAIGHT TO SLEEP TONIGHT!! I SHALL DO THE SAME!!

UH...

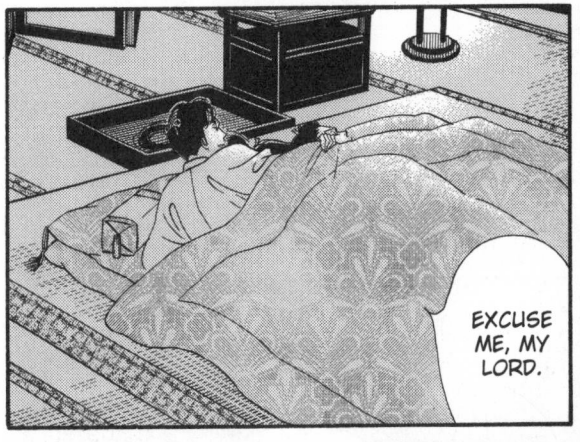

INDEED, IT WAS A VERY LONG DAY. WITH YOUR LEAVE, I SHALL GO TO SLEEP NOW.

YES.

EXCUSE ME, MY LORD.

HYAGH

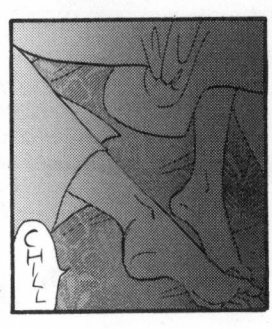

CHILL

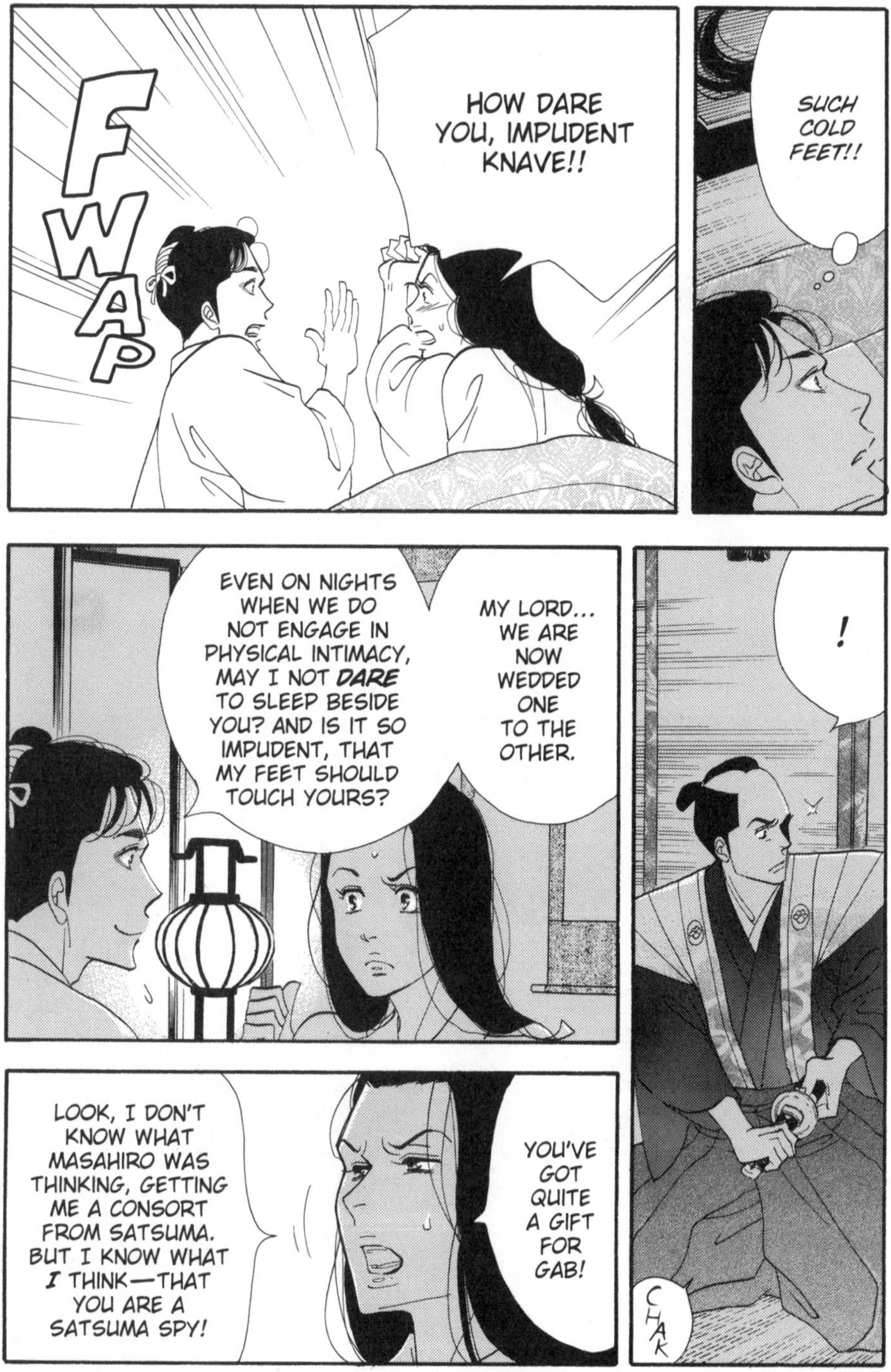
SUCH COLD FEET!!
FWAP
HOW DARE YOU, IMPUDENT KNAVE!!
!
CHAK
MY LORD... WE ARE NOW WEDDED ONE TO THE OTHER.
EVEN ON NIGHTS WHEN WE DO NOT ENGAGE IN PHYSICAL INTIMACY, MAY I NOT **DARE** TO SLEEP BESIDE YOU? AND IS IT SO IMPUDENT, THAT MY FEET SHOULD TOUCH YOURS?
YOU'VE GOT QUITE A GIFT FOR GAB!
LOOK, I DON'T KNOW WHAT MASAHIRO WAS THINKING, GETTING ME A CONSORT FROM SATSUMA. BUT I KNOW WHAT *I* THINK—THAT YOU ARE A SATSUMA SPY!

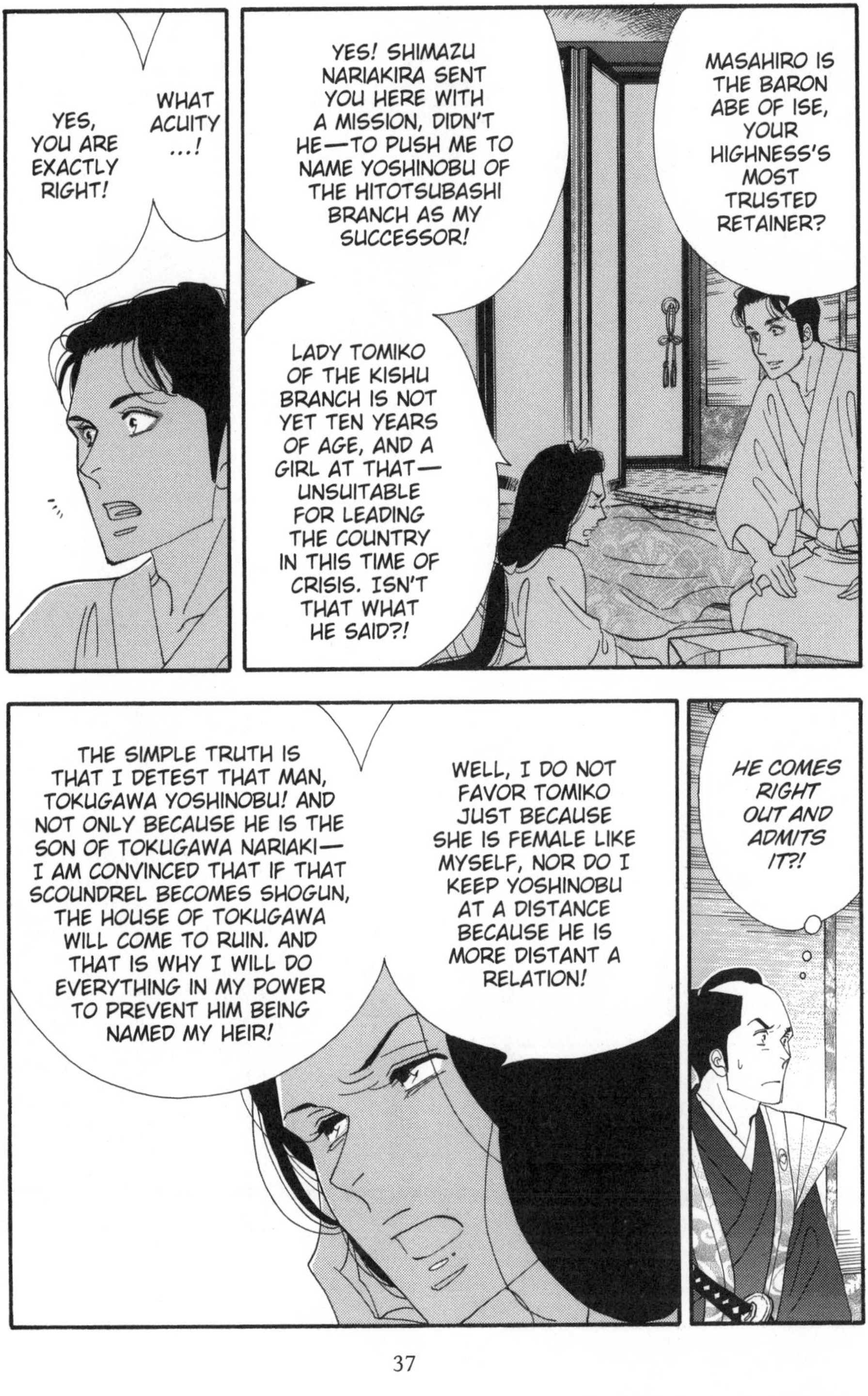

MASAHIRO IS THE BARON ABE OF ISE, YOUR HIGHNESS'S MOST TRUSTED RETAINER?
YES! SHIMAZU NARIAKIRA SENT YOU HERE WITH A MISSION, DIDN'T HE—TO PUSH ME TO NAME YOSHINOBU OF THE HITOTSUBASHI BRANCH AS MY SUCCESSOR!
LADY TOMIKO OF THE KISHU BRANCH IS NOT YET TEN YEARS OF AGE, AND A GIRL AT THAT—UNSUITABLE FOR LEADING THE COUNTRY IN THIS TIME OF CRISIS. ISN'T THAT WHAT HE SAID?!
WHAT ACUITY ...!
YES, YOU ARE EXACTLY RIGHT!
HE COMES RIGHT OUT AND ADMITS IT?!
WELL, I DO NOT FAVOR TOMIKO JUST BECAUSE SHE IS FEMALE LIKE MYSELF, NOR DO I KEEP YOSHINOBU AT A DISTANCE BECAUSE HE IS MORE DISTANT A RELATION!
THE SIMPLE TRUTH IS THAT I DETEST THAT MAN, TOKUGAWA YOSHINOBU! AND NOT ONLY BECAUSE HE IS THE SON OF TOKUGAWA NARIAKI—I AM CONVINCED THAT IF THAT SCOUNDREL BECOMES SHOGUN, THE HOUSE OF TOKUGAWA WILL COME TO RUIN. AND THAT IS WHY I WILL DO EVERYTHING IN MY POWER TO PREVENT HIM BEING NAMED MY HEIR!

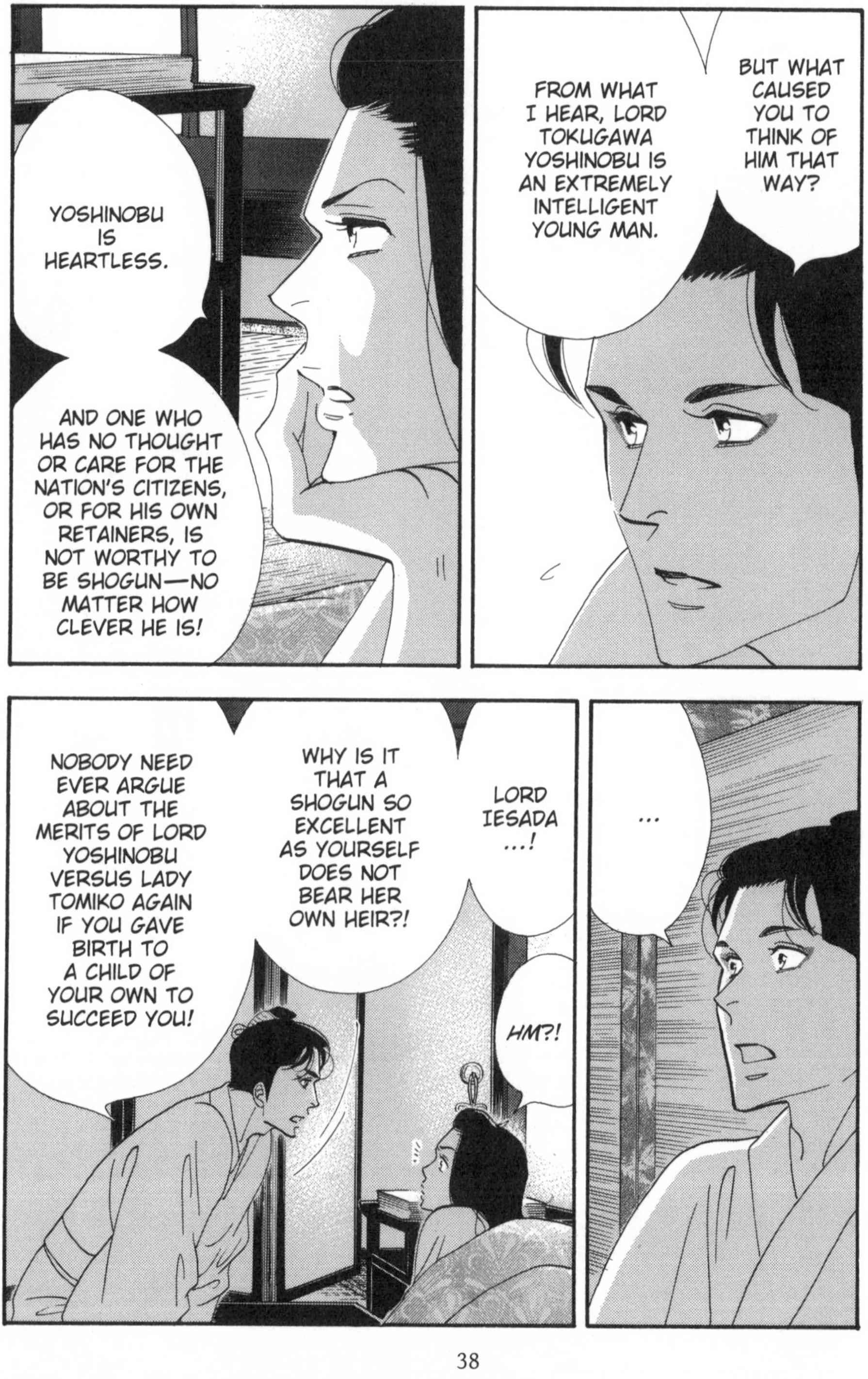
BUT WHAT CAUSED YOU TO THINK OF HIM THAT WAY?
FROM WHAT I HEAR, LORD TOKUGAWA YOSHINOBU IS AN EXTREMELY INTELLIGENT YOUNG MAN.
YOSHINOBU IS HEARTLESS.
AND ONE WHO HAS NO THOUGHT OR CARE FOR THE NATION'S CITIZENS, OR FOR HIS OWN RETAINERS, IS NOT WORTHY TO BE SHOGUN—NO MATTER HOW CLEVER HE IS!
...
LORD IESADA ...!
HM?!
WHY IS IT THAT A SHOGUN SO EXCELLENT AS YOURSELF DOES NOT BEAR HER OWN HEIR?!
NOBODY NEED EVER ARGUE ABOUT THE MERITS OF LORD YOSHINOBU VERSUS LADY TOMIKO AGAIN IF YOU GAVE BIRTH TO A CHILD OF YOUR OWN TO SUCCEED YOU!

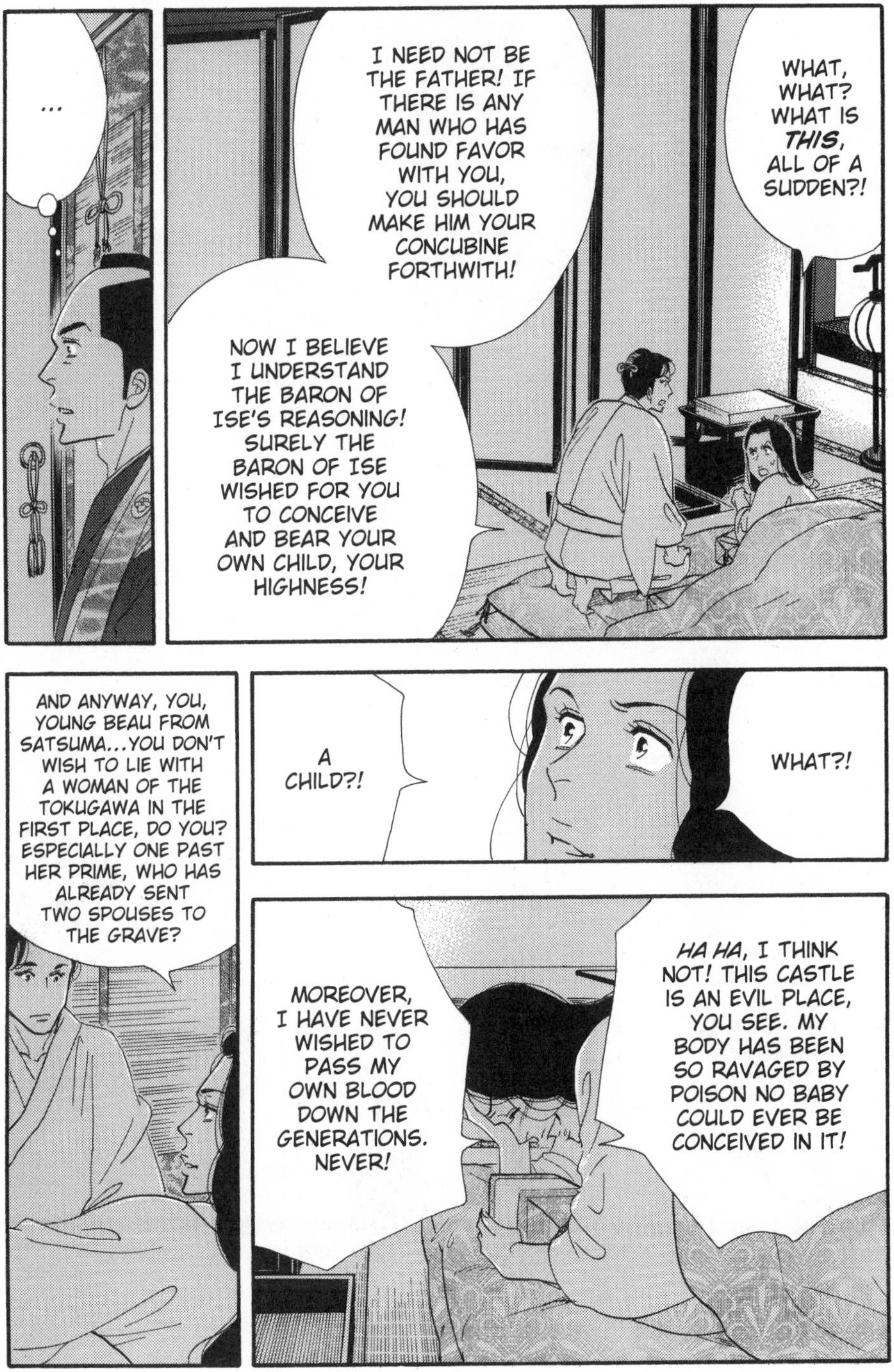
WHAT, WHAT? WHAT IS *THIS*, ALL OF A SUDDEN?!
I NEED NOT BE THE FATHER! IF THERE IS ANY MAN WHO HAS FOUND FAVOR WITH YOU, YOU SHOULD MAKE HIM YOUR CONCUBINE FORTHWITH!
NOW I BELIEVE I UNDERSTAND THE BARON OF ISE'S REASONING! SURELY THE BARON OF ISE WISHED FOR YOU TO CONCEIVE AND BEAR YOUR OWN CHILD, YOUR HIGHNESS!
...
WHAT?!
A CHILD?!
HA HA, I THINK NOT! THIS CASTLE IS AN EVIL PLACE, YOU SEE. MY BODY HAS BEEN SO RAVAGED BY POISON NO BABY COULD EVER BE CONCEIVED IN IT!
MOREOVER, I HAVE NEVER WISHED TO PASS MY OWN BLOOD DOWN THE GENERATIONS. NEVER!
AND ANYWAY, YOU, YOUNG BEAU FROM SATSUMA...YOU DON'T WISH TO LIE WITH A WOMAN OF THE TOKUGAWA IN THE FIRST PLACE, DO YOU? ESPECIALLY ONE PAST HER PRIME, WHO HAS ALREADY SENT TWO SPOUSES TO THE GRAVE?

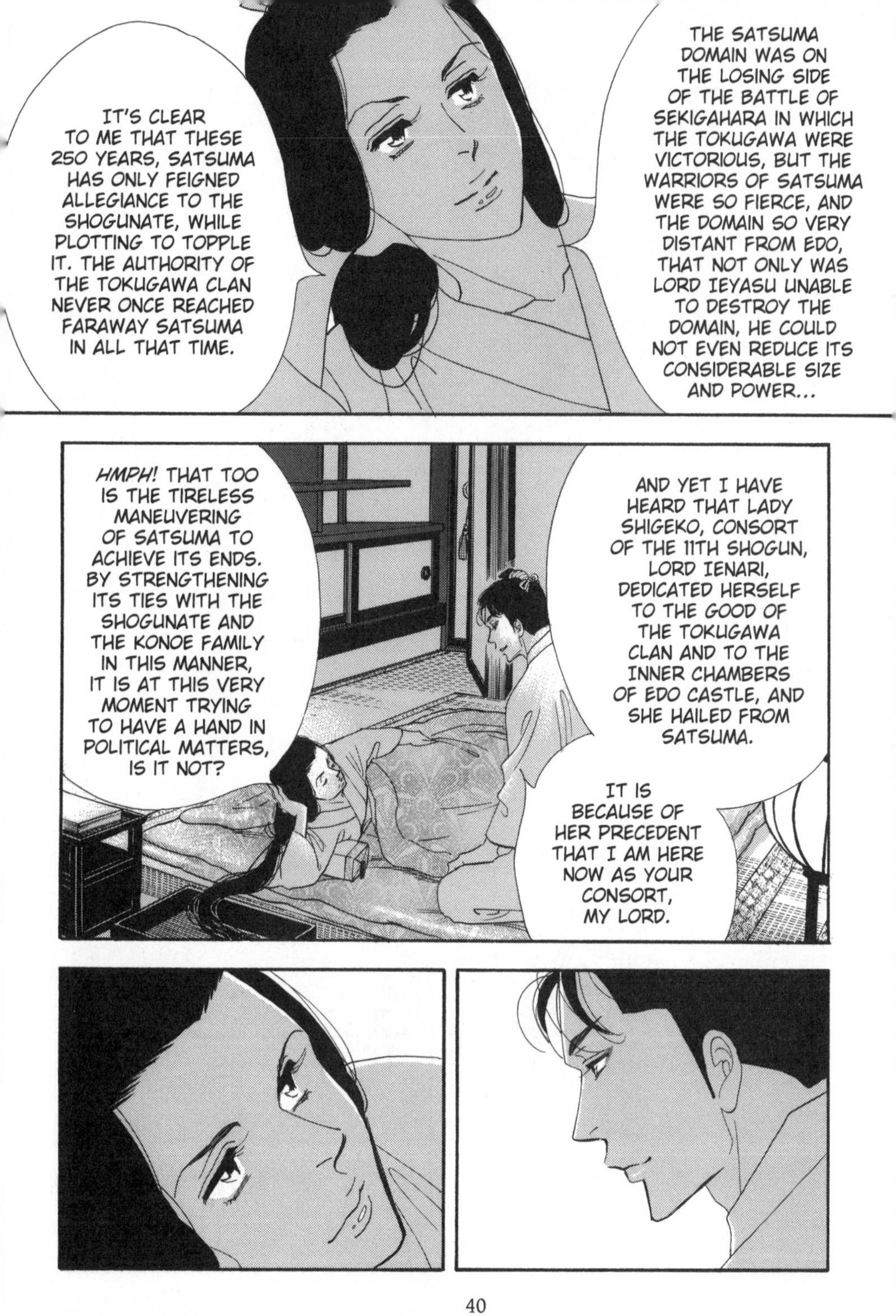
THE SATSUMA DOMAIN WAS ON THE LOSING SIDE OF THE BATTLE OF SEKIGAHARA IN WHICH THE TOKUGAWA WERE VICTORIOUS, BUT THE WARRIORS OF SATSUMA WERE SO FIERCE, AND THE DOMAIN SO VERY DISTANT FROM EDO, THAT NOT ONLY WAS LORD IEYASU UNABLE TO DESTROY THE DOMAIN, HE COULD NOT EVEN REDUCE ITS CONSIDERABLE SIZE AND POWER...
IT'S CLEAR TO ME THAT THESE 250 YEARS, SATSUMA HAS ONLY FEIGNED ALLEGIANCE TO THE SHOGUNATE, WHILE PLOTTING TO TOPPLE IT. THE AUTHORITY OF THE TOKUGAWA CLAN NEVER ONCE REACHED FARAWAY SATSUMA IN ALL THAT TIME.
AND YET I HAVE HEARD THAT LADY SHIGEKO, CONSORT OF THE 11TH SHOGUN, LORD IENARI, DEDICATED HERSELF TO THE GOOD OF THE TOKUGAWA CLAN AND TO THE INNER CHAMBERS OF EDO CASTLE, AND SHE HAILED FROM SATSUMA.
IT IS BECAUSE OF HER PRECEDENT THAT I AM HERE NOW AS YOUR CONSORT, MY LORD.
HMPH! THAT TOO IS THE TIRELESS MANEUVERING OF SATSUMA TO ACHIEVE ITS ENDS. BY STRENGTHENING ITS TIES WITH THE SHOGUNATE AND THE KONOE FAMILY IN THIS MANNER, IT IS AT THIS VERY MOMENT TRYING TO HAVE A HAND IN POLITICAL MATTERS, IS IT NOT?

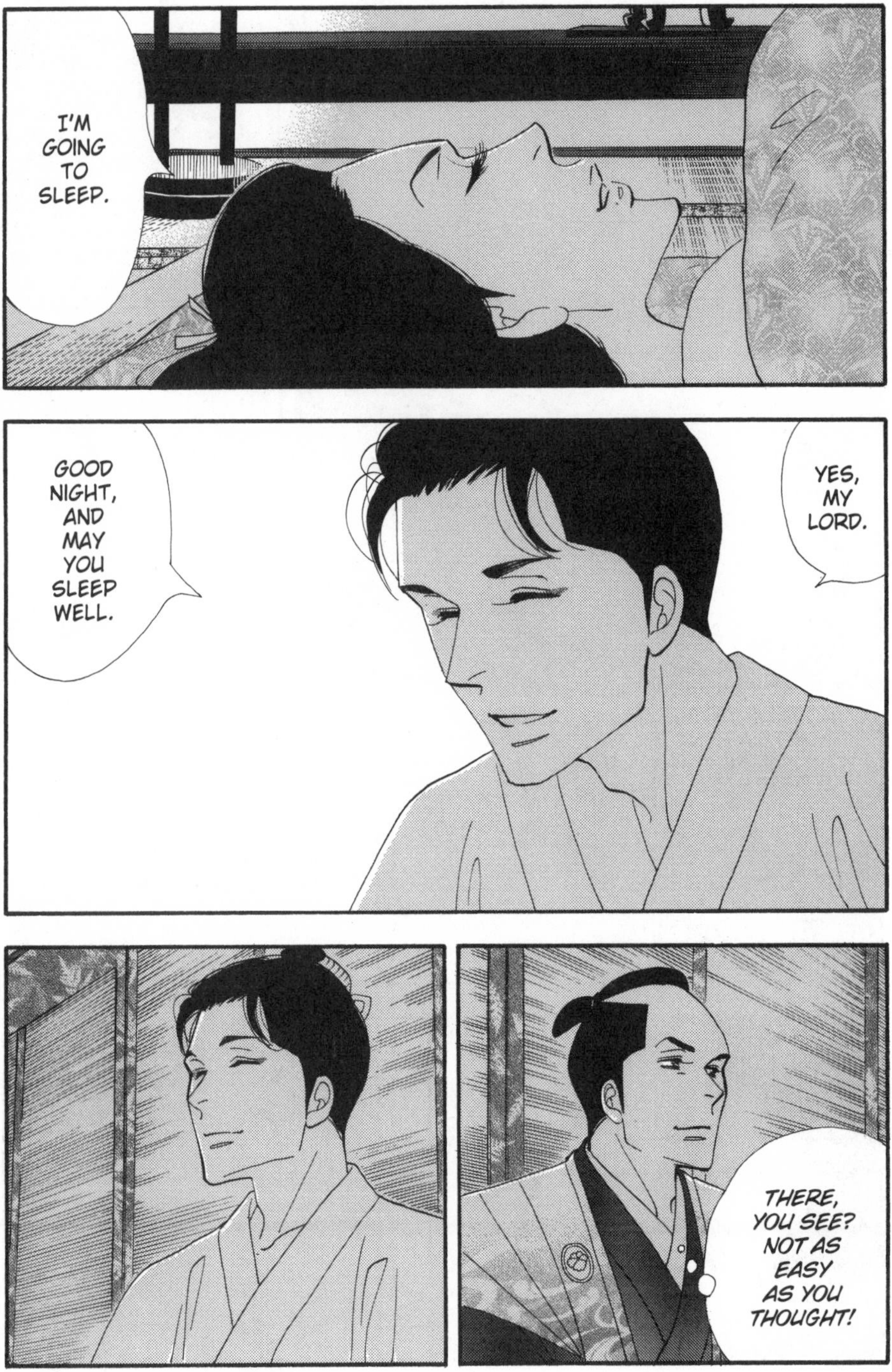

I'M GOING TO SLEEP.
YES, MY LORD.
GOOD NIGHT, AND MAY YOU SLEEP WELL.
THERE, YOU SEE? NOT AS EASY AS YOU THOUGHT!

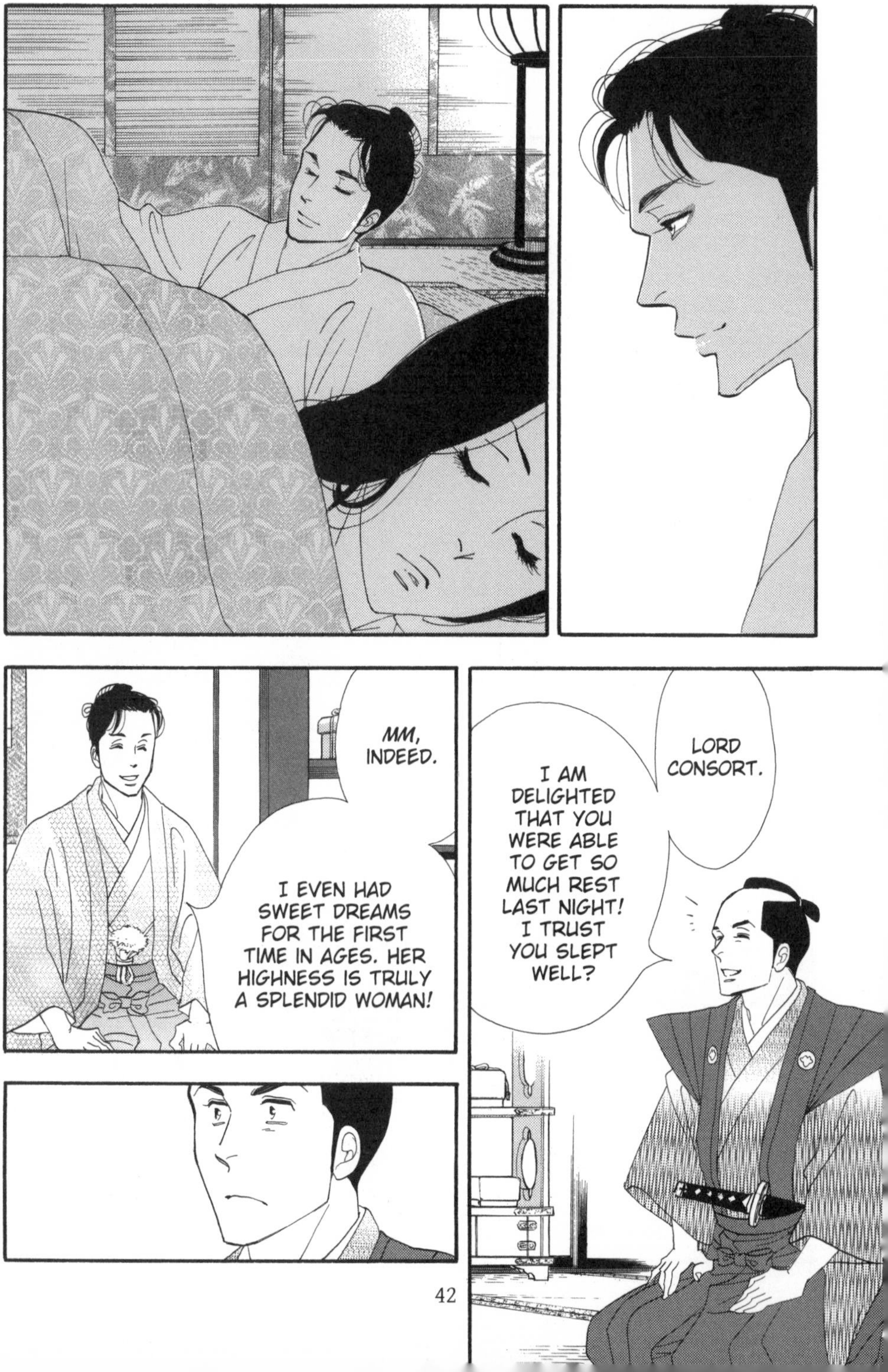
LORD CONSORT.
I AM DELIGHTED THAT YOU WERE ABLE TO GET SO MUCH REST LAST NIGHT! I TRUST YOU SLEPT WELL?
MM, INDEED.
I EVEN HAD SWEET DREAMS FOR THE FIRST TIME IN AGES. HER HIGHNESS IS TRULY A SPLENDID WOMAN!

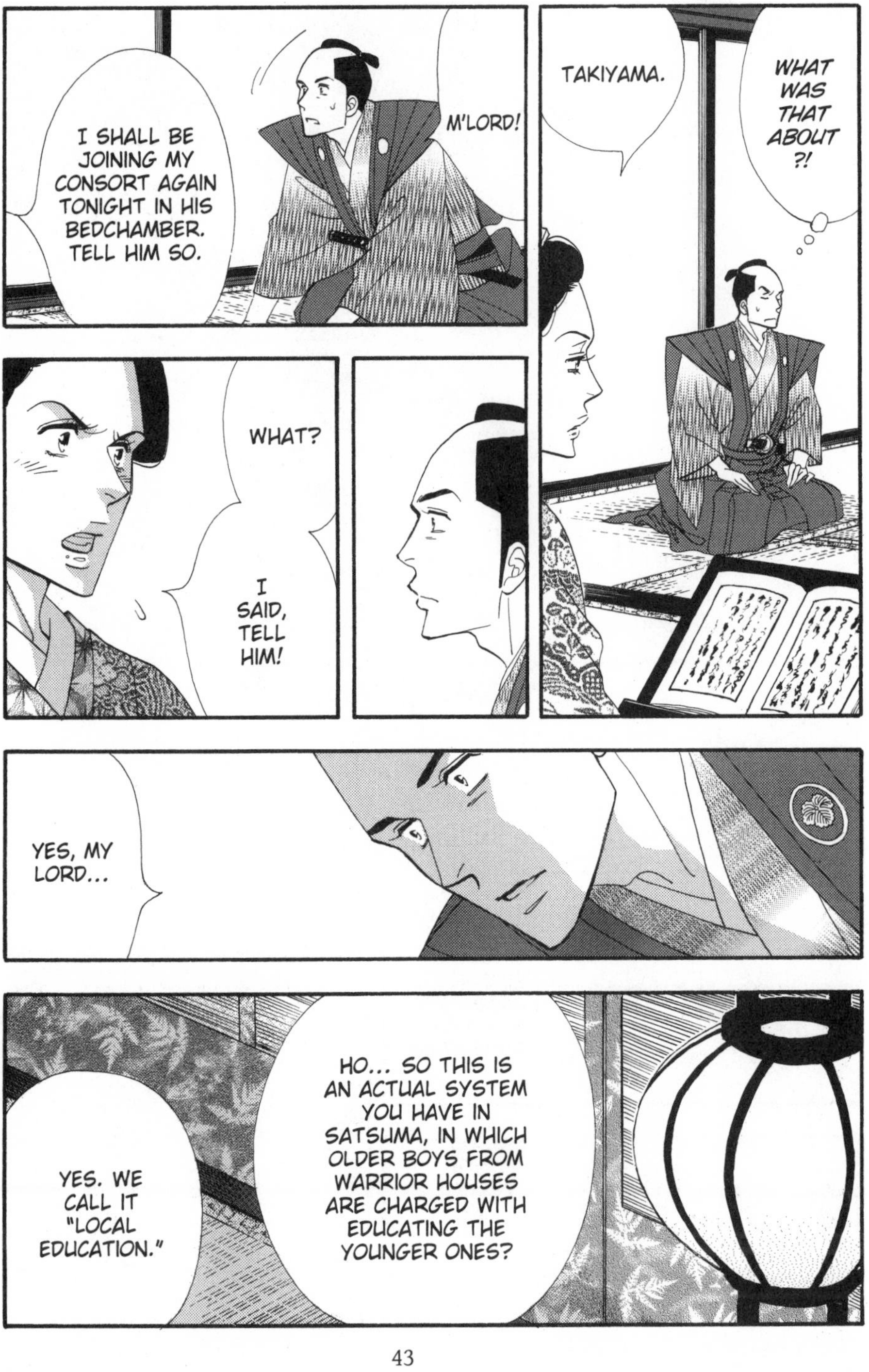
WHAT WAS THAT ABOUT ?!
TAKIYAMA.
M'LORD!
I SHALL BE JOINING MY CONSORT AGAIN TONIGHT IN HIS BEDCHAMBER. TELL HIM SO.
WHAT?
I SAID, TELL HIM!
YES, MY LORD...
HO... SO THIS IS AN ACTUAL SYSTEM YOU HAVE IN SATSUMA, IN WHICH OLDER BOYS FROM WARRIOR HOUSES ARE CHARGED WITH EDUCATING THE YOUNGER ONES?
YES. WE CALL IT "LOCAL EDUCATION."

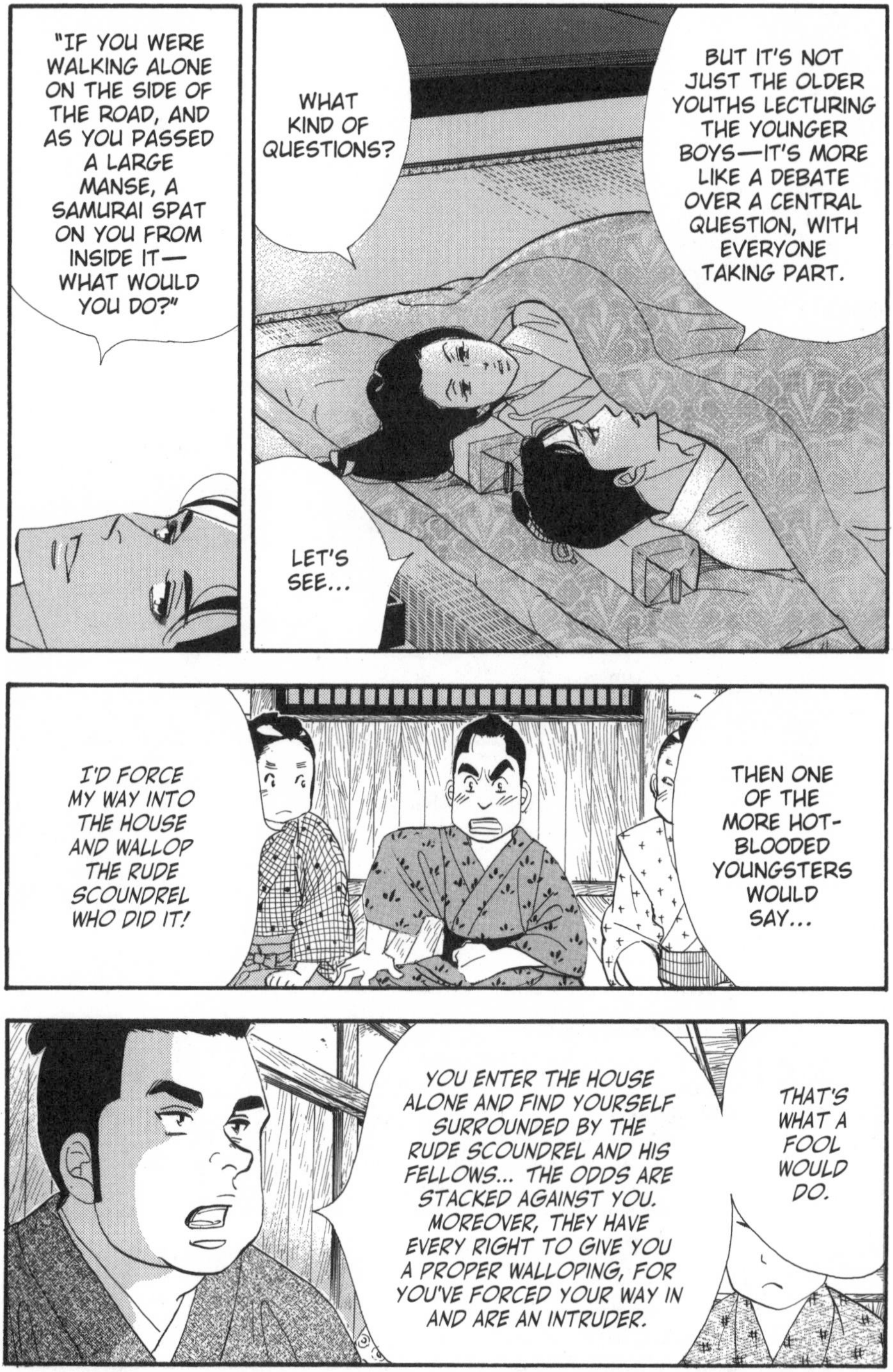
BUT IT'S NOT JUST THE OLDER YOUTHS LECTURING THE YOUNGER BOYS—IT'S MORE LIKE A DEBATE OVER A CENTRAL QUESTION, WITH EVERYONE TAKING PART.
WHAT KIND OF QUESTIONS?
LET'S SEE...
"IF YOU WERE WALKING ALONE ON THE SIDE OF THE ROAD, AND AS YOU PASSED A LARGE MANSE, A SAMURAI SPAT ON YOU FROM INSIDE IT—WHAT WOULD YOU DO?"
THEN ONE OF THE MORE HOT-BLOODED YOUNGSTERS WOULD SAY...
I'D FORCE MY WAY INTO THE HOUSE AND WALLOP THE RUDE SCOUNDREL WHO DID IT!
THAT'S WHAT A FOOL WOULD DO.
YOU ENTER THE HOUSE ALONE AND FIND YOURSELF SURROUNDED BY THE RUDE SCOUNDREL AND HIS FELLOWS... THE ODDS ARE STACKED AGAINST YOU. MOREOVER, THEY HAVE EVERY RIGHT TO GIVE YOU A PROPER WALLOPING, FOR YOU'VE FORCED YOUR WAY IN AND ARE AN INTRUDER.

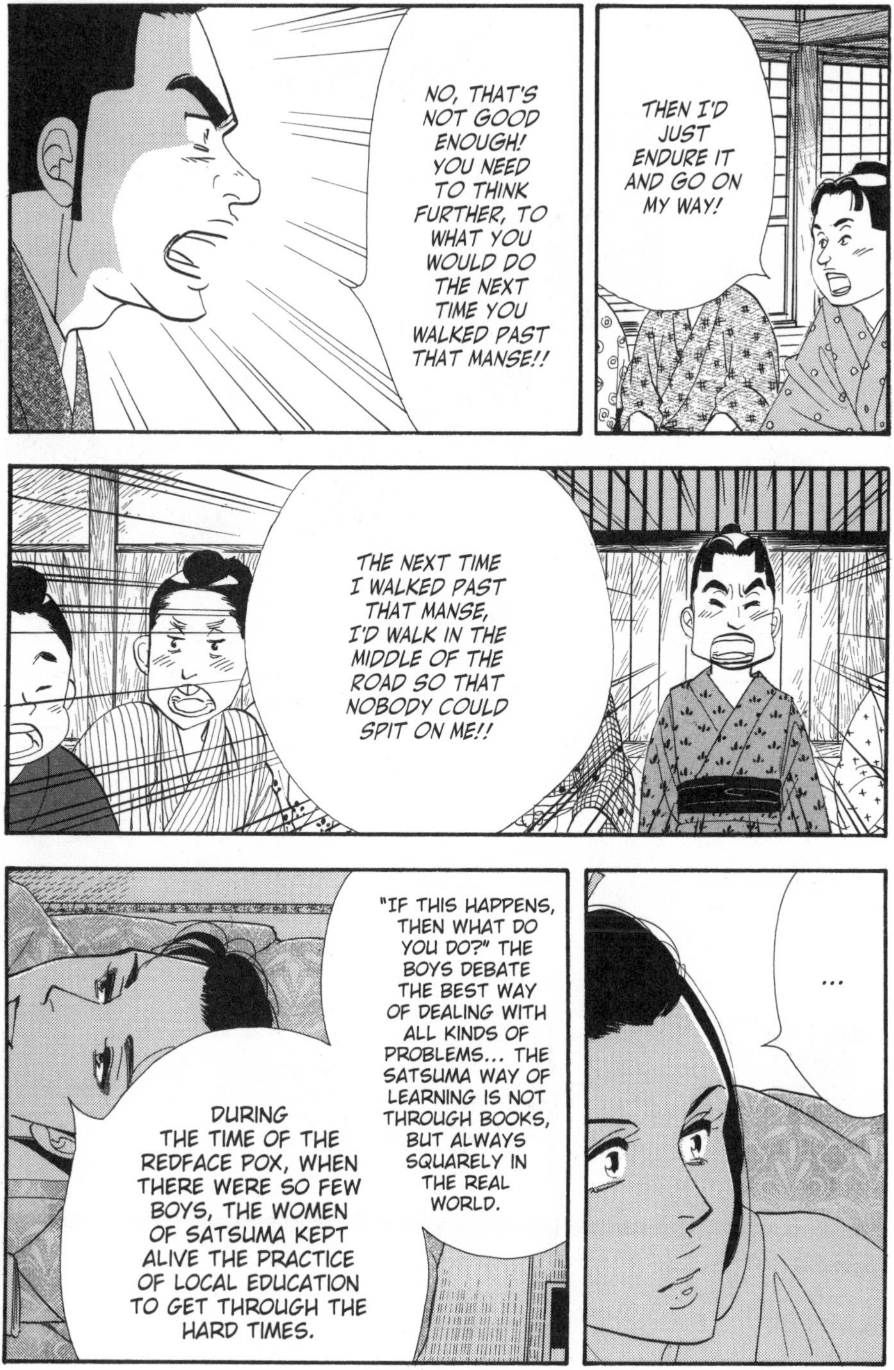
THEN I'D JUST ENDURE IT AND GO ON MY WAY!
NO, THAT'S NOT GOOD ENOUGH! YOU NEED TO THINK FURTHER, TO WHAT YOU WOULD DO THE NEXT TIME YOU WALKED PAST THAT MANSE!!
THE NEXT TIME I WALKED PAST THAT MANSE, I'D WALK IN THE MIDDLE OF THE ROAD SO THAT NOBODY COULD SPIT ON ME!!
...
"IF THIS HAPPENS, THEN WHAT DO YOU DO?" THE BOYS DEBATE THE BEST WAY OF DEALING WITH ALL KINDS OF PROBLEMS... THE SATSUMA WAY OF LEARNING IS NOT THROUGH BOOKS, BUT ALWAYS SQUARELY IN THE REAL WORLD.
DURING THE TIME OF THE REDFACE POX, WHEN THERE WERE SO FEW BOYS, THE WOMEN OF SATSUMA KEPT ALIVE THE PRACTICE OF LOCAL EDUCATION TO GET THROUGH THE HARD TIMES.

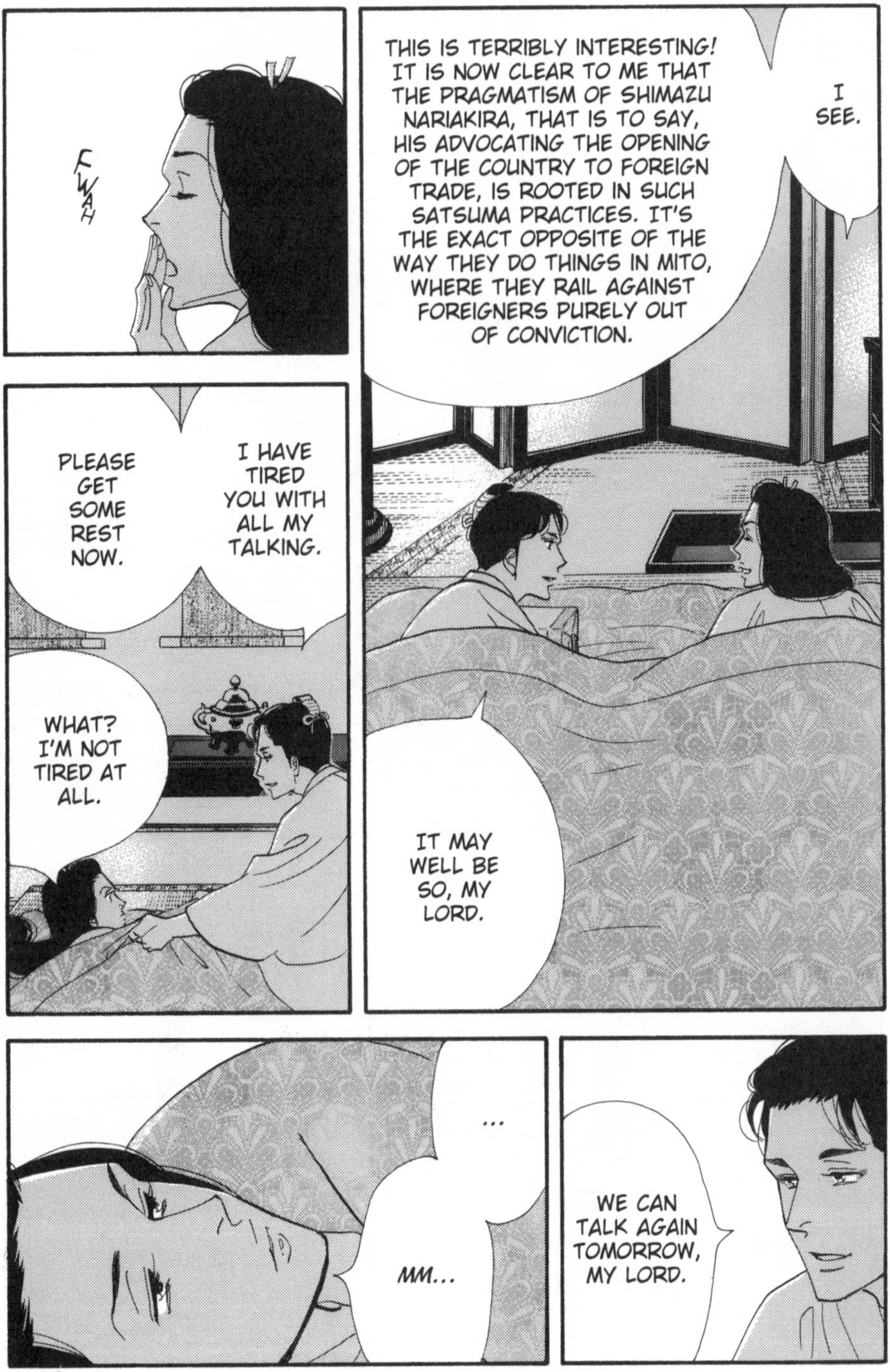
I SEE.
THIS IS TERRIBLY INTERESTING! IT IS NOW CLEAR TO ME THAT THE PRAGMATISM OF SHIMAZU NARIAKIRA, THAT IS TO SAY, HIS ADVOCATING THE OPENING OF THE COUNTRY TO FOREIGN TRADE, IS ROOTED IN SUCH SATSUMA PRACTICES. IT'S THE EXACT OPPOSITE OF THE WAY THEY DO THINGS IN MITO, WHERE THEY RAIL AGAINST FOREIGNERS PURELY OUT OF CONVICTION.
IT MAY WELL BE SO, MY LORD.
FWAH
I HAVE TIRED YOU WITH ALL MY TALKING.
PLEASE GET SOME REST NOW.
WHAT? I'M NOT TIRED AT ALL.
WE CAN TALK AGAIN TOMORROW, MY LORD.
...
MM...

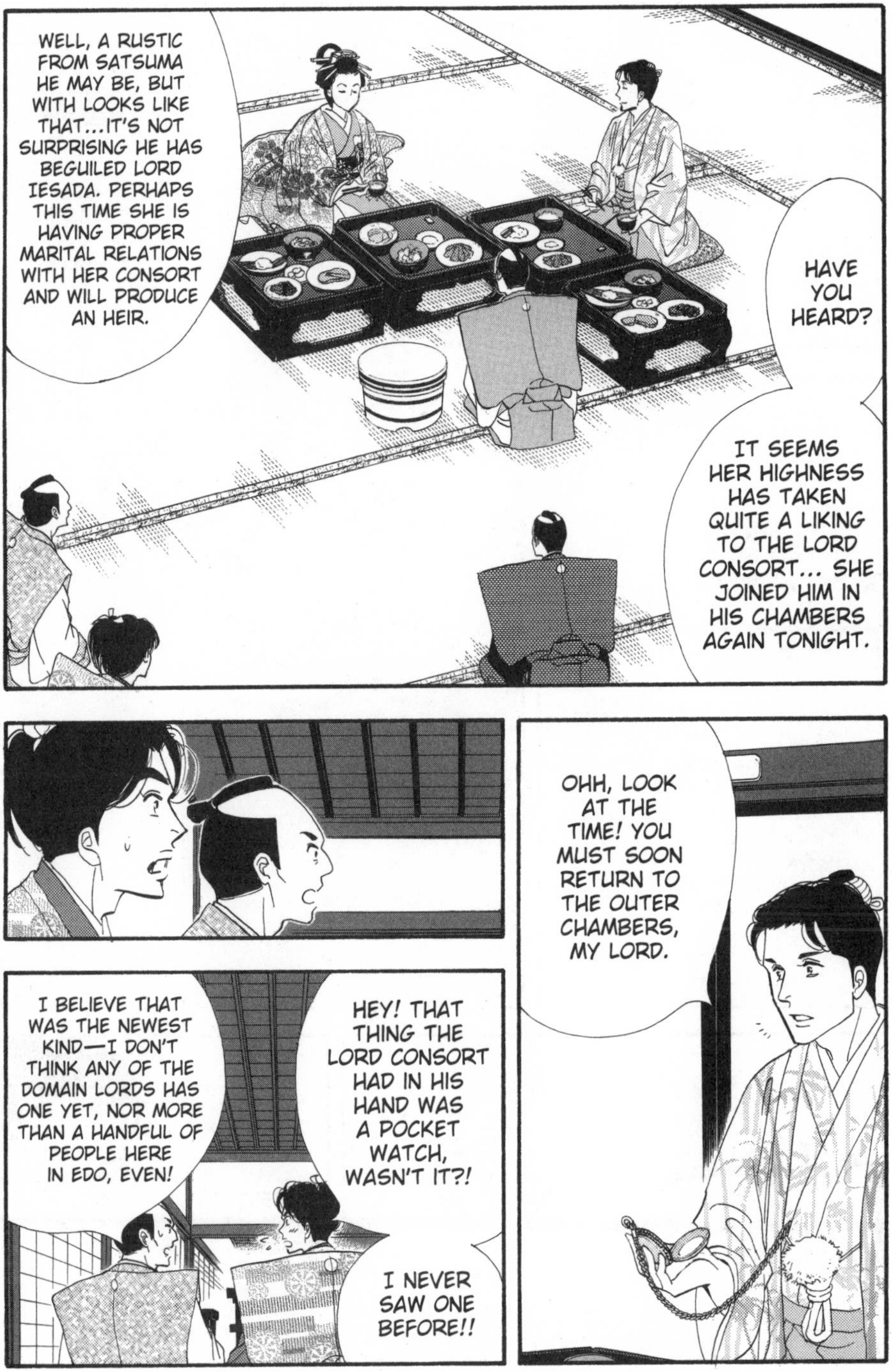
HAVE YOU HEARD?
IT SEEMS HER HIGHNESS HAS TAKEN QUITE A LIKING TO THE LORD CONSORT... SHE JOINED HIM IN HIS CHAMBERS AGAIN TONIGHT.
WELL, A RUSTIC FROM SATSUMA HE MAY BE, BUT WITH LOOKS LIKE THAT...IT'S NOT SURPRISING HE HAS BEGUILED LORD IESADA. PERHAPS THIS TIME SHE IS HAVING PROPER MARITAL RELATIONS WITH HER CONSORT AND WILL PRODUCE AN HEIR.
OHH, LOOK AT THE TIME! YOU MUST SOON RETURN TO THE OUTER CHAMBERS, MY LORD.
HEY! THAT THING THE LORD CONSORT HAD IN HIS HAND WAS A POCKET WATCH, WASN'T IT?!
I NEVER SAW ONE BEFORE!!
I BELIEVE THAT WAS THE NEWEST KIND—I DON'T THINK ANY OF THE DOMAIN LORDS HAS ONE YET, NOR MORE THAN A HANDFUL OF PEOPLE HERE IN EDO, EVEN!

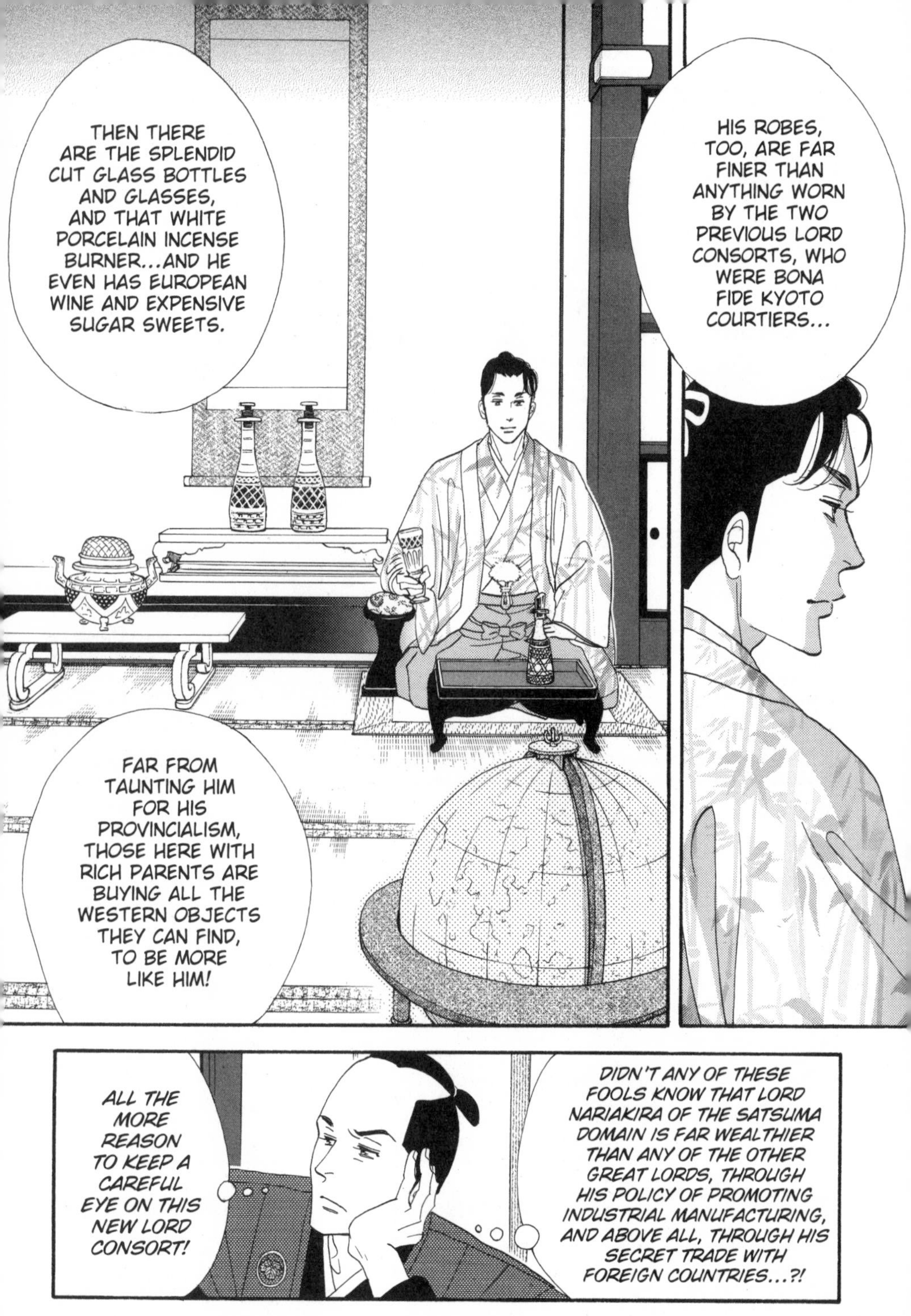
HIS ROBES, TOO, ARE FAR FINER THAN ANYTHING WORN BY THE TWO PREVIOUS LORD CONSORTS, WHO WERE BONA FIDE KYOTO COURTIERS...
THEN THERE ARE THE SPLENDID CUT GLASS BOTTLES AND GLASSES, AND THAT WHITE PORCELAIN INCENSE BURNER...AND HE EVEN HAS EUROPEAN WINE AND EXPENSIVE SUGAR SWEETS.
FAR FROM TAUNTING HIM FOR HIS PROVINCIALISM, THOSE HERE WITH RICH PARENTS ARE BUYING ALL THE WESTERN OBJECTS THEY CAN FIND, TO BE MORE LIKE HIM!
DIDN'T ANY OF THESE FOOLS KNOW THAT LORD NARIAKIRA OF THE SATSUMA DOMAIN IS FAR WEALTHIER THAN ANY OF THE OTHER GREAT LORDS, THROUGH HIS POLICY OF PROMOTING INDUSTRIAL MANUFACTURING, AND ABOVE ALL, THROUGH HIS SECRET TRADE WITH FOREIGN COUNTRIES...?!
ALL THE MORE REASON TO KEEP A CAREFUL EYE ON THIS NEW LORD CONSORT!

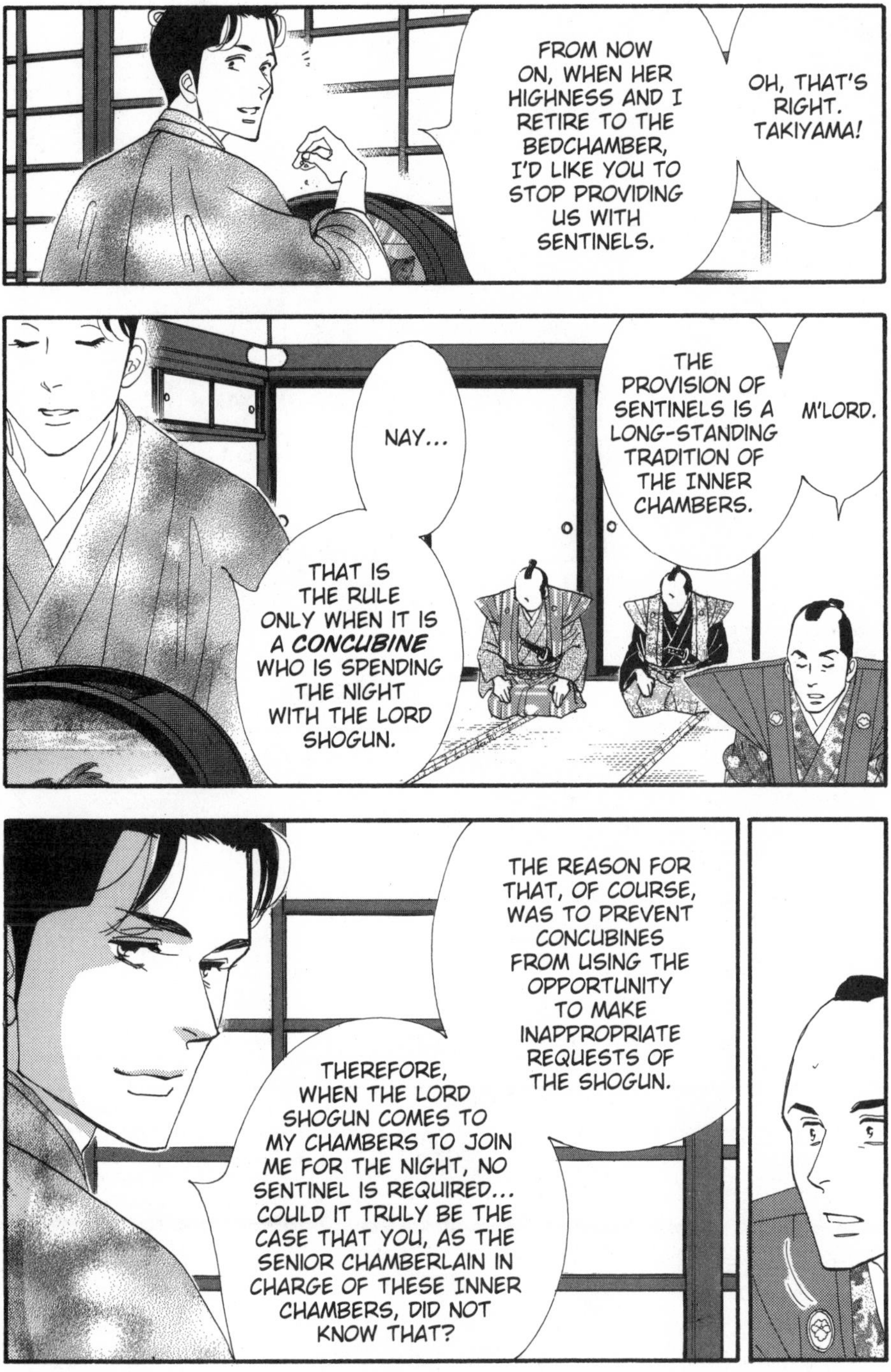
OH, THAT'S RIGHT. TAKIYAMA!
FROM NOW ON, WHEN HER HIGHNESS AND I RETIRE TO THE BEDCHAMBER, I'D LIKE YOU TO STOP PROVIDING US WITH SENTINELS.
M'LORD.
THE PROVISION OF SENTINELS IS A LONG-STANDING TRADITION OF THE INNER CHAMBERS.
NAY...
THAT IS THE RULE ONLY WHEN IT IS A *CONCUBINE* WHO IS SPENDING THE NIGHT WITH THE LORD SHOGUN.
THE REASON FOR THAT, OF COURSE, WAS TO PREVENT CONCUBINES FROM USING THE OPPORTUNITY TO MAKE INAPPROPRIATE REQUESTS OF THE SHOGUN.
THEREFORE, WHEN THE LORD SHOGUN COMES TO MY CHAMBERS TO JOIN ME FOR THE NIGHT, NO SENTINEL IS REQUIRED... COULD IT TRULY BE THE CASE THAT YOU, AS THE SENIOR CHAMBERLAIN IN CHARGE OF THESE INNER CHAMBERS, DID NOT KNOW THAT?

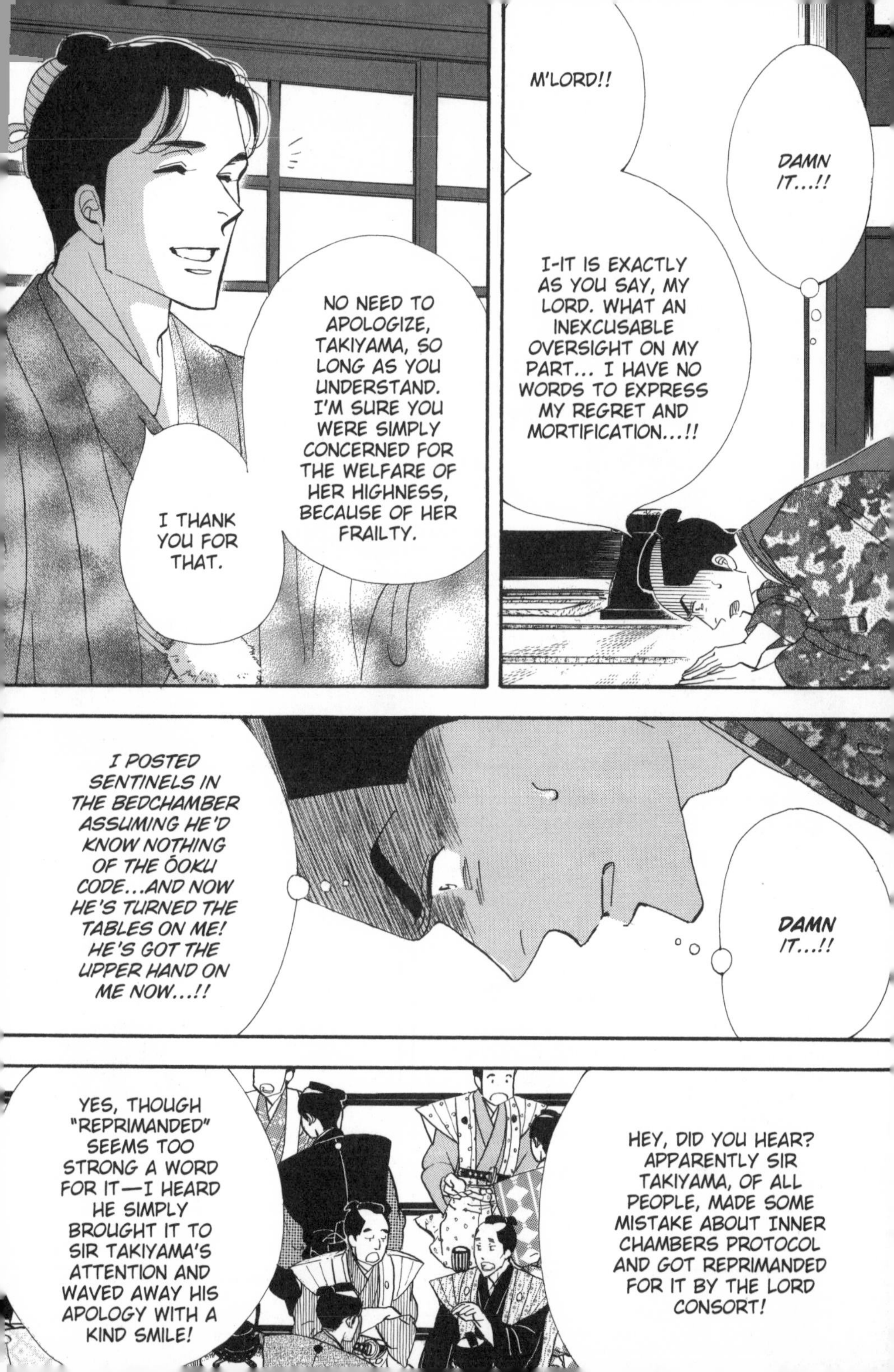
M'LORD!!
DAMN IT...!!
I-IT IS EXACTLY AS YOU SAY, MY LORD. WHAT AN INEXCUSABLE OVERSIGHT ON MY PART... I HAVE NO WORDS TO EXPRESS MY REGRET AND MORTIFICATION...!!
NO NEED TO APOLOGIZE, TAKIYAMA, SO LONG AS YOU UNDERSTAND. I'M SURE YOU WERE SIMPLY CONCERNED FOR THE WELFARE OF HER HIGHNESS, BECAUSE OF HER FRAILTY.
I THANK YOU FOR THAT.
DAMN IT...!!
I POSTED SENTINELS IN THE BEDCHAMBER ASSUMING HE'D KNOW NOTHING OF THE ŌOKU CODE...AND NOW HE'S TURNED THE TABLES ON ME! HE'S GOT THE UPPER HAND ON ME NOW...!!
HEY, DID YOU HEAR? APPARENTLY SIR TAKIYAMA, OF ALL PEOPLE, MADE SOME MISTAKE ABOUT INNER CHAMBERS PROTOCOL AND GOT REPRIMANDED FOR IT BY THE LORD CONSORT!
YES, THOUGH "REPRIMANDED" SEEMS TOO STRONG A WORD FOR IT—I HEARD HE SIMPLY BROUGHT IT TO SIR TAKIYAMA'S ATTENTION AND WAVED AWAY HIS APOLOGY WITH A KIND SMILE!

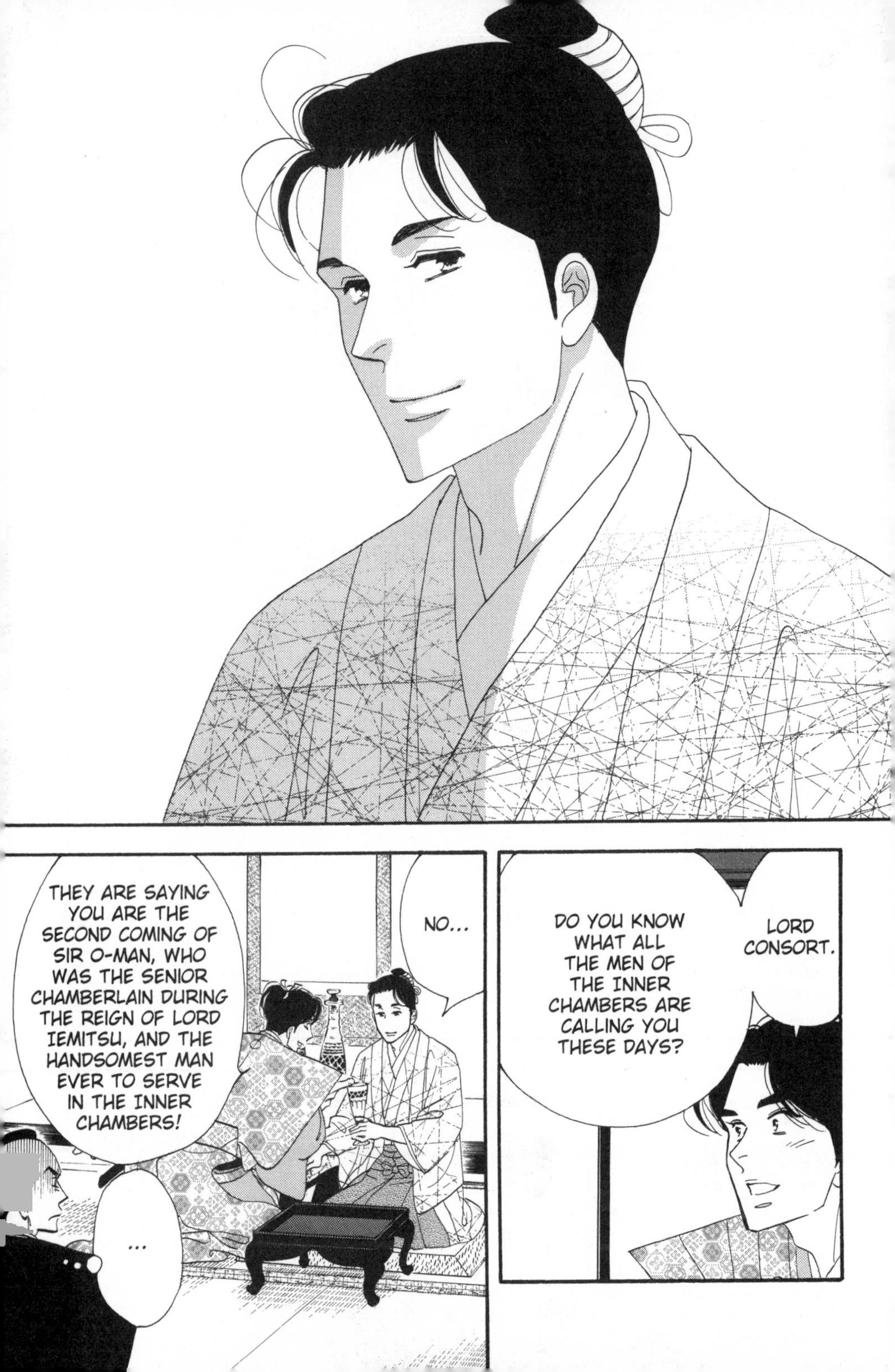
LORD CONSORT.
DO YOU KNOW WHAT ALL THE MEN OF THE INNER CHAMBERS ARE CALLING YOU THESE DAYS?
NO...
THEY ARE SAYING YOU ARE THE SECOND COMING OF SIR O-MAN, WHO WAS THE SENIOR CHAMBERLAIN DURING THE REIGN OF LORD IEMITSU, AND THE HANDSOMEST MAN EVER TO SERVE IN THE INNER CHAMBERS!
...

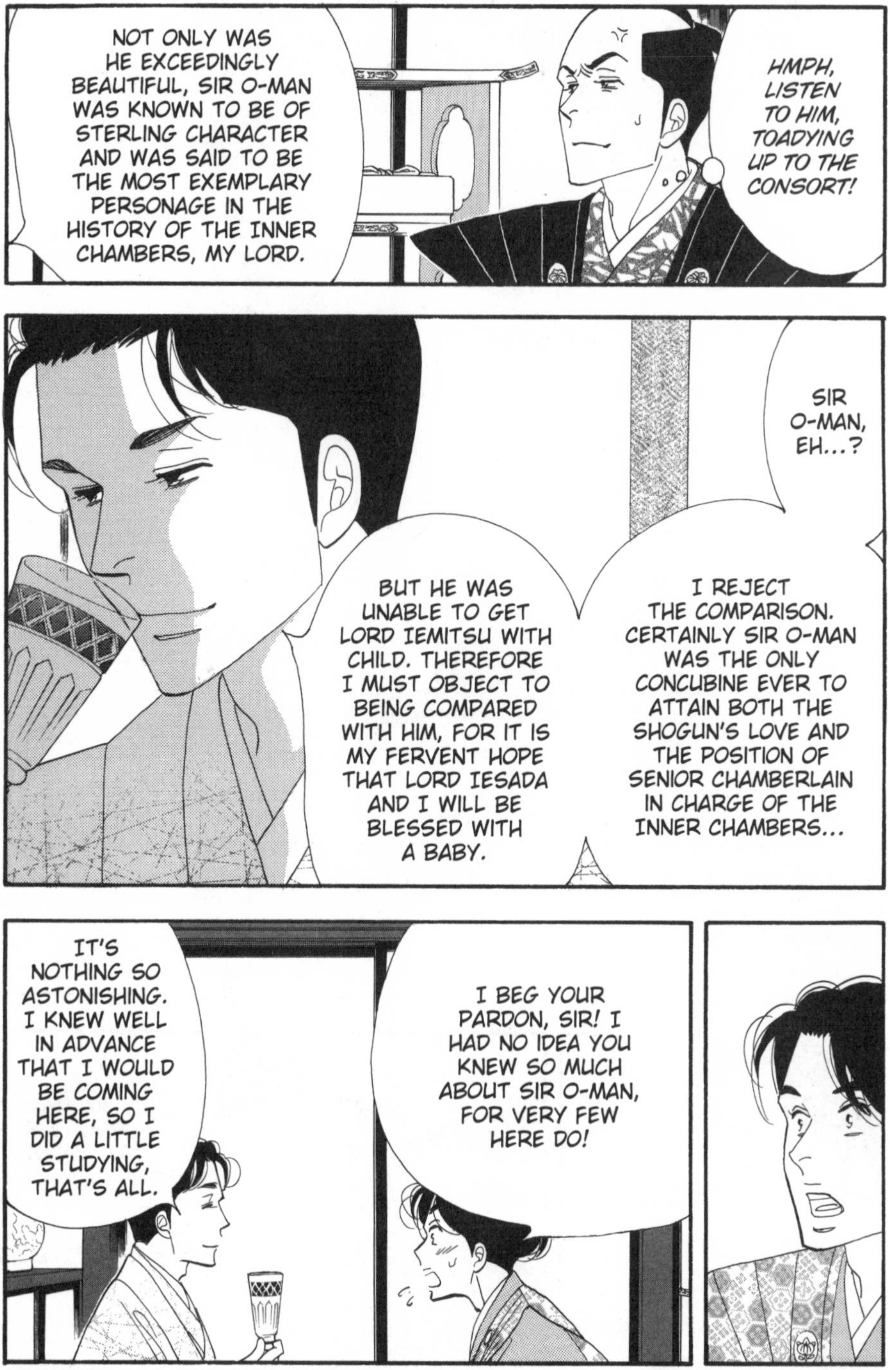
HMPH, LISTEN TO HIM, TOADYING UP TO THE CONSORT!
NOT ONLY WAS HE EXCEEDINGLY BEAUTIFUL, SIR O-MAN WAS KNOWN TO BE OF STERLING CHARACTER AND WAS SAID TO BE THE MOST EXEMPLARY PERSONAGE IN THE HISTORY OF THE INNER CHAMBERS, MY LORD.
SIR O-MAN, EH...?
I REJECT THE COMPARISON. CERTAINLY SIR O-MAN WAS THE ONLY CONCUBINE EVER TO ATTAIN BOTH THE SHOGUN'S LOVE AND THE POSITION OF SENIOR CHAMBERLAIN IN CHARGE OF THE INNER CHAMBERS...
BUT HE WAS UNABLE TO GET LORD IEMITSU WITH CHILD. THEREFORE I MUST OBJECT TO BEING COMPARED WITH HIM, FOR IT IS MY FERVENT HOPE THAT LORD IESADA AND I WILL BE BLESSED WITH A BABY.
I BEG YOUR PARDON, SIR! I HAD NO IDEA YOU KNEW SO MUCH ABOUT SIR O-MAN, FOR VERY FEW HERE DO!
IT'S NOTHING SO ASTONISHING. I KNEW WELL IN ADVANCE THAT I WOULD BE COMING HERE, SO I DID A LITTLE STUDYING, THAT'S ALL.

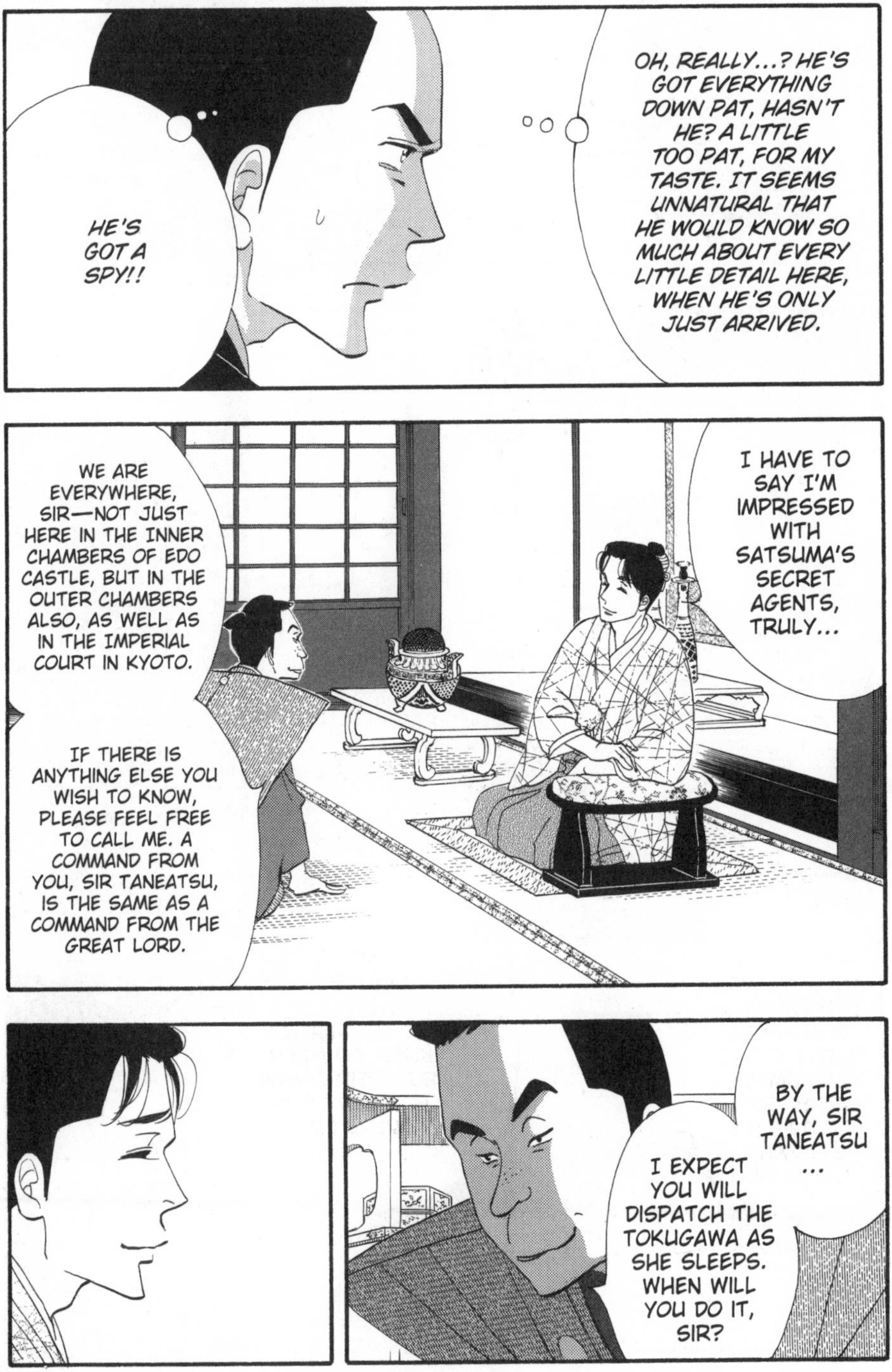
OH, REALLY...? HE'S GOT EVERYTHING DOWN PAT, HASN'T HE? A LITTLE TOO PAT, FOR MY TASTE. IT SEEMS UNNATURAL THAT HE WOULD KNOW SO MUCH ABOUT EVERY LITTLE DETAIL HERE, WHEN HE'S ONLY JUST ARRIVED.
HE'S GOT A SPY!!
I HAVE TO SAY I'M IMPRESSED WITH SATSUMA'S SECRET AGENTS, TRULY...
WE ARE EVERYWHERE, SIR—NOT JUST HERE IN THE INNER CHAMBERS OF EDO CASTLE, BUT IN THE OUTER CHAMBERS ALSO, AS WELL AS IN THE IMPERIAL COURT IN KYOTO.
IF THERE IS ANYTHING ELSE YOU WISH TO KNOW, PLEASE FEEL FREE TO CALL ME. A COMMAND FROM YOU, SIR TANEATSU, IS THE SAME AS A COMMAND FROM THE GREAT LORD.
BY THE WAY, SIR TANEATSU ...
I EXPECT YOU WILL DISPATCH THE TOKUGAWA AS SHE SLEEPS. WHEN WILL YOU DO IT, SIR?

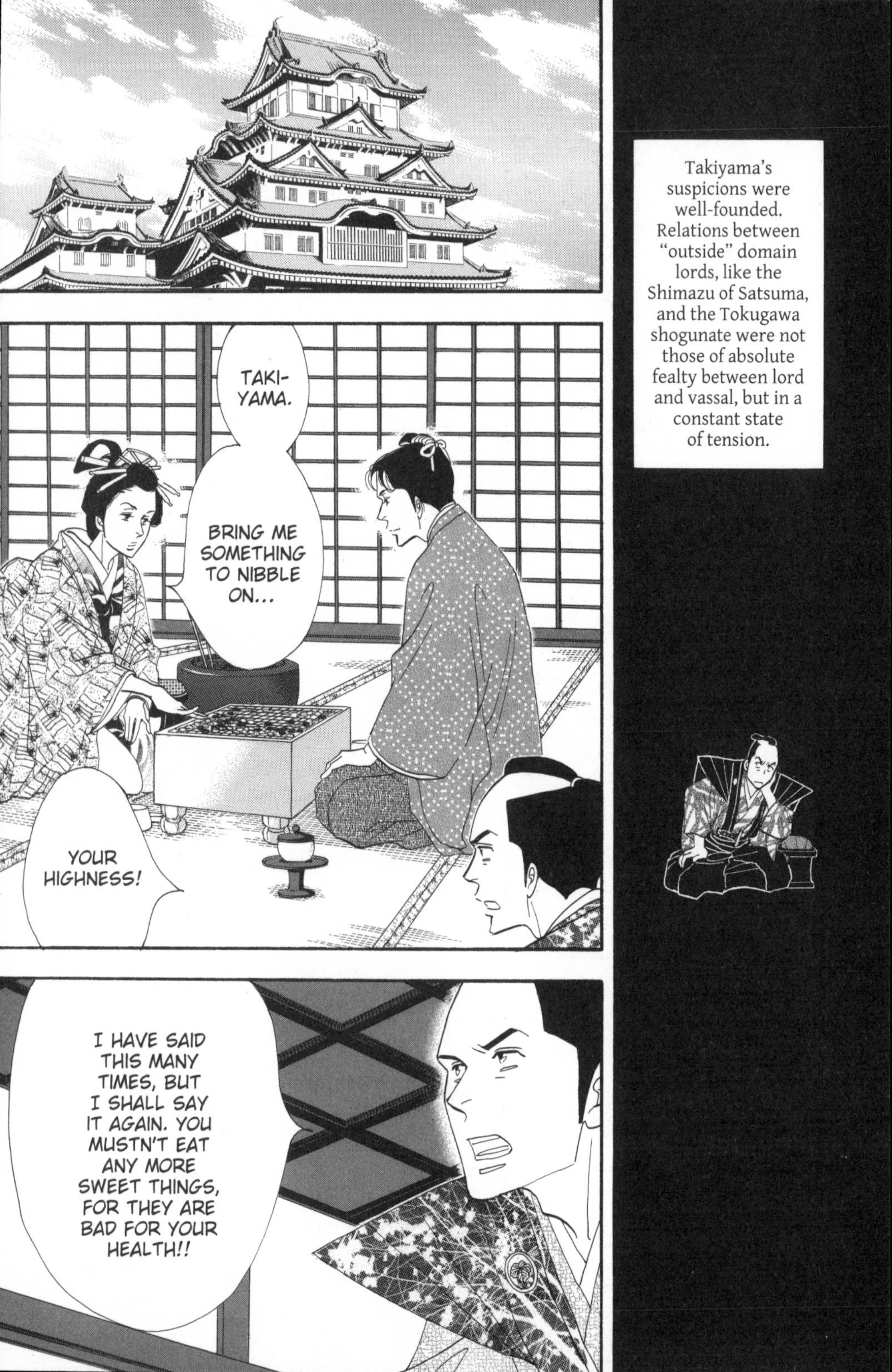
Takiyama's suspicions were well-founded. Relations between "outside" domain lords, like the Shimazu of Satsuma, and the Tokugawa shogunate were not those of absolute fealty between lord and vassal, but in a constant state of tension.
TAKI-YAMA.
BRING ME SOMETHING TO NIBBLE ON...
YOUR HIGHNESS!
I HAVE SAID THIS MANY TIMES, BUT I SHALL SAY IT AGAIN. YOU MUSTN'T EAT ANY MORE SWEET THINGS, FOR THEY ARE BAD FOR YOUR HEALTH!!

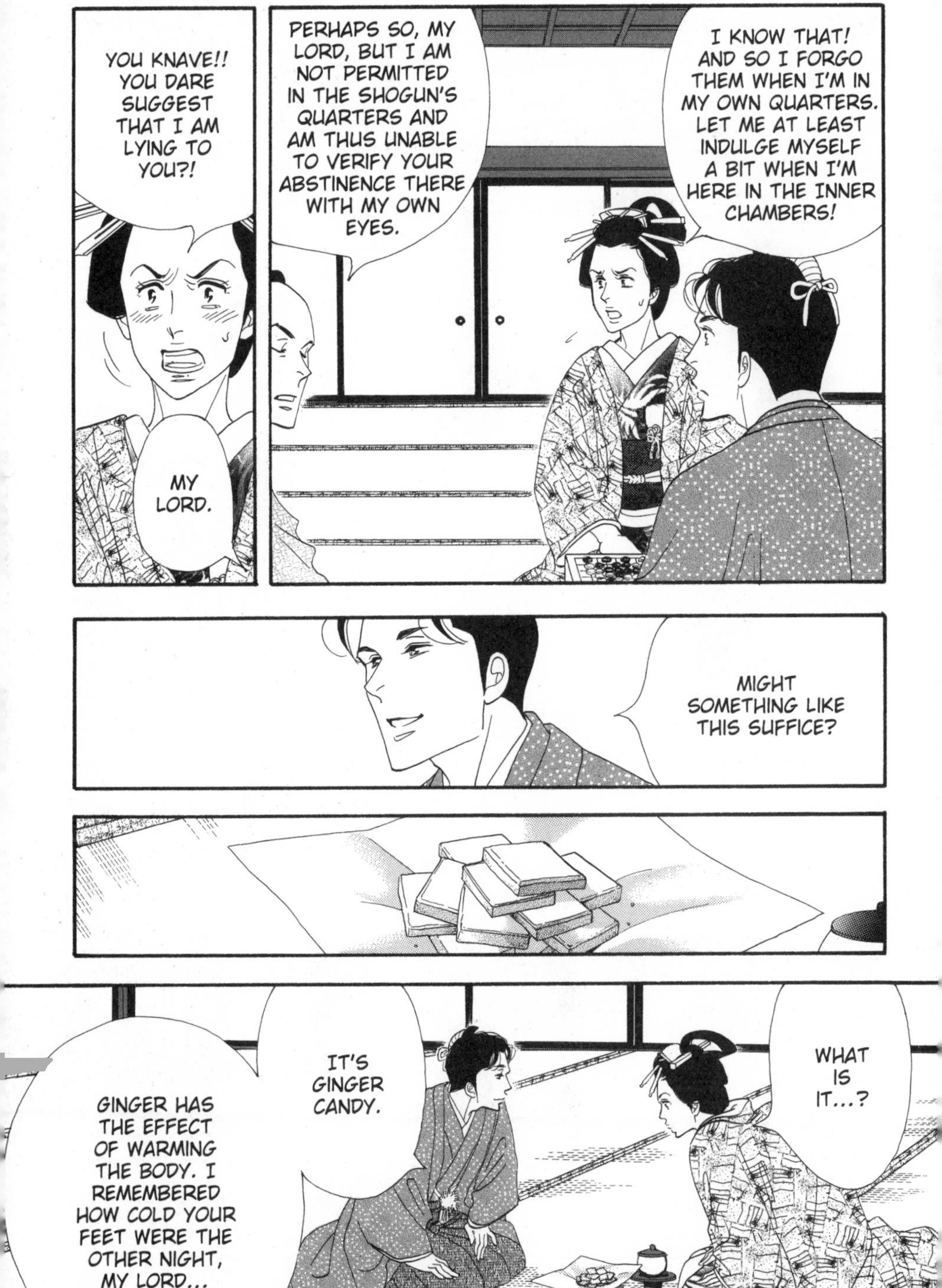
I KNOW THAT! AND SO I FORGO THEM WHEN I'M IN MY OWN QUARTERS. LET ME AT LEAST INDULGE MYSELF A BIT WHEN I'M HERE IN THE INNER CHAMBERS!
PERHAPS SO, MY LORD, BUT I AM NOT PERMITTED IN THE SHOGUN'S QUARTERS AND AM THUS UNABLE TO VERIFY YOUR ABSTINENCE THERE WITH MY OWN EYES.
YOU KNAVE!! YOU DARE SUGGEST THAT I AM LYING TO YOU?!
MY LORD.
MIGHT SOMETHING LIKE THIS SUFFICE?
WHAT IS IT...?
IT'S GINGER CANDY.
GINGER HAS THE EFFECT OF WARMING THE BODY. I REMEMBERED HOW COLD YOUR FEET WERE THE OTHER NIGHT, MY LORD...

NO, M'LORD!

WHAT DO YOU SAY, TAKIYAMA? YOU CAN'T OBJECT TO HER HIGHNESS NIBBLING ON THESE?

OH!

KRNCH KRNCH

MM! IT'S SWEET, BUT WITHIN THE SWEETNESS IS A SPICY HEAT...

I LIKE IT!

I AM VERY HAPPY TO HEAR IT.

KRNCH

IT'S LIKE I'M SOME KIND OF HECTORING OLD UNCLE OR SOMETHING!!

WELL, HELL!!

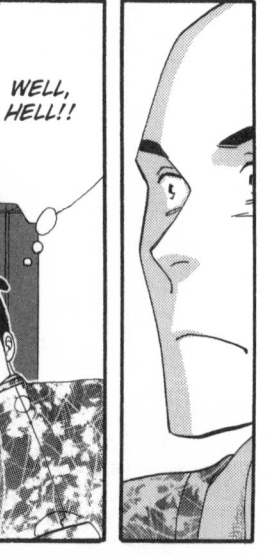

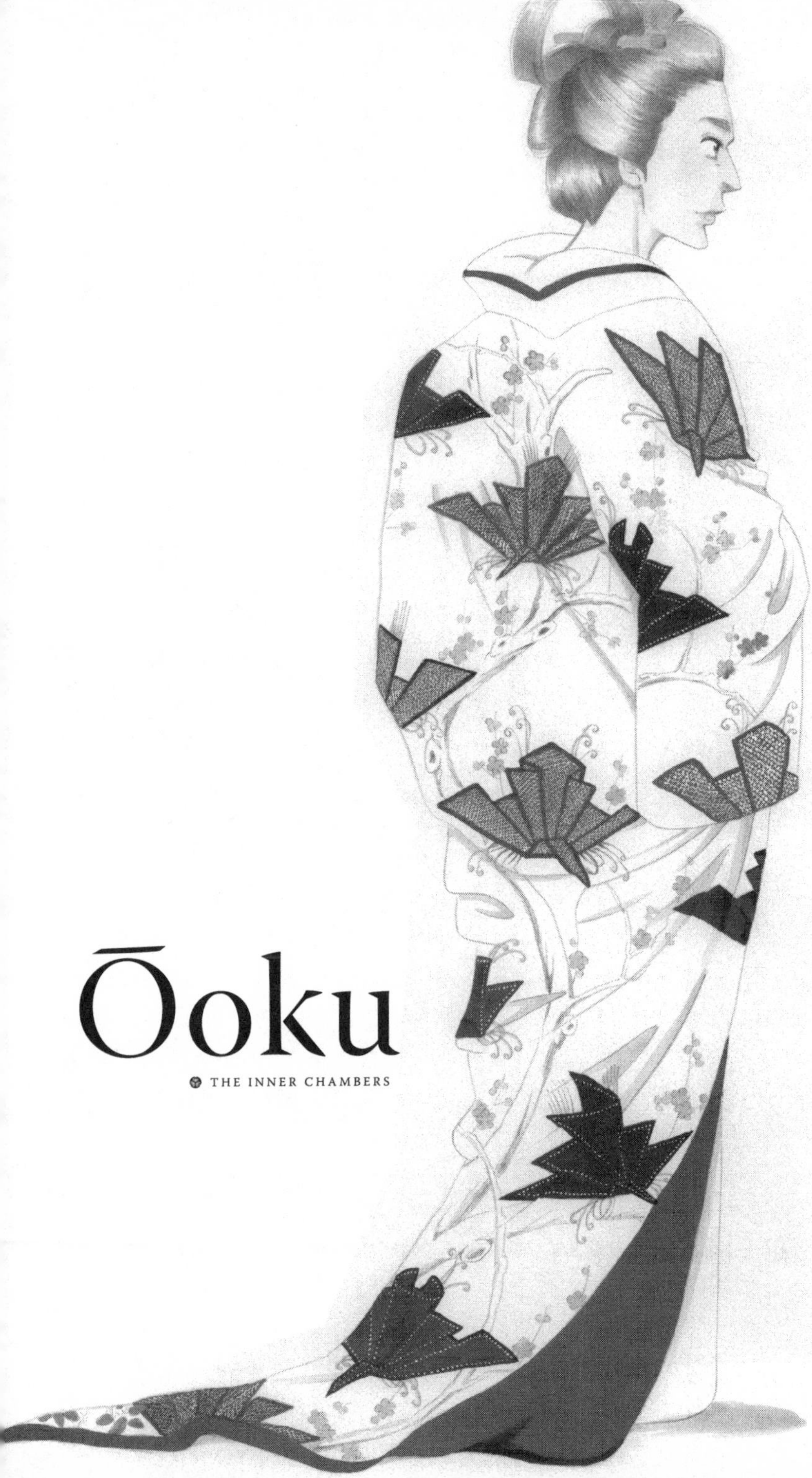

Ōoku

THE INNER CHAMBERS

Ōoku

🏵 THE INNER CHAMBERS

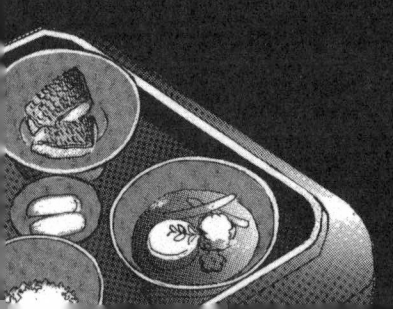

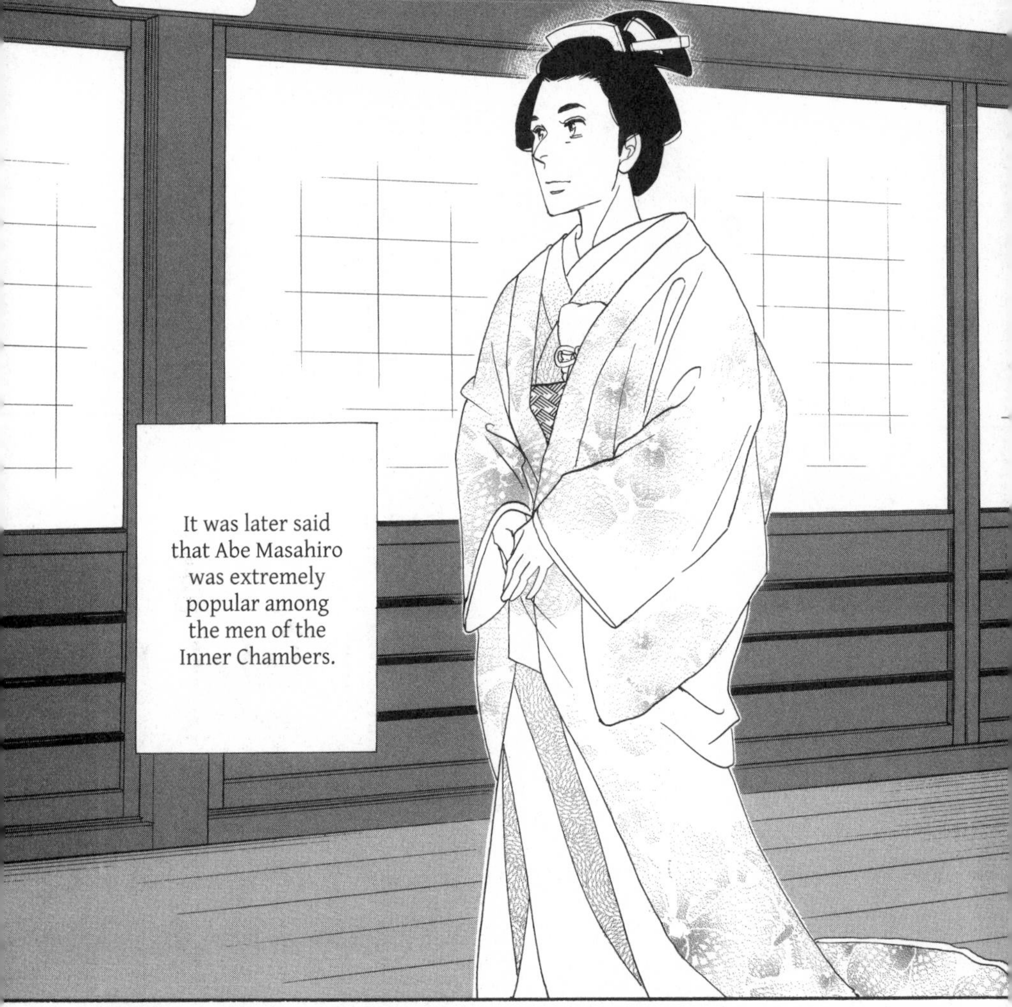
It was later said that Abe Masahiro was extremely popular among the men of the Inner Chambers.

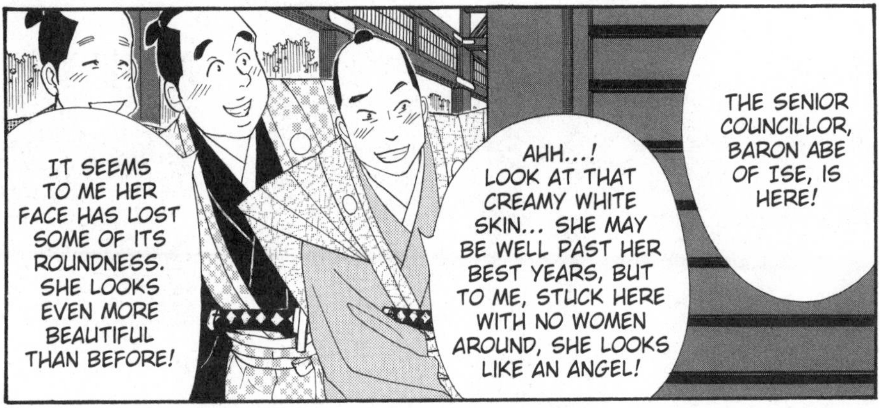
THE SENIOR COUNCILLOR, BARON ABE OF ISE, IS HERE!
AHH...! LOOK AT THAT CREAMY WHITE SKIN... SHE MAY BE WELL PAST HER BEST YEARS, BUT TO ME, STUCK HERE WITH NO WOMEN AROUND, SHE LOOKS LIKE AN ANGEL!
IT SEEMS TO ME HER FACE HAS LOST SOME OF ITS ROUNDNESS. SHE LOOKS EVEN MORE BEAUTIFUL THAN BEFORE!

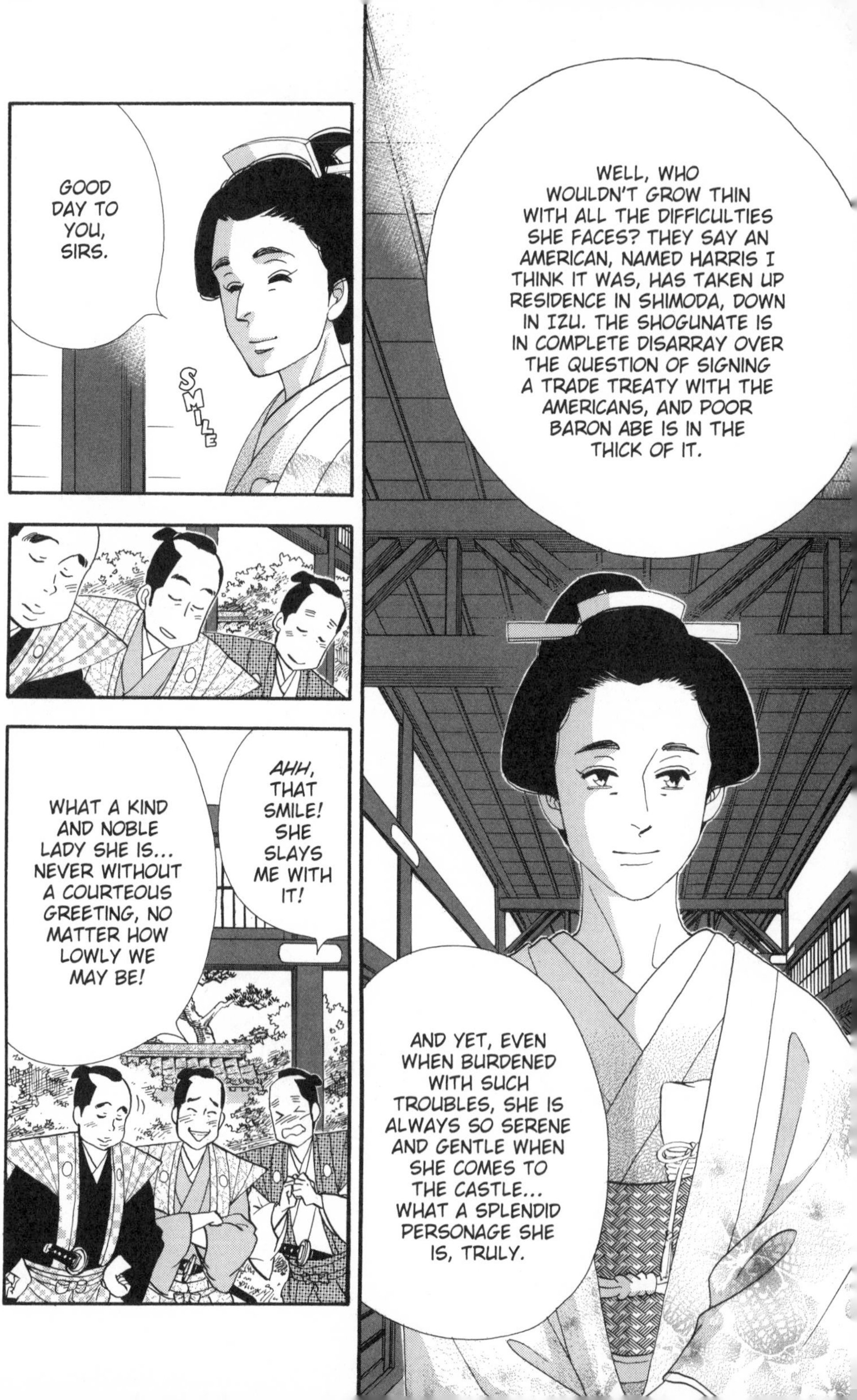
WELL, WHO WOULDN'T GROW THIN WITH ALL THE DIFFICULTIES SHE FACES? THEY SAY AN AMERICAN, NAMED HARRIS I THINK IT WAS, HAS TAKEN UP RESIDENCE IN SHIMODA, DOWN IN IZU. THE SHOGUNATE IS IN COMPLETE DISARRAY OVER THE QUESTION OF SIGNING A TRADE TREATY WITH THE AMERICANS, AND POOR BARON ABE IS IN THE THICK OF IT.
AND YET, EVEN WHEN BURDENED WITH SUCH TROUBLES, SHE IS ALWAYS SO SERENE AND GENTLE WHEN SHE COMES TO THE CASTLE... WHAT A SPLENDID PERSONAGE SHE IS, TRULY.
GOOD DAY TO YOU, SIRS.
SMILE
AHH, THAT SMILE! SHE SLAYS ME WITH IT!
WHAT A KIND AND NOBLE LADY SHE IS... NEVER WITHOUT A COURTEOUS GREETING, NO MATTER HOW LOWLY WE MAY BE!

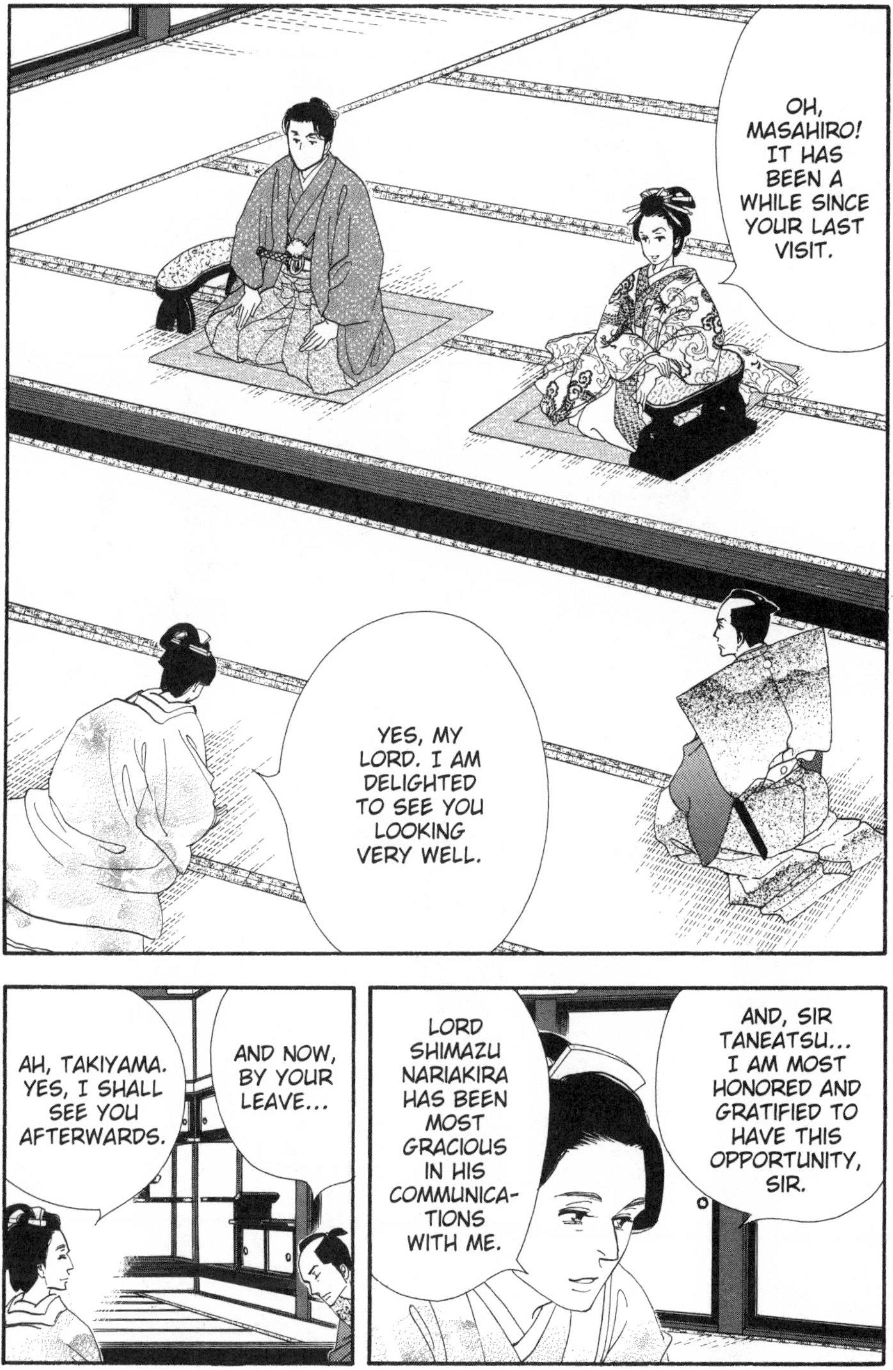
OH, MASAHIRO! IT HAS BEEN A WHILE SINCE YOUR LAST VISIT.
YES, MY LORD. I AM DELIGHTED TO SEE YOU LOOKING VERY WELL.
AND, SIR TANEATSU... I AM MOST HONORED AND GRATIFIED TO HAVE THIS OPPORTUNITY, SIR.
LORD SHIMAZU NARIAKIRA HAS BEEN MOST GRACIOUS IN HIS COMMUNICA-TIONS WITH ME.
AND NOW, BY YOUR LEAVE...
AH, TAKIYAMA. YES, I SHALL SEE YOU AFTERWARDS.

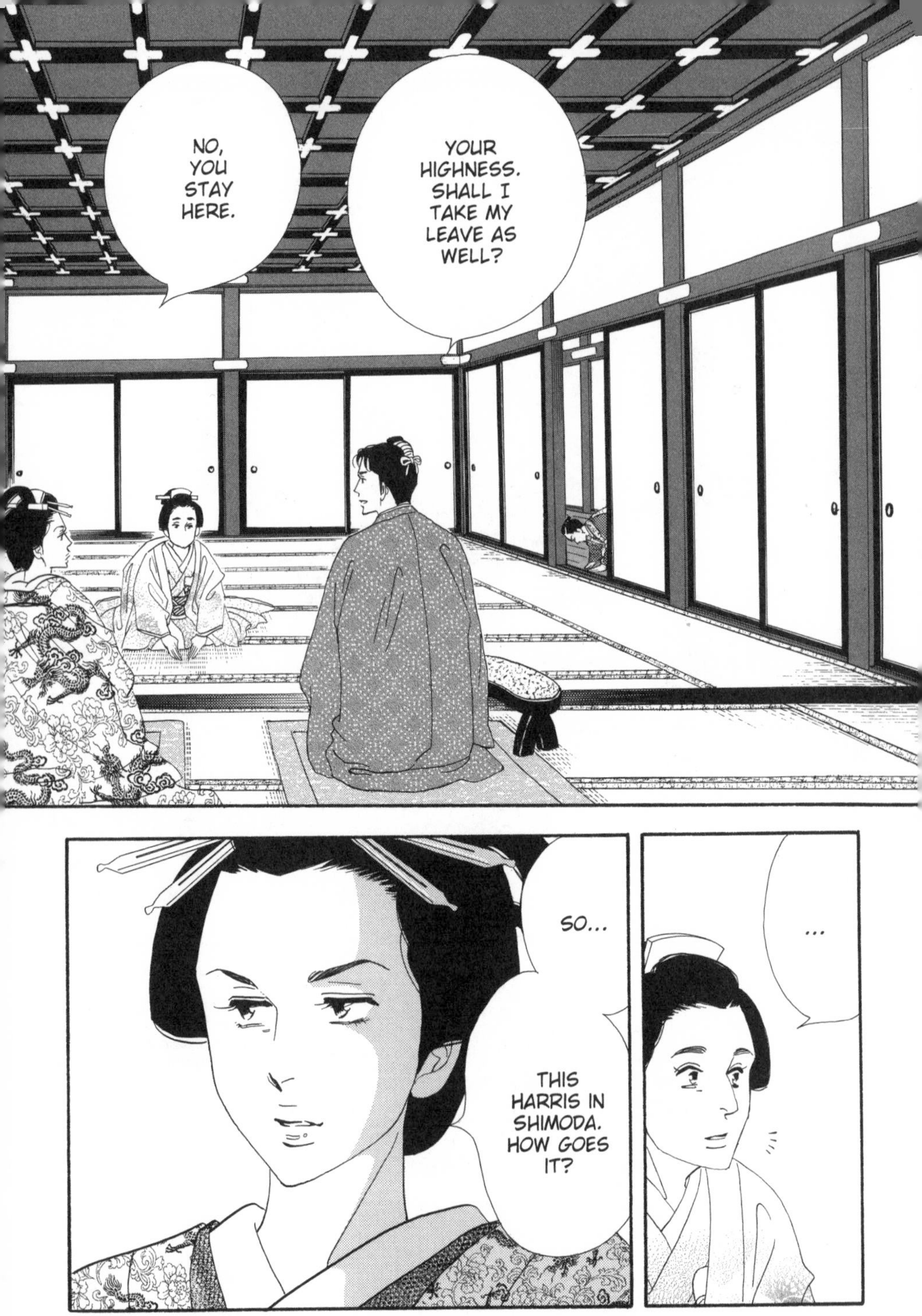
YOUR HIGHNESS. SHALL I TAKE MY LEAVE AS WELL?
NO, YOU STAY HERE.
...
SO...
THIS HARRIS IN SHIMODA. HOW GOES IT?

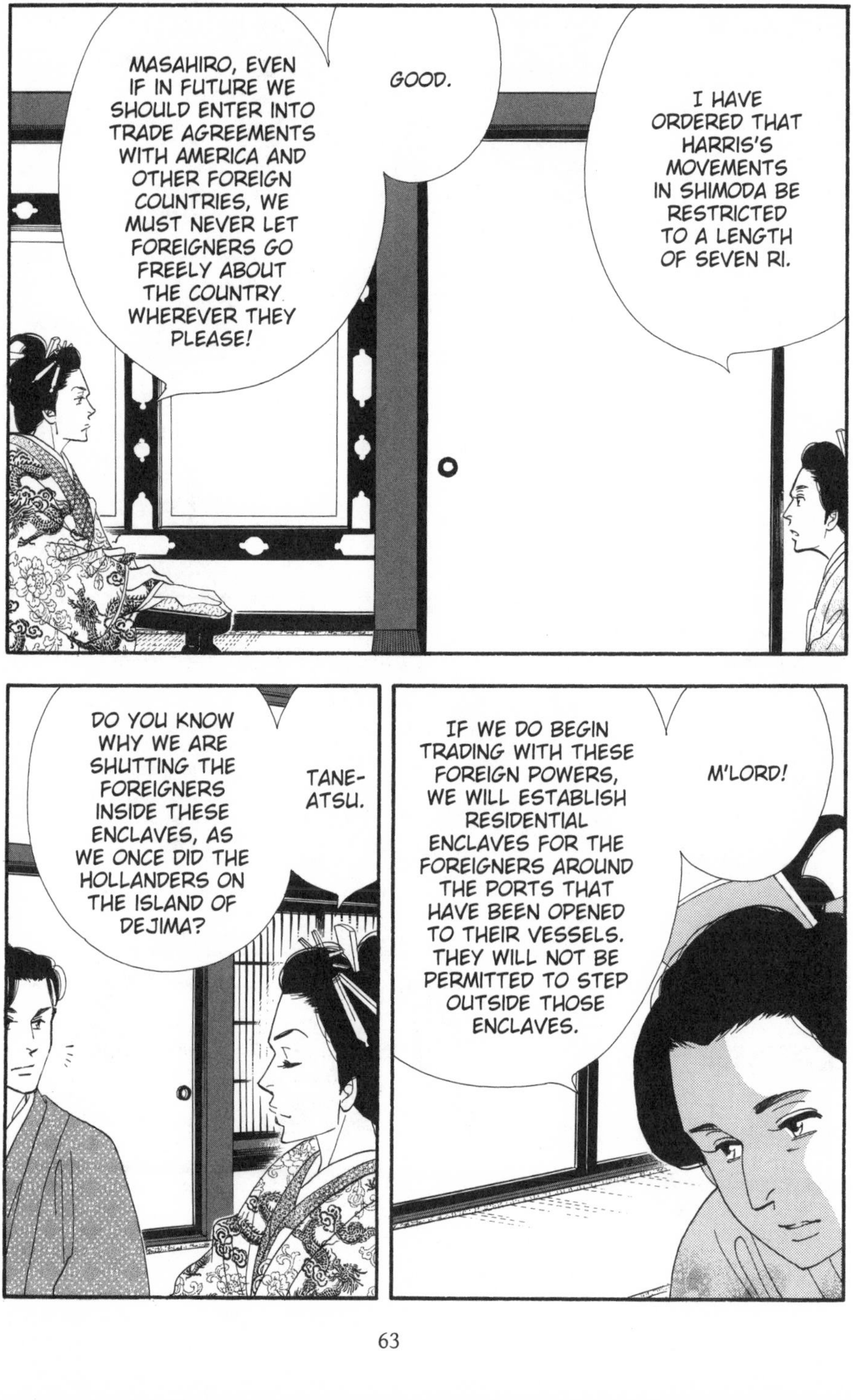
I HAVE ORDERED THAT HARRIS'S MOVEMENTS IN SHIMODA BE RESTRICTED TO A LENGTH OF SEVEN RI.
GOOD.
MASAHIRO, EVEN IF IN FUTURE WE SHOULD ENTER INTO TRADE AGREEMENTS WITH AMERICA AND OTHER FOREIGN COUNTRIES, WE MUST NEVER LET FOREIGNERS GO FREELY ABOUT THE COUNTRY WHEREVER THEY PLEASE!
M'LORD!
IF WE DO BEGIN TRADING WITH THESE FOREIGN POWERS, WE WILL ESTABLISH RESIDENTIAL ENCLAVES FOR THE FOREIGNERS AROUND THE PORTS THAT HAVE BEEN OPENED TO THEIR VESSELS. THEY WILL NOT BE PERMITTED TO STEP OUTSIDE THOSE ENCLAVES.
TANE-ATSU.
DO YOU KNOW WHY WE ARE SHUTTING THE FOREIGNERS INSIDE THESE ENCLAVES, AS WE ONCE DID THE HOLLANDERS ON THE ISLAND OF DEJIMA?

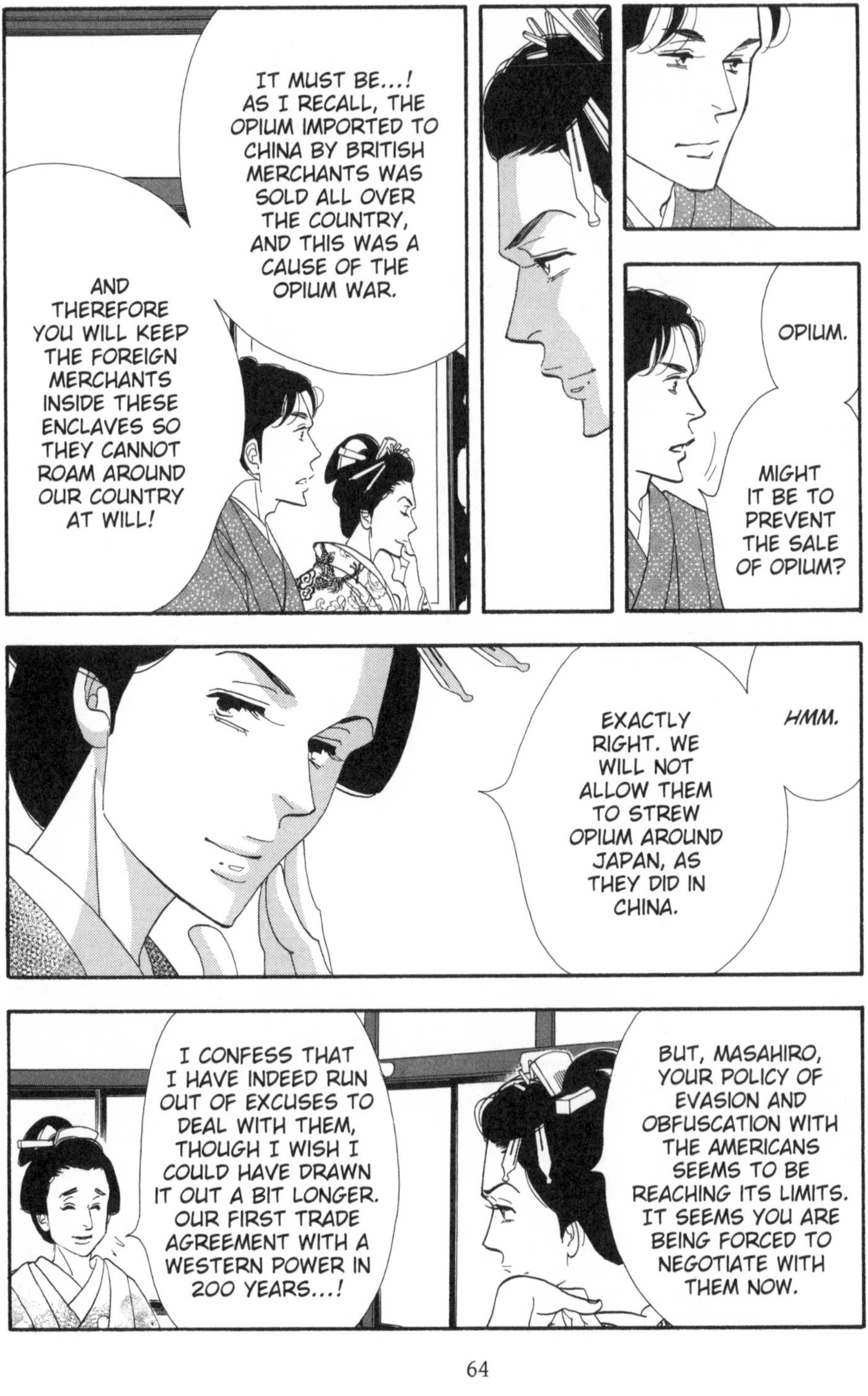
OPIUM.
MIGHT IT BE TO PREVENT THE SALE OF OPIUM?
IT MUST BE...! AS I RECALL, THE OPIUM IMPORTED TO CHINA BY BRITISH MERCHANTS WAS SOLD ALL OVER THE COUNTRY, AND THIS WAS A CAUSE OF THE OPIUM WAR.
AND THEREFORE YOU WILL KEEP THE FOREIGN MERCHANTS INSIDE THESE ENCLAVES SO THEY CANNOT ROAM AROUND OUR COUNTRY AT WILL!
HMM.
EXACTLY RIGHT. WE WILL NOT ALLOW THEM TO STREW OPIUM AROUND JAPAN, AS THEY DID IN CHINA.
BUT, MASAHIRO, YOUR POLICY OF EVASION AND OBFUSCATION WITH THE AMERICANS SEEMS TO BE REACHING ITS LIMITS. IT SEEMS YOU ARE BEING FORCED TO NEGOTIATE WITH THEM NOW.
I CONFESS THAT I HAVE INDEED RUN OUT OF EXCUSES TO DEAL WITH THEM, THOUGH I WISH I COULD HAVE DRAWN IT OUT A BIT LONGER. OUR FIRST TRADE AGREEMENT WITH A WESTERN POWER IN 200 YEARS...!

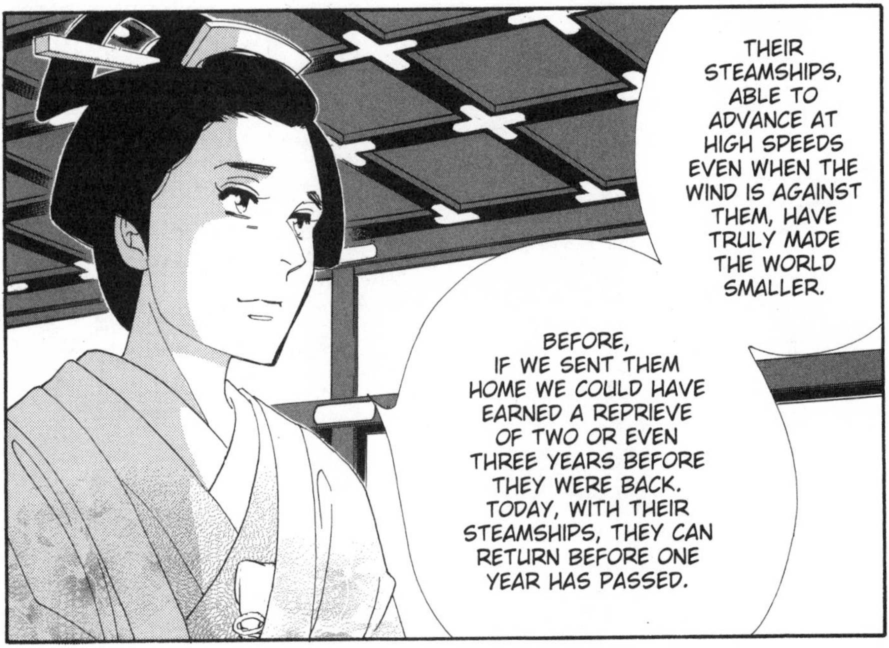
THEIR STEAMSHIPS, ABLE TO ADVANCE AT HIGH SPEEDS EVEN WHEN THE WIND IS AGAINST THEM, HAVE TRULY MADE THE WORLD SMALLER.
BEFORE, IF WE SENT THEM HOME WE COULD HAVE EARNED A REPRIEVE OF TWO OR EVEN THREE YEARS BEFORE THEY WERE BACK. TODAY, WITH THEIR STEAMSHIPS, THEY CAN RETURN BEFORE ONE YEAR HAS PASSED.
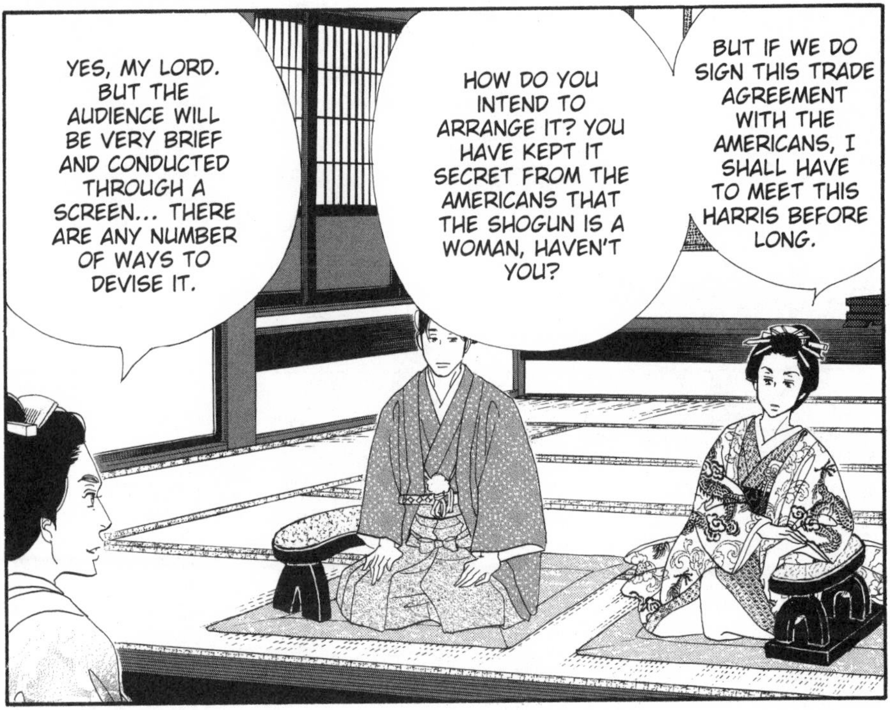
BUT IF WE DO SIGN THIS TRADE AGREEMENT WITH THE AMERICANS, I SHALL HAVE TO MEET THIS HARRIS BEFORE LONG.
HOW DO YOU INTEND TO ARRANGE IT? YOU HAVE KEPT IT SECRET FROM THE AMERICANS THAT THE SHOGUN IS A WOMAN, HAVEN'T YOU?
YES, MY LORD. BUT THE AUDIENCE WILL BE VERY BRIEF AND CONDUCTED THROUGH A SCREEN... THERE ARE ANY NUMBER OF WAYS TO DEVISE IT.

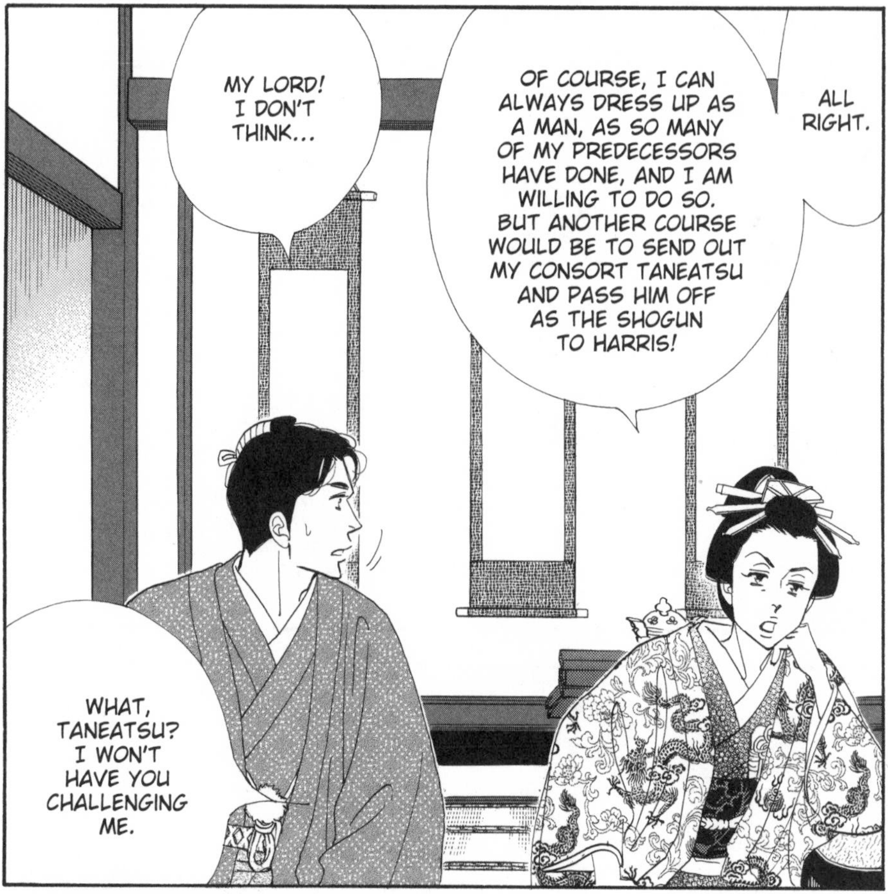
ALL RIGHT.
OF COURSE, I CAN ALWAYS DRESS UP AS A MAN, AS SO MANY OF MY PREDECESSORS HAVE DONE, AND I AM WILLING TO DO SO. BUT ANOTHER COURSE WOULD BE TO SEND OUT MY CONSORT TANEATSU AND PASS HIM OFF AS THE SHOGUN TO HARRIS!
MY LORD! I DON'T THINK...
WHAT, TANEATSU? I WON'T HAVE YOU CHALLENGING ME.

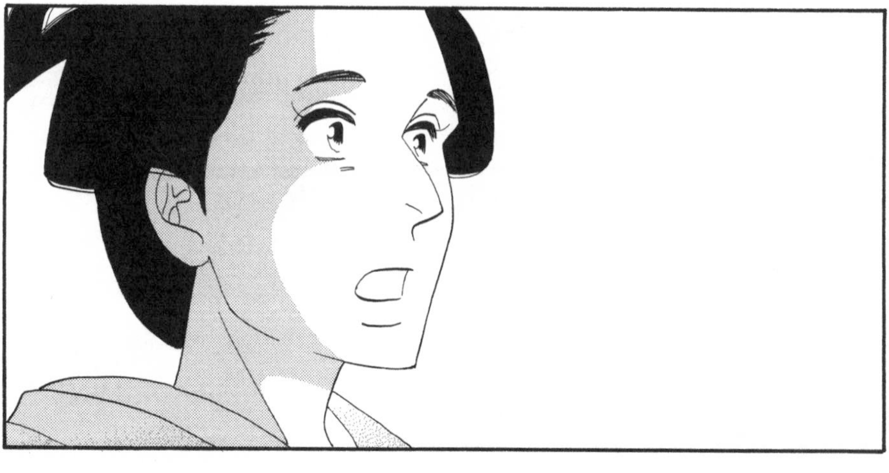

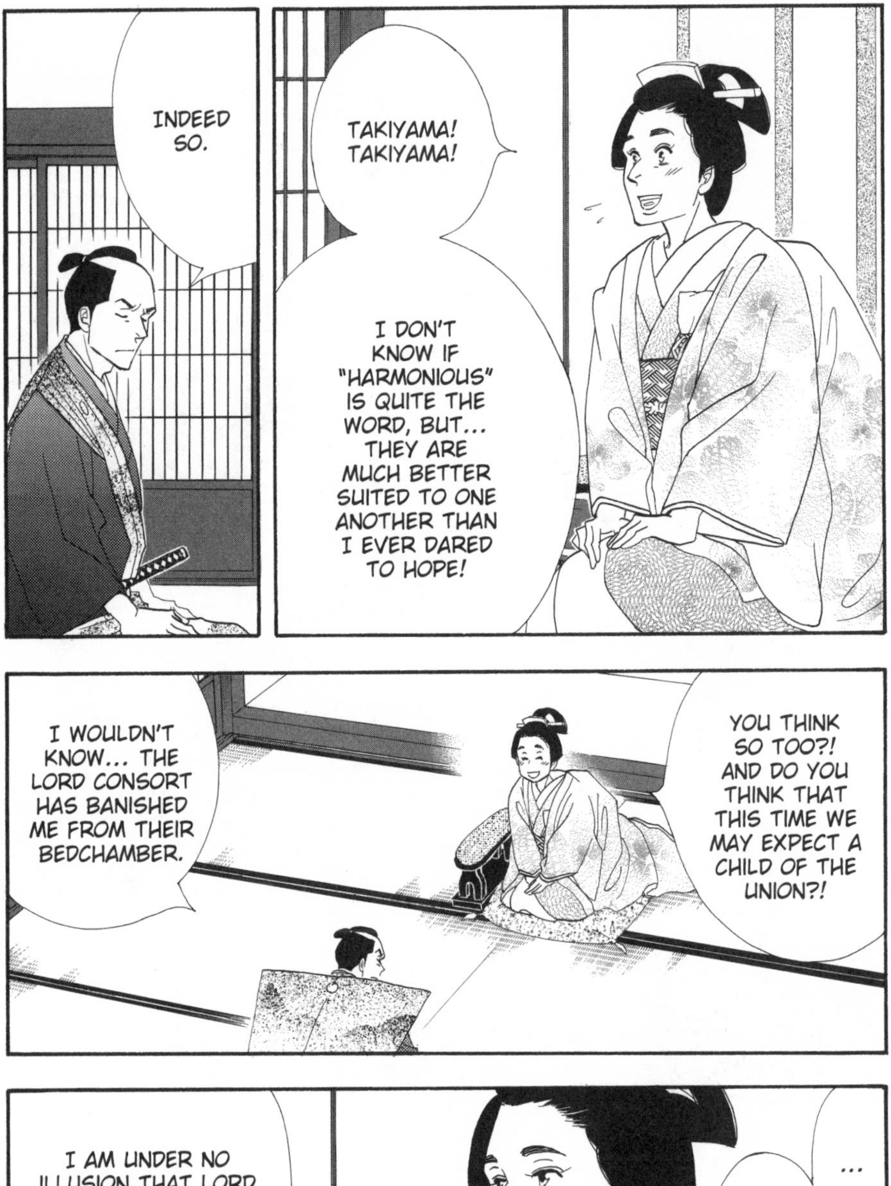
TAKIYAMA! TAKIYAMA!
I DON'T KNOW IF "HARMONIOUS" IS QUITE THE WORD, BUT... THEY ARE MUCH BETTER SUITED TO ONE ANOTHER THAN I EVER DARED TO HOPE!
INDEED SO.
YOU THINK SO TOO?! AND DO YOU THINK THAT THIS TIME WE MAY EXPECT A CHILD OF THE UNION?!
I WOULDN'T KNOW... THE LORD CONSORT HAS BANISHED ME FROM THEIR BEDCHAMBER.
...
TAKIYAMA.
I AM UNDER NO ILLUSION THAT LORD SHIMAZU NARIAKIRA OF SATSUMA SENT SIR TANEATSU HERE TO EDO WITH NO DESIGNS OF HIS OWN.

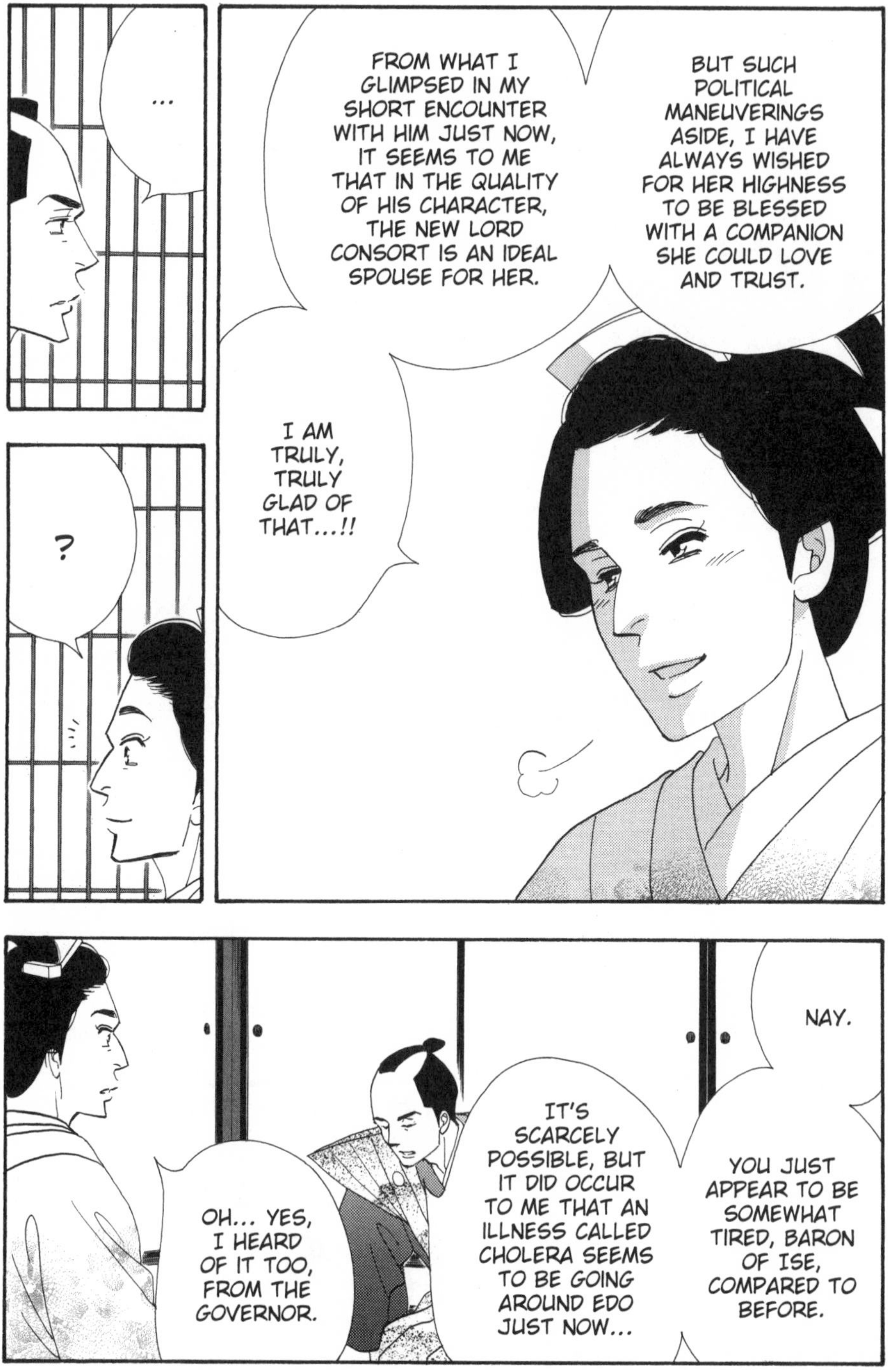
BUT SUCH POLITICAL MANEUVERINGS ASIDE, I HAVE ALWAYS WISHED FOR HER HIGHNESS TO BE BLESSED WITH A COMPANION SHE COULD LOVE AND TRUST.
FROM WHAT I GLIMPSED IN MY SHORT ENCOUNTER WITH HIM JUST NOW, IT SEEMS TO ME THAT IN THE QUALITY OF HIS CHARACTER, THE NEW LORD CONSORT IS AN IDEAL SPOUSE FOR HER.
I AM TRULY, TRULY GLAD OF THAT...!!
...
?
NAY.
YOU JUST APPEAR TO BE SOMEWHAT TIRED, BARON OF ISE, COMPARED TO BEFORE.
IT'S SCARCELY POSSIBLE, BUT IT DID OCCUR TO ME THAT AN ILLNESS CALLED CHOLERA SEEMS TO BE GOING AROUND EDO JUST NOW...
OH... YES, I HEARD OF IT TOO, FROM THE GOVERNOR.

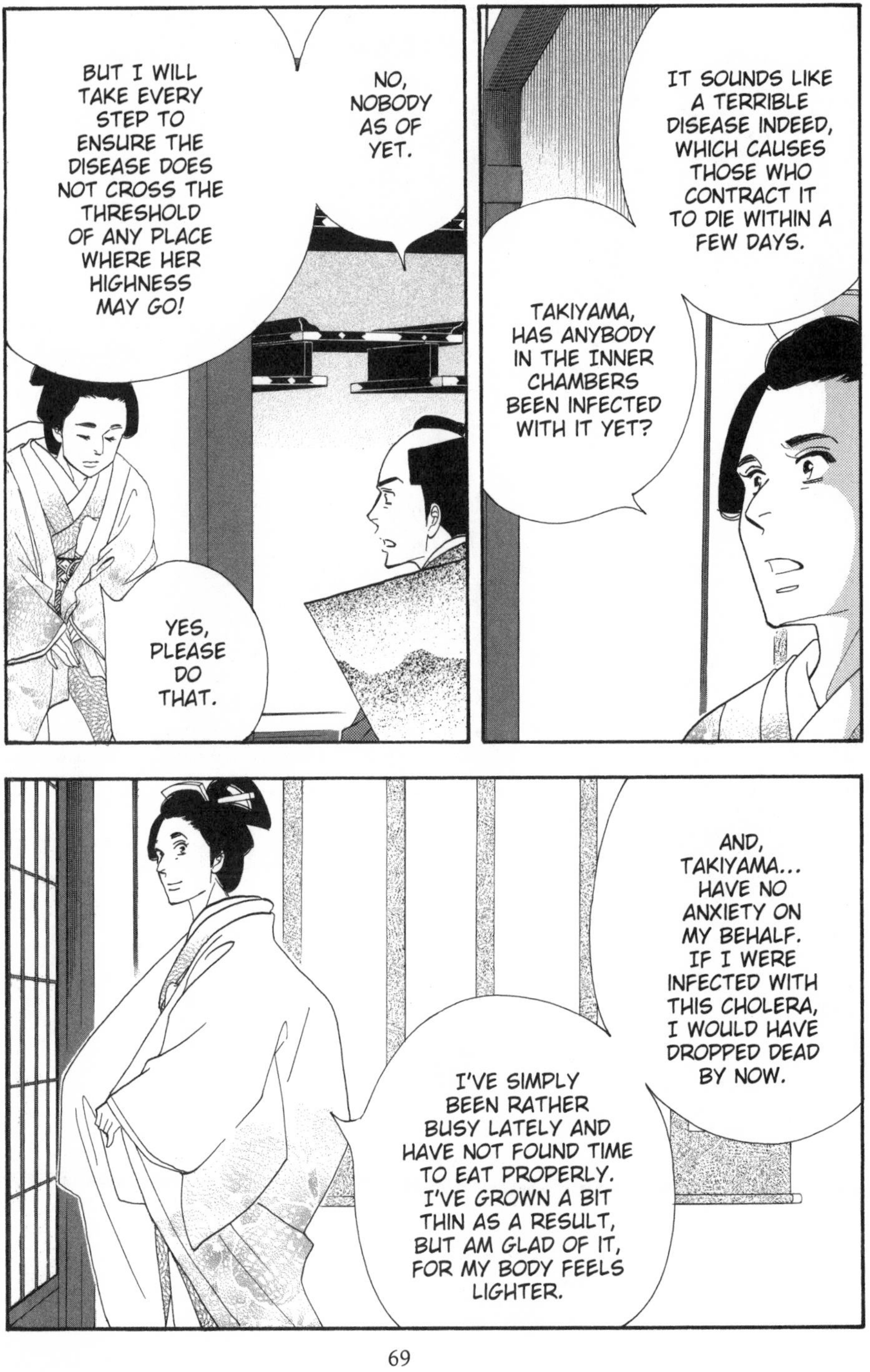
IT SOUNDS LIKE A TERRIBLE DISEASE INDEED, WHICH CAUSES THOSE WHO CONTRACT IT TO DIE WITHIN A FEW DAYS.
TAKIYAMA, HAS ANYBODY IN THE INNER CHAMBERS BEEN INFECTED WITH IT YET?
NO, NOBODY AS OF YET.
BUT I WILL TAKE EVERY STEP TO ENSURE THE DISEASE DOES NOT CROSS THE THRESHOLD OF ANY PLACE WHERE HER HIGHNESS MAY GO!
YES, PLEASE DO THAT.
AND, TAKIYAMA... HAVE NO ANXIETY ON MY BEHALF. IF I WERE INFECTED WITH THIS CHOLERA, I WOULD HAVE DROPPED DEAD BY NOW.
I'VE SIMPLY BEEN RATHER BUSY LATELY AND HAVE NOT FOUND TIME TO EAT PROPERLY. I'VE GROWN A BIT THIN AS A RESULT, BUT AM GLAD OF IT, FOR MY BODY FEELS LIGHTER.

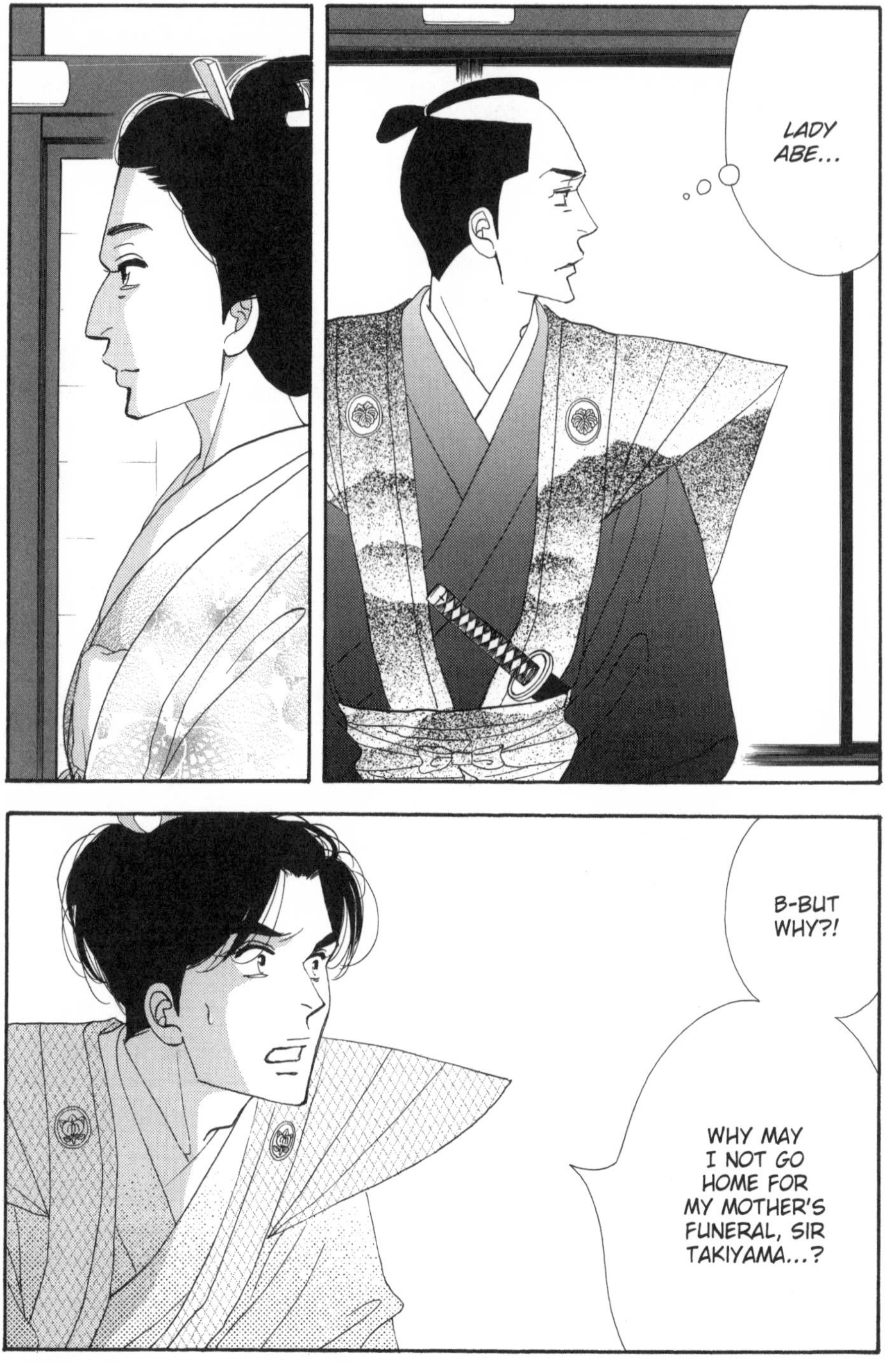
LADY ABE...
B-BUT WHY?!
WHY MAY I NOT GO HOME FOR MY MOTHER'S FUNERAL, SIR TAKIYAMA...?

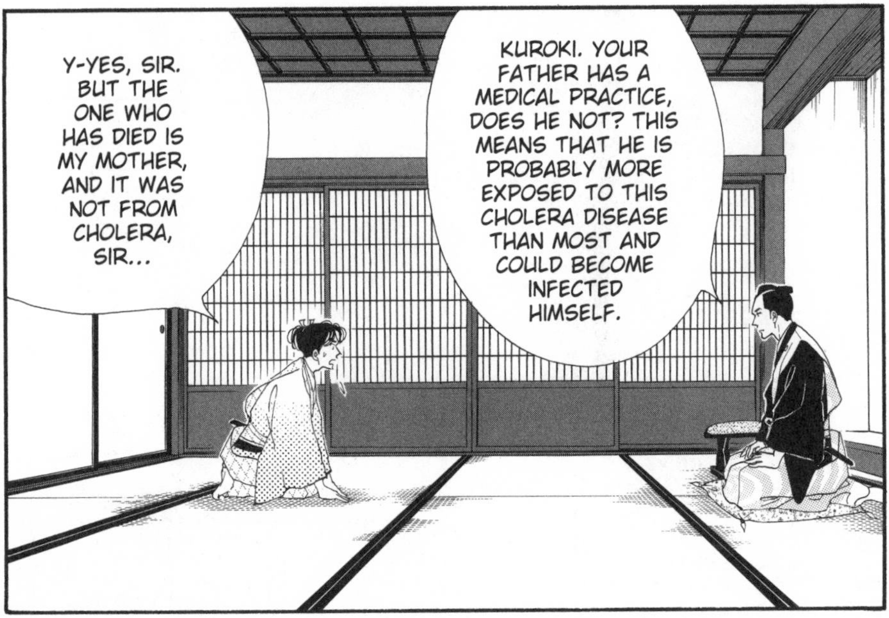
KUROKI. YOUR FATHER HAS A MEDICAL PRACTICE, DOES HE NOT? THIS MEANS THAT HE IS PROBABLY MORE EXPOSED TO THIS CHOLERA DISEASE THAN MOST AND COULD BECOME INFECTED HIMSELF.
Y-YES, SIR. BUT THE ONE WHO HAS DIED IS MY MOTHER, AND IT WAS NOT FROM CHOLERA, SIR...
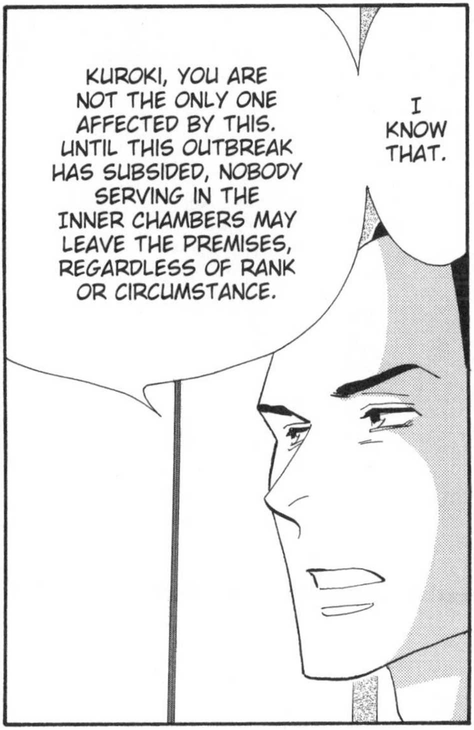
KUROKI, YOU ARE NOT THE ONLY ONE AFFECTED BY THIS. UNTIL THIS OUTBREAK HAS SUBSIDED, NOBODY SERVING IN THE INNER CHAMBERS MAY LEAVE THE PREMISES, REGARDLESS OF RANK OR CIRCUMSTANCE.
I KNOW THAT.
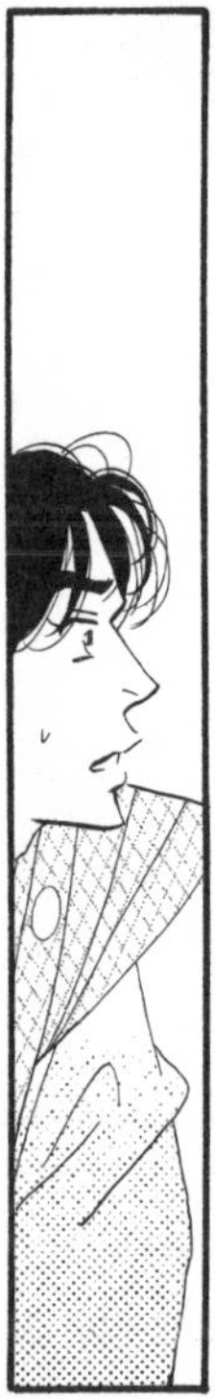
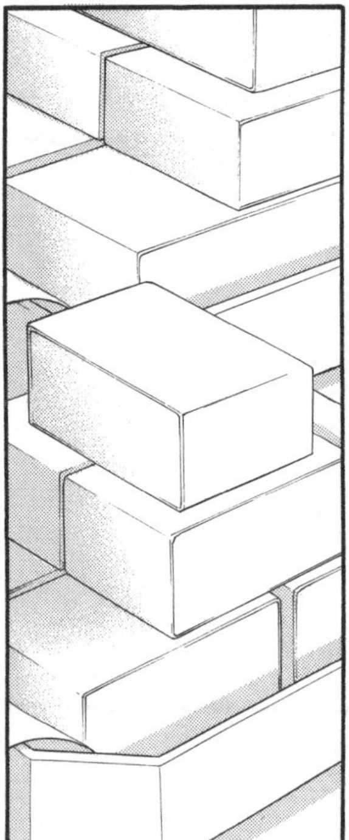

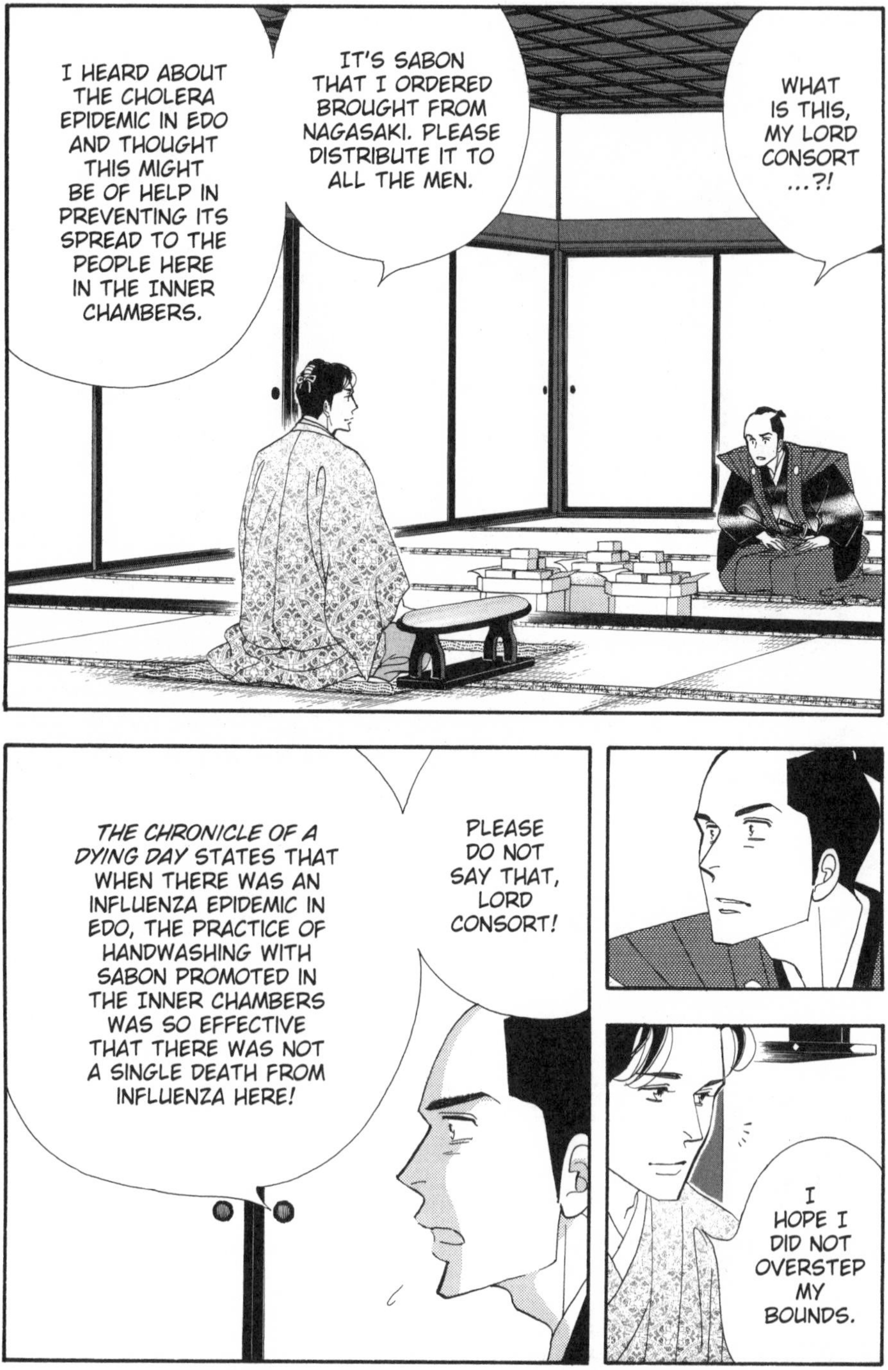
WHAT IS THIS, MY LORD CONSORT ...?!
IT'S SABON THAT I ORDERED BROUGHT FROM NAGASAKI. PLEASE DISTRIBUTE IT TO ALL THE MEN.
I HEARD ABOUT THE CHOLERA EPIDEMIC IN EDO AND THOUGHT THIS MIGHT BE OF HELP IN PREVENTING ITS SPREAD TO THE PEOPLE HERE IN THE INNER CHAMBERS.
I HOPE I DID NOT OVERSTEP MY BOUNDS.
PLEASE DO NOT SAY THAT, LORD CONSORT!
THE CHRONICLE OF A DYING DAY STATES THAT WHEN THERE WAS AN INFLUENZA EPIDEMIC IN EDO, THE PRACTICE OF HANDWASHING WITH SABON PROMOTED IN THE INNER CHAMBERS WAS SO EFFECTIVE THAT THERE WAS NOT A SINGLE DEATH FROM INFLUENZA HERE!

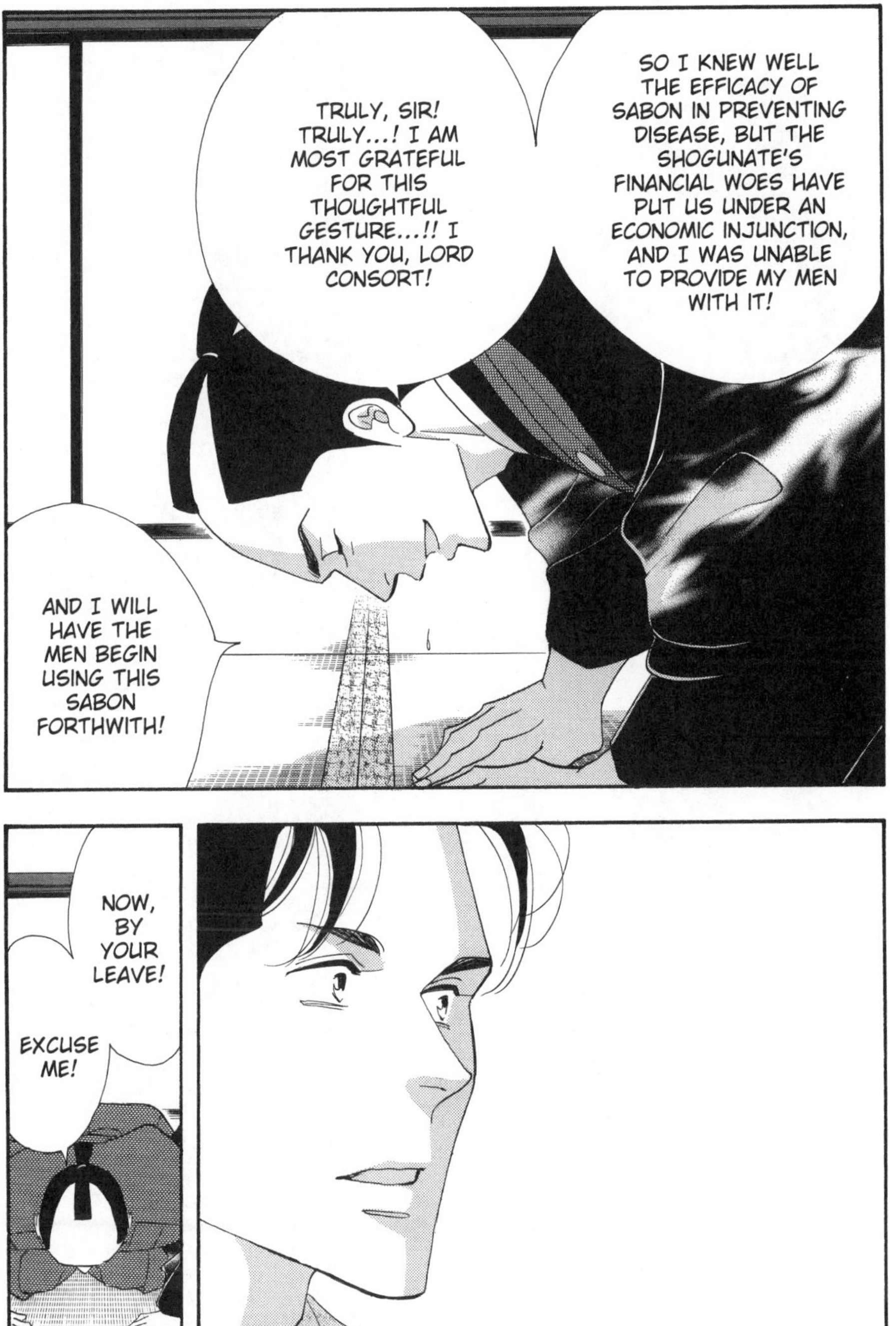
SO I KNEW WELL THE EFFICACY OF SABON IN PREVENTING DISEASE, BUT THE SHOGUNATE'S FINANCIAL WOES HAVE PUT US UNDER AN ECONOMIC INJUNCTION, AND I WAS UNABLE TO PROVIDE MY MEN WITH IT!
TRULY, SIR! TRULY...! I AM MOST GRATEFUL FOR THIS THOUGHTFUL GESTURE...!! I THANK YOU, LORD CONSORT!
AND I WILL HAVE THE MEN BEGIN USING THIS SABON FORTHWITH!
NOW, BY YOUR LEAVE!
EXCUSE ME!

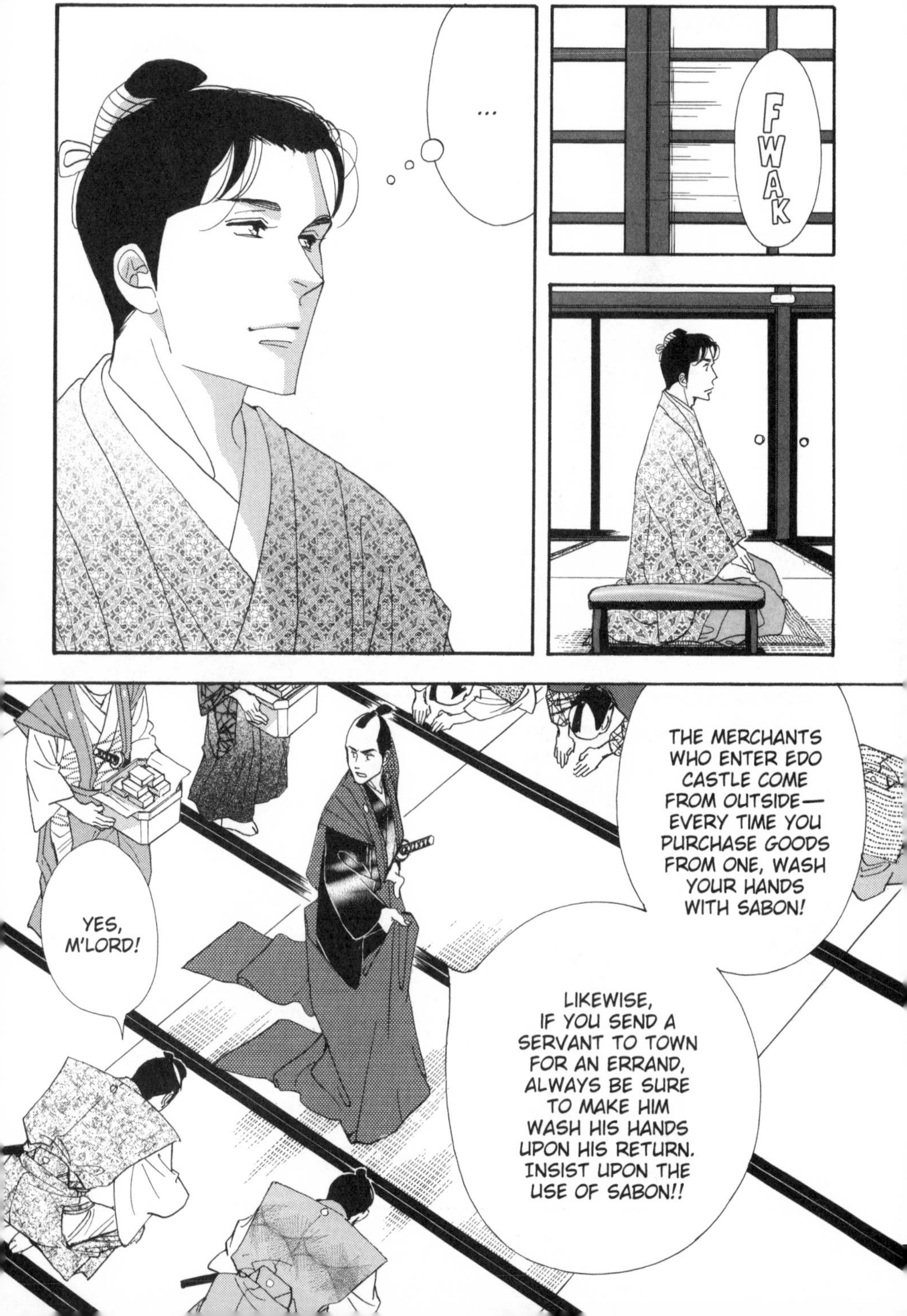
FWAK
...
THE MERCHANTS WHO ENTER EDO CASTLE COME FROM OUTSIDE— EVERY TIME YOU PURCHASE GOODS FROM ONE, WASH YOUR HANDS WITH SABON!
LIKEWISE, IF YOU SEND A SERVANT TO TOWN FOR AN ERRAND, ALWAYS BE SURE TO MAKE HIM WASH HIS HANDS UPON HIS RETURN. INSIST UPON THE USE OF SABON!!
YES, M'LORD!

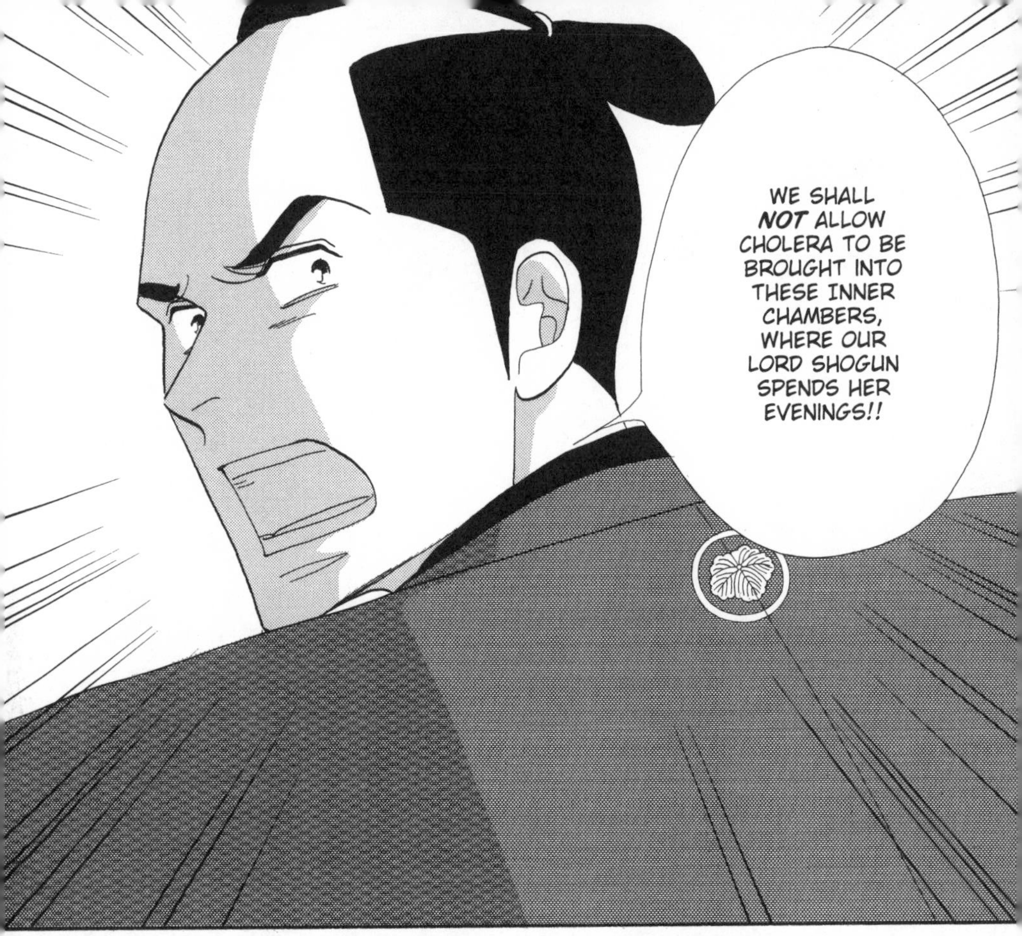
WE SHALL **NOT** ALLOW CHOLERA TO BE BROUGHT INTO THESE INNER CHAMBERS, WHERE OUR LORD SHOGUN SPENDS HER EVENINGS!!

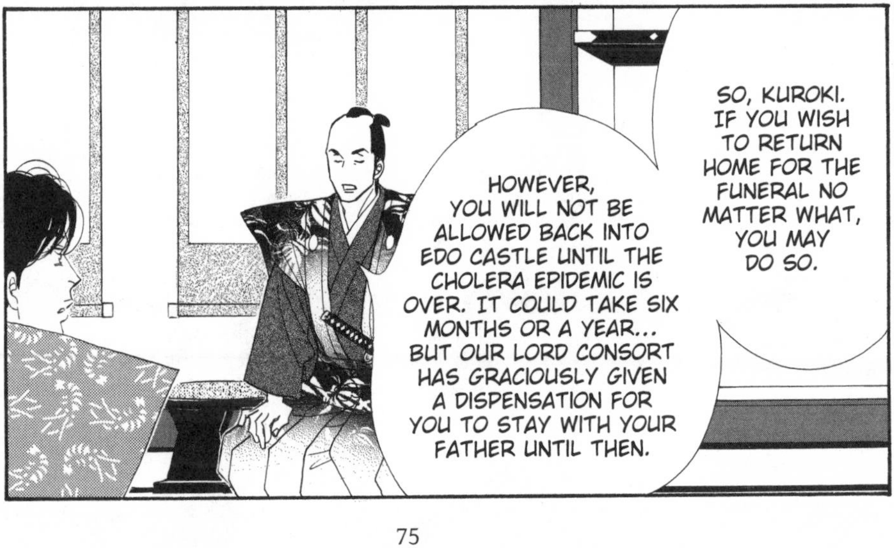
SO, KUROKI. IF YOU WISH TO RETURN HOME FOR THE FUNERAL NO MATTER WHAT, YOU MAY DO SO.
HOWEVER, YOU WILL NOT BE ALLOWED BACK INTO EDO CASTLE UNTIL THE CHOLERA EPIDEMIC IS OVER. IT COULD TAKE SIX MONTHS OR A YEAR... BUT OUR LORD CONSORT HAS GRACIOUSLY GIVEN A DISPENSATION FOR YOU TO STAY WITH YOUR FATHER UNTIL THEN.

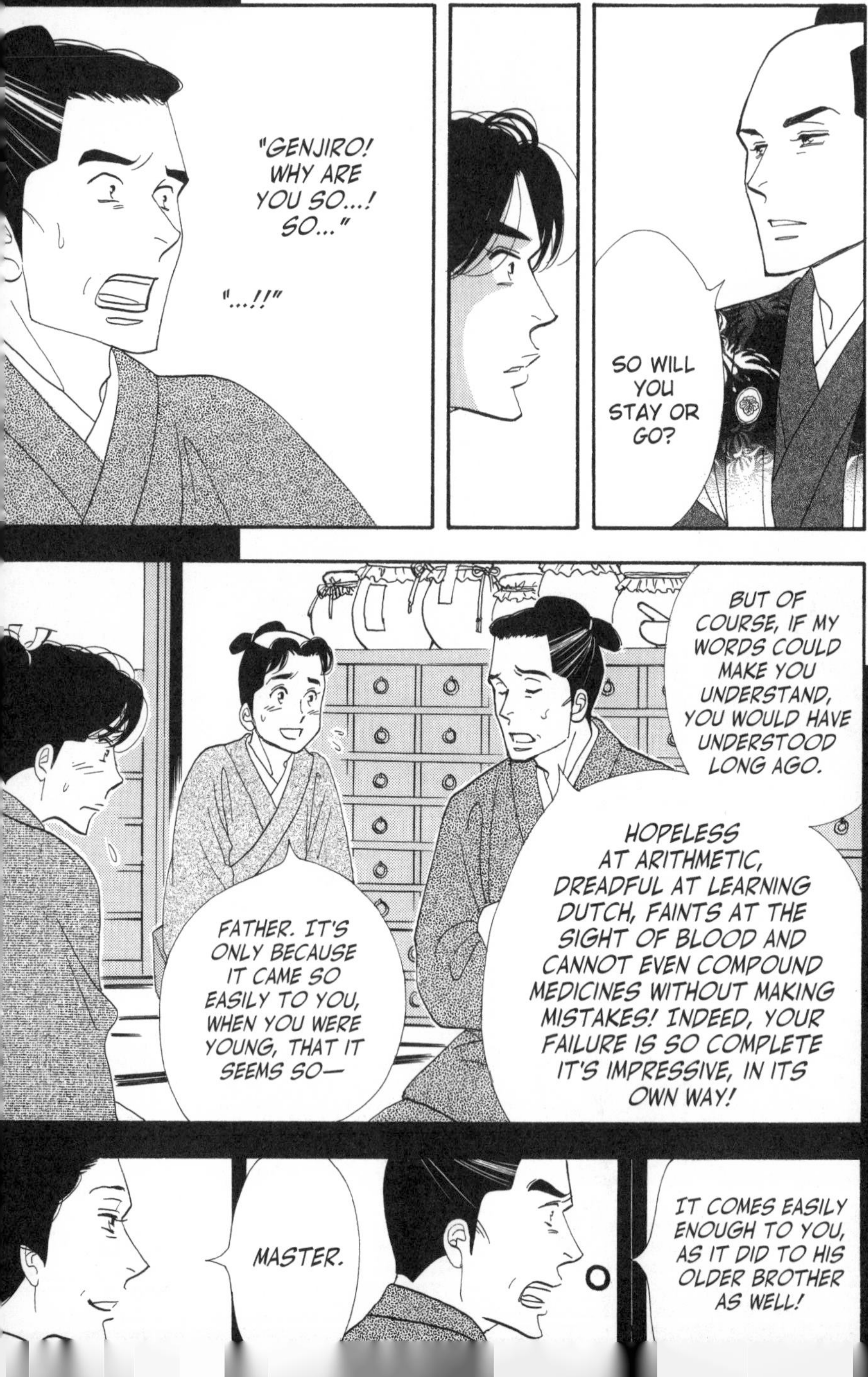
SO WILL YOU STAY OR GO?
"GENJIRO! WHY ARE YOU SO...! SO..."
"...!!"
BUT OF COURSE, IF MY WORDS COULD MAKE YOU UNDERSTAND, YOU WOULD HAVE UNDERSTOOD LONG AGO.
HOPELESS AT ARITHMETIC, DREADFUL AT LEARNING DUTCH, FAINTS AT THE SIGHT OF BLOOD AND CANNOT EVEN COMPOUND MEDICINES WITHOUT MAKING MISTAKES! INDEED, YOUR FAILURE IS SO COMPLETE IT'S IMPRESSIVE, IN ITS OWN WAY!
FATHER. IT'S ONLY BECAUSE IT CAME SO EASILY TO YOU, WHEN YOU WERE YOUNG, THAT IT SEEMS SO—
IT COMES EASILY ENOUGH TO YOU, AS IT DID TO HIS OLDER BROTHER AS WELL!
MASTER.

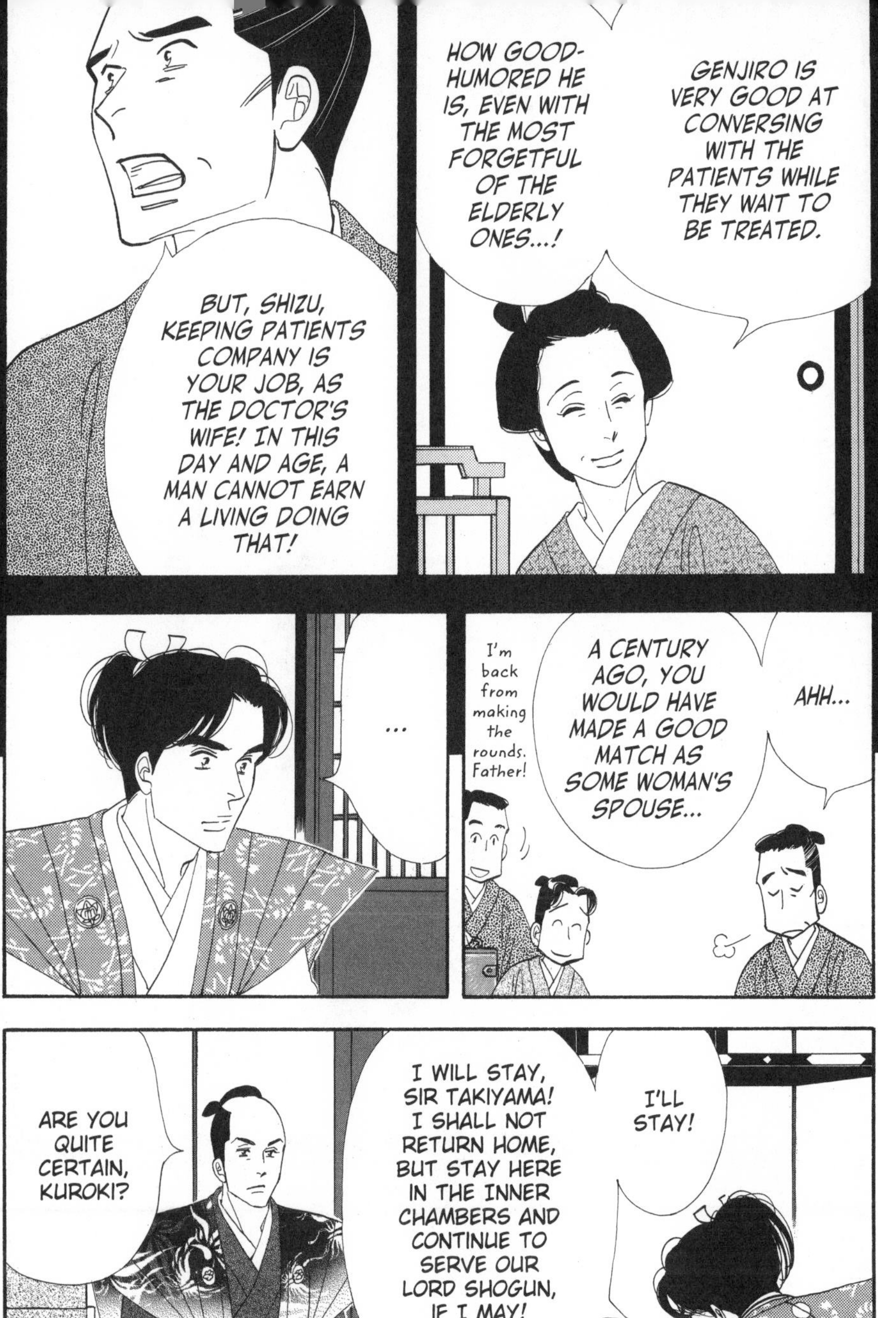
GENJIRO IS VERY GOOD AT CONVERSING WITH THE PATIENTS WHILE THEY WAIT TO BE TREATED.
HOW GOOD-HUMORED HE IS, EVEN WITH THE MOST FORGETFUL OF THE ELDERLY ONES...!
BUT, SHIZU, KEEPING PATIENTS COMPANY IS YOUR JOB, AS THE DOCTOR'S WIFE! IN THIS DAY AND AGE, A MAN CANNOT EARN A LIVING DOING THAT!
AHH...
A CENTURY AGO, YOU WOULD HAVE MADE A GOOD MATCH AS SOME WOMAN'S SPOUSE...
I'm back from making the rounds. Father!
...
I'LL STAY!
I WILL STAY, SIR TAKIYAMA! I SHALL NOT RETURN HOME, BUT STAY HERE IN THE INNER CHAMBERS AND CONTINUE TO SERVE OUR LORD SHOGUN, IF I MAY!
ARE YOU QUITE CERTAIN, KUROKI?

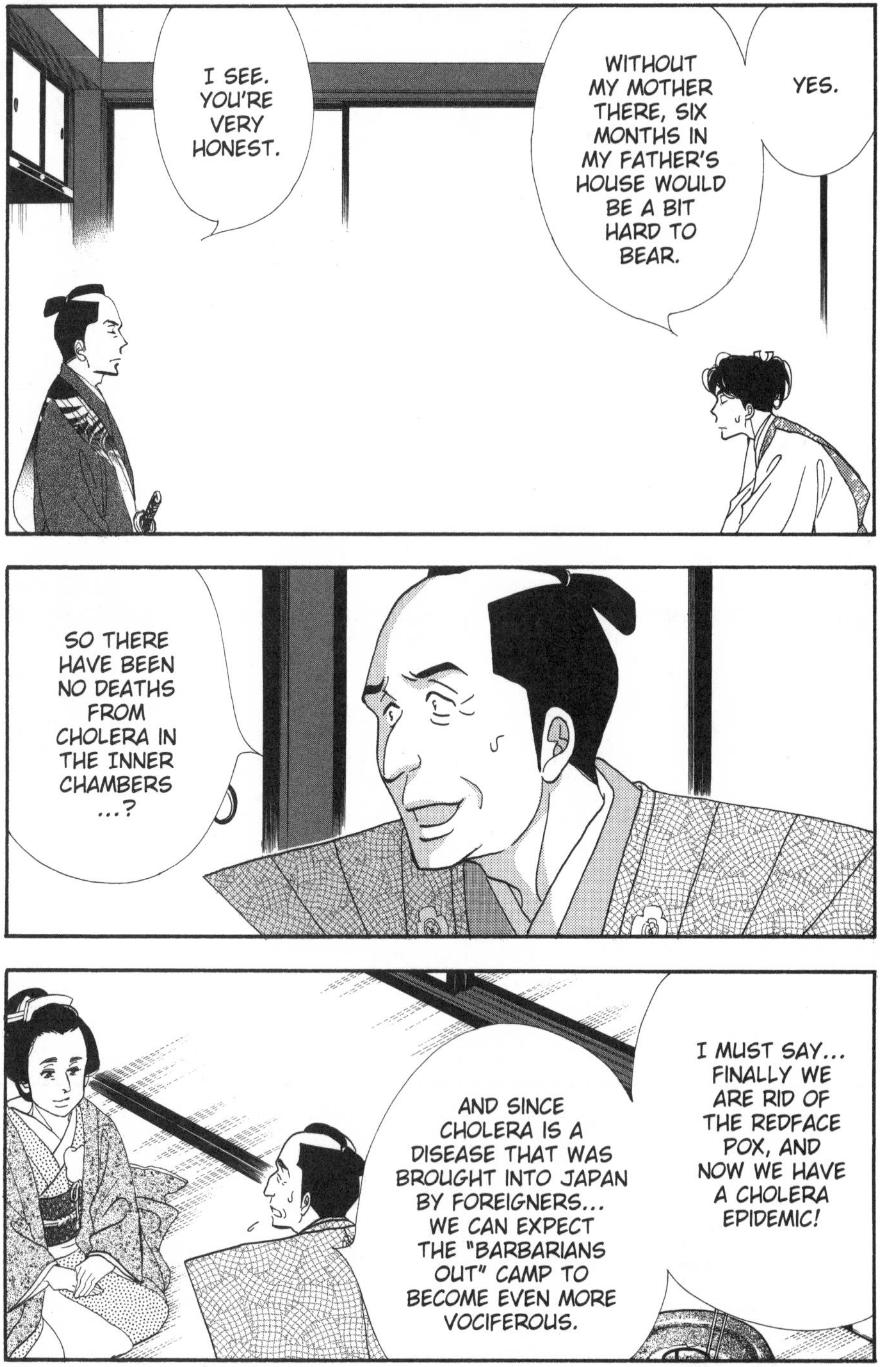
YES.
WITHOUT MY MOTHER THERE, SIX MONTHS IN MY FATHER'S HOUSE WOULD BE A BIT HARD TO BEAR.
I SEE. YOU'RE VERY HONEST.
SO THERE HAVE BEEN NO DEATHS FROM CHOLERA IN THE INNER CHAMBERS ...?
I MUST SAY... FINALLY WE ARE RID OF THE REDFACE POX, AND NOW WE HAVE A CHOLERA EPIDEMIC!
AND SINCE CHOLERA IS A DISEASE THAT WAS BROUGHT INTO JAPAN BY FOREIGNERS... WE CAN EXPECT THE "BARBARIANS OUT" CAMP TO BECOME EVEN MORE VOCIFEROUS.

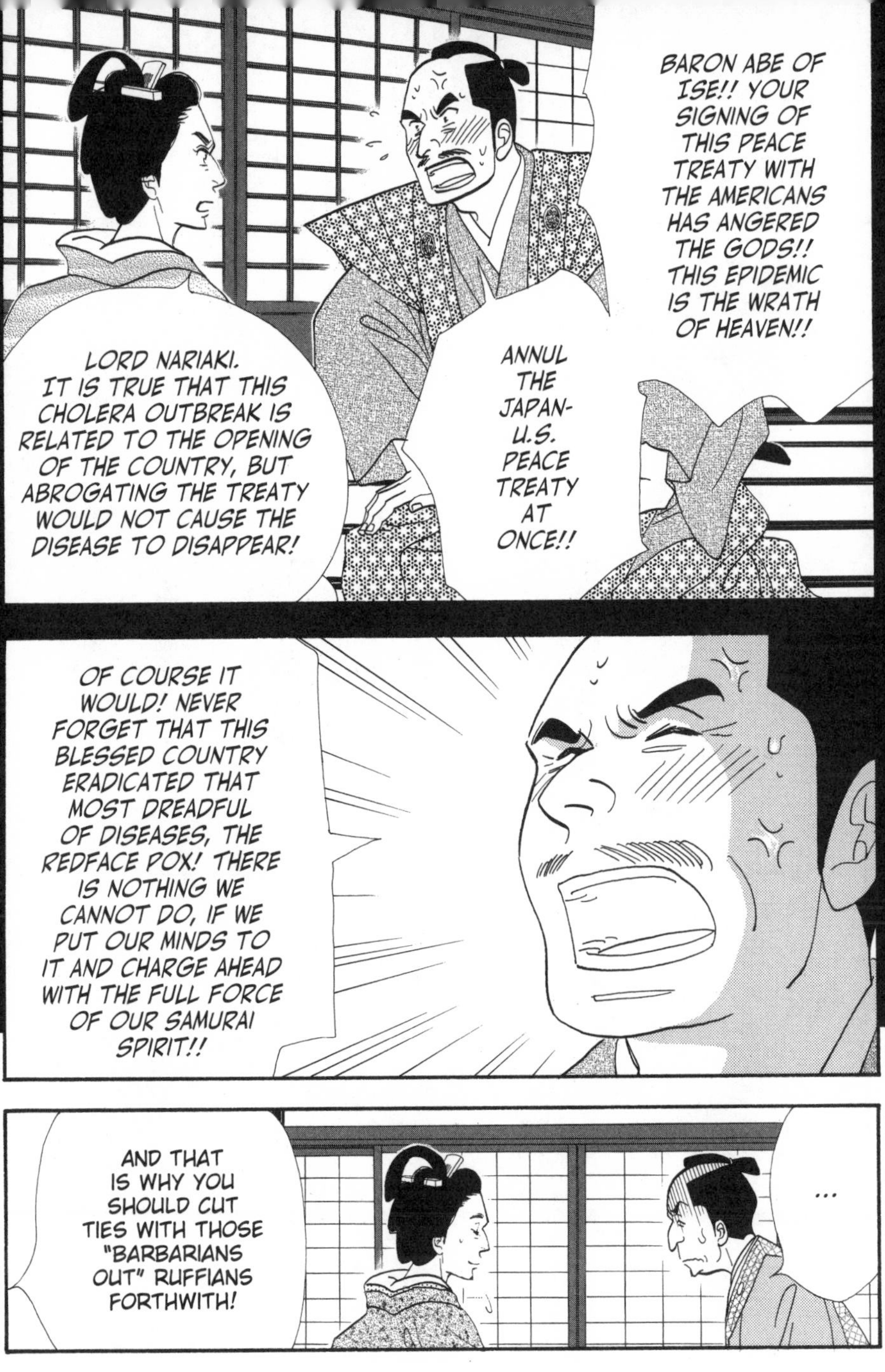
BARON ABE OF ISE!! YOUR SIGNING OF THIS PEACE TREATY WITH THE AMERICANS HAS ANGERED THE GODS!! THIS EPIDEMIC IS THE WRATH OF HEAVEN!!
ANNUL THE JAPAN-U.S. PEACE TREATY AT ONCE!!
LORD NARIAKI. IT IS TRUE THAT THIS CHOLERA OUTBREAK IS RELATED TO THE OPENING OF THE COUNTRY, BUT ABROGATING THE TREATY WOULD NOT CAUSE THE DISEASE TO DISAPPEAR!
OF COURSE IT WOULD! NEVER FORGET THAT THIS BLESSED COUNTRY ERADICATED THAT MOST DREADFUL OF DISEASES, THE REDFACE POX! THERE IS NOTHING WE CANNOT DO, IF WE PUT OUR MINDS TO IT AND CHARGE AHEAD WITH THE FULL FORCE OF OUR SAMURAI SPIRIT!!
AND THAT IS WHY YOU SHOULD CUT TIES WITH THOSE "BARBARIANS OUT" RUFFIANS FORTHWITH!
...

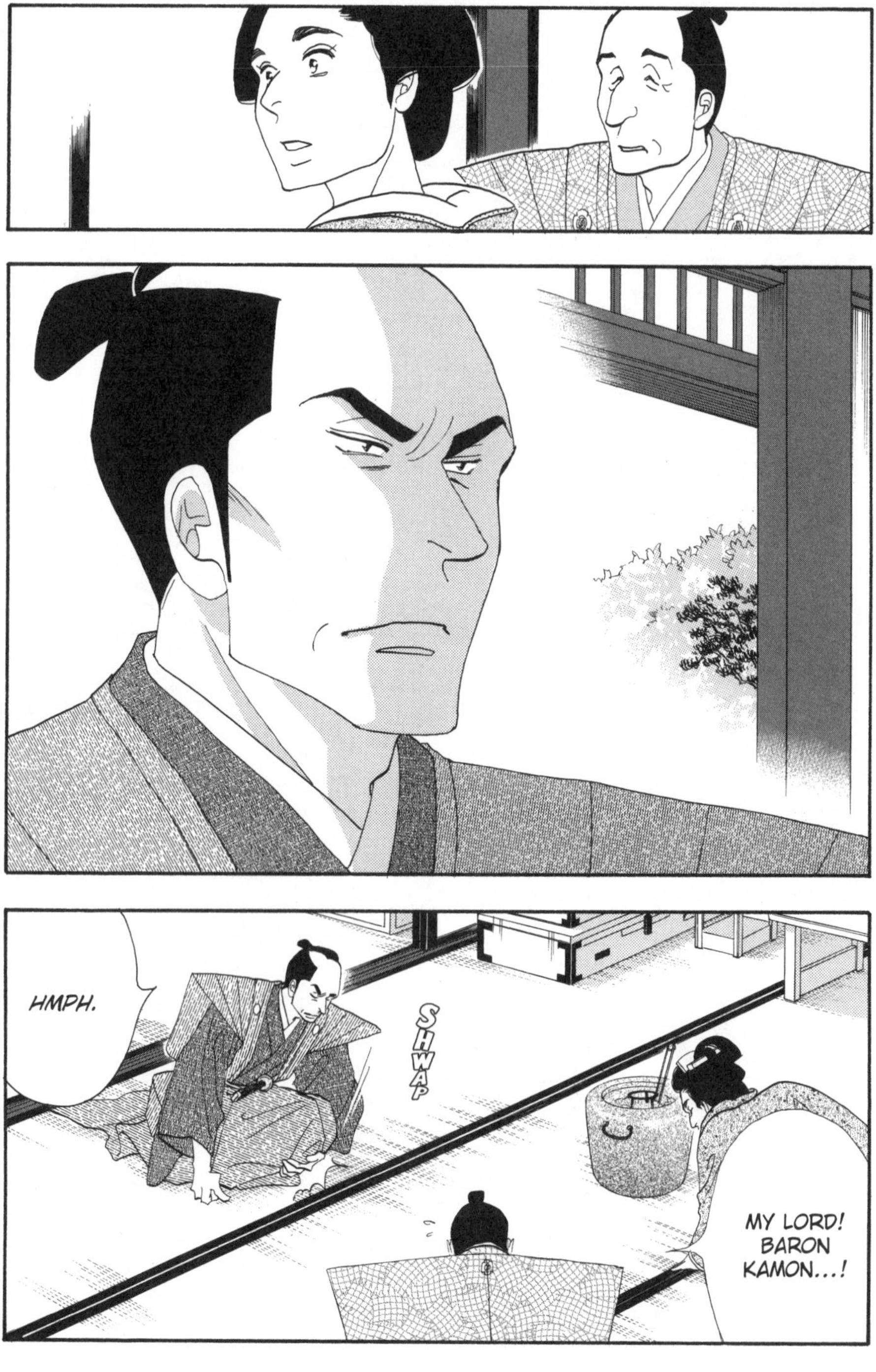
MY LORD! BARON KAMON...!
SHWAP
HMPH.

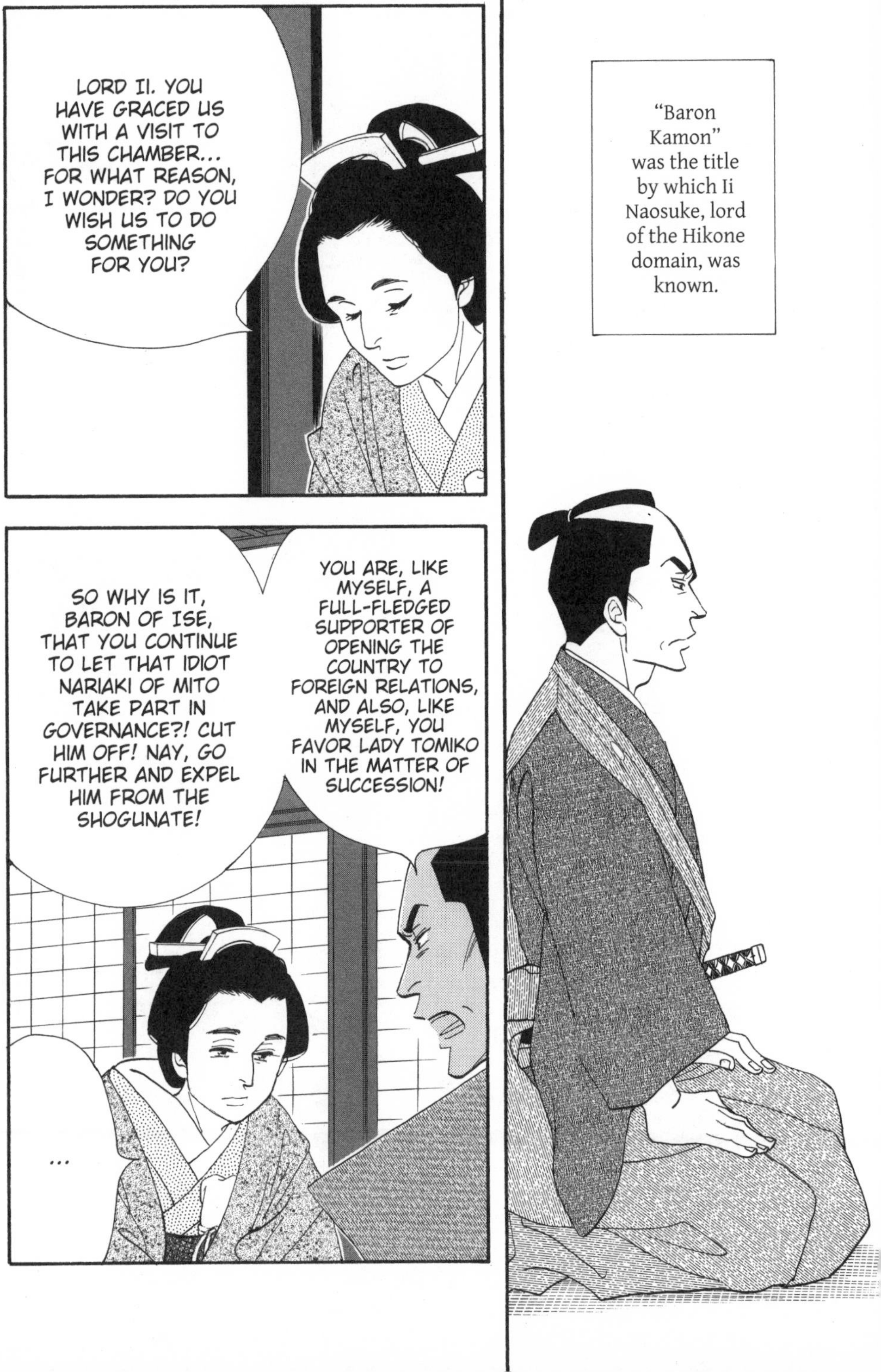
"Baron Kamon" was the title by which Ii Naosuke, lord of the Hikone domain, was known.
LORD II. YOU HAVE GRACED US WITH A VISIT TO THIS CHAMBER... FOR WHAT REASON, I WONDER? DO YOU WISH US TO DO SOMETHING FOR YOU?
YOU ARE, LIKE MYSELF, A FULL-FLEDGED SUPPORTER OF OPENING THE COUNTRY TO FOREIGN RELATIONS, AND ALSO, LIKE MYSELF, YOU FAVOR LADY TOMIKO IN THE MATTER OF SUCCESSION!
SO WHY IS IT, BARON OF ISE, THAT YOU CONTINUE TO LET THAT IDIOT NARIAKI OF MITO TAKE PART IN GOVERNANCE?! CUT HIM OFF! NAY, GO FURTHER AND EXPEL HIM FROM THE SHOGUNATE!
...

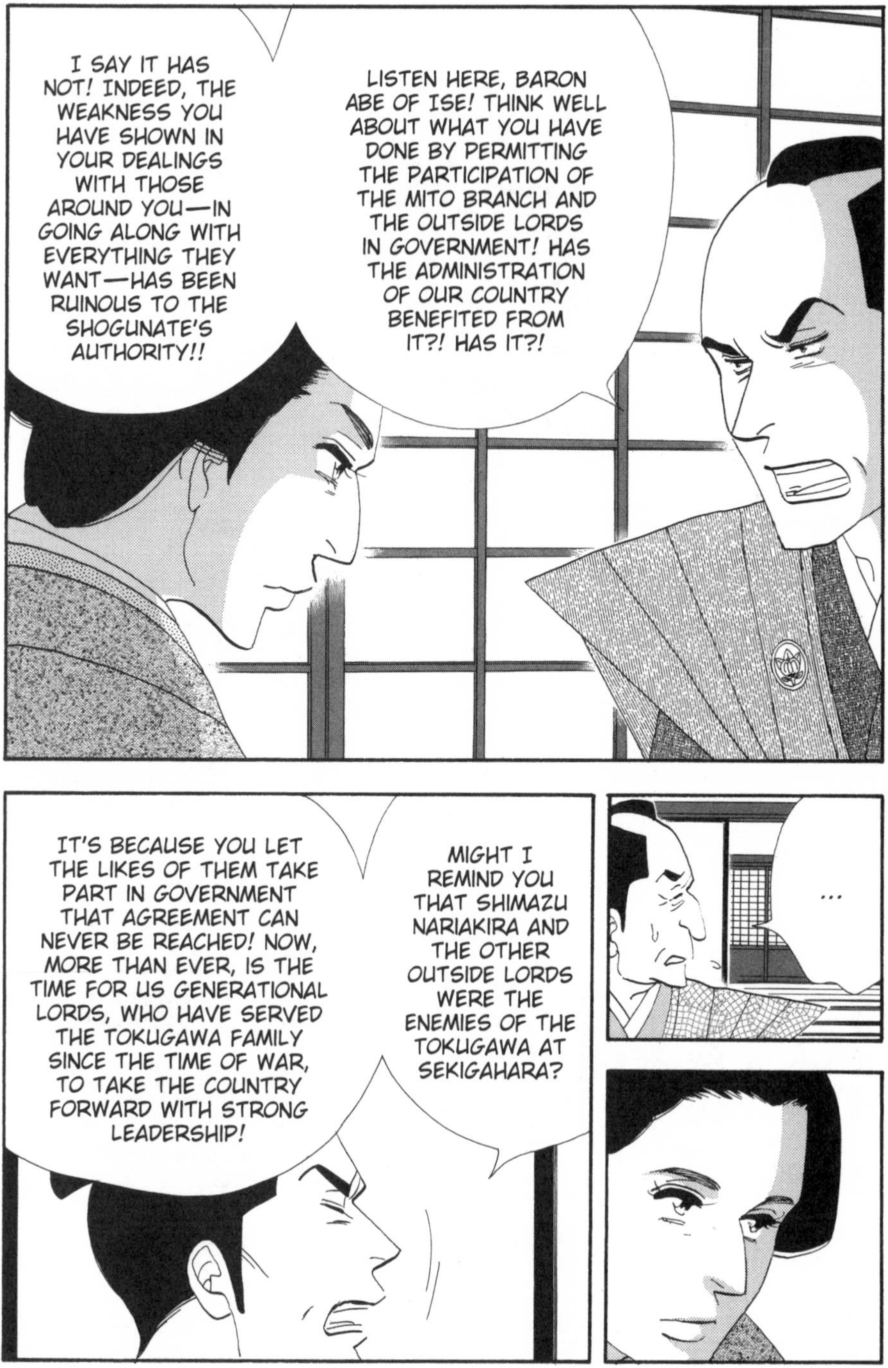
LISTEN HERE, BARON ABE OF ISE! THINK WELL ABOUT WHAT YOU HAVE DONE BY PERMITTING THE PARTICIPATION OF THE MITO BRANCH AND THE OUTSIDE LORDS IN GOVERNMENT! HAS THE ADMINISTRATION OF OUR COUNTRY BENEFITED FROM IT?! HAS IT?!
I SAY IT HAS NOT! INDEED, THE WEAKNESS YOU HAVE SHOWN IN YOUR DEALINGS WITH THOSE AROUND YOU—IN GOING ALONG WITH EVERYTHING THEY WANT—HAS BEEN RUINOUS TO THE SHOGUNATE'S AUTHORITY!!
...
MIGHT I REMIND YOU THAT SHIMAZU NARIAKIRA AND THE OTHER OUTSIDE LORDS WERE THE ENEMIES OF THE TOKUGAWA AT SEKIGAHARA?
IT'S BECAUSE YOU LET THE LIKES OF THEM TAKE PART IN GOVERNMENT THAT AGREEMENT CAN NEVER BE REACHED! NOW, MORE THAN EVER, IS THE TIME FOR US GENERATIONAL LORDS, WHO HAVE SERVED THE TOKUGAWA FAMILY SINCE THE TIME OF WAR, TO TAKE THE COUNTRY FORWARD WITH STRONG LEADERSHIP!

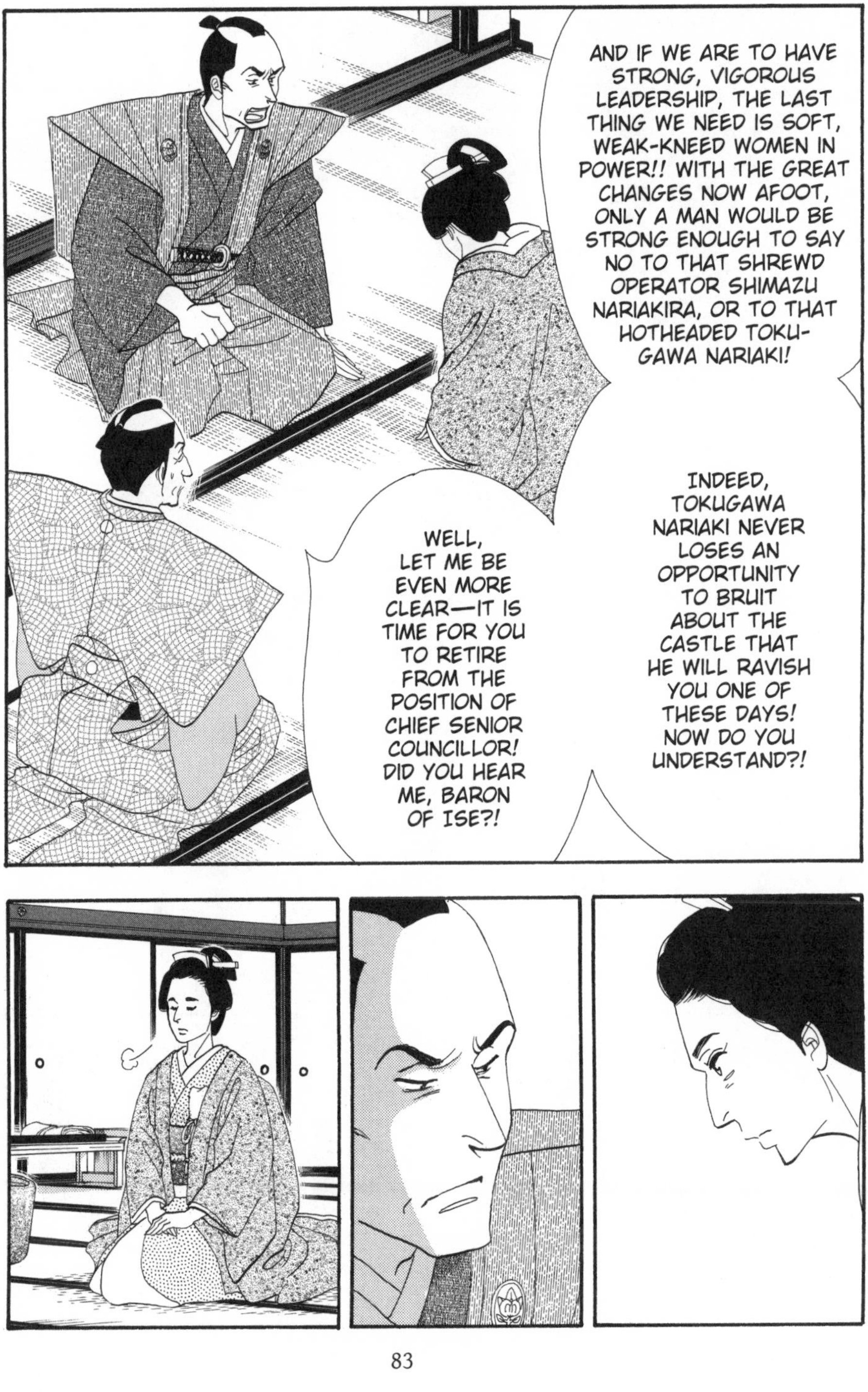
AND IF WE ARE TO HAVE STRONG, VIGOROUS LEADERSHIP, THE LAST THING WE NEED IS SOFT, WEAK-KNEED WOMEN IN POWER!! WITH THE GREAT CHANGES NOW AFOOT, ONLY A MAN WOULD BE STRONG ENOUGH TO SAY NO TO THAT SHREWD OPERATOR SHIMAZU NARIAKIRA, OR TO THAT HOTHEADED TOKU-GAWA NARIAKI!
INDEED, TOKUGAWA NARIAKI NEVER LOSES AN OPPORTUNITY TO BRUIT ABOUT THE CASTLE THAT HE WILL RAVISH YOU ONE OF THESE DAYS! NOW DO YOU UNDERSTAND?!
WELL, LET ME BE EVEN MORE CLEAR—IT IS TIME FOR YOU TO RETIRE FROM THE POSITION OF CHIEF SENIOR COUNCILLOR! DID YOU HEAR ME, BARON OF ISE?!

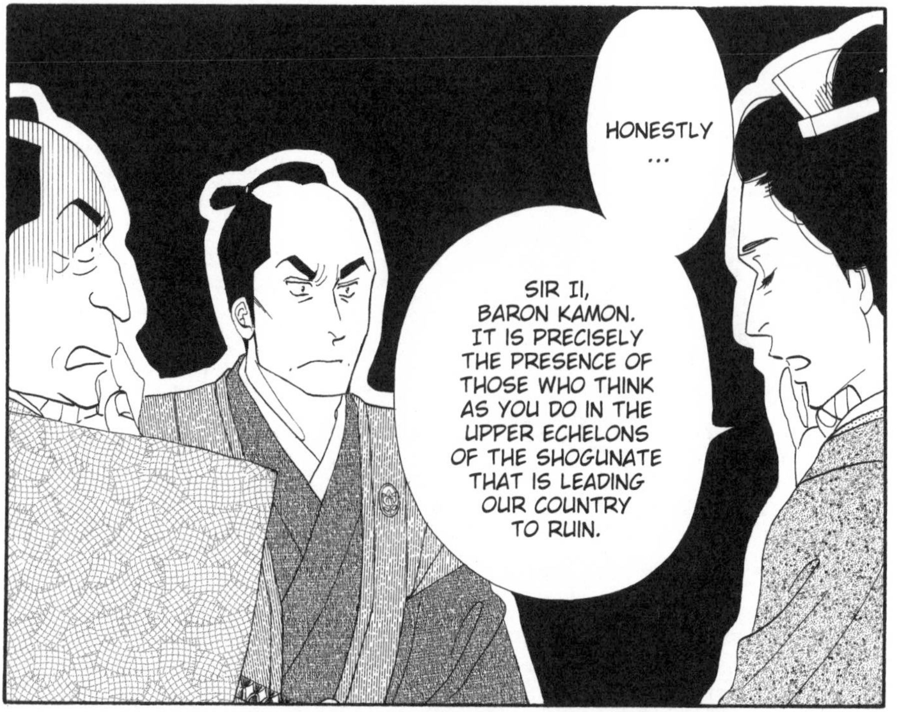
HONESTLY ...
SIR II, BARON KAMON. IT IS PRECISELY THE PRESENCE OF THOSE WHO THINK AS YOU DO IN THE UPPER ECHELONS OF THE SHOGUNATE THAT IS LEADING OUR COUNTRY TO RUIN.

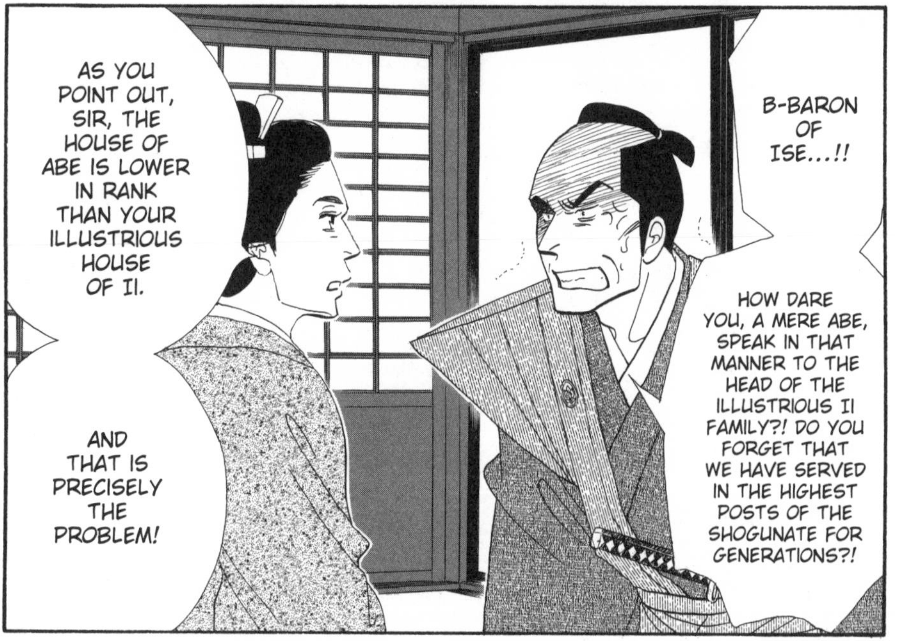
B-BARON OF ISE...!!
AS YOU POINT OUT, SIR, THE HOUSE OF ABE IS LOWER IN RANK THAN YOUR ILLUSTRIOUS HOUSE OF II.
HOW DARE YOU, A MERE ABE, SPEAK IN THAT MANNER TO THE HEAD OF THE ILLUSTRIOUS II FAMILY?! DO YOU FORGET THAT WE HAVE SERVED IN THE HIGHEST POSTS OF THE SHOGUNATE FOR GENERATIONS?!
AND THAT IS PRECISELY THE PROBLEM!

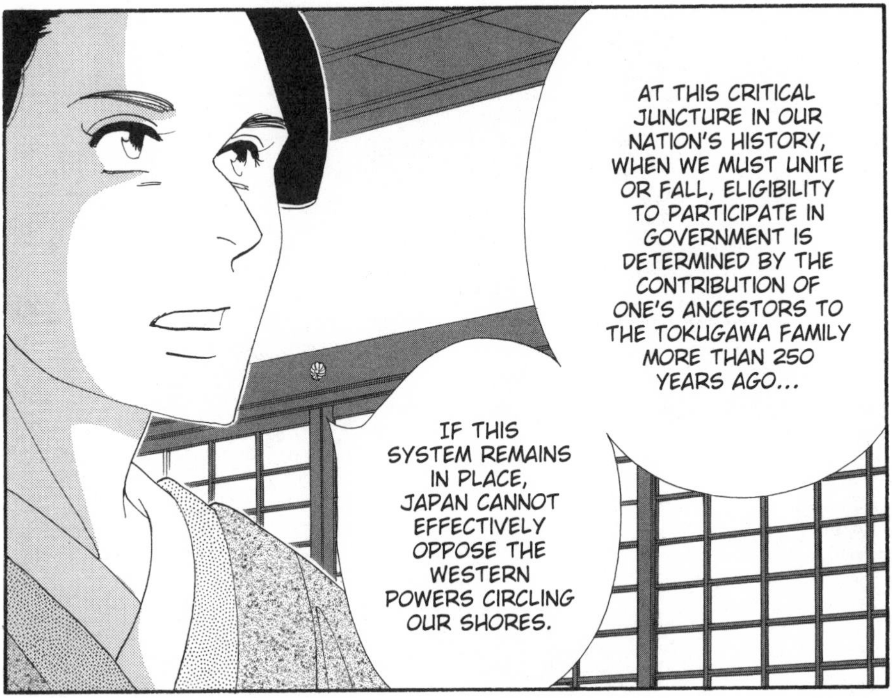
AT THIS CRITICAL JUNCTURE IN OUR NATION'S HISTORY, WHEN WE MUST UNITE OR FALL, ELIGIBILITY TO PARTICIPATE IN GOVERNMENT IS DETERMINED BY THE CONTRIBUTION OF ONE'S ANCESTORS TO THE TOKUGAWA FAMILY MORE THAN 250 YEARS AGO...
IF THIS SYSTEM REMAINS IN PLACE, JAPAN CANNOT EFFECTIVELY OPPOSE THE WESTERN POWERS CIRCLING OUR SHORES.

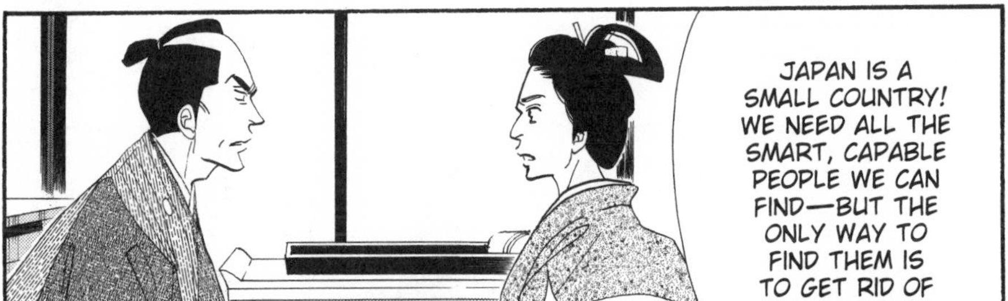
JAPAN IS A SMALL COUNTRY! WE NEED ALL THE SMART, CAPABLE PEOPLE WE CAN FIND—BUT THE ONLY WAY TO FIND THEM IS TO GET RID OF THE BARRIERS OF RANK AND DOMAIN.
YOU YOURSELF, SIR NAOSUKE, WERE FORCED TO LANGUISH FOR YEARS DOING LITTLE, IN SPITE OF YOUR RECOGNIZED INTELLECT, FOR NO REASON OTHER THAN THAT YOU WERE NOT THE FIRSTBORN SON OF THE II FAMILY!
THEREFORE, YOU OUGHT TO UNDERSTAND BETTER THAN MOST THE TERRIBLE FRUSTRATION OF HAVING THE AMBITION AND ABILITY TO ACHIEVE GREAT THINGS, YET HAVING NO AVENUE TO DO SO!

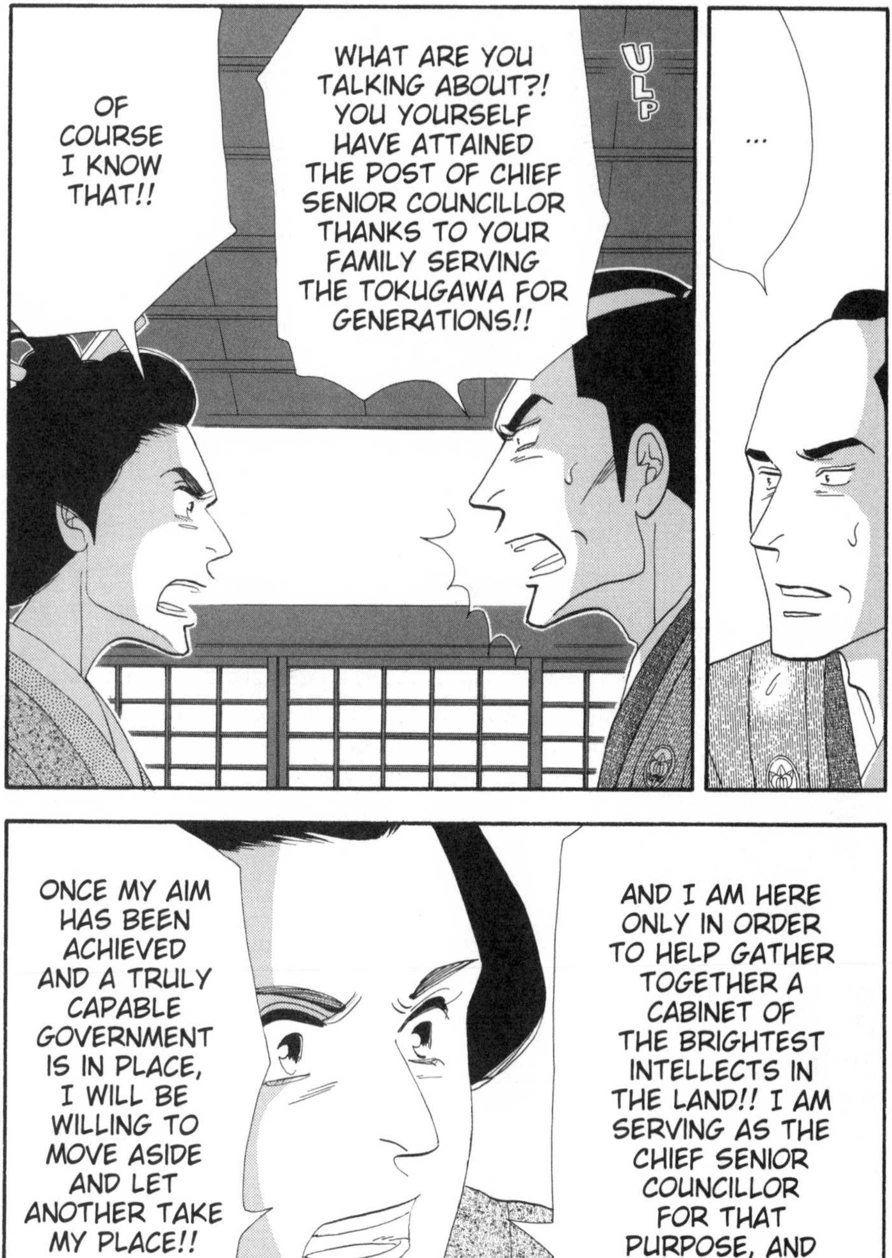
...
ULP
WHAT ARE YOU TALKING ABOUT?! YOU YOURSELF HAVE ATTAINED THE POST OF CHIEF SENIOR COUNCILLOR THANKS TO YOUR FAMILY SERVING THE TOKUGAWA FOR GENERATIONS!!
OF COURSE I KNOW THAT!!
AND I AM HERE ONLY IN ORDER TO HELP GATHER TOGETHER A CABINET OF THE BRIGHTEST INTELLECTS IN THE LAND!! I AM SERVING AS THE CHIEF SENIOR COUNCILLOR FOR THAT PURPOSE, AND THAT PURPOSE ALONE!!
ONCE MY AIM HAS BEEN ACHIEVED AND A TRULY CAPABLE GOVERNMENT IS IN PLACE, I WILL BE WILLING TO MOVE ASIDE AND LET ANOTHER TAKE MY PLACE!!

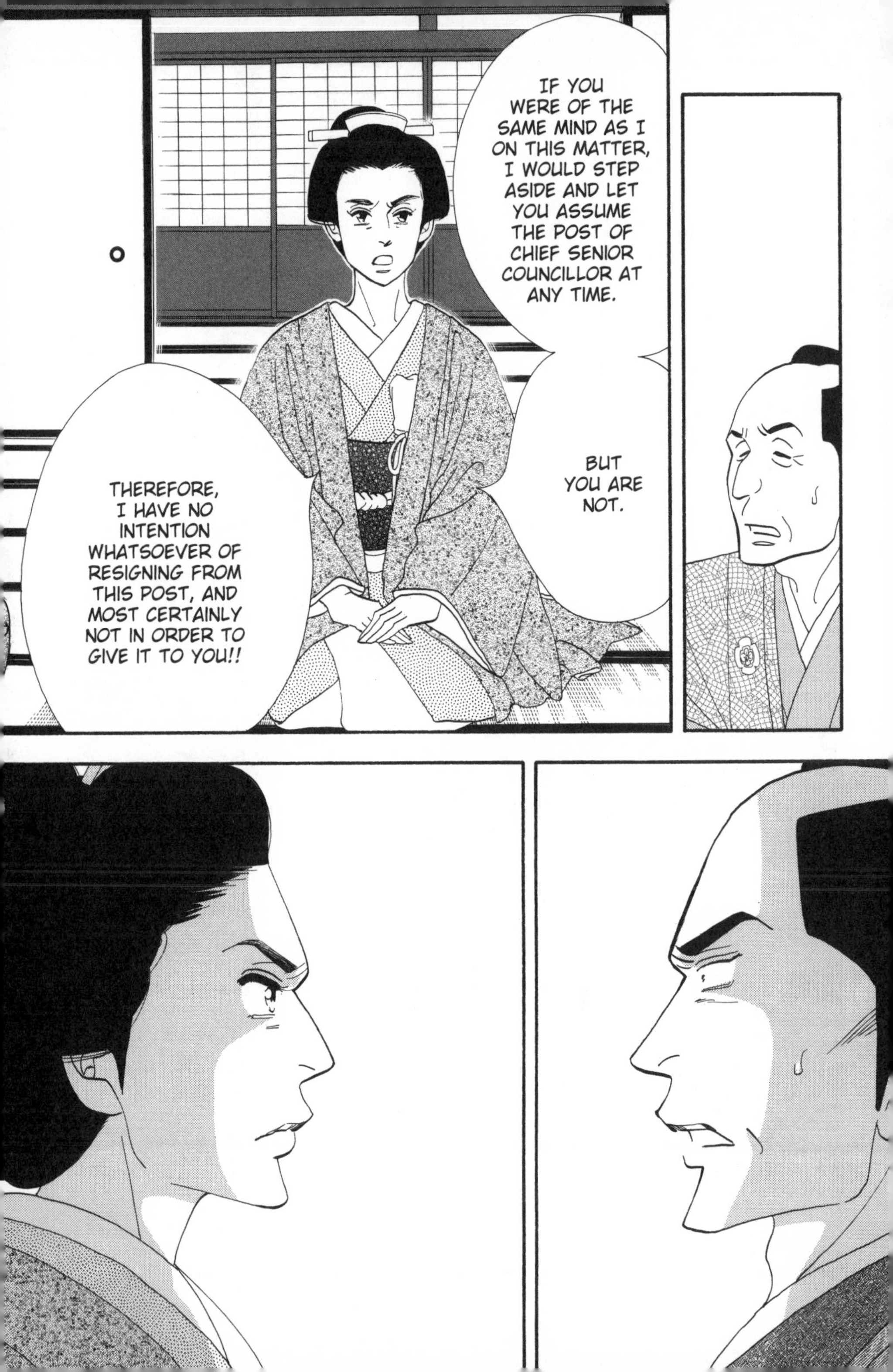
IF YOU WERE OF THE SAME MIND AS I ON THIS MATTER, I WOULD STEP ASIDE AND LET YOU ASSUME THE POST OF CHIEF SENIOR COUNCILLOR AT ANY TIME.
BUT YOU ARE NOT.
THEREFORE, I HAVE NO INTENTION WHATSOEVER OF RESIGNING FROM THIS POST, AND MOST CERTAINLY NOT IN ORDER TO GIVE IT TO YOU!!

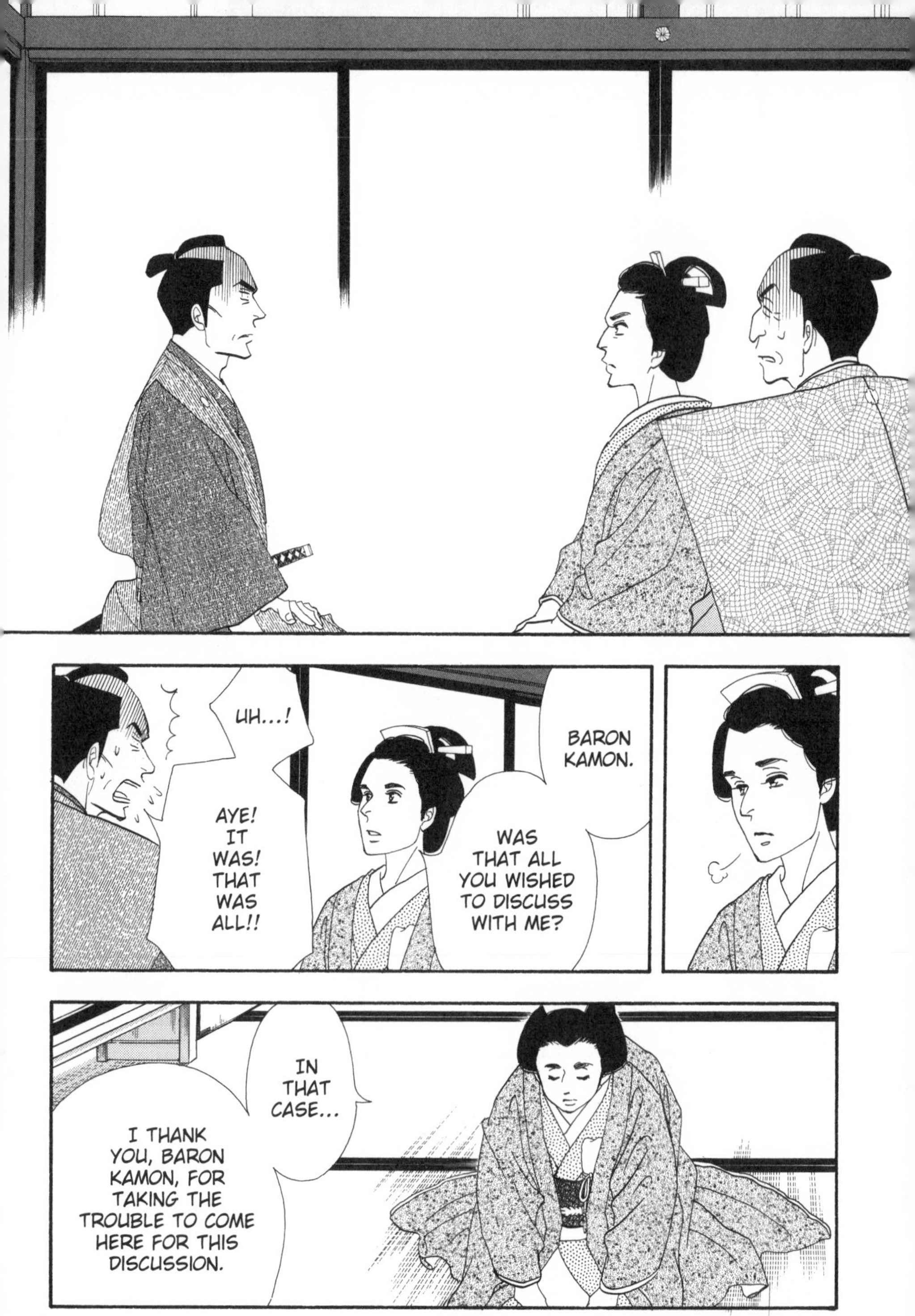
BARON KAMON.
WAS THAT ALL YOU WISHED TO DISCUSS WITH ME?
UH...!
AYE! IT WAS! THAT WAS ALL!!
IN THAT CASE...
I THANK YOU, BARON KAMON, FOR TAKING THE TROUBLE TO COME HERE FOR THIS DISCUSSION.

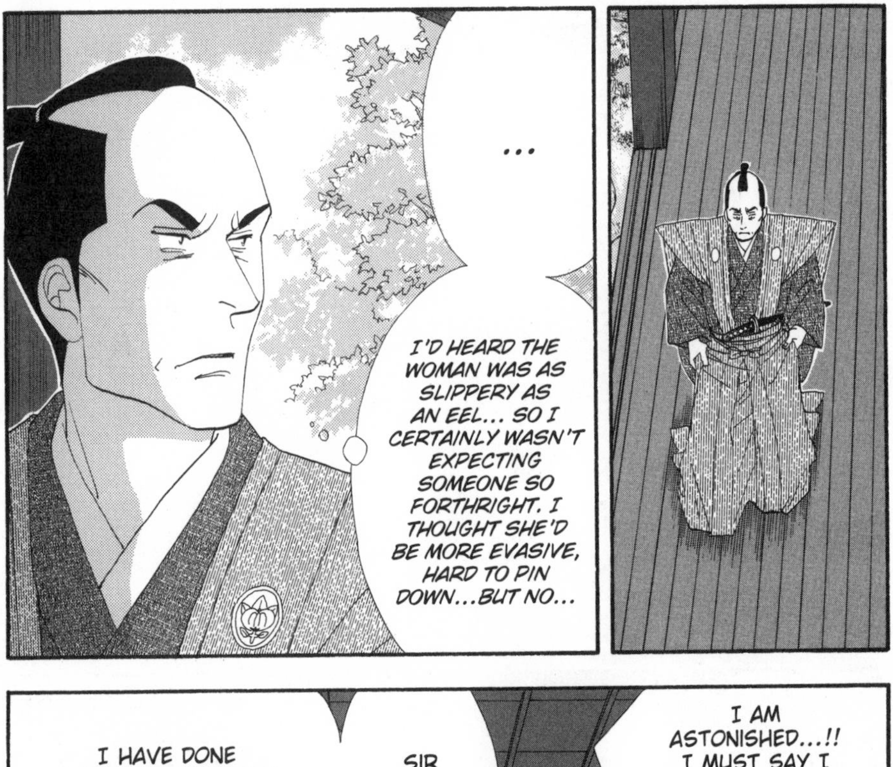
...
I'D HEARD THE WOMAN WAS AS SLIPPERY AS AN EEL... SO I CERTAINLY WASN'T EXPECTING SOMEONE SO FORTHRIGHT. I THOUGHT SHE'D BE MORE EVASIVE, HARD TO PIN DOWN...BUT NO...
I AM ASTONISHED...!! I MUST SAY I NEVER EXPECTED SOMEONE SO CALM AND GENTLE AS YOURSELF TO SPEAK LIKE THAT TO ANYONE, MUCH LESS A POWERFUL MINISTER LIKE SIR II.
SIR HOTTA MASA-YOSHI...
I HAVE DONE EVERYTHING I COULD TO THE UTMOST OF MY POWERS, AND YET A MOUNTAIN OF PROBLEMS REMAINS TO BE SOLVED, STARTING WITH THE TRADE TREATY DEMANDED BY THE AMERICANS.
IT WAS EXHILARATING TO HEAR, I MUST ADMIT, BUT WILL IT NOT MAKE THINGS DIFFICULT FOR YOU FROM NOW ON?

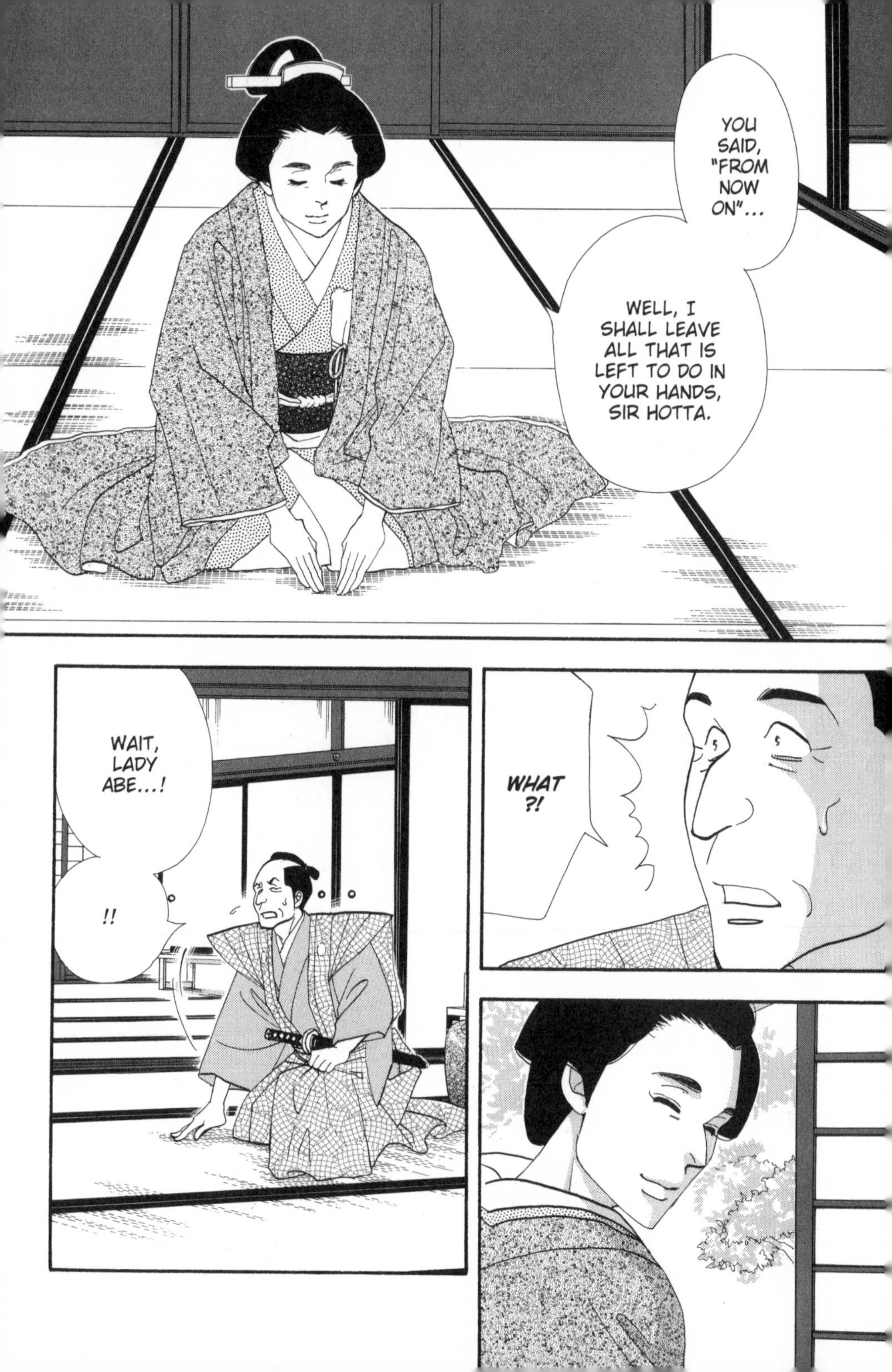
YOU SAID, "FROM NOW ON"...
WELL, I SHALL LEAVE ALL THAT IS LEFT TO DO IN YOUR HANDS, SIR HOTTA.
WHAT?!
WAIT, LADY ABE...!
!!

...!!

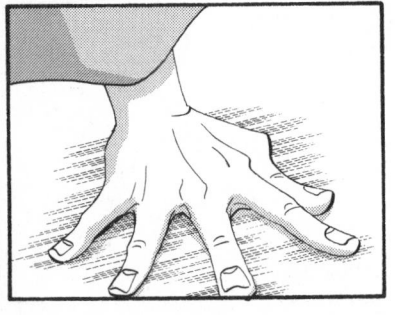

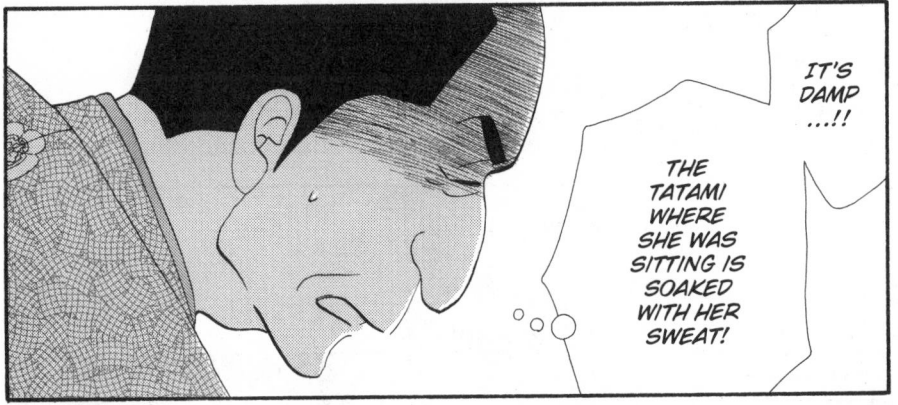

IT'S DAMP ...!!

THE TATAMI WHERE SHE WAS SITTING IS SOAKED WITH HER SWEAT!

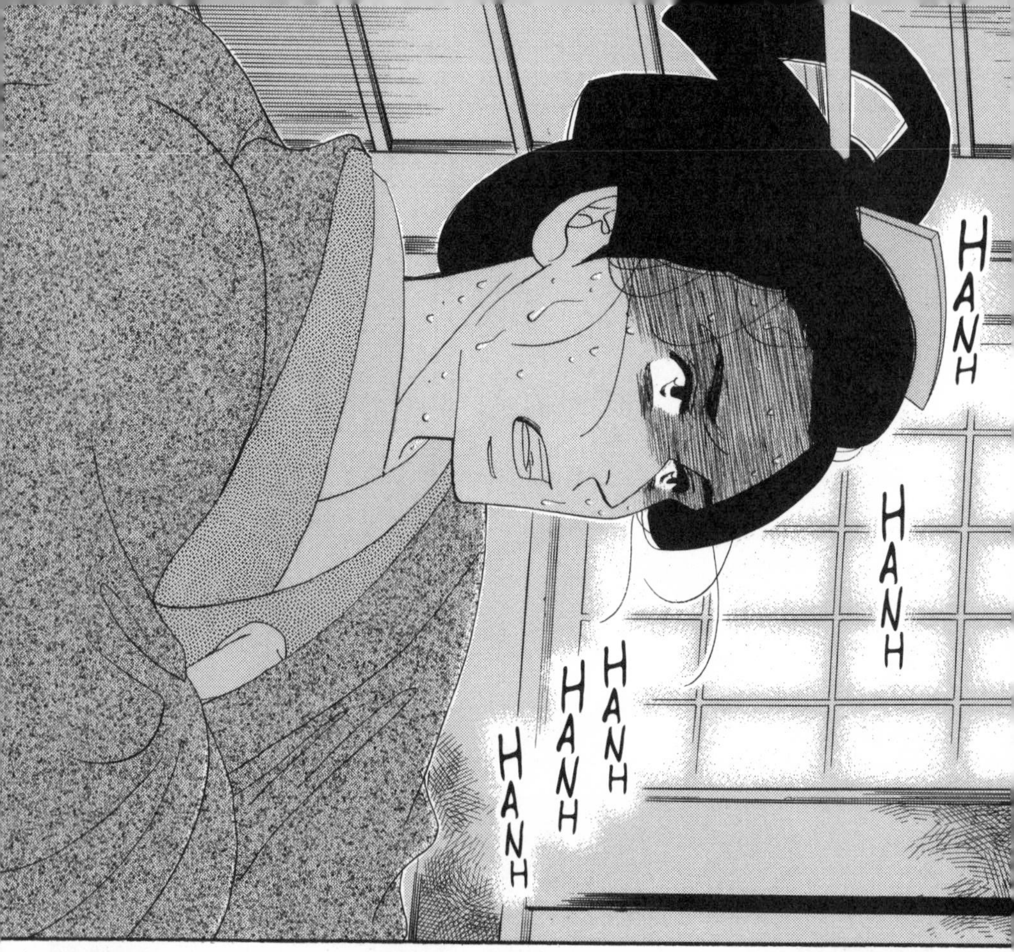
HANH
HANH
HANH
HANH
HANH

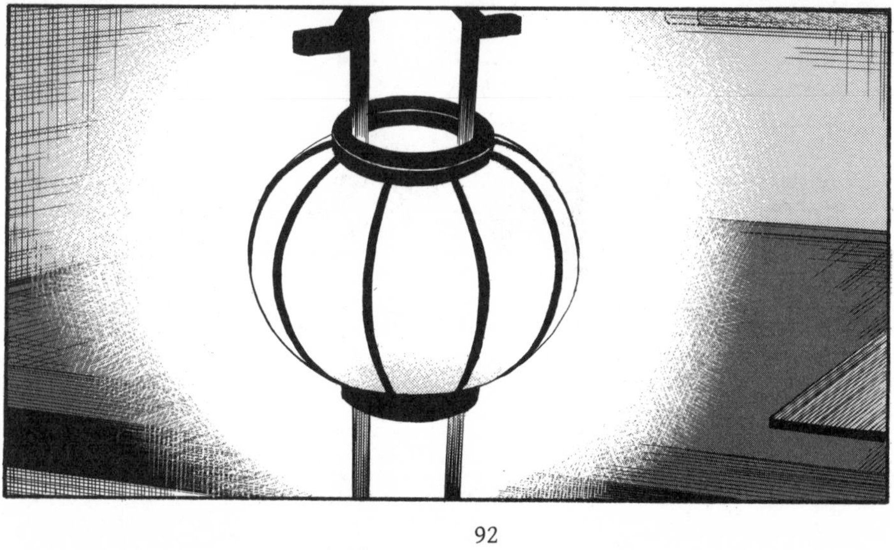

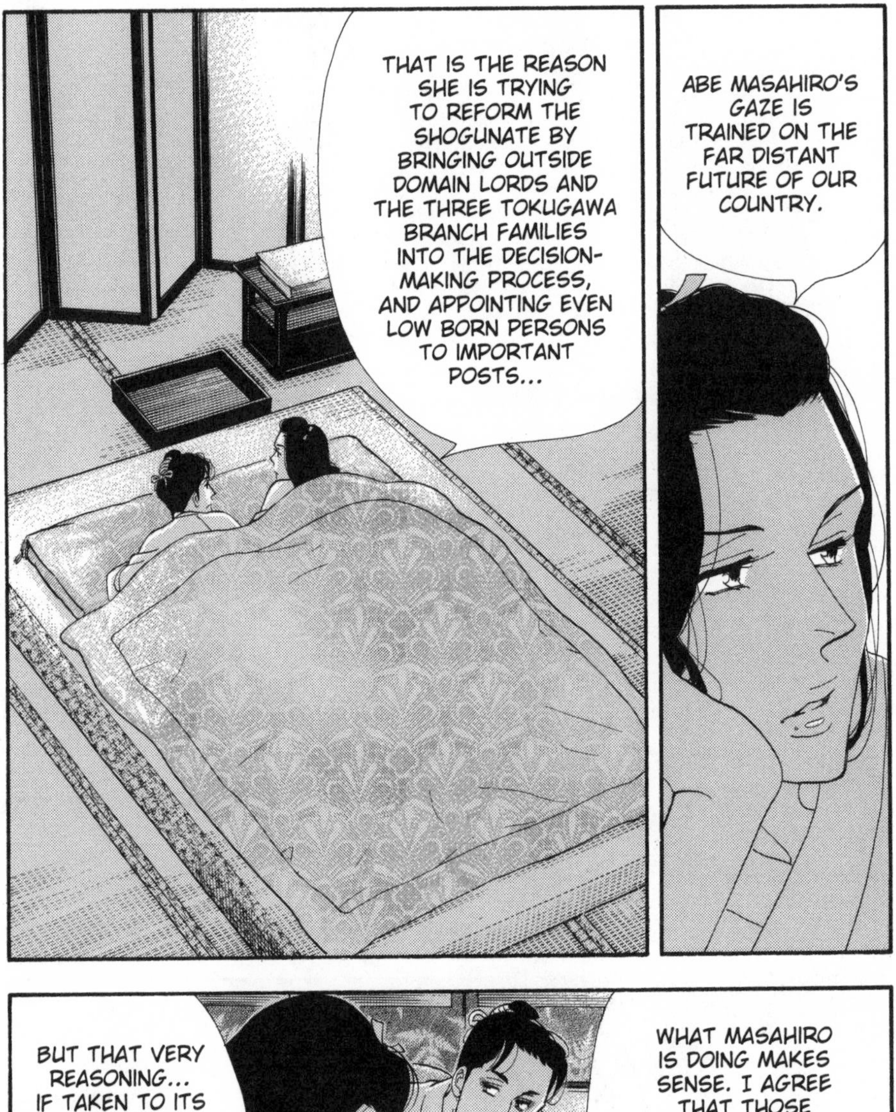
ABE MASAHIRO'S GAZE IS TRAINED ON THE FAR DISTANT FUTURE OF OUR COUNTRY.
THAT IS THE REASON SHE IS TRYING TO REFORM THE SHOGUNATE BY BRINGING OUTSIDE DOMAIN LORDS AND THE THREE TOKUGAWA BRANCH FAMILIES INTO THE DECISION-MAKING PROCESS, AND APPOINTING EVEN LOW BORN PERSONS TO IMPORTANT POSTS...
WHAT MASAHIRO IS DOING MAKES SENSE. I AGREE THAT THOSE WHO ARE BEST QUALIFIED TO MAKE THINGS MOVE IN THIS COUNTRY SHOULD BE GIVEN KEY POSITIONS, REGARDLESS OF THEIR SOCIAL STATUS.
BUT THAT VERY REASONING... IF TAKEN TO ITS LOGICAL END, MEANS THE CURRENT SYSTEM OF RULE, GIVING POWER ONLY TO THOSE WHO WERE BORN INTO THE TOKUGAWA FAMILY, IS SENSELESS.

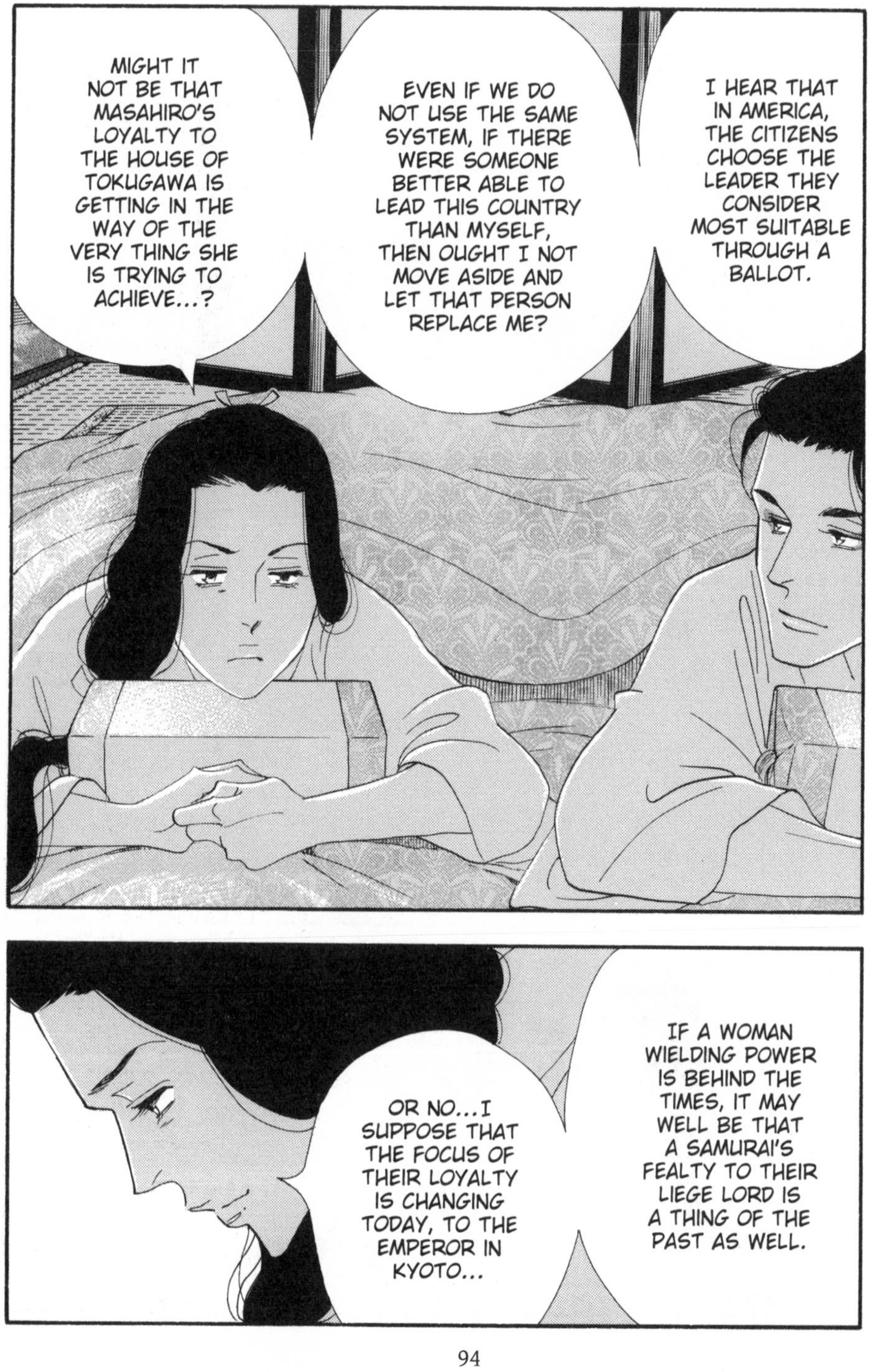
I HEAR THAT IN AMERICA, THE CITIZENS CHOOSE THE LEADER THEY CONSIDER MOST SUITABLE THROUGH A BALLOT.
EVEN IF WE DO NOT USE THE SAME SYSTEM, IF THERE WERE SOMEONE BETTER ABLE TO LEAD THIS COUNTRY THAN MYSELF, THEN OUGHT I NOT MOVE ASIDE AND LET THAT PERSON REPLACE ME?
MIGHT IT NOT BE THAT MASAHIRO'S LOYALTY TO THE HOUSE OF TOKUGAWA IS GETTING IN THE WAY OF THE VERY THING SHE IS TRYING TO ACHIEVE...?
IF A WOMAN WIELDING POWER IS BEHIND THE TIMES, IT MAY WELL BE THAT A SAMURAI'S FEALTY TO THEIR LIEGE LORD IS A THING OF THE PAST AS WELL.
OR NO...I SUPPOSE THAT THE FOCUS OF THEIR LOYALTY IS CHANGING TODAY, TO THE EMPEROR IN KYOTO...

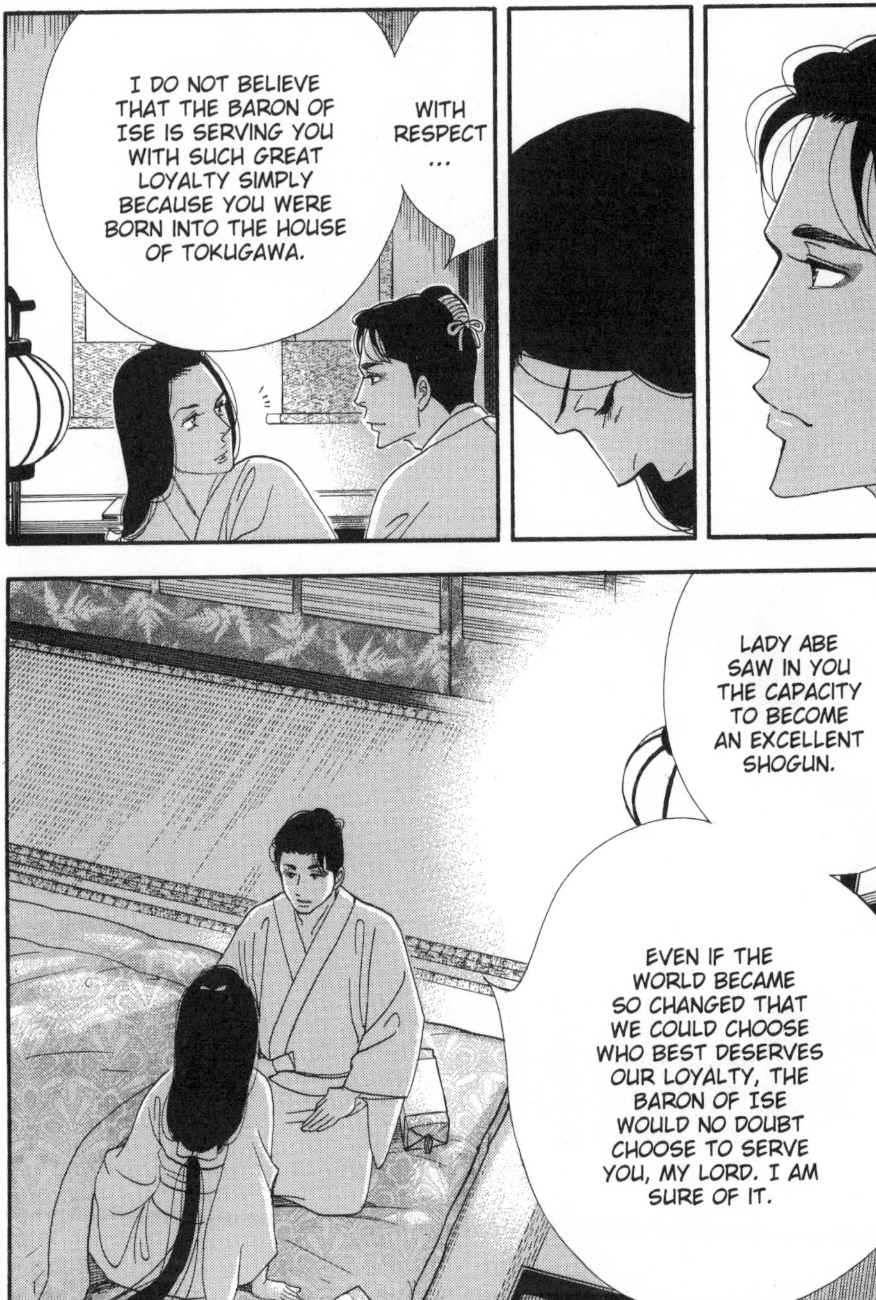
WITH RESPECT ...
I DO NOT BELIEVE THAT THE BARON OF ISE IS SERVING YOU WITH SUCH GREAT LOYALTY SIMPLY BECAUSE YOU WERE BORN INTO THE HOUSE OF TOKUGAWA.
LADY ABE SAW IN YOU THE CAPACITY TO BECOME AN EXCELLENT SHOGUN.
EVEN IF THE WORLD BECAME SO CHANGED THAT WE COULD CHOOSE WHO BEST DESERVES OUR LOYALTY, THE BARON OF ISE WOULD NO DOUBT CHOOSE TO SERVE YOU, MY LORD. I AM SURE OF IT.

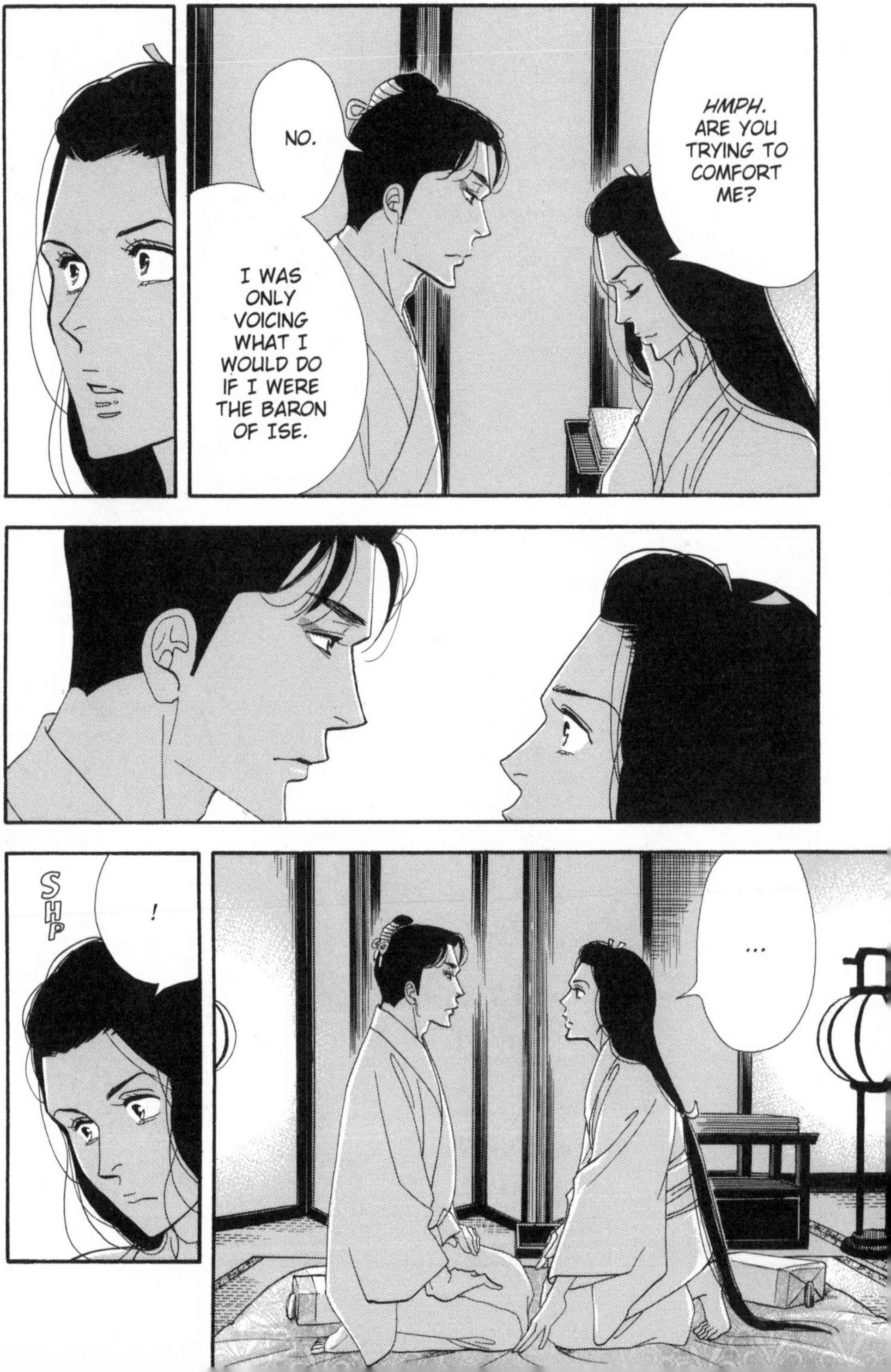
HMPH. ARE YOU TRYING TO COMFORT ME?
NO.
I WAS ONLY VOICING WHAT I WOULD DO IF I WERE THE BARON OF ISE.
...
!
SHP

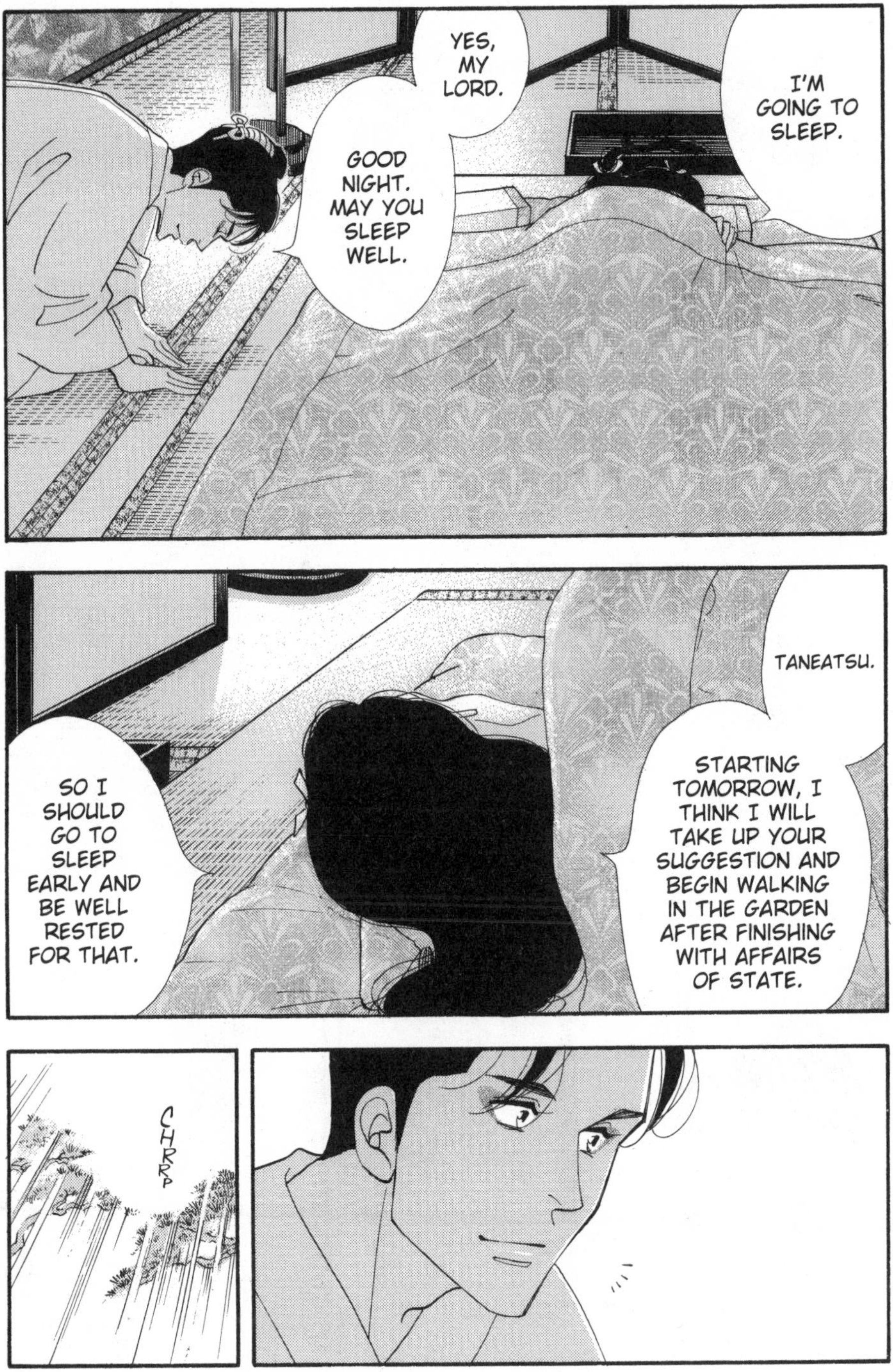
I'M GOING TO SLEEP.
YES, MY LORD.
GOOD NIGHT. MAY YOU SLEEP WELL.
TANEATSU.
STARTING TOMORROW, I THINK I WILL TAKE UP YOUR SUGGESTION AND BEGIN WALKING IN THE GARDEN AFTER FINISHING WITH AFFAIRS OF STATE.
SO I SHOULD GO TO SLEEP EARLY AND BE WELL RESTED FOR THAT.
CHRRP

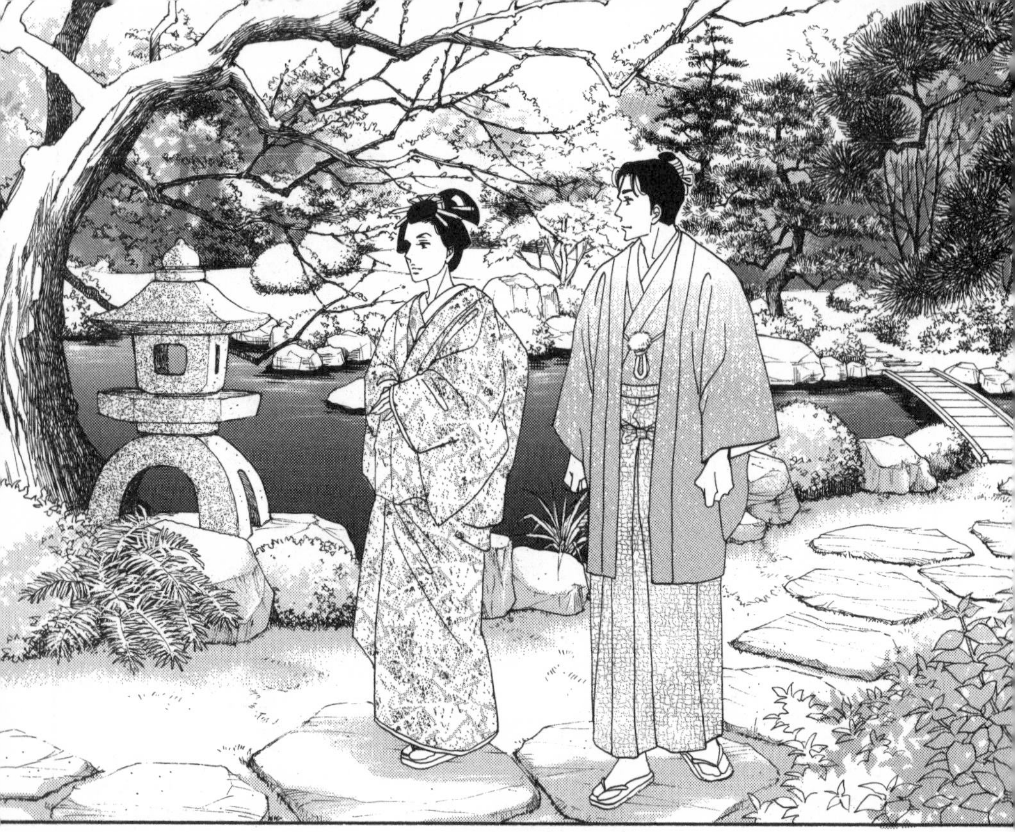
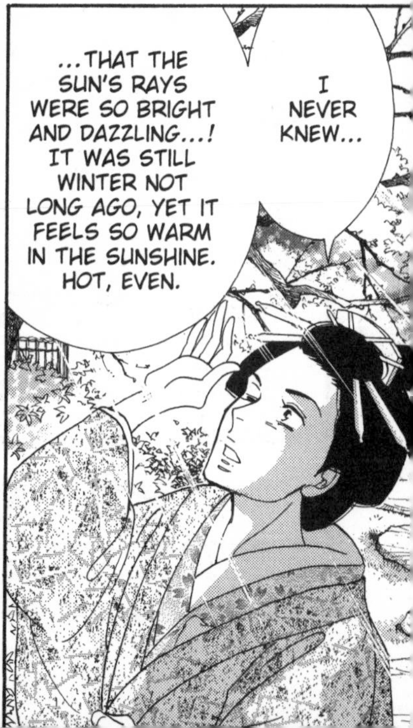
I NEVER KNEW...
...THAT THE SUN'S RAYS WERE SO BRIGHT AND DAZZLING...! IT WAS STILL WINTER NOT LONG AGO, YET IT FEELS SO WARM IN THE SUNSHINE. HOT, EVEN.
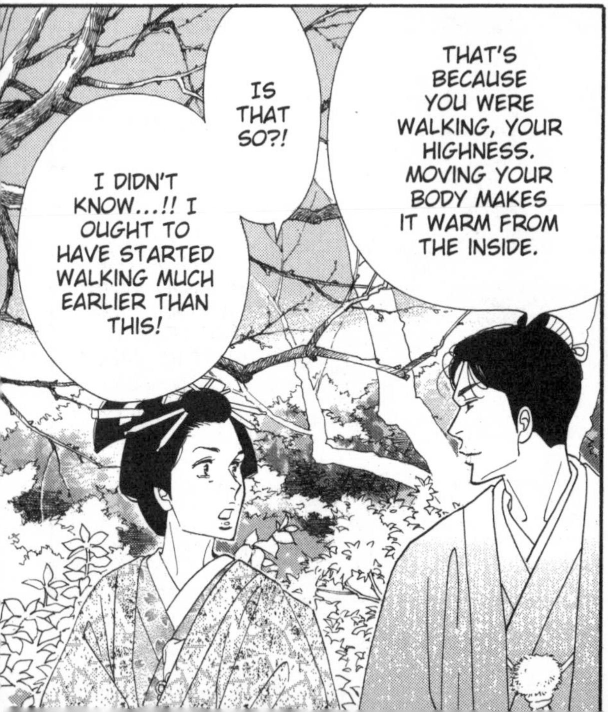
THAT'S BECAUSE YOU WERE WALKING, YOUR HIGHNESS. MOVING YOUR BODY MAKES IT WARM FROM THE INSIDE.
IS THAT SO?!
I DIDN'T KNOW...!! I OUGHT TO HAVE STARTED WALKING MUCH EARLIER THAN THIS!

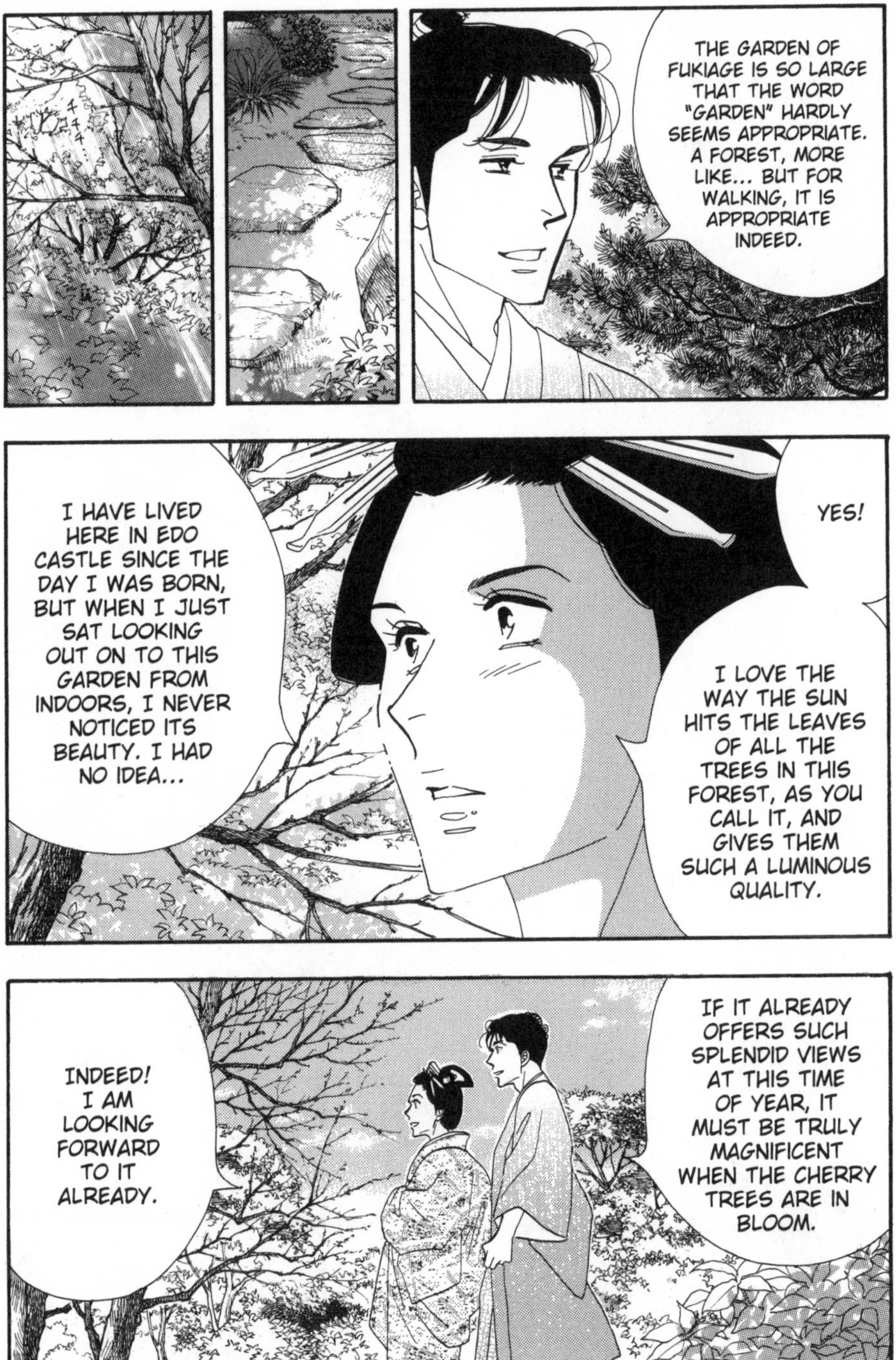
THE GARDEN OF FUKIAGE IS SO LARGE THAT THE WORD "GARDEN" HARDLY SEEMS APPROPRIATE. A FOREST, MORE LIKE... BUT FOR WALKING, IT IS APPROPRIATE INDEED.
YES!
I LOVE THE WAY THE SUN HITS THE LEAVES OF ALL THE TREES IN THIS FOREST, AS YOU CALL IT, AND GIVES THEM SUCH A LUMINOUS QUALITY.
I HAVE LIVED HERE IN EDO CASTLE SINCE THE DAY I WAS BORN, BUT WHEN I JUST SAT LOOKING OUT ON TO THIS GARDEN FROM INDOORS, I NEVER NOTICED ITS BEAUTY. I HAD NO IDEA...
IF IT ALREADY OFFERS SUCH SPLENDID VIEWS AT THIS TIME OF YEAR, IT MUST BE TRULY MAGNIFICENT WHEN THE CHERRY TREES ARE IN BLOOM.
INDEED! I AM LOOKING FORWARD TO IT ALREADY.

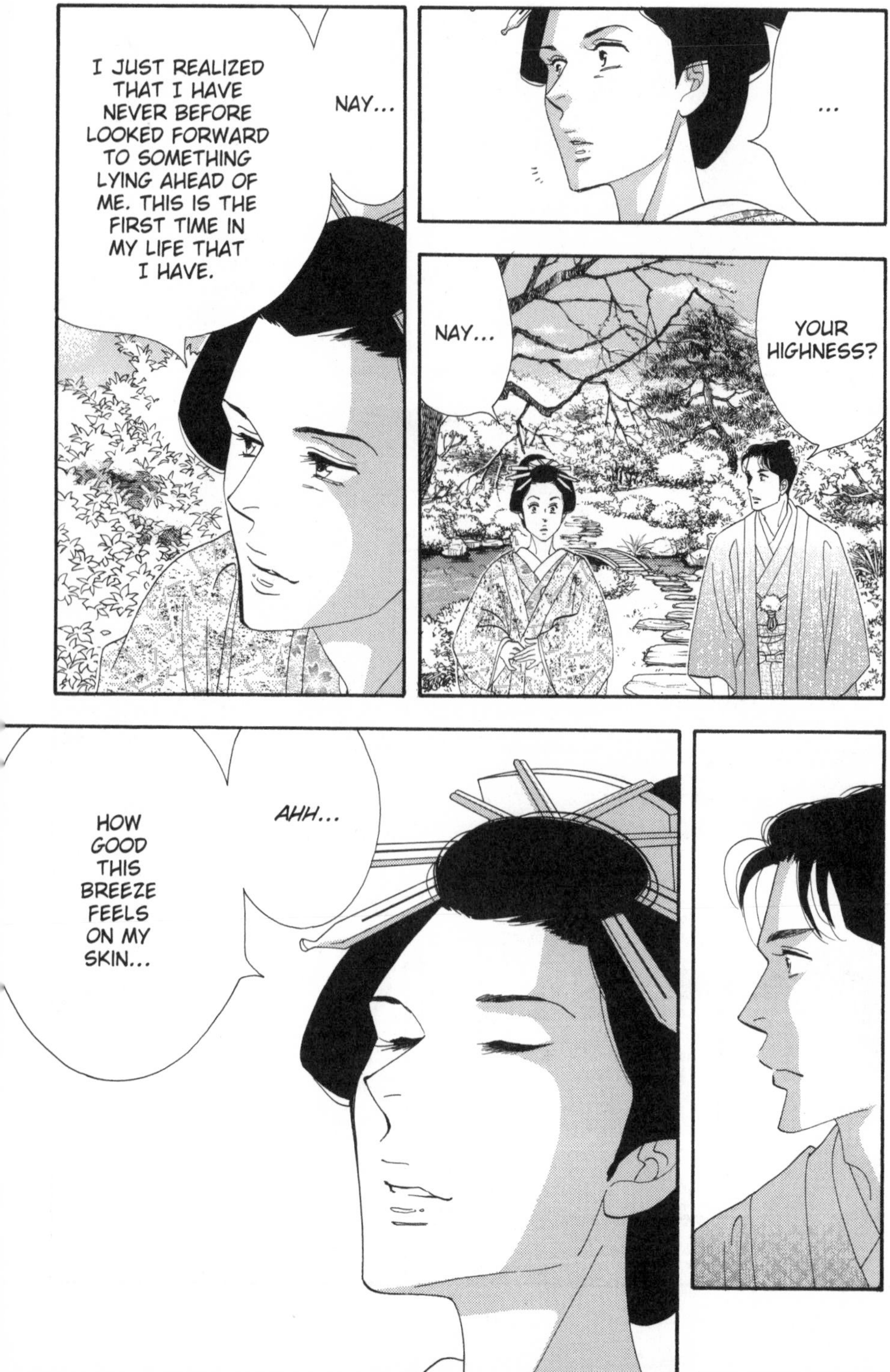
...
YOUR HIGHNESS?
NAY...
NAY...
I JUST REALIZED THAT I HAVE NEVER BEFORE LOOKED FORWARD TO SOMETHING LYING AHEAD OF ME. THIS IS THE FIRST TIME IN MY LIFE THAT I HAVE.
AHH...
HOW GOOD THIS BREEZE FEELS ON MY SKIN...

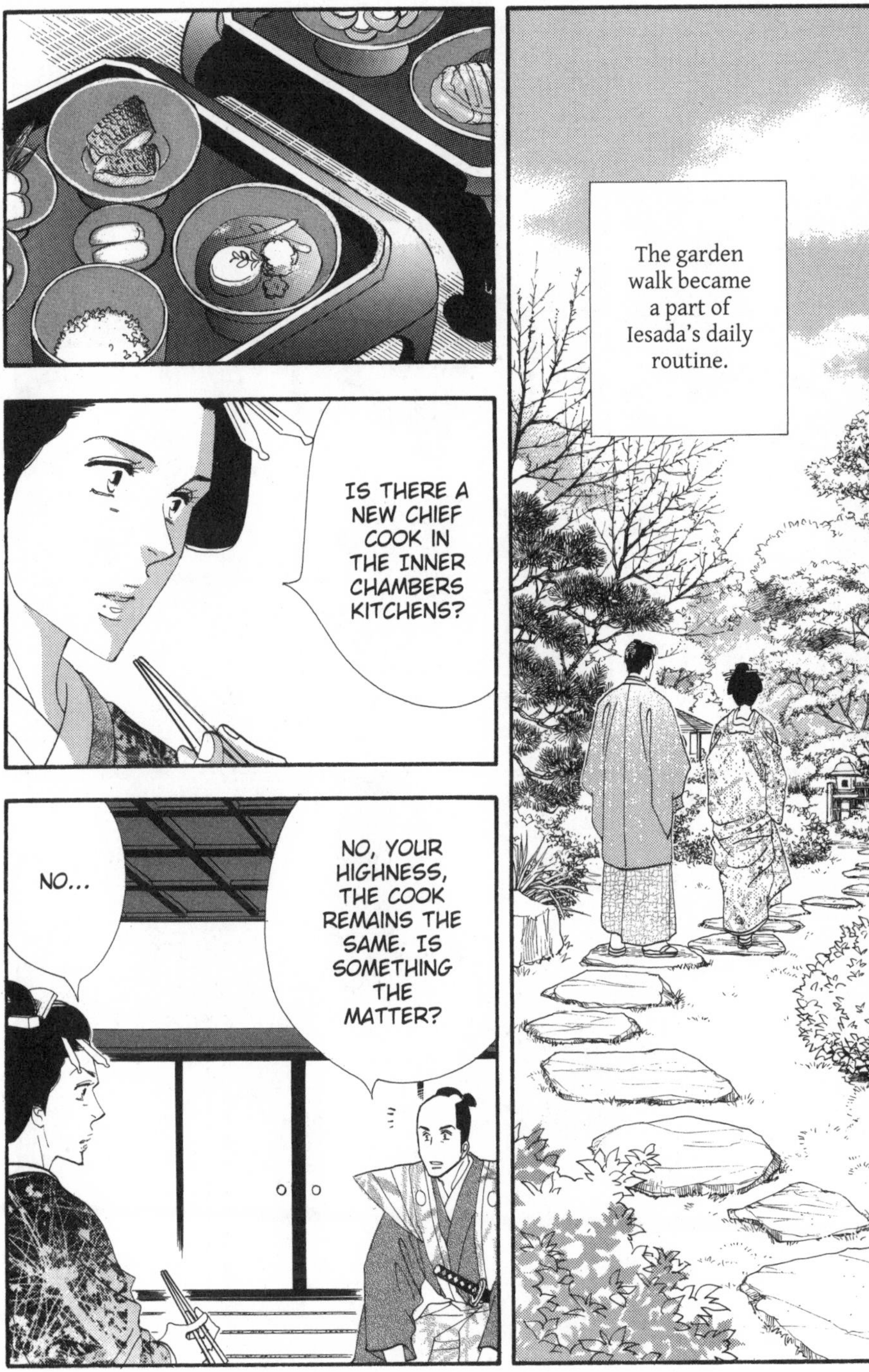
The garden walk became a part of Iesada's daily routine.
IS THERE A NEW CHIEF COOK IN THE INNER CHAMBERS KITCHENS?
NO, YOUR HIGHNESS, THE COOK REMAINS THE SAME. IS SOMETHING THE MATTER?
NO...

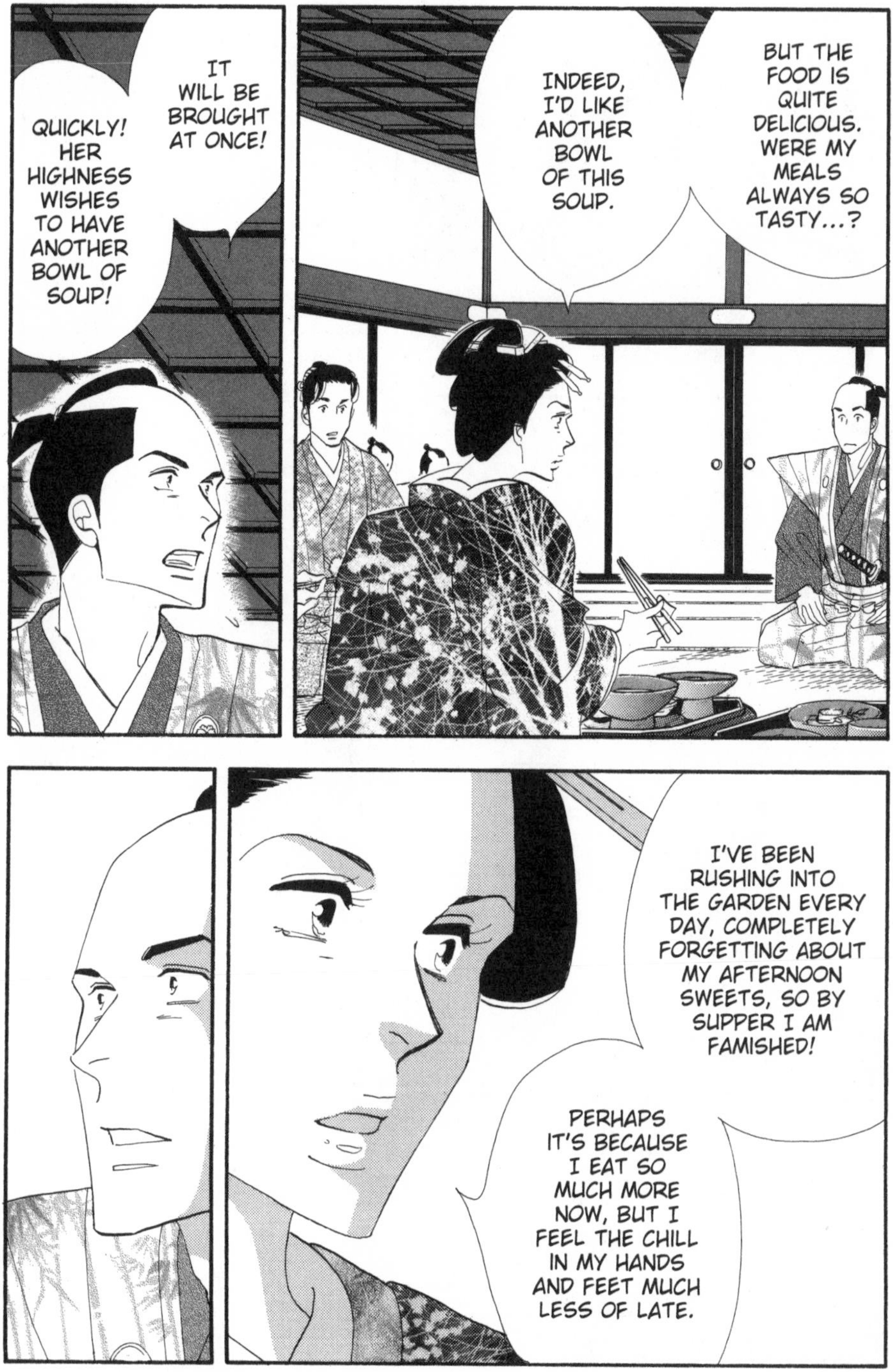
BUT THE FOOD IS QUITE DELICIOUS. WERE MY MEALS ALWAYS SO TASTY...?
INDEED, I'D LIKE ANOTHER BOWL OF THIS SOUP.
IT WILL BE BROUGHT AT ONCE!
QUICKLY! HER HIGHNESS WISHES TO HAVE ANOTHER BOWL OF SOUP!
I'VE BEEN RUSHING INTO THE GARDEN EVERY DAY, COMPLETELY FORGETTING ABOUT MY AFTERNOON SWEETS, SO BY SUPPER I AM FAMISHED!
PERHAPS IT'S BECAUSE I EAT SO MUCH MORE NOW, BUT I FEEL THE CHILL IN MY HANDS AND FEET MUCH LESS OF LATE.

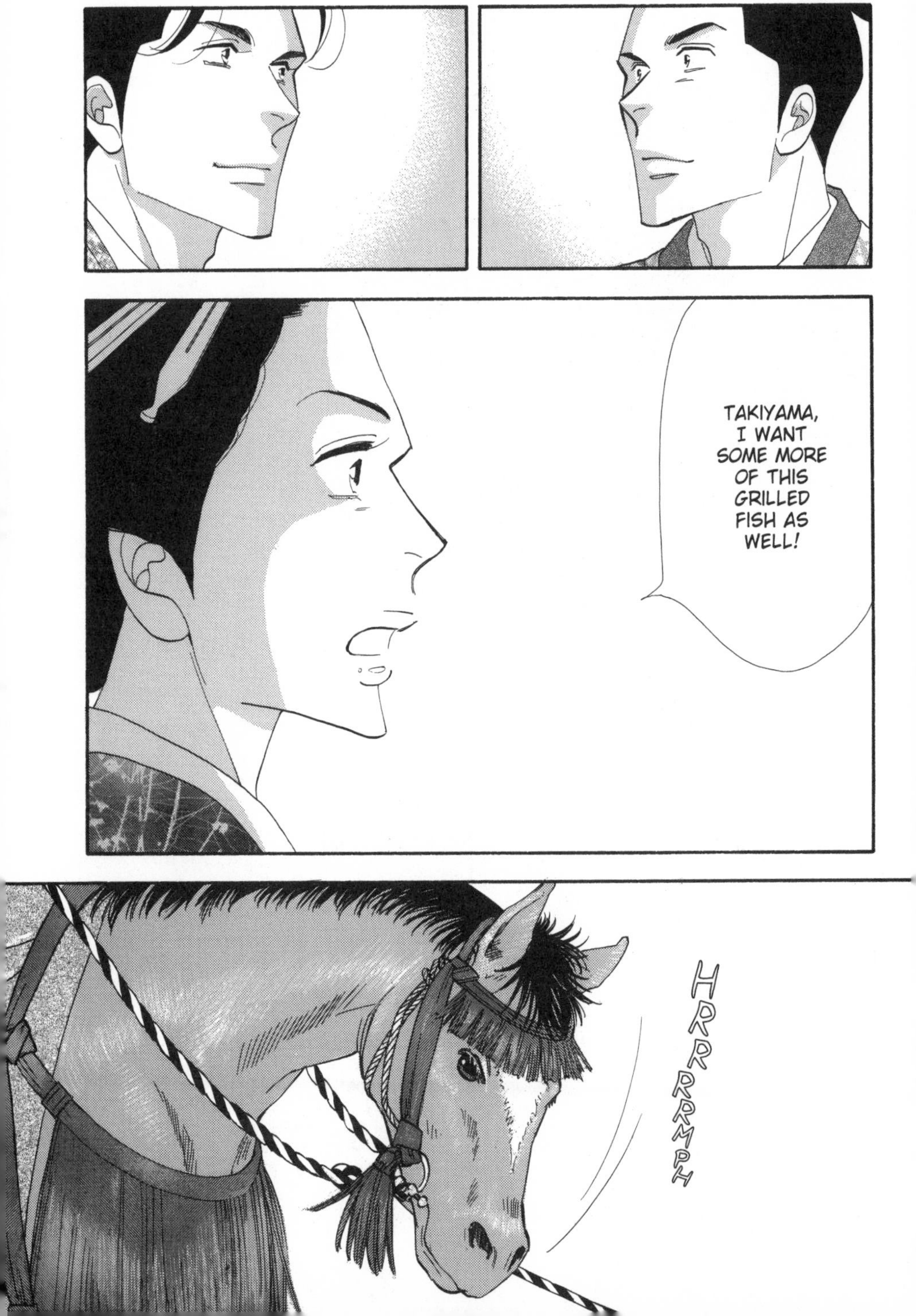
TAKIYAMA, I WANT SOME MORE OF THIS GRILLED FISH AS WELL!
HRRRRRMPH

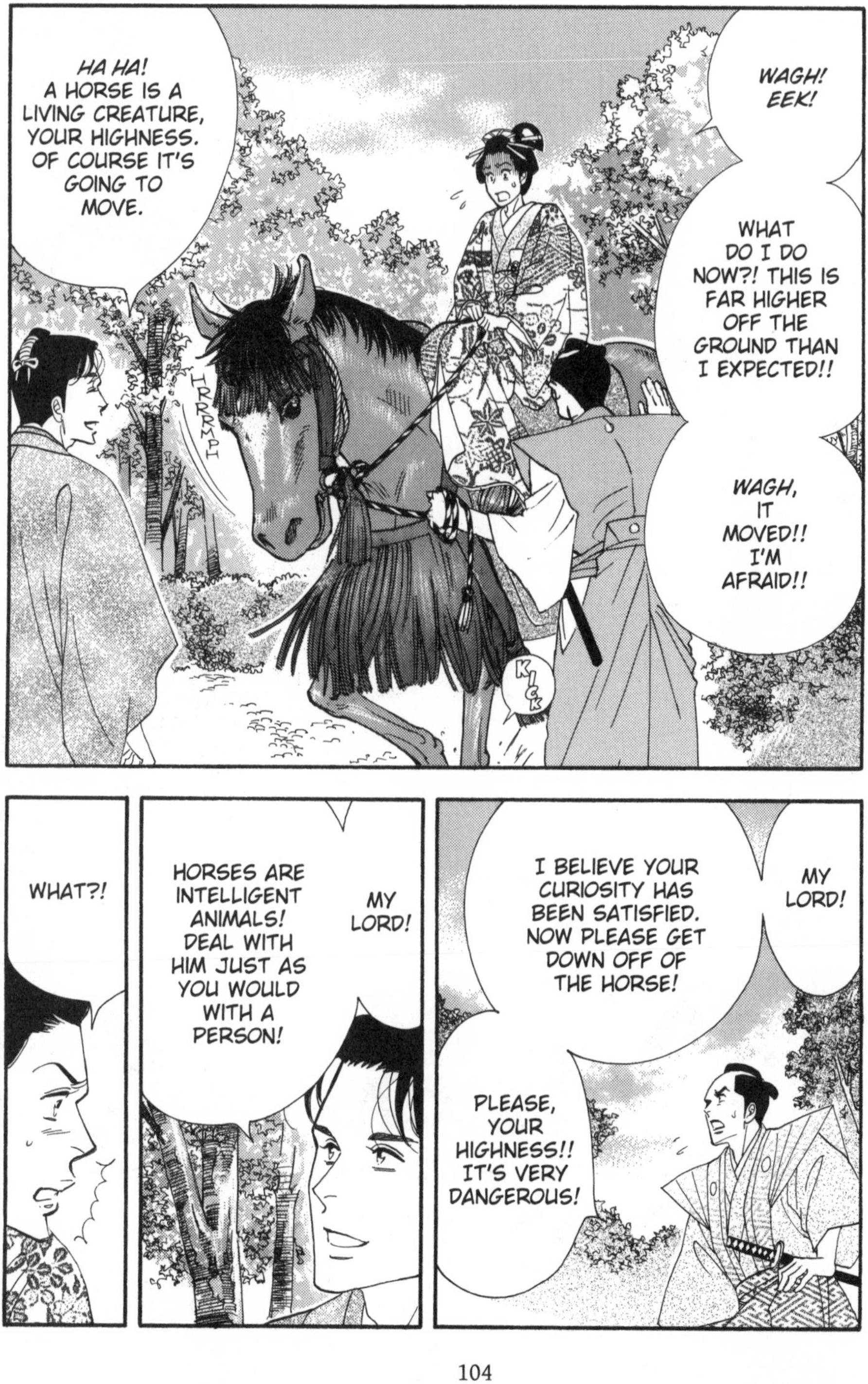
WAGH! EEK!
WHAT DO I DO NOW?! THIS IS FAR HIGHER OFF THE GROUND THAN I EXPECTED!!
WAGH, IT MOVED!! I'M AFRAID!!
KICK
HRRRMPH
HA HA! A HORSE IS A LIVING CREATURE, YOUR HIGHNESS. OF COURSE IT'S GOING TO MOVE.
MY LORD!
I BELIEVE YOUR CURIOSITY HAS BEEN SATISFIED. NOW PLEASE GET DOWN OFF OF THE HORSE!
PLEASE, YOUR HIGHNESS!! IT'S VERY DANGEROUS!
MY LORD!
HORSES ARE INTELLIGENT ANIMALS! DEAL WITH HIM JUST AS YOU WOULD WITH A PERSON!
WHAT?!

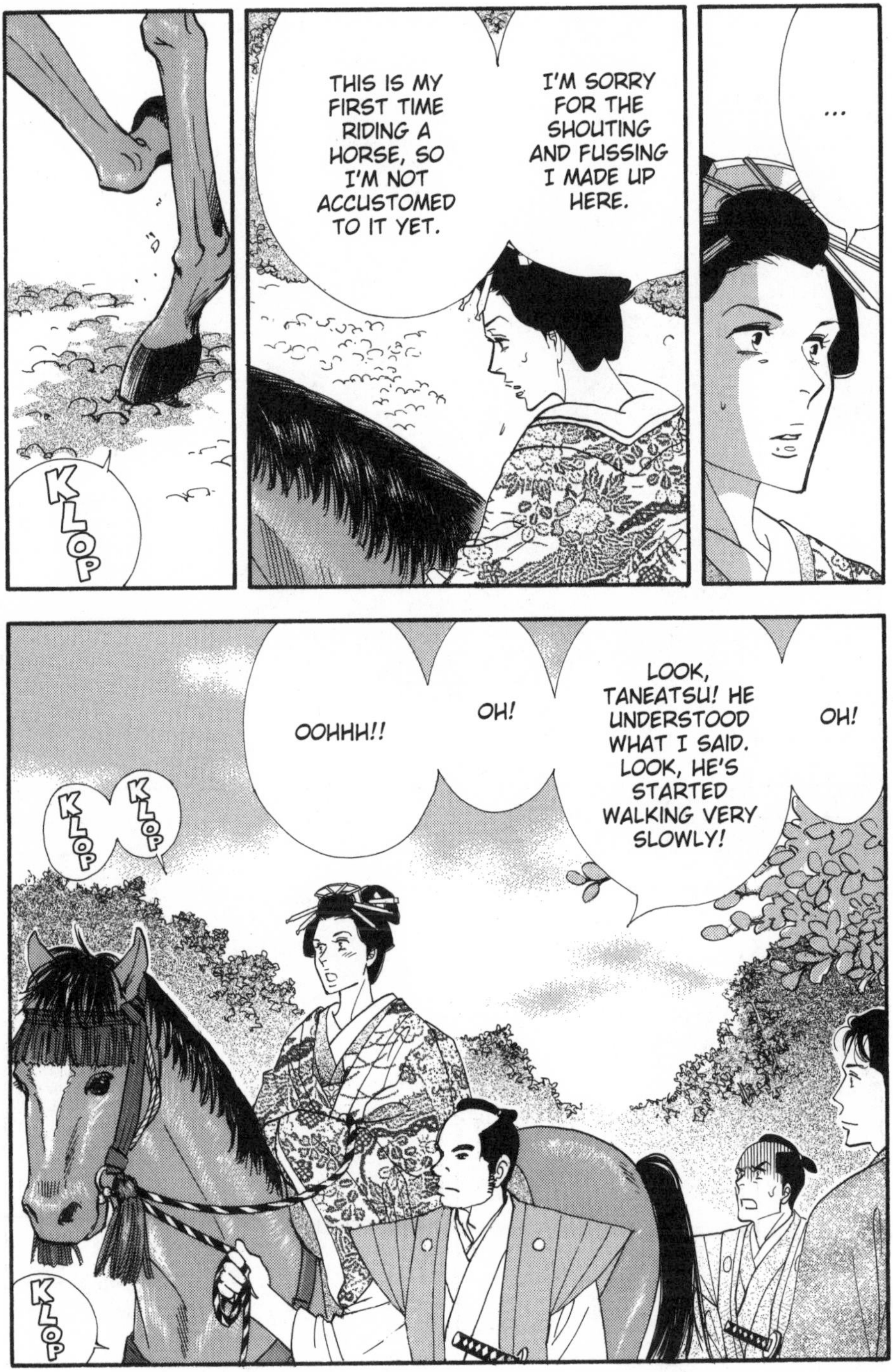
...
I'M SORRY FOR THE SHOUTING AND FUSSING I MADE UP HERE.
THIS IS MY FIRST TIME RIDING A HORSE, SO I'M NOT ACCUSTOMED TO IT YET.
KLOP
OH!
LOOK, TANEATSU! HE UNDERSTOOD WHAT I SAID. LOOK, HE'S STARTED WALKING VERY SLOWLY!
OH!
OOHHH!!
KLOP
KLOP
KLOP

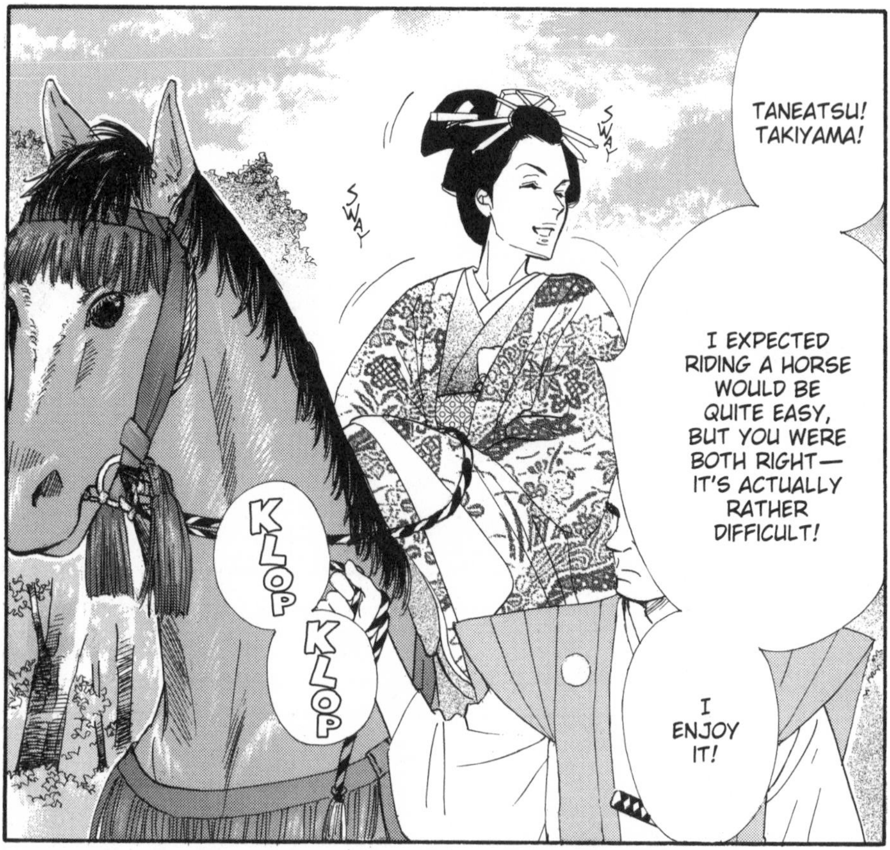
TANEATSU! TAKIYAMA!
SWAY
SWAY
I EXPECTED RIDING A HORSE WOULD BE QUITE EASY, BUT YOU WERE BOTH RIGHT—IT'S ACTUALLY RATHER DIFFICULT!
KLOP
KLOP
I ENJOY IT!
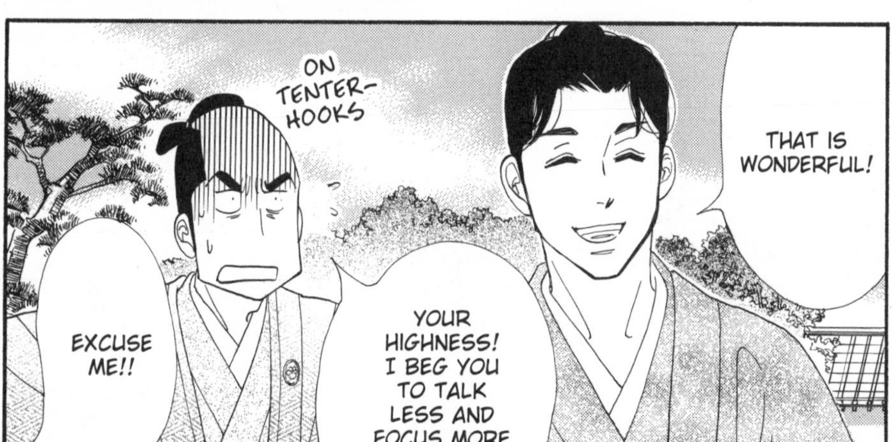
THAT IS WONDERFUL!
ON TENTER-HOOKS
YOUR HIGHNESS! I BEG YOU TO TALK LESS AND FOCUS MORE ON RIDING!
EXCUSE ME!!

WHAT IS IT?!
DO NOT SHOUT LIKE THAT WHEN OUR LORD IS RIDING, FOR YOU MAY FRIGHTEN THE HORSE!
M'LORD! I BEG YOUR PARDON! BUT I HAVE BEEN SENT WITH NEWS OF GREAT URGENCY THAT OUR LORD THE SHOGUN MUST HEAR AT ONCE!
!
LET ME DOWN.
YOU ARE FROM THE OUTER CHAMBERS, ARE YOU NOT? WHAT IS IT?
I AM SORRY TO REPORT...
...THAT BARON ABE OF ISE HAS BEEN TAKEN GRAVELY ILL AND WILL BE UNABLE TO COME TO THE CASTLE TOMORROW AND HENCEFORWARD!

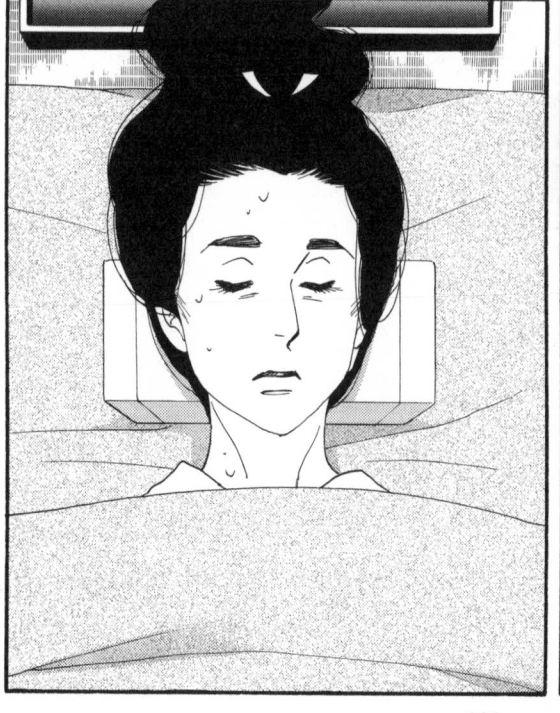

Ōoku

THE INNER CHAMBERS

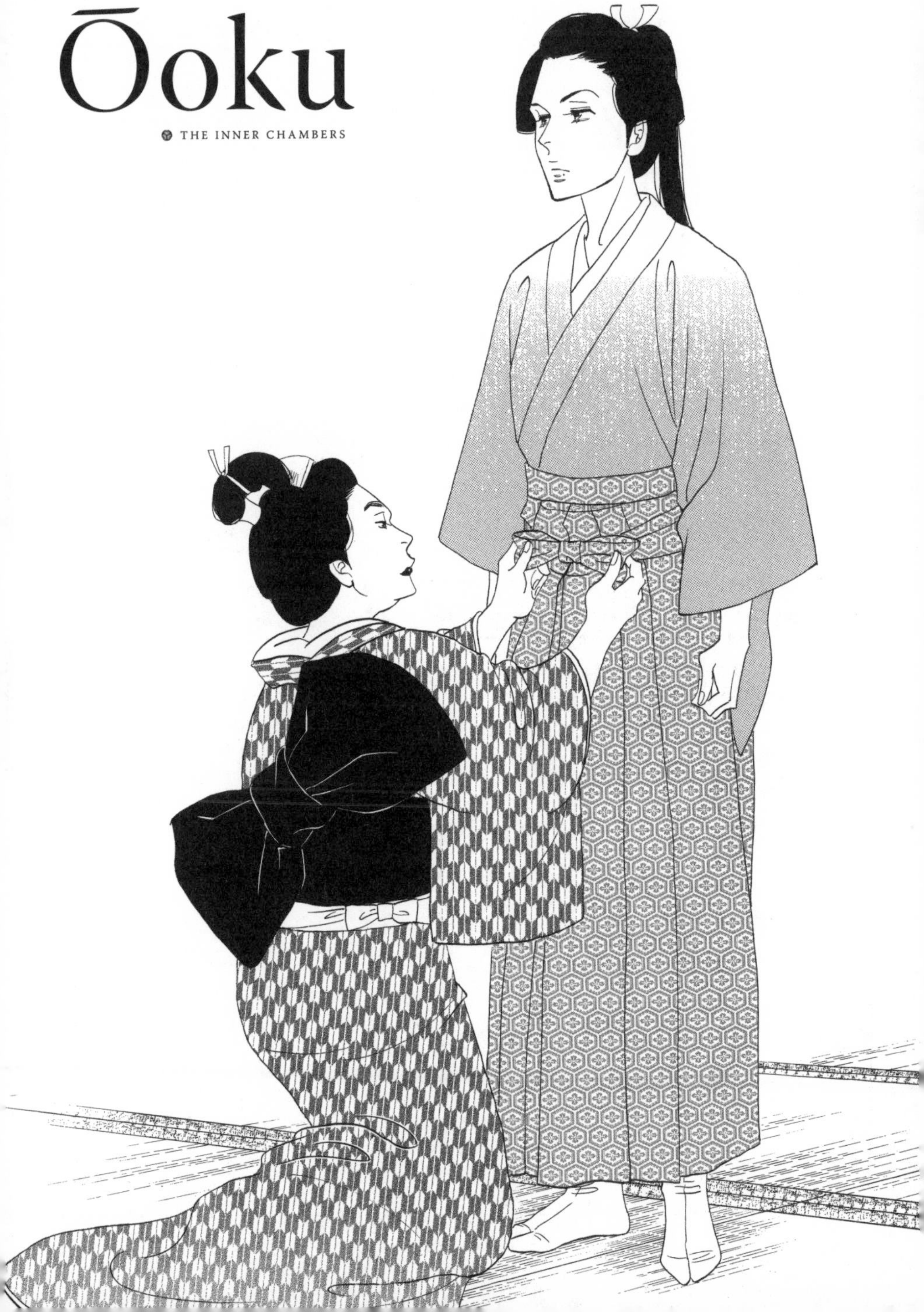

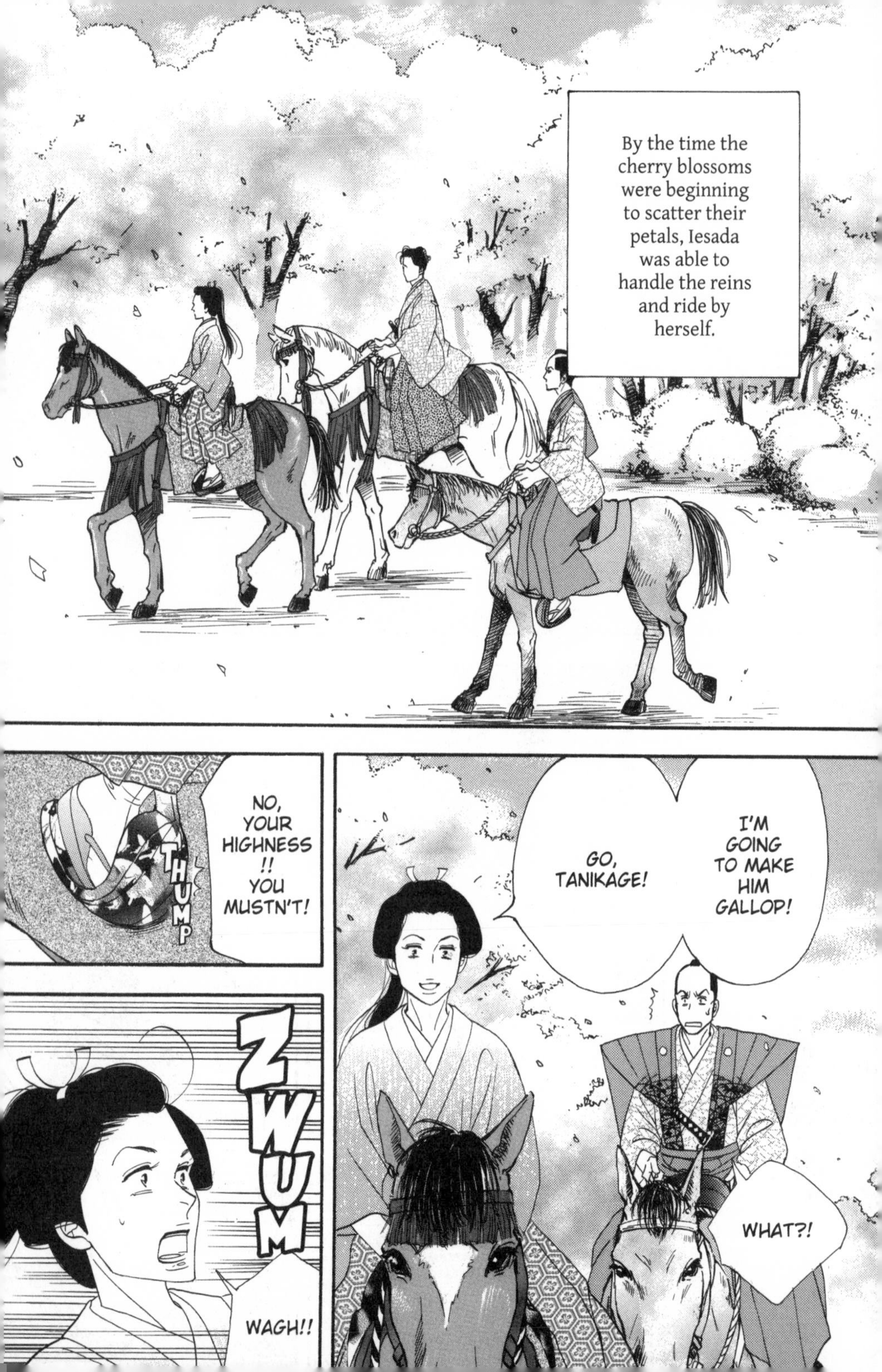
By the time the cherry blossoms were beginning to scatter their petals, Iesada was able to handle the reins and ride by herself.
GO, TANIKAGE!
I'M GOING TO MAKE HIM GALLOP!
WHAT?!
NO, YOUR HIGHNESS!! YOU MUSTN'T!
THUMP
ZWUM
WAGH!!

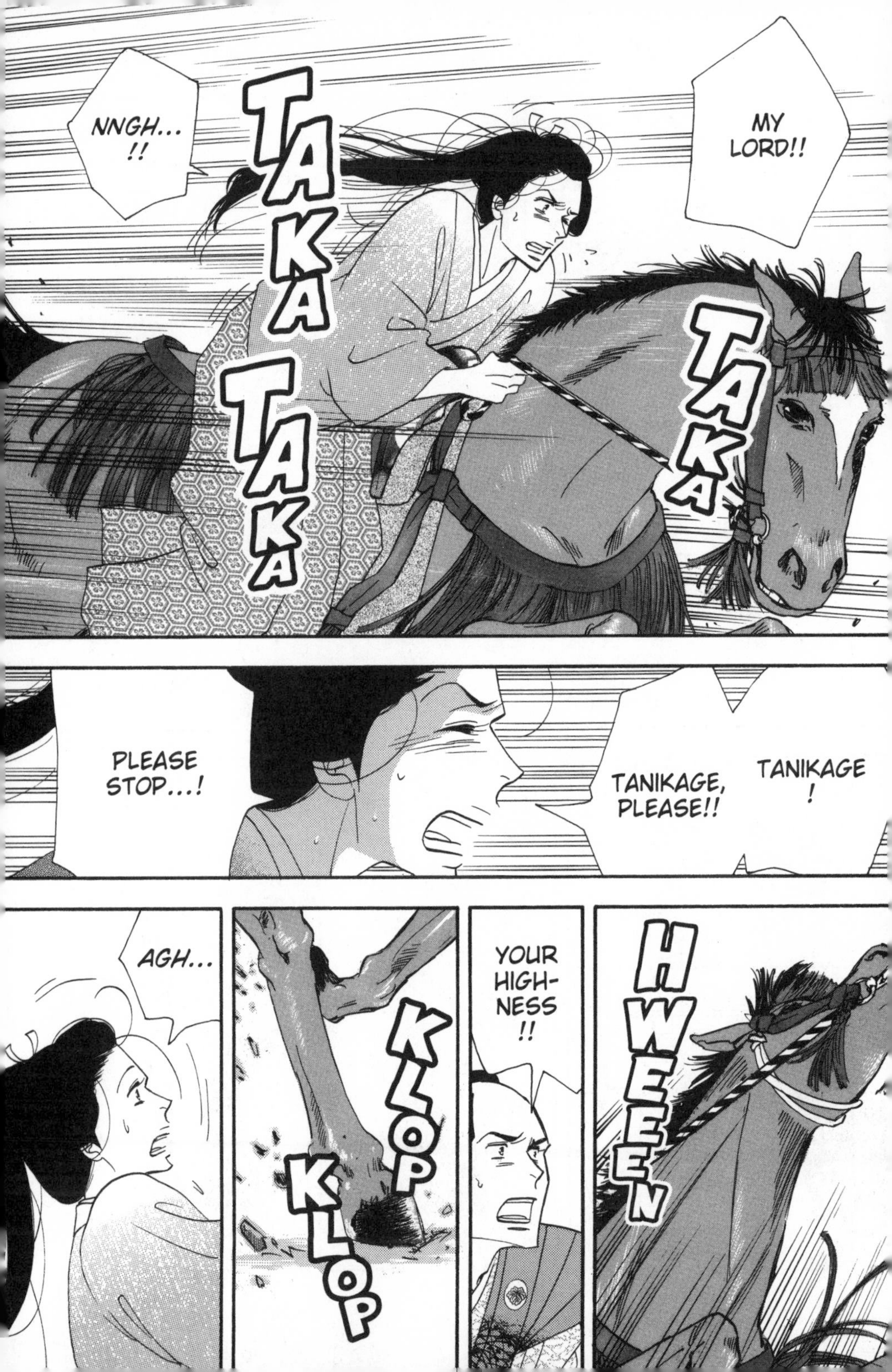
MY LORD!!
TAKA
TAKA TAKA
NNGH... !!
TANIKAGE !
TANIKAGE, PLEASE!!
PLEASE STOP...!
HWEEEN
YOUR HIGH-NESS !!
KLOP KLOP
AGH...

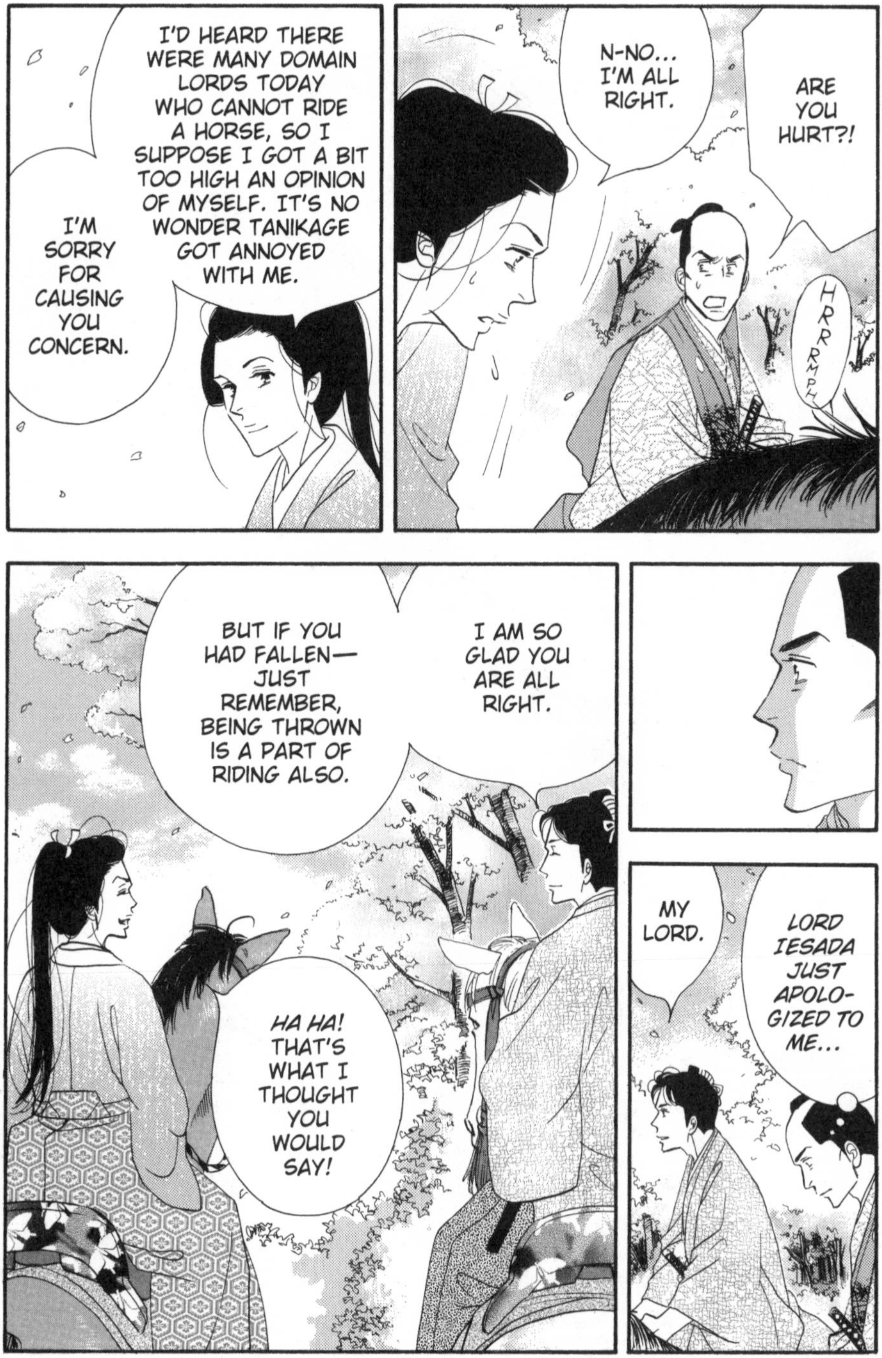
ARE YOU HURT?!
HRRRMPH
N-NO... I'M ALL RIGHT.
I'D HEARD THERE WERE MANY DOMAIN LORDS TODAY WHO CANNOT RIDE A HORSE, SO I SUPPOSE I GOT A BIT TOO HIGH AN OPINION OF MYSELF. IT'S NO WONDER TANIKAGE GOT ANNOYED WITH ME.
I'M SORRY FOR CAUSING YOU CONCERN.
I AM SO GLAD YOU ARE ALL RIGHT.
BUT IF YOU HAD FALLEN— JUST REMEMBER, BEING THROWN IS A PART OF RIDING ALSO.
HA HA! THAT'S WHAT I THOUGHT YOU WOULD SAY!
LORD IESADA JUST APOLOGIZED TO ME...
MY LORD.

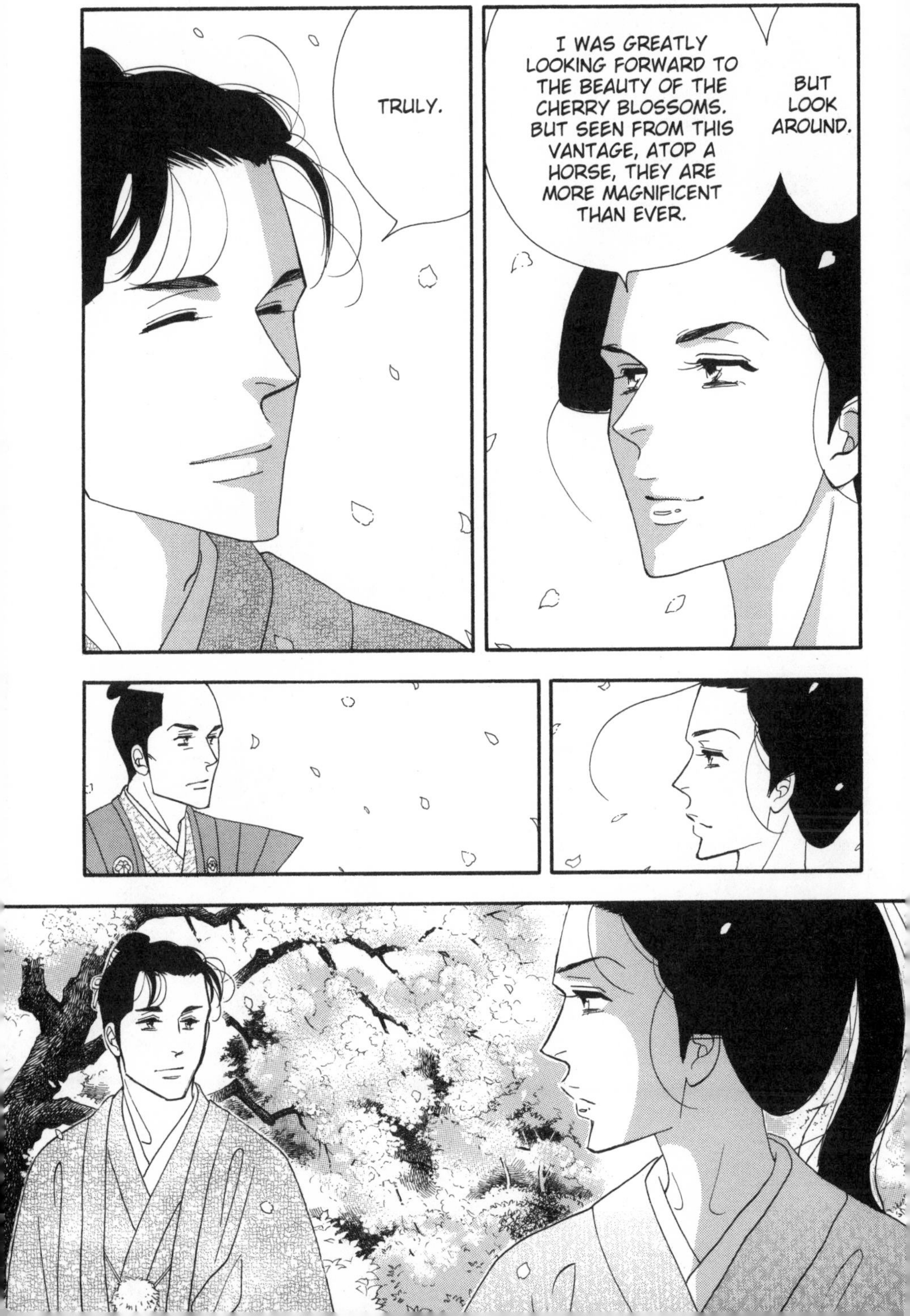
BUT LOOK AROUND.
I WAS GREATLY LOOKING FORWARD TO THE BEAUTY OF THE CHERRY BLOSSOMS. BUT SEEN FROM THIS VANTAGE, ATOP A HORSE, THEY ARE MORE MAGNIFICENT THAN EVER.
TRULY.

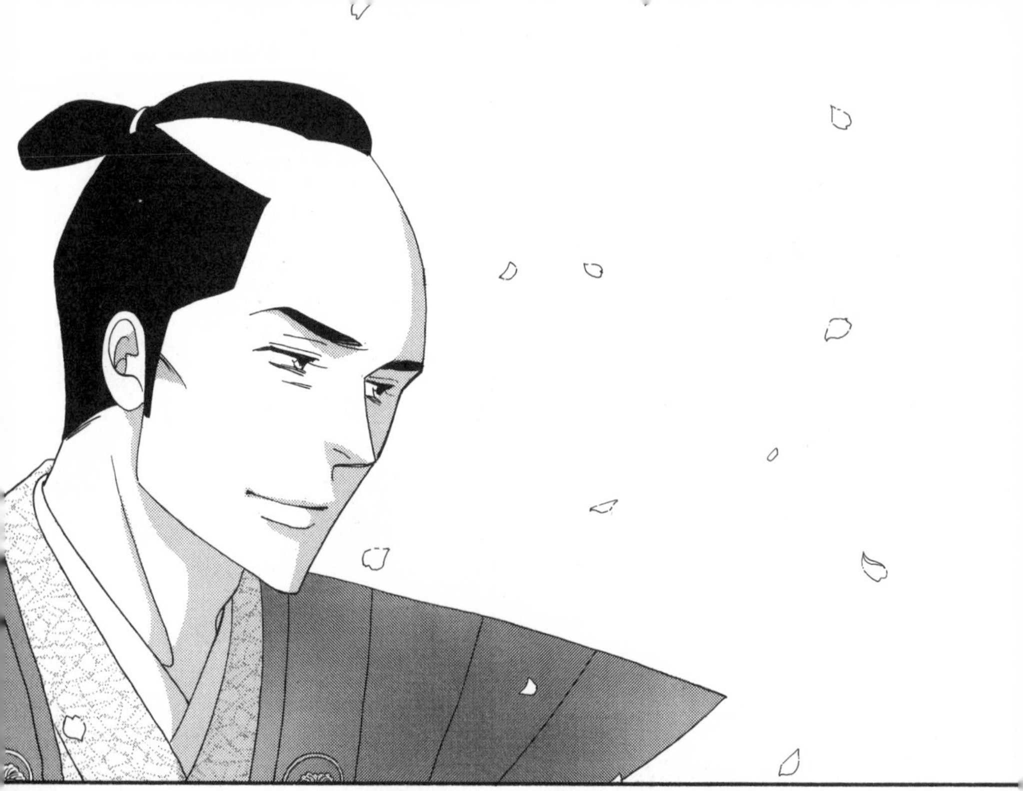

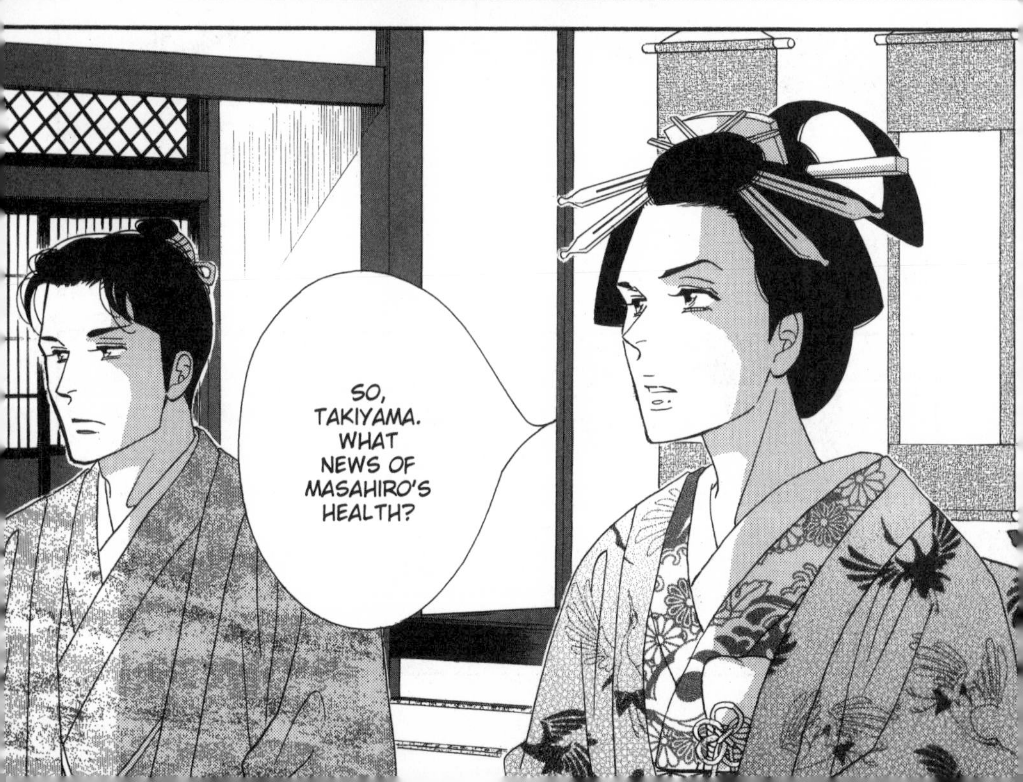
SO, TAKIYAMA. WHAT NEWS OF MASAHIRO'S HEALTH?

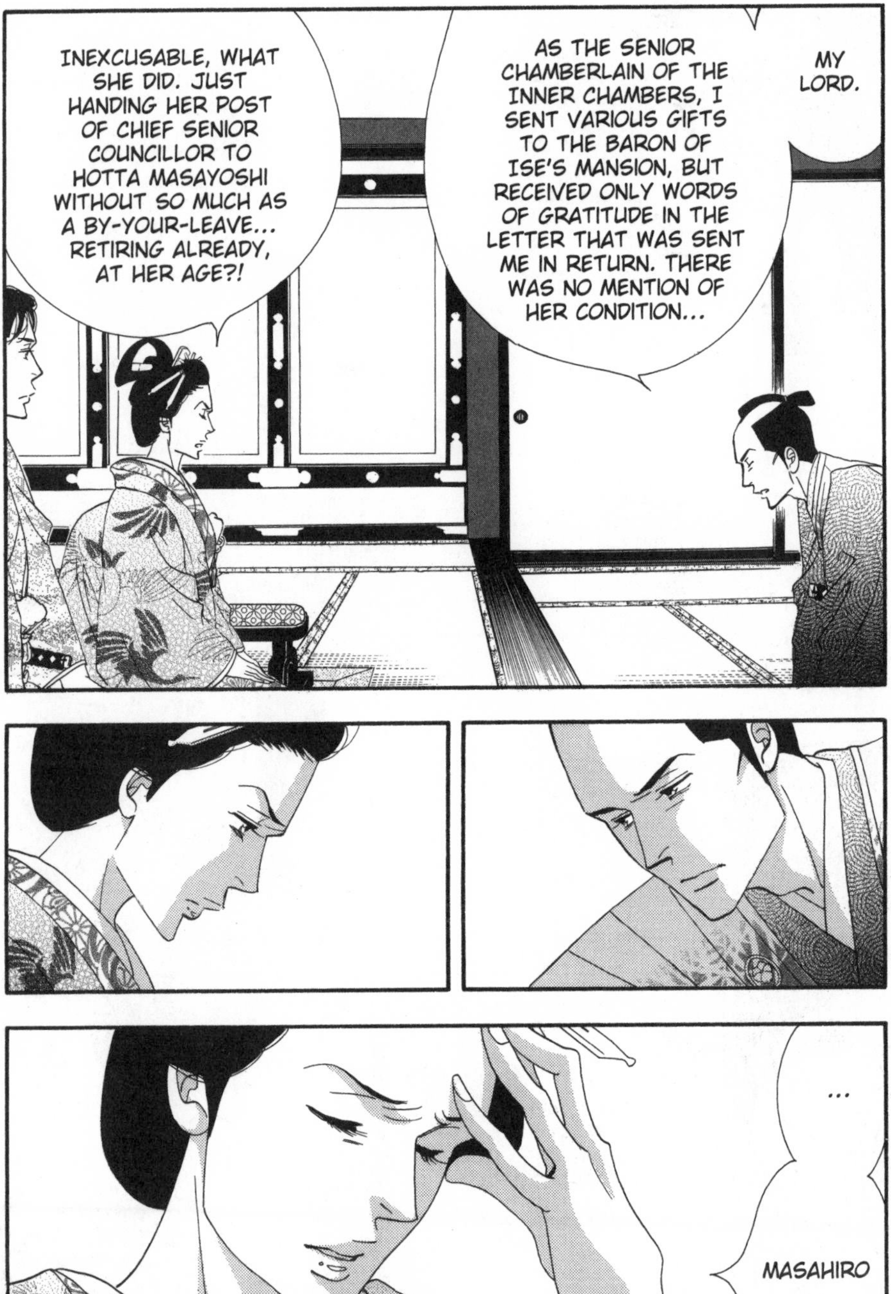
MY LORD.
AS THE SENIOR CHAMBERLAIN OF THE INNER CHAMBERS, I SENT VARIOUS GIFTS TO THE BARON OF ISE'S MANSION, BUT RECEIVED ONLY WORDS OF GRATITUDE IN THE LETTER THAT WAS SENT ME IN RETURN. THERE WAS NO MENTION OF HER CONDITION...
INEXCUSABLE, WHAT SHE DID. JUST HANDING HER POST OF CHIEF SENIOR COUNCILLOR TO HOTTA MASAYOSHI WITHOUT SO MUCH AS A BY-YOUR-LEAVE... RETIRING ALREADY, AT HER AGE?!
...
MASAHIRO ...

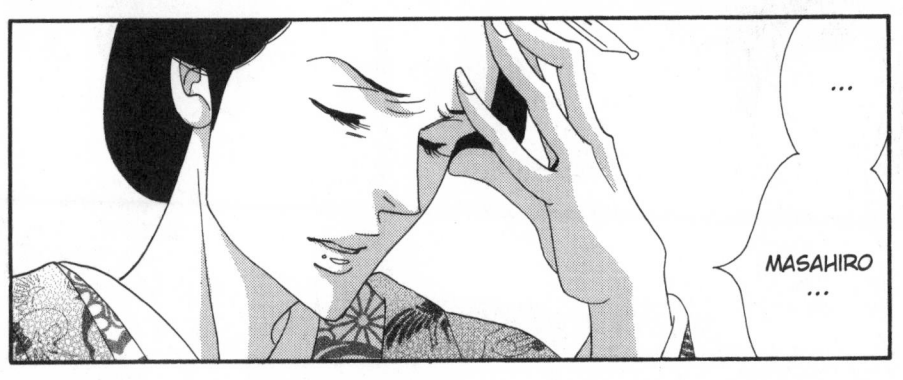

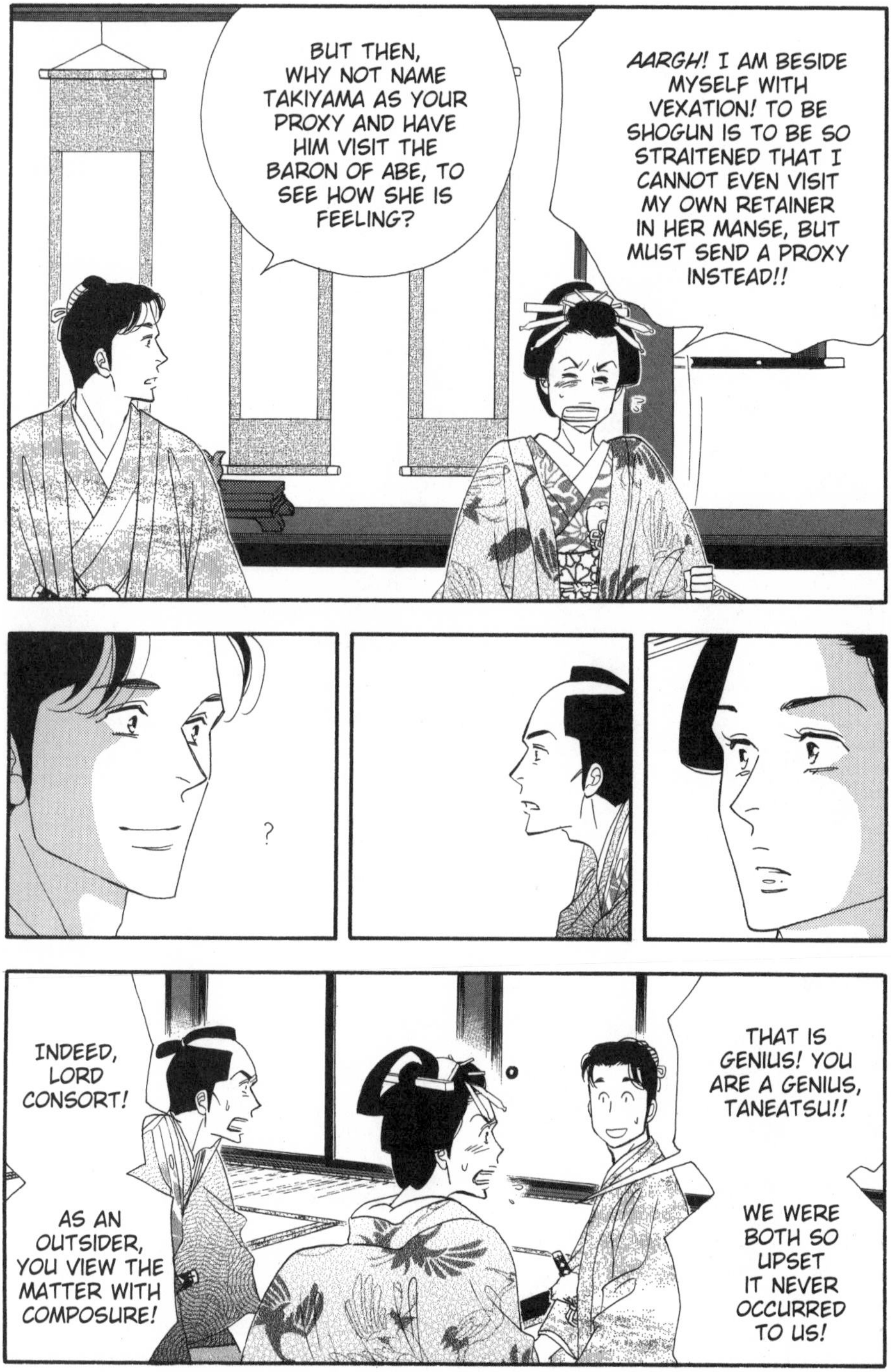
AARGH! I AM BESIDE MYSELF WITH VEXATION! TO BE SHOGUN IS TO BE SO STRAITENED THAT I CANNOT EVEN VISIT MY OWN RETAINER IN HER MANSE, BUT MUST SEND A PROXY INSTEAD!!
BUT THEN, WHY NOT NAME TAKIYAMA AS YOUR PROXY AND HAVE HIM VISIT THE BARON OF ABE, TO SEE HOW SHE IS FEELING?
?
THAT IS GENIUS! YOU ARE A GENIUS, TANEATSU!!
WE WERE BOTH SO UPSET IT NEVER OCCURRED TO US!
INDEED, LORD CONSORT!
AS AN OUTSIDER, YOU VIEW THE MATTER WITH COMPOSURE!

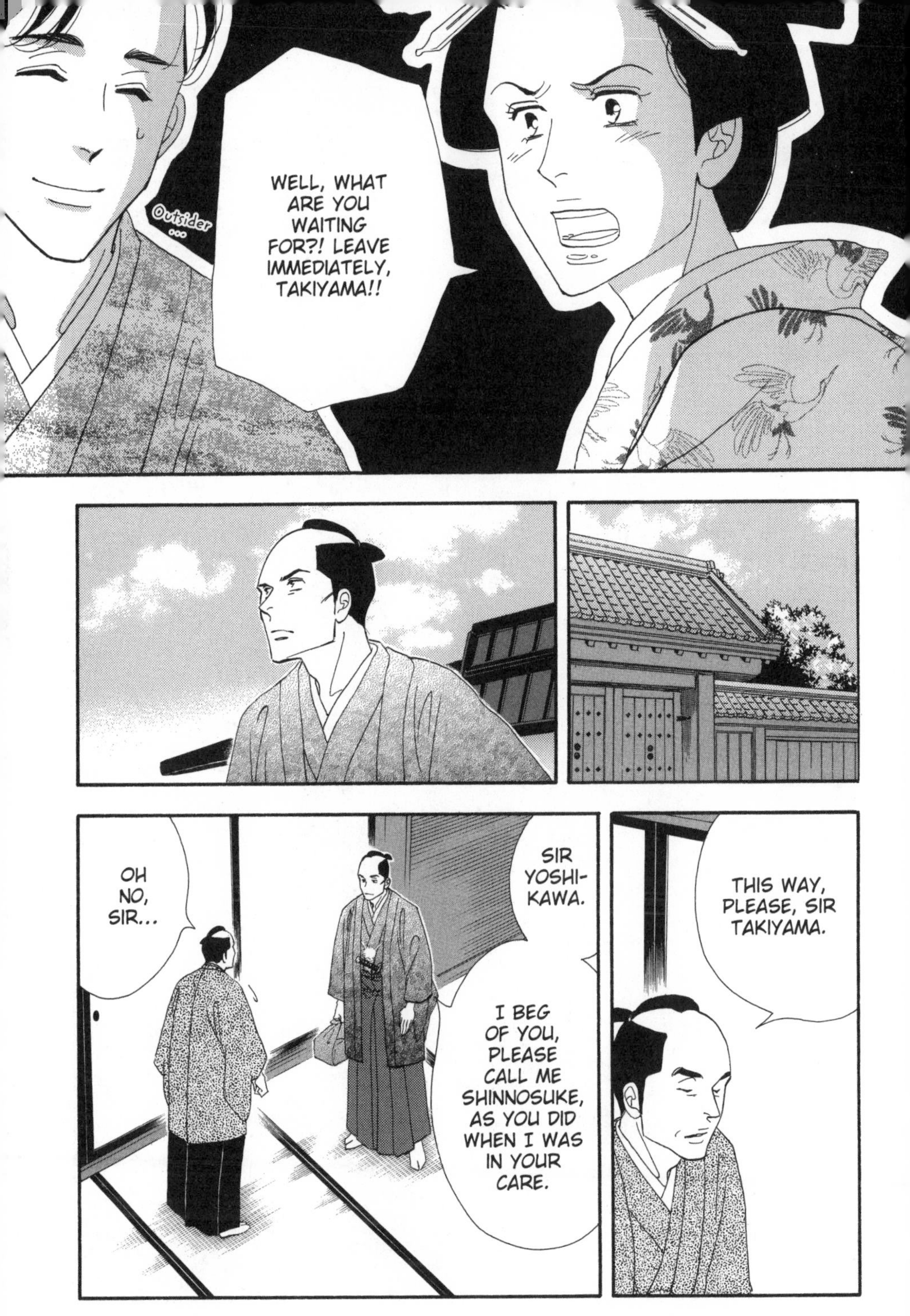
WELL, WHAT ARE YOU WAITING FOR?! LEAVE IMMEDIATELY, TAKIYAMA!!
Outsider...
THIS WAY, PLEASE, SIR TAKIYAMA.
SIR YOSHI-KAWA.
I BEG OF YOU, PLEASE CALL ME SHINNOSUKE, AS YOU DID WHEN I WAS IN YOUR CARE.
OH NO, SIR...

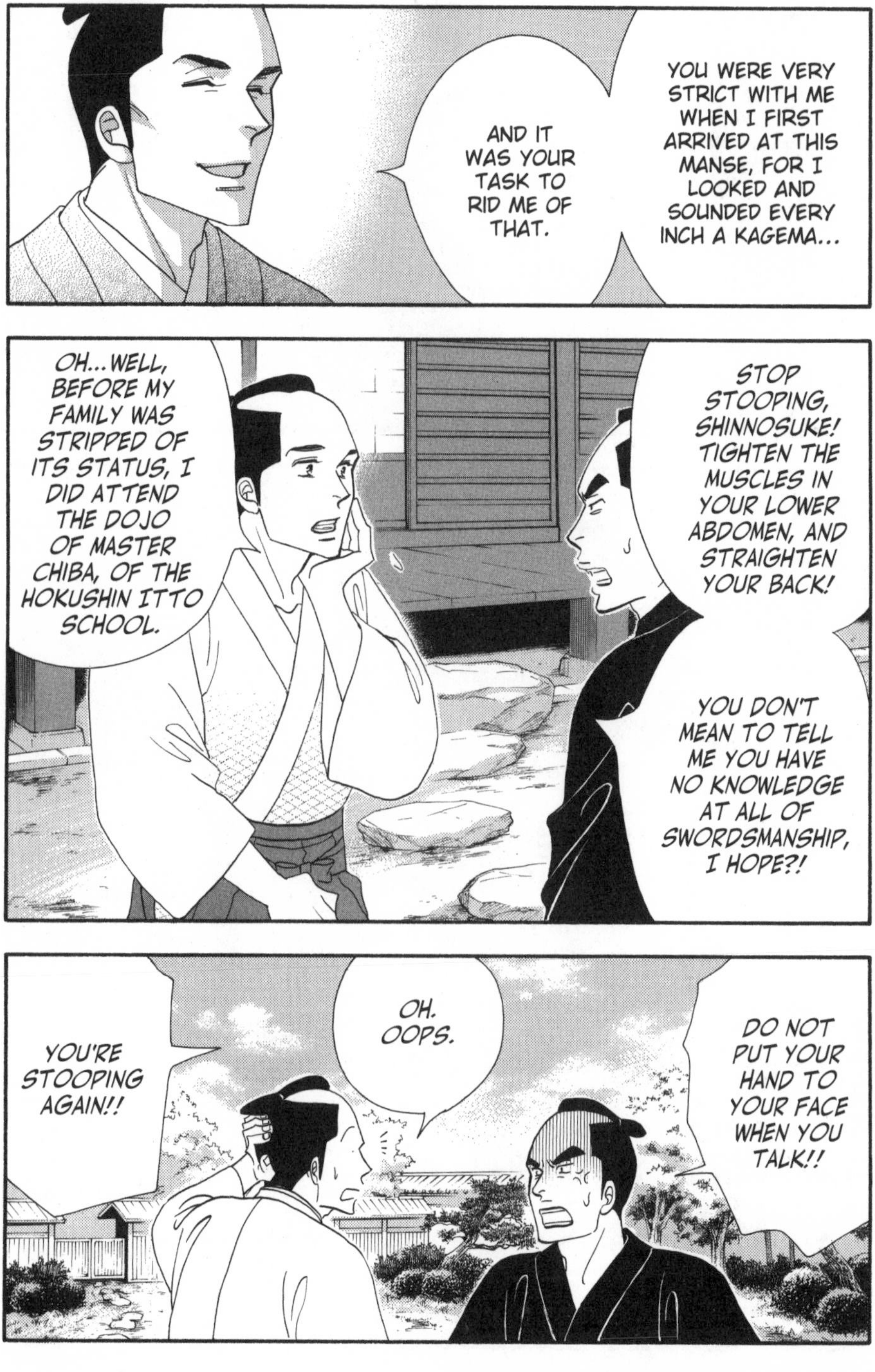

YOU WERE VERY STRICT WITH ME WHEN I FIRST ARRIVED AT THIS MANSE, FOR I LOOKED AND SOUNDED EVERY INCH A KAGEMA...
AND IT WAS YOUR TASK TO RID ME OF THAT.
STOP STOOPING, SHINNOSUKE! TIGHTEN THE MUSCLES IN YOUR LOWER ABDOMEN, AND STRAIGHTEN YOUR BACK!
YOU DON'T MEAN TO TELL ME YOU HAVE NO KNOWLEDGE AT ALL OF SWORDSMANSHIP, I HOPE?!
OH...WELL, BEFORE MY FAMILY WAS STRIPPED OF ITS STATUS, I DID ATTEND THE DOJO OF MASTER CHIBA, OF THE HOKUSHIN ITTO SCHOOL.
DO NOT PUT YOUR HAND TO YOUR FACE WHEN YOU TALK!!
OH. OOPS.
YOU'RE STOOPING AGAIN!!

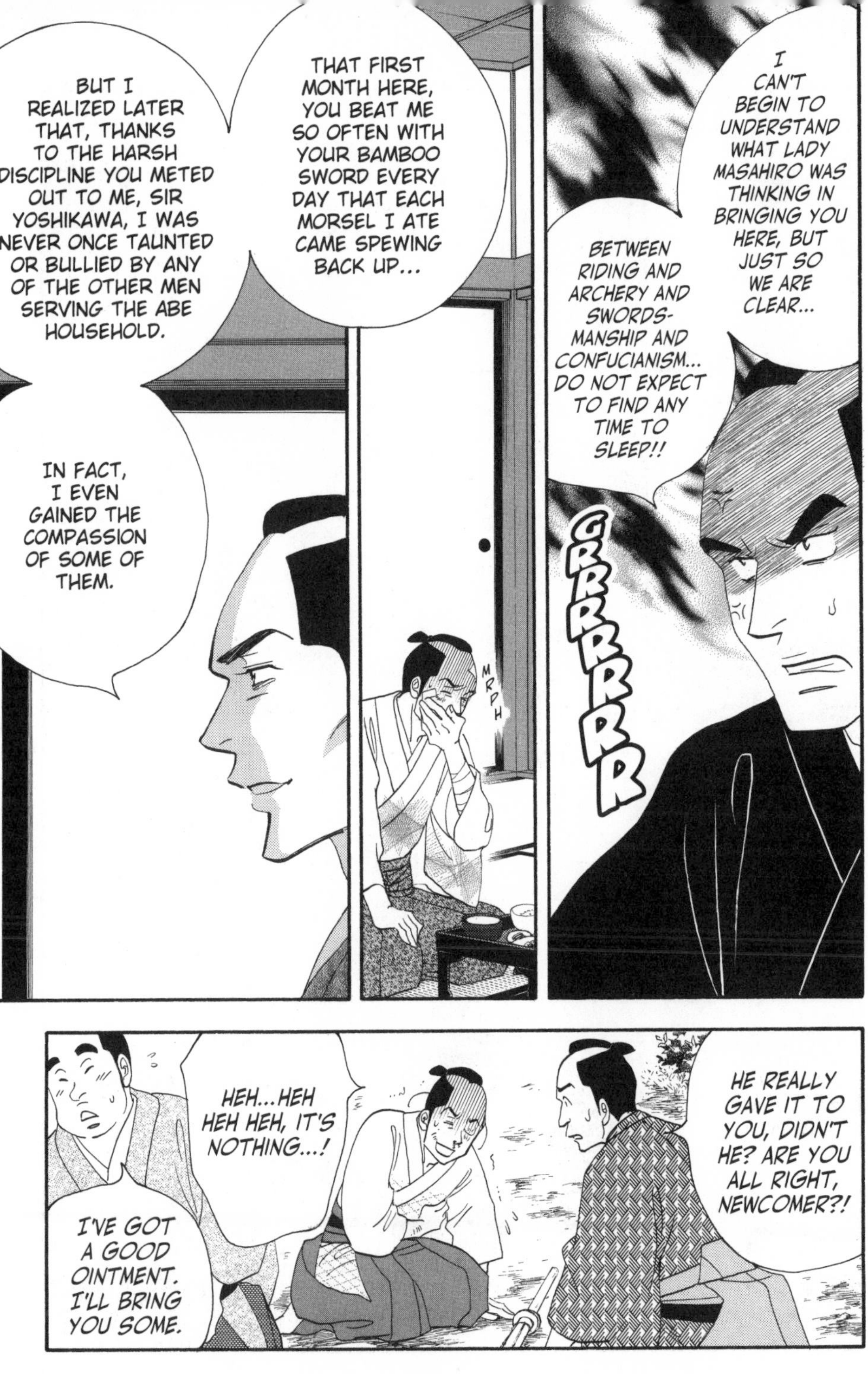
I CAN'T BEGIN TO UNDERSTAND WHAT LADY MASAHIRO WAS THINKING IN BRINGING YOU HERE, BUT JUST SO WE ARE CLEAR...
BETWEEN RIDING AND ARCHERY AND SWORDS-MANSHIP AND CONFUCIANISM... DO NOT EXPECT TO FIND ANY TIME TO SLEEP!!
GRRRRRRR
MRPH
THAT FIRST MONTH HERE, YOU BEAT ME SO OFTEN WITH YOUR BAMBOO SWORD EVERY DAY THAT EACH MORSEL I ATE CAME SPEWING BACK UP...
BUT I REALIZED LATER THAT, THANKS TO THE HARSH DISCIPLINE YOU METED OUT TO ME, SIR YOSHIKAWA, I WAS NEVER ONCE TAUNTED OR BULLIED BY ANY OF THE OTHER MEN SERVING THE ABE HOUSEHOLD.
IN FACT, I EVEN GAINED THE COMPASSION OF SOME OF THEM.
HE REALLY GAVE IT TO YOU, DIDN'T HE? ARE YOU ALL RIGHT, NEWCOMER?!
HEH...HEH HEH HEH, IT'S NOTHING...!
I'VE GOT A GOOD OINTMENT. I'LL BRING YOU SOME.

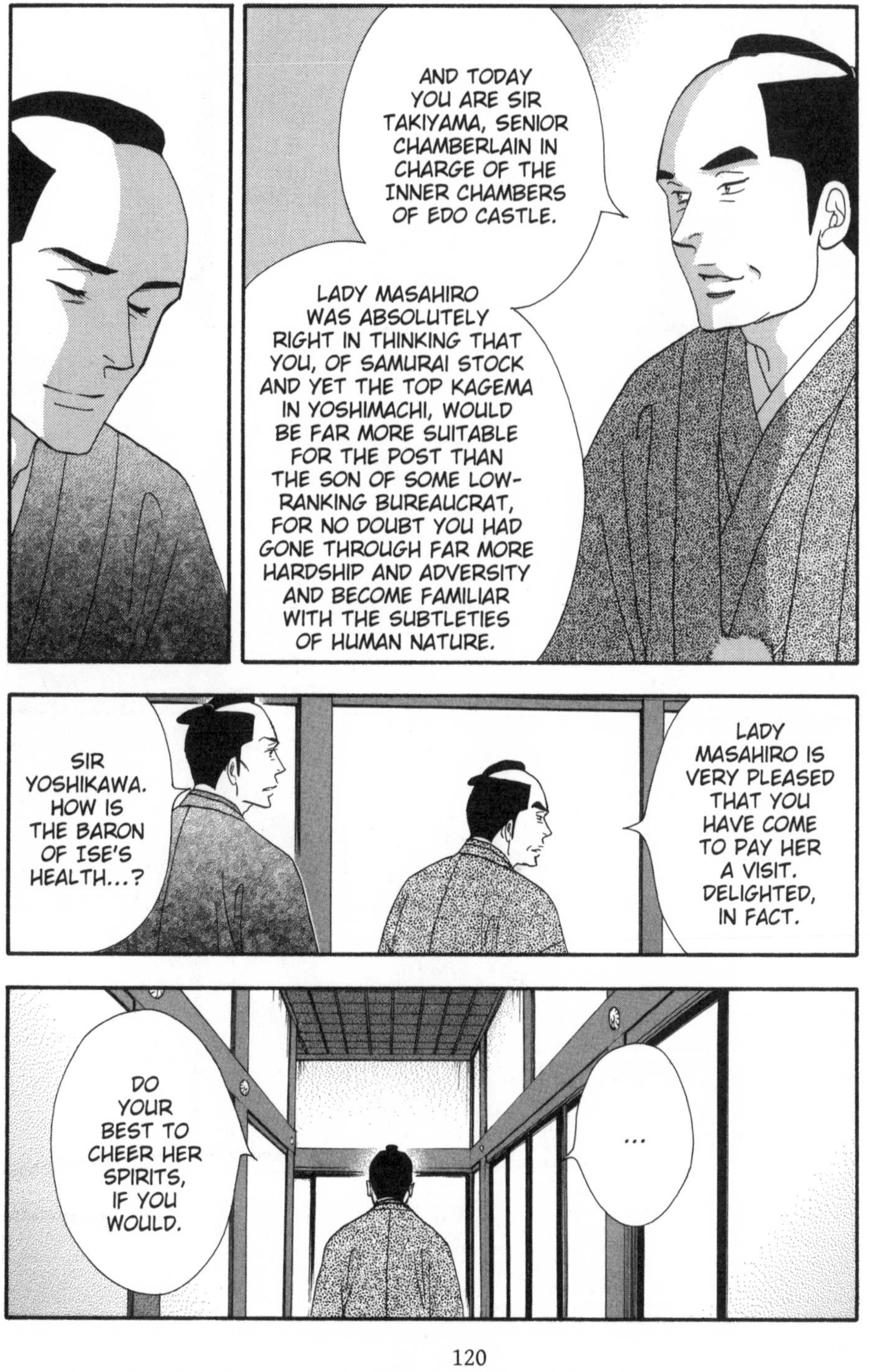
AND TODAY YOU ARE SIR TAKIYAMA, SENIOR CHAMBERLAIN IN CHARGE OF THE INNER CHAMBERS OF EDO CASTLE.
LADY MASAHIRO WAS ABSOLUTELY RIGHT IN THINKING THAT YOU, OF SAMURAI STOCK AND YET THE TOP KAGEMA IN YOSHIMACHI, WOULD BE FAR MORE SUITABLE FOR THE POST THAN THE SON OF SOME LOW-RANKING BUREAUCRAT, FOR NO DOUBT YOU HAD GONE THROUGH FAR MORE HARDSHIP AND ADVERSITY AND BECOME FAMILIAR WITH THE SUBTLETIES OF HUMAN NATURE.
LADY MASAHIRO IS VERY PLEASED THAT YOU HAVE COME TO PAY HER A VISIT. DELIGHTED, IN FACT.
SIR YOSHIKAWA. HOW IS THE BARON OF ISE'S HEALTH...?
...
DO YOUR BEST TO CHEER HER SPIRITS, IF YOU WOULD.

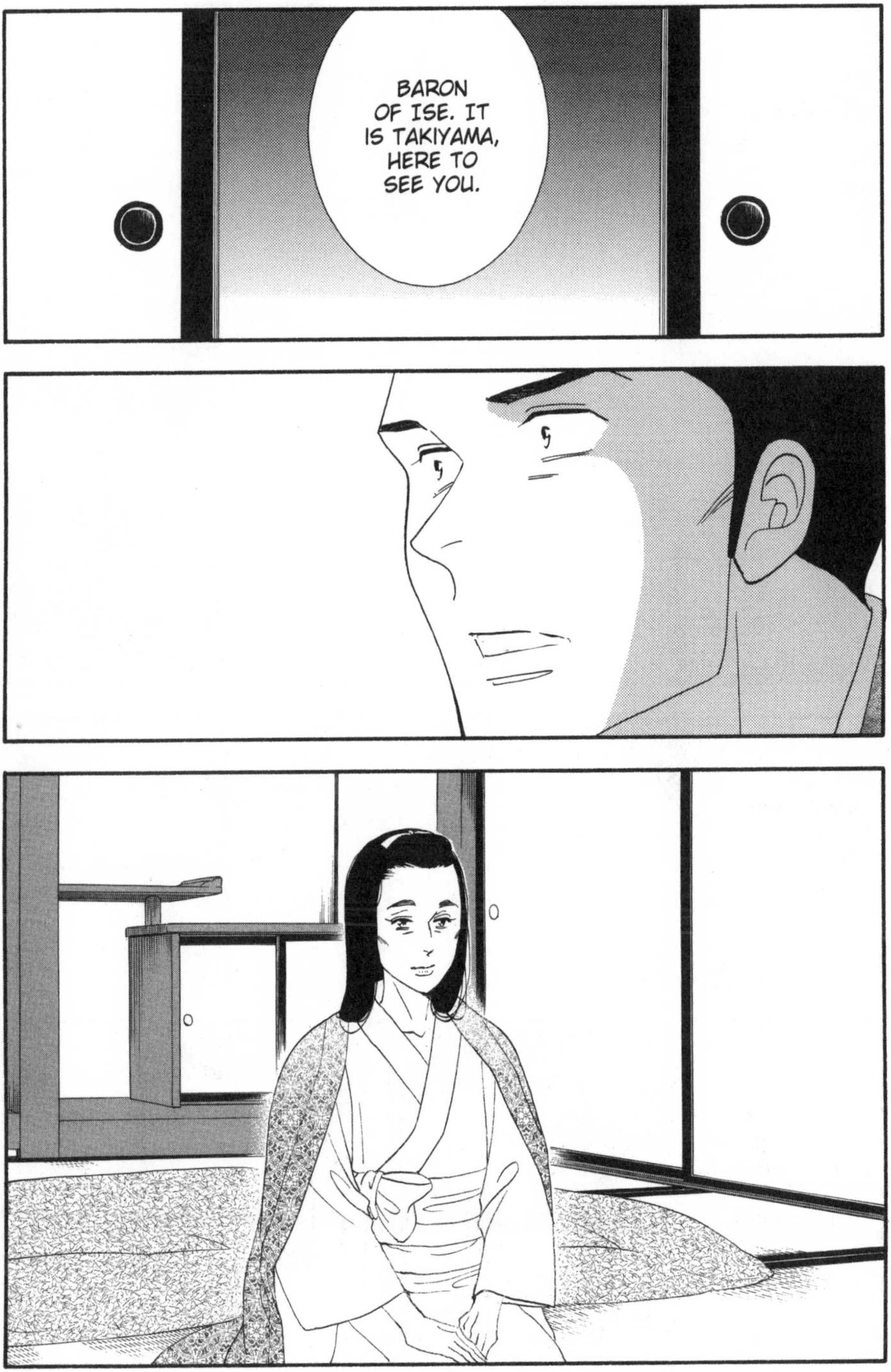
BARON OF ISE. IT IS TAKIYAMA, HERE TO SEE YOU.

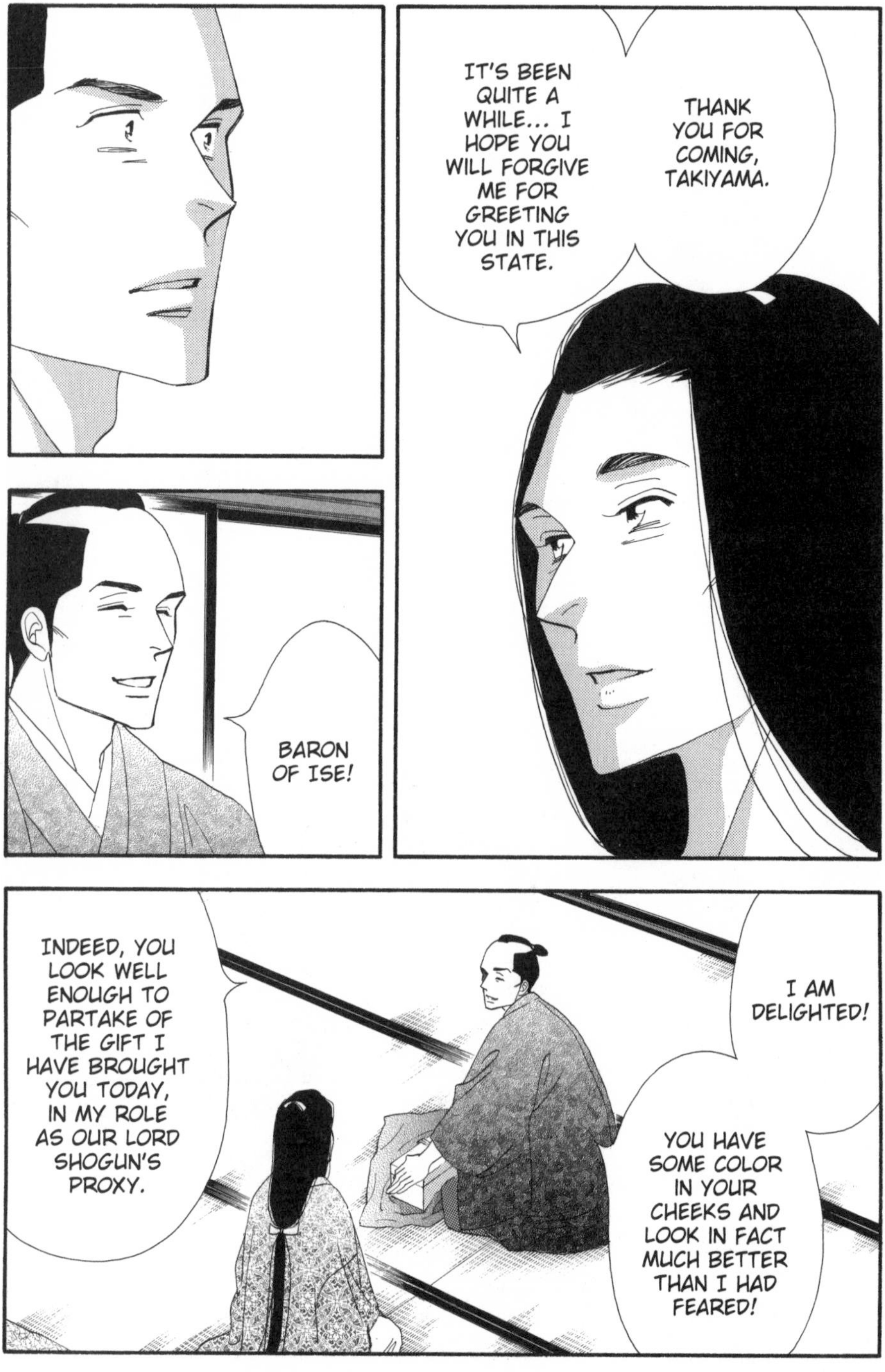
THANK YOU FOR COMING, TAKIYAMA.
IT'S BEEN QUITE A WHILE... I HOPE YOU WILL FORGIVE ME FOR GREETING YOU IN THIS STATE.
BARON OF ISE!
I AM DELIGHTED!
YOU HAVE SOME COLOR IN YOUR CHEEKS AND LOOK IN FACT MUCH BETTER THAN I HAD FEARED!
INDEED, YOU LOOK WELL ENOUGH TO PARTAKE OF THE GIFT I HAVE BROUGHT YOU TODAY, IN MY ROLE AS OUR LORD SHOGUN'S PROXY.

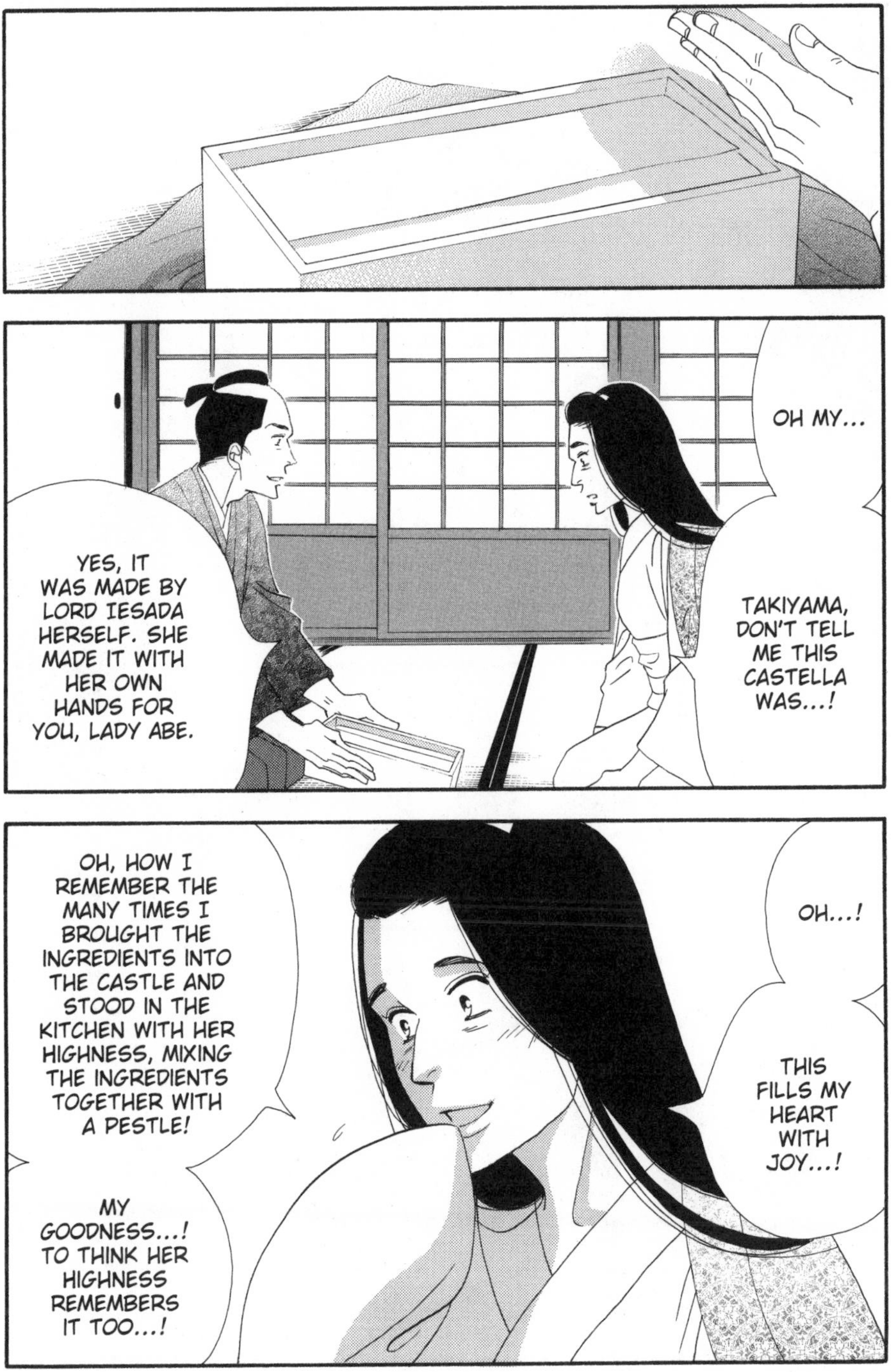
OH MY...
TAKIYAMA, DON'T TELL ME THIS CASTELLA WAS...!
YES, IT WAS MADE BY LORD IESADA HERSELF. SHE MADE IT WITH HER OWN HANDS FOR YOU, LADY ABE.
OH...!
THIS FILLS MY HEART WITH JOY...!
OH, HOW I REMEMBER THE MANY TIMES I BROUGHT THE INGREDIENTS INTO THE CASTLE AND STOOD IN THE KITCHEN WITH HER HIGHNESS, MIXING THE INGREDIENTS TOGETHER WITH A PESTLE!
MY GOODNESS...! TO THINK HER HIGHNESS REMEMBERS IT TOO...!

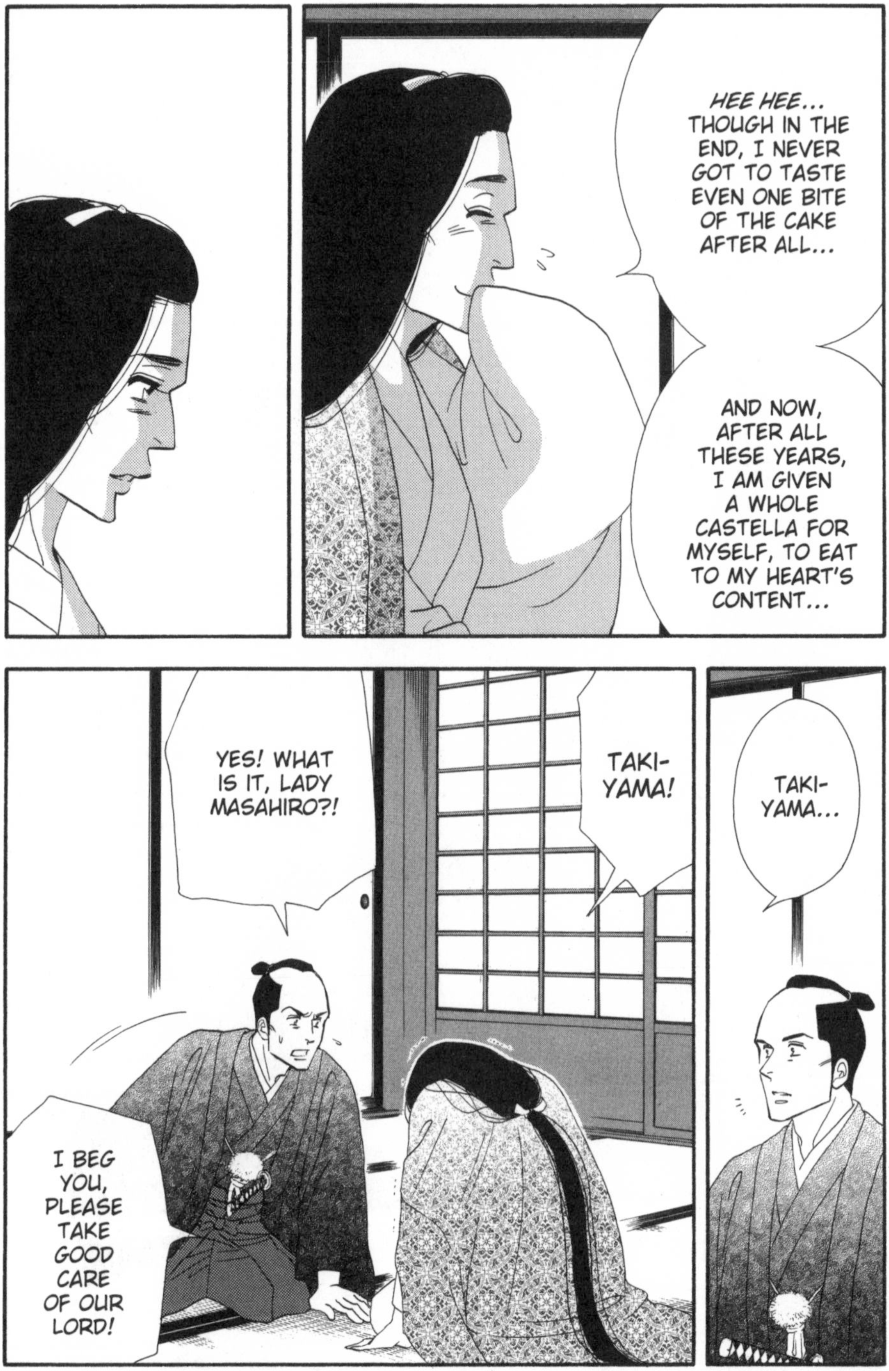
HEE HEE... THOUGH IN THE END, I NEVER GOT TO TASTE EVEN ONE BITE OF THE CAKE AFTER ALL...
AND NOW, AFTER ALL THESE YEARS, I AM GIVEN A WHOLE CASTELLA FOR MYSELF, TO EAT TO MY HEART'S CONTENT...
TAKI-YAMA...
TAKI-YAMA!
YES! WHAT IS IT, LADY MASAHIRO?!
I BEG YOU, PLEASE TAKE GOOD CARE OF OUR LORD!

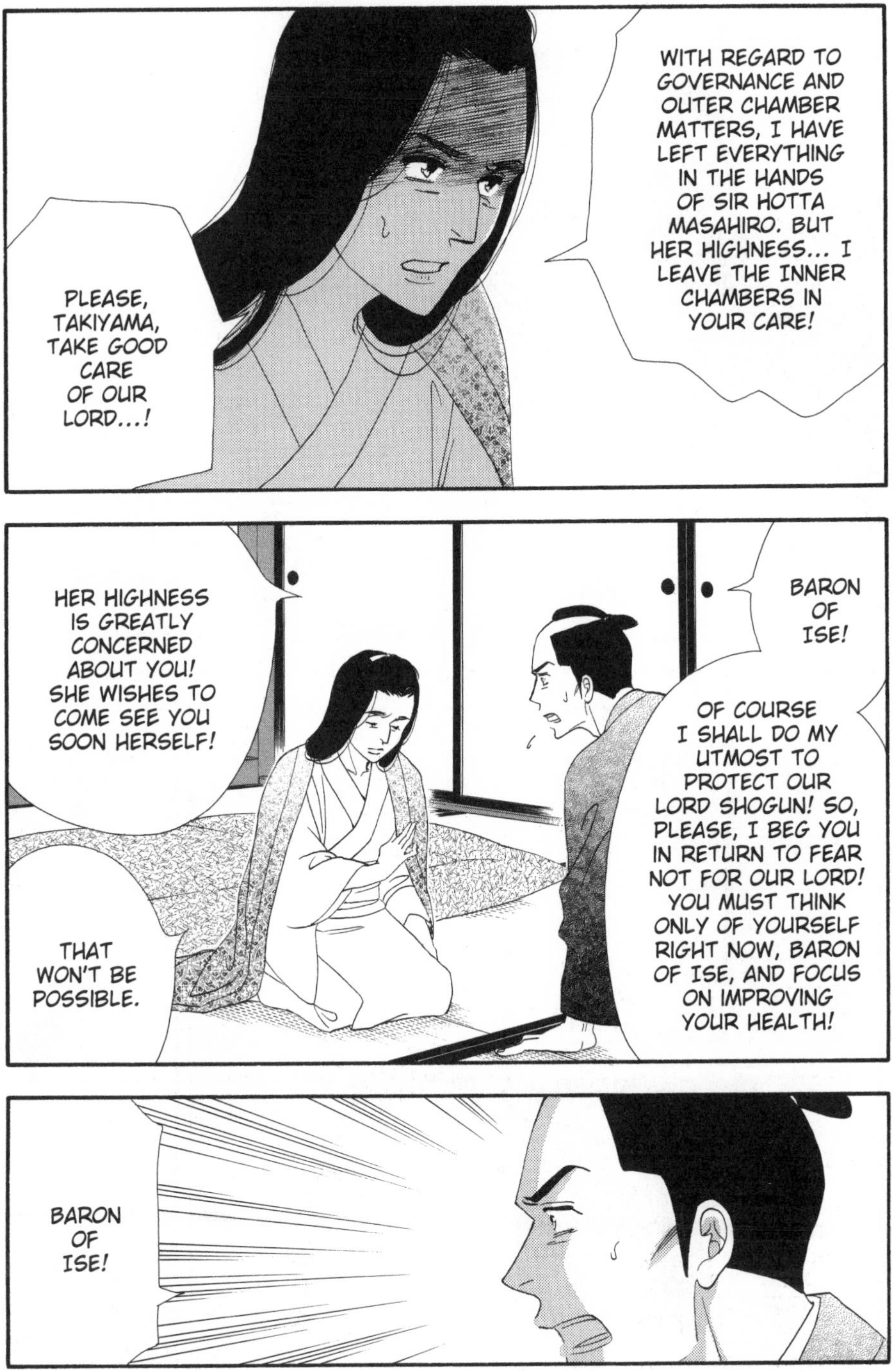
WITH REGARD TO GOVERNANCE AND OUTER CHAMBER MATTERS, I HAVE LEFT EVERYTHING IN THE HANDS OF SIR HOTTA MASAHIRO. BUT HER HIGHNESS... I LEAVE THE INNER CHAMBERS IN YOUR CARE!
PLEASE, TAKIYAMA, TAKE GOOD CARE OF OUR LORD...!
BARON OF ISE!
OF COURSE I SHALL DO MY UTMOST TO PROTECT OUR LORD SHOGUN! SO, PLEASE, I BEG YOU IN RETURN TO FEAR NOT FOR OUR LORD! YOU MUST THINK ONLY OF YOURSELF RIGHT NOW, BARON OF ISE, AND FOCUS ON IMPROVING YOUR HEALTH!
HER HIGHNESS IS GREATLY CONCERNED ABOUT YOU! SHE WISHES TO COME SEE YOU SOON HERSELF!
THAT WON'T BE POSSIBLE.
BARON OF ISE!

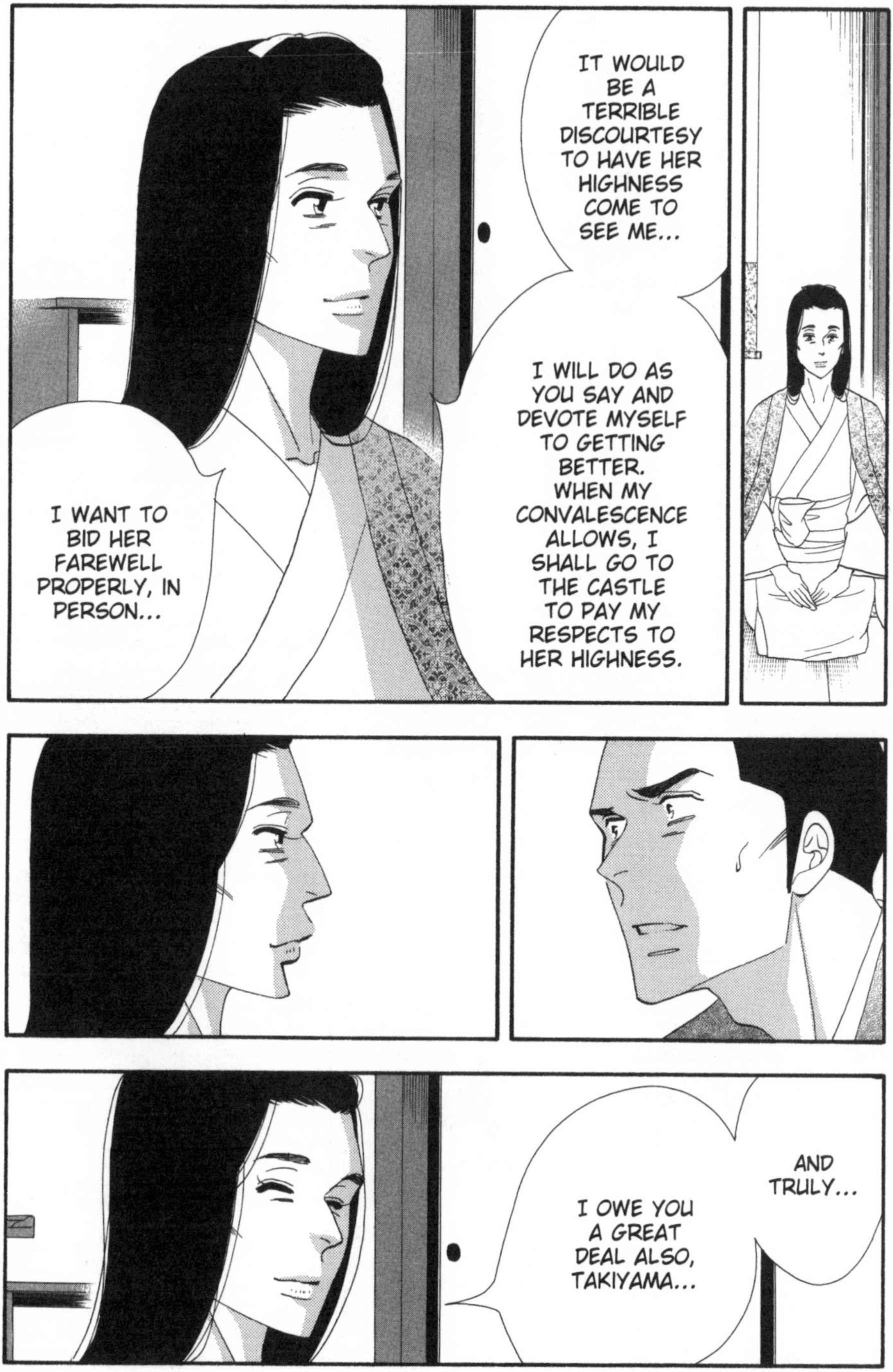
IT WOULD BE A TERRIBLE DISCOURTESY TO HAVE HER HIGHNESS COME TO SEE ME...
I WILL DO AS YOU SAY AND DEVOTE MYSELF TO GETTING BETTER. WHEN MY CONVALESCENCE ALLOWS, I SHALL GO TO THE CASTLE TO PAY MY RESPECTS TO HER HIGHNESS.
I WANT TO BID HER FAREWELL PROPERLY, IN PERSON...
AND TRULY...
I OWE YOU A GREAT DEAL ALSO, TAKIYAMA...

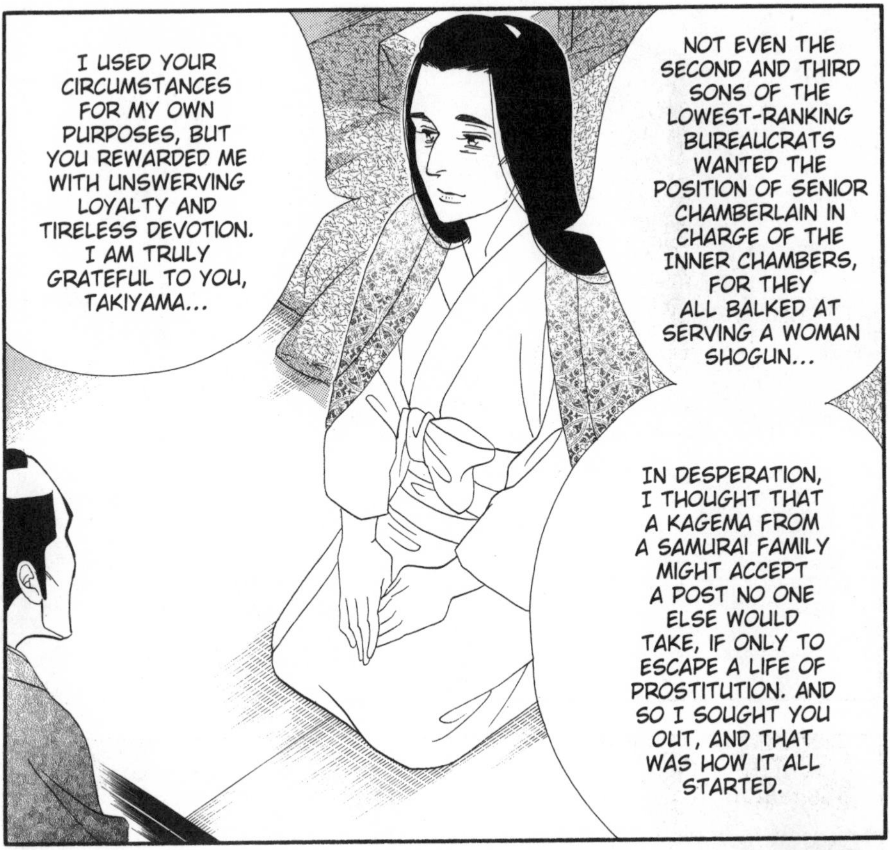
NOT EVEN THE SECOND AND THIRD SONS OF THE LOWEST-RANKING BUREAUCRATS WANTED THE POSITION OF SENIOR CHAMBERLAIN IN CHARGE OF THE INNER CHAMBERS, FOR THEY ALL BALKED AT SERVING A WOMAN SHOGUN...
IN DESPERATION, I THOUGHT THAT A KAGEMA FROM A SAMURAI FAMILY MIGHT ACCEPT A POST NO ONE ELSE WOULD TAKE, IF ONLY TO ESCAPE A LIFE OF PROSTITUTION. AND SO I SOUGHT YOU OUT, AND THAT WAS HOW IT ALL STARTED.
I USED YOUR CIRCUMSTANCES FOR MY OWN PURPOSES, BUT YOU REWARDED ME WITH UNSWERVING LOYALTY AND TIRELESS DEVOTION. I AM TRULY GRATEFUL TO YOU, TAKIYAMA...
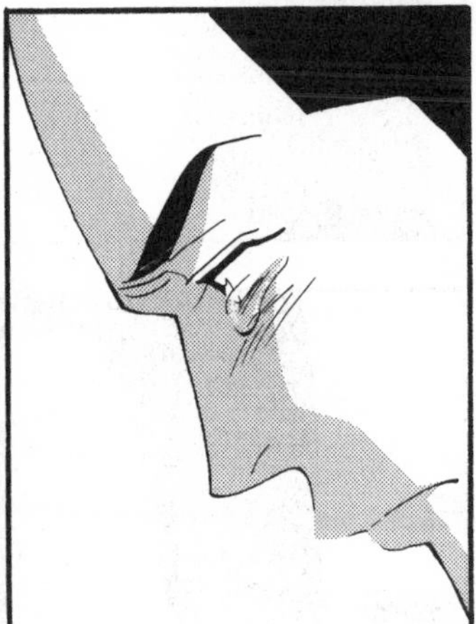
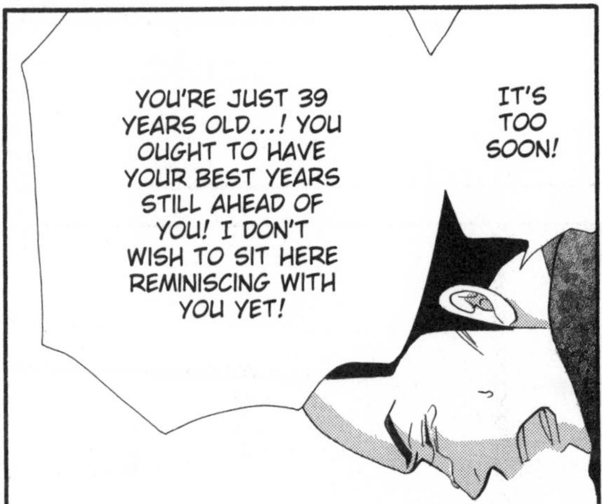
IT'S TOO SOON!
YOU'RE JUST 39 YEARS OLD...! YOU OUGHT TO HAVE YOUR BEST YEARS STILL AHEAD OF YOU! I DON'T WISH TO SIT HERE REMINISCING WITH YOU YET!

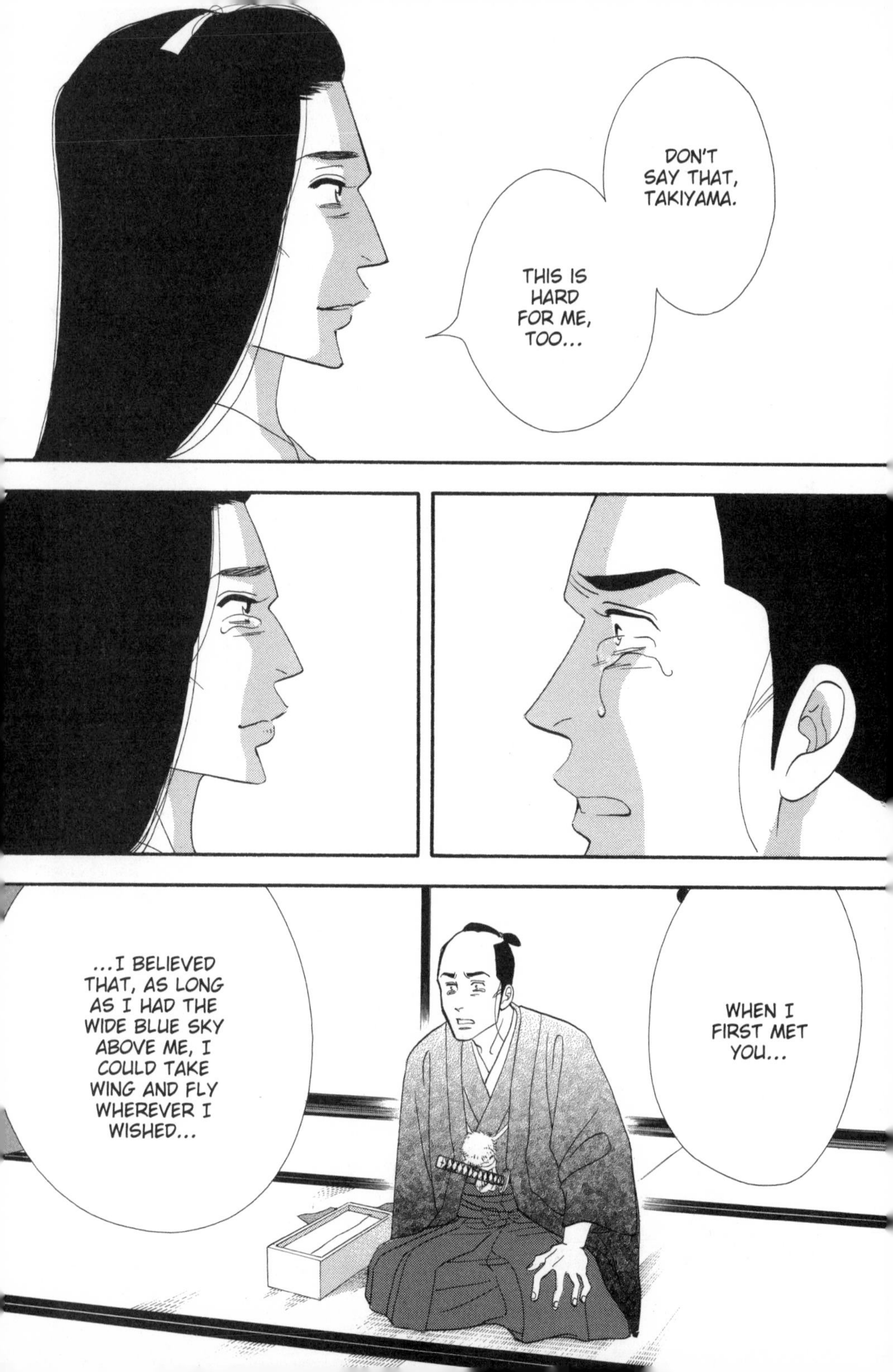
DON'T SAY THAT, TAKIYAMA.
THIS IS HARD FOR ME, TOO...
WHEN I FIRST MET YOU...
...I BELIEVED THAT, AS LONG AS I HAD THE WIDE BLUE SKY ABOVE ME, I COULD TAKE WING AND FLY WHEREVER I WISHED...

IT NEVER OCCURRED TO ME THAT MY WINGS MIGHT BECOME BROKEN AND THAT THE DAY WOULD COME WHEN I COULD FLY NO MORE...

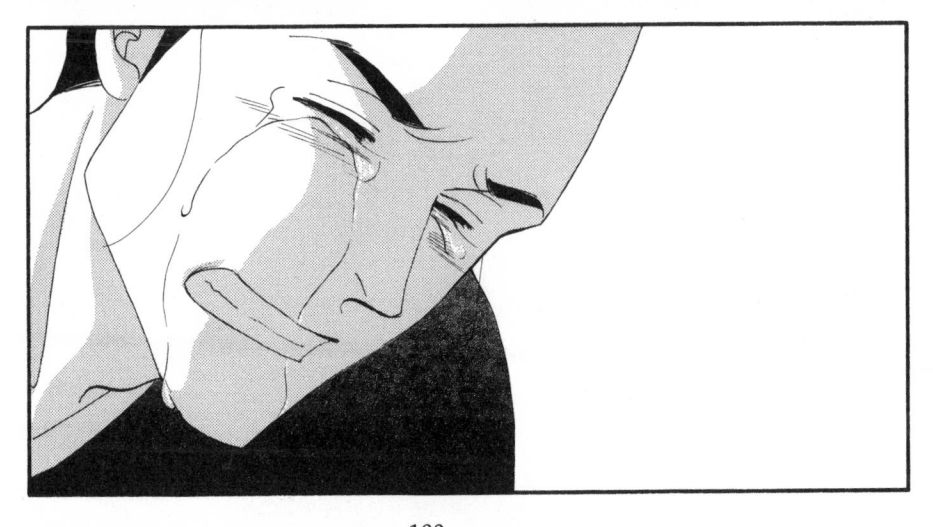

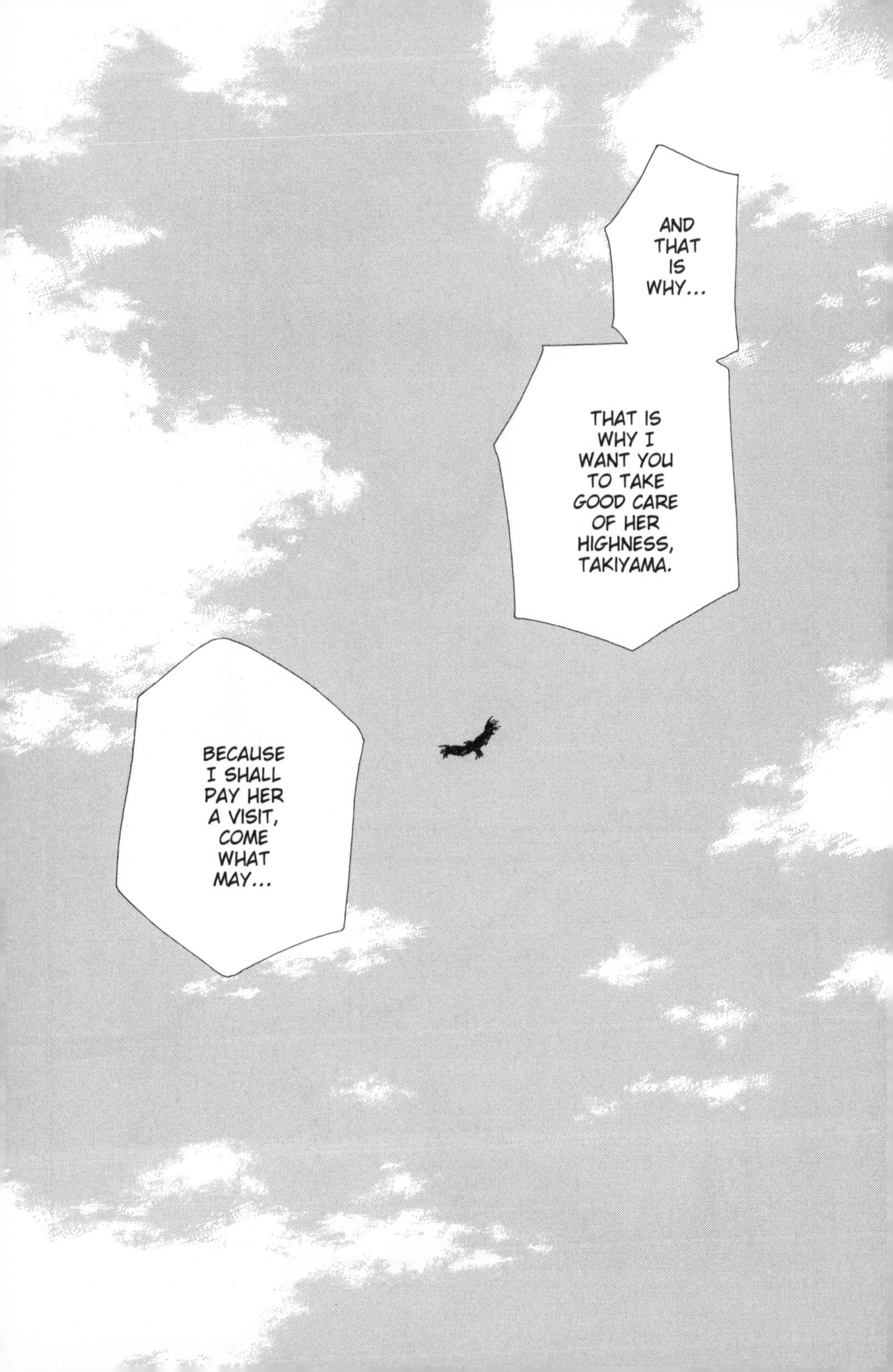
AND THAT IS WHY...
THAT IS WHY I WANT YOU TO TAKE GOOD CARE OF HER HIGHNESS, TAKIYAMA.
BECAUSE I SHALL PAY HER A VISIT, COME WHAT MAY...

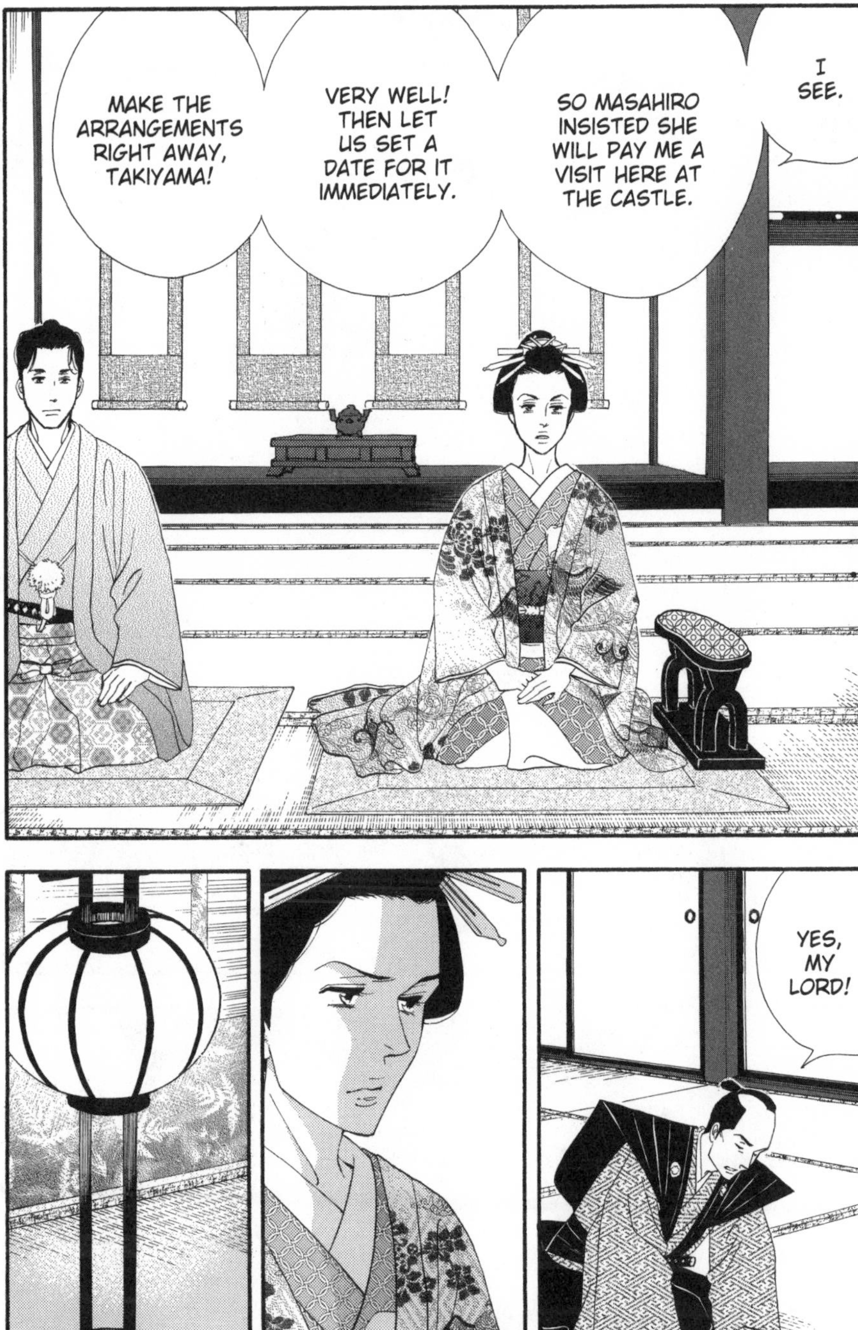
I SEE.
SO MASAHIRO INSISTED SHE WILL PAY ME A VISIT HERE AT THE CASTLE.
VERY WELL! THEN LET US SET A DATE FOR IT IMMEDIATELY.
MAKE THE ARRANGEMENTS RIGHT AWAY, TAKIYAMA!
YES, MY LORD!

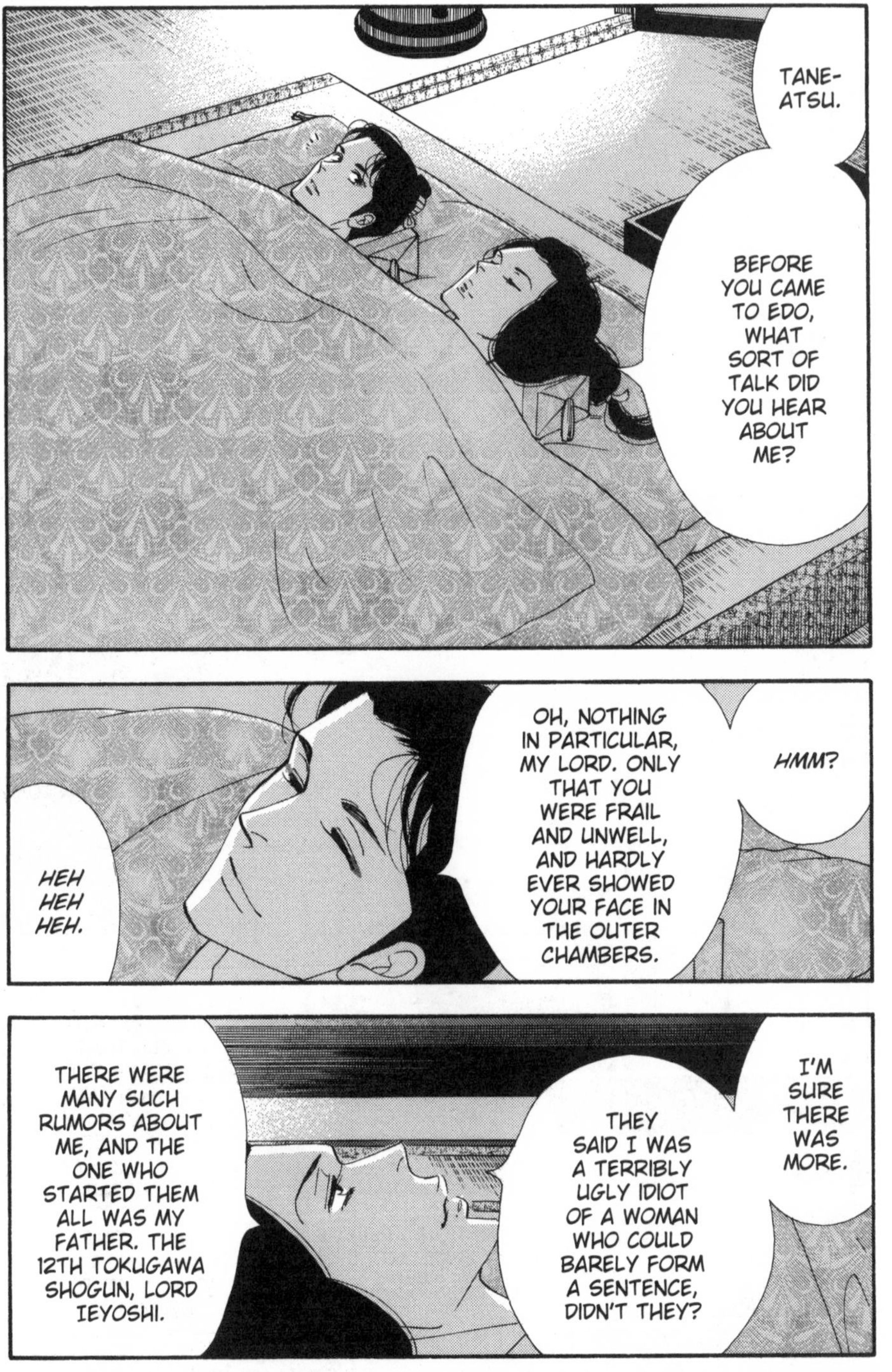
TANE-ATSU.
BEFORE YOU CAME TO EDO, WHAT SORT OF TALK DID YOU HEAR ABOUT ME?
HMM?
OH, NOTHING IN PARTICULAR, MY LORD. ONLY THAT YOU WERE FRAIL AND UNWELL, AND HARDLY EVER SHOWED YOUR FACE IN THE OUTER CHAMBERS.
HEH HEH HEH.
I'M SURE THERE WAS MORE.
THEY SAID I WAS A TERRIBLY UGLY IDIOT OF A WOMAN WHO COULD BARELY FORM A SENTENCE, DIDN'T THEY?
THERE WERE MANY SUCH RUMORS ABOUT ME, AND THE ONE WHO STARTED THEM ALL WAS MY FATHER. THE 12TH TOKUGAWA SHOGUN, LORD IEYOSHI.

FOR MANY YEARS I WAS MY FATHER'S PLAYTHING, AND HE WANTED TO KEEP IT THAT WAY. HE KEPT SPREADING THOSE MALICIOUS RUMORS ABOUT ME TO RUIN MY CHANCES OF FINDING A SPOUSE.
EVEN SO, A CONSORT WAS FOUND FOR ME... TWICE. BOTH OF THEM WERE GIVEN POISON BY MY FATHER AND DIED. I MYSELF WAS POISONED BY HIM, AND BY MY MOTHER AS WELL...
WHEN, IN SPITE OF ALL THAT, I BECAME THE SHOGUN AND WAS GIVEN MY OWN INNER CHAMBERS, MY FATHER FINALLY STOPPED MOLESTING ME. AND I OWE THAT TO MASAHIRO.
IF MASAHIRO HAD NOT BEEN THERE TO SAVE ME, I WOULD HAVE REMAINED IN THAT HELL UNTIL MY FATHER'S DEATH.

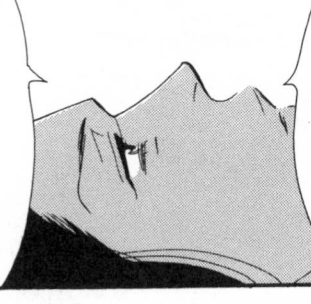

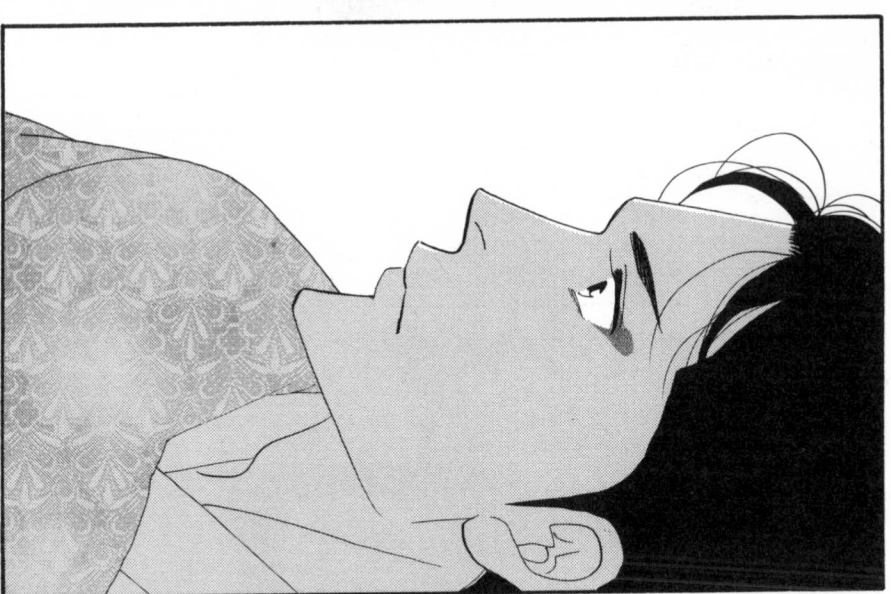

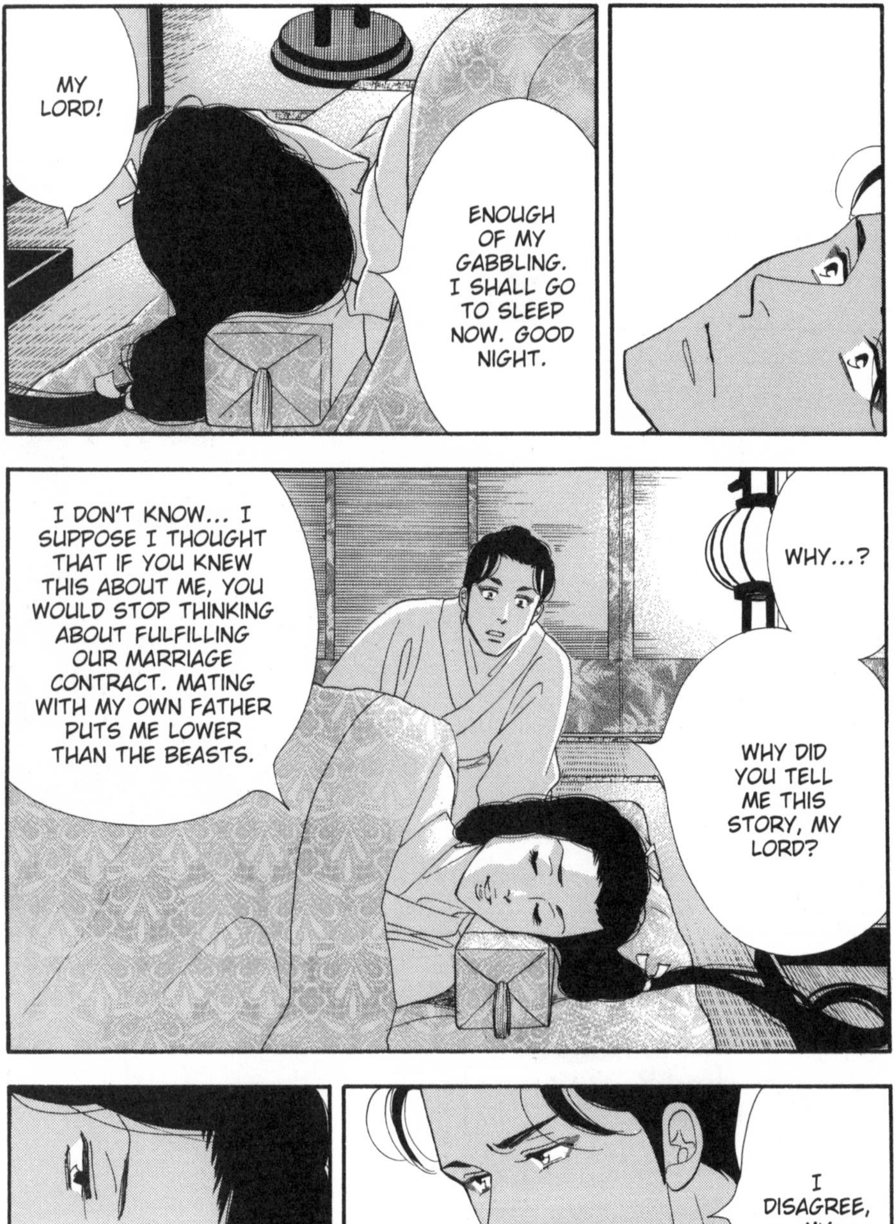
ENOUGH OF MY GABBLING. I SHALL GO TO SLEEP NOW. GOOD NIGHT.
MY LORD!
WHY...?
WHY DID YOU TELL ME THIS STORY, MY LORD?
I DON'T KNOW... I SUPPOSE I THOUGHT THAT IF YOU KNEW THIS ABOUT ME, YOU WOULD STOP THINKING ABOUT FULFILLING OUR MARRIAGE CONTRACT. MATING WITH MY OWN FATHER PUTS ME LOWER THAN THE BEASTS.
I DISAGREE, MY LORD!

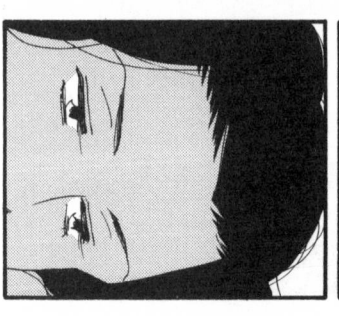

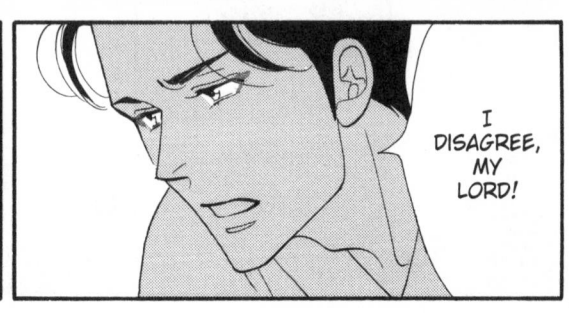

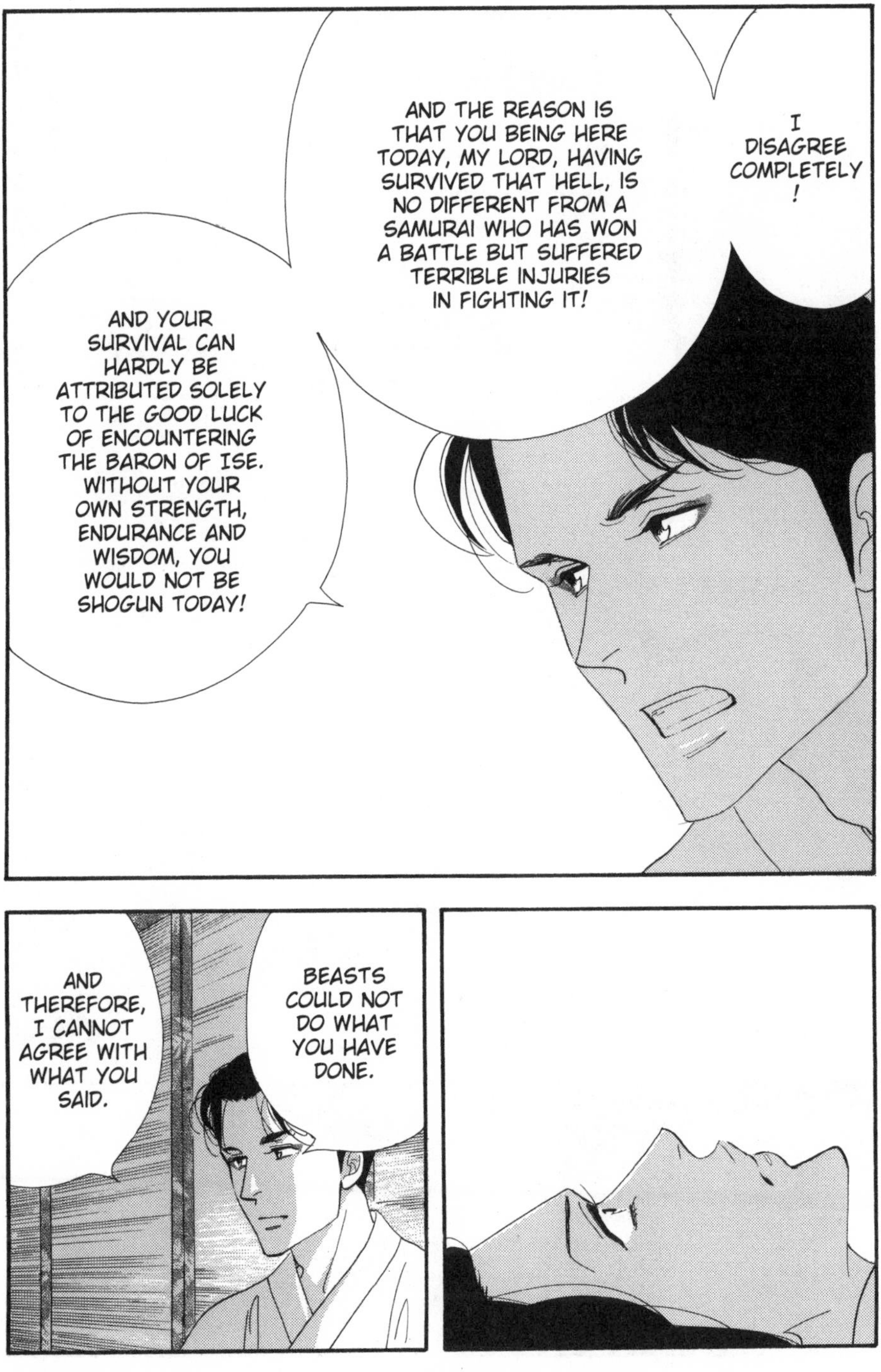
I DISAGREE COMPLETELY!
AND THE REASON IS THAT YOU BEING HERE TODAY, MY LORD, HAVING SURVIVED THAT HELL, IS NO DIFFERENT FROM A SAMURAI WHO HAS WON A BATTLE BUT SUFFERED TERRIBLE INJURIES IN FIGHTING IT!
AND YOUR SURVIVAL CAN HARDLY BE ATTRIBUTED SOLELY TO THE GOOD LUCK OF ENCOUNTERING THE BARON OF ISE. WITHOUT YOUR OWN STRENGTH, ENDURANCE AND WISDOM, YOU WOULD NOT BE SHOGUN TODAY!
BEASTS COULD NOT DO WHAT YOU HAVE DONE.
AND THEREFORE, I CANNOT AGREE WITH WHAT YOU SAID.

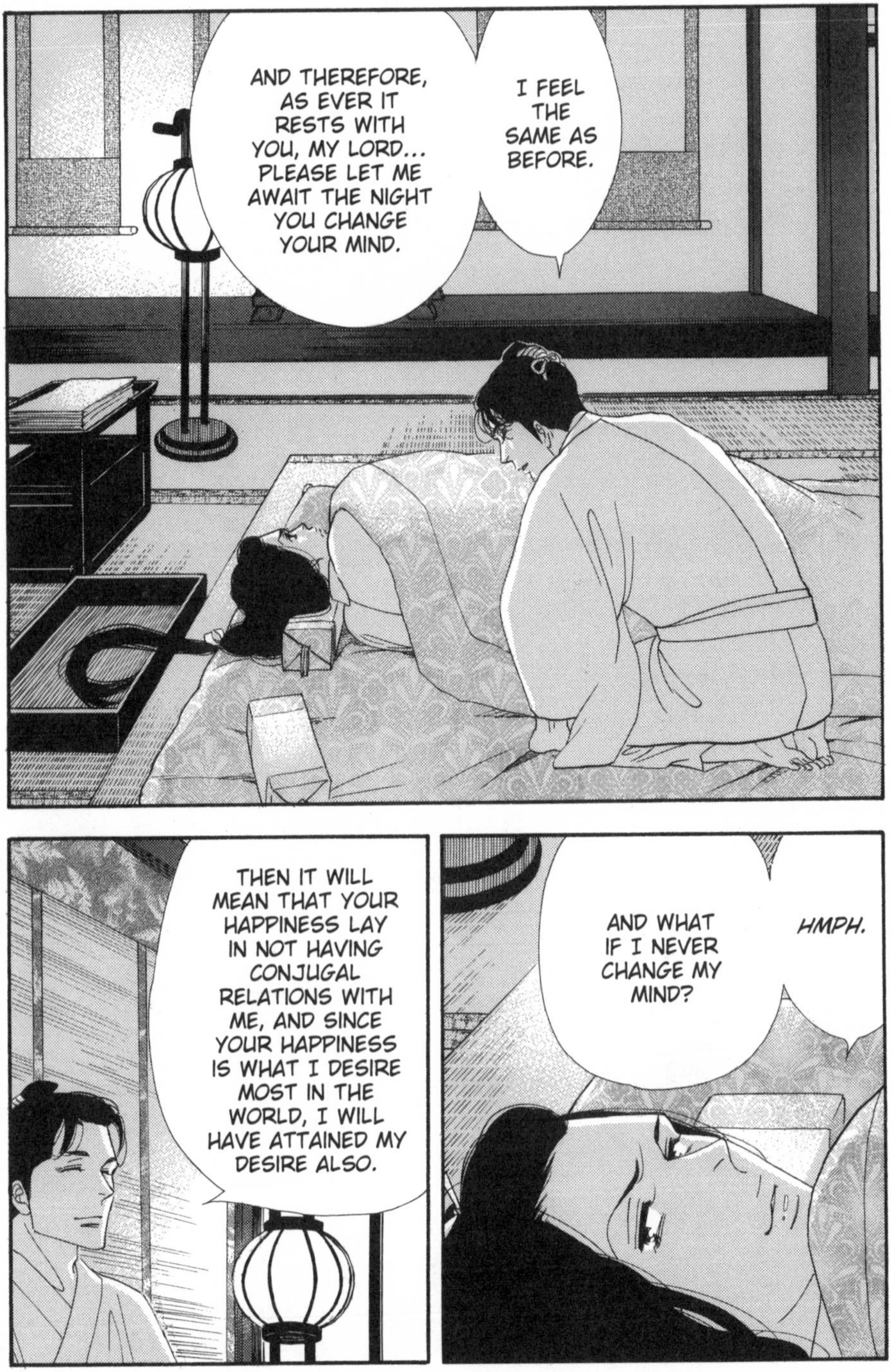
I FEEL THE SAME AS BEFORE.
AND THEREFORE, AS EVER IT RESTS WITH YOU, MY LORD... PLEASE LET ME AWAIT THE NIGHT YOU CHANGE YOUR MIND.
HMPH.
AND WHAT IF I NEVER CHANGE MY MIND?
THEN IT WILL MEAN THAT YOUR HAPPINESS LAY IN NOT HAVING CONJUGAL RELATIONS WITH ME, AND SINCE YOUR HAPPINESS IS WHAT I DESIRE MOST IN THE WORLD, I WILL HAVE ATTAINED MY DESIRE ALSO.

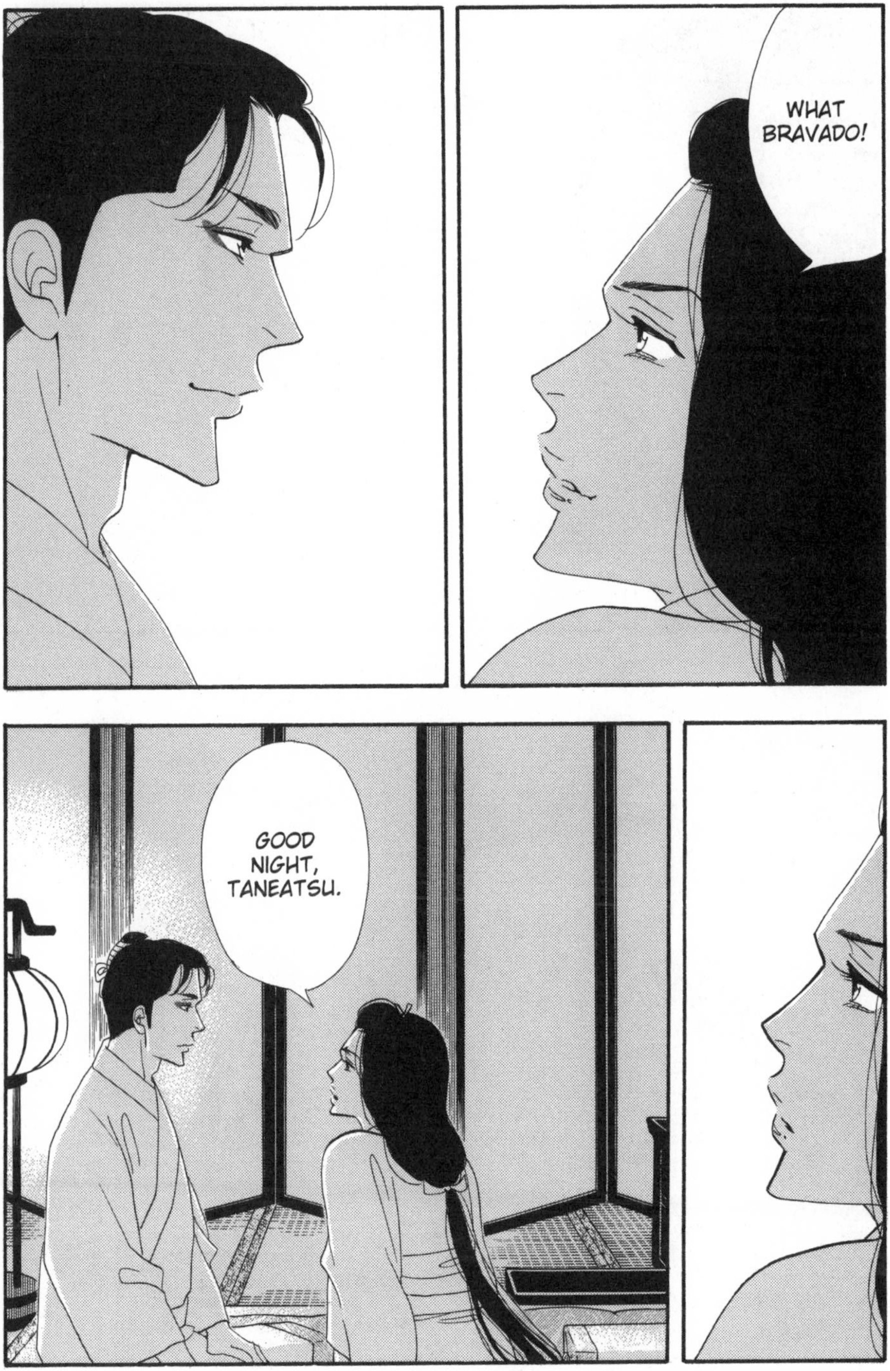
WHAT BRAVADO!
GOOD NIGHT, TANEATSU.

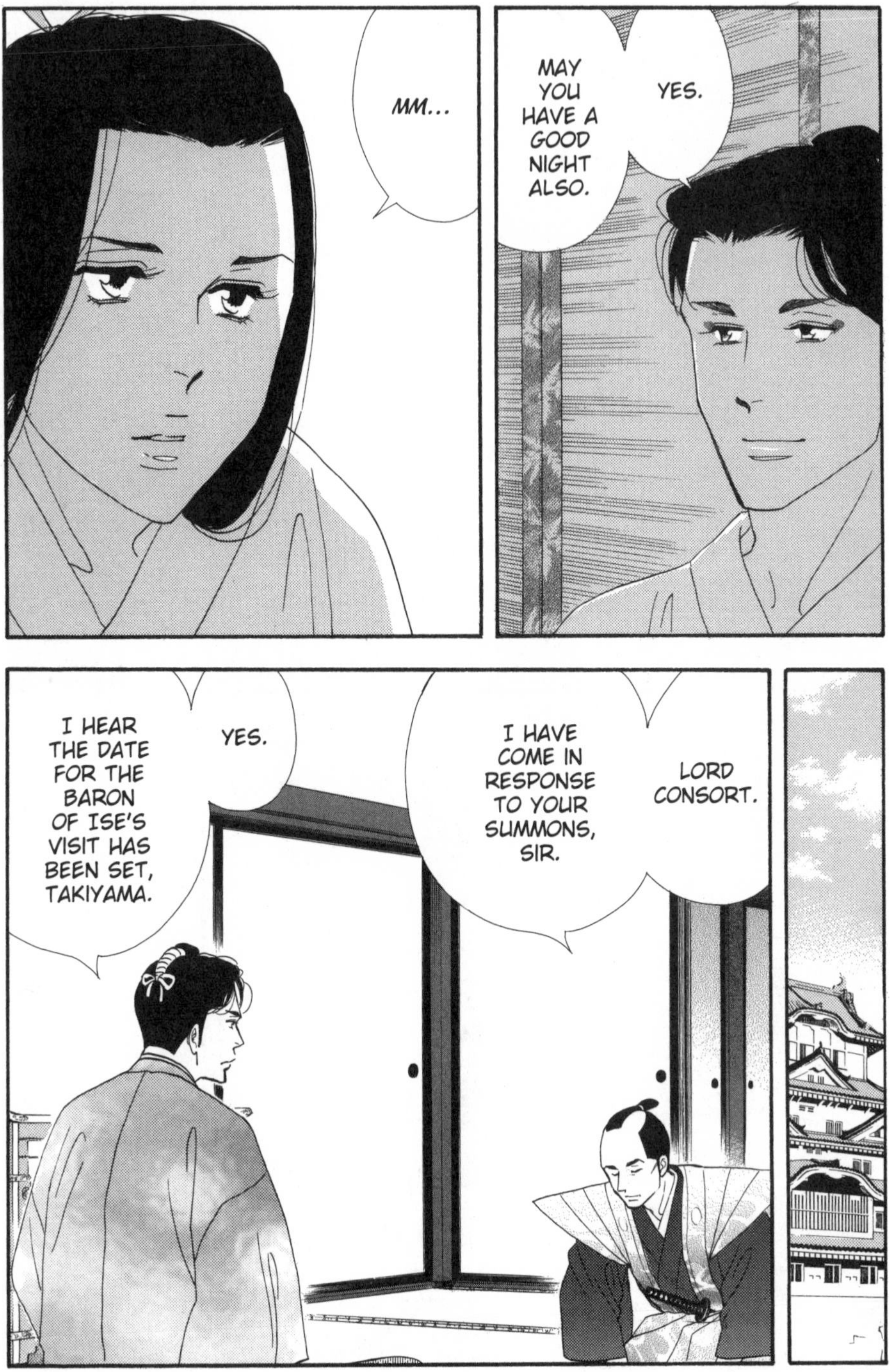
YES.
MAY YOU HAVE A GOOD NIGHT ALSO.
MM...
LORD CONSORT.
I HAVE COME IN RESPONSE TO YOUR SUMMONS, SIR.
YES.
I HEAR THE DATE FOR THE BARON OF ISE'S VISIT HAS BEEN SET, TAKIYAMA.

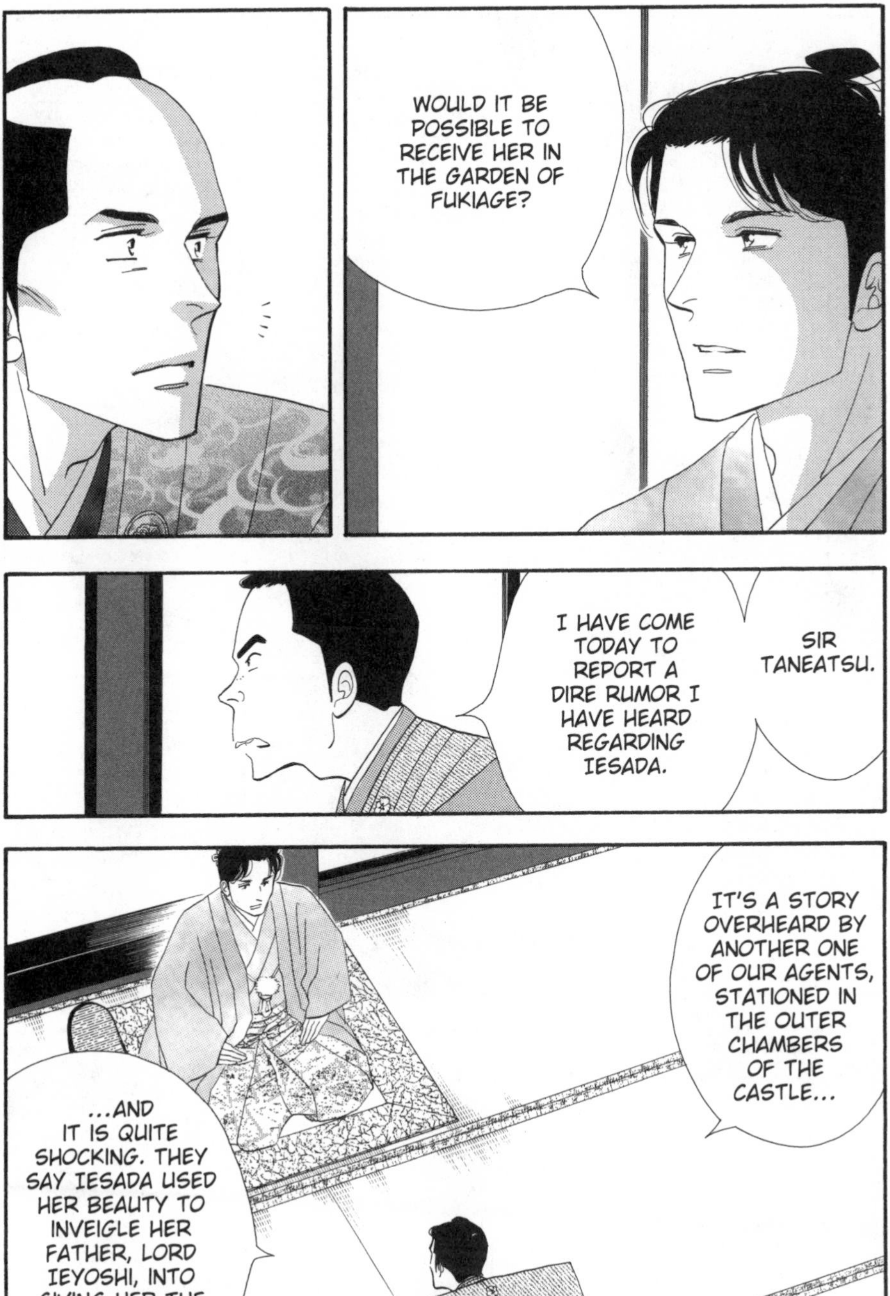
WOULD IT BE POSSIBLE TO RECEIVE HER IN THE GARDEN OF FUKIAGE?
SIR TANEATSU.
I HAVE COME TODAY TO REPORT A DIRE RUMOR I HAVE HEARD REGARDING IESADA.
IT'S A STORY OVERHEARD BY ANOTHER ONE OF OUR AGENTS, STATIONED IN THE OUTER CHAMBERS OF THE CASTLE...
...AND IT IS QUITE SHOCKING. THEY SAY IESADA USED HER BEAUTY TO INVEIGLE HER FATHER, LORD IEYOSHI, INTO GIVING HER THE SHOGUN'S SEAT.

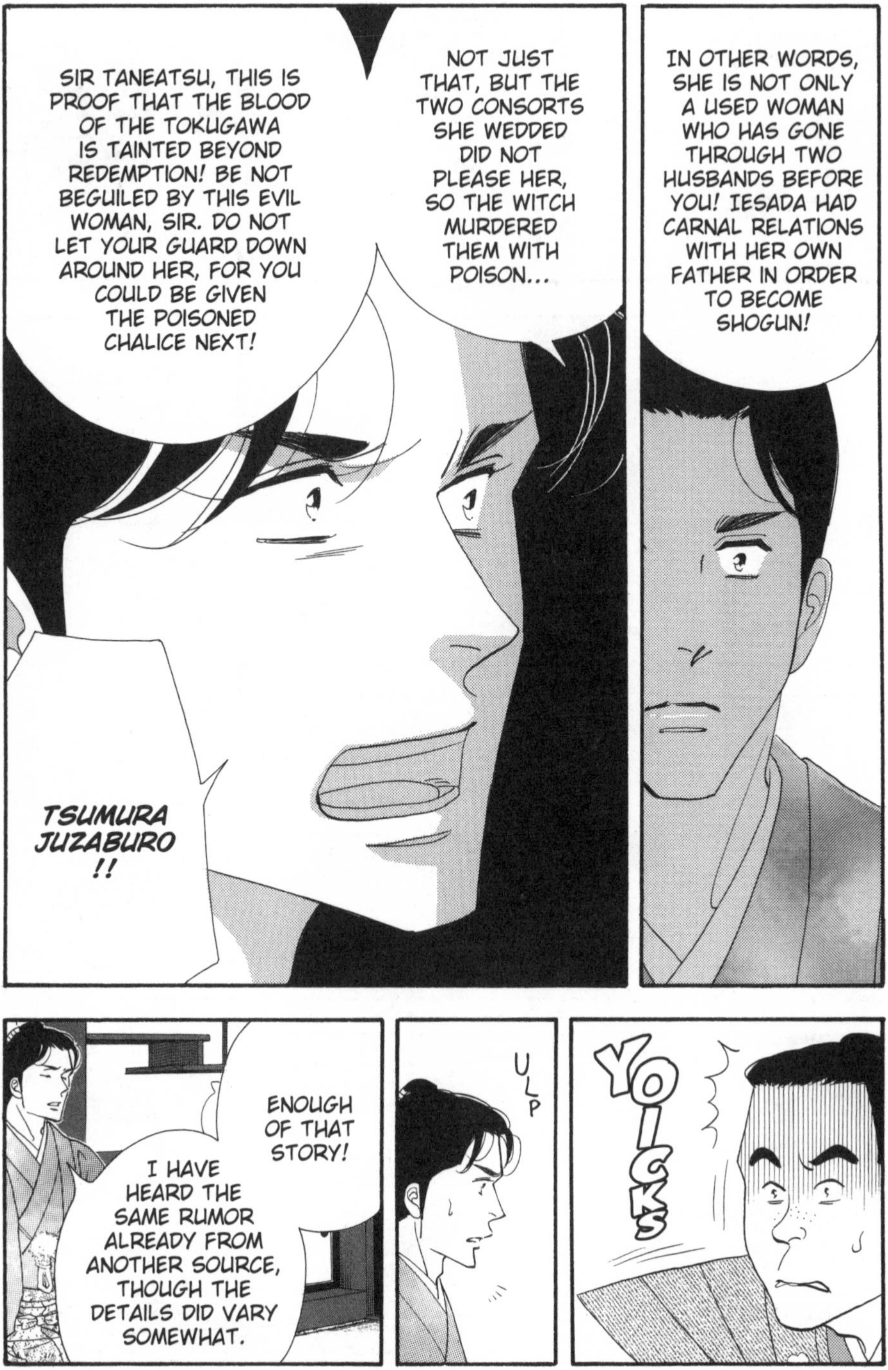
IN OTHER WORDS, SHE IS NOT ONLY A USED WOMAN WHO HAS GONE THROUGH TWO HUSBANDS BEFORE YOU! IESADA HAD CARNAL RELATIONS WITH HER OWN FATHER IN ORDER TO BECOME SHOGUN!
NOT JUST THAT, BUT THE TWO CONSORTS SHE WEDDED DID NOT PLEASE HER, SO THE WITCH MURDERED THEM WITH POISON...
SIR TANEATSU, THIS IS PROOF THAT THE BLOOD OF THE TOKUGAWA IS TAINTED BEYOND REDEMPTION! BE NOT BEGUILED BY THIS EVIL WOMAN, SIR. DO NOT LET YOUR GUARD DOWN AROUND HER, FOR YOU COULD BE GIVEN THE POISONED CHALICE NEXT!
TSUMURA JUZABURO !!
YOICKS
ULP
ENOUGH OF THAT STORY!
I HAVE HEARD THE SAME RUMOR ALREADY FROM ANOTHER SOURCE, THOUGH THE DETAILS DID VARY SOMEWHAT.

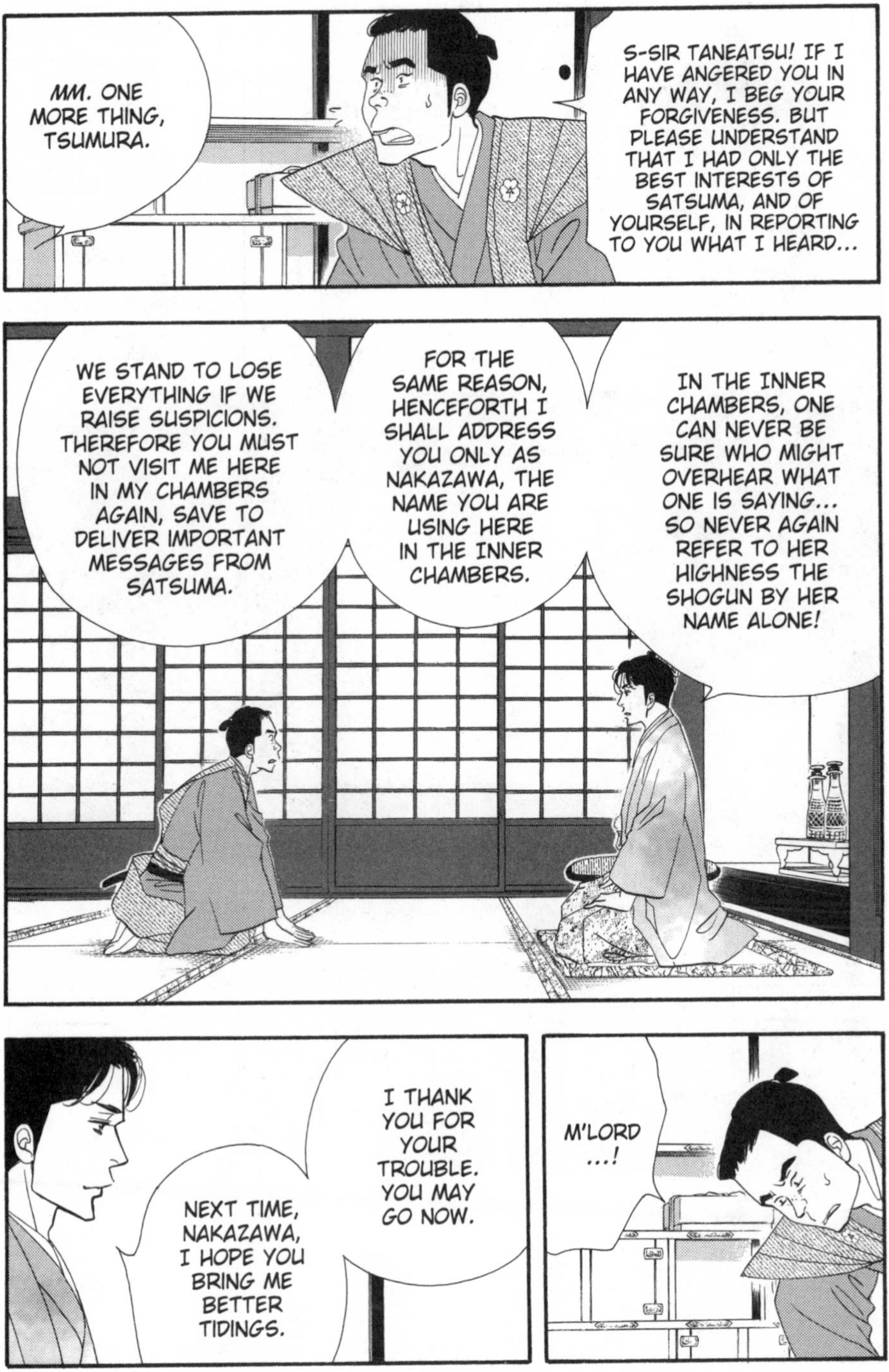
S-SIR TANEATSU! IF I HAVE ANGERED YOU IN ANY WAY, I BEG YOUR FORGIVENESS. BUT PLEASE UNDERSTAND THAT I HAD ONLY THE BEST INTERESTS OF SATSUMA, AND OF YOURSELF, IN REPORTING TO YOU WHAT I HEARD...
MM. ONE MORE THING, TSUMURA.
IN THE INNER CHAMBERS, ONE CAN NEVER BE SURE WHO MIGHT OVERHEAR WHAT ONE IS SAYING... SO NEVER AGAIN REFER TO HER HIGHNESS THE SHOGUN BY HER NAME ALONE!
FOR THE SAME REASON, HENCEFORTH I SHALL ADDRESS YOU ONLY AS NAKAZAWA, THE NAME YOU ARE USING HERE IN THE INNER CHAMBERS.
WE STAND TO LOSE EVERYTHING IF WE RAISE SUSPICIONS. THEREFORE YOU MUST NOT VISIT ME HERE IN MY CHAMBERS AGAIN, SAVE TO DELIVER IMPORTANT MESSAGES FROM SATSUMA.
M'LORD ...!
I THANK YOU FOR YOUR TROUBLE. YOU MAY GO NOW.
NEXT TIME, NAKAZAWA, I HOPE YOU BRING ME BETTER TIDINGS.

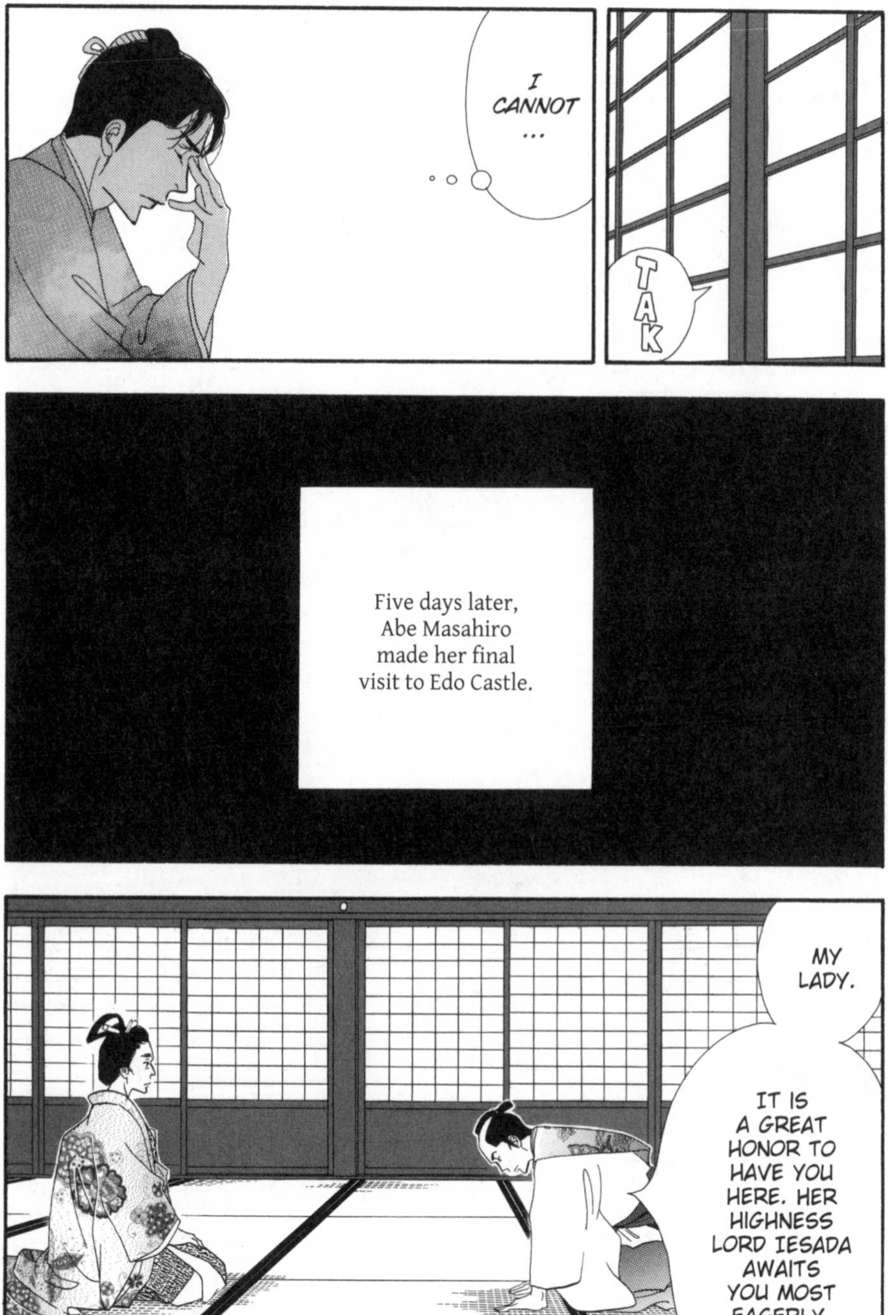
TAK
I CANNOT ...
Five days later, Abe Masahiro made her final visit to Edo Castle.
MY LADY.
IT IS A GREAT HONOR TO HAVE YOU HERE. HER HIGHNESS LORD IESADA AWAITS YOU MOST EAGERLY.

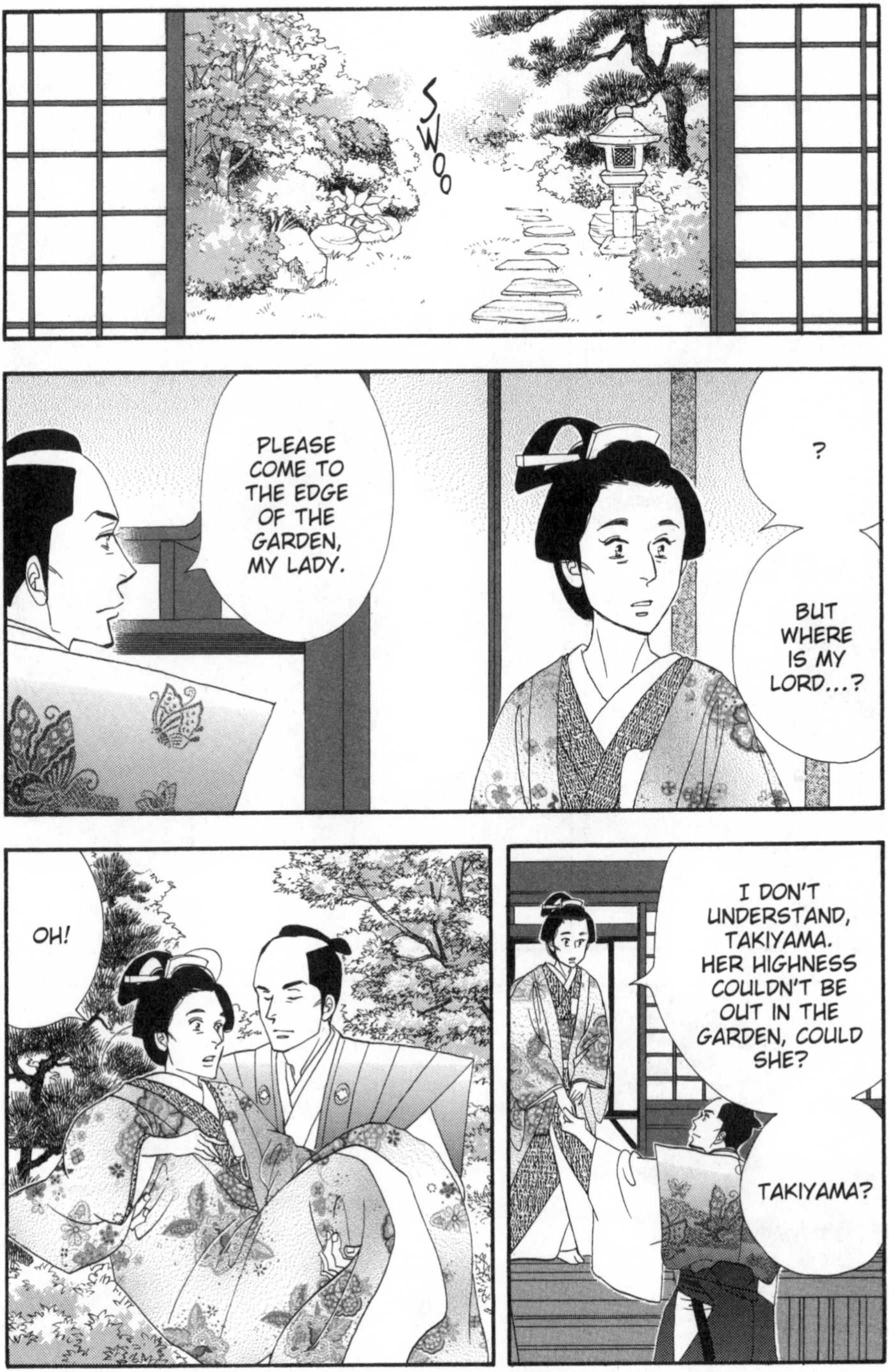
SWOO
?
BUT WHERE IS MY LORD...?
PLEASE COME TO THE EDGE OF THE GARDEN, MY LADY.
I DON'T UNDERSTAND, TAKIYAMA. HER HIGHNESS COULDN'T BE OUT IN THE GARDEN, COULD SHE?
TAKIYAMA?
OH!

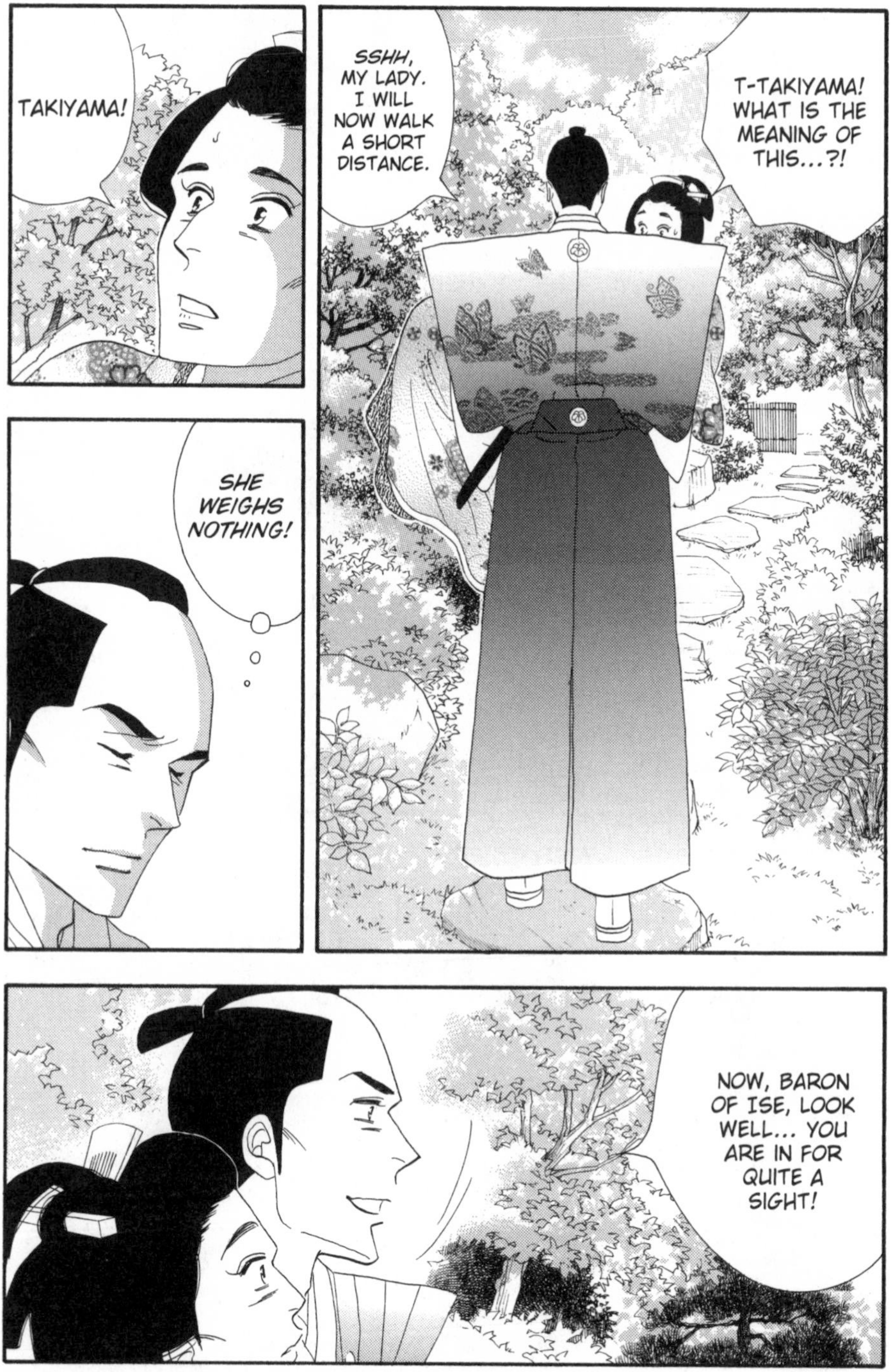
T-TAKIYAMA! WHAT IS THE MEANING OF THIS...?!
SSHH, MY LADY. I WILL NOW WALK A SHORT DISTANCE.
TAKIYAMA!
SHE WEIGHS NOTHING!
NOW, BARON OF ISE, LOOK WELL... YOU ARE IN FOR QUITE A SIGHT!

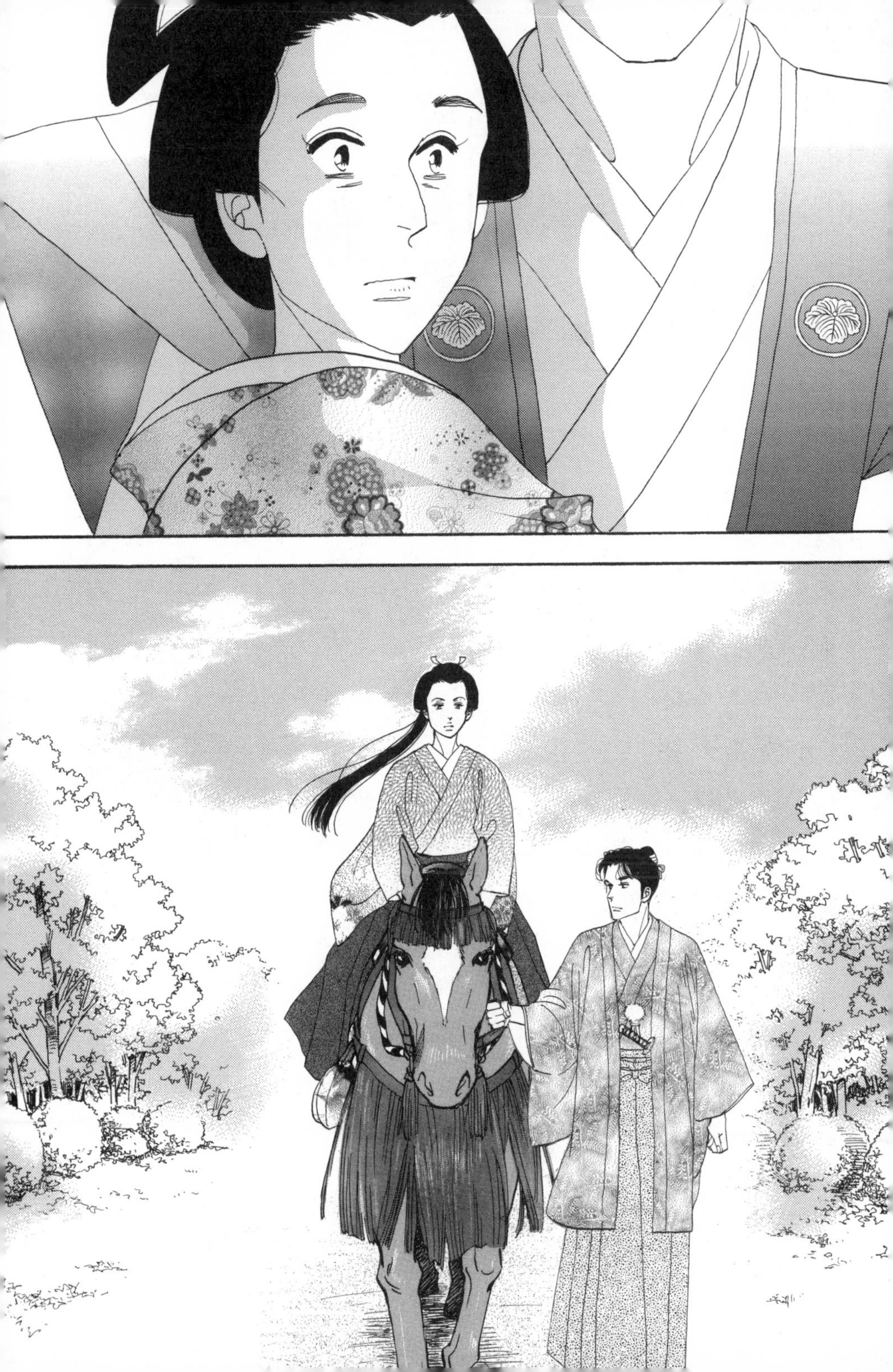

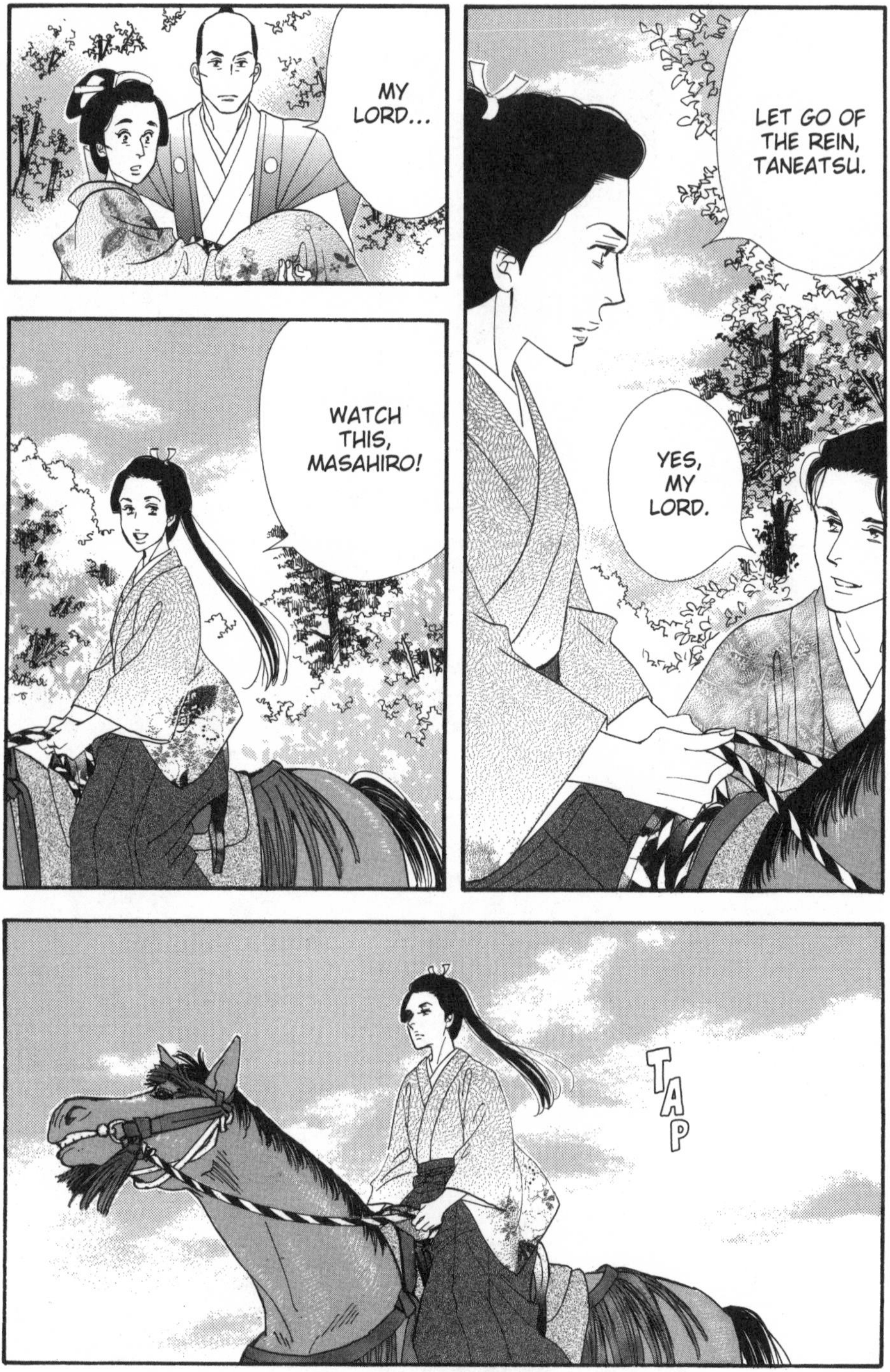

LET GO OF THE REIN, TANEATSU.
YES, MY LORD.
MY LORD...
WATCH THIS, MASAHIRO!
TAP

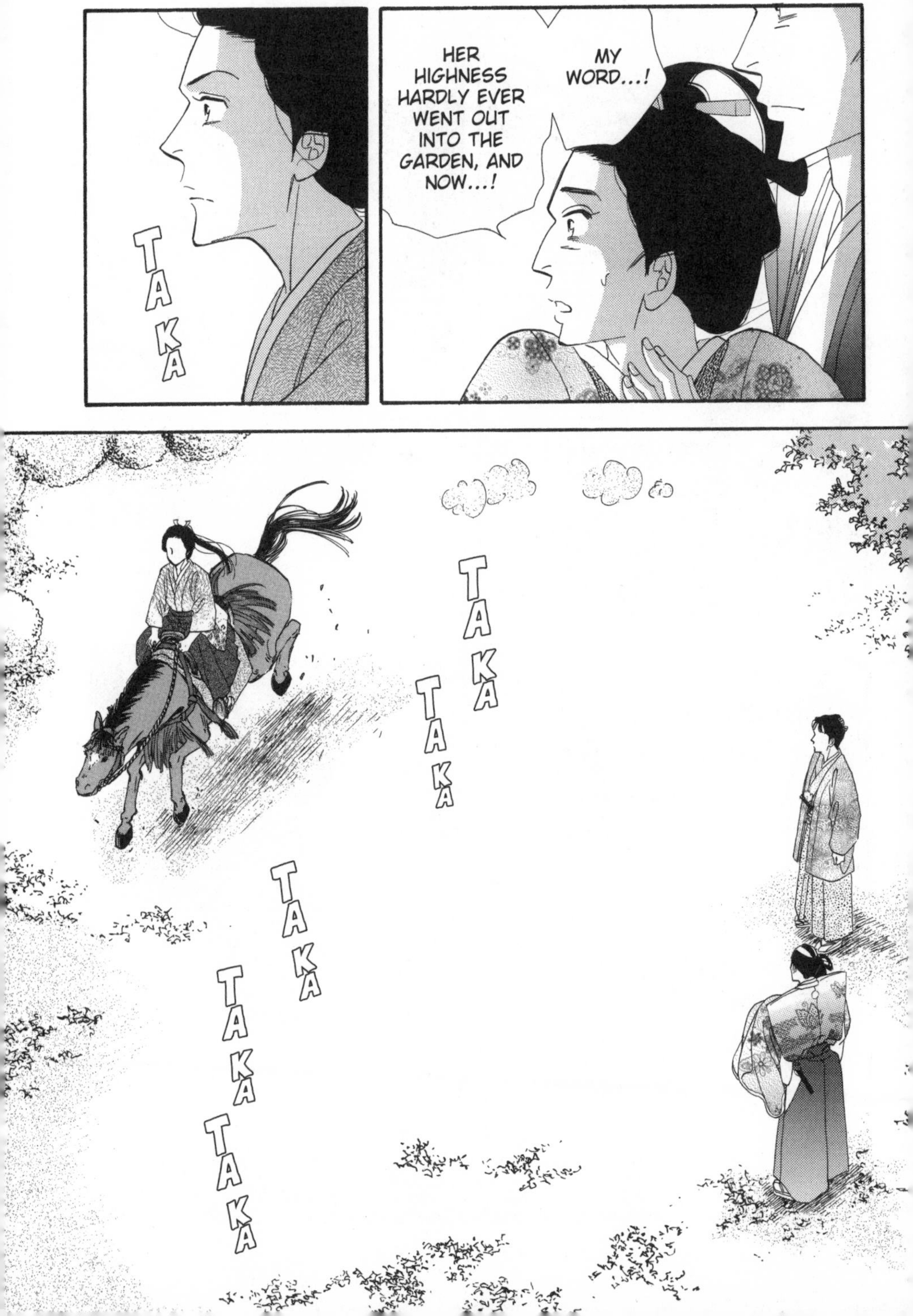
MY WORD...!
HER HIGHNESS HARDLY EVER WENT OUT INTO THE GARDEN, AND NOW...!
TAKA
TAKA
TAKA
TAKA
TAKA
TAKA

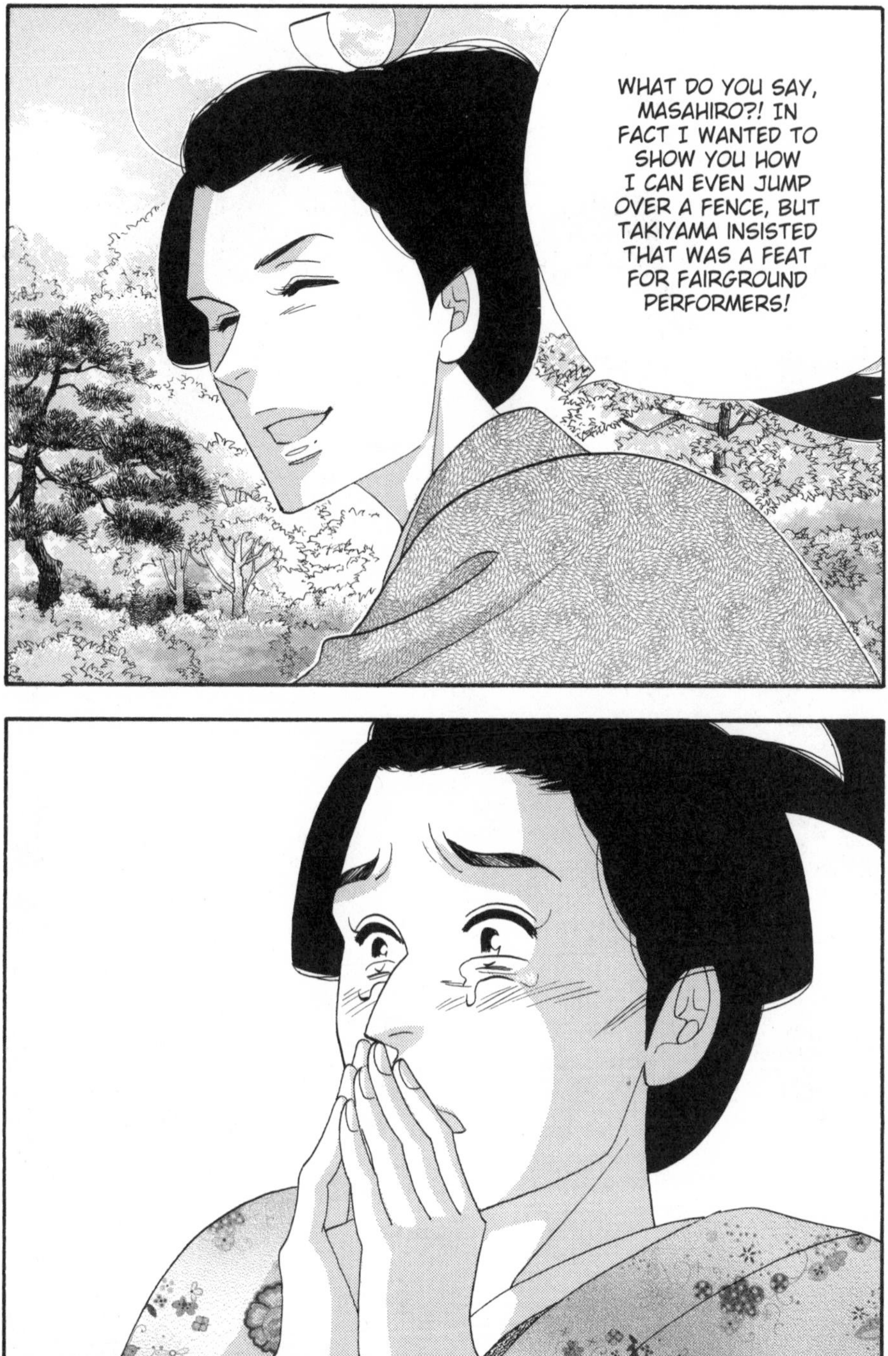
WHAT DO YOU SAY, MASAHIRO?! IN FACT I WANTED TO SHOW YOU HOW I CAN EVEN JUMP OVER A FENCE, BUT TAKIYAMA INSISTED THAT WAS A FEAT FOR FAIRGROUND PERFORMERS!

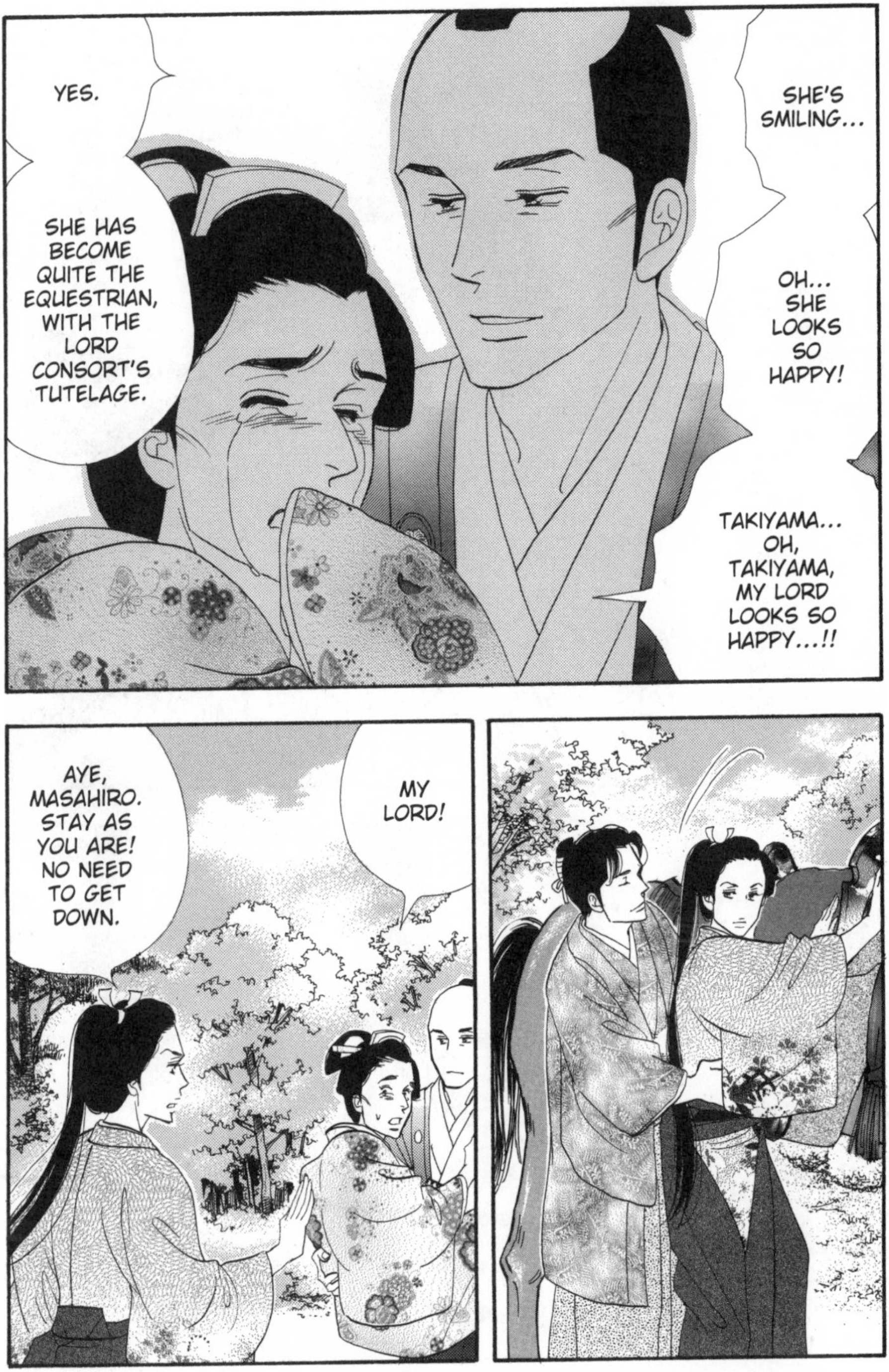
SHE'S SMILING...
OH... SHE LOOKS SO HAPPY!
TAKIYAMA... OH, TAKIYAMA, MY LORD LOOKS SO HAPPY...!!
YES.
SHE HAS BECOME QUITE THE EQUESTRIAN, WITH THE LORD CONSORT'S TUTELAGE.
MY LORD!
AYE, MASAHIRO. STAY AS YOU ARE! NO NEED TO GET DOWN.

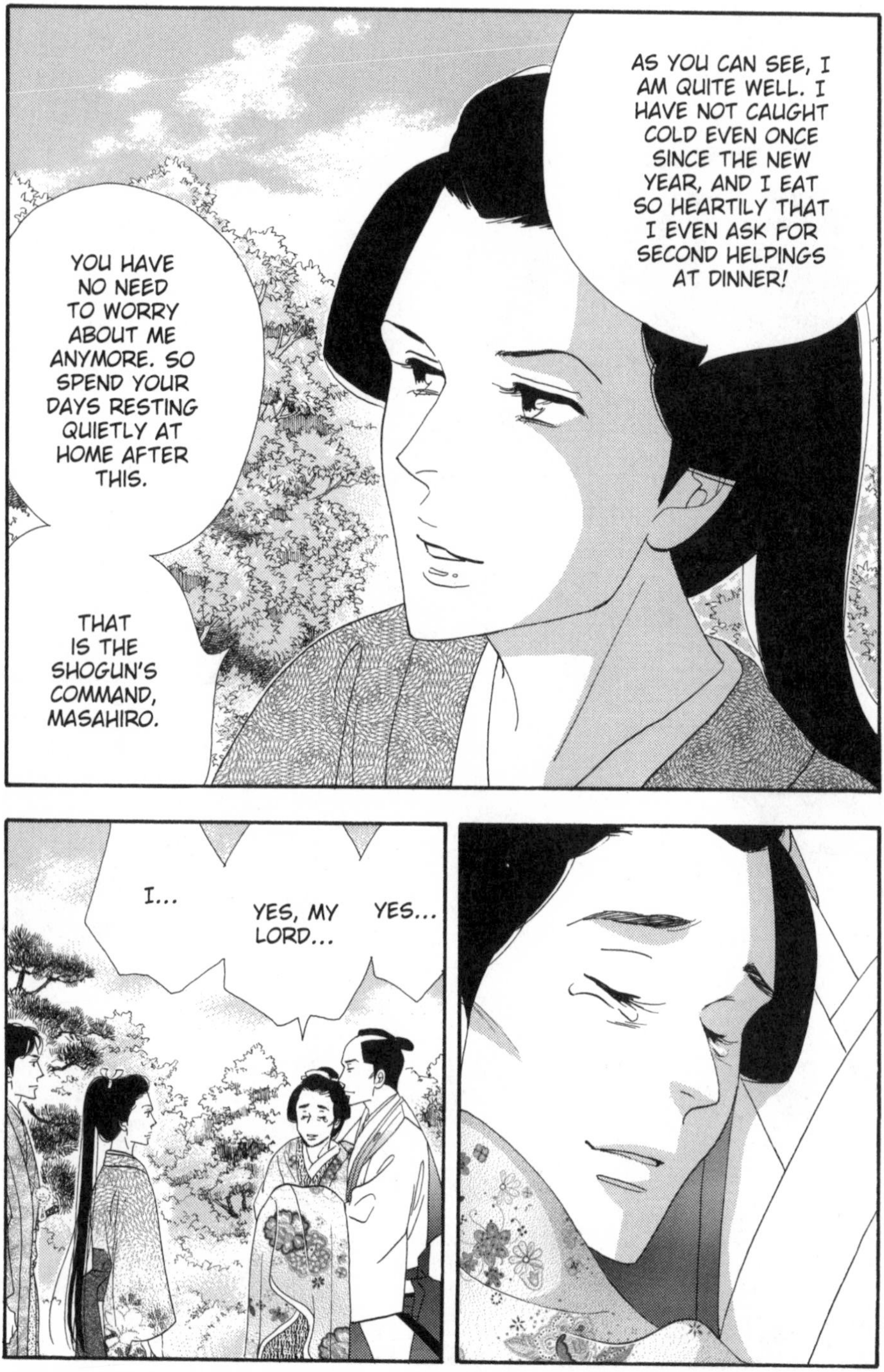
AS YOU CAN SEE, I AM QUITE WELL. I HAVE NOT CAUGHT COLD EVEN ONCE SINCE THE NEW YEAR, AND I EAT SO HEARTILY THAT I EVEN ASK FOR SECOND HELPINGS AT DINNER!
YOU HAVE NO NEED TO WORRY ABOUT ME ANYMORE. SO SPEND YOUR DAYS RESTING QUIETLY AT HOME AFTER THIS.
THAT IS THE SHOGUN'S COMMAND, MASAHIRO.
YES...
YES, MY LORD...
I...

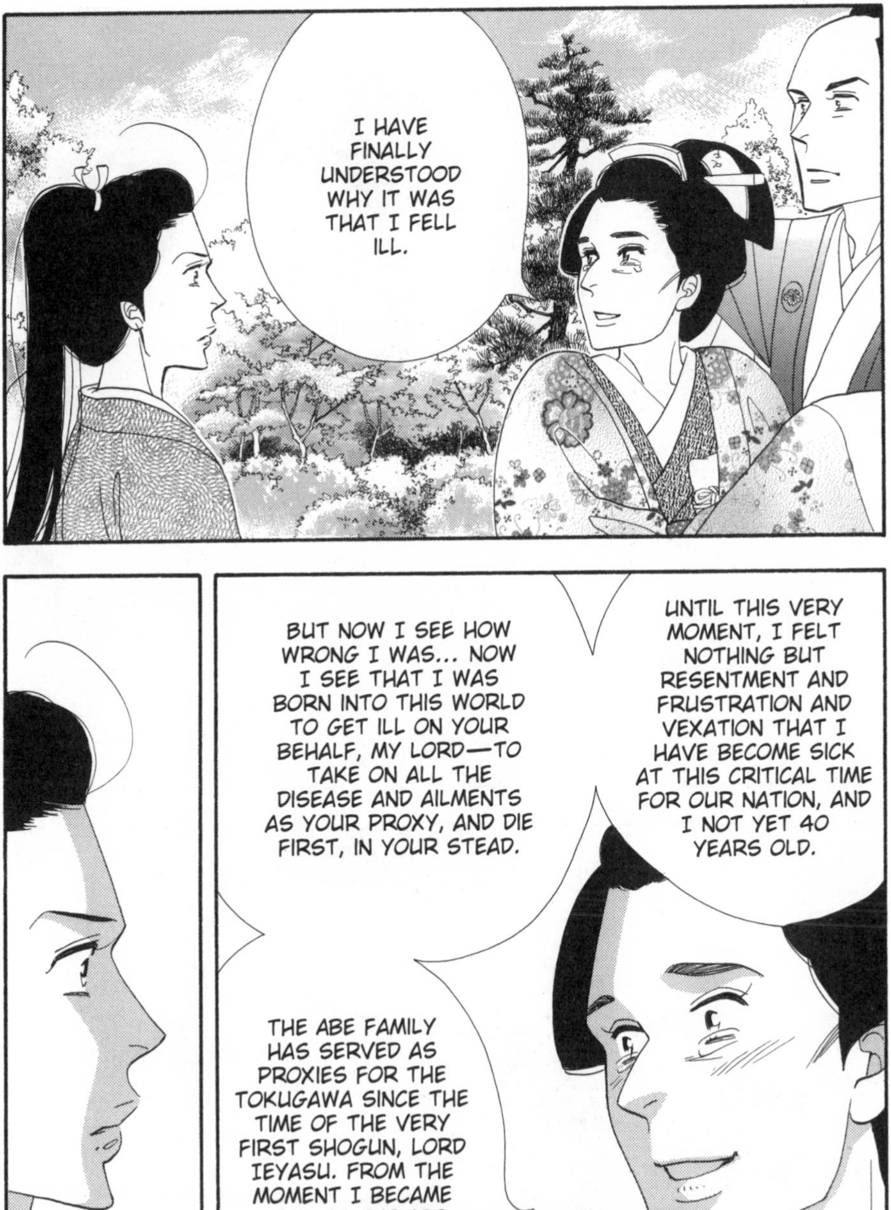
I HAVE FINALLY UNDERSTOOD WHY IT WAS THAT I FELL ILL.
UNTIL THIS VERY MOMENT, I FELT NOTHING BUT RESENTMENT AND FRUSTRATION AND VEXATION THAT I HAVE BECOME SICK AT THIS CRITICAL TIME FOR OUR NATION, AND I NOT YET 40 YEARS OLD.
BUT NOW I SEE HOW WRONG I WAS... NOW I SEE THAT I WAS BORN INTO THIS WORLD TO GET ILL ON YOUR BEHALF, MY LORD—TO TAKE ON ALL THE DISEASE AND AILMENTS AS YOUR PROXY, AND DIE FIRST, IN YOUR STEAD.
THE ABE FAMILY HAS SERVED AS PROXIES FOR THE TOKUGAWA SINCE THE TIME OF THE VERY FIRST SHOGUN, LORD IEYASU. FROM THE MOMENT I BECAME HEAD OF THE ABE FAMILY, I SHOULD HAVE KNOWN THAT THIS WAS MY ROLE...!

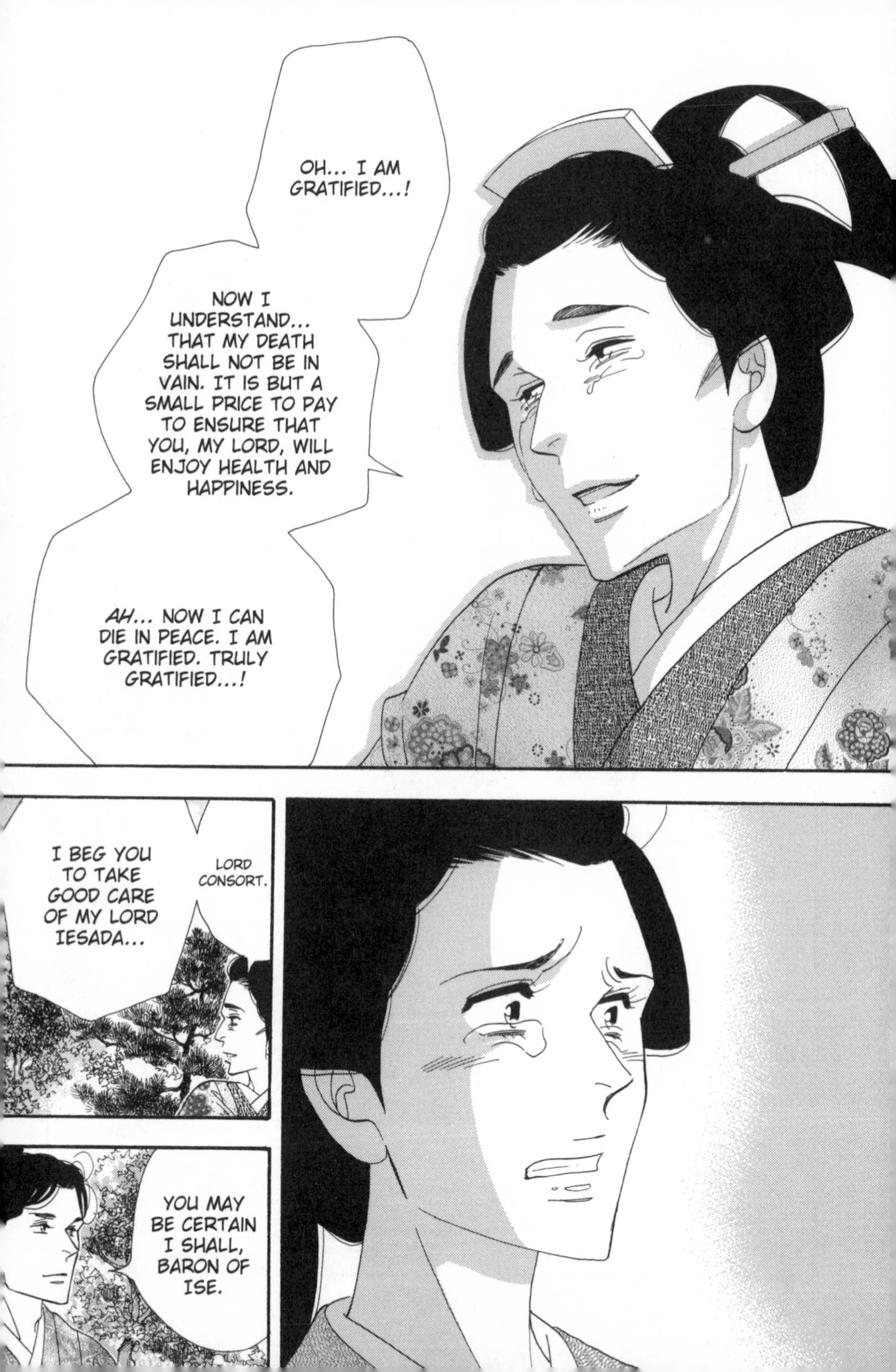
OH... I AM GRATIFIED...!
NOW I UNDERSTAND... THAT MY DEATH SHALL NOT BE IN VAIN. IT IS BUT A SMALL PRICE TO PAY TO ENSURE THAT YOU, MY LORD, WILL ENJOY HEALTH AND HAPPINESS.
AH... NOW I CAN DIE IN PEACE. I AM GRATIFIED. TRULY GRATIFIED...!
LORD CONSORT.
I BEG YOU TO TAKE GOOD CARE OF MY LORD IESADA...
YOU MAY BE CERTAIN I SHALL, BARON OF ISE.

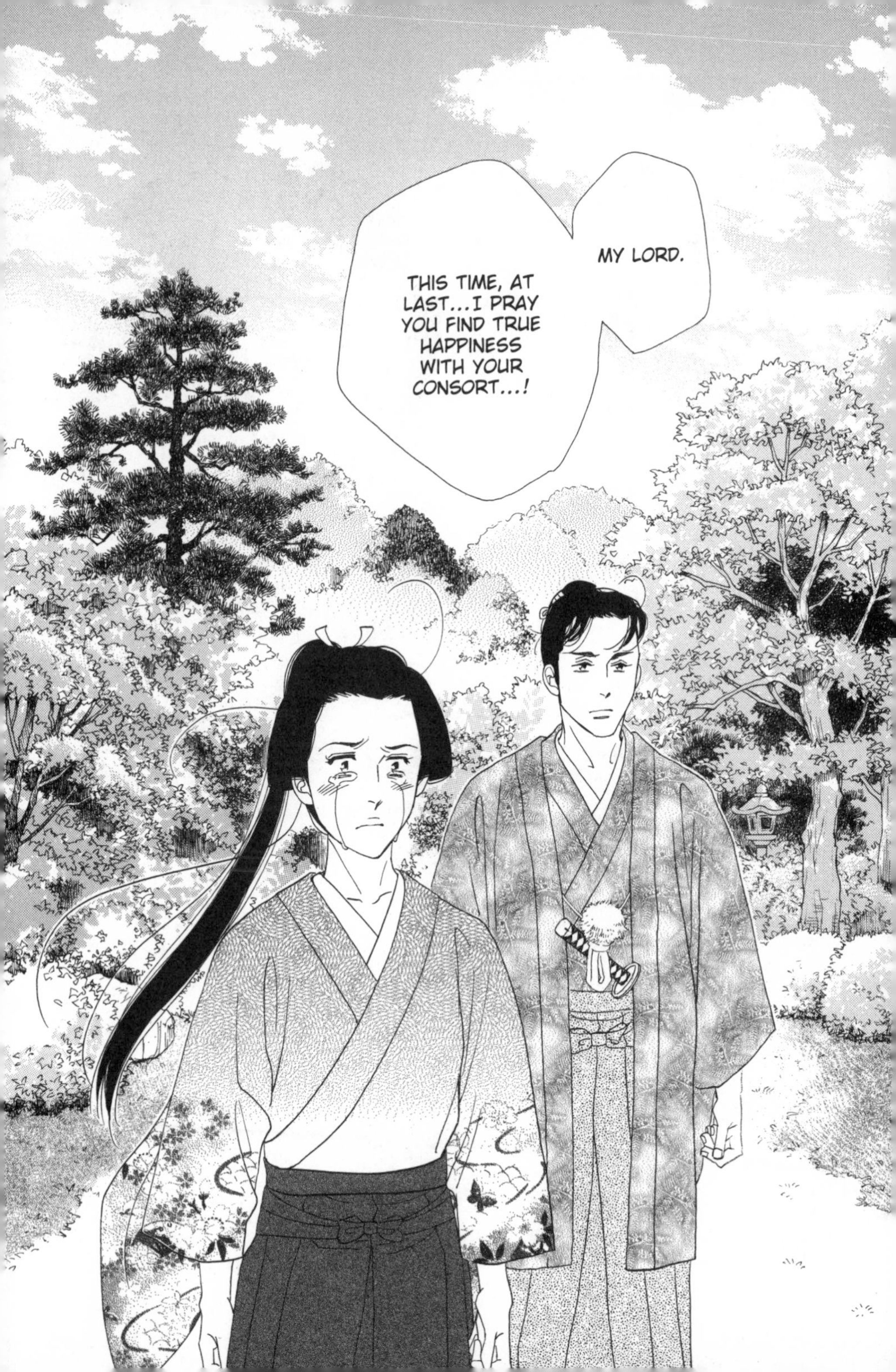
MY LORD.
THIS TIME, AT LAST...I PRAY YOU FIND TRUE HAPPINESS WITH YOUR CONSORT...!

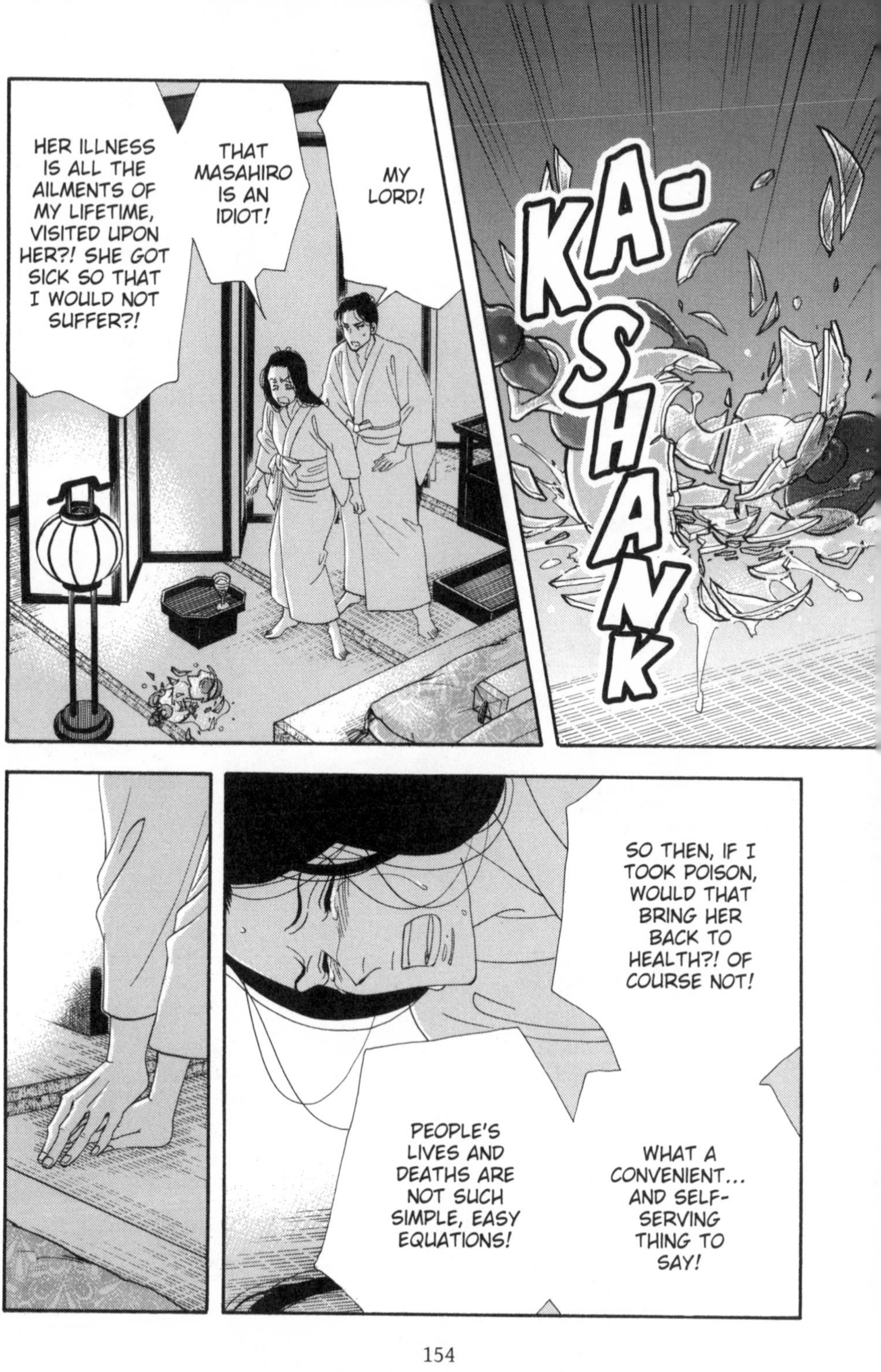

KA-SHANK
MY LORD!
THAT MASAHIRO IS AN IDIOT!
HER ILLNESS IS ALL THE AILMENTS OF MY LIFETIME, VISITED UPON HER?! SHE GOT SICK SO THAT I WOULD NOT SUFFER?!
SO THEN, IF I TOOK POISON, WOULD THAT BRING HER BACK TO HEALTH?! OF COURSE NOT!
WHAT A CONVENIENT... AND SELF-SERVING THING TO SAY!
PEOPLE'S LIVES AND DEATHS ARE NOT SUCH SIMPLE, EASY EQUATIONS!

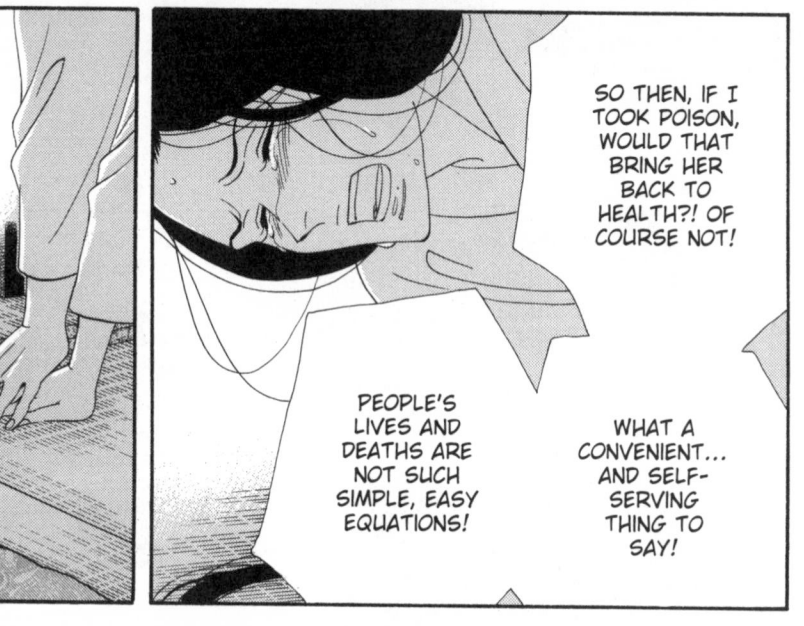

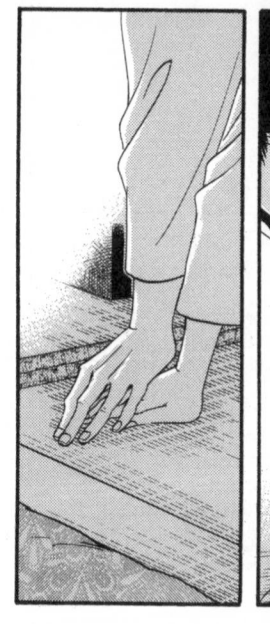

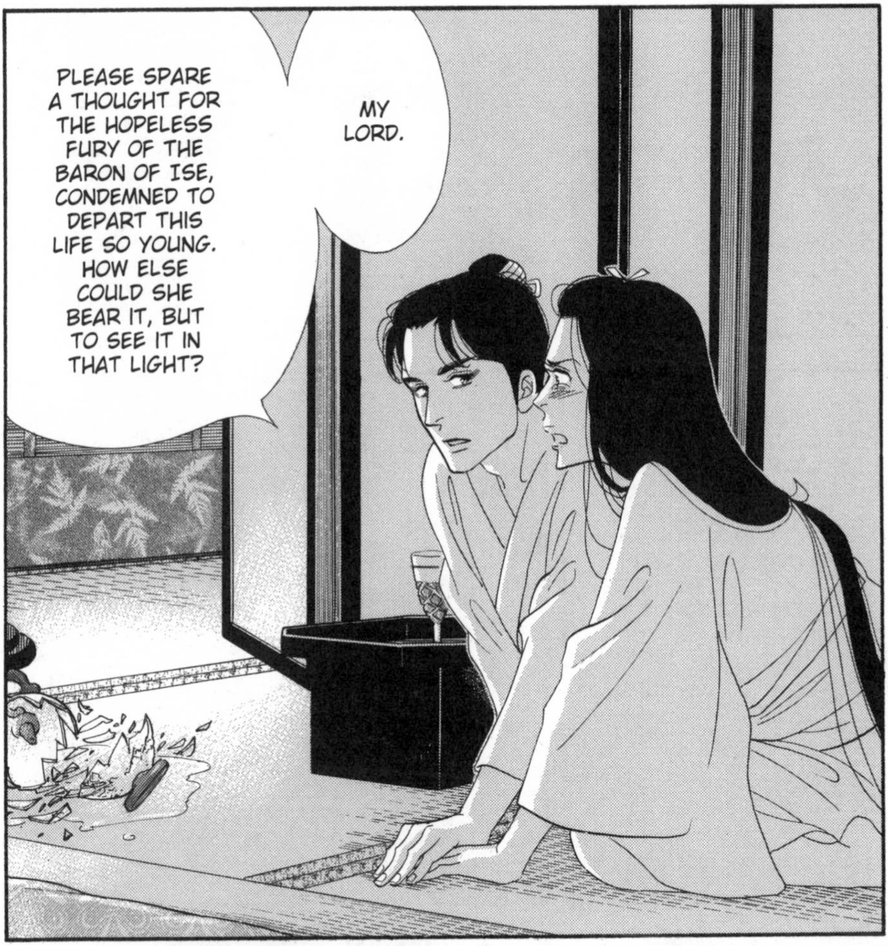
MY LORD.
PLEASE SPARE A THOUGHT FOR THE HOPELESS FURY OF THE BARON OF ISE, CONDEMNED TO DEPART THIS LIFE SO YOUNG. HOW ELSE COULD SHE BEAR IT, BUT TO SEE IT IN THAT LIGHT?
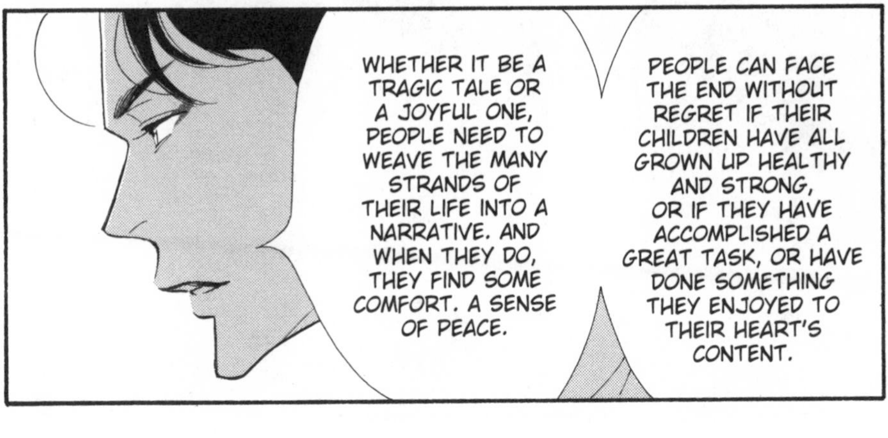
PEOPLE CAN FACE THE END WITHOUT REGRET IF THEIR CHILDREN HAVE ALL GROWN UP HEALTHY AND STRONG, OR IF THEY HAVE ACCOMPLISHED A GREAT TASK, OR HAVE DONE SOMETHING THEY ENJOYED TO THEIR HEART'S CONTENT.
WHETHER IT BE A TRAGIC TALE OR A JOYFUL ONE, PEOPLE NEED TO WEAVE THE MANY STRANDS OF THEIR LIFE INTO A NARRATIVE. AND WHEN THEY DO, THEY FIND SOME COMFORT. A SENSE OF PEACE.

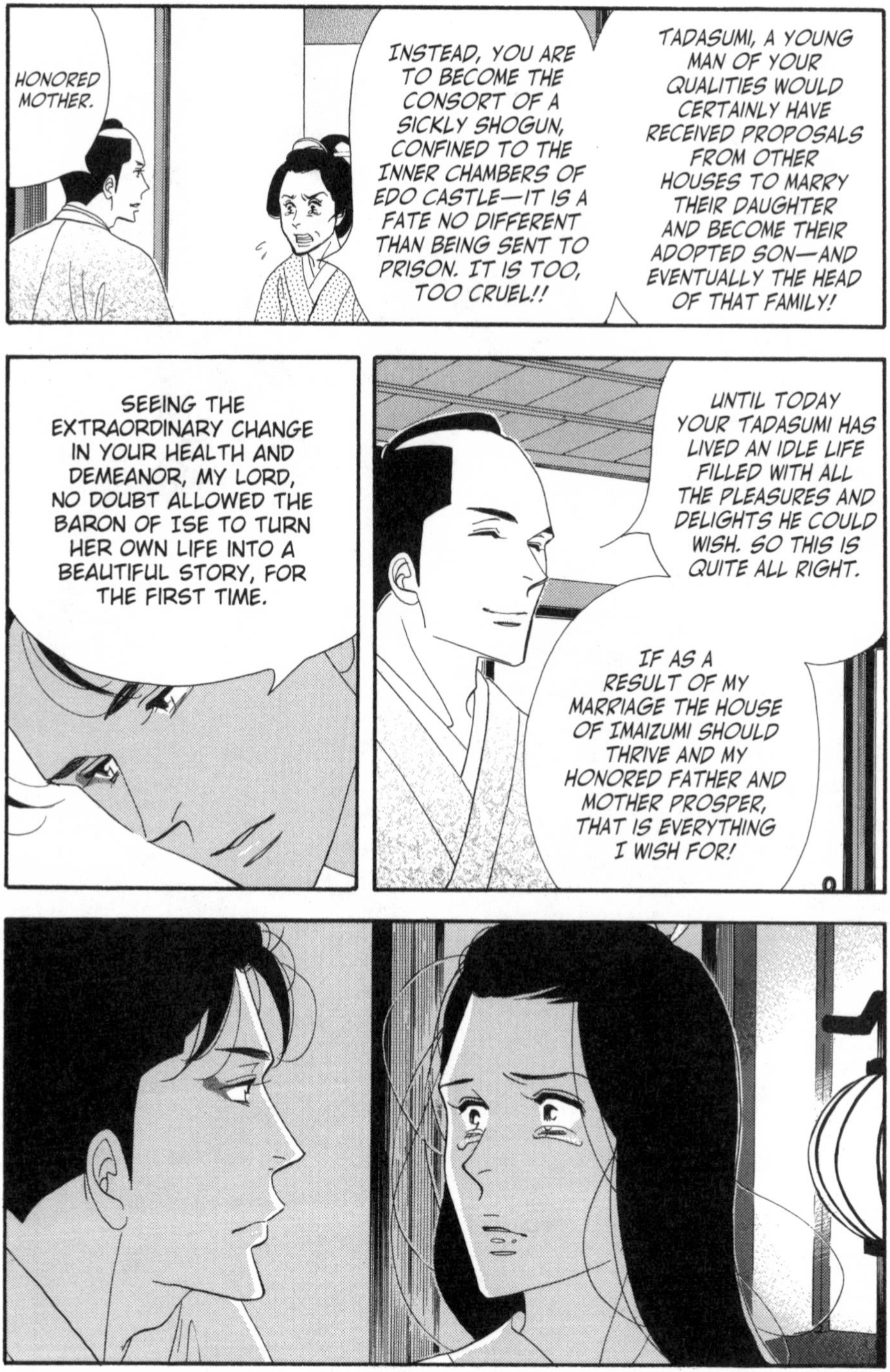
TADASUMI, A YOUNG MAN OF YOUR QUALITIES WOULD CERTAINLY HAVE RECEIVED PROPOSALS FROM OTHER HOUSES TO MARRY THEIR DAUGHTER AND BECOME THEIR ADOPTED SON—AND EVENTUALLY THE HEAD OF THAT FAMILY!
INSTEAD, YOU ARE TO BECOME THE CONSORT OF A SICKLY SHOGUN, CONFINED TO THE INNER CHAMBERS OF EDO CASTLE—IT IS A FATE NO DIFFERENT THAN BEING SENT TO PRISON. IT IS TOO, TOO CRUEL!!
HONORED MOTHER.
UNTIL TODAY YOUR TADASUMI HAS LIVED AN IDLE LIFE FILLED WITH ALL THE PLEASURES AND DELIGHTS HE COULD WISH. SO THIS IS QUITE ALL RIGHT.
IF AS A RESULT OF MY MARRIAGE THE HOUSE OF IMAIZUMI SHOULD THRIVE AND MY HONORED FATHER AND MOTHER PROSPER, THAT IS EVERYTHING I WISH FOR!
SEEING THE EXTRAORDINARY CHANGE IN YOUR HEALTH AND DEMEANOR, MY LORD, NO DOUBT ALLOWED THE BARON OF ISE TO TURN HER OWN LIFE INTO A BEAUTIFUL STORY, FOR THE FIRST TIME.

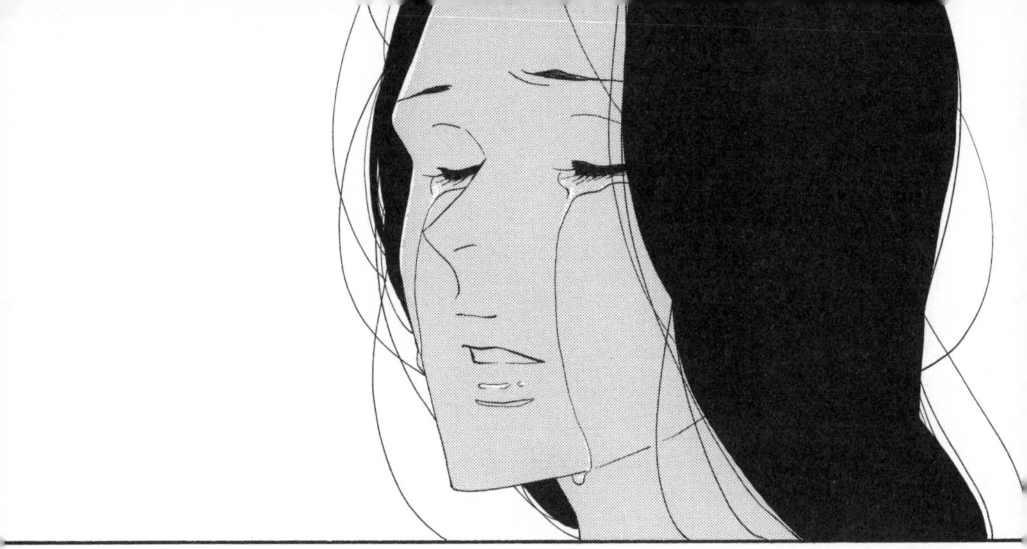
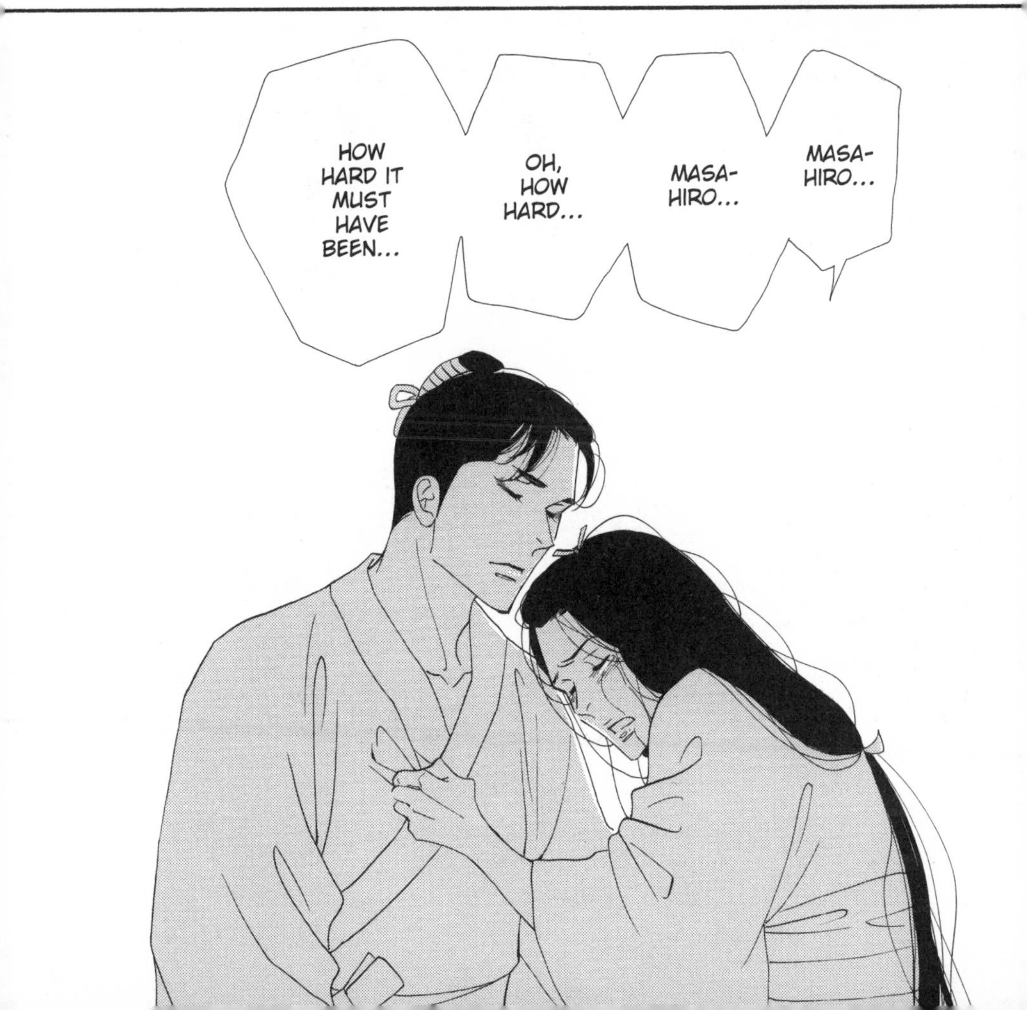
MASA-HIRO...
MASA-HIRO...
OH, HOW HARD...
HOW HARD IT MUST HAVE BEEN...

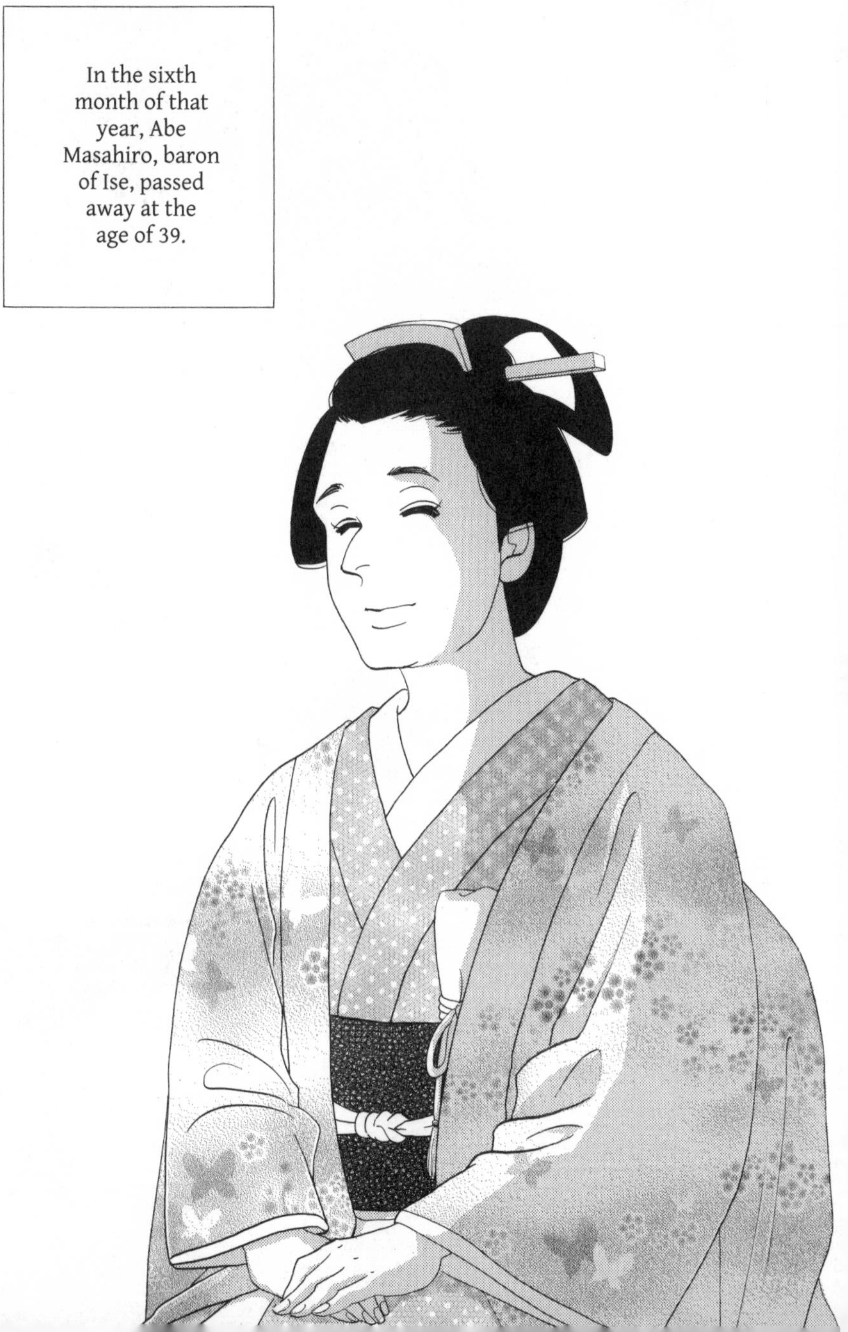
In the sixth month of that year, Abe Masahiro, baron of Ise, passed away at the age of 39.

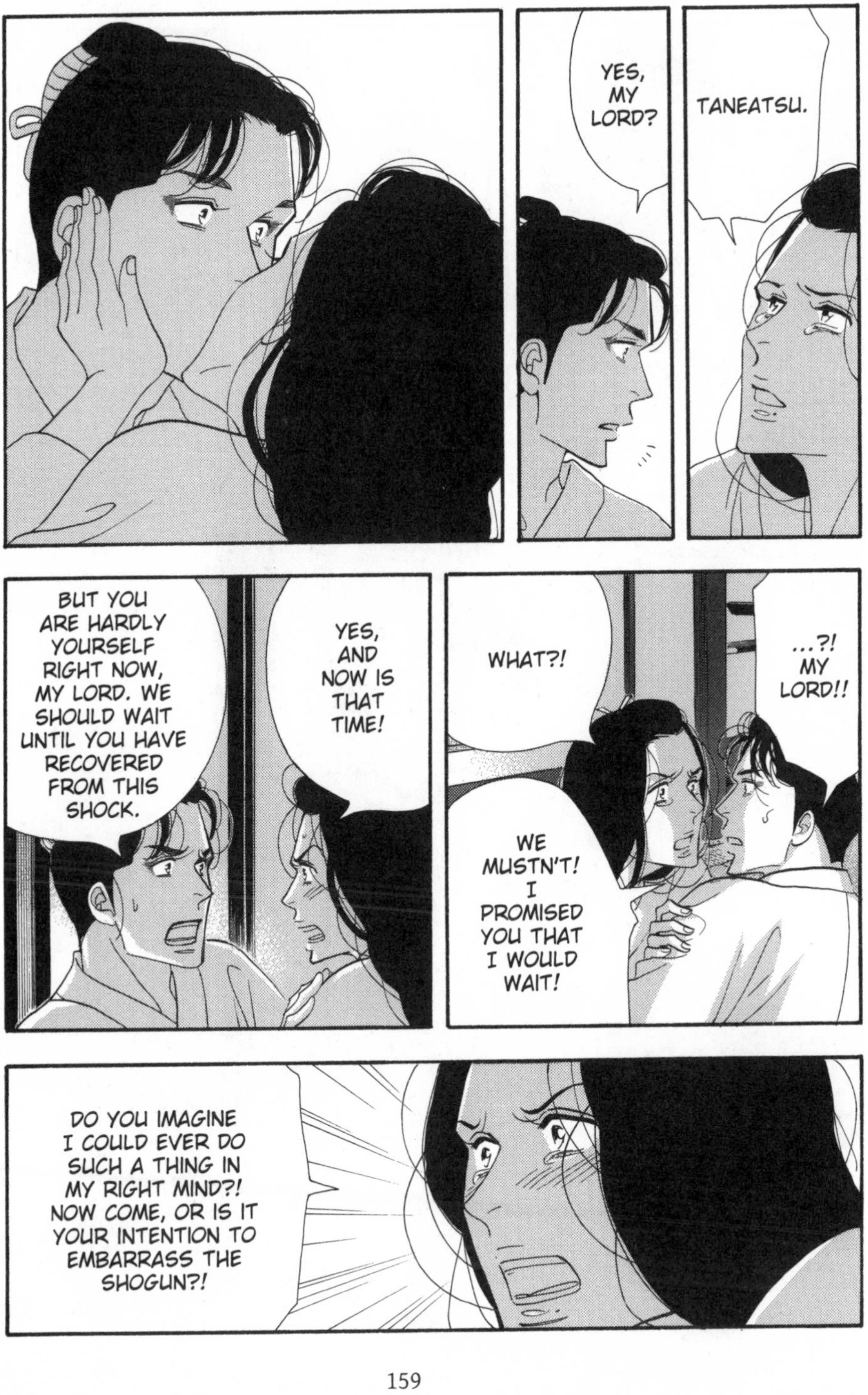
TANEATSU.
YES, MY LORD?
...?! MY LORD!!
WHAT?!
WE MUSTN'T! I PROMISED YOU THAT I WOULD WAIT!
YES, AND NOW IS THAT TIME!
BUT YOU ARE HARDLY YOURSELF RIGHT NOW, MY LORD. WE SHOULD WAIT UNTIL YOU HAVE RECOVERED FROM THIS SHOCK.
DO YOU IMAGINE I COULD EVER DO SUCH A THING IN MY RIGHT MIND?! NOW COME, OR IS IT YOUR INTENTION TO EMBARRASS THE SHOGUN?!

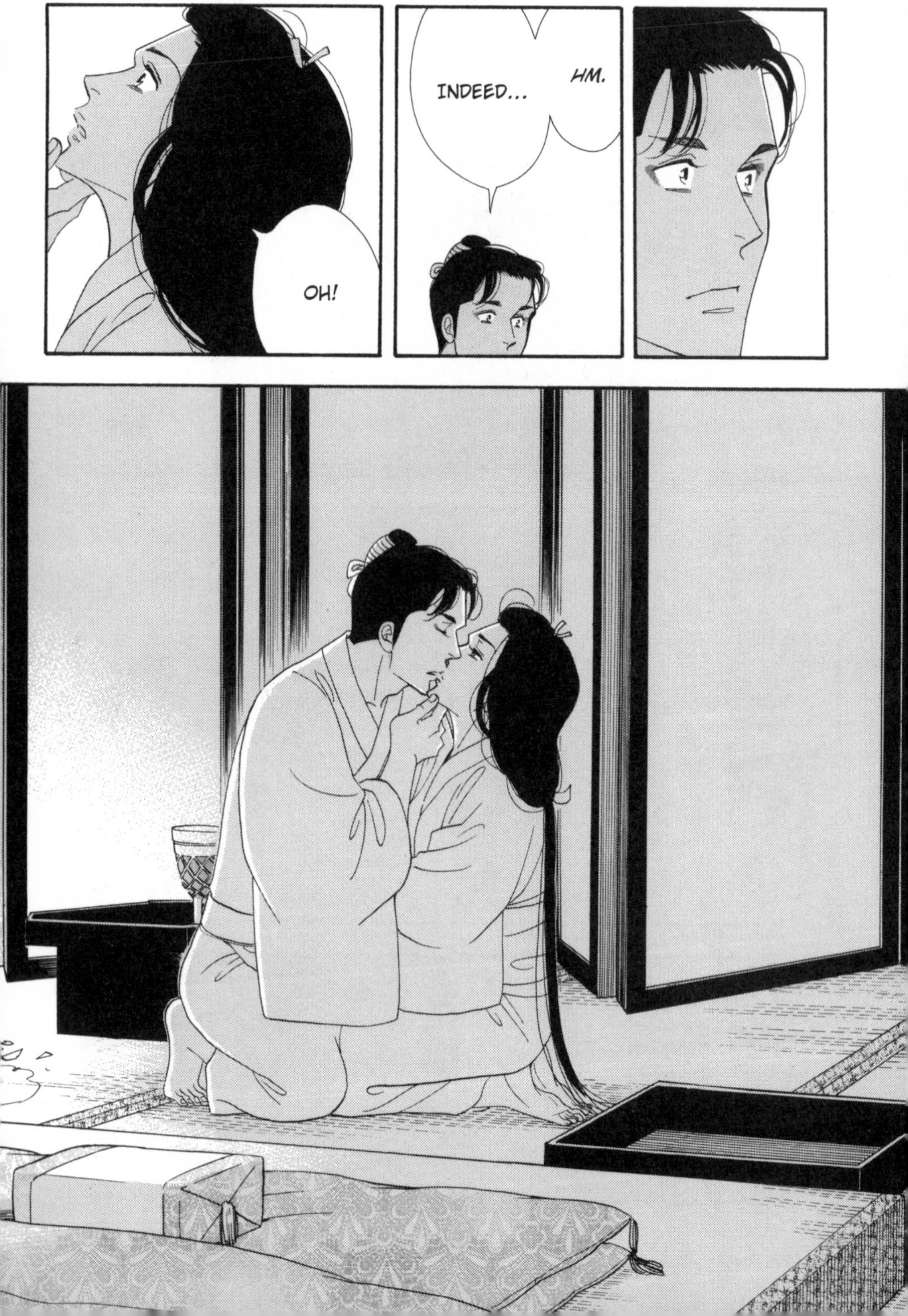
HM.
INDEED...
OH!

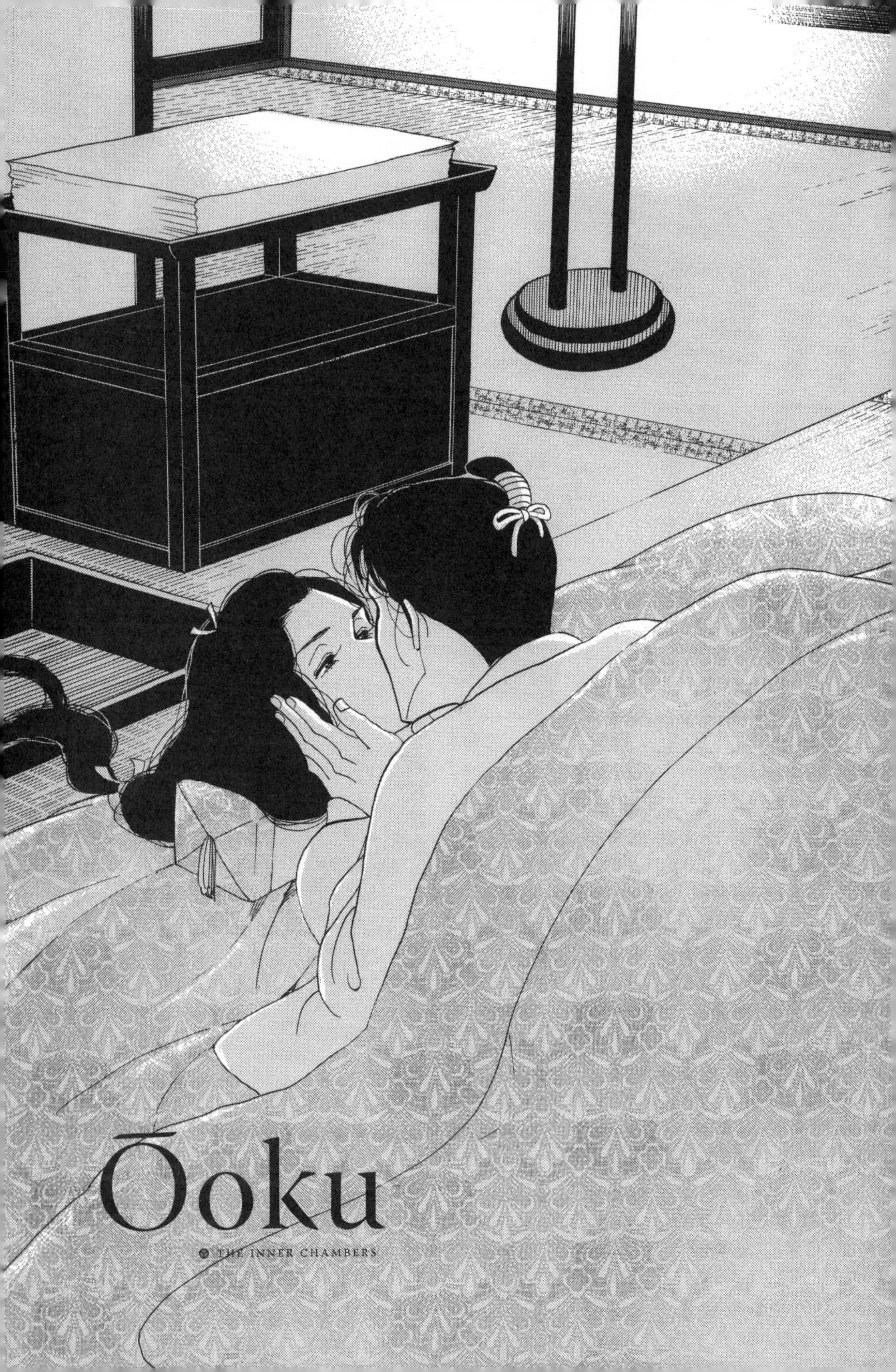
Ōoku
THE INNER CHAMBERS

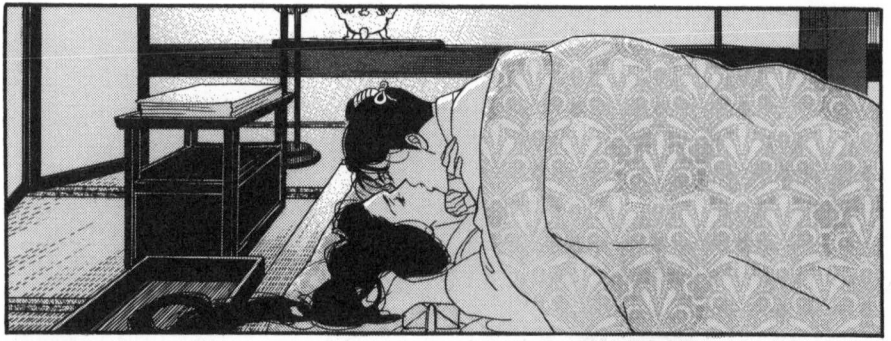

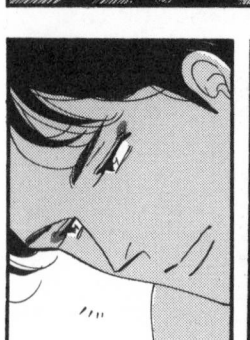

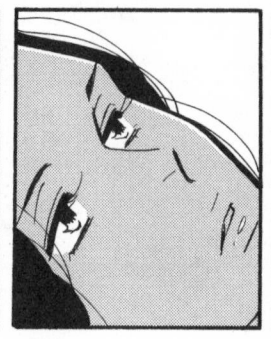

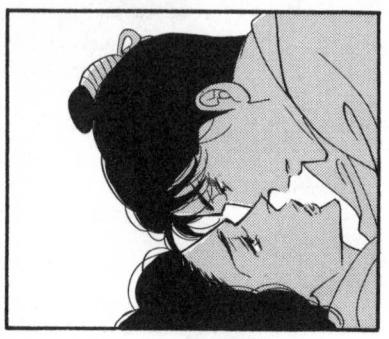

...
SIR SUMI...
P-PLEASE DON'T GAZE AT ME LIKE THAT...
IT MAKES ME NERVOUS...

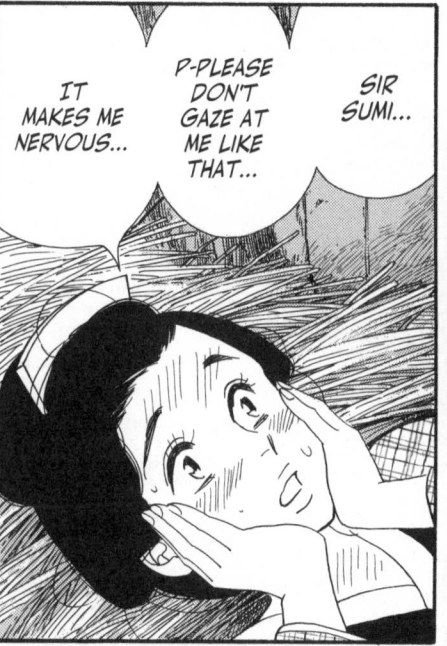

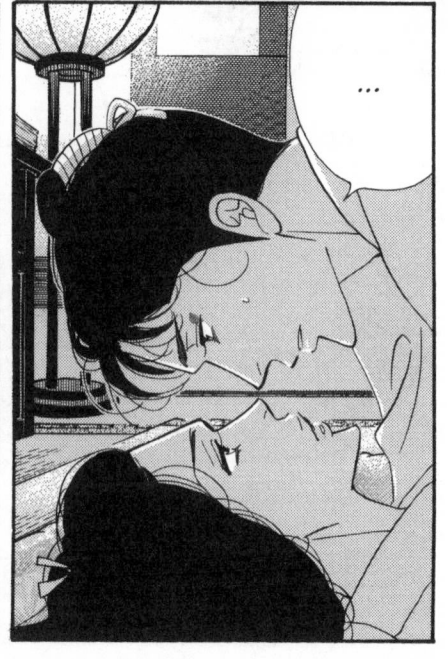

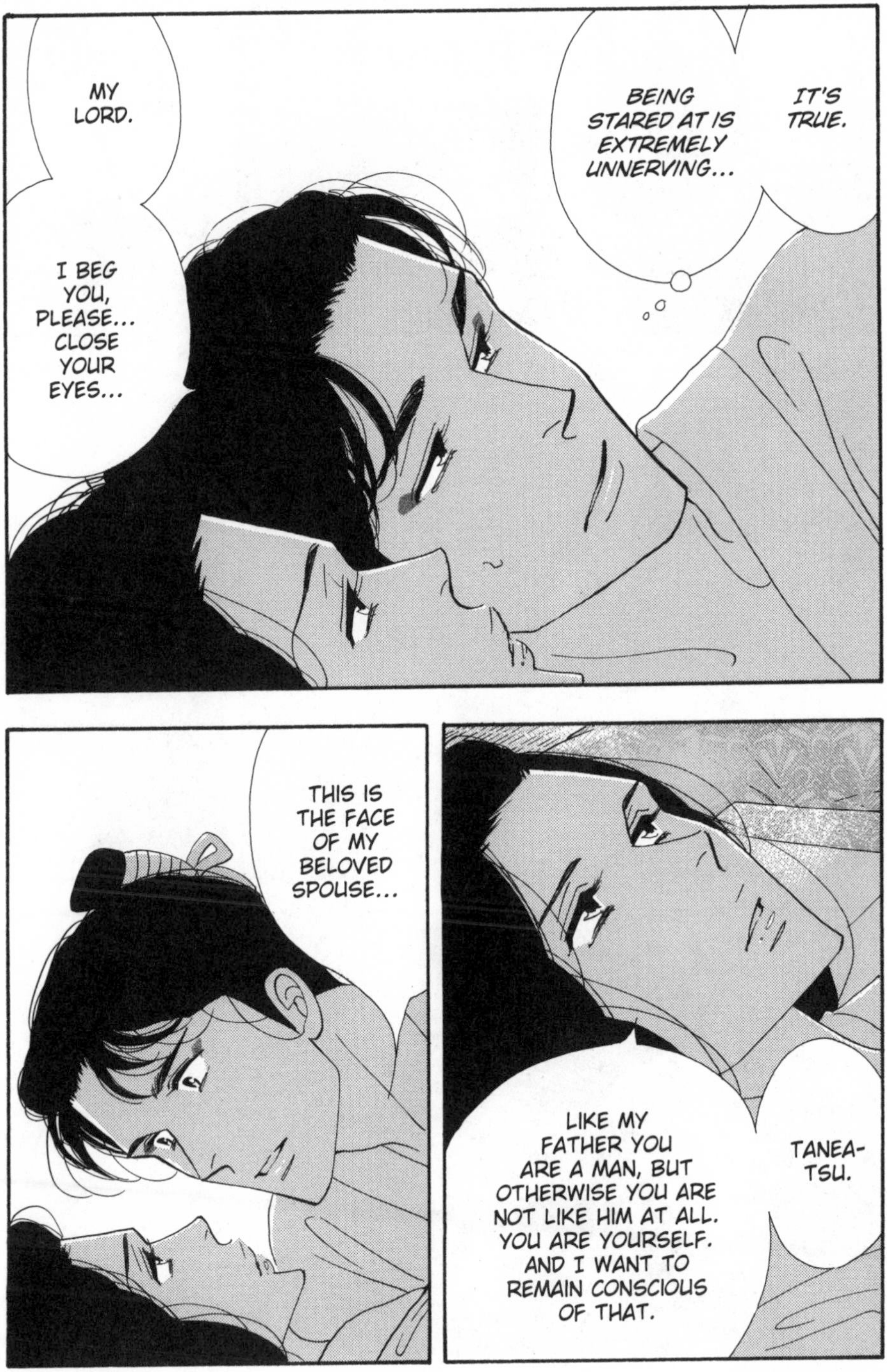
IT'S TRUE.
BEING STARED AT IS EXTREMELY UNNERVING...
MY LORD.
I BEG YOU, PLEASE... CLOSE YOUR EYES...
TANEA-TSU.
LIKE MY FATHER YOU ARE A MAN, BUT OTHERWISE YOU ARE NOT LIKE HIM AT ALL. YOU ARE YOURSELF. AND I WANT TO REMAIN CONSCIOUS OF THAT.
THIS IS THE FACE OF MY BELOVED SPOUSE...

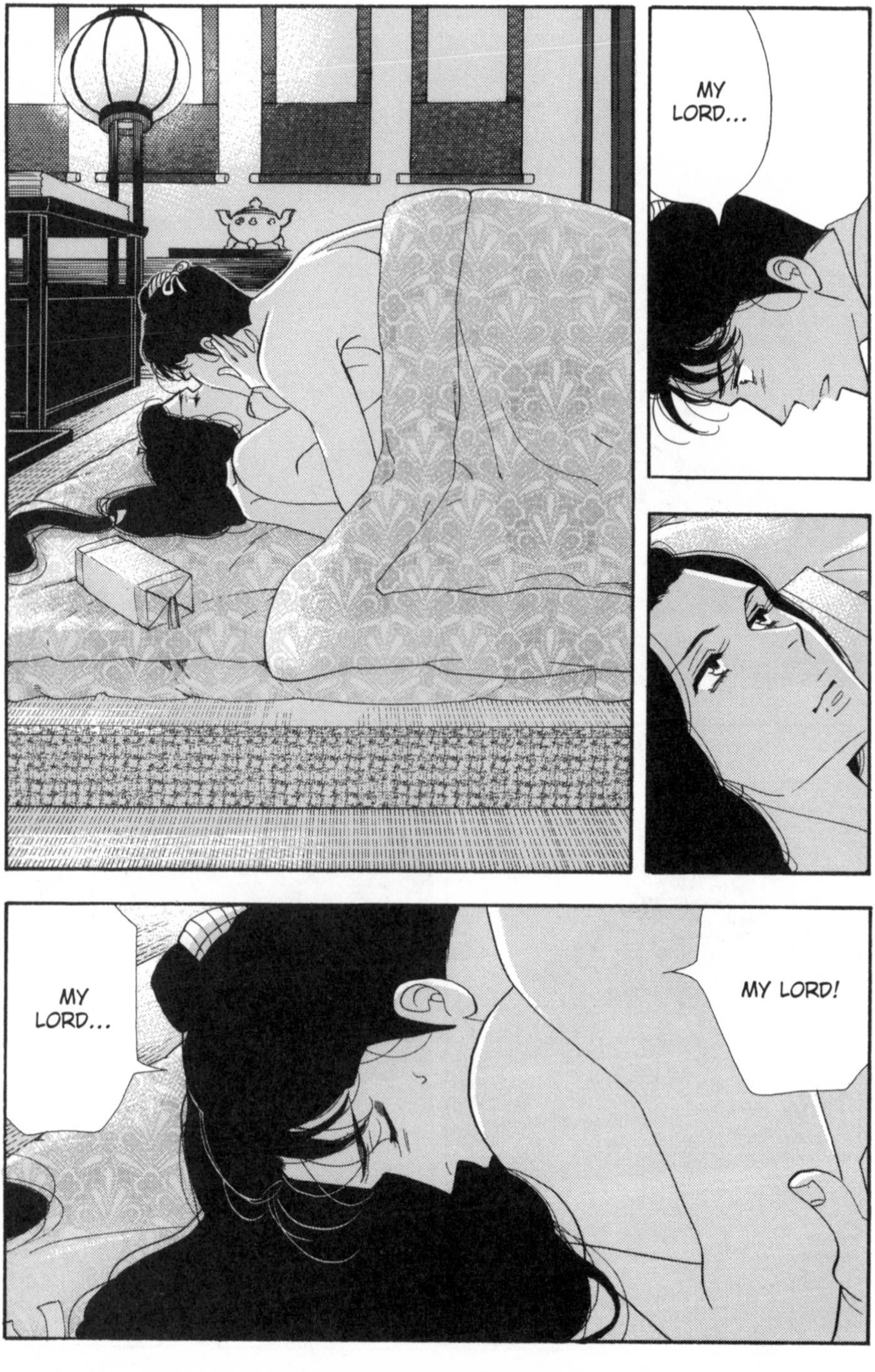
MY LORD...
MY LORD!
MY LORD...

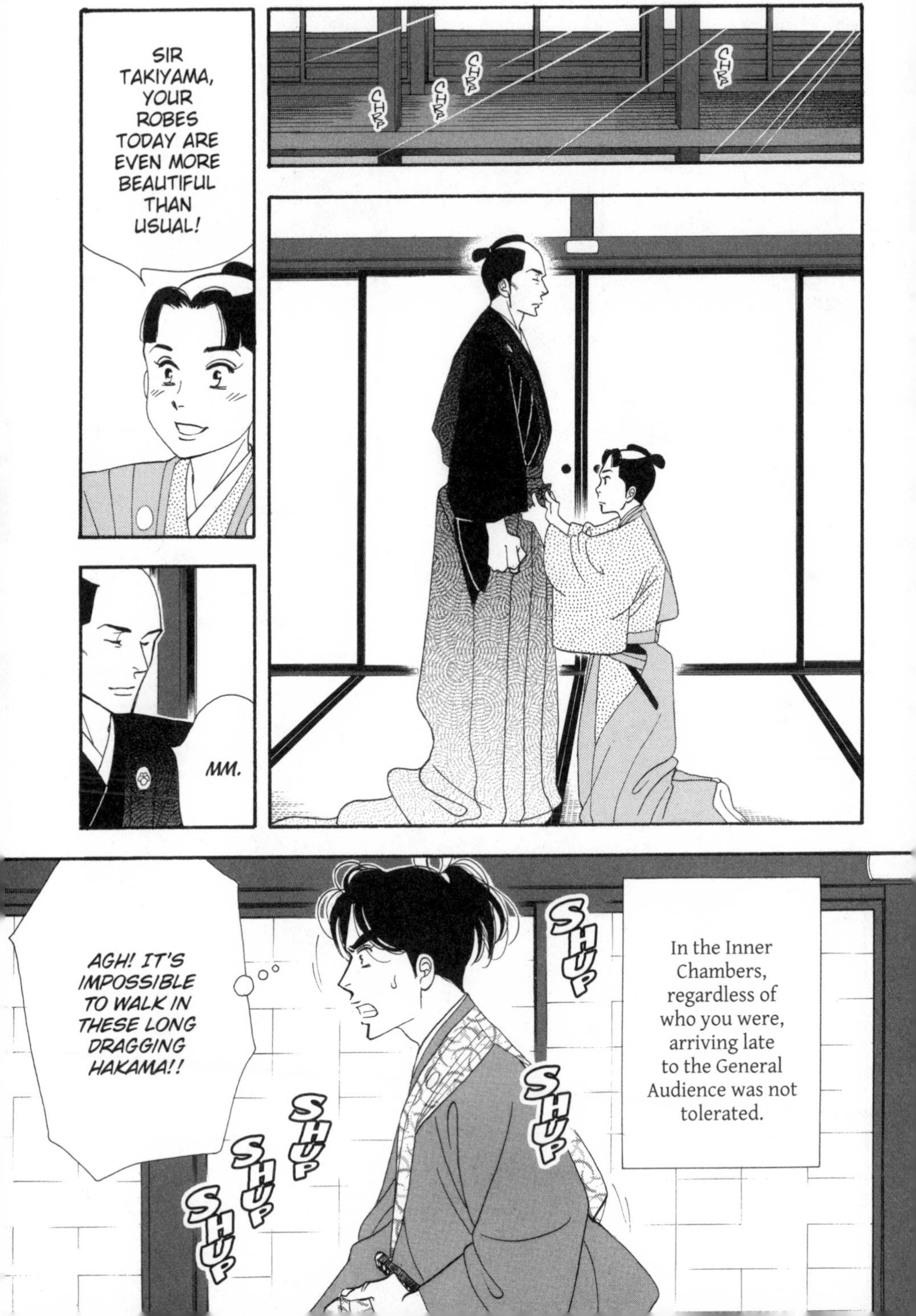
CHRP
CHRP
CHRP
CHRP
SIR TAKIYAMA, YOUR ROBES TODAY ARE EVEN MORE BEAUTIFUL THAN USUAL!
MM.
In the Inner Chambers, regardless of who you were, arriving late to the General Audience was not tolerated.
SHUP
SHUP
AGH! IT'S IMPOSSIBLE TO WALK IN THESE LONG DRAGGING HAKAMA!!
SHUP
SHUP
SHUP

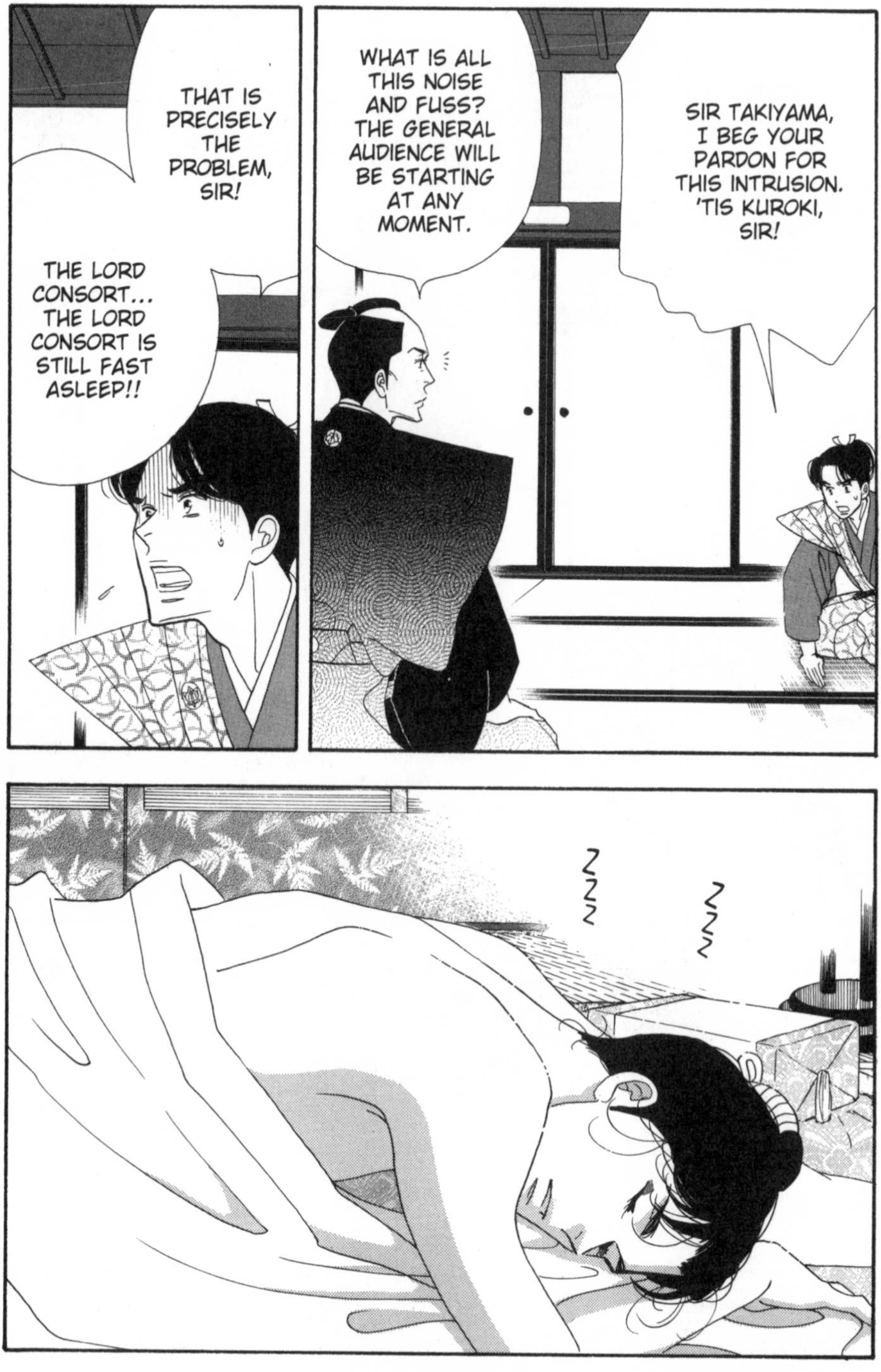
SIR TAKIYAMA, I BEG YOUR PARDON FOR THIS INTRUSION. 'TIS KUROKI, SIR!
WHAT IS ALL THIS NOISE AND FUSS? THE GENERAL AUDIENCE WILL BE STARTING AT ANY MOMENT.
THAT IS PRECISELY THE PROBLEM, SIR!
THE LORD CONSORT... THE LORD CONSORT IS STILL FAST ASLEEP!!
ZZZ
ZZZ

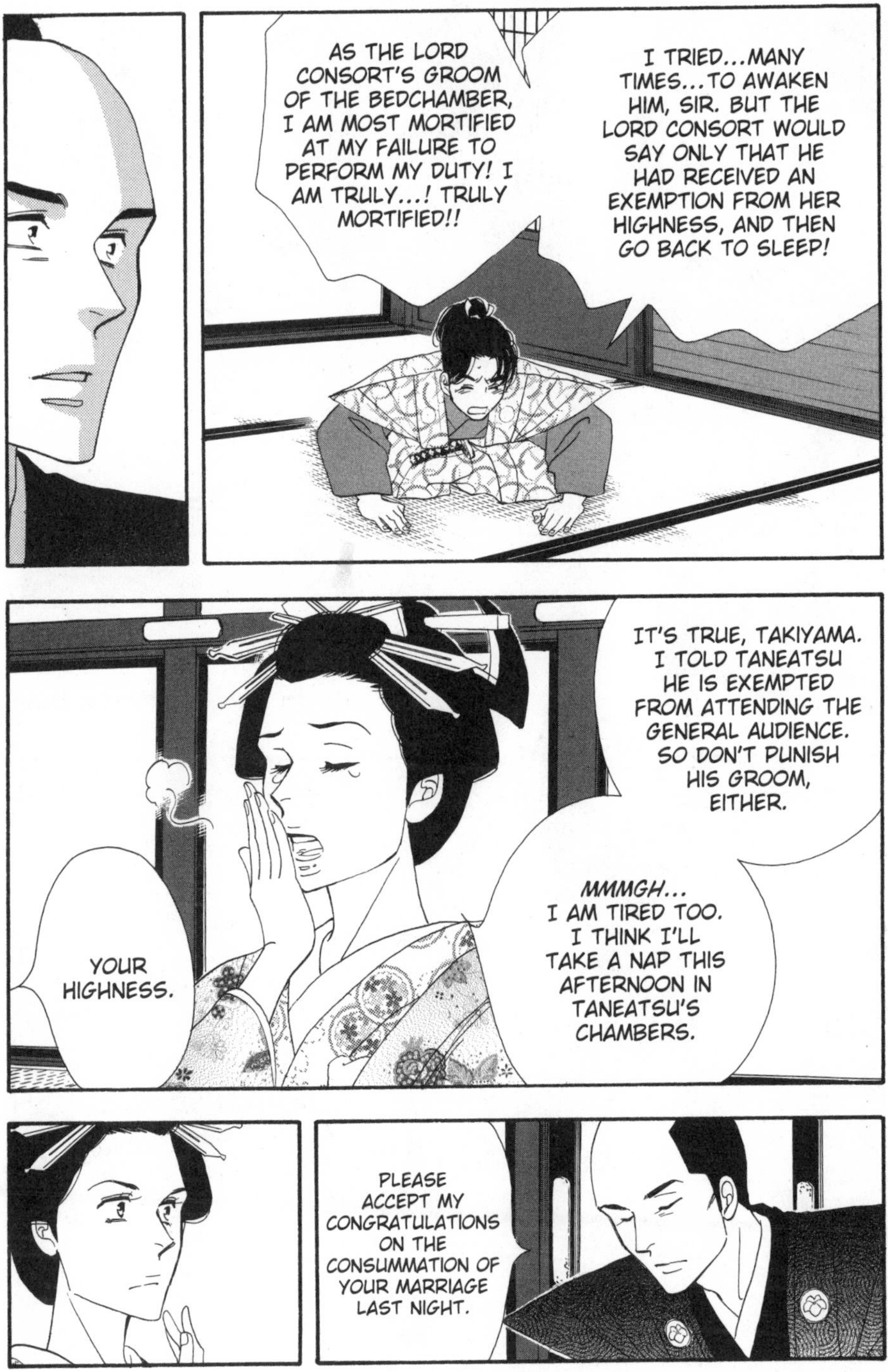

I TRIED...MANY TIMES...TO AWAKEN HIM, SIR. BUT THE LORD CONSORT WOULD SAY ONLY THAT HE HAD RECEIVED AN EXEMPTION FROM HER HIGHNESS, AND THEN GO BACK TO SLEEP!
AS THE LORD CONSORT'S GROOM OF THE BEDCHAMBER, I AM MOST MORTIFIED AT MY FAILURE TO PERFORM MY DUTY! I AM TRULY...! TRULY MORTIFIED!!
IT'S TRUE, TAKIYAMA. I TOLD TANEATSU HE IS EXEMPTED FROM ATTENDING THE GENERAL AUDIENCE. SO DON'T PUNISH HIS GROOM, EITHER.
MMMGH... I AM TIRED TOO. I THINK I'LL TAKE A NAP THIS AFTERNOON IN TANEATSU'S CHAMBERS.
YOUR HIGHNESS.
PLEASE ACCEPT MY CONGRATULATIONS ON THE CONSUMMATION OF YOUR MARRIAGE LAST NIGHT.

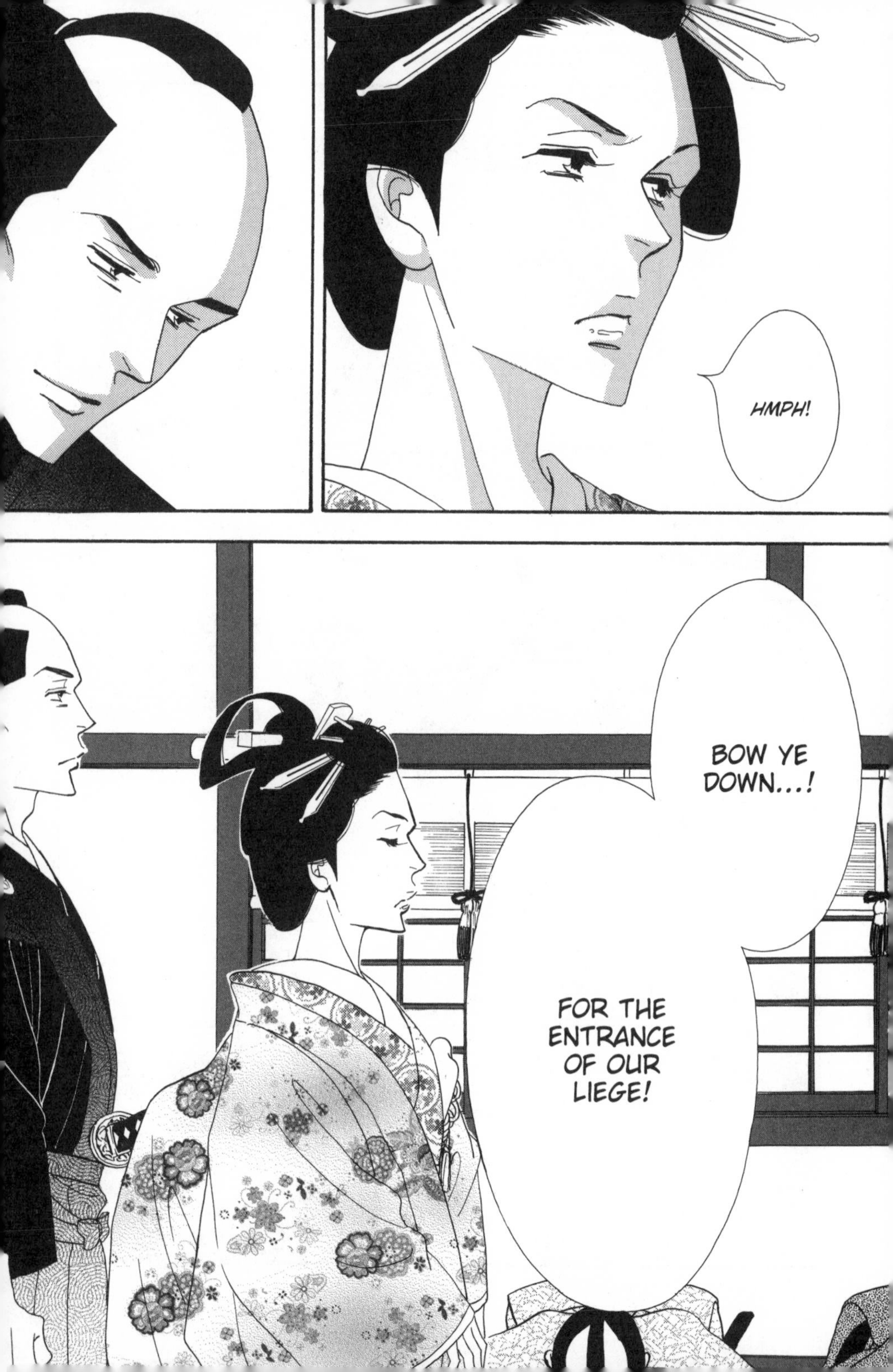
HMPH!
BOW YE DOWN...!
FOR THE ENTRANCE OF OUR LIEGE!

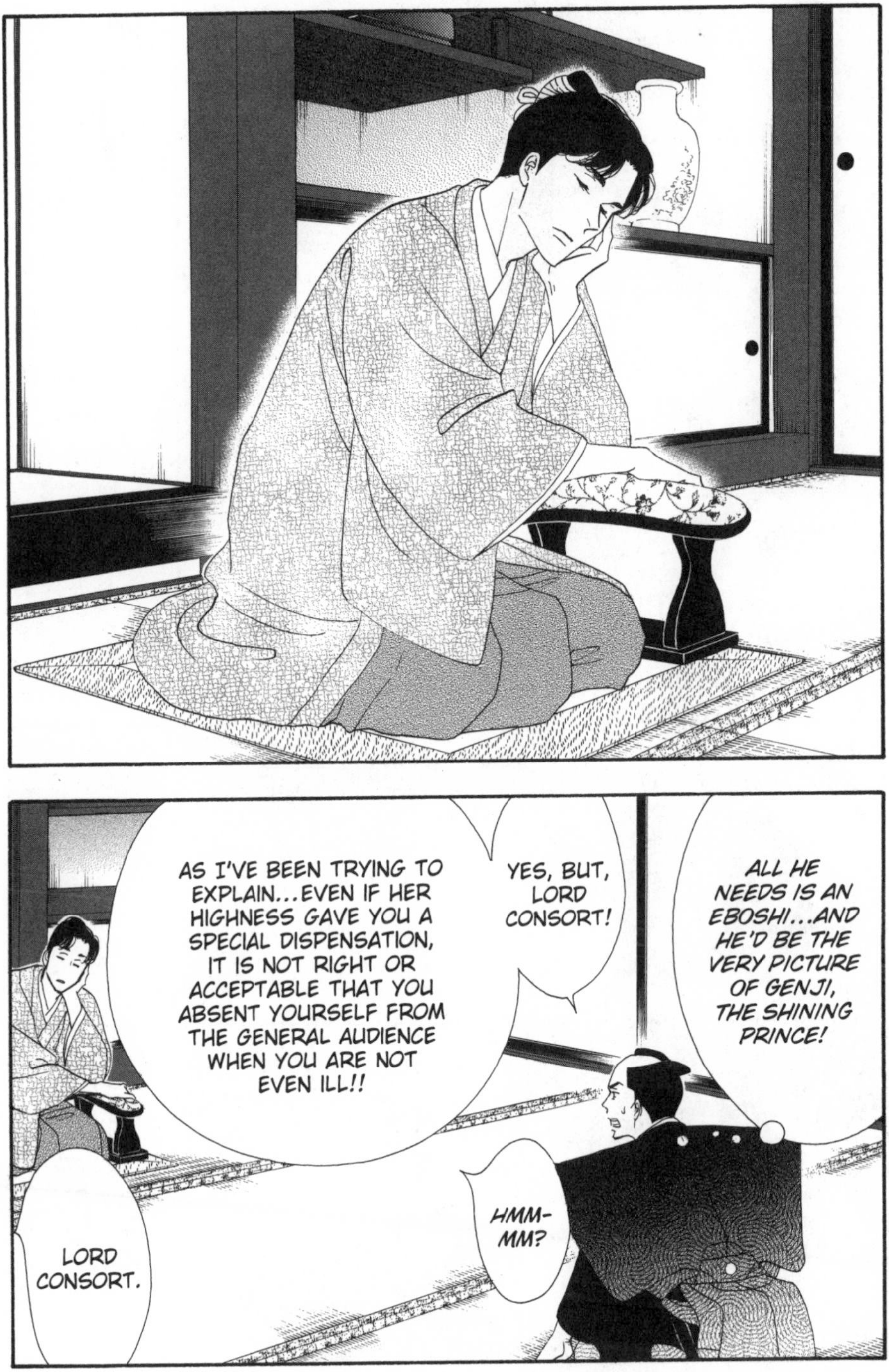
ALL HE NEEDS IS AN EBOSHI...AND HE'D BE THE VERY PICTURE OF GENJI, THE SHINING PRINCE!
YES, BUT, LORD CONSORT!
AS I'VE BEEN TRYING TO EXPLAIN...EVEN IF HER HIGHNESS GAVE YOU A SPECIAL DISPENSATION, IT IS NOT RIGHT OR ACCEPTABLE THAT YOU ABSENT YOURSELF FROM THE GENERAL AUDIENCE WHEN YOU ARE NOT EVEN ILL!!
HMM-MM?
LORD CONSORT.

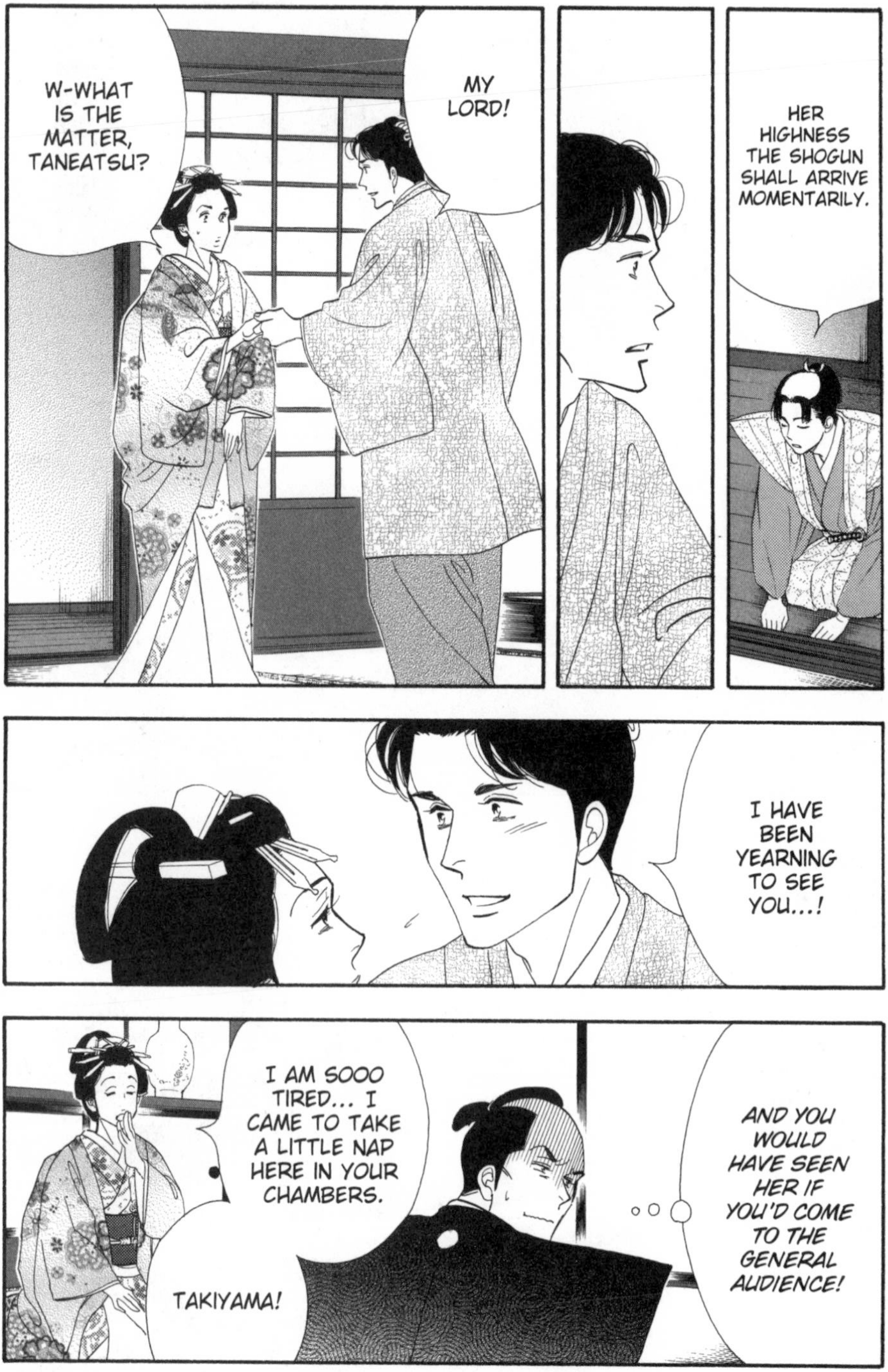
HER HIGHNESS THE SHOGUN SHALL ARRIVE MOMENTARILY.
MY LORD!
W-WHAT IS THE MATTER, TANEATSU?
I HAVE BEEN YEARNING TO SEE YOU...!
AND YOU WOULD HAVE SEEN HER IF YOU'D COME TO THE GENERAL AUDIENCE!
I AM SOOO TIRED... I CAME TO TAKE A LITTLE NAP HERE IN YOUR CHAMBERS.
TAKIYAMA!

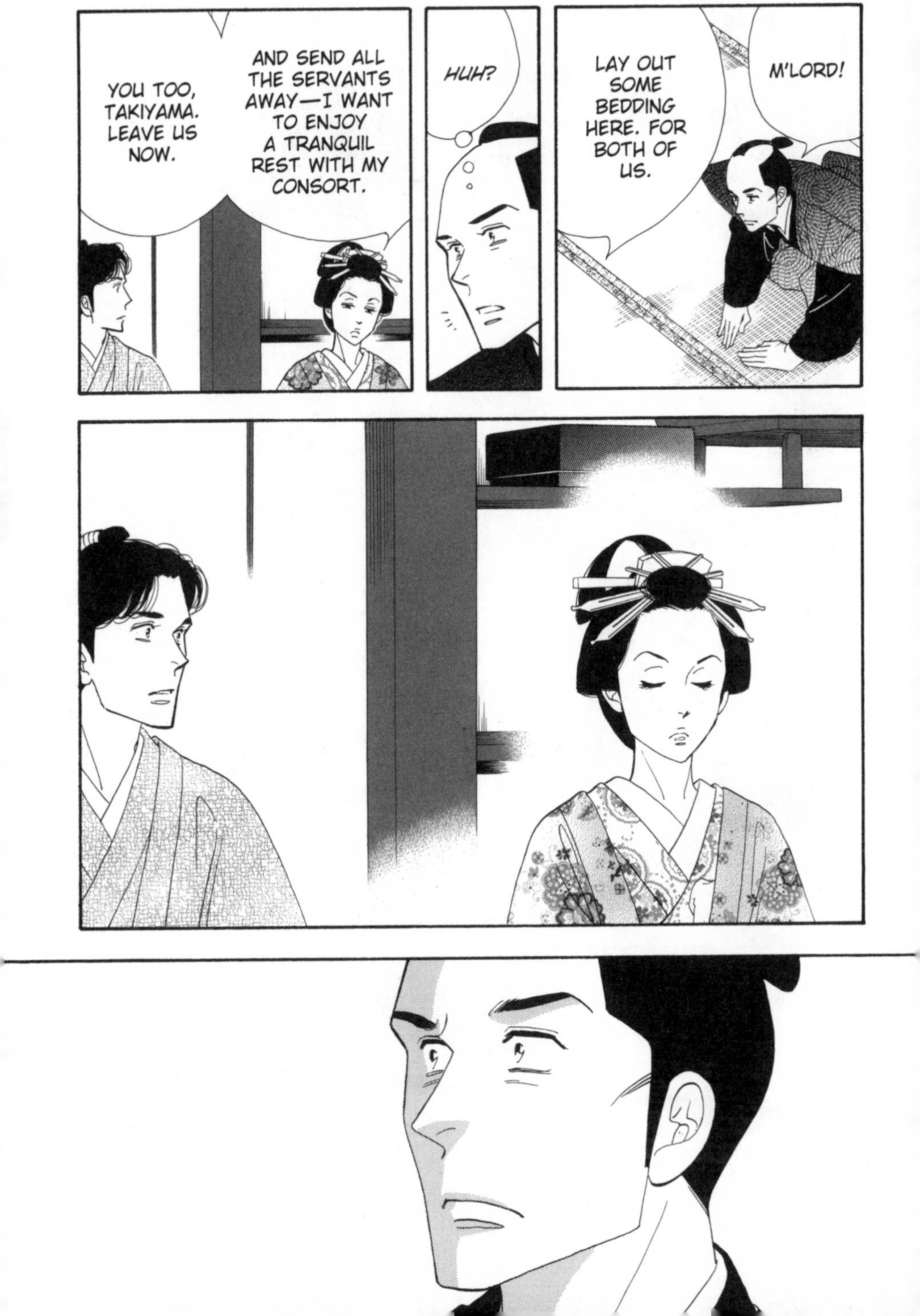
M'LORD!
LAY OUT SOME BEDDING HERE. FOR BOTH OF US.
HUH?
AND SEND ALL THE SERVANTS AWAY—I WANT TO ENJOY A TRANQUIL REST WITH MY CONSORT.
YOU TOO, TAKIYAMA. LEAVE US NOW.

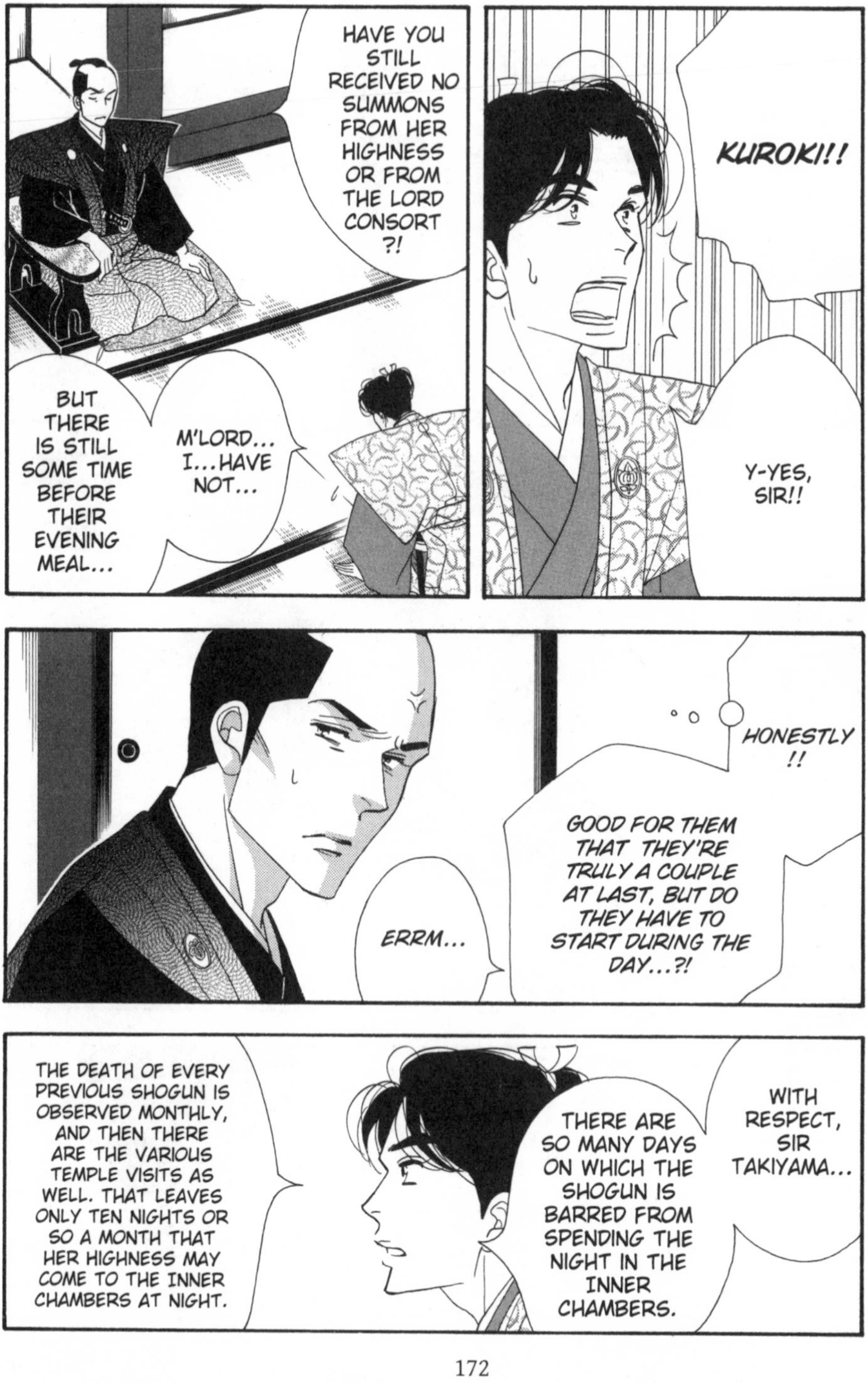
KUROKI!!
Y-YES, SIR!!
HAVE YOU STILL RECEIVED NO SUMMONS FROM HER HIGHNESS OR FROM THE LORD CONSORT ?!
M'LORD... I...HAVE NOT...
BUT THERE IS STILL SOME TIME BEFORE THEIR EVENING MEAL...
HONESTLY !!
GOOD FOR THEM THAT THEY'RE TRULY A COUPLE AT LAST, BUT DO THEY HAVE TO START DURING THE DAY...?!
ERRM...
WITH RESPECT, SIR TAKIYAMA...
THERE ARE SO MANY DAYS ON WHICH THE SHOGUN IS BARRED FROM SPENDING THE NIGHT IN THE INNER CHAMBERS.
THE DEATH OF EVERY PREVIOUS SHOGUN IS OBSERVED MONTHLY, AND THEN THERE ARE THE VARIOUS TEMPLE VISITS AS WELL. THAT LEAVES ONLY TEN NIGHTS OR SO A MONTH THAT HER HIGHNESS MAY COME TO THE INNER CHAMBERS AT NIGHT.

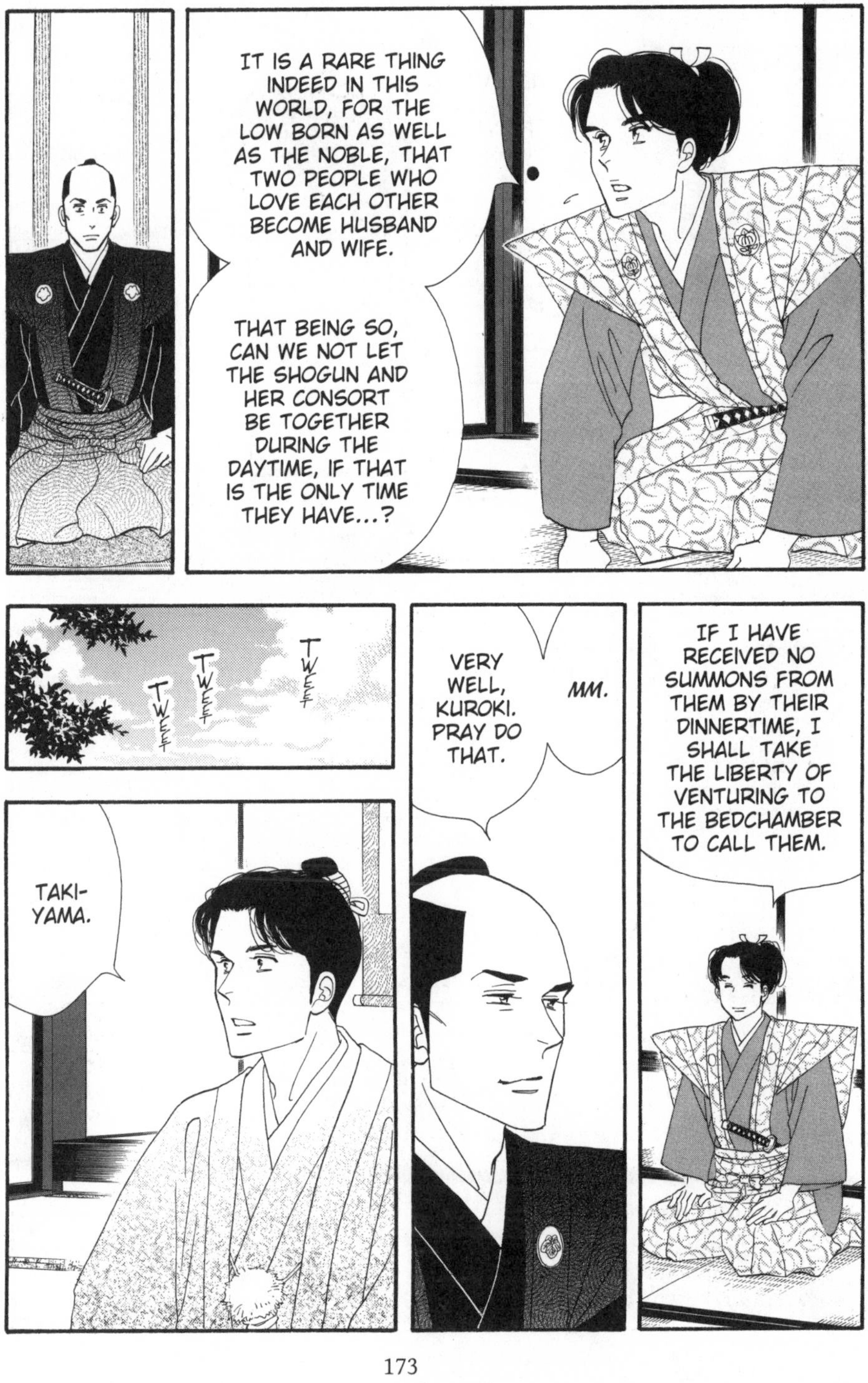
IT IS A RARE THING INDEED IN THIS WORLD, FOR THE LOW BORN AS WELL AS THE NOBLE, THAT TWO PEOPLE WHO LOVE EACH OTHER BECOME HUSBAND AND WIFE.
THAT BEING SO, CAN WE NOT LET THE SHOGUN AND HER CONSORT BE TOGETHER DURING THE DAYTIME, IF THAT IS THE ONLY TIME THEY HAVE...?
IF I HAVE RECEIVED NO SUMMONS FROM THEM BY THEIR DINNERTIME, I SHALL TAKE THE LIBERTY OF VENTURING TO THE BEDCHAMBER TO CALL THEM.
MM.
VERY WELL, KUROKI. PRAY DO THAT.
TWEET
TWEET
TWEET
TAKI-YAMA.

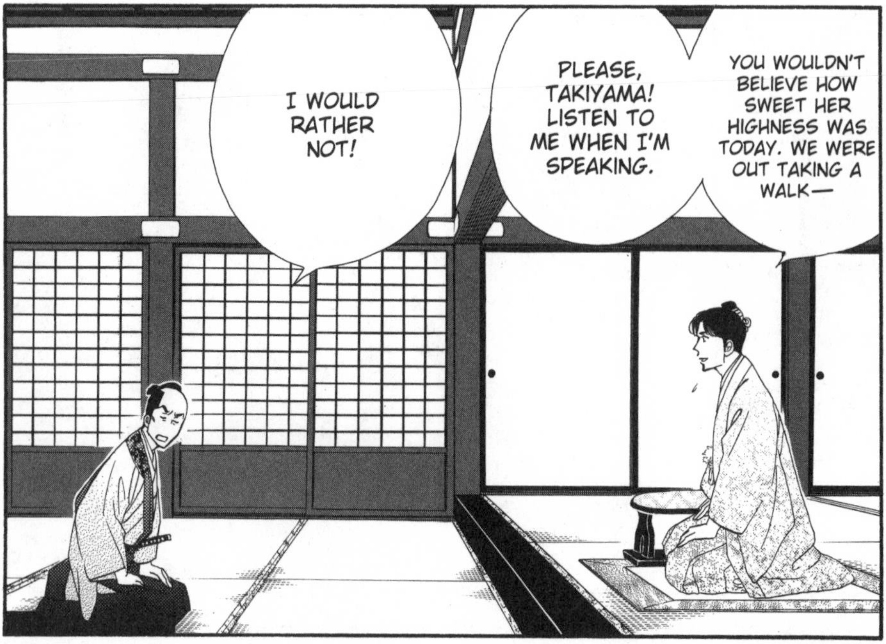
YOU WOULDN'T BELIEVE HOW SWEET HER HIGHNESS WAS TODAY. WE WERE OUT TAKING A WALK—
PLEASE, TAKIYAMA! LISTEN TO ME WHEN I'M SPEAKING.
I WOULD RATHER NOT!
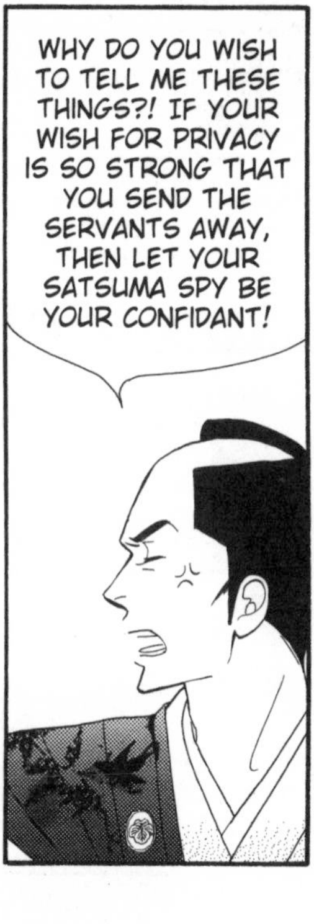
WHY DO YOU WISH TO TELL ME THESE THINGS?! IF YOUR WISH FOR PRIVACY IS SO STRONG THAT YOU SEND THE SERVANTS AWAY, THEN LET YOUR SATSUMA SPY BE YOUR CONFIDANT!
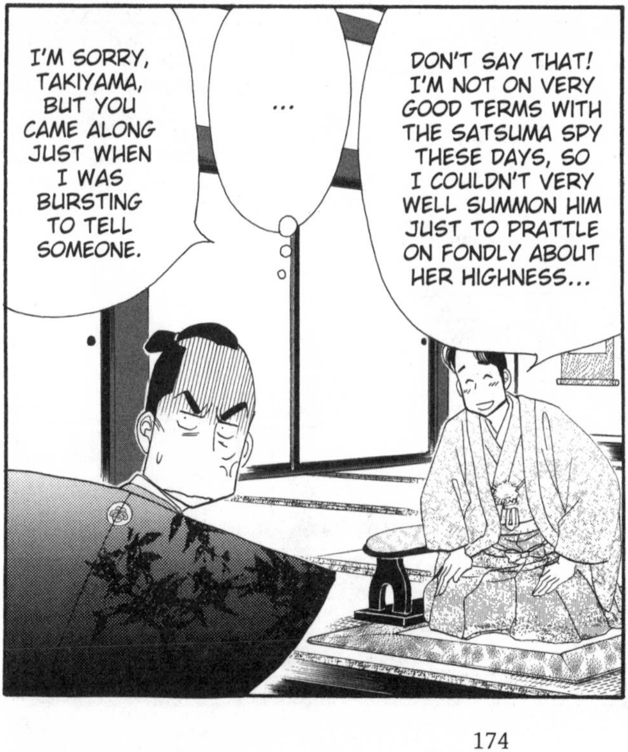
DON'T SAY THAT! I'M NOT ON VERY GOOD TERMS WITH THE SATSUMA SPY THESE DAYS, SO I COULDN'T VERY WELL SUMMON HIM JUST TO PRATTLE ON FONDLY ABOUT HER HIGHNESS...
...
I'M SORRY, TAKIYAMA, BUT YOU CAME ALONG JUST WHEN I WAS BURSTING TO TELL SOMEONE.

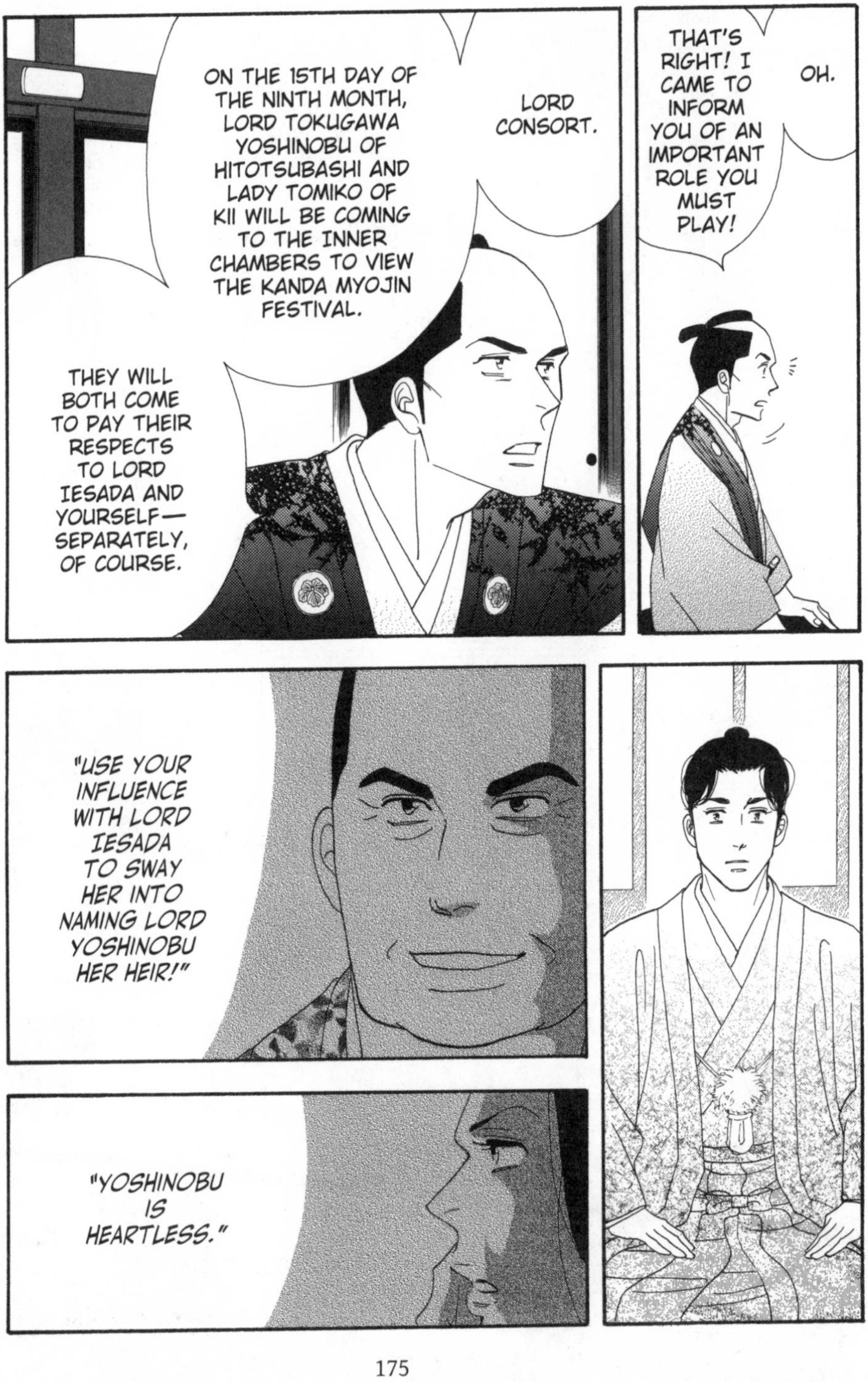
OH.
THAT'S RIGHT! I CAME TO INFORM YOU OF AN IMPORTANT ROLE YOU MUST PLAY!
LORD CONSORT.
ON THE 15TH DAY OF THE NINTH MONTH, LORD TOKUGAWA YOSHINOBU OF HITOTSUBASHI AND LADY TOMIKO OF KII WILL BE COMING TO THE INNER CHAMBERS TO VIEW THE KANDA MYOJIN FESTIVAL.
THEY WILL BOTH COME TO PAY THEIR RESPECTS TO LORD IESADA AND YOURSELF— SEPARATELY, OF COURSE.
"USE YOUR INFLUENCE WITH LORD IESADA TO SWAY HER INTO NAMING LORD YOSHINOBU HER HEIR!"
"YOSHINOBU IS HEARTLESS."

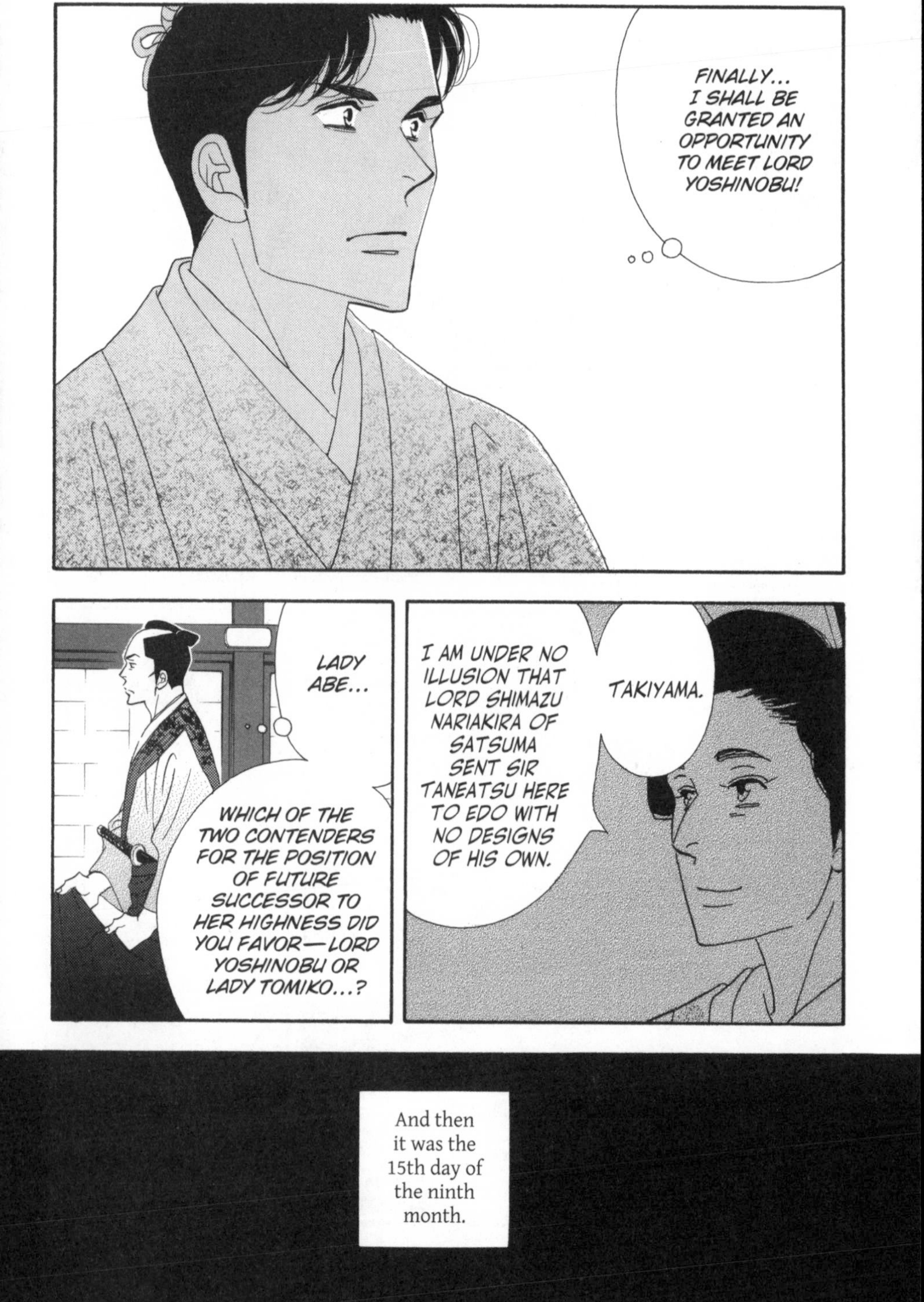
FINALLY... I SHALL BE GRANTED AN OPPORTUNITY TO MEET LORD YOSHINOBU!
TAKIYAMA.
I AM UNDER NO ILLUSION THAT LORD SHIMAZU NARIAKIRA OF SATSUMA SENT SIR TANEATSU HERE TO EDO WITH NO DESIGNS OF HIS OWN.
LADY ABE...
WHICH OF THE TWO CONTENDERS FOR THE POSITION OF FUTURE SUCCESSOR TO HER HIGHNESS DID YOU FAVOR—LORD YOSHINOBU OR LADY TOMIKO...?
And then it was the 15th day of the ninth month.

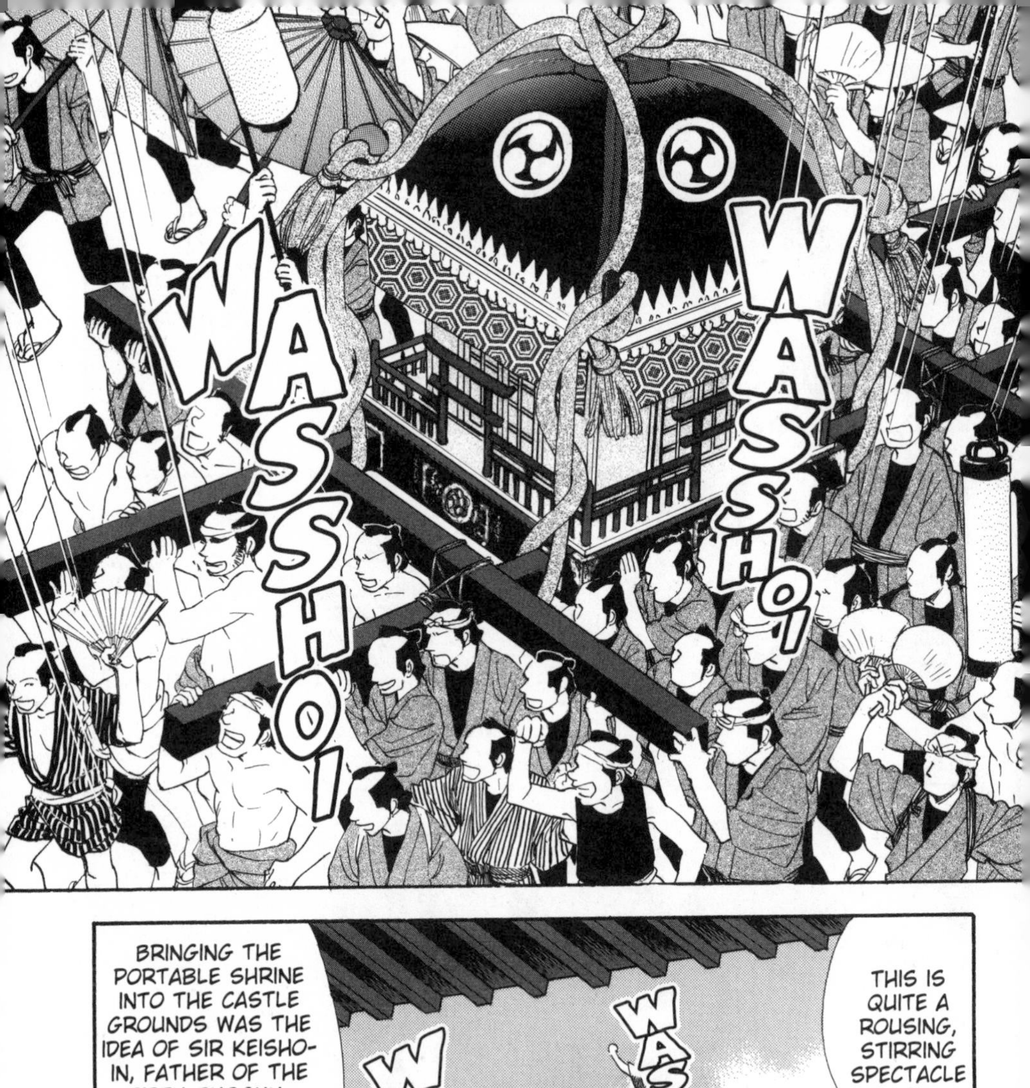
WASSHOI
WASSHOI

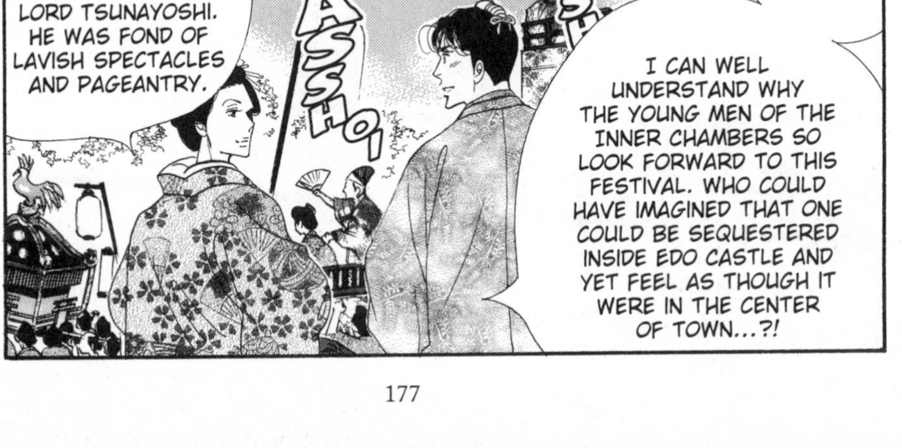
THIS IS QUITE A ROUSING, STIRRING SPECTACLE!
WASSH
WASSHOI
BRINGING THE PORTABLE SHRINE INTO THE CASTLE GROUNDS WAS THE IDEA OF SIR KEISHO-IN, FATHER OF THE FIFTH SHOGUN, LORD TSUNAYOSHI. HE WAS FOND OF LAVISH SPECTACLES AND PAGEANTRY.
I CAN WELL UNDERSTAND WHY THE YOUNG MEN OF THE INNER CHAMBERS SO LOOK FORWARD TO THIS FESTIVAL. WHO COULD HAVE IMAGINED THAT ONE COULD BE SEQUESTERED INSIDE EDO CASTLE AND YET FEEL AS THOUGH IT WERE IN THE CENTER OF TOWN...?!

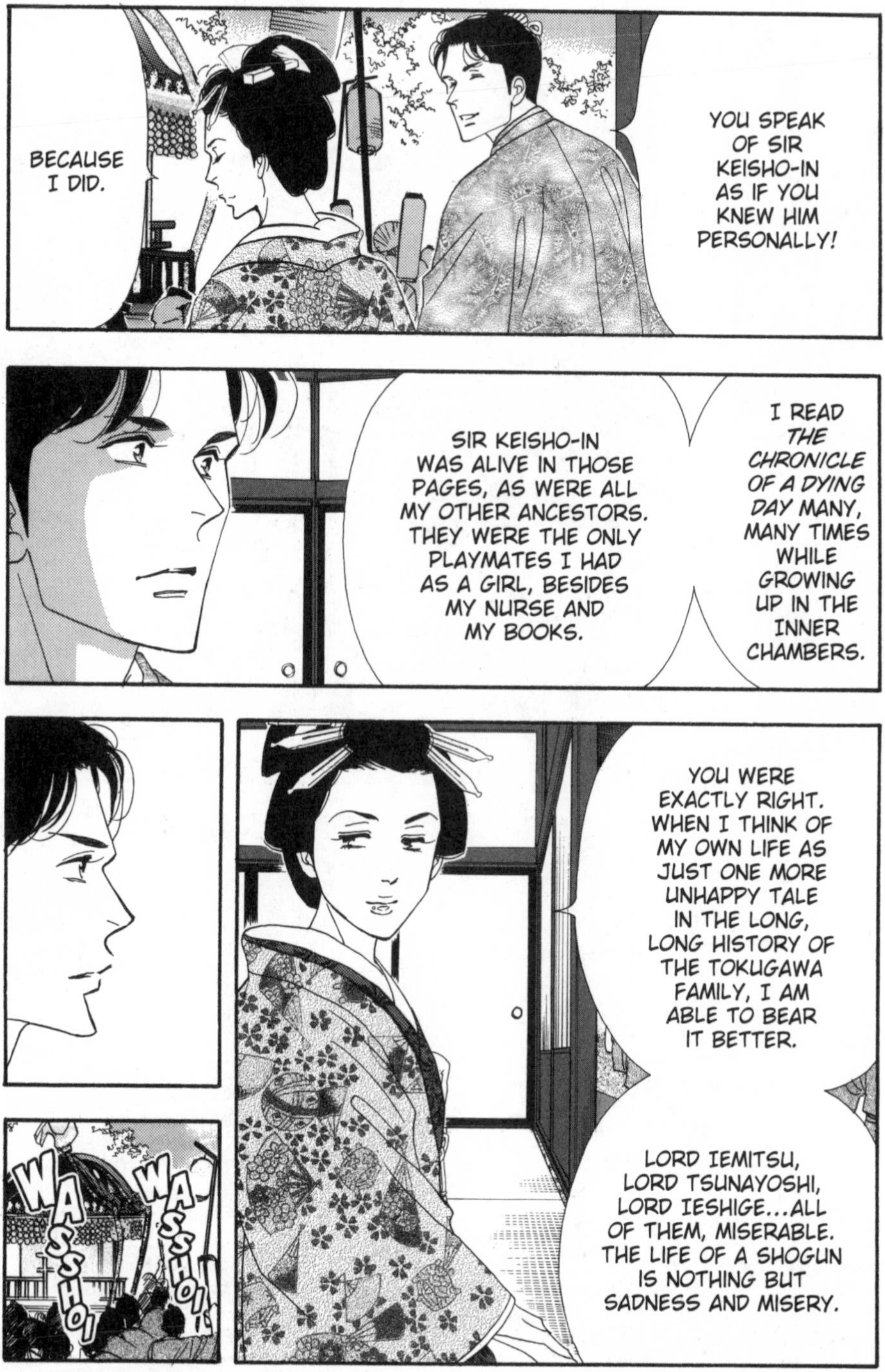
YOU SPEAK OF SIR KEISHO-IN AS IF YOU KNEW HIM PERSONALLY!
BECAUSE I DID.
I READ *THE CHRONICLE OF A DYING DAY* MANY, MANY TIMES WHILE GROWING UP IN THE INNER CHAMBERS.
SIR KEISHO-IN WAS ALIVE IN THOSE PAGES, AS WERE ALL MY OTHER ANCESTORS. THEY WERE THE ONLY PLAYMATES I HAD AS A GIRL, BESIDES MY NURSE AND MY BOOKS.
YOU WERE EXACTLY RIGHT. WHEN I THINK OF MY OWN LIFE AS JUST ONE MORE UNHAPPY TALE IN THE LONG, LONG HISTORY OF THE TOKUGAWA FAMILY, I AM ABLE TO BEAR IT BETTER.
LORD IEMITSU, LORD TSUNAYOSHI, LORD IESHIGE...ALL OF THEM, MISERABLE. THE LIFE OF A SHOGUN IS NOTHING BUT SADNESS AND MISERY.
WASSHOI
WASSHOI

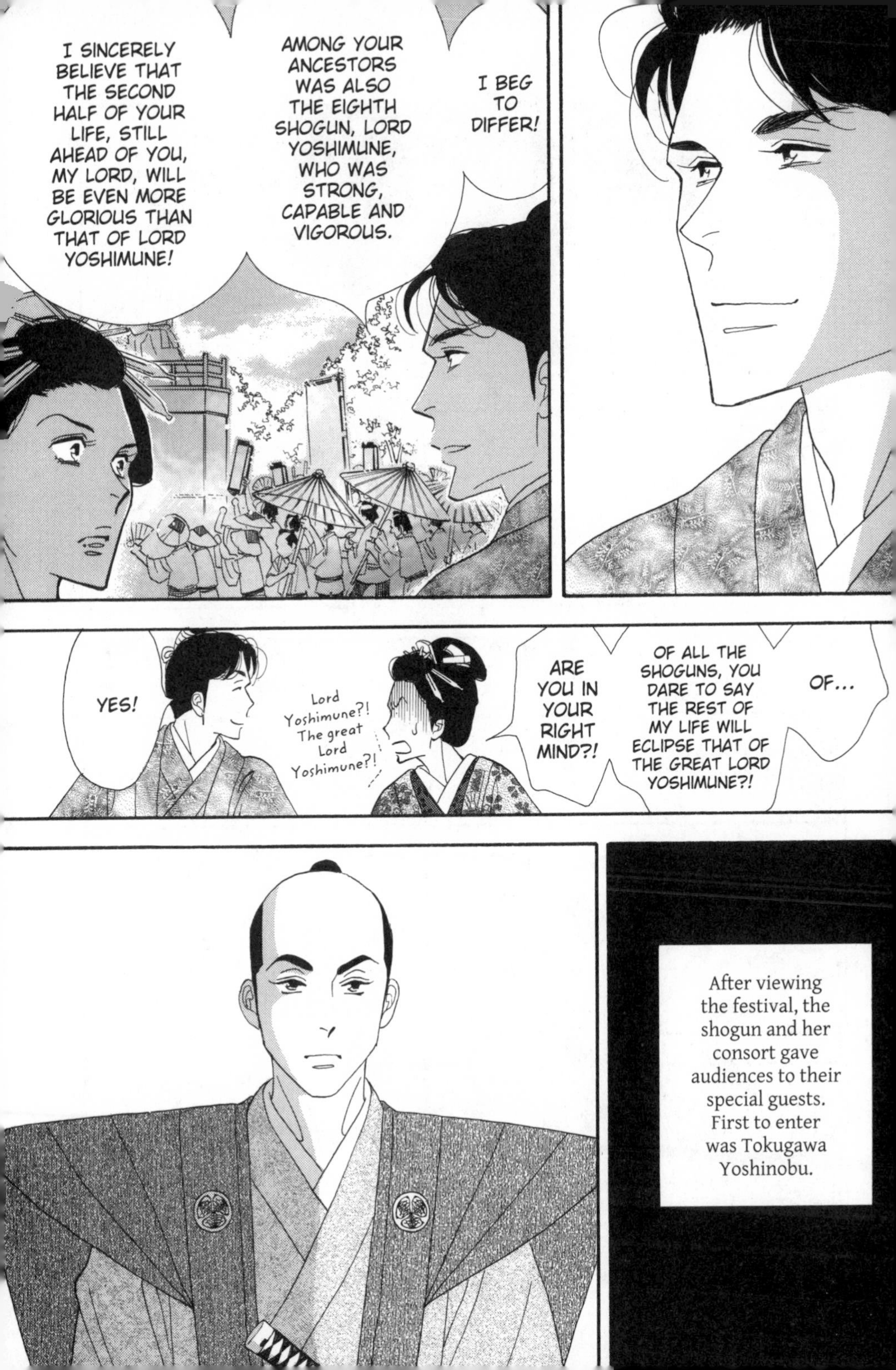
I BEG TO DIFFER!
AMONG YOUR ANCESTORS WAS ALSO THE EIGHTH SHOGUN, LORD YOSHIMUNE, WHO WAS STRONG, CAPABLE AND VIGOROUS.
I SINCERELY BELIEVE THAT THE SECOND HALF OF YOUR LIFE, STILL AHEAD OF YOU, MY LORD, WILL BE EVEN MORE GLORIOUS THAN THAT OF LORD YOSHIMUNE!
OF...
OF ALL THE SHOGUNS, YOU DARE TO SAY THE REST OF MY LIFE WILL ECLIPSE THAT OF THE GREAT LORD YOSHIMUNE?!
ARE YOU IN YOUR RIGHT MIND?!
Lord Yoshimune?! The great Lord Yoshimune?!
YES!
After viewing the festival, the shogun and her consort gave audiences to their special guests. First to enter was Tokugawa Yoshinobu.

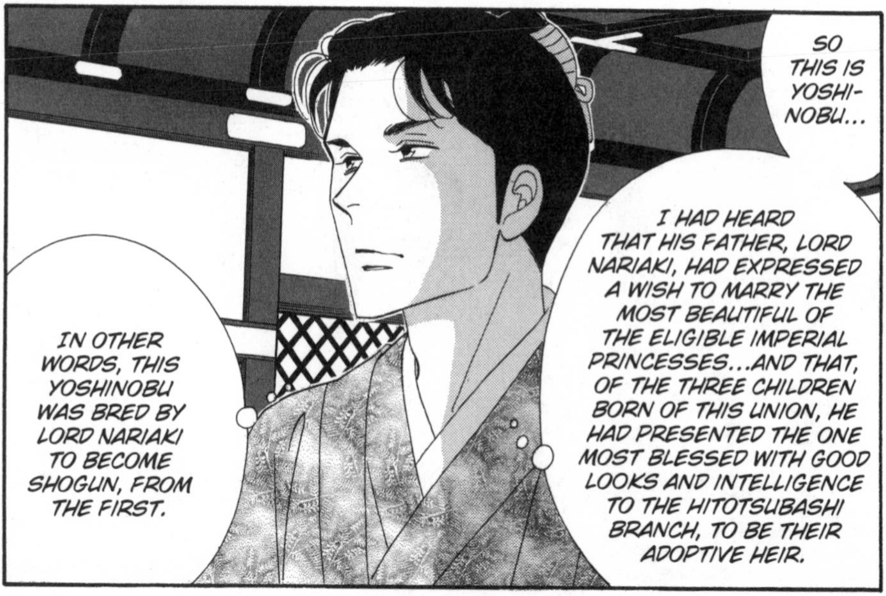
SO THIS IS YOSHI-NOBU...
I HAD HEARD THAT HIS FATHER, LORD NARIAKI, HAD EXPRESSED A WISH TO MARRY THE MOST BEAUTIFUL OF THE ELIGIBLE IMPERIAL PRINCESSES...AND THAT, OF THE THREE CHILDREN BORN OF THIS UNION, HE HAD PRESENTED THE ONE MOST BLESSED WITH GOOD LOOKS AND INTELLIGENCE TO THE HITOTSUBASHI BRANCH, TO BE THEIR ADOPTIVE HEIR.
IN OTHER WORDS, THIS YOSHINOBU WAS BRED BY LORD NARIAKI TO BECOME SHOGUN, FROM THE FIRST.

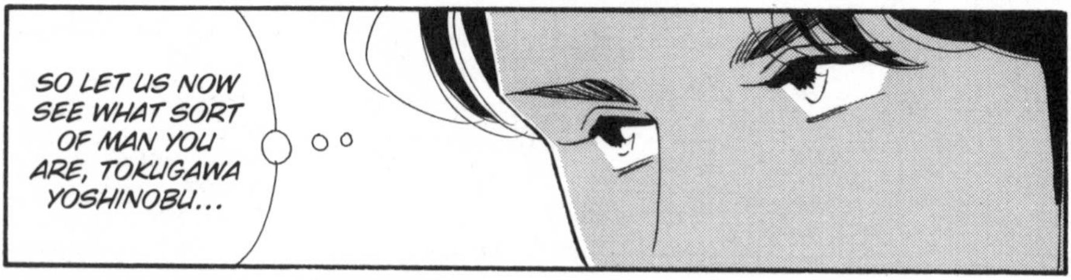
SO LET US NOW SEE WHAT SORT OF MAN YOU ARE, TOKUGAWA YOSHINOBU...

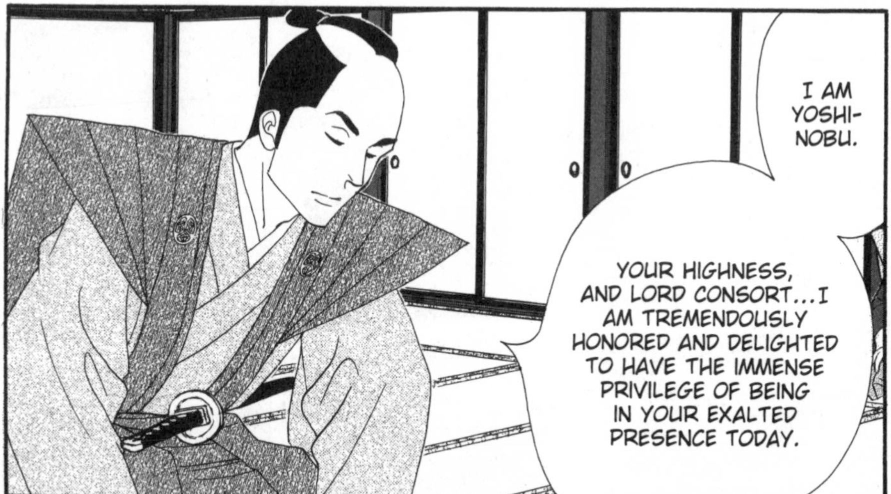
I AM YOSHI-NOBU.
YOUR HIGHNESS, AND LORD CONSORT...I AM TREMENDOUSLY HONORED AND DELIGHTED TO HAVE THE IMMENSE PRIVILEGE OF BEING IN YOUR EXALTED PRESENCE TODAY.

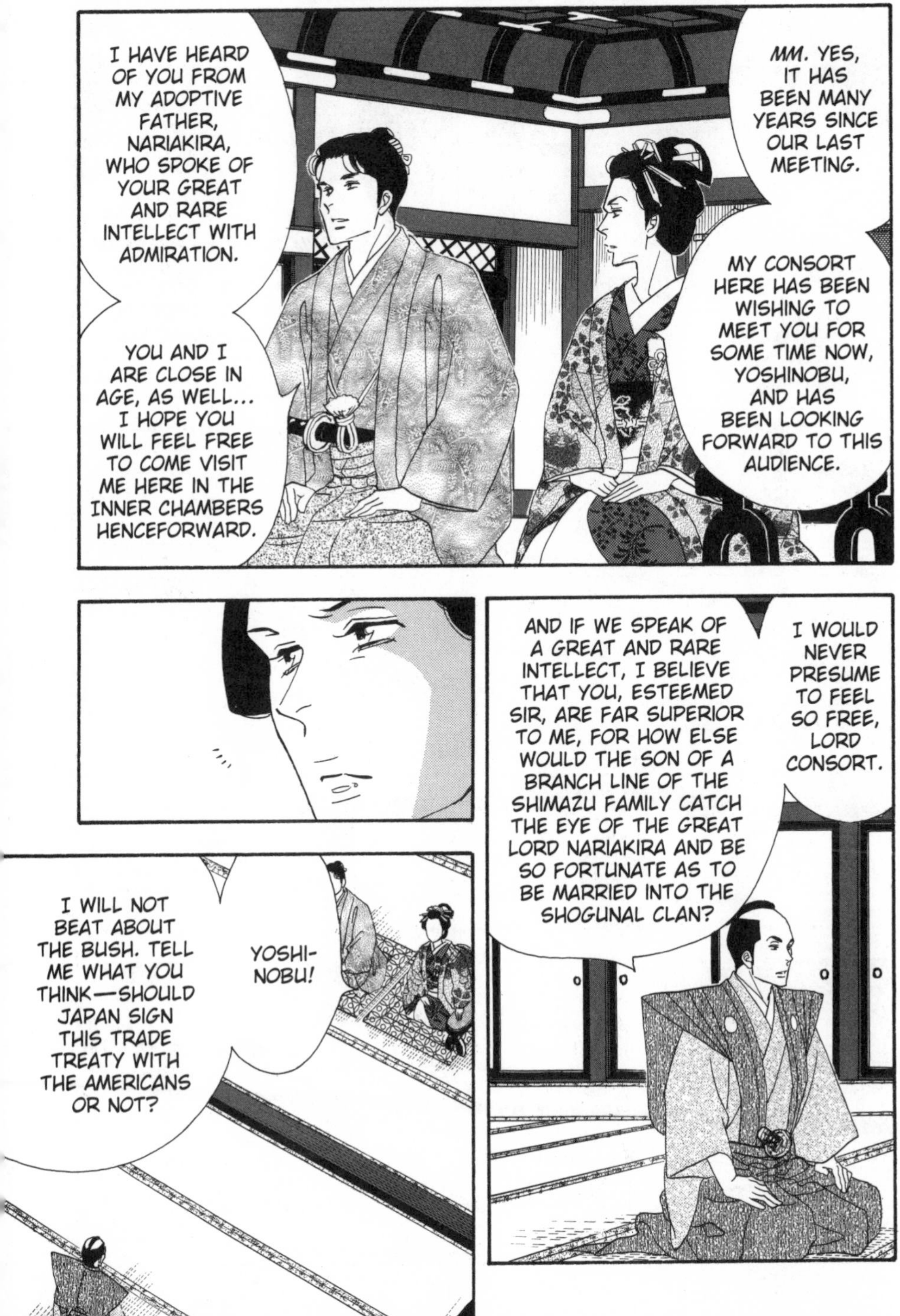
MM. YES, IT HAS BEEN MANY YEARS SINCE OUR LAST MEETING.
MY CONSORT HERE HAS BEEN WISHING TO MEET YOU FOR SOME TIME NOW, YOSHINOBU, AND HAS BEEN LOOKING FORWARD TO THIS AUDIENCE.
I HAVE HEARD OF YOU FROM MY ADOPTIVE FATHER, NARIAKIRA, WHO SPOKE OF YOUR GREAT AND RARE INTELLECT WITH ADMIRATION.
YOU AND I ARE CLOSE IN AGE, AS WELL... I HOPE YOU WILL FEEL FREE TO COME VISIT ME HERE IN THE INNER CHAMBERS HENCEFORWARD.
I WOULD NEVER PRESUME TO FEEL SO FREE, LORD CONSORT.
AND IF WE SPEAK OF A GREAT AND RARE INTELLECT, I BELIEVE THAT YOU, ESTEEMED SIR, ARE FAR SUPERIOR TO ME, FOR HOW ELSE WOULD THE SON OF A BRANCH LINE OF THE SHIMAZU FAMILY CATCH THE EYE OF THE GREAT LORD NARIAKIRA AND BE SO FORTUNATE AS TO BE MARRIED INTO THE SHOGUNAL CLAN?
YOSHI-NOBU!
I WILL NOT BEAT ABOUT THE BUSH. TELL ME WHAT YOU THINK—SHOULD JAPAN SIGN THIS TRADE TREATY WITH THE AMERICANS OR NOT?

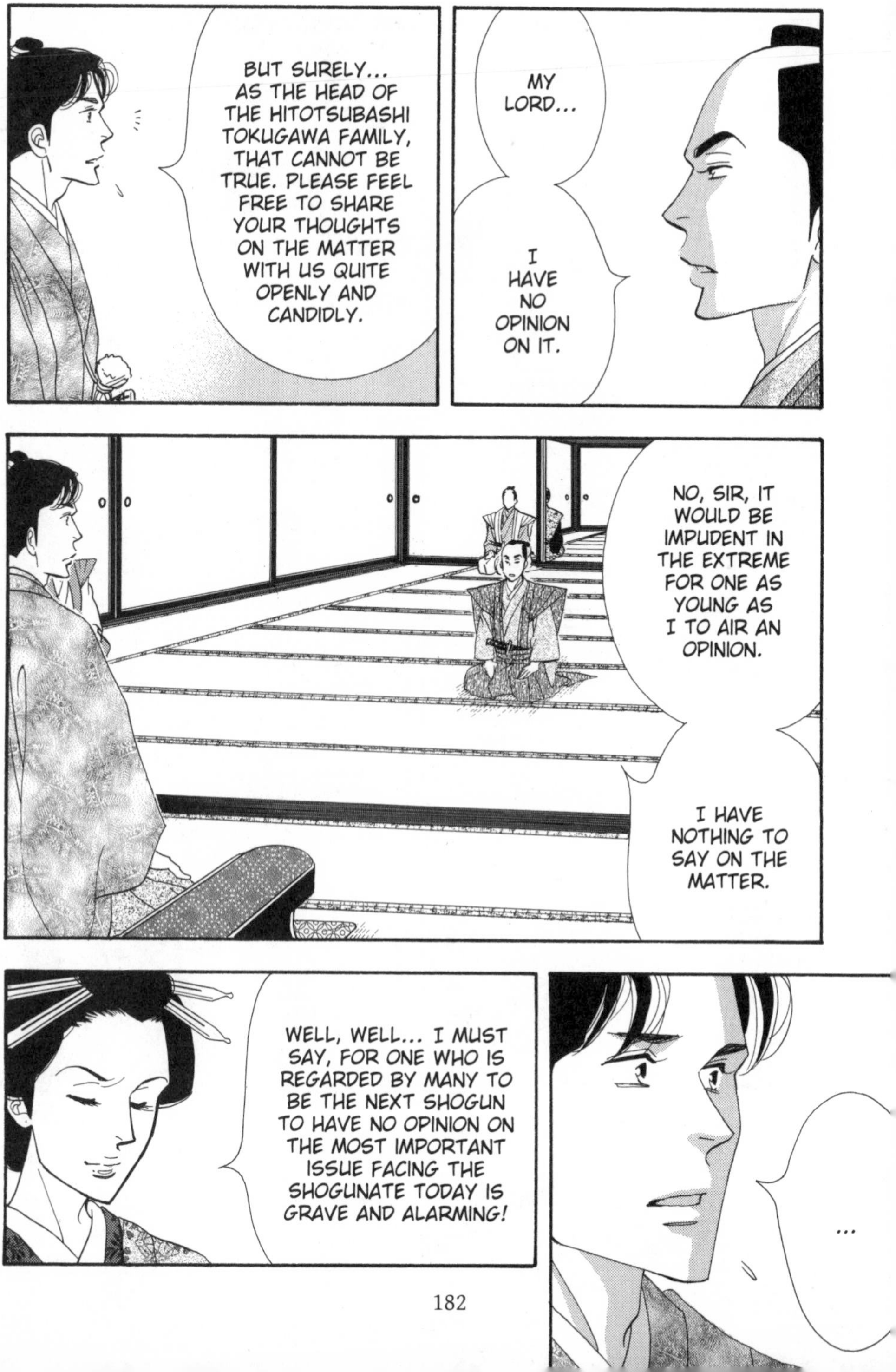
MY LORD...
I HAVE NO OPINION ON IT.
BUT SURELY... AS THE HEAD OF THE HITOTSUBASHI TOKUGAWA FAMILY, THAT CANNOT BE TRUE. PLEASE FEEL FREE TO SHARE YOUR THOUGHTS ON THE MATTER WITH US QUITE OPENLY AND CANDIDLY.
NO, SIR, IT WOULD BE IMPUDENT IN THE EXTREME FOR ONE AS YOUNG AS I TO AIR AN OPINION.
I HAVE NOTHING TO SAY ON THE MATTER.
...
WELL, WELL... I MUST SAY, FOR ONE WHO IS REGARDED BY MANY TO BE THE NEXT SHOGUN TO HAVE NO OPINION ON THE MOST IMPORTANT ISSUE FACING THE SHOGUNATE TODAY IS GRAVE AND ALARMING!

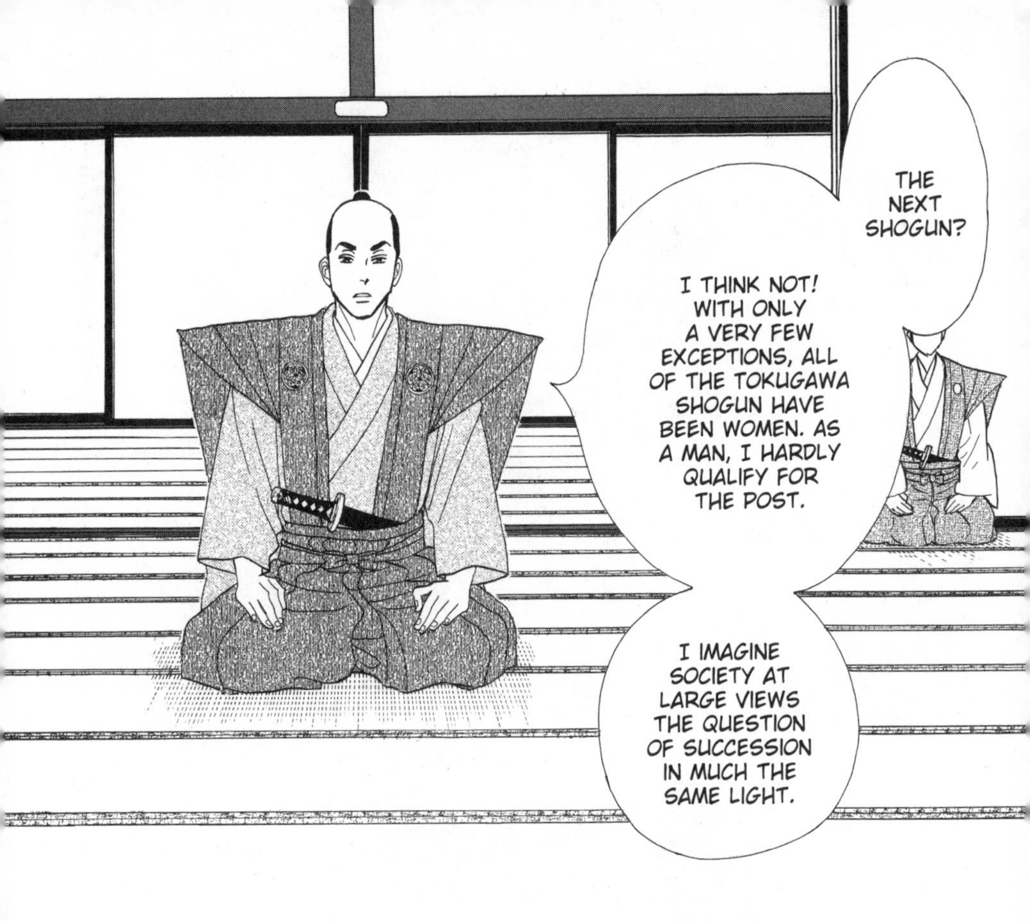
THE NEXT SHOGUN?
I THINK NOT! WITH ONLY A VERY FEW EXCEPTIONS, ALL OF THE TOKUGAWA SHOGUN HAVE BEEN WOMEN. AS A MAN, I HARDLY QUALIFY FOR THE POST.
I IMAGINE SOCIETY AT LARGE VIEWS THE QUESTION OF SUCCESSION IN MUCH THE SAME LIGHT.

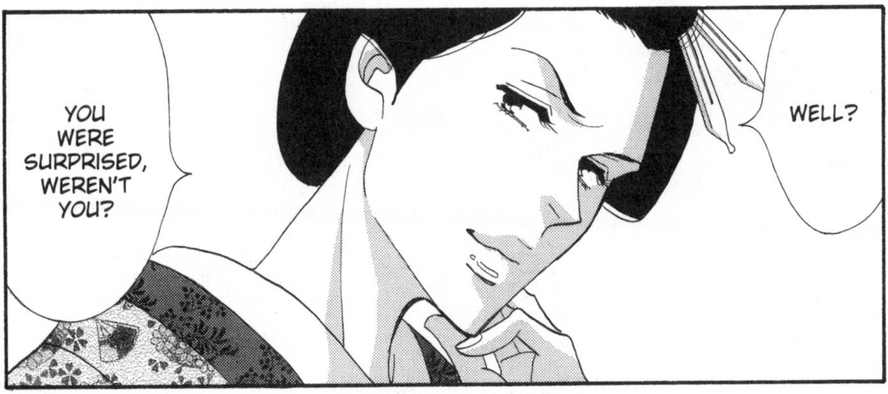
WELL?
YOU WERE SURPRISED, WEREN'T YOU?

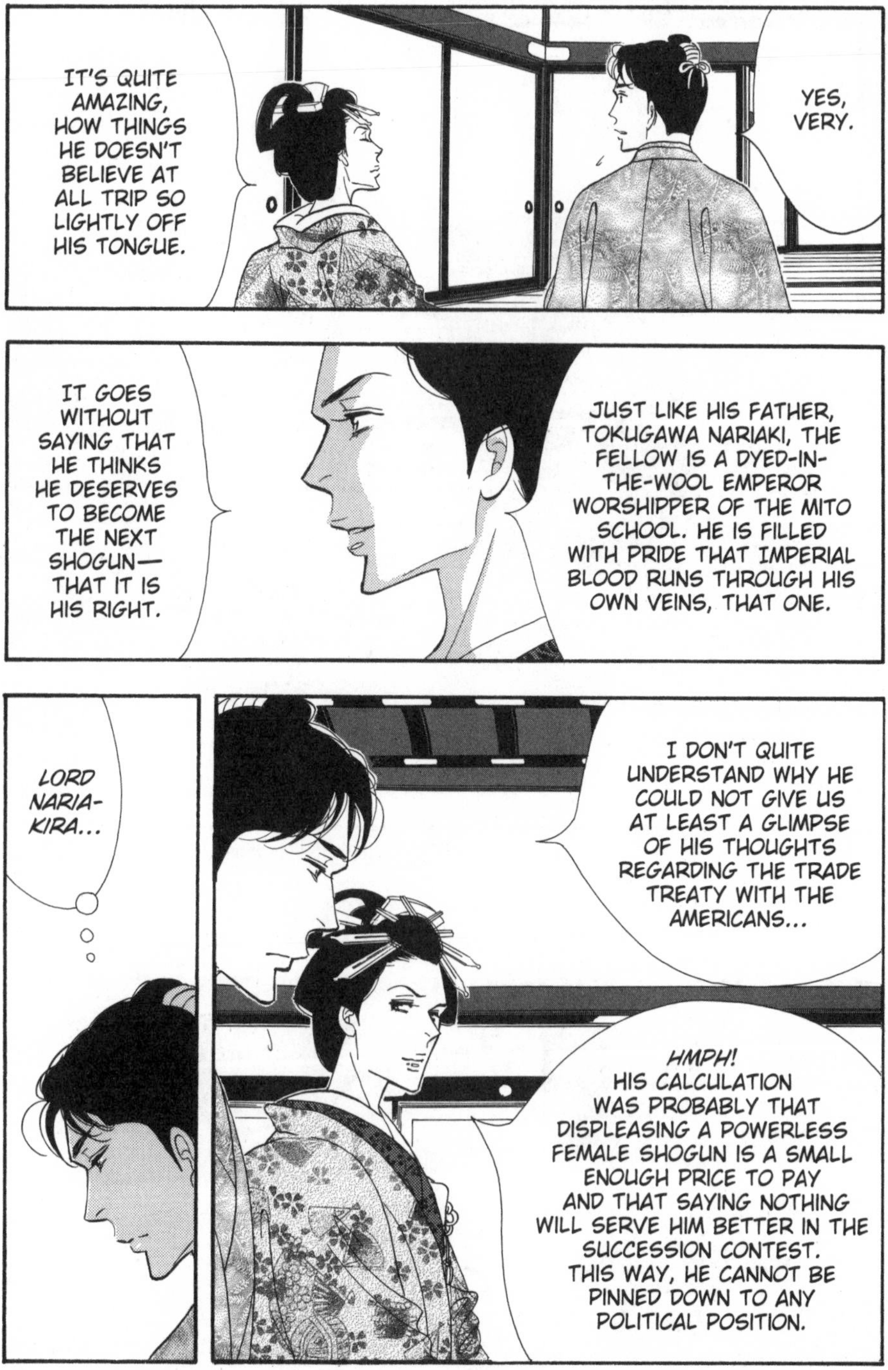
IT'S QUITE AMAZING, HOW THINGS HE DOESN'T BELIEVE AT ALL TRIP SO LIGHTLY OFF HIS TONGUE.
YES, VERY.
JUST LIKE HIS FATHER, TOKUGAWA NARIAKI, THE FELLOW IS A DYED-IN-THE-WOOL EMPEROR WORSHIPPER OF THE MITO SCHOOL. HE IS FILLED WITH PRIDE THAT IMPERIAL BLOOD RUNS THROUGH HIS OWN VEINS, THAT ONE.
IT GOES WITHOUT SAYING THAT HE THINKS HE DESERVES TO BECOME THE NEXT SHOGUN—THAT IT IS HIS RIGHT.
I DON'T QUITE UNDERSTAND WHY HE COULD NOT GIVE US AT LEAST A GLIMPSE OF HIS THOUGHTS REGARDING THE TRADE TREATY WITH THE AMERICANS...
HMPH! HIS CALCULATION WAS PROBABLY THAT DISPLEASING A POWERLESS FEMALE SHOGUN IS A SMALL ENOUGH PRICE TO PAY AND THAT SAYING NOTHING WILL SERVE HIM BETTER IN THE SUCCESSION CONTEST. THIS WAY, HE CANNOT BE PINNED DOWN TO ANY POLITICAL POSITION.
LORD NARIA-KIRA...

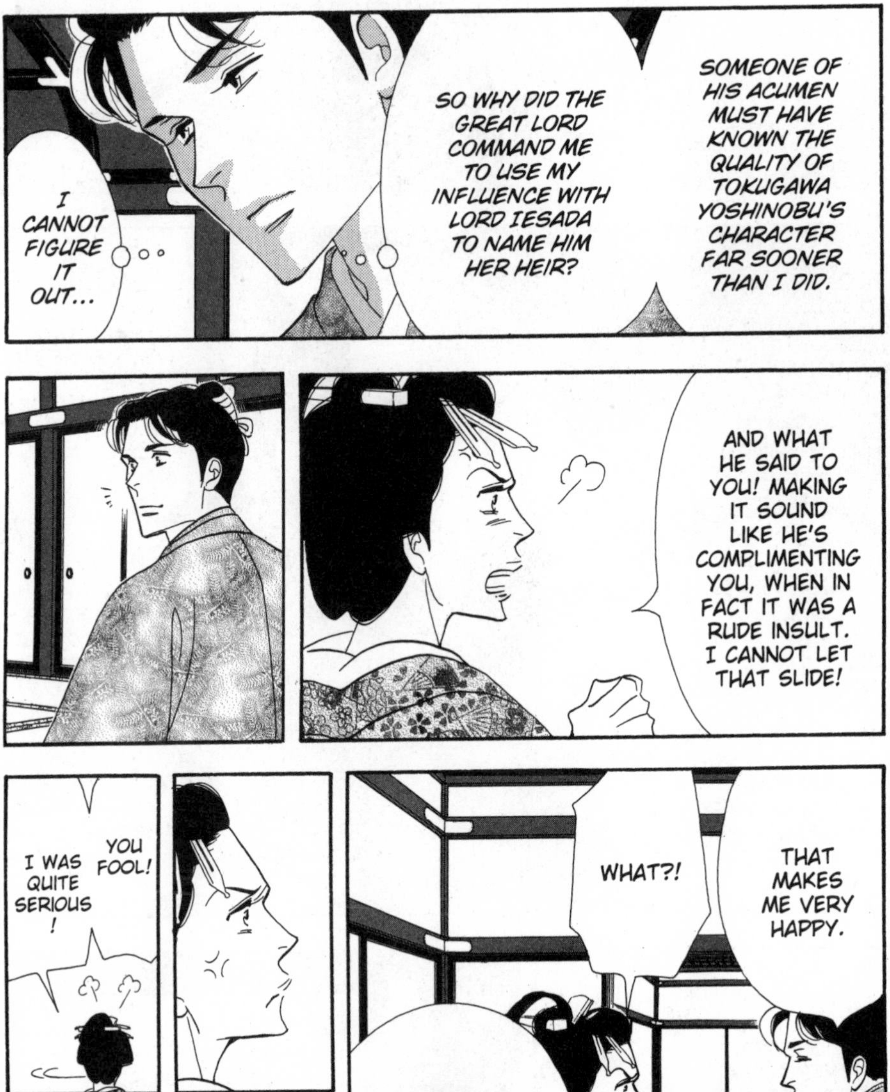
SOMEONE OF HIS ACUMEN MUST HAVE KNOWN THE QUALITY OF TOKUGAWA YOSHINOBU'S CHARACTER FAR SOONER THAN I DID.
SO WHY DID THE GREAT LORD COMMAND ME TO USE MY INFLUENCE WITH LORD IESADA TO NAME HIM HER HEIR?
I CANNOT FIGURE IT OUT...
AND WHAT HE SAID TO YOU! MAKING IT SOUND LIKE HE'S COMPLIMENTING YOU, WHEN IN FACT IT WAS A RUDE INSULT. I CANNOT LET THAT SLIDE!
THAT MAKES ME VERY HAPPY.
WHAT?!
YOU ARE SO ANGERED ON MY BEHALF. AN INSULT TO ME HAS YOU FUMING! HOW COULD I NOT BE DELIGHTED BY THAT?
YOU FOOL!
I WAS QUITE SERIOUS!

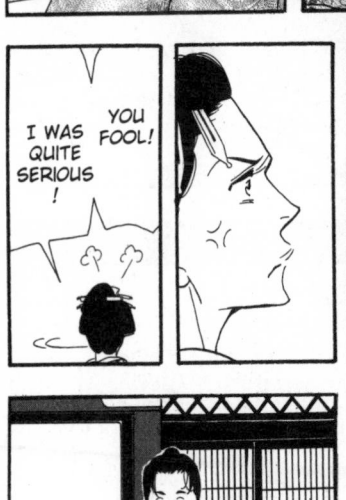

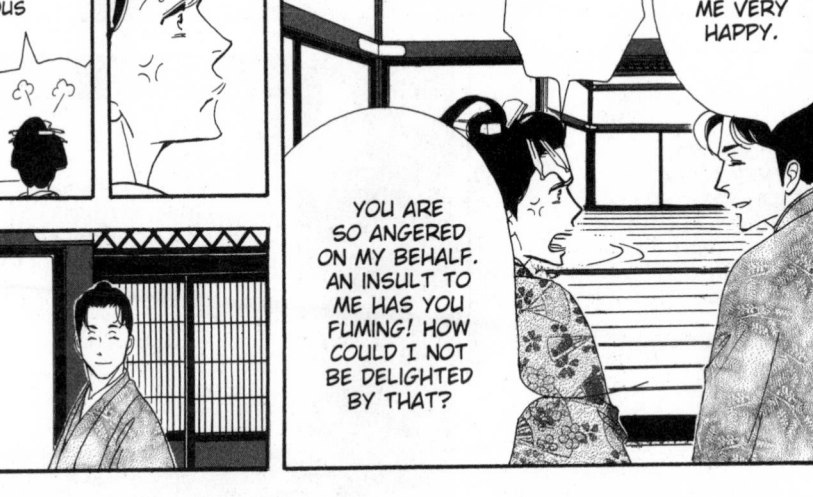

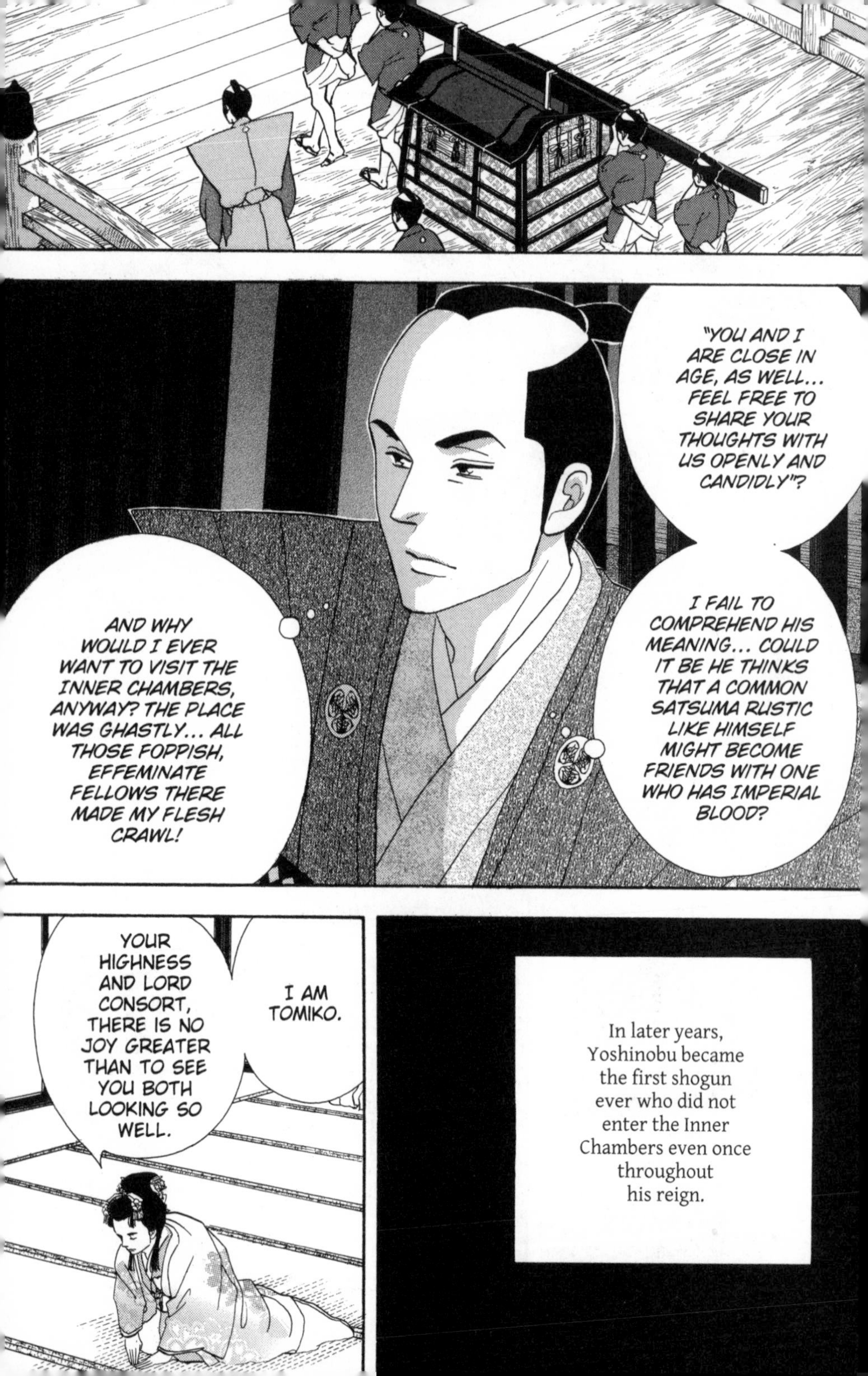
"YOU AND I ARE CLOSE IN AGE, AS WELL... FEEL FREE TO SHARE YOUR THOUGHTS WITH US OPENLY AND CANDIDLY"?
I FAIL TO COMPREHEND HIS MEANING... COULD IT BE HE THINKS THAT A COMMON SATSUMA RUSTIC LIKE HIMSELF MIGHT BECOME FRIENDS WITH ONE WHO HAS IMPERIAL BLOOD?
AND WHY WOULD I EVER WANT TO VISIT THE INNER CHAMBERS, ANYWAY? THE PLACE WAS GHASTLY... ALL THOSE FOPPISH, EFFEMINATE FELLOWS THERE MADE MY FLESH CRAWL!
In later years, Yoshinobu became the first shogun ever who did not enter the Inner Chambers even once throughout his reign.
I AM TOMIKO.
YOUR HIGHNESS AND LORD CONSORT, THERE IS NO JOY GREATER THAN TO SEE YOU BOTH LOOKING SO WELL.

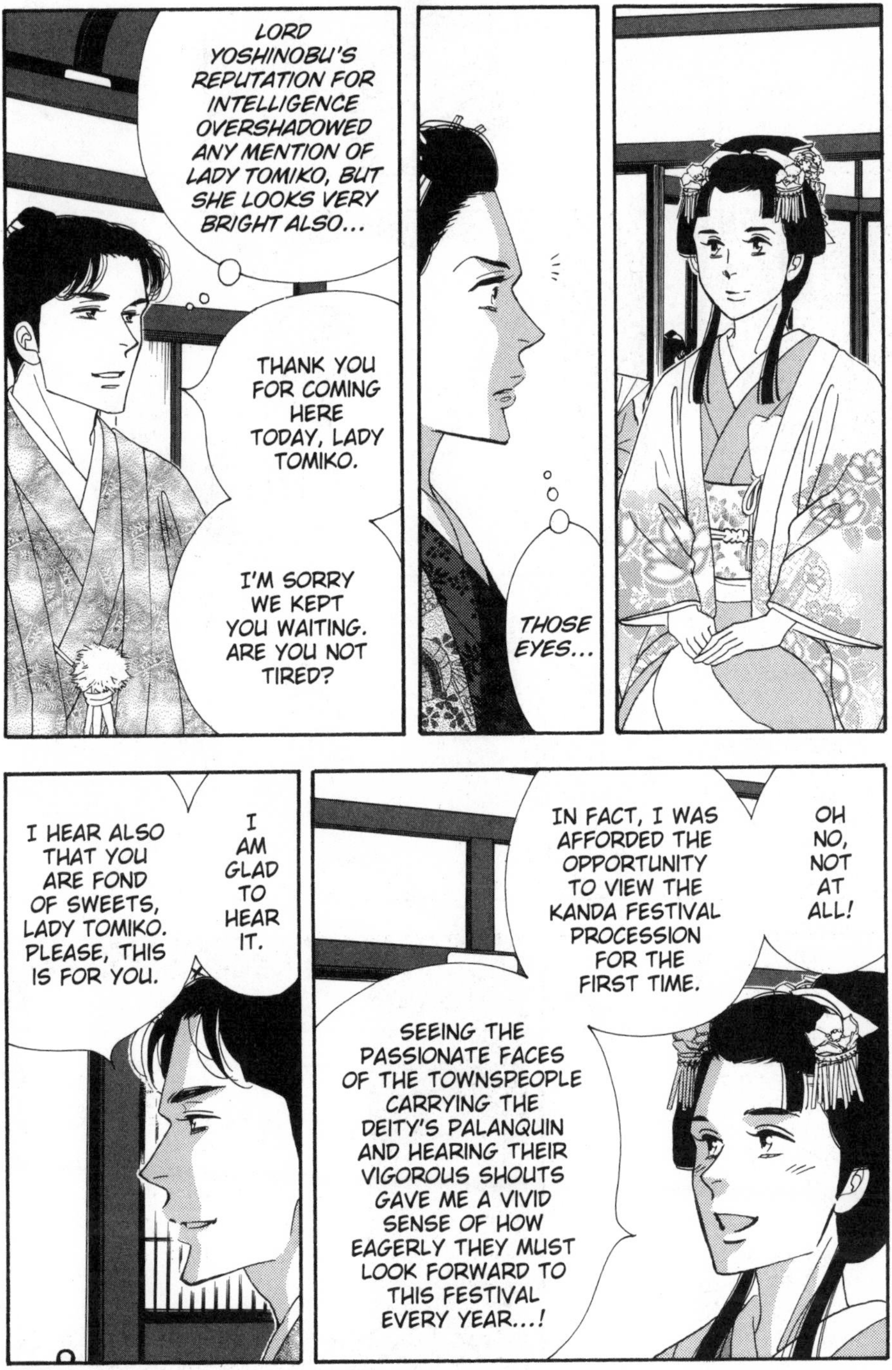
THOSE EYES...
LORD YOSHINOBU'S REPUTATION FOR INTELLIGENCE OVERSHADOWED ANY MENTION OF LADY TOMIKO, BUT SHE LOOKS VERY BRIGHT ALSO...
THANK YOU FOR COMING HERE TODAY, LADY TOMIKO.
I'M SORRY WE KEPT YOU WAITING. ARE YOU NOT TIRED?
OH NO, NOT AT ALL!
IN FACT, I WAS AFFORDED THE OPPORTUNITY TO VIEW THE KANDA FESTIVAL PROCESSION FOR THE FIRST TIME.
SEEING THE PASSIONATE FACES OF THE TOWNSPEOPLE CARRYING THE DEITY'S PALANQUIN AND HEARING THEIR VIGOROUS SHOUTS GAVE ME A VIVID SENSE OF HOW EAGERLY THEY MUST LOOK FORWARD TO THIS FESTIVAL EVERY YEAR...!
I AM GLAD TO HEAR IT.
I HEAR ALSO THAT YOU ARE FOND OF SWEETS, LADY TOMIKO. PLEASE, THIS IS FOR YOU.

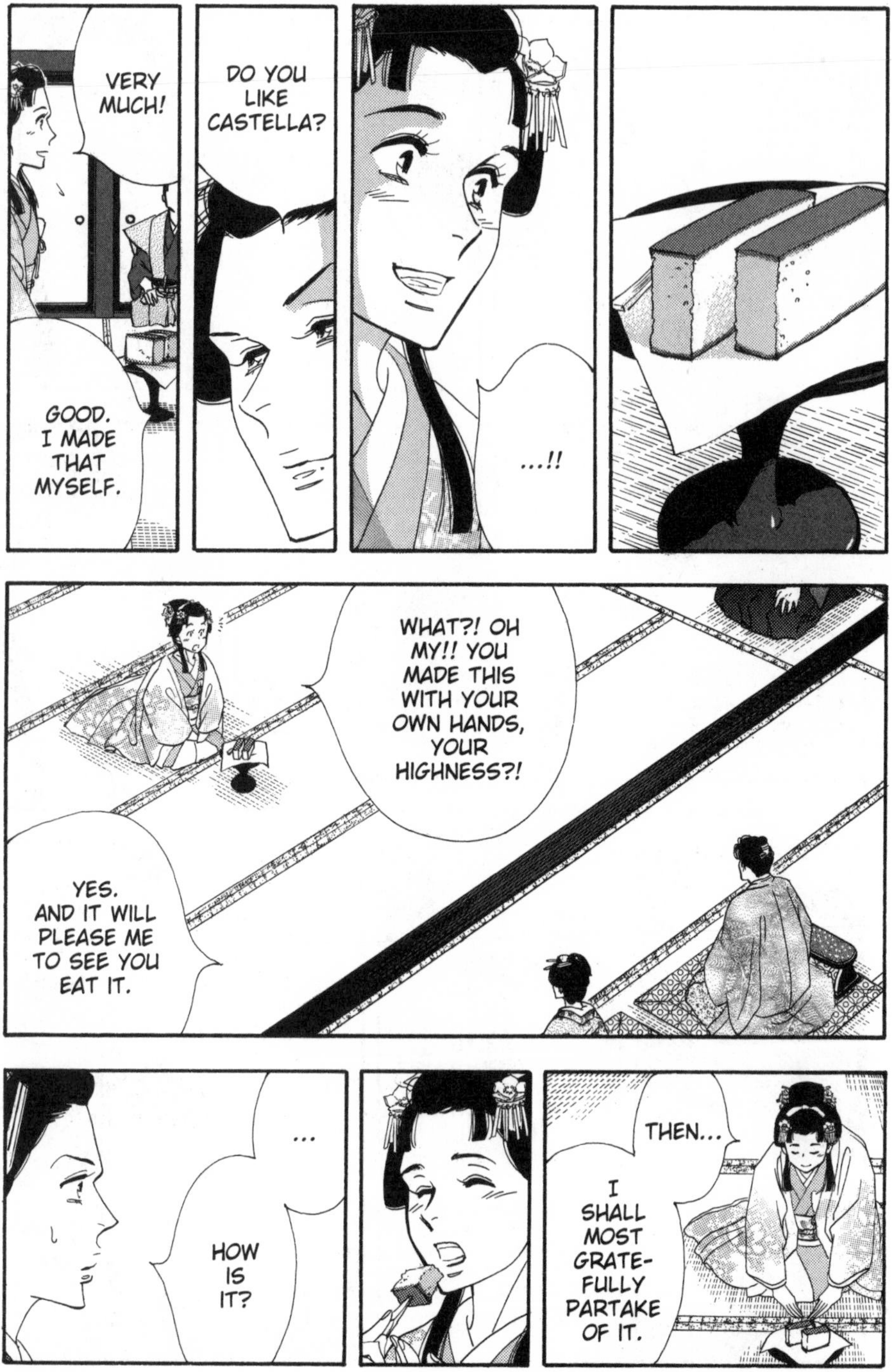

...!!
DO YOU LIKE CASTELLA?
VERY MUCH!
GOOD. I MADE THAT MYSELF.
WHAT?! OH MY!! YOU MADE THIS WITH YOUR OWN HANDS, YOUR HIGHNESS?!
YES. AND IT WILL PLEASE ME TO SEE YOU EAT IT.
THEN...
I SHALL MOST GRATE-FULLY PARTAKE OF IT.
HOW IS IT?
...

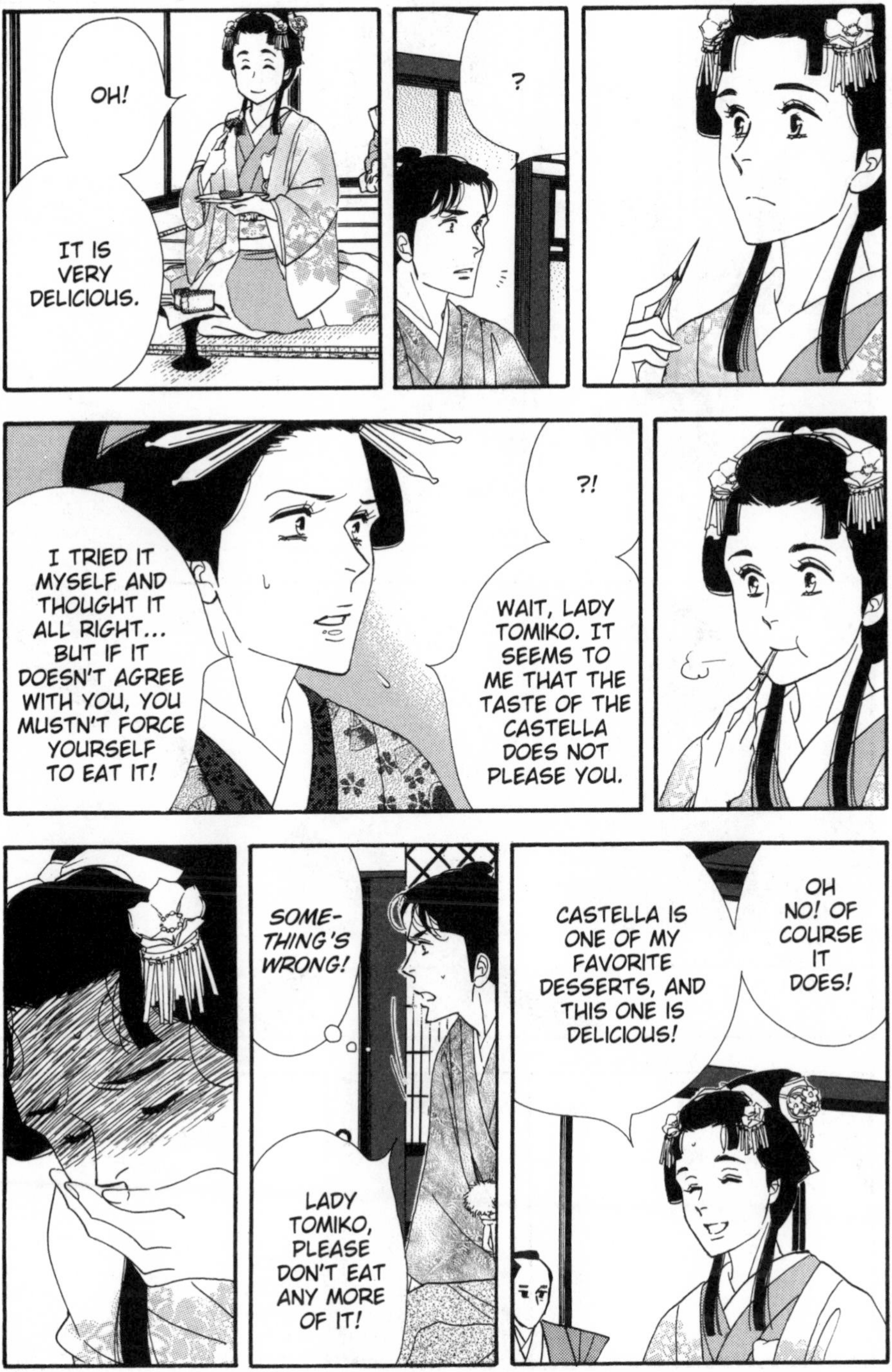
?
OH!
IT IS VERY DELICIOUS.
?!
WAIT, LADY TOMIKO. IT SEEMS TO ME THAT THE TASTE OF THE CASTELLA DOES NOT PLEASE YOU.
I TRIED IT MYSELF AND THOUGHT IT ALL RIGHT... BUT IF IT DOESN'T AGREE WITH YOU, YOU MUSTN'T FORCE YOURSELF TO EAT IT!
OH NO! OF COURSE IT DOES!
CASTELLA IS ONE OF MY FAVORITE DESSERTS, AND THIS ONE IS DELICIOUS!
SOME-THING'S WRONG!
LADY TOMIKO, PLEASE DON'T EAT ANY MORE OF IT!

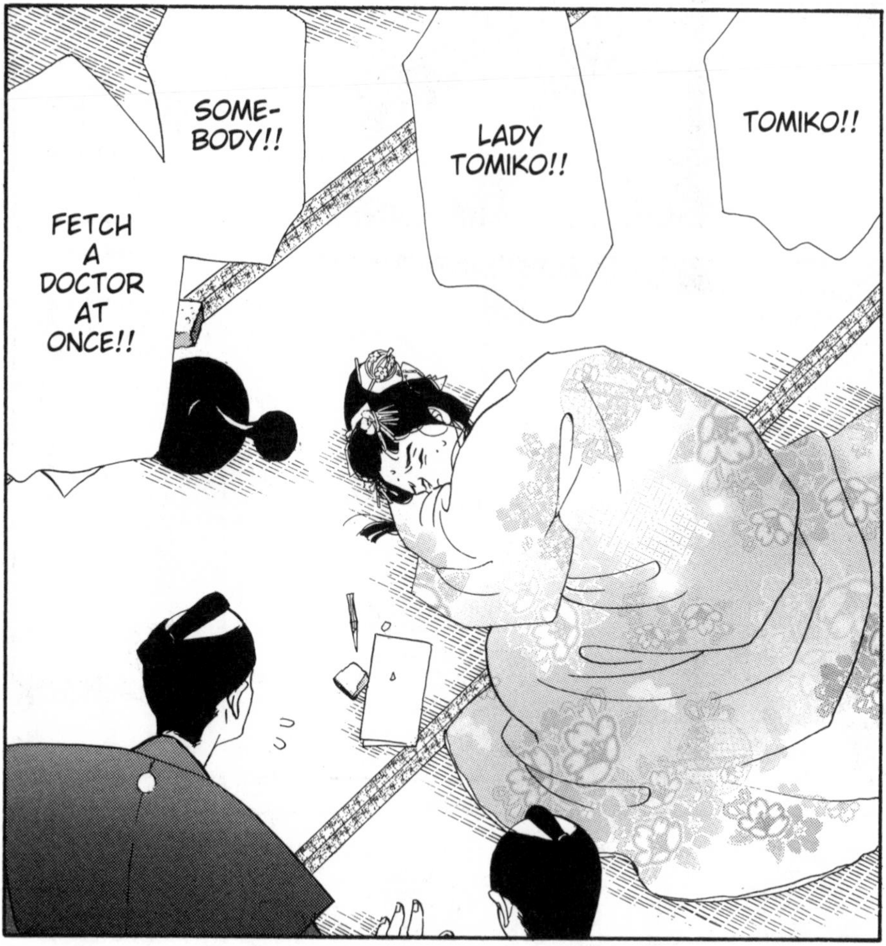
TOMIKO!!
LADY TOMIKO!!
SOME-BODY!!
FETCH A DOCTOR AT ONCE!!

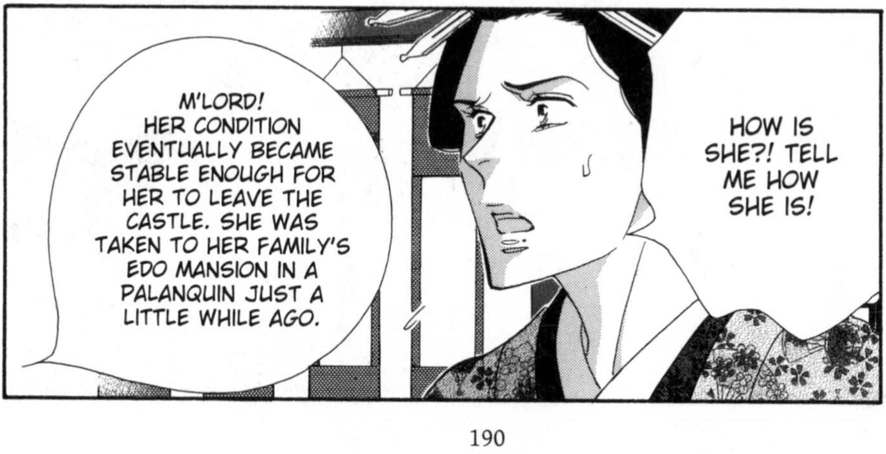
HOW IS SHE?! TELL ME HOW SHE IS!
M'LORD! HER CONDITION EVENTUALLY BECAME STABLE ENOUGH FOR HER TO LEAVE THE CASTLE. SHE WAS TAKEN TO HER FAMILY'S EDO MANSION IN A PALANQUIN JUST A LITTLE WHILE AGO.

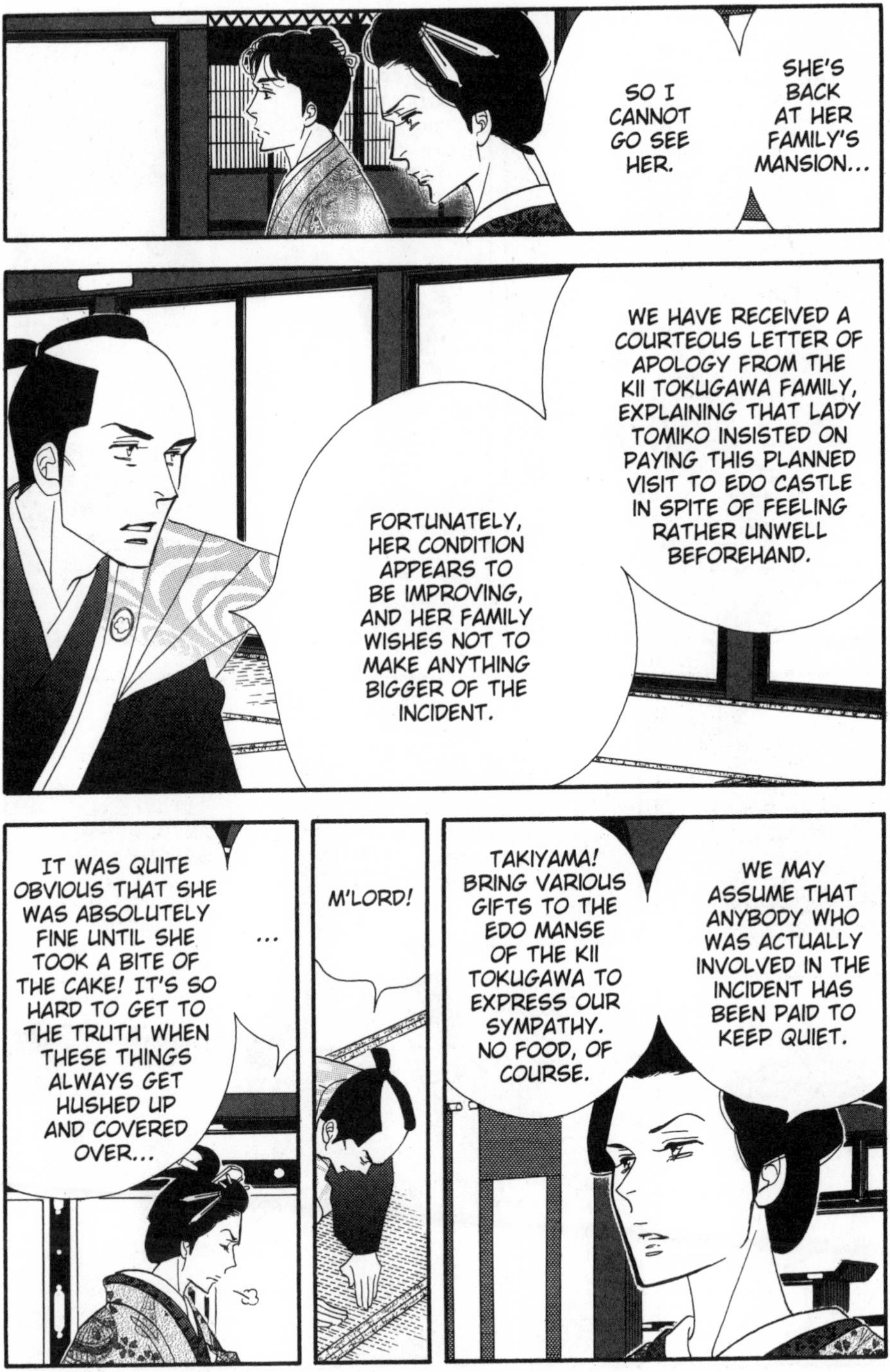
SHE'S BACK AT HER FAMILY'S MANSION...
SO I CANNOT GO SEE HER.
WE HAVE RECEIVED A COURTEOUS LETTER OF APOLOGY FROM THE KII TOKUGAWA FAMILY, EXPLAINING THAT LADY TOMIKO INSISTED ON PAYING THIS PLANNED VISIT TO EDO CASTLE IN SPITE OF FEELING RATHER UNWELL BEFOREHAND.
FORTUNATELY, HER CONDITION APPEARS TO BE IMPROVING, AND HER FAMILY WISHES NOT TO MAKE ANYTHING BIGGER OF THE INCIDENT.
WE MAY ASSUME THAT ANYBODY WHO WAS ACTUALLY INVOLVED IN THE INCIDENT HAS BEEN PAID TO KEEP QUIET.
TAKIYAMA! BRING VARIOUS GIFTS TO THE EDO MANSE OF THE KII TOKUGAWA TO EXPRESS OUR SYMPATHY. NO FOOD, OF COURSE.
M'LORD!
...
IT WAS QUITE OBVIOUS THAT SHE WAS ABSOLUTELY FINE UNTIL SHE TOOK A BITE OF THE CAKE! IT'S SO HARD TO GET TO THE TRUTH WHEN THESE THINGS ALWAYS GET HUSHED UP AND COVERED OVER...

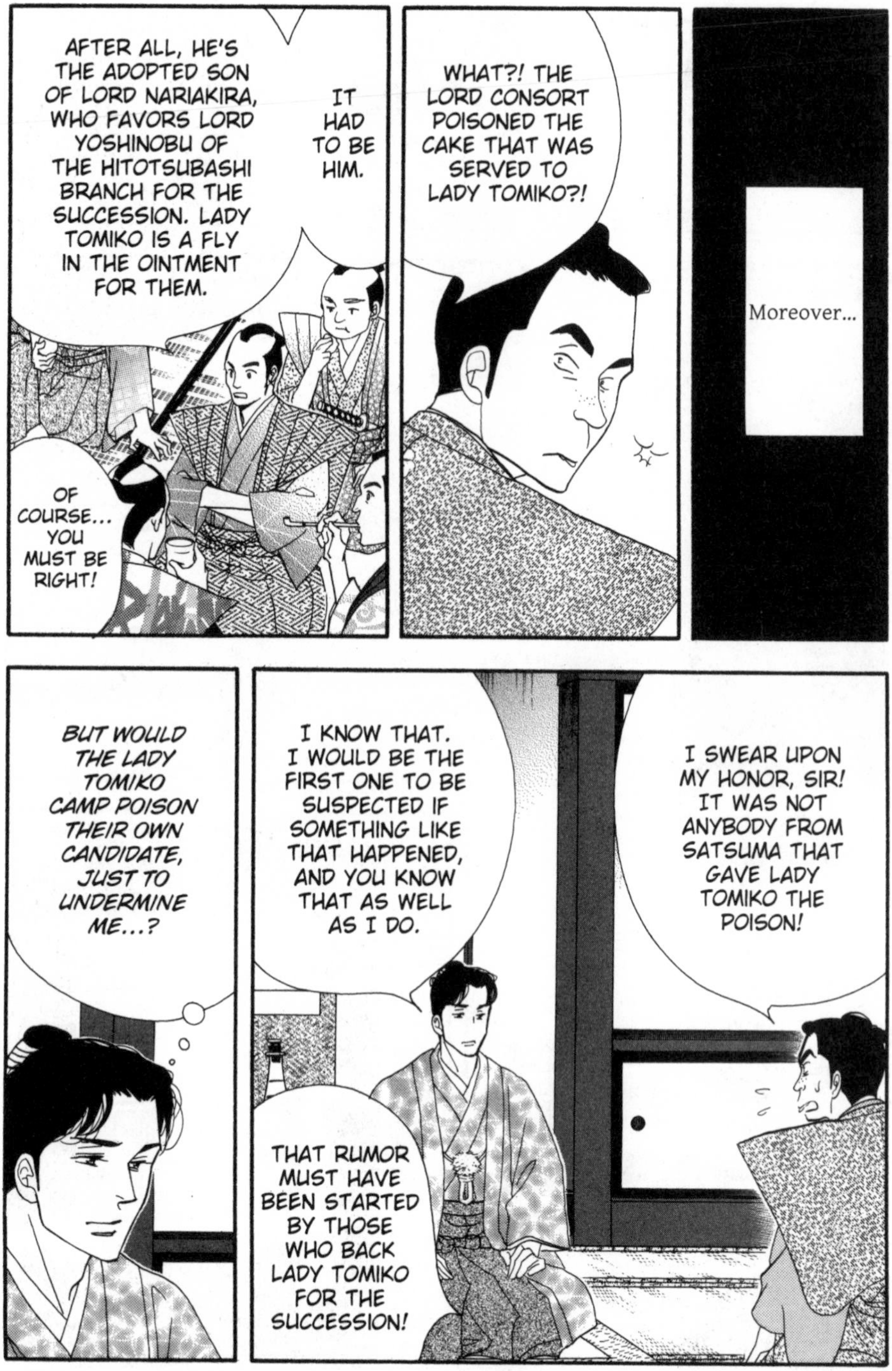
Moreover...
WHAT?! THE LORD CONSORT POISONED THE CAKE THAT WAS SERVED TO LADY TOMIKO?!
AFTER ALL, HE'S THE ADOPTED SON OF LORD NARIAKIRA, WHO FAVORS LORD YOSHINOBU OF THE HITOTSUBASHI BRANCH FOR THE SUCCESSION. LADY TOMIKO IS A FLY IN THE OINTMENT FOR THEM.
IT HAD TO BE HIM.
OF COURSE... YOU MUST BE RIGHT!
I SWEAR UPON MY HONOR, SIR! IT WAS NOT ANYBODY FROM SATSUMA THAT GAVE LADY TOMIKO THE POISON!
I KNOW THAT. I WOULD BE THE FIRST ONE TO BE SUSPECTED IF SOMETHING LIKE THAT HAPPENED, AND YOU KNOW THAT AS WELL AS I DO.
THAT RUMOR MUST HAVE BEEN STARTED BY THOSE WHO BACK LADY TOMIKO FOR THE SUCCESSION!
BUT WOULD THE LADY TOMIKO CAMP POISON THEIR OWN CANDIDATE, JUST TO UNDERMINE ME...?

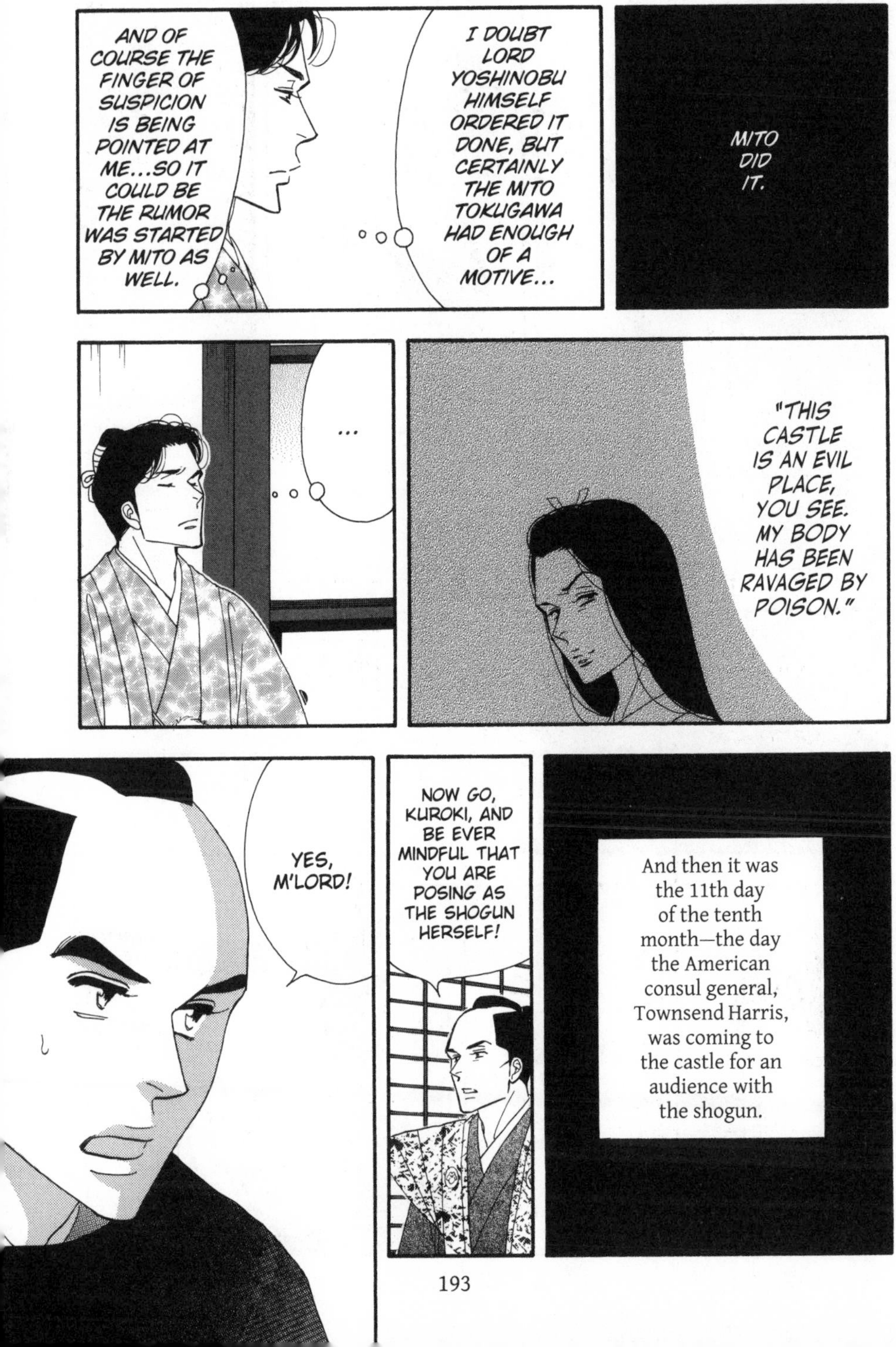
MITO DID IT.
I DOUBT LORD YOSHINOBU HIMSELF ORDERED IT DONE, BUT CERTAINLY THE MITO TOKUGAWA HAD ENOUGH OF A MOTIVE...
AND OF COURSE THE FINGER OF SUSPICION IS BEING POINTED AT ME...SO IT COULD BE THE RUMOR WAS STARTED BY MITO AS WELL.
"THIS CASTLE IS AN EVIL PLACE, YOU SEE. MY BODY HAS BEEN RAVAGED BY POISON."
...
And then it was the 11th day of the tenth month—the day the American consul general, Townsend Harris, was coming to the castle for an audience with the shogun.
NOW GO, KUROKI, AND BE EVER MINDFUL THAT YOU ARE POSING AS THE SHOGUN HERSELF!
YES, M'LORD!

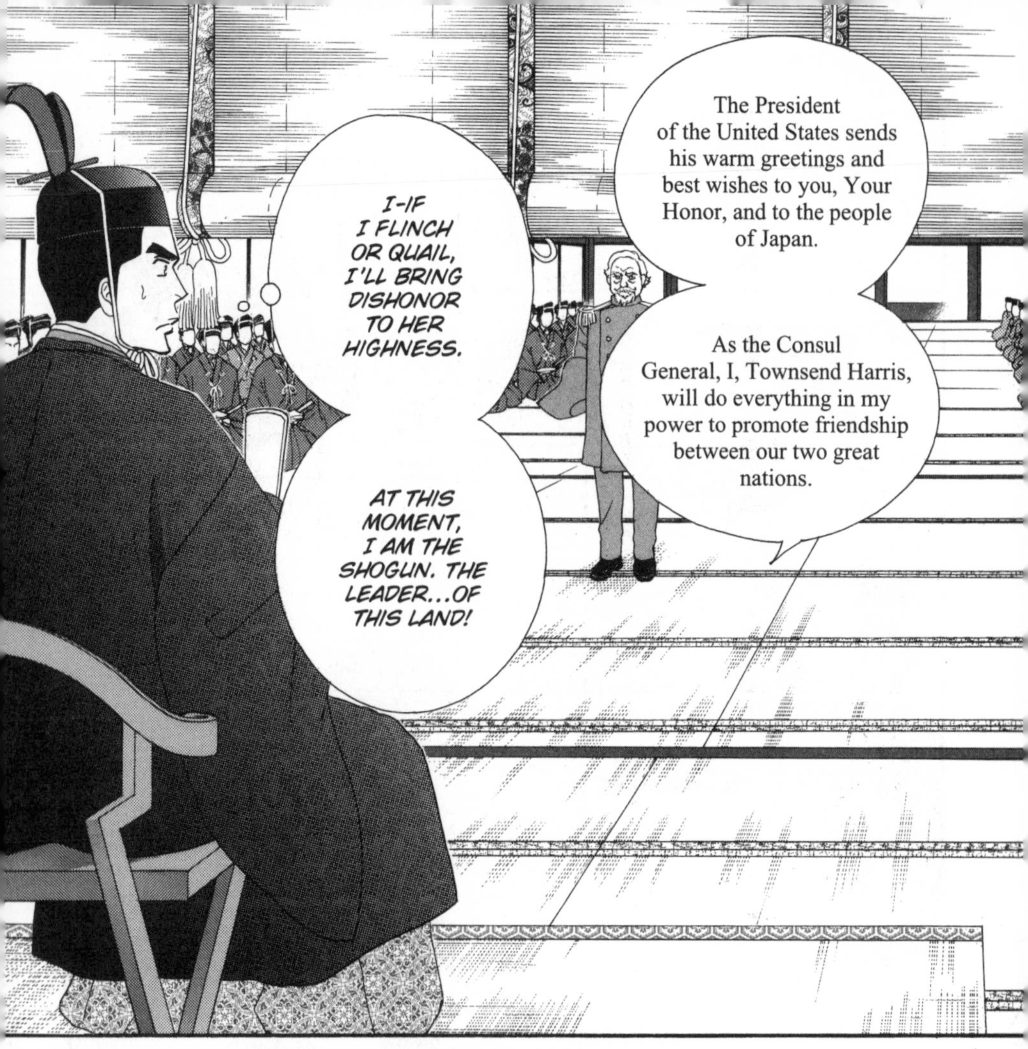
The President of the United States sends his warm greetings and best wishes to you, Your Honor, and to the people of Japan.
As the Consul General, I, Townsend Harris, will do everything in my power to promote friendship between our two great nations.
I-IF I FLINCH OR QUAIL, I'LL BRING DISHONOR TO HER HIGHNESS.
AT THIS MOMENT, I AM THE SHOGUN. THE LEADER...OF THIS LAND!
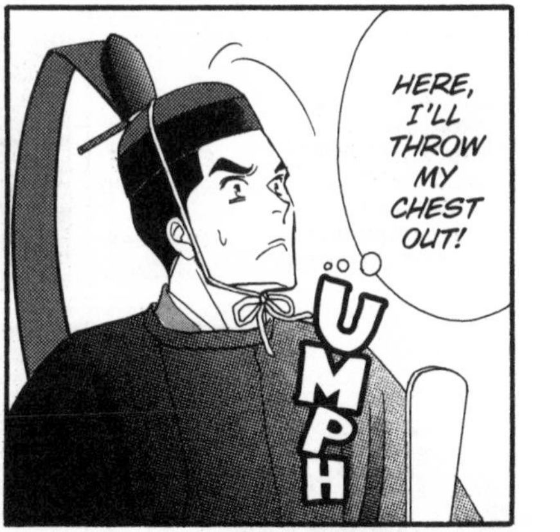
HERE, I'LL THROW MY CHEST OUT!
UMPH
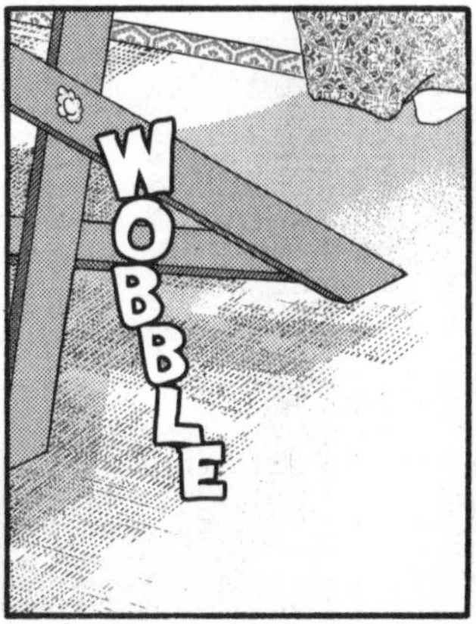
WOBBLE
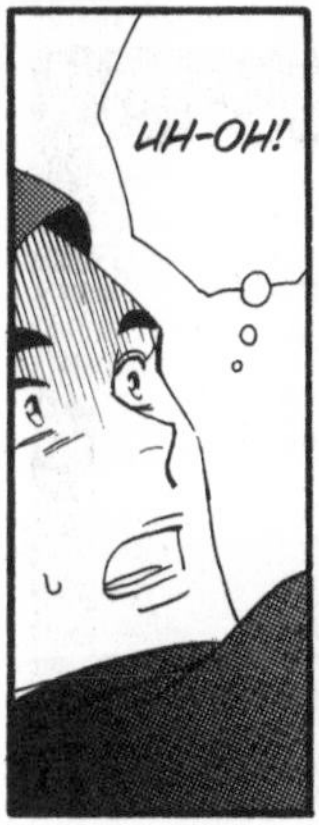
UH-OH!

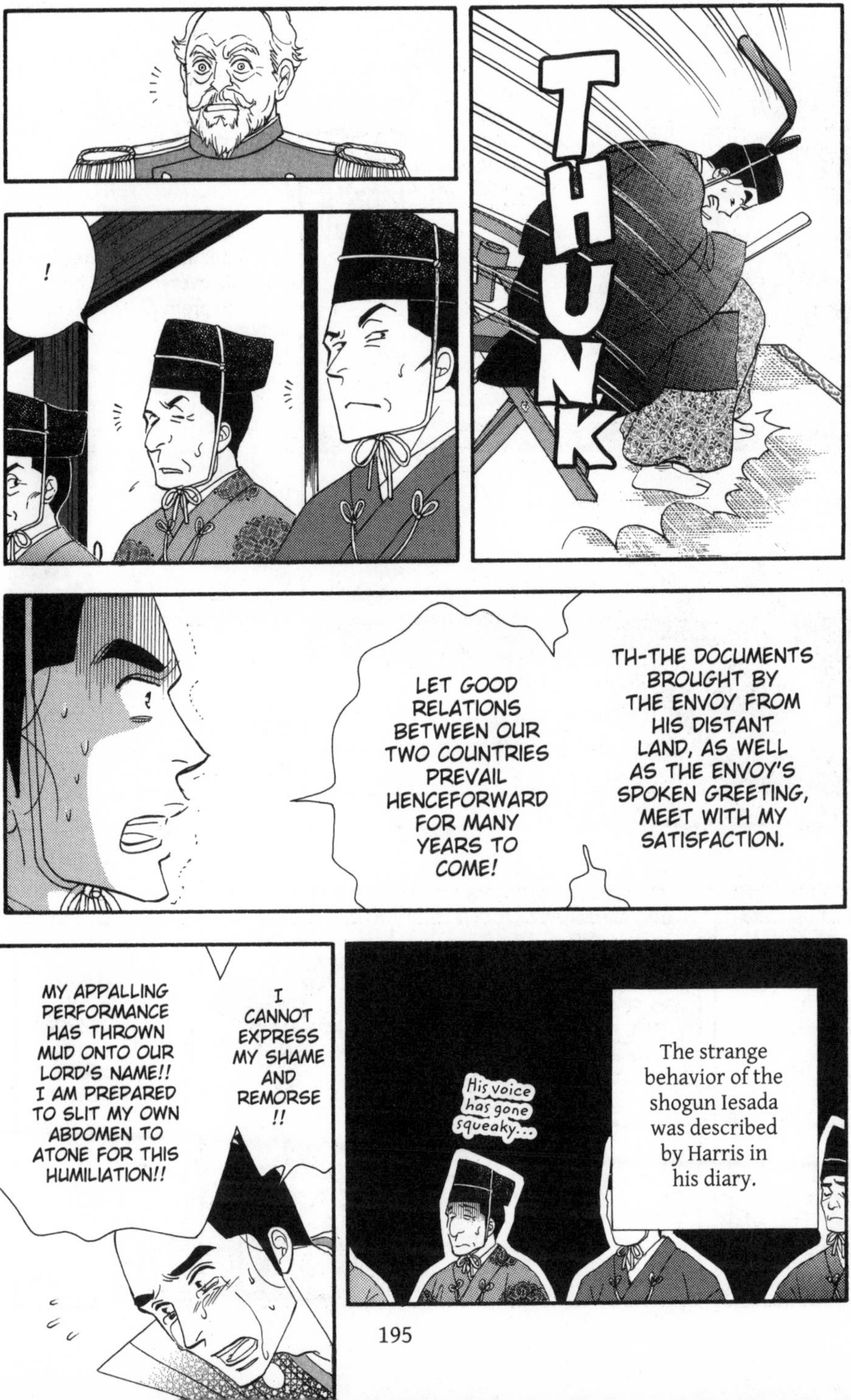
THUNK
!
TH-THE DOCUMENTS BROUGHT BY THE ENVOY FROM HIS DISTANT LAND, AS WELL AS THE ENVOY'S SPOKEN GREETING, MEET WITH MY SATISFACTION.
LET GOOD RELATIONS BETWEEN OUR TWO COUNTRIES PREVAIL HENCEFORWARD FOR MANY YEARS TO COME!
The strange behavior of the shogun Iesada was described by Harris in his diary.
His voice has gone squeaky...
I CANNOT EXPRESS MY SHAME AND REMORSE!!
MY APPALLING PERFORMANCE HAS THROWN MUD ONTO OUR LORD'S NAME!! I AM PREPARED TO SLIT MY OWN ABDOMEN TO ATONE FOR THIS HUMILIATION!!

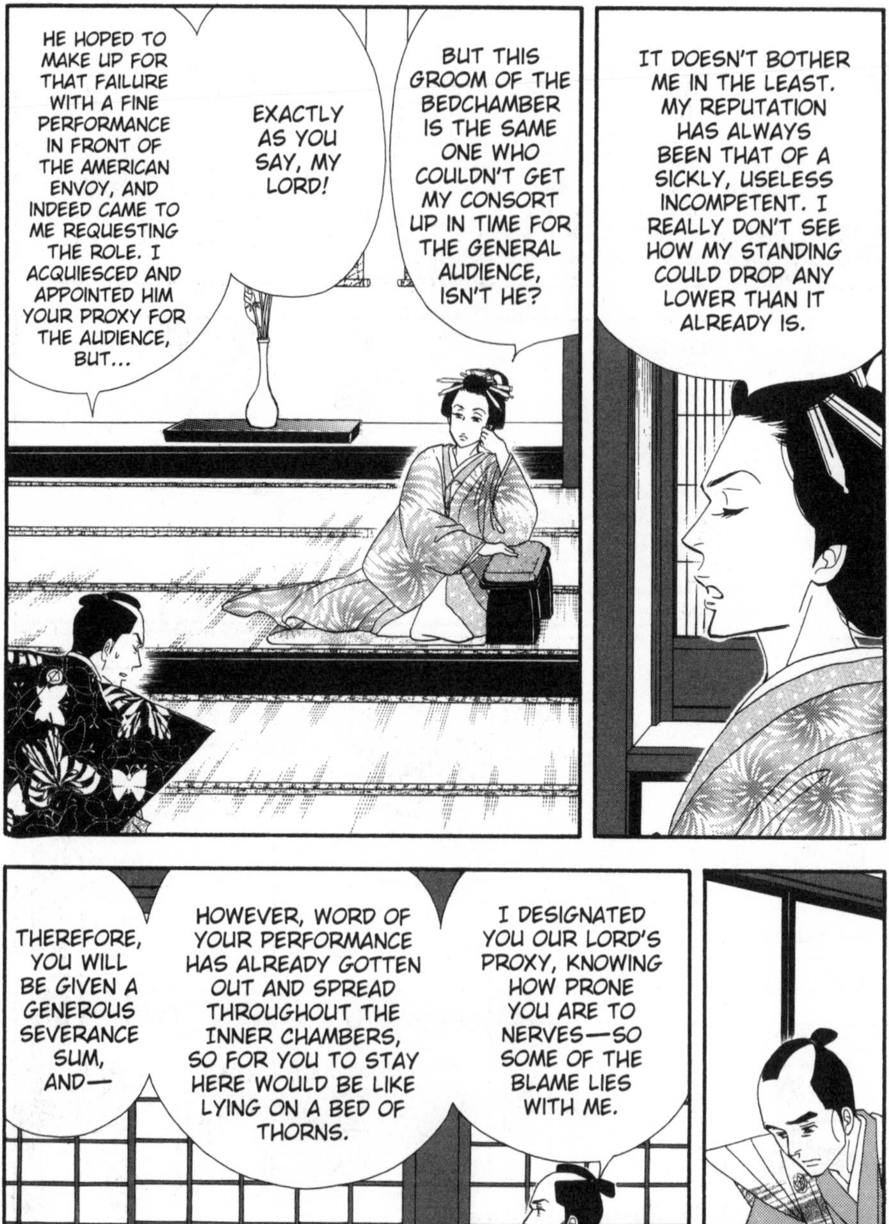
IT DOESN'T BOTHER ME IN THE LEAST. MY REPUTATION HAS ALWAYS BEEN THAT OF A SICKLY, USELESS INCOMPETENT. I REALLY DON'T SEE HOW MY STANDING COULD DROP ANY LOWER THAN IT ALREADY IS.
BUT THIS GROOM OF THE BEDCHAMBER IS THE SAME ONE WHO COULDN'T GET MY CONSORT UP IN TIME FOR THE GENERAL AUDIENCE, ISN'T HE?
EXACTLY AS YOU SAY, MY LORD!
HE HOPED TO MAKE UP FOR THAT FAILURE WITH A FINE PERFORMANCE IN FRONT OF THE AMERICAN ENVOY, AND INDEED CAME TO ME REQUESTING THE ROLE. I ACQUIESCED AND APPOINTED HIM YOUR PROXY FOR THE AUDIENCE, BUT...
I DESIGNATED YOU OUR LORD'S PROXY, KNOWING HOW PRONE YOU ARE TO NERVES—SO SOME OF THE BLAME LIES WITH ME.
HOWEVER, WORD OF YOUR PERFORMANCE HAS ALREADY GOTTEN OUT AND SPREAD THROUGHOUT THE INNER CHAMBERS, SO FOR YOU TO STAY HERE WOULD BE LIKE LYING ON A BED OF THORNS.
THEREFORE, YOU WILL BE GIVEN A GENEROUS SEVERANCE SUM, AND—
!

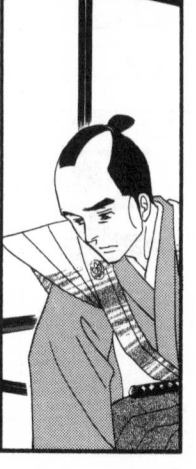

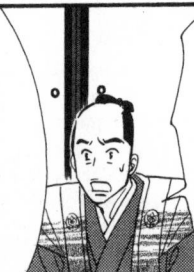

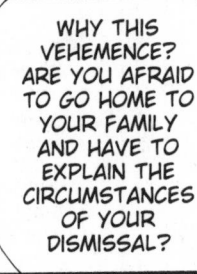

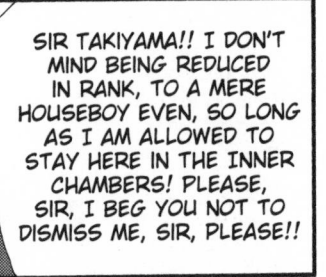

SIR TAKIYAMA!! I DON'T MIND BEING REDUCED IN RANK, TO A MERE HOUSEBOY EVEN, SO LONG AS I AM ALLOWED TO STAY HERE IN THE INNER CHAMBERS! PLEASE, SIR, I BEG YOU NOT TO DISMISS ME, SIR, PLEASE!!
WHY THIS VEHEMENCE? ARE YOU AFRAID TO GO HOME TO YOUR FAMILY AND HAVE TO EXPLAIN THE CIRCUMSTANCES OF YOUR DISMISSAL?
NO, SIR, THAT IS NOT THE REASON!
I WAS SPARED THE PUNISHMENT OF COMMITTING SEPPUKU BY THE GRACE AND KINDNESS OF OUR LORD SHOGUN. THEREFORE, I WISH TO SPEND MY REMAINING DAYS HERE IN THE INNER CHAMBERS, DOING WHATEVER I CAN TO REPAY MY DEBT TO HER HIGHNESS AND TO YOU, SIR TAKIYAMA!
...
IT WILL NOT BE EASY AT FIRST. BE READY.
SPLASH
I GUESS ...
...HE SHAVED OFF ALL SENSE OF SHAME WITH HIS FORELOCKS.

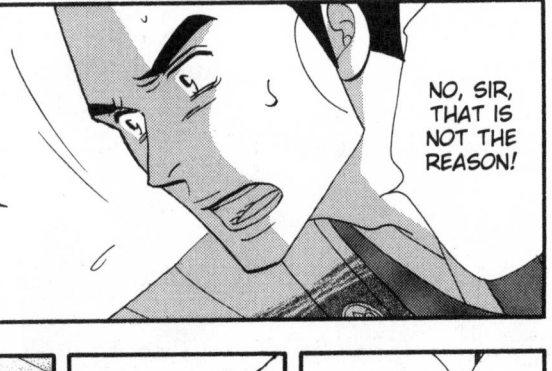

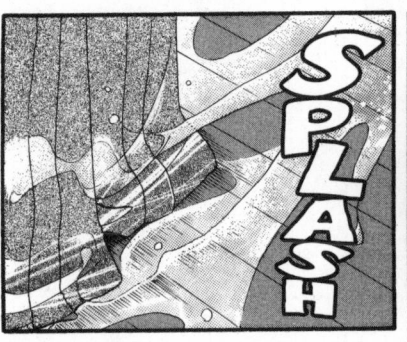

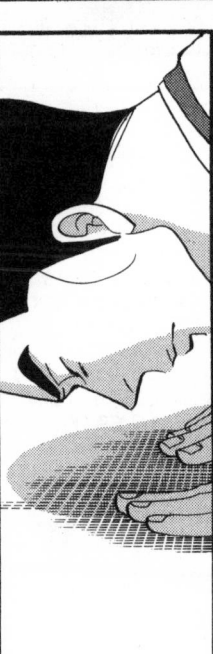

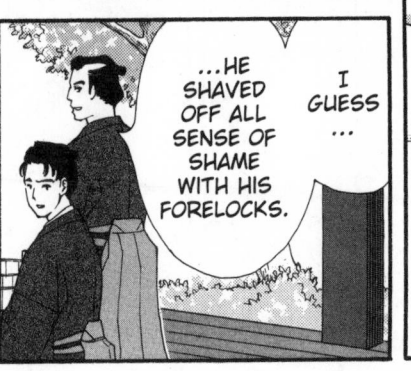

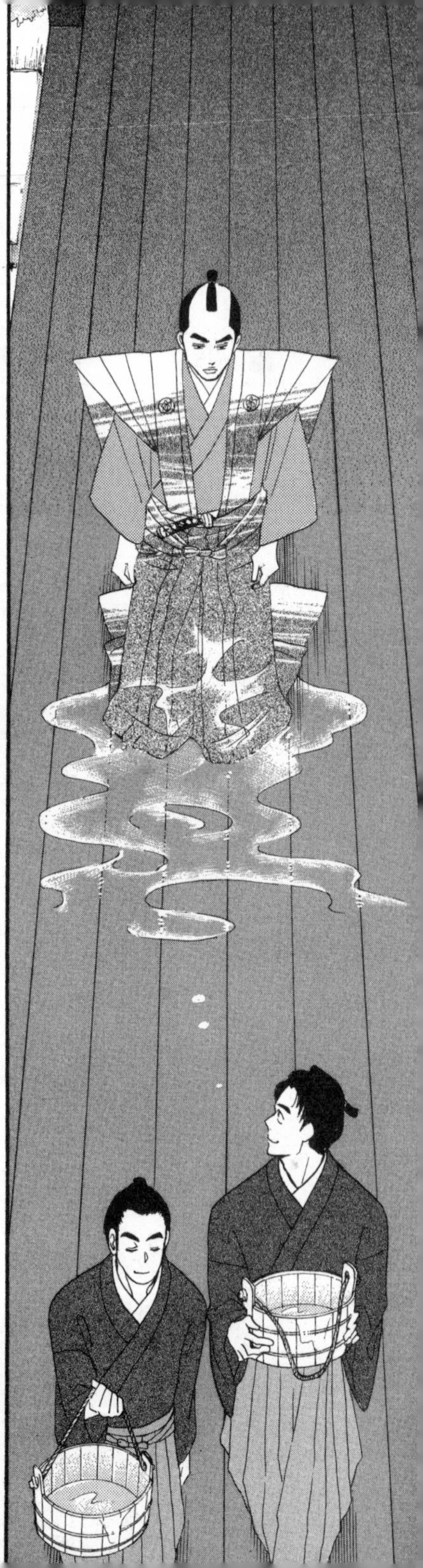

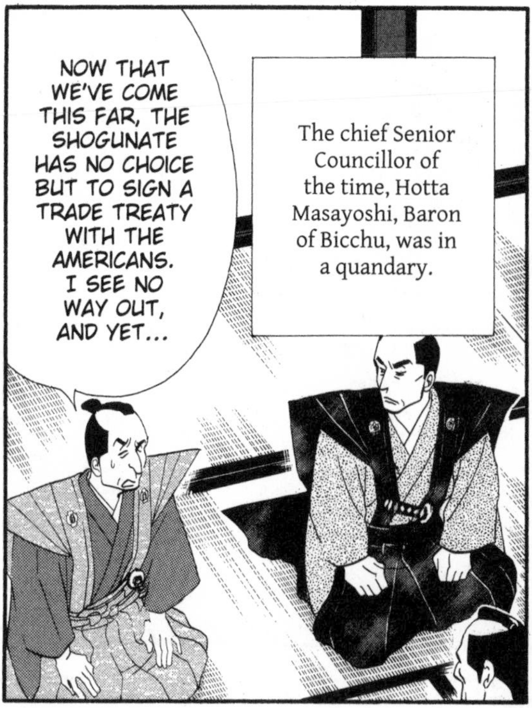
The chief Senior Councillor of the time, Hotta Masayoshi, Baron of Bicchu, was in a quandary.
NOW THAT WE'VE COME THIS FAR, THE SHOGUNATE HAS NO CHOICE BUT TO SIGN A TRADE TREATY WITH THE AMERICANS. I SEE NO WAY OUT, AND YET...

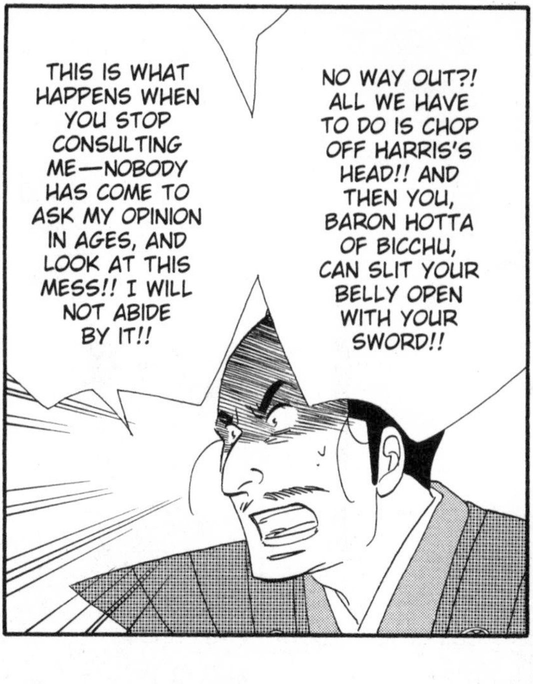
NO WAY OUT?! ALL WE HAVE TO DO IS CHOP OFF HARRIS'S HEAD!! AND THEN YOU, BARON HOTTA OF BICCHU, CAN SLIT YOUR BELLY OPEN WITH YOUR SWORD!!
THIS IS WHAT HAPPENS WHEN YOU STOP CONSULTING ME—NOBODY HAS COME TO ASK MY OPINION IN AGES, AND LOOK AT THIS MESS!! I WILL NOT ABIDE BY IT!!

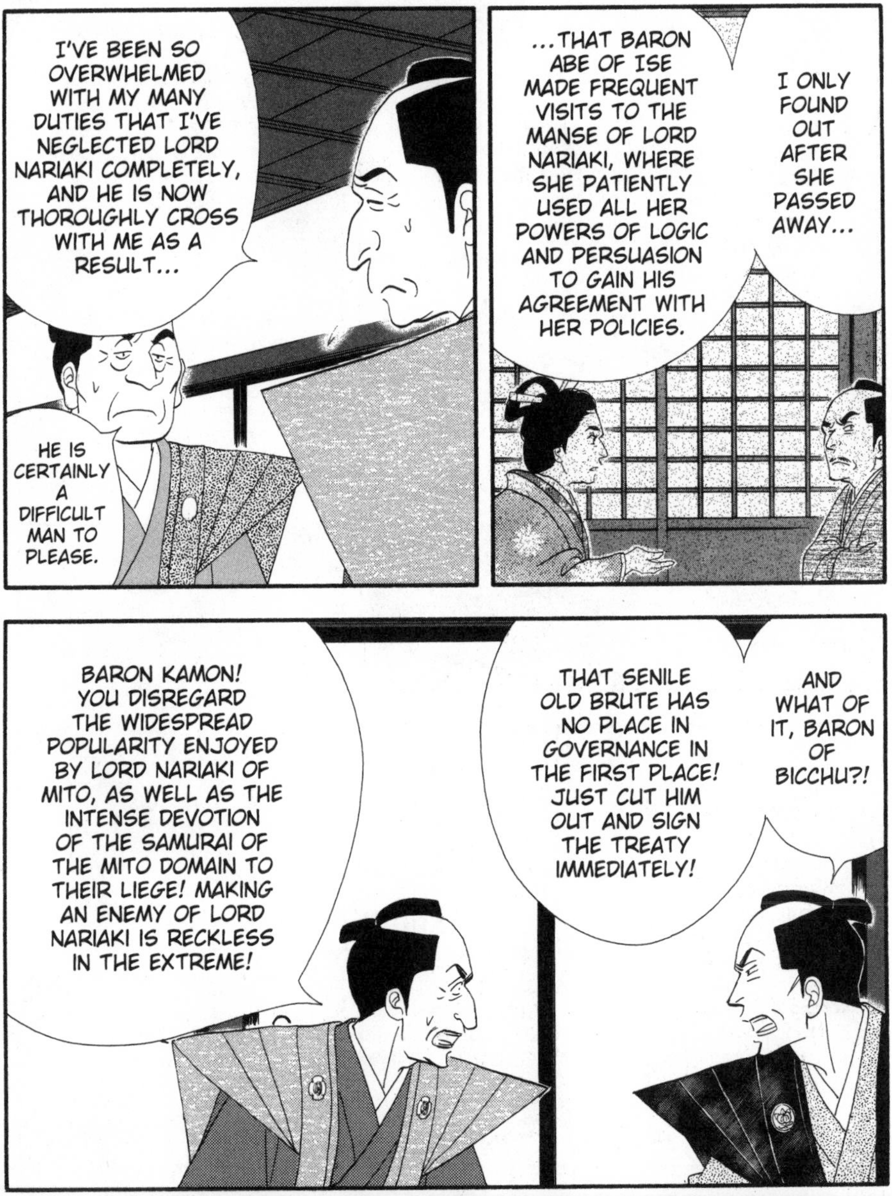
I ONLY FOUND OUT AFTER SHE PASSED AWAY...
...THAT BARON ABE OF ISE MADE FREQUENT VISITS TO THE MANSE OF LORD NARIAKI, WHERE SHE PATIENTLY USED ALL HER POWERS OF LOGIC AND PERSUASION TO GAIN HIS AGREEMENT WITH HER POLICIES.
I'VE BEEN SO OVERWHELMED WITH MY MANY DUTIES THAT I'VE NEGLECTED LORD NARIAKI COMPLETELY, AND HE IS NOW THOROUGHLY CROSS WITH ME AS A RESULT...
HE IS CERTAINLY A DIFFICULT MAN TO PLEASE.
AND WHAT OF IT, BARON OF BICCHU?!
THAT SENILE OLD BRUTE HAS NO PLACE IN GOVERNANCE IN THE FIRST PLACE! JUST CUT HIM OUT AND SIGN THE TREATY IMMEDIATELY!
BARON KAMON! YOU DISREGARD THE WIDESPREAD POPULARITY ENJOYED BY LORD NARIAKI OF MITO, AS WELL AS THE INTENSE DEVOTION OF THE SAMURAI OF THE MITO DOMAIN TO THEIR LIEGE! MAKING AN ENEMY OF LORD NARIAKI IS RECKLESS IN THE EXTREME!

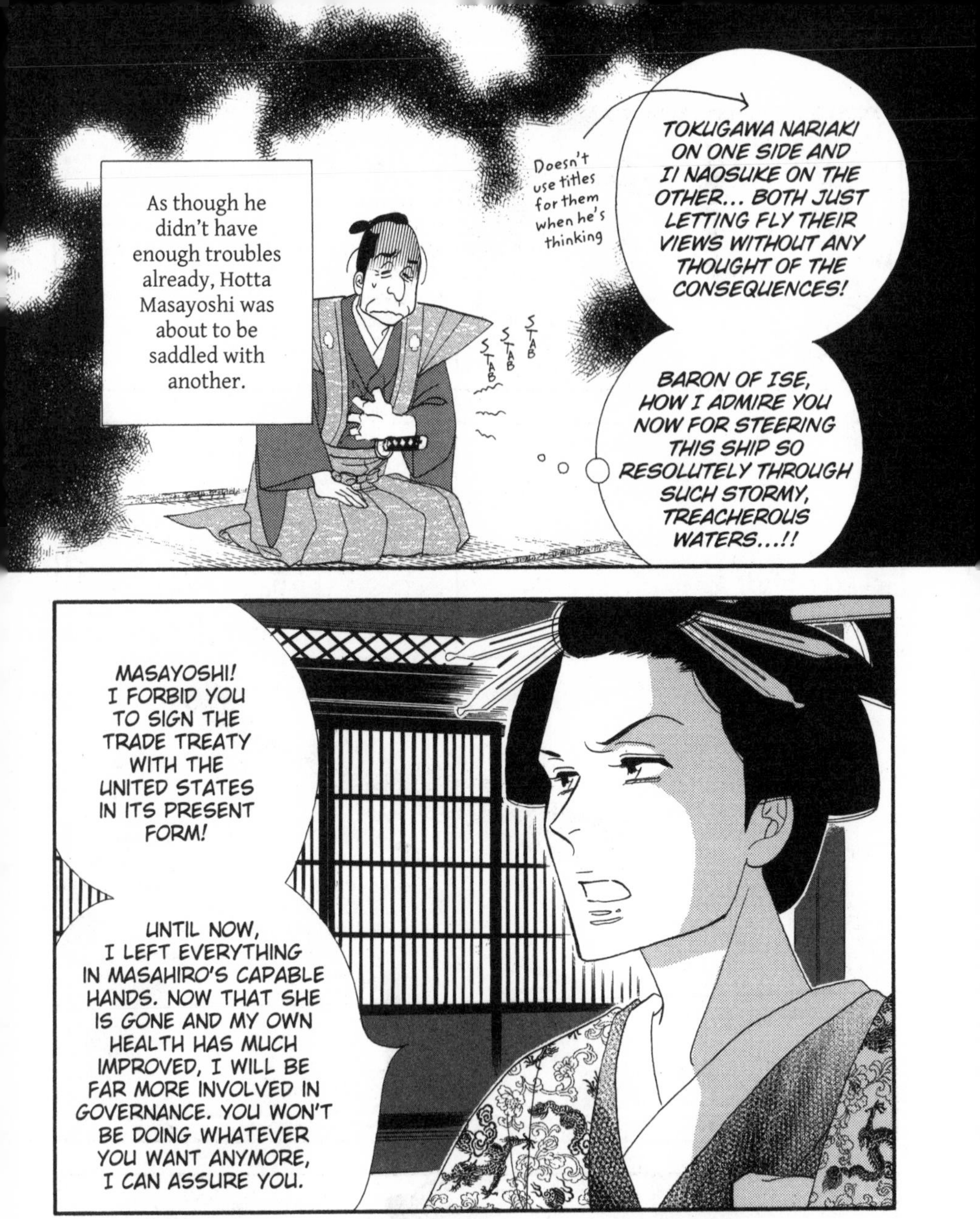
TOKUGAWA NARIAKI ON ONE SIDE AND II NAOSUKE ON THE OTHER… BOTH JUST LETTING FLY THEIR VIEWS WITHOUT ANY THOUGHT OF THE CONSEQUENCES!
Doesn't use titles for them when he's thinking
BARON OF ISE, HOW I ADMIRE YOU NOW FOR STEERING THIS SHIP SO RESOLUTELY THROUGH SUCH STORMY, TREACHEROUS WATERS…!!
STAB STAB STAB
As though he didn't have enough troubles already, Hotta Masayoshi was about to be saddled with another.
MASAYOSHI! I FORBID YOU TO SIGN THE TRADE TREATY WITH THE UNITED STATES IN ITS PRESENT FORM!
UNTIL NOW, I LEFT EVERYTHING IN MASAHIRO'S CAPABLE HANDS. NOW THAT SHE IS GONE AND MY OWN HEALTH HAS MUCH IMPROVED, I WILL BE FAR MORE INVOLVED IN GOVERNANCE. YOU WON'T BE DOING WHATEVER YOU WANT ANYMORE, I CAN ASSURE YOU.

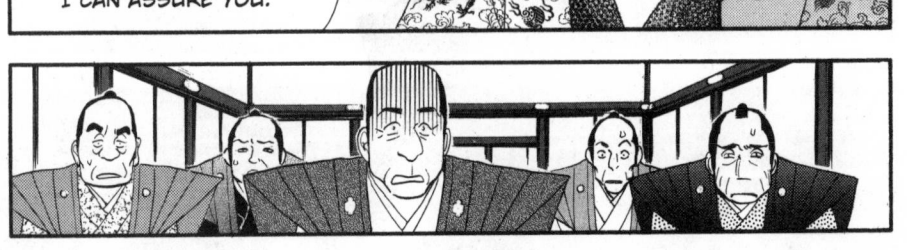

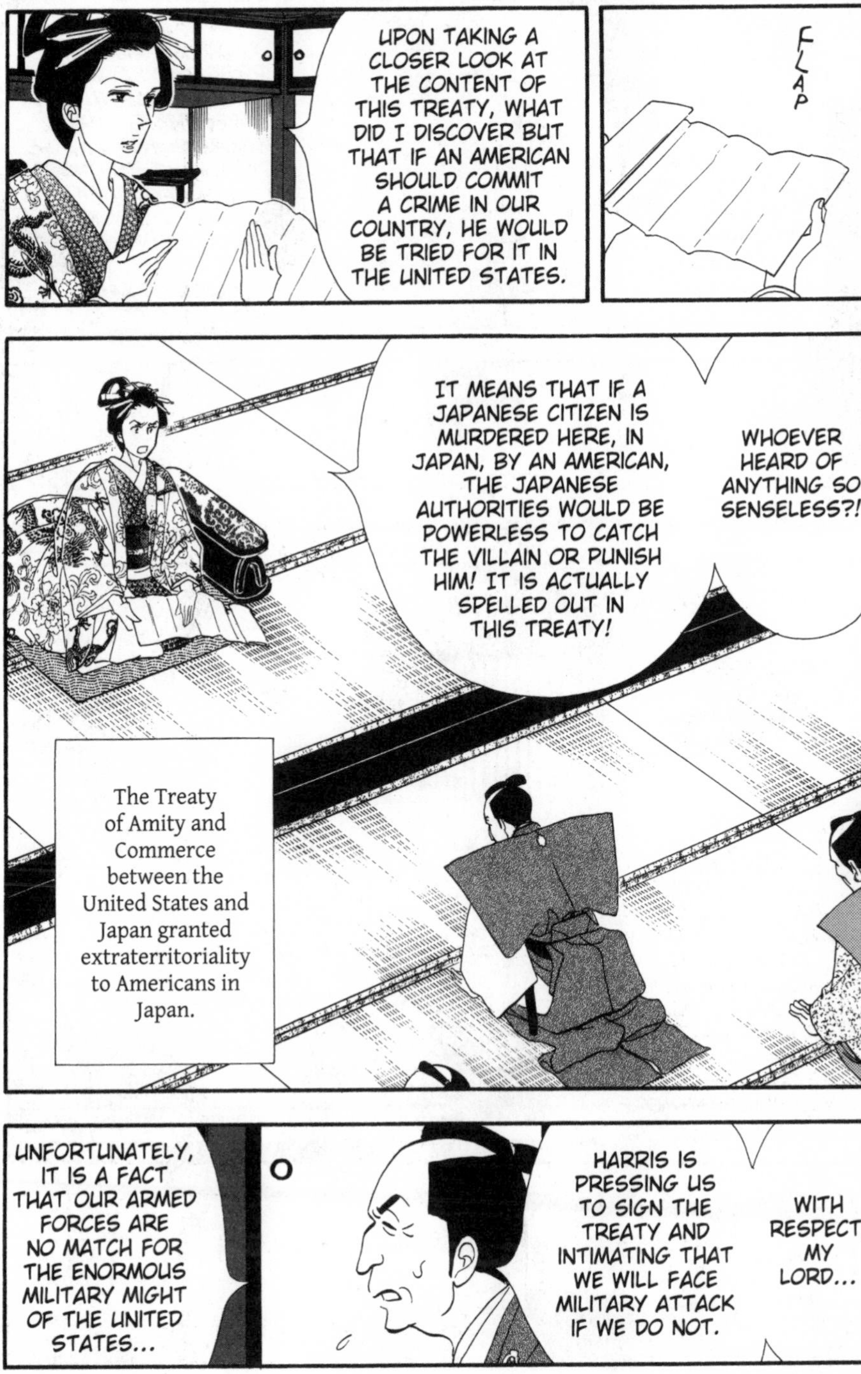
FLAP
UPON TAKING A CLOSER LOOK AT THE CONTENT OF THIS TREATY, WHAT DID I DISCOVER BUT THAT IF AN AMERICAN SHOULD COMMIT A CRIME IN OUR COUNTRY, HE WOULD BE TRIED FOR IT IN THE UNITED STATES.
IT MEANS THAT IF A JAPANESE CITIZEN IS MURDERED HERE, IN JAPAN, BY AN AMERICAN, THE JAPANESE AUTHORITIES WOULD BE POWERLESS TO CATCH THE VILLAIN OR PUNISH HIM! IT IS ACTUALLY SPELLED OUT IN THIS TREATY!
WHOEVER HEARD OF ANYTHING SO SENSELESS?!
The Treaty of Amity and Commerce between the United States and Japan granted extraterritoriality to Americans in Japan.
WITH RESPECT, MY LORD...
HARRIS IS PRESSING US TO SIGN THE TREATY AND INTIMATING THAT WE WILL FACE MILITARY ATTACK IF WE DO NOT.
O
UNFORTUNATELY, IT IS A FACT THAT OUR ARMED FORCES ARE NO MATCH FOR THE ENORMOUS MILITARY MIGHT OF THE UNITED STATES...

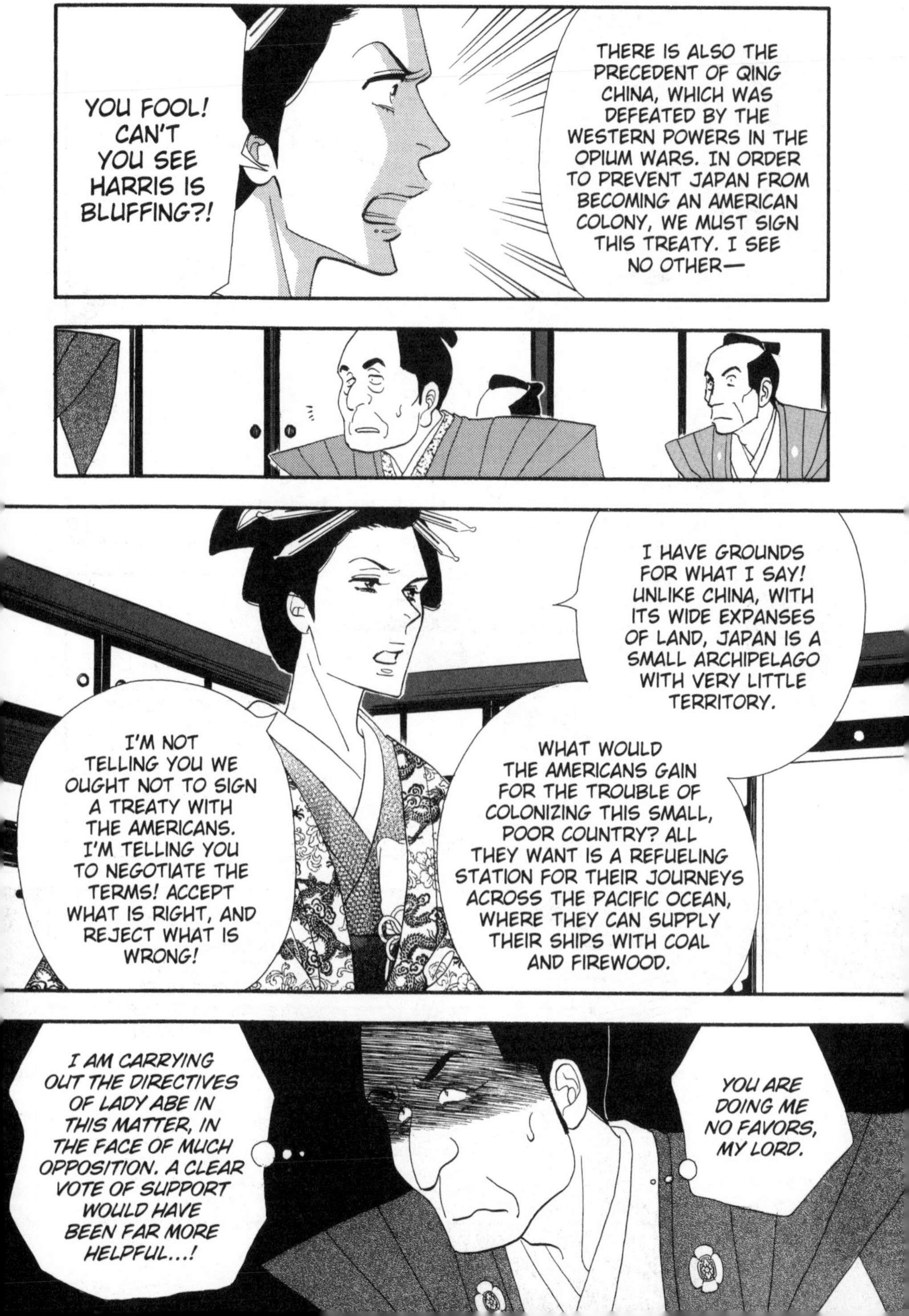
THERE IS ALSO THE PRECEDENT OF QING CHINA, WHICH WAS DEFEATED BY THE WESTERN POWERS IN THE OPIUM WARS. IN ORDER TO PREVENT JAPAN FROM BECOMING AN AMERICAN COLONY, WE MUST SIGN THIS TREATY. I SEE NO OTHER—
YOU FOOL! CAN'T YOU SEE HARRIS IS BLUFFING?!
I HAVE GROUNDS FOR WHAT I SAY! UNLIKE CHINA, WITH ITS WIDE EXPANSES OF LAND, JAPAN IS A SMALL ARCHIPELAGO WITH VERY LITTLE TERRITORY.
WHAT WOULD THE AMERICANS GAIN FOR THE TROUBLE OF COLONIZING THIS SMALL, POOR COUNTRY? ALL THEY WANT IS A REFUELING STATION FOR THEIR JOURNEYS ACROSS THE PACIFIC OCEAN, WHERE THEY CAN SUPPLY THEIR SHIPS WITH COAL AND FIREWOOD.
I'M NOT TELLING YOU WE OUGHT NOT TO SIGN A TREATY WITH THE AMERICANS. I'M TELLING YOU TO NEGOTIATE THE TERMS! ACCEPT WHAT IS RIGHT, AND REJECT WHAT IS WRONG!
YOU ARE DOING ME NO FAVORS, MY LORD.
I AM CARRYING OUT THE DIRECTIVES OF LADY ABE IN THIS MATTER, IN THE FACE OF MUCH OPPOSITION. A CLEAR VOTE OF SUPPORT WOULD HAVE BEEN FAR MORE HELPFUL...!

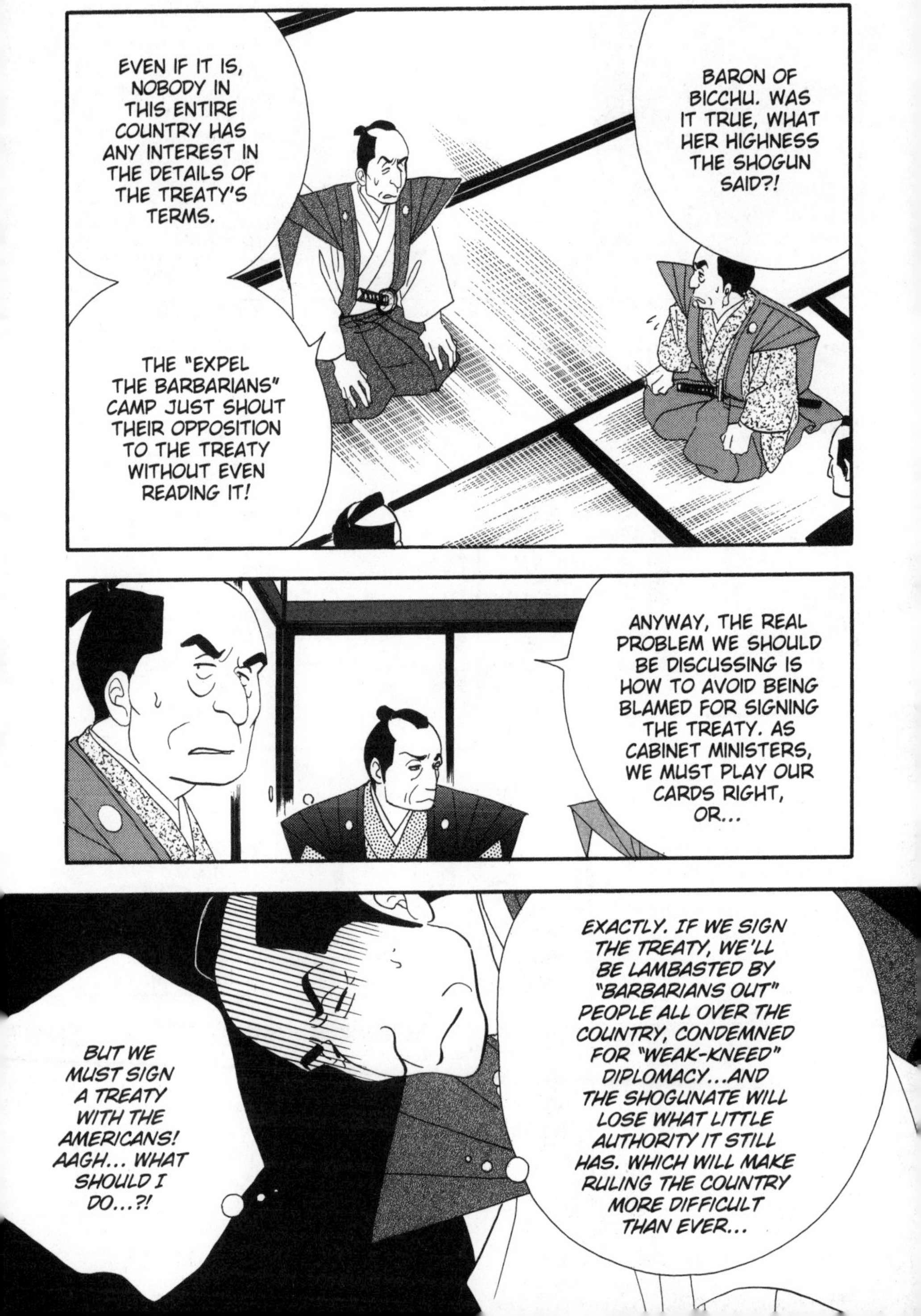
BARON OF BICCHU. WAS IT TRUE, WHAT HER HIGHNESS THE SHOGUN SAID?!
EVEN IF IT IS, NOBODY IN THIS ENTIRE COUNTRY HAS ANY INTEREST IN THE DETAILS OF THE TREATY'S TERMS.
THE "EXPEL THE BARBARIANS" CAMP JUST SHOUT THEIR OPPOSITION TO THE TREATY WITHOUT EVEN READING IT!
ANYWAY, THE REAL PROBLEM WE SHOULD BE DISCUSSING IS HOW TO AVOID BEING BLAMED FOR SIGNING THE TREATY. AS CABINET MINISTERS, WE MUST PLAY OUR CARDS RIGHT, OR...
EXACTLY. IF WE SIGN THE TREATY, WE'LL BE LAMBASTED BY "BARBARIANS OUT" PEOPLE ALL OVER THE COUNTRY, CONDEMNED FOR "WEAK-KNEED" DIPLOMACY...AND THE SHOGUNATE WILL LOSE WHAT LITTLE AUTHORITY IT STILL HAS. WHICH WILL MAKE RULING THE COUNTRY MORE DIFFICULT THAN EVER...
BUT WE MUST SIGN A TREATY WITH THE AMERICANS! AAGH... WHAT SHOULD I DO...?!

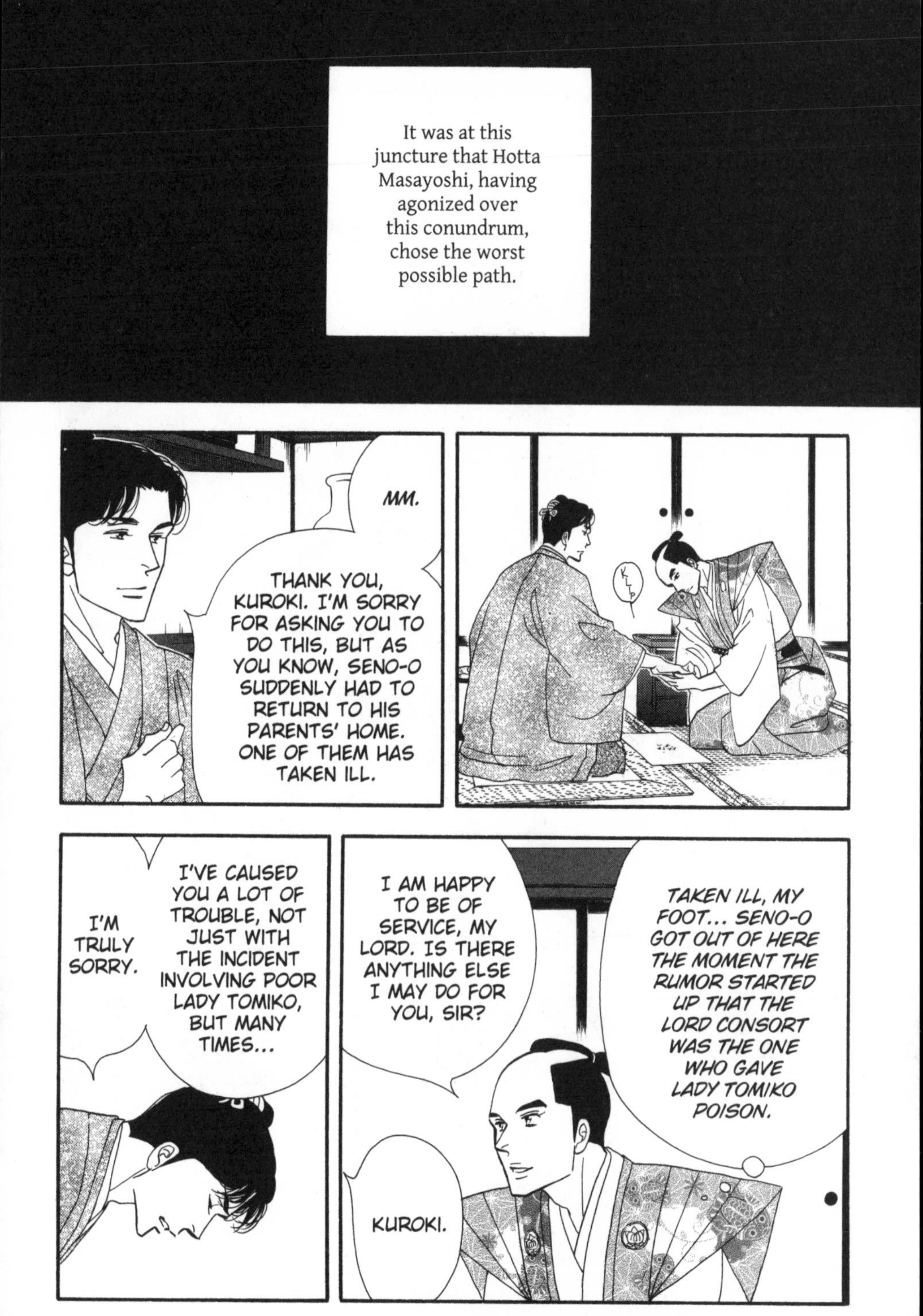
It was at this juncture that Hotta Masayoshi, having agonized over this conundrum, chose the worst possible path.
MM.
THANK YOU, KUROKI. I'M SORRY FOR ASKING YOU TO DO THIS, BUT AS YOU KNOW, SENO-O SUDDENLY HAD TO RETURN TO HIS PARENTS' HOME. ONE OF THEM HAS TAKEN ILL.
TAKEN ILL, MY FOOT... SENO-O GOT OUT OF HERE THE MOMENT THE RUMOR STARTED UP THAT THE LORD CONSORT WAS THE ONE WHO GAVE LADY TOMIKO POISON.
I AM HAPPY TO BE OF SERVICE, MY LORD. IS THERE ANYTHING ELSE I MAY DO FOR YOU, SIR?
KUROKI.
I'VE CAUSED YOU A LOT OF TROUBLE, NOT JUST WITH THE INCIDENT INVOLVING POOR LADY TOMIKO, BUT MANY TIMES...
I'M TRULY SORRY.

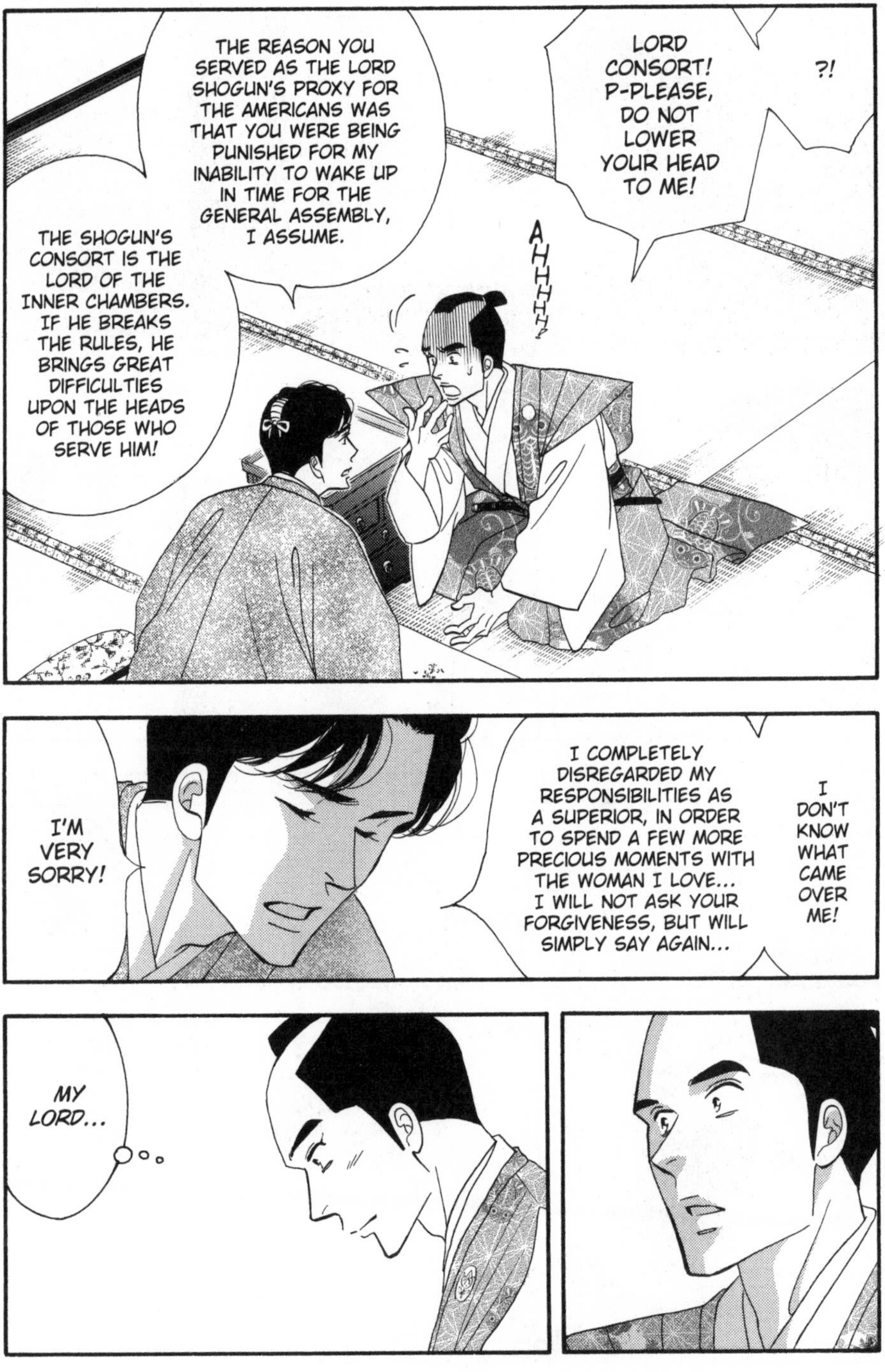
?!
LORD CONSORT! P-PLEASE, DO NOT LOWER YOUR HEAD TO ME!
AHHHHH!
THE REASON YOU SERVED AS THE LORD SHOGUN'S PROXY FOR THE AMERICANS WAS THAT YOU WERE BEING PUNISHED FOR MY INABILITY TO WAKE UP IN TIME FOR THE GENERAL ASSEMBLY, I ASSUME.
THE SHOGUN'S CONSORT IS THE LORD OF THE INNER CHAMBERS. IF HE BREAKS THE RULES, HE BRINGS GREAT DIFFICULTIES UPON THE HEADS OF THOSE WHO SERVE HIM!
I DON'T KNOW WHAT CAME OVER ME!
I COMPLETELY DISREGARDED MY RESPONSIBILITIES AS A SUPERIOR, IN ORDER TO SPEND A FEW MORE PRECIOUS MOMENTS WITH THE WOMAN I LOVE... I WILL NOT ASK YOUR FORGIVENESS, BUT WILL SIMPLY SAY AGAIN...
I'M VERY SORRY!
MY LORD...

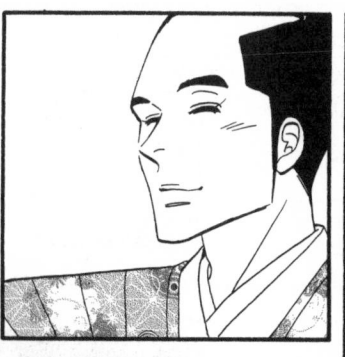

I AM VERY GLAD THAT I DID NOT LEAVE THE INNER CHAMBERS AFTER ALL... IT IS A PRIVILEGE TO SERVE YOU, LORD CONSORT, AND I AM DEEPLY GRATEFUL FOR IT.
NOW PLEASE RAISE YOUR HEAD, SIR. I AM A BUNGLER WHO QUITE OFTEN MAKES MISTAKES, SO IF MY LORD SHOULD OCCASIONALLY SHOW SUCH SIGNS OF BEING LESS THAN PERFECT, IT IS REASSURING TO ME, MORE THAN ANYTHING ELSE.
...
THANK YOU, KUROKI.
AHH...

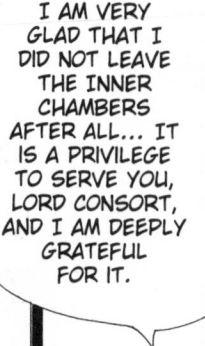

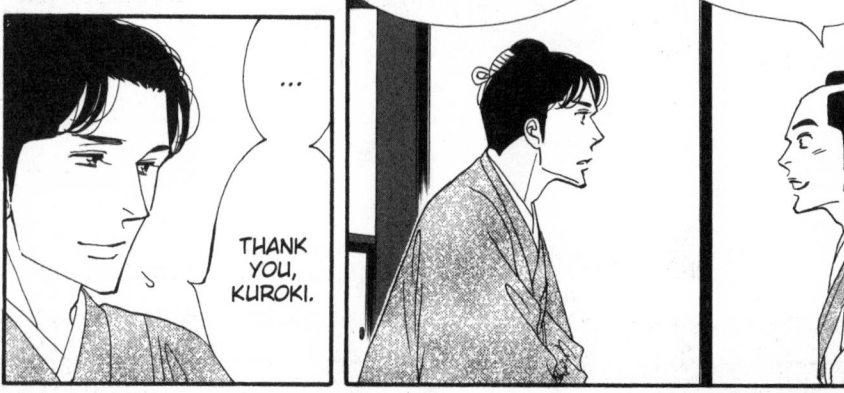

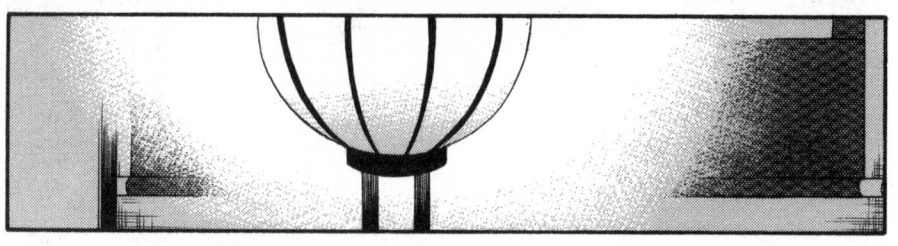

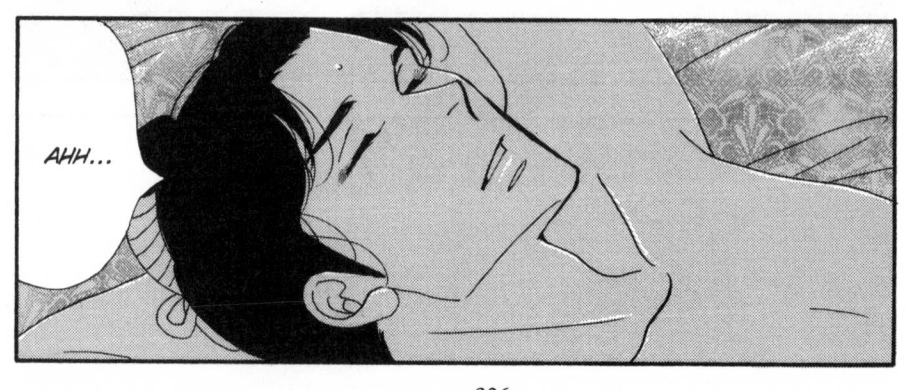

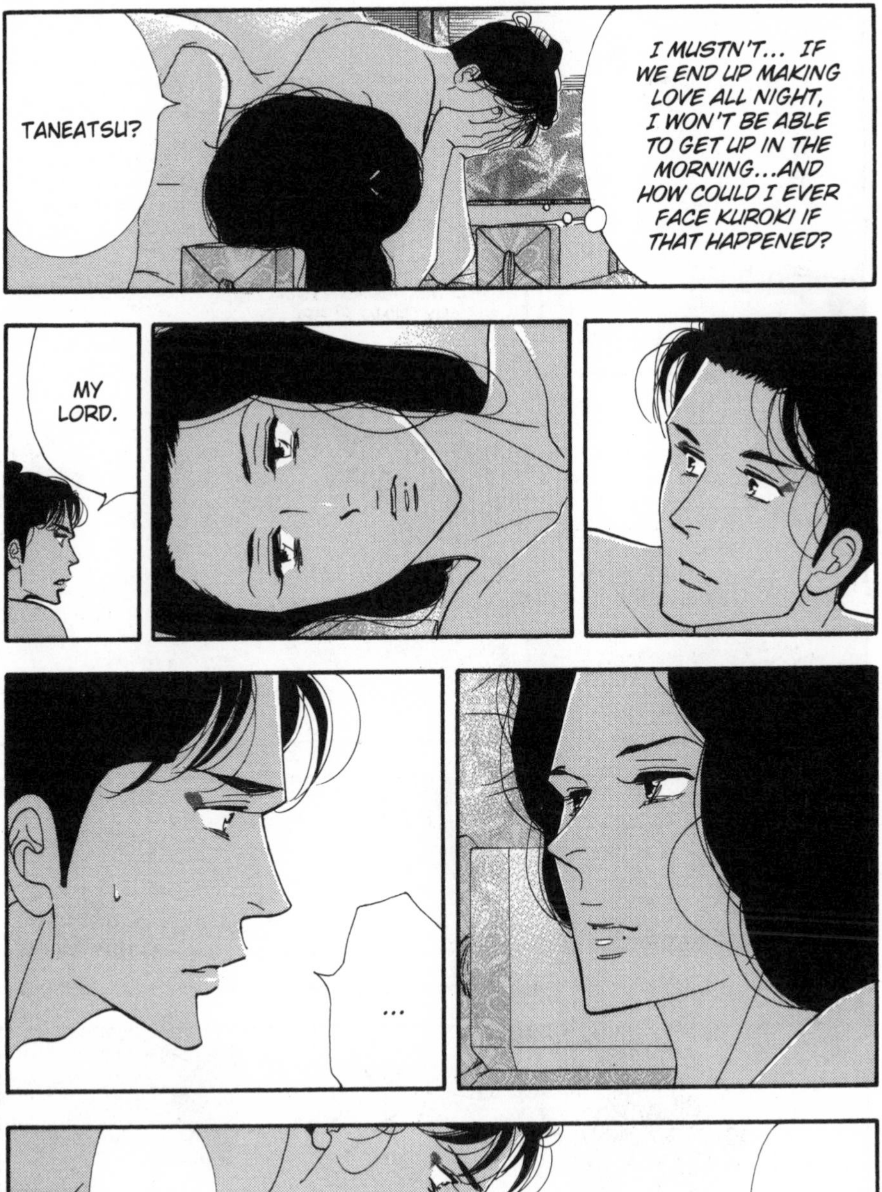
I MUSTN'T... IF WE END UP MAKING LOVE ALL NIGHT, I WON'T BE ABLE TO GET UP IN THE MORNING...AND HOW COULD I EVER FACE KUROKI IF THAT HAPPENED?
TANEATSU?
MY LORD.
...
TANEATSU.
MY LORD!

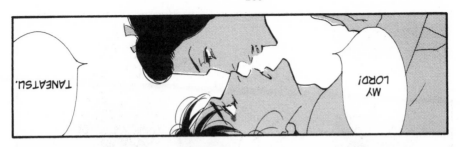

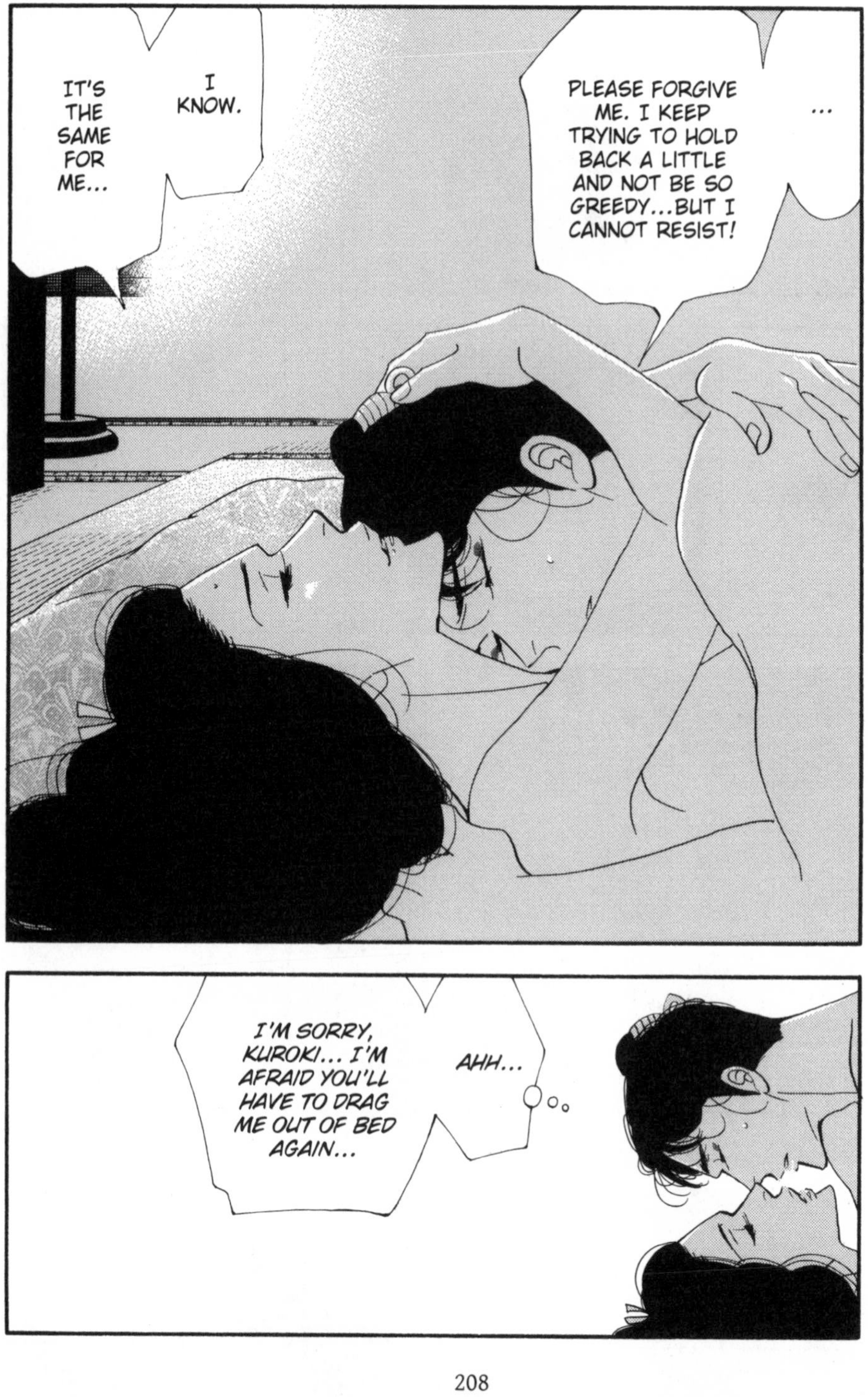
...
PLEASE FORGIVE ME. I KEEP TRYING TO HOLD BACK A LITTLE AND NOT BE SO GREEDY...BUT I CANNOT RESIST!
I KNOW.
IT'S THE SAME FOR ME...
AHH...
I'M SORRY, KUROKI... I'M AFRAID YOU'LL HAVE TO DRAG ME OUT OF BED AGAIN...

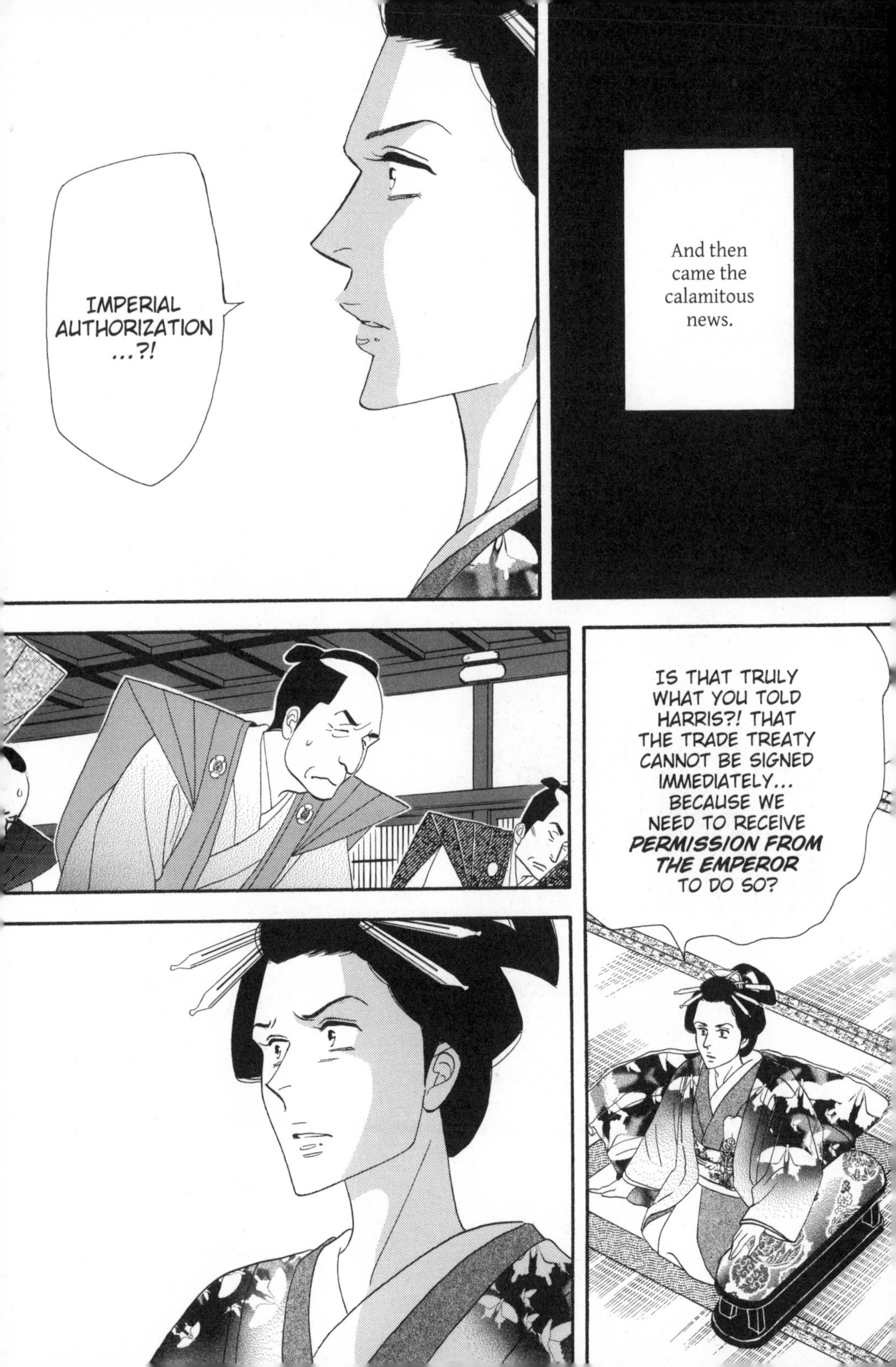
And then came the calamitous news.
IMPERIAL AUTHORIZATION ...?!
IS THAT TRULY WHAT YOU TOLD HARRIS?! THAT THE TRADE TREATY CANNOT BE SIGNED IMMEDIATELY... BECAUSE WE NEED TO RECEIVE ***PERMISSION FROM THE EMPEROR*** TO DO SO?

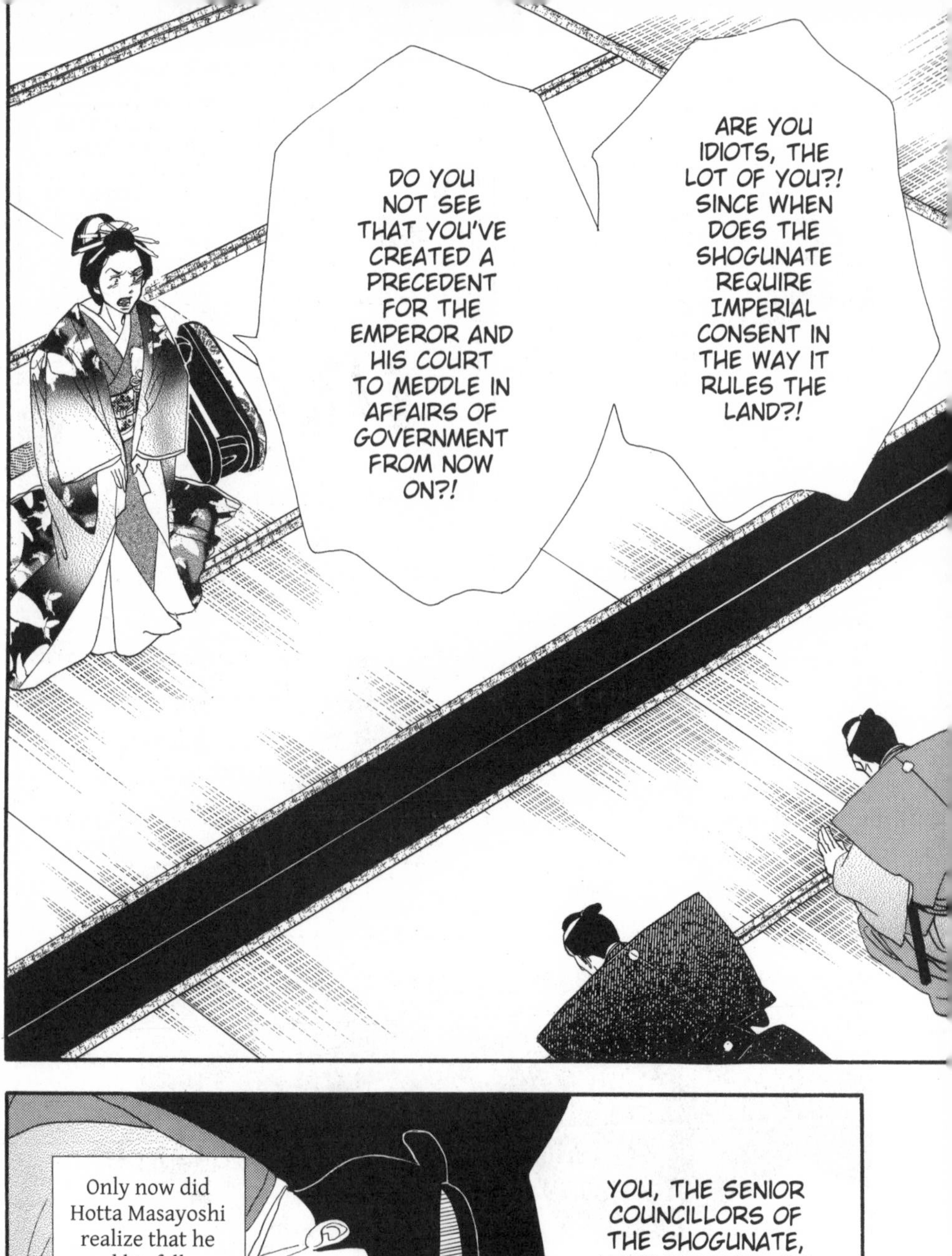
ARE YOU IDIOTS, THE LOT OF YOU?! SINCE WHEN DOES THE SHOGUNATE REQUIRE IMPERIAL CONSENT IN THE WAY IT RULES THE LAND?!
DO YOU NOT SEE THAT YOU'VE CREATED A PRECEDENT FOR THE EMPEROR AND HIS COURT TO MEDDLE IN AFFAIRS OF GOVERNMENT FROM NOW ON?!

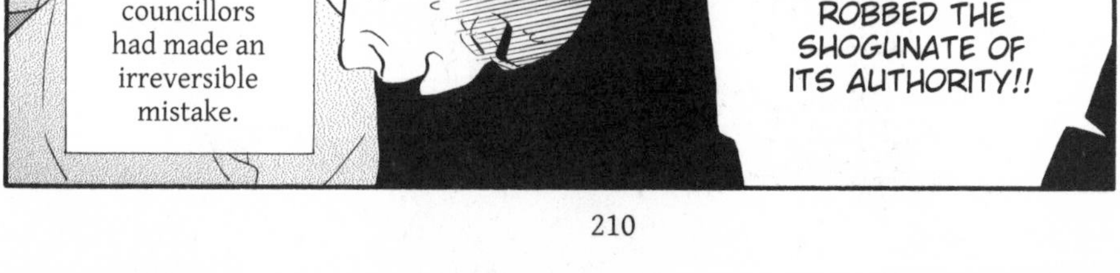
YOU, THE SENIOR COUNCILLORS OF THE SHOGUNATE, HAVE YOURSELVES ROBBED THE SHOGUNATE OF ITS AUTHORITY!!
Only now did Hotta Masayoshi realize that he and his fellow councillors had made an irreversible mistake.

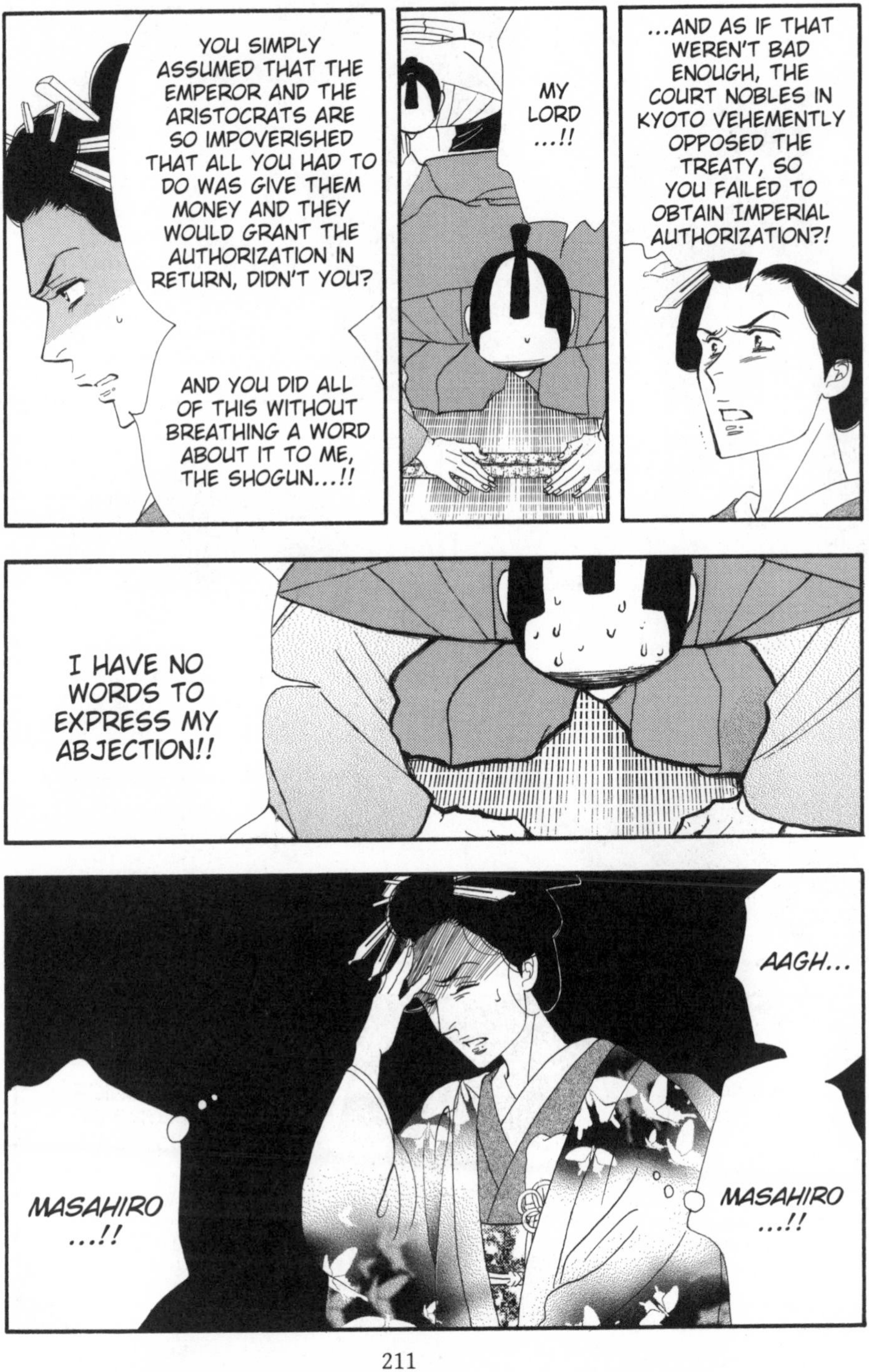
...AND AS IF THAT WEREN'T BAD ENOUGH, THE COURT NOBLES IN KYOTO VEHEMENTLY OPPOSED THE TREATY, SO YOU FAILED TO OBTAIN IMPERIAL AUTHORIZATION?!
MY LORD ...!!
YOU SIMPLY ASSUMED THAT THE EMPEROR AND THE ARISTOCRATS ARE SO IMPOVERISHED THAT ALL YOU HAD TO DO WAS GIVE THEM MONEY AND THEY WOULD GRANT THE AUTHORIZATION IN RETURN, DIDN'T YOU?
AND YOU DID ALL OF THIS WITHOUT BREATHING A WORD ABOUT IT TO ME, THE SHOGUN...!!
I HAVE NO WORDS TO EXPRESS MY ABJECTION!!
AAGH...
MASAHIRO ...!!
MASAHIRO ...!!

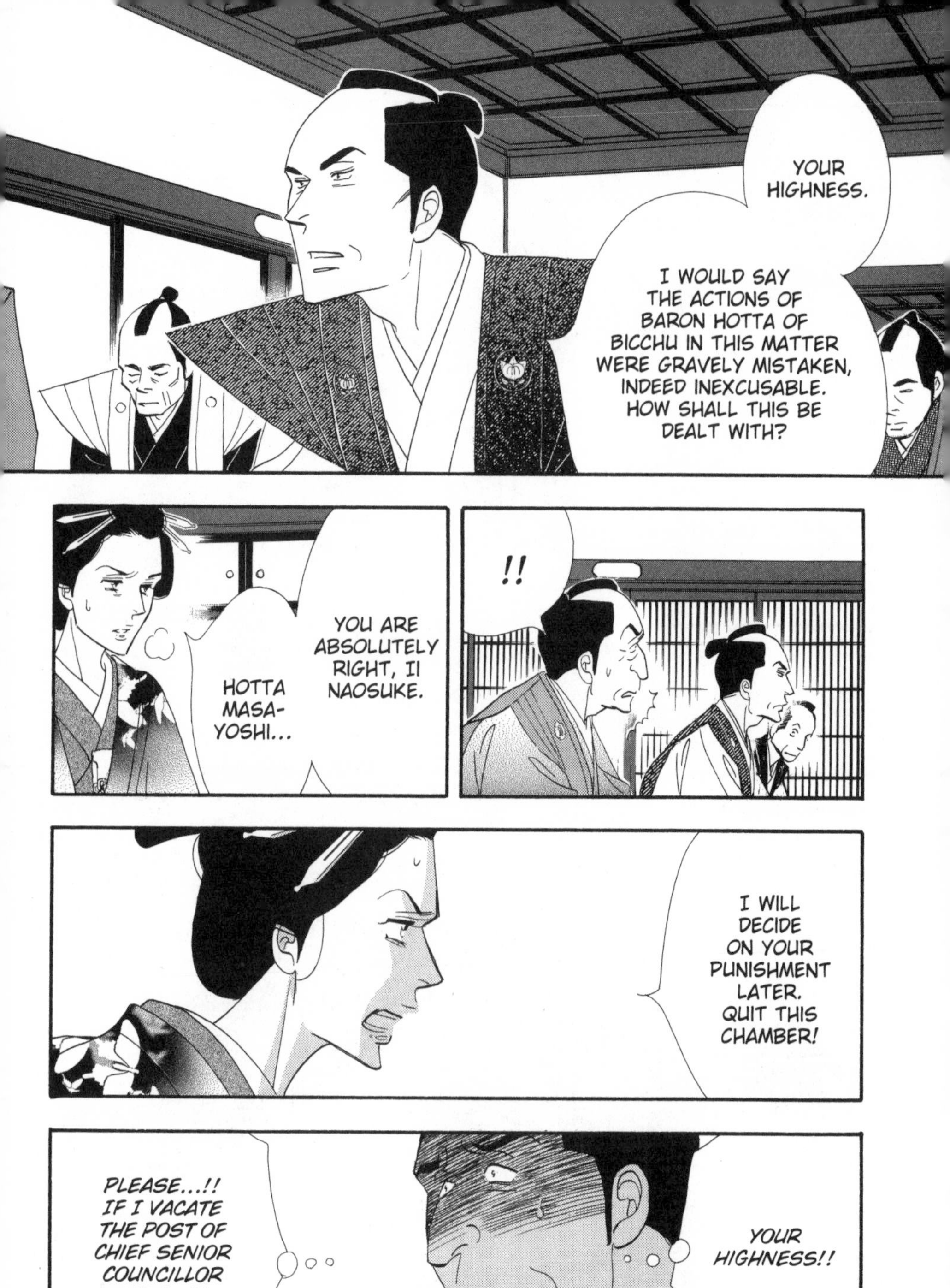
YOUR HIGHNESS.
I WOULD SAY THE ACTIONS OF BARON HOTTA OF BICCHU IN THIS MATTER WERE GRAVELY MISTAKEN, INDEED INEXCUSABLE. HOW SHALL THIS BE DEALT WITH?
!!
YOU ARE ABSOLUTELY RIGHT, II NAOSUKE.
HOTTA MASA-YOSHI...
I WILL DECIDE ON YOUR PUNISHMENT LATER. QUIT THIS CHAMBER!
YOUR HIGHNESS!!
PLEASE...!! IF I VACATE THE POST OF CHIEF SENIOR COUNCILLOR NOW...!!

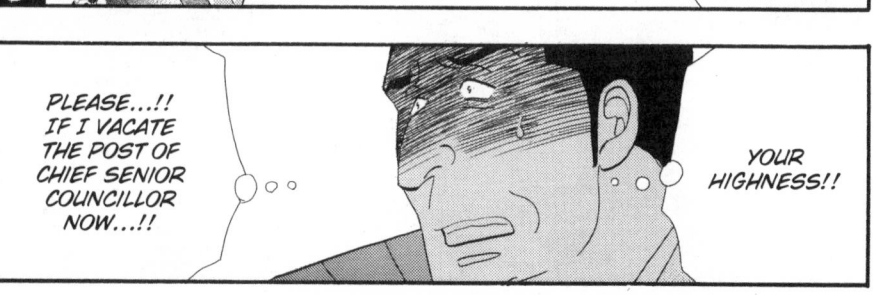

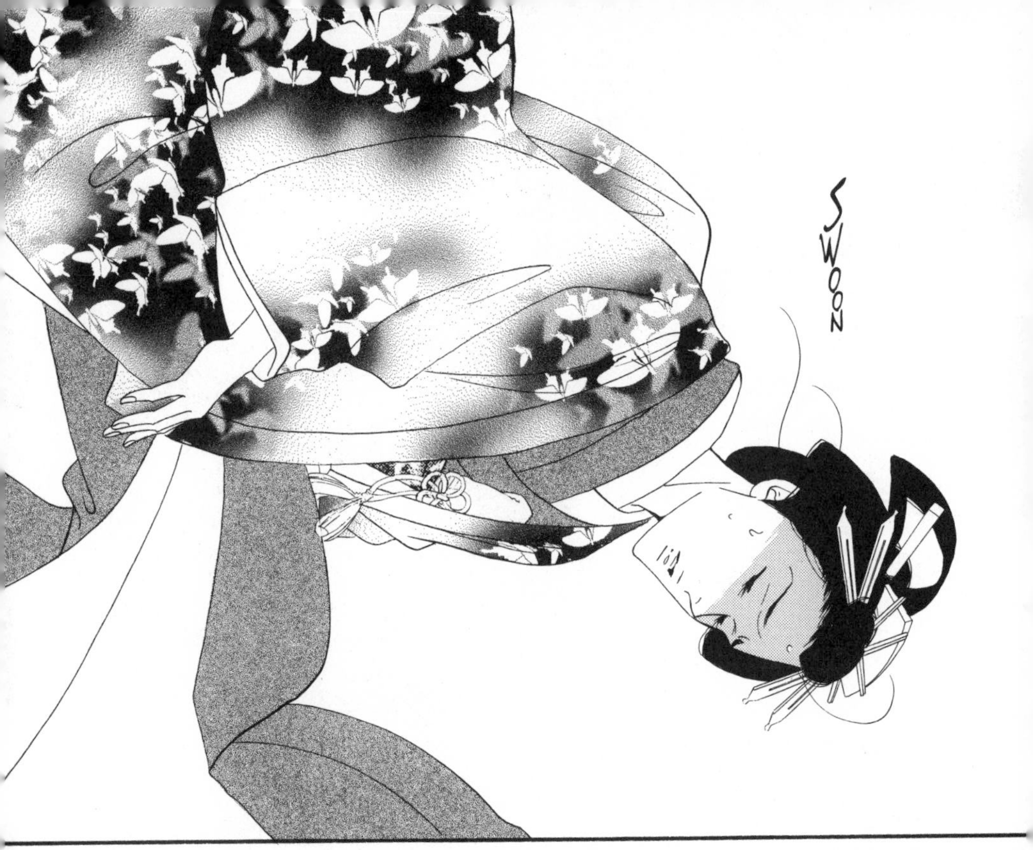
SWOON

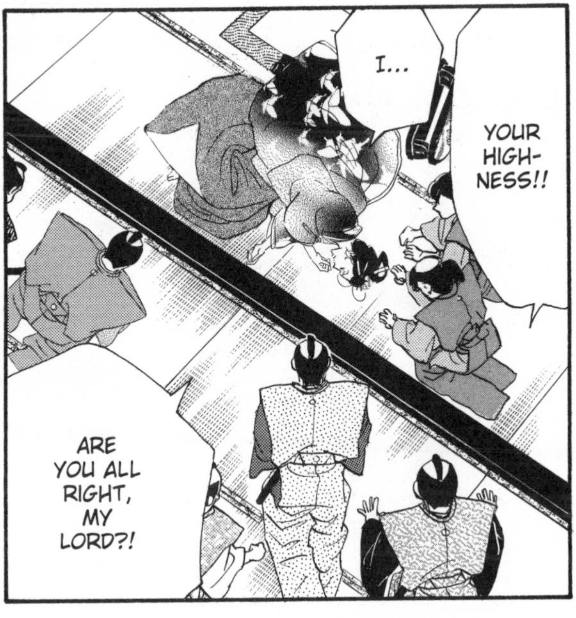
I...
YOUR HIGH-NESS!!
ARE YOU ALL RIGHT, MY LORD?!

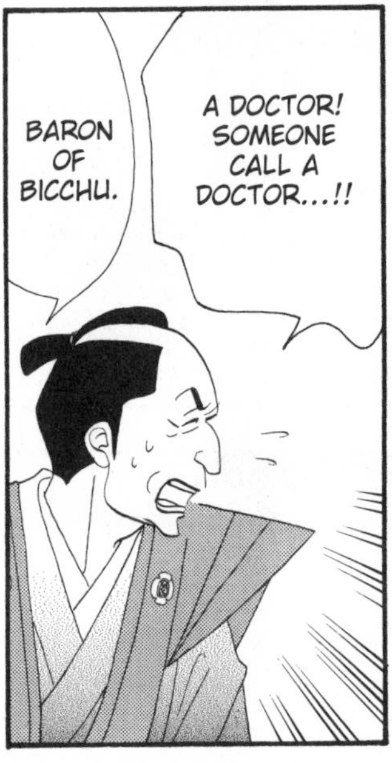
A DOCTOR! SOMEONE CALL A DOCTOR...!!
BARON OF BICCHU.

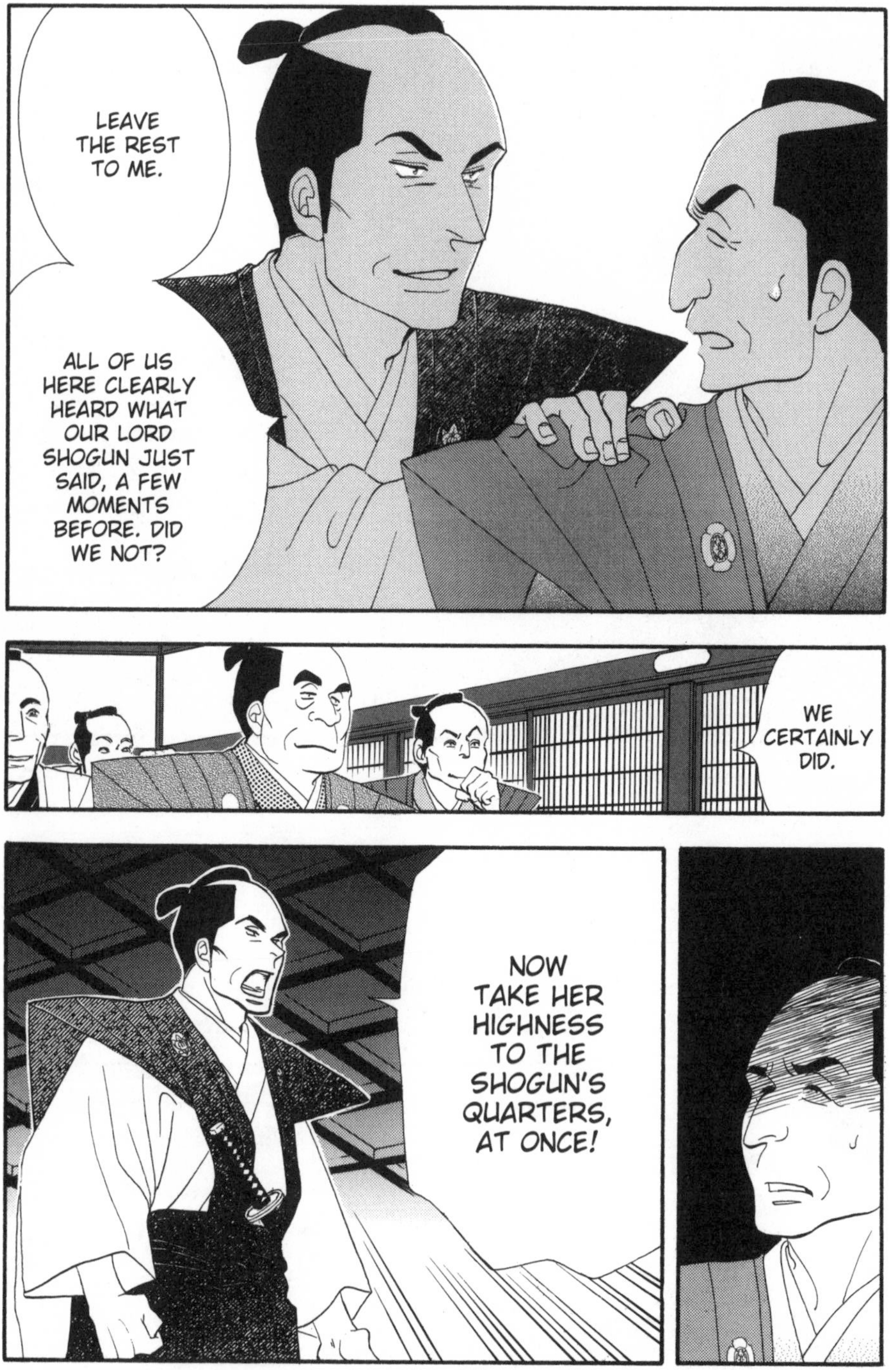
LEAVE THE REST TO ME.
ALL OF US HERE CLEARLY HEARD WHAT OUR LORD SHOGUN JUST SAID, A FEW MOMENTS BEFORE. DID WE NOT?
WE CERTAINLY DID.
NOW TAKE HER HIGHNESS TO THE SHOGUN'S QUARTERS, AT ONCE!

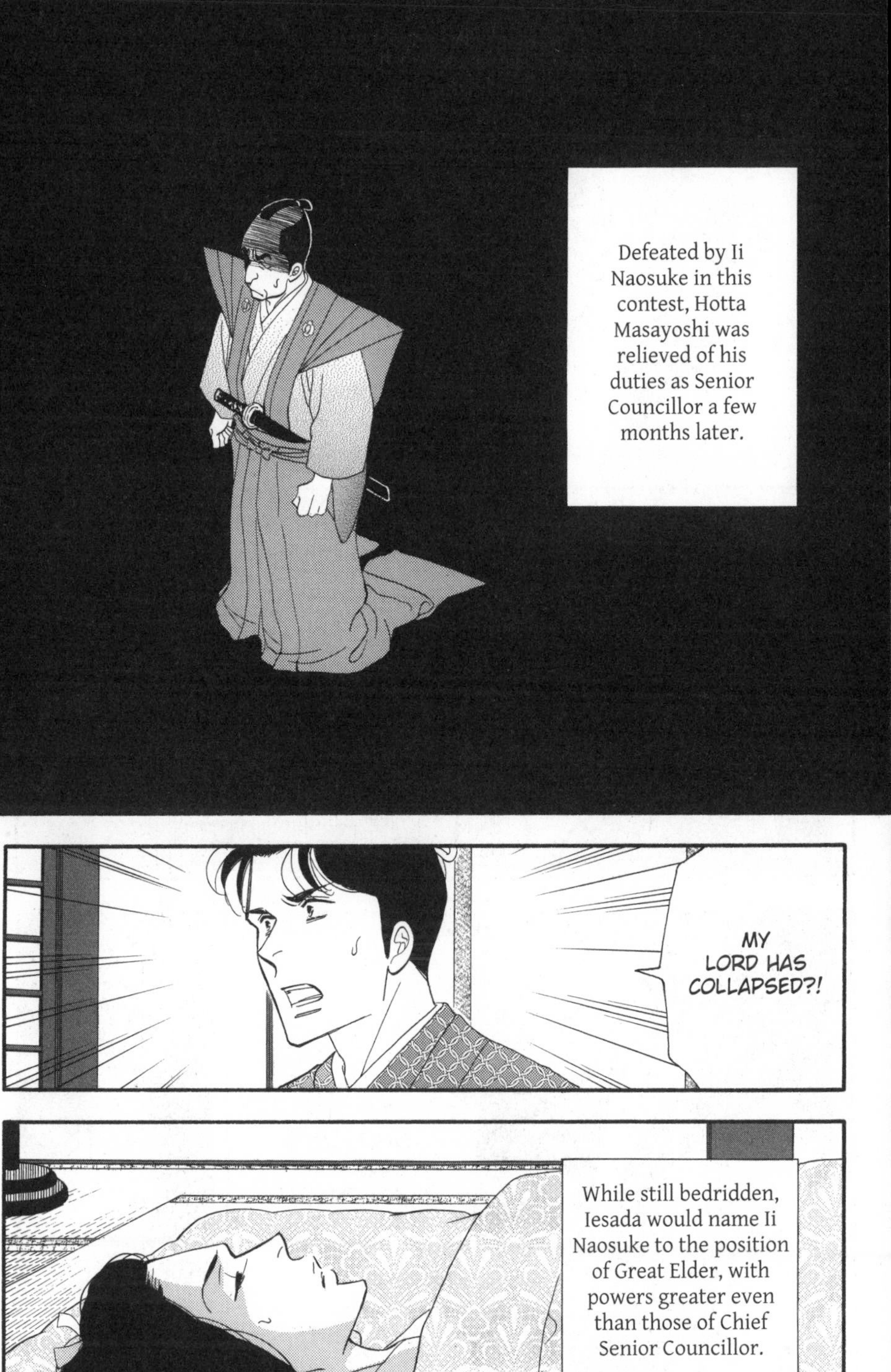
Defeated by Ii Naosuke in this contest, Hotta Masayoshi was relieved of his duties as Senior Councillor a few months later.
MY LORD HAS COLLAPSED?!
While still bedridden, Iesada would name Ii Naosuke to the position of Great Elder, with powers greater even than those of Chief Senior Councillor.

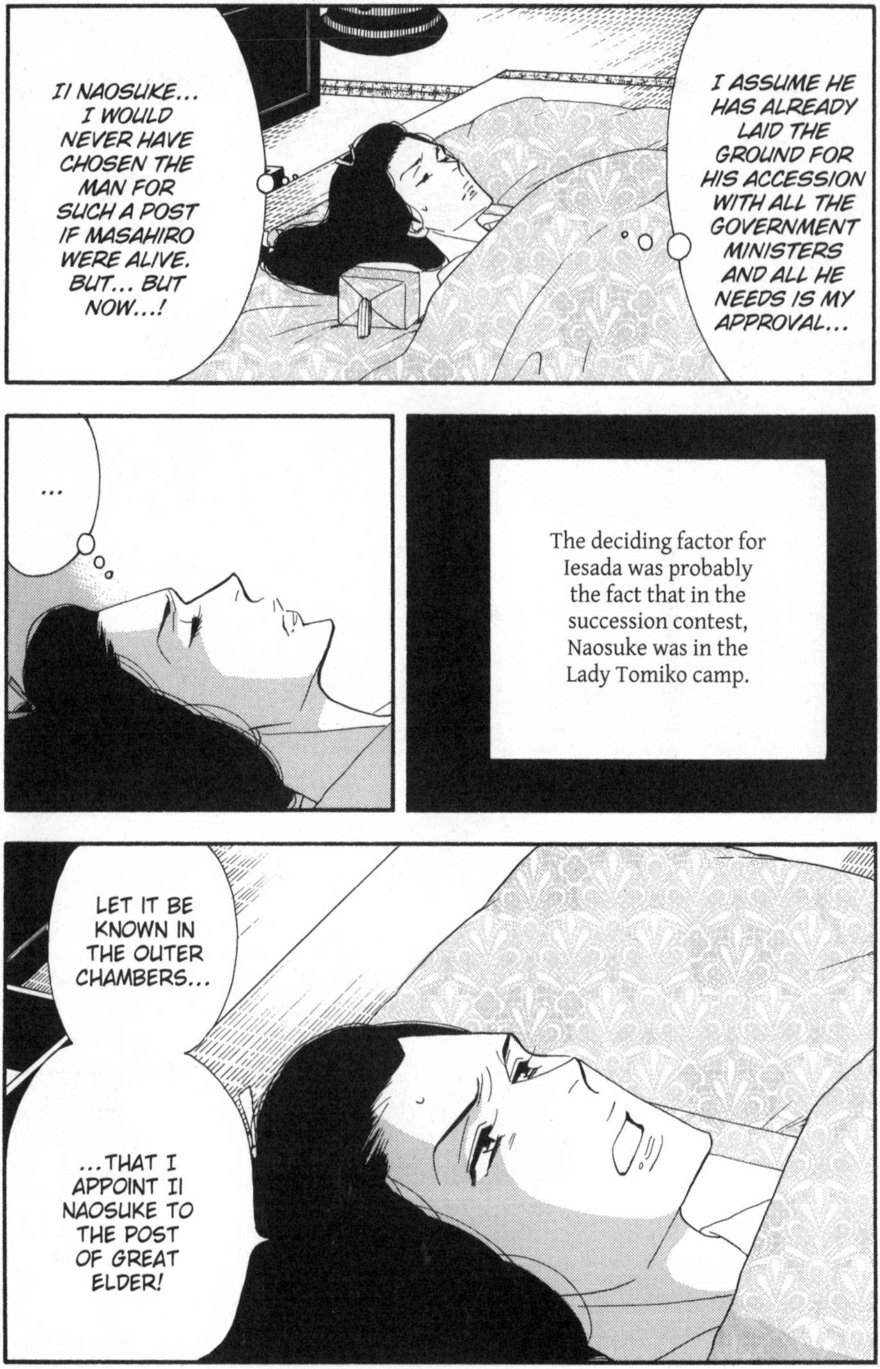
I ASSUME HE HAS ALREADY LAID THE GROUND FOR HIS ACCESSION WITH ALL THE GOVERNMENT MINISTERS AND ALL HE NEEDS IS MY APPROVAL...
II NAOSUKE... I WOULD NEVER HAVE CHOSEN THE MAN FOR SUCH A POST IF MASAHIRO WERE ALIVE. BUT... BUT NOW...!
The deciding factor for Iesada was probably the fact that in the succession contest, Naosuke was in the Lady Tomiko camp.
...
LET IT BE KNOWN IN THE OUTER CHAMBERS...
...THAT I APPOINT II NAOSUKE TO THE POST OF GREAT ELDER!

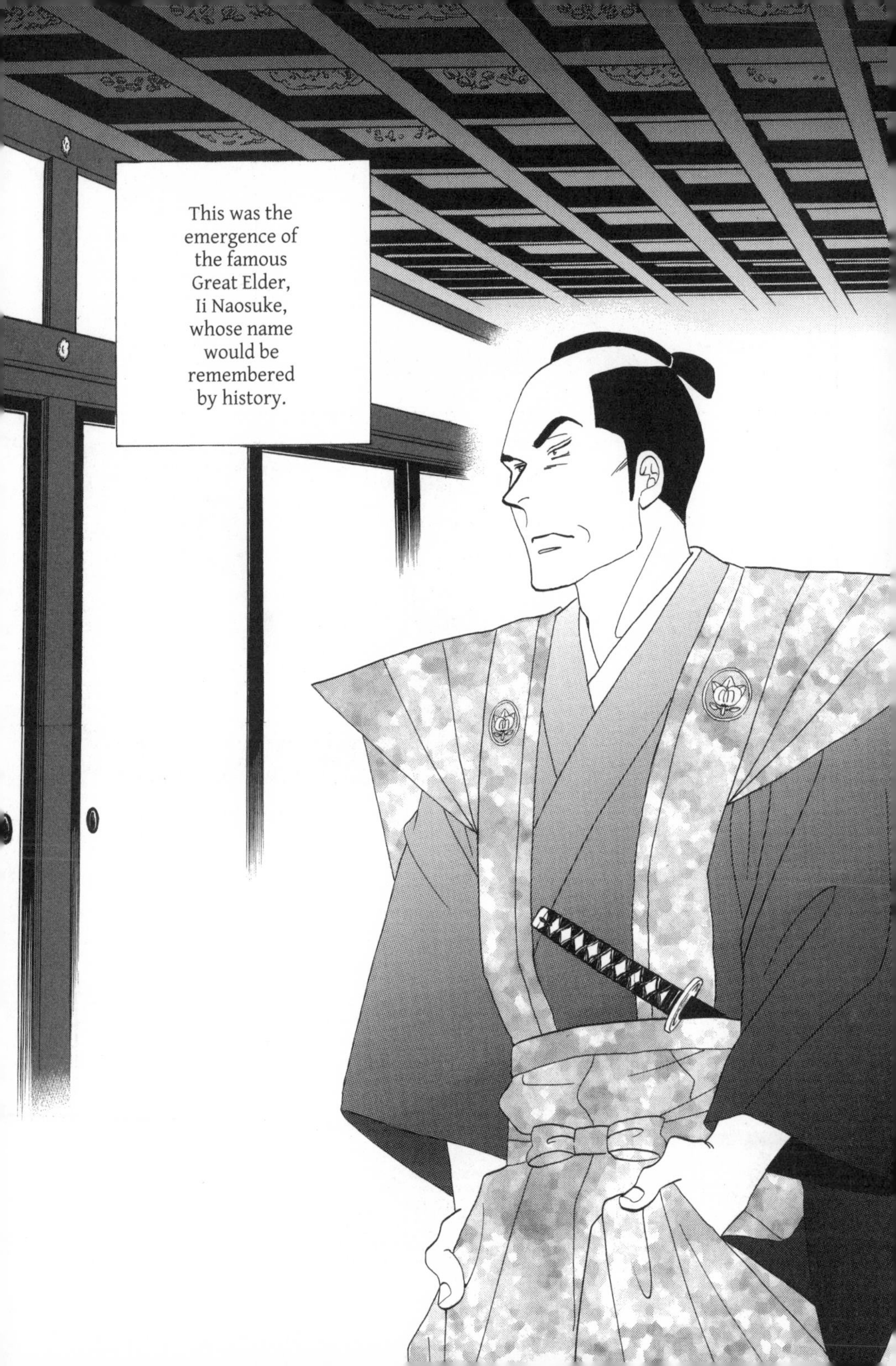
This was the emergence of the famous Great Elder, Ii Naosuke, whose name would be remembered by history.

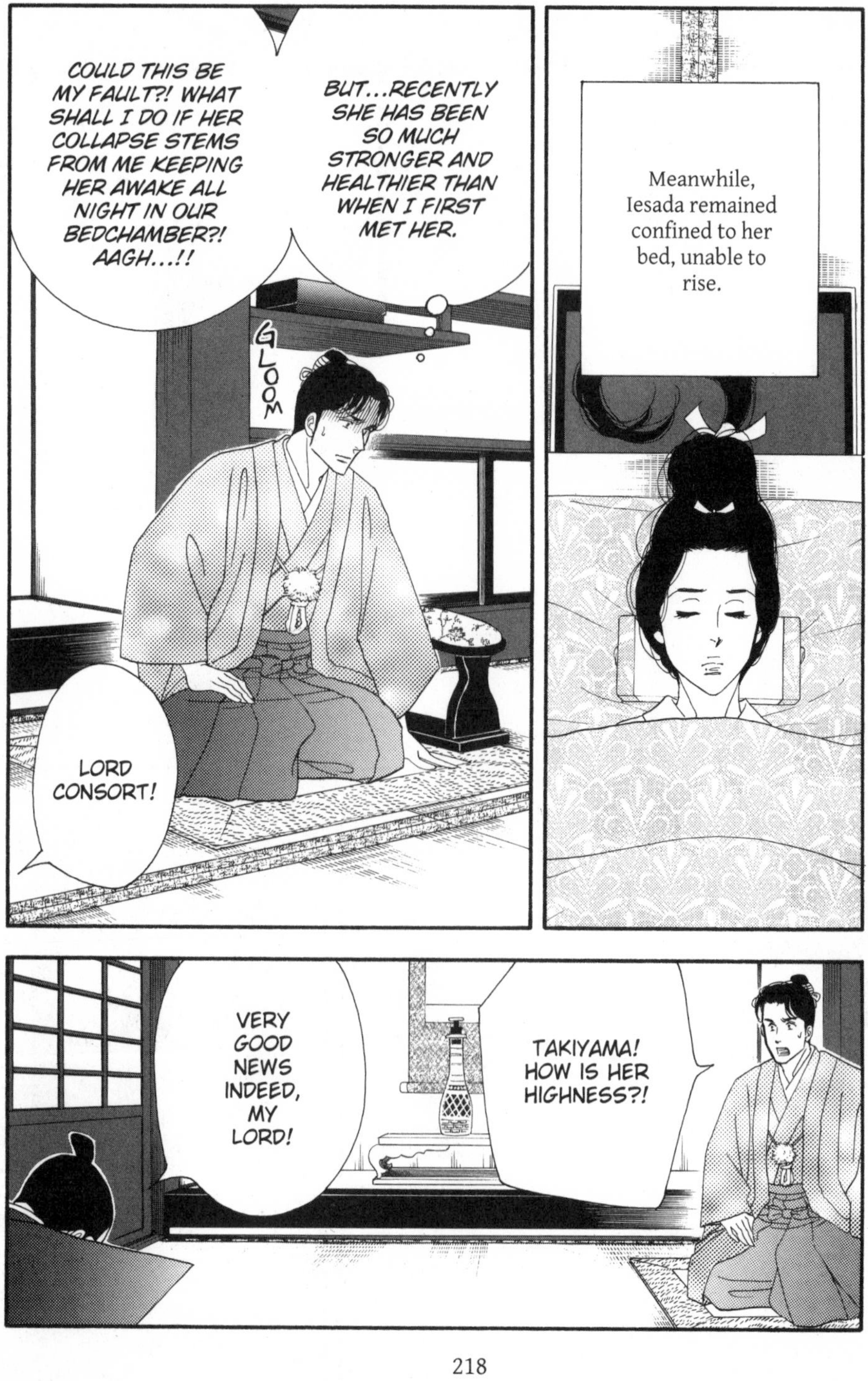
Meanwhile, Iesada remained confined to her bed, unable to rise.
BUT...RECENTLY SHE HAS BEEN SO MUCH STRONGER AND HEALTHIER THAN WHEN I FIRST MET HER.
COULD THIS BE MY FAULT?! WHAT SHALL I DO IF HER COLLAPSE STEMS FROM ME KEEPING HER AWAKE ALL NIGHT IN OUR BEDCHAMBER?! AAGH...!!
GLOOM
LORD CONSORT!
TAKIYAMA! HOW IS HER HIGHNESS?!
VERY GOOD NEWS INDEED, MY LORD!

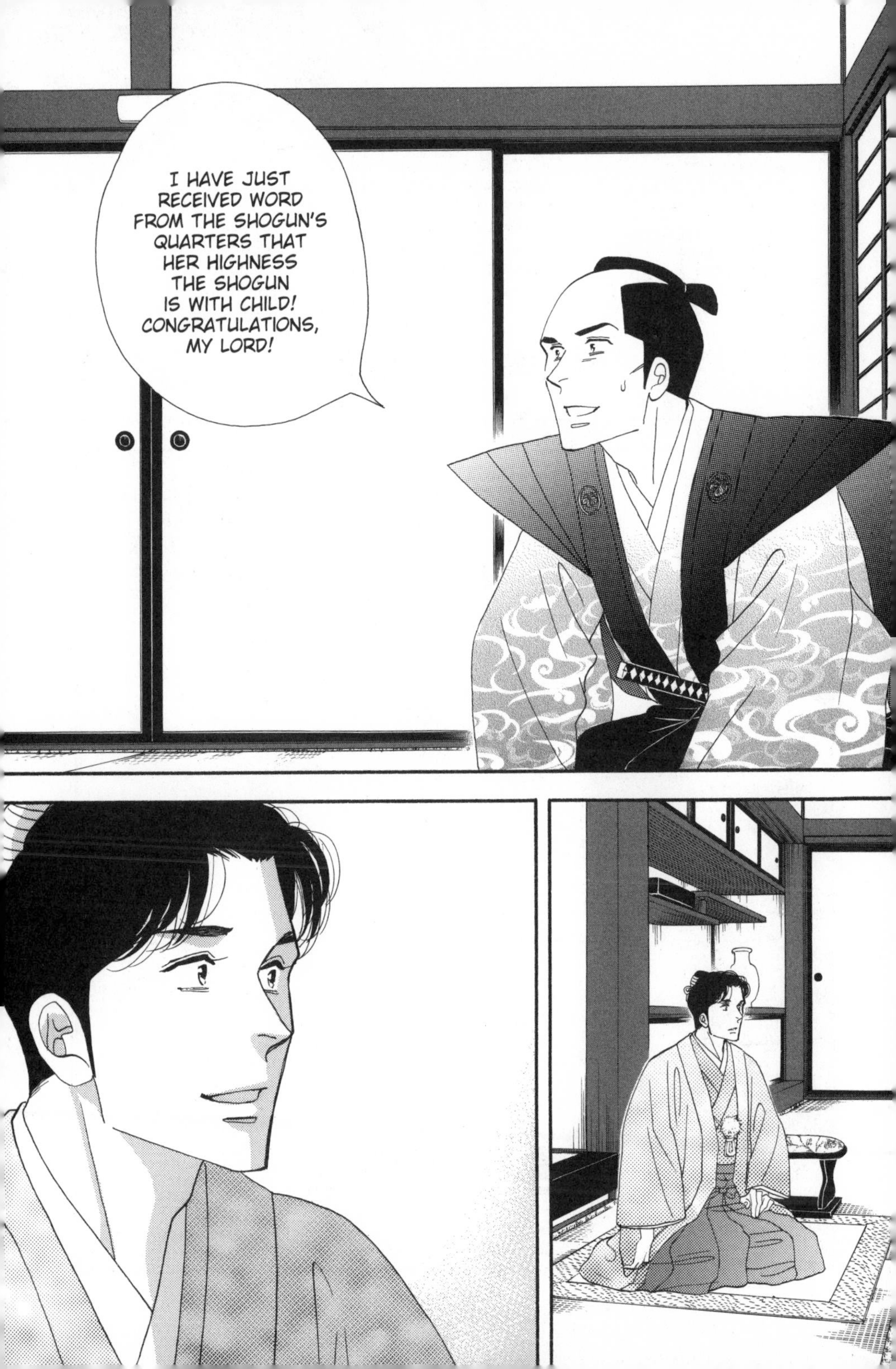
I HAVE JUST RECEIVED WORD FROM THE SHOGUN'S QUARTERS THAT HER HIGHNESS THE SHOGUN IS WITH CHILD! CONGRATULATIONS, MY LORD!

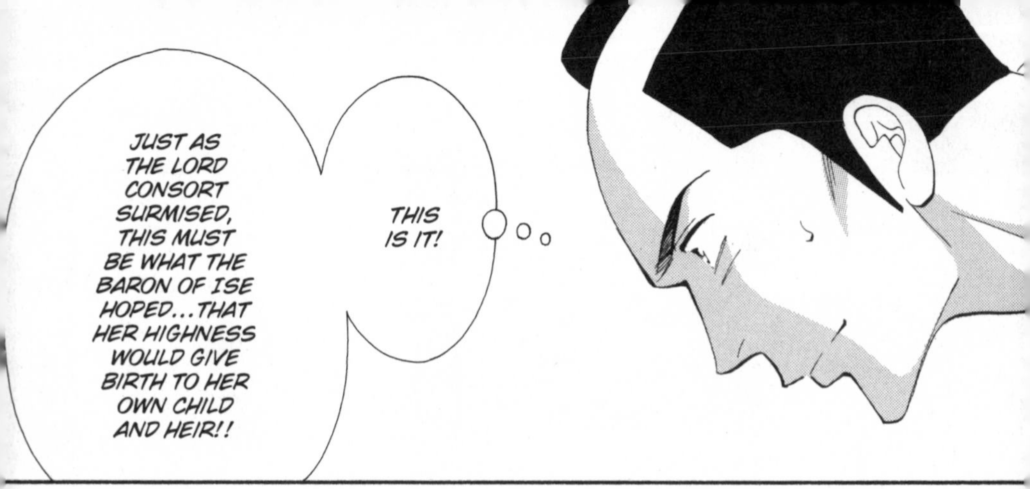
THIS IS IT!
JUST AS THE LORD CONSORT SURMISED, THIS MUST BE WHAT THE BARON OF ISE HOPED...THAT HER HIGHNESS WOULD GIVE BIRTH TO HER OWN CHILD AND HEIR!!
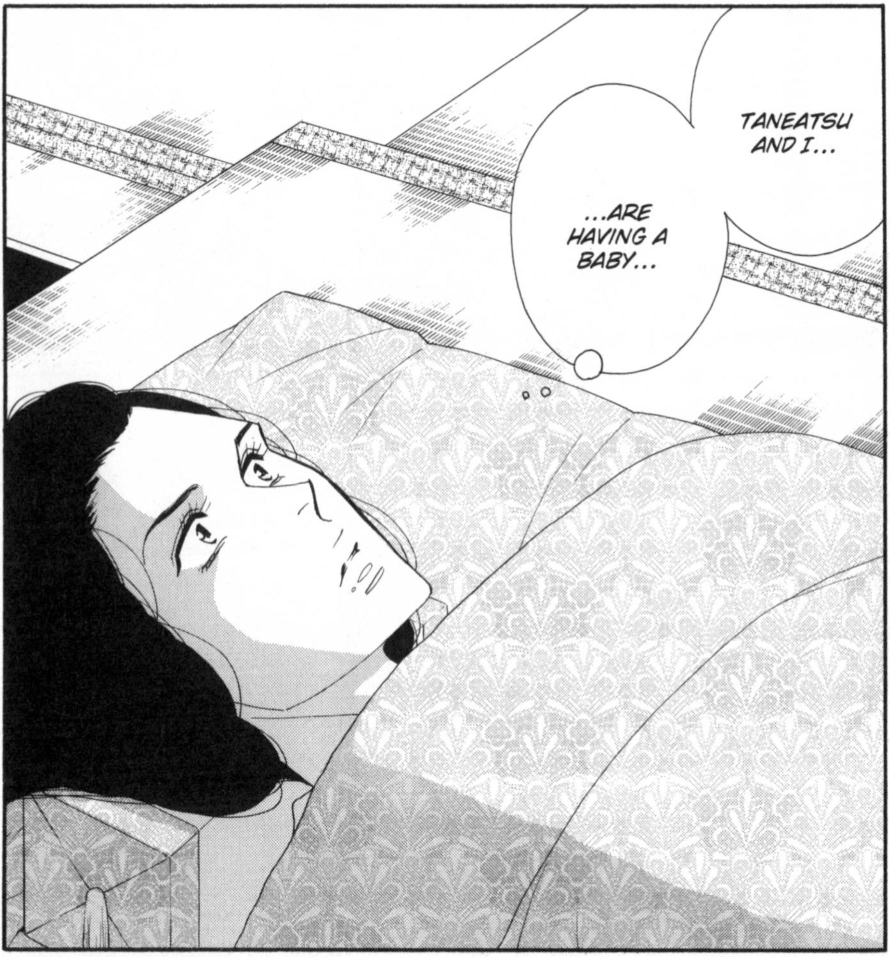
TANEATSU AND I...
...ARE HAVING A BABY...

Ōoku
THE INNER CHAMBERS

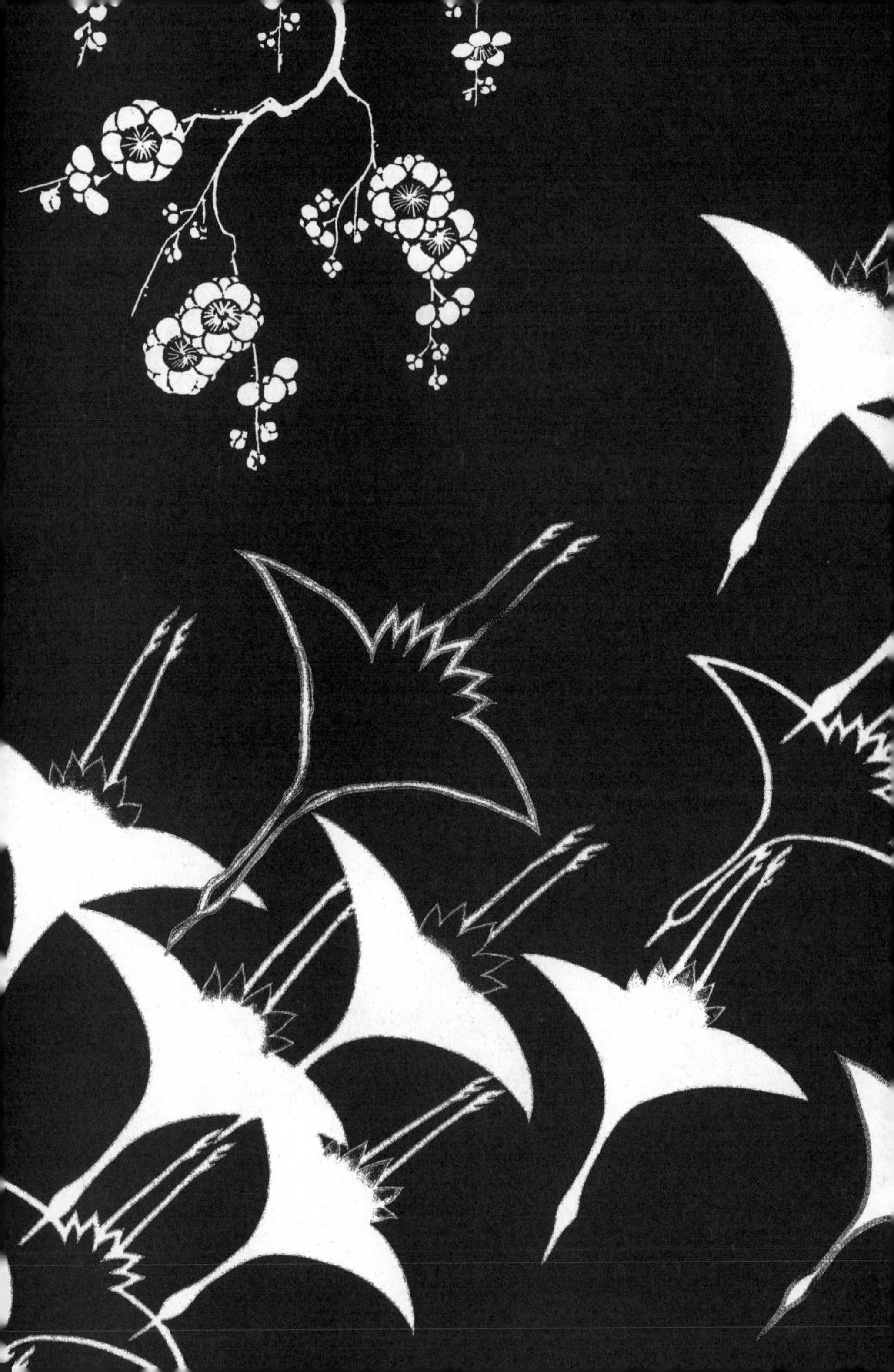

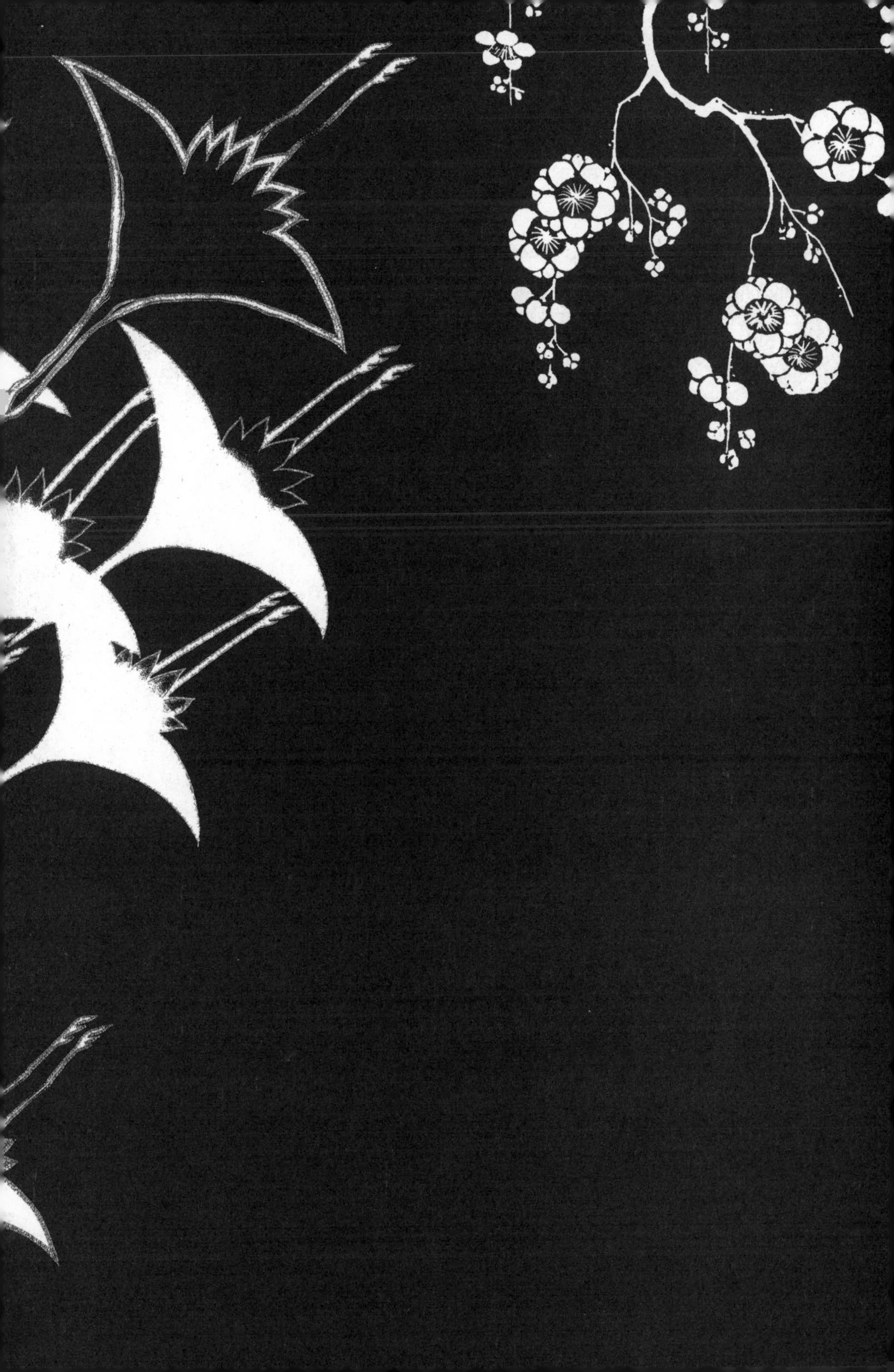

Ōoku: The Inner Chambers

VOLUME 14 · END NOTES

by Akemi Wegmüller

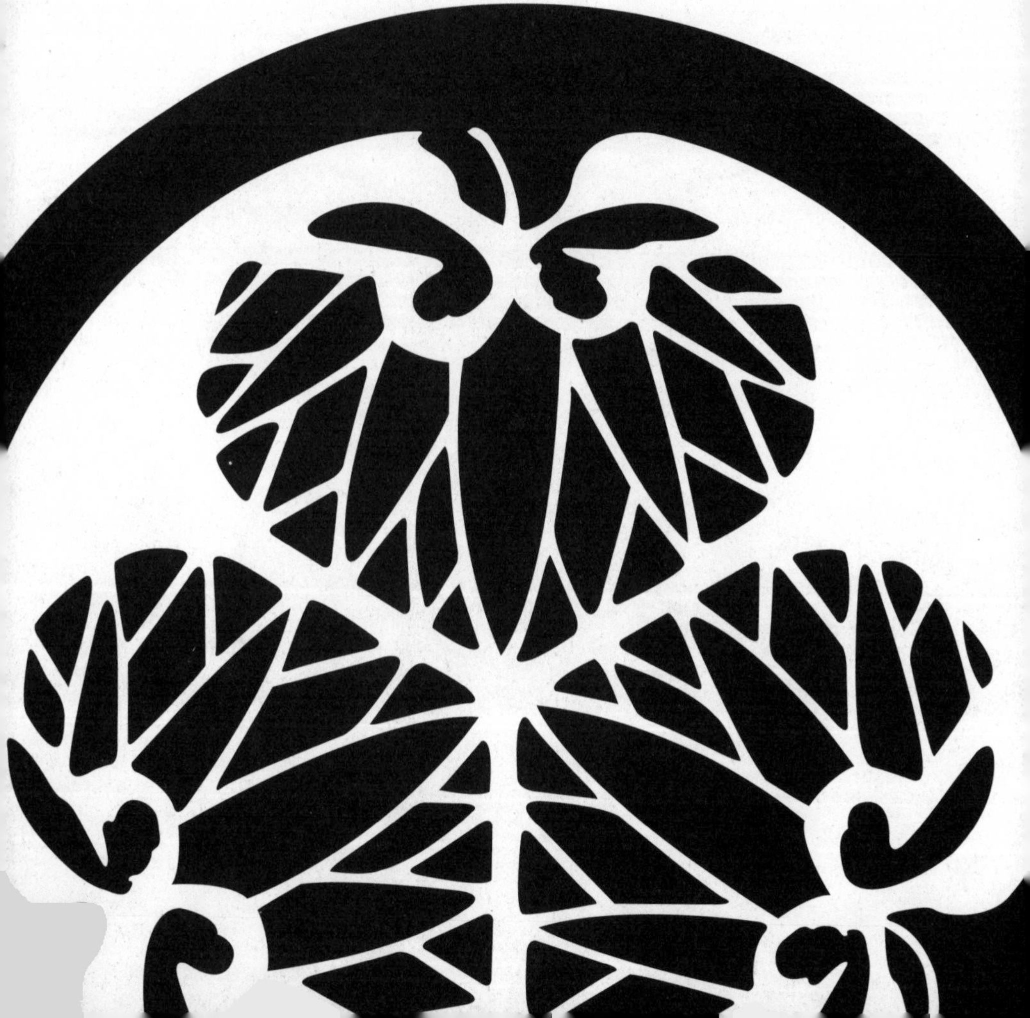

Page 11, panel 1 · RYUKYU KINGDOM
A kingdom from the 15th to 19th centuries that included modern Okinawa.

Page 21, panel 3 · OUTSIDE LORDS
Known as *tozama daimyo* in Japanese, they were domain lords who declared fealty to the shogunate after the Battle of Sekigahara and were therefore never considered true vassals.

Page 63, panel 1 · SEVEN RI
One ri is about 3.9 kilometers, so seven ri is roughly 27 kilometers, or 17 miles.

Page 118, panel 1 · KAGEMA
Young male prostitutes who served both male and female clients, and appeared in either masculine or feminine attire.

Page 165, panel 5 · HAKAMA
A Japanese garment tied at the waist and worn over kimono. Divided hakama were worn when riding horses and resemble pants in that they have two separate legs. Undivided hakama do not have separate legs.

Page 169, panel 1 · EBOSHI, GENJI
Eboshi are the black lacquered headdresses worn by court nobility in the Heian era. Genji is the main character in *The Tale of Genji*, a Heian-era tale of Don Juan-like escapades.

CREATOR BIOGRAPHY

FUMI YOSHINAGA

Fumi Yoshinaga is a Tokyo-born manga creator who debuted in 1994 with *Tsuki to Sandaru* (*The Moon and the Sandals*). Yoshinaga has won numerous awards, including the 2009 Osamu Tezuka Cultural Prize for *Ōoku*, the 2002 Kodansha Manga Award for her series *Antique Bakery* and the 2006 Japan Media Arts Festival Excellence Award for *Ōoku*. She was also nominated for the 2008 Eisner Award for Best Writer/Artist.

Ōoku

THE INNER CHAMBERS

THIS IS THE LAST PAGE.

Ōoku: The Inner Chambers has been printed in
the original Japanese format in order to preserve
the orientation of the original artwork.

Ōoku

THE INNER CHAMBERS

Ōoku: The Inner Chambers
Vol. 14

VIZ Signature Edition

Story and Art by Fumi Yoshinaga

Translation & Adaptation/Akemi Wegmüller
Touch-up Art & Lettering/Monalisa De Asis
Design/Yukiko Whitley
Editor/Pancha Diaz

Ōoku by Fumi Yoshinaga © Fumi Yoshinaga 2017
All rights reserved. First published in Japan in 2017 by
HAKUSENSHA, Inc., Tokyo. English language translation
rights arranged with HAKUSENSHA, Inc., Tokyo.

Printed in Canada

Published by VIZ Media, LLC
P.O. Box 77010
San Francisco, CA 94107

10 9 8 7 6 5 4 3 2 1
First printing, November 2018

VIZ MEDIA
viz.com

VIZ SIGNATURE
vizsignature.com